PERSONAL INJURY HANDBOOK

The College of Law
of England and Wales

Birmingham • Chester • Guildford • London • York

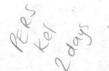

AUSTRALIA
LBC Information Services
Sydney

CANADA AND USA
Carswell
Toronto, Ontario

NEW ZEALAND
Brooker's
Auckland

SINGAPORE AND MALAYSIA
Sweet & Maxwell (Asia)
Singapore and Kuala Lumpur

PERSONAL INJURY HANDBOOK

SECOND EDITION

LONDON · SWEET & MAXWELL ·2001

Published in 2001 by
Sweet & Maxwell Limited of
100 Avenue Road, Swiss Cottage, London NW3 3PF
(*http://www.sweetandmaxwell*.co.uk)

Reprinted 2003

Typeset by LBJ Typesetting Ltd
of Kingsclere
Printed in Great Britain by
MPG Books Ltd, Bodmin

No natural forests were destroyed to make this product;
only farmed timber was used and replanted

ISBN 0 421 739 207

A catalogue record for this book
is available from the British Library

Foreword

When the first edition of this Handbook was first published my distinguished predecessor Lord Justice Beldam wrote that it "can play an important part in maintaining respect for the law". It turned out to be so. The Personal Injury Bar Association had assembled the talent within its ranks and produced a book of inestimable value.

In only three years since the work appeared there have been momentous changes in the law of personal injury. The Civil Procedure Rules have not only changed the playing field but have also moved the goal posts by encouraging a more co-operative and cost effective approach to bringing cases before the Courts. We are still adapting to the brave new CPR world where there is only one expert and judicial case management demands strict adherence to timetables. We are grappling with the limits of disclosure as they are redefined in the endeavour to reconcile relevance to the seeker and with oppression of those against whom it is sought.

These changes coincide with the emergence of conditional fee arrangements.

The substantive law continues to develop. We have not heard the last of the expanding liability of public authorities, such as the police and local education authorities. European Directives and Protocols continue to re-shape our traditional concepts of English Law. We may yet have a reversal of the burden of proof where personal injury results from the provision of medical services. The claimant proves that he was a patient and the condition complained of.

The defence has to prove the absence of negligence or that the condition complained of was not occasioned by the treatment or the withholding of treatment but due to the condition for which the treatment was given or the natural ageing process.

As the authors correctly assess, the changes in the area of quantum have had the most dramatic effect. Following the recommendations of the Law Commission the decision of the five judge Court of Appeal in *Heil v. Rankin* and the associated cases resulted in guidelines for the levels of awards across the whole of the personal injury spectrum. Other seminal decisions have determined the multipliers for future losses based on discount rates. These are still minefields for the unwary.

Finally, the European Convention on Human Rights has already had a significant influence on our domestic law. This effect will be enhanced by the coming into effect of the Human Rights Act. Wisely the editors have included new chapters to accommodate the changes.

The outstanding merit of this book is the fact that it is the result of collaboration between the most senior and distinguished practitioners in this field. I know of no other publication (save for Halsbury's Laws of England) where each of the contributors is an acknowledged expert in the subject about which he or she writes. As a result the book has an unique authority and reliability which will be particularly appreciated by the judiciary and practitioners alike.

Without reservation I recommend this book to the professional and lay people alike. There can be no doubt that it will remain compulsory reading and trusted companion for all those interested in this ever growing field of English Law. If this book is not on his shelves the practitioner will find his tasks more daunting then they need be.

THE RIGHT HONOURABLE LORD JUSTICE OTTON
Honorary President of the Personal
Injuries Bar Association
October 2000.

Preface

If the first edition was a necessary companion, to give a point of handy reference, in the increasingly technical world of personal injury practice, then the second edition is all the more so. The sceptic might be forgiven for thinking that changes between one edition, and another, are largely cosmetic.

Wholesale changes have affected the whole substance, practice, and context of personal injury litigation within the last two years as to add substantially to this handbook, and to cause much to be re-written.

Procedurally, the Civil Procedure Rules have come into effect. The old law is no longer reliable (see *Biguzzi*). Yet the procedures affect every part of our practice. There may be tension between some of the provisions of the Rules, and the requirements imposed upon the Courts by the Human Rights Act 1998, which comes into force within days of my writing this Preface. Will there, for instance, be limits upon the disclosure of medical records (see *MS v. Sweden*). Equally surely, though, tension may await a barrister who takes a human rights point too casually, or inappropriately (see what the Master of the Rolls had to say in *Walker v. Daniels*).

The substantive law continues to develop. The implications of *Phelps v. Hillingdon* and *Waters v. Metropolitan Police* remain to be worked out. Quite apart from common law, the Courts are now beginning to apply the plethora of statutory regulation that derives from Europe (see for example *Hawkes v. Southwark*). Keeping up-to-date with the applicable decisions is, perhaps, more difficult now than it ever has been.

Despite the fundamental and far-reaching changes in procedure, and in the substantial law relating to liability, it is perhaps in the area of quantum that the changes have been more dramatic still. We are fortunate in this edition to have contributors who were centrally involved in the keynote cases of *Wells v. Wells* (in relation to multipliers), and *Heil v. Rankin* (in relation to the quantum in respect of pain, suffering and loss of amenity). The most up-to-date material in respect of the calculation of future loss is contained within this handbook (well ahead, I believe, of any comparable publication) owing to the involvement of members of the PIBA in the relevant working parties and committees. Such headlong change cannot come without a warning. The Lord Chancellor may yet exercise his powers under the Damages Act to alter the discount rate upon the basis of which multipliers are calculated. The rate of interest recoverable on an award for pain, suffering and loss of amenity may yet vary from the 2 per cent at which the Court of Appeal have recently placed it. A reader needs to be aware of those changes, and that the law is dated as at September 1, 2000.

However, I am proud that so many senior members of the Association have had the enthusiasm, despite their busy practices, to make the benefits of their knowledge and experience available to members of the Personal Injury Bar Association and others, to expand upon the changes to procedure, liability, and quantum, and to comment upon the impact of the Human Rights Act 1998. Each of our contributors is an acknowledged expert in the field in which he or she writes. Although this book is not a replacement for the standard practitioner's work where detail requires it, and time allows, it nonetheless provides a handy, quick, and accurate conspectus of the fields where most problems are likely to arise in practice.

I am proud to associate the Personal Injuries Bar Association with the second edition of this work: and I feel confident that personal injury advocates will find it every bit as useful as the first, if not more so . . .

BRIAN LANGSTAFF Q.C.
September 2000
Cloisters
1 Pump Court
Temple
London

Contents

Section 1—Liability

Section 2—Damages

Section 3—Procedure

Section 4—Funding

Contents

Section 5—Human Rights

Table of Cases

Table of Cases

Table of Cases

Table of Cases

Table of Statutes

Table of Statutory Instruments

Table of Rules of the Supreme Court, Civil Procedure Rules and Practice Directions

Table of European Legislation

Table of European Cases

Section 1

LIABILITY

1. Duty of Care

For a duty of care to arise in Common Law negligence a three-part test 1–01
must be satisfied. There must be sufficient proximity between the parties, it
must be just, fair and reasonable to impose a duty of care, and injury to the
claimant must be reasonably foreseeable: see *Caparo Industries plc v.
Dickman*.[1] The three-part test is a flexible test in that there is a large degree
of overlap between the parts which provide a useful structure to simplify
the problem of identifying whether or not there is a duty of care: see *Marc
Rich & Co. v. Bishop Rock Marine*.[2]

Employers

An employer of workmen clearly satisfies the proximity test and the just, 1–02
fair and reasonable test so far as his employees are concerned. Thus, the
third element of reasonable foreseeability of injury is the important test
which needs to be satisfied in order to establish that in the particular
circumstances the employer owes a duty of care to his employees. To
establish liability it is then necessary to prove breach of the duty and that
the breach caused personal injury.

There may be a duty of care implied in a contract of service between an
employer and an employee, but the precise scope is unclear and most
commentators consider that the tortious duty is more extensive.

Employee on Loan

Where an employee is loaned to another employer, the temporary 1–03
employer may so take over the control of how the employee does his work
that the employee becomes part of the temporary employer's organisation
and the temporary employer is thus liable to the employee: see *Garrard v.
A.E. Soutbey & Co. and Standard Telephones and Cables*.[3] However, if an
employer has delegated to another party one of his duties to his employees,
such as the duty to provide and operate a safe system of work, that
delegation does not allow the employer to escape liability if the duty has
not been properly performed: see *McDermid v. Nash Dredging Co. Ltd*,[4]

---

[1] [1990] 2 A.C. 605.
[2] [1996] 1 A.C. 211.
[3] [1952] 2 Q.B. 174; [1992] 2 Q.B. 174.
[4] [1987] A.C. 906.

and also *Morris v. Breaveglen Ltd.*[5] In such situations it may well be that both the employer and the temporary employer owe a duty of care to the employee. Although the duty may exist and be non-delegable, it is a question of fact and degree as to whether there has been a breach: see *Cook v. Square Deal Ltd and others*[6] where the employee was injured by a defective floor in Saudi Arabia and could not recover against his employer who was based in England.

Self-employed Workers

1–04   A self-employed workman will satisfy the proximity and "just, fair and reasonable" tests in respect of those who might be affected by his actions in carrying out his work. Again, the test of foreseeability is the vital third element.

Where a self-employed worker is engaged by an "employer" if it is a genuine labour-only sub-contract, the common law duties of an employer to his employee are not owed to the self-employed workman: see *Quinn v. Birch Bros. (Builders) Ltd.*[7] The true status of the workman will be examined so that a builder's labourer "on the lump" can be held to be an employee: see *Ferguson v. John Dawson & Partners (Contractors) Ltd.*[8] The element of control is important, but not decisive, and the question of "whose business is it?" is important in determining whether the workman is an employee to whom a duty of care is owed: see *Lane v. The Shire Roofing Company (Oxford) Ltd.*[9]

Road Users

1–05   Road users, whether drivers or pedestrians, owe a duty of care to other road users: see *Nance v. British Columbia Electric Rly Co. Ltd.*[10]

Other Parties

1–06   A few examples help to illustrate the point. A passenger in an aircraft on a test flight was owed a duty of care by the authorities who certified the airworthiness of the aircraft: see *Perrett v. Collins.*[11] A fire brigade does not

---

[5] [1993] I.C.R. 766, CA; [1993] P.I.Q.R. P294.
[6] [1992] I.C.R. 262, CA; [1992] P.I.Q.R. P33, CA.
[7] [1966] 2 Q.B. 370, CA.
[8] [1976] 1 W.L.R. 1213.
[9] [1995] P.I.Q.R. P417.
[10] [1951] A.C. 601.
[11] [1998] 2 Lloyd's Rep. 255, CA.

owe a duty of care to the owner of premises: see *Capital Counties plc v. Hampshire County Council.*[12]

Foreseeability

The test of foreseeability is flexible. It contains two distinct elements: the incidence of risk and the degree of severity of risk created. This is not always identified in the reported cases. The difficulty arises in making the judgment between the risk that is so small that a reasonable man would disregard it and the risk, which although small, would not be disregarded. In *Bolton v. Stone,*[13] the chance of the cricket ball hitting someone in the road was a risk of such small magnitude that it could be disregarded. In *Gerrard v. Staffordshire Potteries*[14] the risk of a ceramic fragment flying up into the eye of a worker when glaze was applied by compressed air was held to be sufficiently great to found liability.

1–07

In *Gerrard*, there had never been a previous injury, but the risk was of permanent damage to eyesight. In *Bolton v. Stone*, the road was an ordinary side road giving access to private houses in Cheetham Hill, Manchester. If the cricket ground had abutted the M6, where a ball could shatter a windscreen and cause multiple collisions, the decision might have been different.

The fact that the event has not occurred previously may have evidential force but is not decisive: see, for example, *Gerrard v. Staffordshire Potteries*.

Foreseeability is often said to be an objective test, but this can be misleading. The objective test is the degree of knowledge to be expected of the ordinary prudent employer: see *Stokes v. Guest Keen & Nettlefold (Bolts and Nuts) Ltd.*[15] It may well be necessary to consider whether the proposed defendant has or should have specialist knowledge of technical or scientific matters. A large corporation with a research department, medical officers and safety officers will be expected to know more than a smaller concern. Access to trade publications or trade knowledge may be a relevant matter. Reports from the Chief Inspector of Factories may help to set the standard: see *Bryce v. Swan Hunter Group*.[16]

Where an employer knows, or ought to have known, that an employee has a vulnerability to injury, whether it be for example a weakened back or a sensitive skin, then the employer is under a duty to take extra precautions: see *Paris v. Stepney Borough Council*.[17] The duty does not necessarily extend to providing complete protection; it is a question of

---

[12] [1997] Q.B. 1004, CA.
[13] [1951] A.C. 850.
[14] [1995] I.C.R. 502, CA; [1995] P.I.Q.R. P169.
[15] [1968] 1 W.L.R. 1776.
[16] [1988] 1 All E.R. 659.
[17] [1951] A.C. 367.

what is reasonable in balancing the risk. It may be sufficient to warn the employee of the risks. There is no duty to provide alternative work, or to dismiss the employee: see *Withers v. Perry Chain Co.*[18]

"Nervous Shock"

1–08   To succeed in a claim for damages for "nervous shock" it is necessary to prove that the claimant has suffered a recognised psychiatric illness: see *Page v. Smith*[19] and *Frost v. Chief Constable of South Yorkshire.*[20]

The law on this topic has undergone recent clarification and some of the earlier cases will need to be treated with care. A key to understanding the topic is to divide the claimant into categories of "primary victims" and "secondary victims".

A primary victim is someone who is involved in an accident, for example the occupant of a car involved in a collision or a factory worker present at an explosion. A duty of care arises if the defendant can, or should, foresee that his conduct will expose the victim to a risk of personal injury, whether physical or psychiatric. Where the primary victim has suffered physical injury, the defendant will be bound to compensate the claimant if psychiatric injury results, even if psychiatric injury was not foreseeable; this is the "eggshell skull" rule: see *Malcolm v. Broadhurst.*[21] Where there is no physical injury, there must be foreseeability of psychiatric injury in a person of reasonable fortitude. Once the duty has arisen it is no defence to the claim that the victim was predisposed to psychiatric illness, or that the psychiatric illness takes a rare form or is of unusual severity: see *Page v. Smith.*

A secondary victim is a person who was no more than a passive and unwilling witness of injury to others. In order to show sufficient proximity to establish a successful claim, the secondary victim must show a close tie of love and affection to the immediate victim, closeness in time and space to the incident or its aftermath, and perception by sight or hearing or its equivalent of the event or its aftermath: see *Alcock v. Chief Constable of West Yorkshire.*[22] Seeing a disaster on television was not sufficiently proximate: see *Alcock v. Chief Constable of West Yorkshire.*

Rescuers are a rather particular hybrid. They were not put in peril by the accident itself, but come to render assistance in the immediate aftermath. They do not have a close tie of love or affection with the victims and so do not qualify for compensation under the secondary victim definition. Where

---

[18] [1961] 1 W.L.R. 1314, CA.
[19] [1996] A.C. 155, HL; [1995] P.I.Q.R. P329, HL.
[20] [1999] 2 A.C. 455.
[21] [1970] 3 All E.R. 508.
[22] [1992] 1 A.C. 310.

they put themselves in physical danger or reasonably believed that they had put themselves in danger, they will establish a duty of care and will be compensated for psychiatric damage: see *Frost v. Chief Constable of South Yorkshire; Chadwick v. British Railways Board*[23]; *McFarlane v. E.E. Caledonia Limited.*[24]

---

[23] [1967] 1 W.L.R. 912.
[24] [1994] 2 All E.R. 1, CA.

2. Foreseeability

The concept of reasonable foreseeability dominates the law of negli- 2–01
gence. It is used in determining the existence of a duty of care, breach of a
duty and the damages that are recoverable. This chapter considers how far
it has become a sufficient as well as a necessary condition, and what exactly
has to be foreseen, in order to establish liability in tort for personal
injuries.

Duty of Care

The modern tripartite test for the determination of a duty of care 2–02
consists of foreseeability, proximity and the fair, just and reasonable
consideration: see *Caparo Industries v. Dickman*.[1] "Proximity" is often
used as an umbrella term to encompass all the circumstances in which a
duty of care arises in tort. In this sense, foreseeability has been a
cornerstone of proximity since the seminal words of Lord Atkin in
Donoghue v. Stevenson[2] that:

> "you must take reasonable care to avoid acts or omissions which you can
> reasonably foresee would be likely to injure your neighbour."

Whilst foreseeability is always a necessary requirement to generate a
duty of care, it is usually sufficient as the only requirement in situations
where physical harm is foreseen.[3] Thus, in most personal injury cases,
reasonable foreseeability of personal injury is the only requirement. It is
unnecessary to consider the other elements of the tripartite test in the
normal running down or accident at work case.

There are exceptions to this general rule. In cases of pure omission, mere
foresight of physical injury is insufficient to impose a duty. Unless there has
been an assumption of responsibility, there is no duty to assist a drowning
person. In cases where there is a power but no duty to act, liability is
denied on grounds of insufficient proximity[4] or more exceptionally because
it is not just and reasonable to impose a duty[5] even though damage from

---

[1] [1990] 2 A.C. 605 at 617–8 *per* Lord Bridge.
[2] [1932] A.C. 562.
[3] *The Hau Lien* [1991] 1 Lloyd's Rep. 309, 328.
[4] See *Capital & Counties plc v. Hampshire County Council* [1997] Q.B. 1004; *Stovin v. Wise*
[1996] A.C. 923.
[5] See *Hill v. Chief Constable of West Yorkshire* [1989] A.C. 53; *X (Minors) v. Bedfordshire
County Council* [1995] 2 A.C. 633. This is likely to be a less easy route to denial of liability
in the future, since the decision in *Osman v. United Kingdom* [2000] 29 E.H.R.R., and with
the advent of the Human Rights Act: see *Barrett v. Enfield LBC* [1999] 3 W.L.R. 79; *Arthur
J.S. Hall & Co. v. Simons, July 21, 2000, HL; Phelps v. London Borough of Hillingdon*, July
27, 2000, HL.

failure to act is reasonably foreseeable. In such cases there is no positive duty to act. Where, however, by reason of the proximity of the relationship between the parties or assumption of responsibility by one party, there is a duty to take positive steps, for instance to prevent the wrongdoing of a third party, the normal test of foreseeability is applied.[6]

The Standard of Foresight

2–03   "Reasonable foresight" consists of more than merely foreseeing the *possibility* of a particular occurrence. A defendant is expected to foresee and guard against only the reasonable and *probable* consequences of a failure to take care.[7] A classic illustration of this point is *Bolton v. Stone*.[8] In that case it was foreseeable that a cricket ball might hit someone passing the cricket ground, but the risk was very small. The House of Lords held that foreseeing the possibility of injury was insufficient and that the reasonable man was only expected to take "precautions against risks which are reasonably likely to happen."[9]

In a modern industrialised society the risk, meaning the possibility, of physical injury is ubiquitous and inescapable. If the risk of being struck by a cricket ball is "extremely small" or "negligible", then it amounts to one of the many risks ordinarily to be expected in modern life. Such risks do not normally create a cause of action for anyone suffering an accidental injury.[10]

Contrast *Bolton v. Stone* with *Miller v. Jackson*,[11] another cricketing case. What distinguishes the two decisions is the degree of foresight of injury. In *Bolton v. Stone*, becuase only six balls in 28 years had been hit into the road, the risk was foreseeable but not likely. In *Miller v. Jackson*, because six to nine balls per season were hit into the housing estate, the risk of injury was not merely foreseeable but likely.

At one time *Bolton v. Stone* was erroneously thought to require foresight of injury as being more likely than not to occur. It is now well established that the probability required to impose a duty of care is that of a "real risk". This was defined by Lord Reid in *Overseas Tankship (U.K.) Ltd v. The Miller Steamship Co. Pty (The Wagon Mound No. 2)*[12] as "one which would occur to the mind of a reasonable man . . . and which he would not brush aside as far-fetched". In that case the Miller Steamship Co. owned

---

[6] See *Smith v. Littlwoods Organisation Ltd* [1987] A.C. 241 and *Kent v. Griffiths* [2000] 2 W.L.R. 1158.
[7] See *Glasgow Corporation v. Muir* [1943] A.C. 448, 454.
[8] [1951] A.C. 850.
[9] *ibid. per* Lord Oaksey, 863.
[10] See *Green v. Building Scene Ltd* [1994] P.I.Q.R. 259 at 269 *per* Staughton L.J.
[11] [1977] Q.B. 966.
[12] [1967] A.C. 617, 643.

two vessels which were moored at a wharf and were undergoing repairs involving oxy-acetylene welding. *The Wagon Mound,* a vessel chartered by Overseas Tankship, carelessly allowed oil to overflow and drift around the wharf and vessels. The oil caught fire and damaged the wharf and vessels. It was held by the Board that as, on the trial judge's findings, the chief engineer of *The Wagon Mound* ought to have known that there was a real risk that the oil would catch fire,[13] there was sufficient probability of damage by fire for a duty to avoid such damage to exist. This is to be contrasted with the opposite finding of fact in *The Wagon Mound No. 1*[14] (in which the wharf owners sued the charterers of *The Wagon Mound*) that an engineer could not reasonably have been expected to know that oil spread on water was capable of catching fire. As a result in that case no liability was established.

Whether a risk is sufficiently serious so as to amount to a "real risk" 2–04 depends on the facts of each case. A small risk may nonetheless be a real risk.[15]

Reasonably foreseeability is an objective test in which events are seen through the eyes of the reasonable man who is imputed with all the facts which the defendant knew or ought to have known at the time of the event. He does not have the benefit of hindsight. Hence a defendant is not liable if at the time an operation is carried out, it is not known that the anaesthetic could be contaminated by disinfectant and cause paralysis.[16] The standard of care is to a large degree a function of what ought to have been foreseen and so is very flexible. For instance, if an employer knows that an employee has a particular vulnerability, such as having only one eye, he ought to foresee the liklihood of a more severe injury and take additional precautions.[17] Similarly, organisers of a disabled persons' sports event will be under a more onerous duty in respect of safety measures than if it were an able bodied event.[18] If the defendant has knowledge and experience which is higher than that to be expected of a reasonable man acting in his position or capacity, then he is judged by that enhanced standard of foresight.[19]

---

[13] "Serious damage to ships or other property was not only foreseeable but very likely", *per* Lord Reid 643C–D.

[14] *Overseas Tankship (U.K.) Ltd v. Morts Dock and Engineering Co. Ltd. (The Wagon Mound No. 1),* [1961] A.C. 388.

[15] *Gerrard v. Staffordshire Potteries* [1995] P.I.Q.R. P169.

[16] See *Roe v. Minister of Health* [1954] 2 Q.B. 66, the court "must not look at the 1947 accident with 1954 spectacles", *per* Denning L.J.

[17] See *Paris v. Stepney Borough Council* [1951] A.C. 376. This has so far been the route to a finding of liability in the stress at work claims, see *Walker v. Northumberland County Council* [1995] 1 All E.R. 747.

[18] See *Morrell v. Owen, The Times,* December 14, 1993.

[19] See *Stokes v. Guest, Keen & Nettlefold (Bolts and Nuts) Ltd* [1968] 1 W.L.R. 1776.

Class of Person

2–05   A duty of care in negligence is not owed to the world, but only to one's neighbours, *i.e.* "persons who are so closely and directly affected by my act that I ought reasonably to have them in contemplation as being affected" by my act or omission.[20] A claimant can only recover if he shows himself to be within the category of victims which was reasonably foreseeable. Another way of putting this is to say there must be proximity in time, space and relationship between the claimant and the tortfeasor. Generally, if a person is within the range of physical danger then he is a foreseeable claimant.

Kind of Damage

2–06   Duties of care in tort do not exist in the abstract.

"But there can be no liability until the damage is done. It is not the act but the consequences on which tortious duty is founded. Just as (as it has been said) there is no such thing as negligence in the air, so there is no such thing as liability in the air."[21]

Thus, in every case it is necessary to analyse whether a duty was owed to the particular claimant to protect him against the damage he has in fact suffered.

"The essential factor in determining liability is whether the damage is of such a kind as the reasonable man should have foreseen."[22]

In a different context (recovery of damages for pure economic loss), Lord Bridge said:

"It is never sufficient to ask simply whether A owes D a duty of care. It is always necessary to determine the scope of the duty by reference to the kind of damage from which A must take care to save B harmless."[23]

The concept of "kind of damage" can be analysed in terms of:

(a) the kind of accident or occurrence,
(b) the kind of injury,

in fact suffered.

---

[20] *Donoghue v. Stevenson, op. cit.* at 580.
[21] *The Wagon Mound No. 1, op. cit.* at 425.
[22] *ibid.* at 426.
[23] *Caparo Industries plc. v. Dickman, op. cit.* at 627.

The Kind of Accident

The kind of accident or occurrence must be reasonably foreseeable.[24] If **2–07** the kind of accident is foreseeable, it matters not that the precise manner of its occurrence is unforeseeable. Thus, in *Hughes v. Lord Advocate*[25] liability was established when paraffin lamps were left unguarded by a hole in a road and boys dropped one down the hole causing an explosion in which one of them suffered burn injuries. A burning accident was foreseeable, although the precise way in which it happened (*i.e.* an explosion) was not.[26]

In contrast, *The Wagon Mound (No. 1)*, on the facts found, pollution damage to the wharf from the spillage of oil was foreseeable but the ignition of the oil was not. Hence the defendants owed no duty to the wharf owners in resepct of damage to the wharf caused when the spilt oil was unexpectedly set on fire. Damage by fire which was unforeseeable was a different kind of damage to damage by spoiling.

More controversially, the Court of Appeal has held that an accident occurring from an explosion caused by the chemical reaction of an asbestos sheet being dropped in a cauldron of molten liquid was a different kind of accident to one caused by the sheet being dropped and splashing molten liquid.[27] Arguably, both were burning accidents. Yet the former was held not to be foreseeable; although the latter was, the danger of such splashing had passed when the asbestos sheet became completely submerged.[28]

In *Jolley v. London Borough of Sutton*,[29] a boat the Local Authority had failed to remove from their land was potentially dangerous to children playing on it because it was rotten. An accident occurred when two teenage boys propped the boat up with a car jack in order to work under it and one was injured when the boat collapsed. The cause of the accident was not the rotten condition of the boat, but the inadequate manner in which it had been jacked and propped up. On those facts the Court of Appeal held that there was no liability because the accident which occurred was of a different kind to the accident which was foreseeable. The House of Lords reversed this decision.[30]

Lord Steyn's speech reversed the decision on the basis that it was foreseeable that teenage boys might try to move or lift the boat and in doing so suffer injury; thus the kind of accident which occurred (a lifting and moving accident) was foreseeable even if the precise circumstances were not.

---

[24] *Hughes v. Lord Advocate* [1963] A.C. 837.
[25] *ibid.*
[26] *ibid.* at 856.
[27] *Doughty v. Turner Manufacturing Company* [1964] 1 Q.B. 518.
[28] *Doughty* can be reconciled with *Hughes* in that in the latter case the known source of danger was the same, namely, the paraffin lamp, in the former case the explosive nature of asbestos was a different and unknown danger to that of splashing hot liquid.
[29] [1998] 1 W.L.R. 1546.
[30] [2000] 1 W.L.R. 1082.

By contrast Lord Hoffman's speech suggested that at least in accidents involving children a very broad description of the kind of accident should be adopted. The extent to which a very broad description of the kind of accident should be adopted. The extent to which this decision has extended the law will no doubt be the subject of future argument.

These cases demonstrate that careful analysis of the kind of accident is required in each case in order to discover whether liability will be established. This involves, in the words of Lord Steyn, "an intense focus on the circumstances of each case".

The Kind of Injury

2–08   For many years it appeared that a distinction might be drawn between physical injury and psychiatric damage as being two separate kinds of damage. However, after the decision of the House of Lords in *Page v. Smith*[31] it seems that personal injuries are an indivisible kind of damage. Lord Lloyd delivered the majority decision in that case and said:

> "Once it is established that the defendant is under a duty of care to avoid causing personal injury to the plaintiff it matters not whether the injury in fact sustained is physical, psychiatric or both."[32]

The *ratio decidendi* of *Page v. Smith* was limited to deciding that if the claimant was within the foreseeable range of the risk of physical injury (a "primary victim") then psychiatric damage was recoverable, even if such damage was itself unforeseeable. Different control mechanisms still apply to secondary victims, *i.e.* those who suffer psychiatric injury but are outside the foreseeable range of physical injury. In such cases, the requirement of witnessing a traumatic or "shocking" event, of close ties of affection with the primary victim and of foreseeability of psychiatric injury remain.[33] In other personal injury cases it is likely that the *Page v. Smith* approach will be applied.[34] Foresight of the "kind of accident" rather than the "kind of injury" will remain as the main control mechanism in all physical harm cases.

Extent of Damage

2–09   Failing to foresee the extent of damage is immaterial. If it was foreseeable that a worker would be burnt by a splash of molten metal, then he can recover for the unforeseeable cancer which ensues.[35] A tortfeasor will be liable in respect of the unforeseeable predispositions and latent

---

[31] [1996] A.C. 155.
[32] *ibid.* at 190 D–E.
[33] *Frost v. Chief Constable of South Yorkshire Police* [1998] 3 W.L.R. 1509.
[34] Thus *Tremain v. Pike* [1969] 3 All E.R. 1303, in which it was held that a disease transmitted by rat urine was a different type of injury to rat bites or injury from contaminated food, would probably now be decided differently.
[35] *Smith v. Leech Brain & Co. Ltd* [1962] 2 Q.B. 405.

conditions, once he foresees some physical injury, because he must take his victim as he finds him (the "egg shell skull" principle).

Breach of Duty

Though foreseeability may be sufficient to impose a duty of care, other 2–10 factors come into play in considering whether there has been a breach of duty. Notwithstanding that a real risk is foreseen, it is not negligent to fail to eliminate it if in all the circumstances a reasonable man would think it right to neglect to do so.[36] This involves a weighing of the magnitude of the risk and potential harm against the difficulty of eliminating it and the benefit of the activity.

Causation and Damage

Since the decision of the Privy Council in *The Wagon Mound No. 1*[37] 2–11 reasonably foreseeability has been the touchstone for determining causation and remoteness of damage. The statement that "the essential factor in determining liability is whether the damage is of such a kind as the reasonable man should have foreseen"[38] applies just as much at this stage of the analysis as at the duty stage. The components which constitute a duty of care, namely foreseeability of a "kind of damage" and a "class of claimant", are mirrored in the elements of causation and remoteness of damage.

The rationale underlying this congruence of test appears to be the acceptance of the principle that the extent of a tortfeasor's liability should reflect his blameworthiness. If the defendant's carelessness consisted of failing to prevent one kind of damage, he should not be held liable if the claimant suffers a different kind of damage. The concept that breach and damage should specifically coincide has sometimes been called the privity of fault doctrine but is better known as the "risk principle".[39] Put shortly, the principle is that if the damage suffered was not within the risk generated by the breach of duty it should not be recoverable.[40]

The principle is justified not by a logical necessity that the test for duty must match the test for damage, but by "current ideas of justice or morality": see *The Wagon Mound No. 1*.[41] The tort of negligence exists to penalise those who failed to act as they should have done. If damage of a

---

[36] *The Wagon Mound No. 2, op. cit. per* Lord Reid 643.
[37] *op. cit.* at 426.
[38] *ibid.*
[39] Glanville Williams provided the classic exposition of this concept in his article, "*The Risk Principle*," 77 L.Q.R. 179.
[40] In *Roe v. Minister of Health* [1954] 2 Q.B. 66, 85, Denning L.J. said, "the extent of his liability is to be found by asking the one question: is the consequence fairly to be regarded as within the risk created by the negligence?"
[41] *op. cit.* at 422 *per* Viscount Simonds.

particular kind could not have been foreseen, it is unreal to expect the defendant to have taken preventative measures to avoid it.

Although the application of the foreseeability test to both duty and causation may appear to favour defendants, its effect depends crucially upon how broadly or narrowly the categories of "kind of accident" are defined. Furthermore, harshness to the claimant is counterbalanced by the "take your victim as you find him" principle. For instance, the risk of a person scratching their finger merits minor preventative measures. The risk of paralysis merits extensive preventative measures. But if a person suffers a rare reaction to a scratch which results in paralysis, the defendant is liable for the full extent of the injury. Under the risk principle the defendant ought to be penalised for the minor injuries which were foreseeable (*i.e.* a scratch) as a result of failing to take minor preventative measures. Instead he is penalised for failing to take the extensive measures when there was no real risk to justify them. This inconsistency illustrates the underlying tension between the conflicting objectives of tort law, on the one hand to compensate the victim for the injury suffered, and on the other to penalise the defendant only to the extent that he has been at fault.

Just as foreseeability is constrained by other criterions (*e.g.* proximity) when the question is whether a duty of care exists and whether a breach of that duty has occurred, so it is with causation. Take the case of fresh intervening acts. Of course, if these were not reasonably foreseeable, causation by the original negligent act is unlikely to be established. However, even where a fresh intervening act is a foreseeable consequence of the original negligent act, it may nonetheless prevent recovery. Thus, it is foreseeable that negligently parking a car on a dual carriageway will lead to a collision, but where that collision is due to the reckless driving of a lorry colliding into the defendant's parked car there is no causation attributable to the defendant.[42] Similarly, the claimant's act may be reasonably foreseeable, but if it is so unreasonable as to eclipse the wrongdoing of the defendant, no liability will attach.[43] The rationale is that causation is a function of blameworthiness as well as simple causative potency.[44]

Conclusion

One is driven to the conclusion that although reasonable foreseeability is a necessary condition of recovery of damages, it is not a sufficient condition. Though it is, doubtless, a subtle instrument, the law requires other tools to achieve "justice or morality" in the face of the countless variants of fact that the cases reveal. "Although the foreseeability test is a handmaiden of the law, it is by no means a maid-of-all-work.[45]

---

[42] See *Wright v. Lodge* [1993] 4 All E.R. 299.
[43] See *Mckew v. Holland & Hannen & Cubitts* [1969] 3 All E.R. 1621, 1623 G.
[44] These are the two values employed by the Courts in assessing contributory negligence see: *Stapley v. Gypsum Mines Ltd* [1953] A.C. 663.
[45] *per* Salmon L.J. in *Quinn v. Burch Bros (Builders Ltd)* [1966] 2 Q.B. 370, 394.

3. Causation

Principles

(a) The claimant must prove on the balance of probabilities that the   **3–01** relevant negligent act or omission caused the damage for which damages are claimed.

(b) The claimant should succeed if he shows that the defendant's negligence or breach of statutory duty materially increased the risk of injury.

(c) If there are two concurrent tortious acts by different tortfeasors, then both tortfeasors will be held fully liable for the loss if both made a material contribution to the injury.

(d) An intervening act by someone other than the defendant may break the chain of causation.

Proof

The claimant has to prove that a particular breach of duty is, on the   **3–02** balance of probabilities, as a matter of law a cause of the relevant damage. Therefore, if the damage would have occurred in any event, even if there was no breach of duty, the claimant cannot recover: see *Barnett v. Chelsea & Kensington Hospital*.[1]

But, subject to questions of remoteness, causation is a matter of fact. It is not usually sufficient to show that a breach of duty was followed by an injury or illness. There has to be clear evidence of *how* the breach caused the injury or illness: see *Reay v. British Nuclear Fuels plc*.[2]

Proof can be established if the claimant adduces strong evidence that the breach of duty materially increased the risk of a particular disease or condition occurring and the claimant then developed that particular disease or condition: see *McGhee v. NCB*.[3]

However, it was held in *Wilsher v. Essex Area Health Authority*,[4] that *McGhee* laid down no new principle of law and the burden of proving causation remained on the claimant. The House of Lords in *Wilsher* did not overrule *McGhee* but held that in that case the Court was entitled to draw

---

[1] [1969] 1 Q.B. 428.
[2] [1994] P.I.Q.R. P171.
[3] [1973] 1 W.L.R. 1.
[4] [1988] A.C. 1074.

an inference of fact that the failure to provide adequate washing facilities had materially increased the risk of the claimant contracting dermatitis and was therefore a "cause" of the dermatitis, even if the precise causative connection in medical terms could not be identified.

In *Hotson v. East Berkshire Area Health Authority*,[5] the claimant lost the chance of a better medical outcome from an operation due to the defendant's negligence. The House of Lords found against the claimant but refused to rule out altogether for the future a claim for the loss of a chance of a better result from a medical procedure. The House nevertheless doubted whether causation could ever be established in such a situation. Their Lordships held that the principle to be applied in deciding causation in relation to liability was not the same as that applied in assessing damages, as in the assessment of the lost prospects of success in a legal action where a solicitor has been negligent: see *Kitchen v. RAF Association*.[6] In practice, unless the claimant can establish that it is more likely than not that the more favourable outcome would have been achieved had the defendant not been negligent, the chances of success are likely to be very low.

Proof of Causation

3–03   In *Allied Maples Group v. Simmons & Simmons* [1995] 1 W.L.R. 1602, the Court of Appeal set out various tests as to what is necessary to establish causation in different circumstances as follows:

(1) What has to be proved to establish a causal link between the negligence of the defendants and the loss sustained by a claimant depends in the first instance on whether the negligence consists of some positive act or misfeasance or an omission or non-feasance. In the former case, the question of causation is one of historical fact. The Court has to determine on the balance of probability whether the defendant's act, for example the careless driving, caused the claimant's loss consisting of his broken leg. Once established on a balance of probability, the fact is taken as true and the claimant recovers his damages in full. There is no discount because the judge considers that the balance is only just tipped in favour of the claimant and the claimant gets nothing if he fails to establish that it is more likely than not that the accident resulted in the injury. The Court of Appeal drew a distinction between that historical situation and issues where the quantification of the claimant's loss depends upon future uncertain events such as whether, but for the accident,

---

[5] [1987] A.C. 750.
[6] [1958] 1 W.L.R. 563.

a claimant might have been promoted where the court will assess, often in percentage terms, the prospect of promotion and award damages accordingly;

(2) If the defendant's negligence consists of an omission, for example to provide proper equipment or give proper instructions or advice, causation depends, not upon a question of historical fact, but on the answer to the hypothetical question, what would the claimant have done if the equipment had been provided or the instruction or advice given? This can only be a matter of inference to be determined from all the circumstances. The claimant's own evidence that he would have acted to obtain the benefit or avoid the risk, while important, may not be believed by the judge especially if there is compelling evidence that he would not do so in the ordinary way. But, where the action required of the claimant is clearly for his benefit, the court will have little difficulty in concluding that he would have taken it. However, in many cases the risk is not obvious and the precaution may be tedious or uncomfortable, for example the need to use ear-defenders in noisy surroundings or breathing apparatus in dusty ones. It is unfortunately not unknown for workmen persistently not to wear such equipment, even if it is available and known to be so. A striking example of this is *McWilliams v. Sir William Arrol & Co. Ltd* [1962] 1 W.L.R. 295. The employers there failed in breach of their statutory duty to provide a safety belt for the deceased steel erector. But the widow failed in her claim under the Factories Act 1937 because there was compelling evidence that, even if it had been provided, the deceased would not have worn it.

The Court of Appeal stated that although the question is a hypothetical one, it is well established that the claimant must prove on the balance of probability that he would have taken action to obtain the benefit or avoid the risk. But again, if he does establish that, there is no discount because the balance is only just tipped in his favour.

(3) The third situation would be where the claimant's loss depends on the hypothetical action of a third party, either in addition to action by the claimant or independently of it. In such a case, the claimant can succeed provided he shows that he had a substantial chance that the third party would have acted so as to confer the benefit or avoid the risk to the claimant with the evaluation of the substantial chance being a question of quantification of damages. The Court of Appeal rejected the appellant's submission in that case that the claimant could only succeed if in fact the chance of success would be rated at over 50 per cent. The Court of Appeal referred to the case of *Davies v. Taylor* [1974] A.C. 207. In that case, the claimant sued under the

Fatal Accidents Acts in respect of her husband's death. Shortly before his death, she deserted her husband and he learnt of her adultery. He had tried to persuade her to return to him but when she refused he instructed solicitors to institute divorce proceedings. The trial judge rejected the claimant's claim on the grounds that she had failed to discharge the onus of proof which was upon her of showing on a balance of probability that she had an expectation of dependency. The House of Lords held that the judge had applied the wrong test, but nevertheless upheld the decision on the ground that the claimant had only a speculative and not a substantial prospect of continuing dependency. In that case, the question whether or not the claimant had such a prospect depended not only on the conduct of the claimant but also that of the deceased. Lord Reid said at page 213:

> "That here we are not and could not be seeking a decision either that the wife would or that she would not have returned to her husband. You can prove that a past event happened but you cannot prove that a future event will happen and I do not think that the law is so foolish as to suppose that you can. All that you can do is to evaluate the chance. Sometimes it is virtually 100 per cent; sometimes virtually nil. But often it is somewhere in between. And if it is somewhere in between I do not see much difference between a probability of 5 per cent and a probability of 49 per cent.

Lord Reid went on to reject the balance of probability as being the test in that situation. In the *Allied Maples Group* case, the Court of Appeal said that that decision means that the claimant must prove as a matter of causation that he has a real or substantial chance as opposed to a speculative one. If he succeeds in doing so, the evaluation of the chance is part of the assessment of the quantum of damages, the range lying somewhere between something that just qualifies as real or substantial on the one hand and near certainty on the other. However, the Court of Appeal refused to lay down in percentage terms what the lower and upper ends of the bracket should be. A slightly different situation may arise in a case where the allegation is one of negligence by a professional person. In the case of *Bolitho v. City & Hackney Health Authority* [1997] 3 W.L.R. 1151, the House of Lords held that, although in the generality of cases the *Bolam* test had no application in deciding questions of causation, where the breach of duty consisted of an omission to do an act which ought to have been done, the question of what would have constituted a continuing exercise of proper care had the initial failure not taken place so as to determine if the injuries would have been avoided, fell to be decided by reference to that test, that in applying the test the court had to be satisfied that the exponents of a body of professional opinion relied upon had demonstrated that such opinion had a logical basis and in particular had directed their mind where appropriate to the question of comparative risks and benefits and had reached a defensible conclusion and that if, in a rare case, it had been demonstrated that the professional opinion was incapable of withstanding logical analysis, the judge was entitled to hold that it could not provide the benchmark by reference to which the doctor's conduct fell to be assessed. However, the court considered that in most cases the fact that distinguished experts in the field were of a particular opinion would be demonstration of the reasonableness of that opinion. In any situation where the issue, therefore, is whether a professional was guilty of negligence because of a failure to act, the first question that a judge should ask is what would have happened as a matter of probability if the relevant professional had not been negligent and if the omission had not occurred and in answering that question, the *Bolam* test has no part to play. But if the answer to the first question is that the relevant professional, even if the omission had not occurred, would still not have taken the action which the claimant claims should have been taken, this does not determine the issue of causation and the judge has to go on to answer the second question, namely does the professional standard of care require the relevant professional to have taken the action that would have prevented the damage occurring. The House of Lords agreed with the analysis of Hobhouse L.J. in *Joyce v. Merton, Sutton & Wandsworth Health Authority* [1996] 7 Med. L.R. 1 where he said at page 20:

"Thus a claimant can discharge the burden of proof on causation by satisfying the Court either that the relevant person would in fact have taken the requisite action (although she would not have been at fault if she had not) or that the proper discharge of the relevant person's duty towards the claimant required that she take that action.

The former alternative calls for no explanation since it is simply the factual proof of the causative effect of the original fault. The latter is slightly more sophisticated: it involves the factual situation that the original fault did not itself cause the injury but that this was because there would have been some further fault on the part of the defendants; the claimant proves his case by proving that his injuries would have been avoided if proper care had continued to be taken."

Concurrent Causes

3–04   The claimant does not need to show that the relevant breach of duty was the sole cause of his injury or illness. It is sufficient if he can show that the breach of duty made a material contribution to the relevant illness or injury: see *Bonnington Castings v. Wardlaw*[7] and *McGhee v. NCB.*[8]

Thus, a claimant may succeed against a number of successive employers who have each exposed him to a dangerous substance if he can show that each exposure is likely to have materially contributed to the development of the relevant illness or disease.

If the acts of two defendants may have caused the damage but the Court is not sure which one was actually responsible, the Court may infer that both are liable: see *Cook v. Lewis*[9]; *Baker v. Market Harborough Industrial Cooperative Society Limited.*[10] But there must be evidence from which the court can infer such liability.

Break in the Chain of Causation

3–05   An intervening, negligent or intentional act by a person other than the defendant may break the chain of causation if it is the real, substantial, direct or effective cause of the damage: see Lord Asquith in *Stapley v. Gypsum Mines.*[11]

The original cause will then be relegated to the background of the causation of injury. If the claimant develops a disease subsequent to the injury which is unrelated to the accident and which, of itself, would have rendered him unfit for work then he cannot recover for loss of earnings: see *Jobling v. Associated Dairies*[12] where subsequent damage was caused by a supervening tort but it was held that this did not reduce the defendant's liability for the original loss.

But if the intervening event is reasonably foreseeable as a result of the defendant's negligence, then this will not break the chain of causation, such as when a rescuer is injured: see *Haynes v. Harwood*[13] where a rescuer intervened to stop a runaway horse and was injured.

Proof of Negligence

3–06   If the facts adduced by the claimant are such that they make it more probable than not that there was negligence on the part of the defendant, then the Judge may infer negligence in the absence of some explanation

---

[7] [1956] A.C. 613.
[8] [1973] 1 W.L.R. 1.
[9] [1952] 1 D.L.R. 1.
[10] [1953] 1 W.L.R. 472.
[11] [1953] A.C. 663 at 687.
[12] [1982] A.C. 794; *cf. Baker v. Willoughby* [1970] A.C. 467.
[13] [1935] 1 K.B. 146.

from the defendant which explains how those facts could occur without there being negligence on his part. The occurrence in question must be one which would not have happened in the ordinary course of things without there being negligence on the part of someone other than the claimant and the facts must be such that they point to the defendant's negligence and not the negligence of another party. The maxim *res ipsa loquitur* is often used but this is no more than a rule of evidence affecting the onus of proof based on common sense: see *Barkway v. South Wales Transport Company Limited*[14]; *Russell v. L&SW Railway*.[15] For example, where something which was under the management of the defendant or his servants or agents fell onto the claimant, this was held to be reasonable evidence, in the absence of an explanation by the defendant, that the accident arose from want of care: see *Scott v. London & St Katherine Docks Company*[16]; *Ward v. Tesco Stores*.[17]

The defendant can rebut the inference of negligence by proving that he was not negligent, even if he cannot prove precisely what the cause of the accident was.

If the accident occurs because of some latent defect in equipment, then the defendant must show that he has taken all reasonable care in these circumstances: see *Henderson v. Henry E. Jenkins & Sons*.[18]

---

[14] [1950] 1 A.E.R. 392.
[15] [1908] 24 T.L.R. 548.
[16] [1865] 3 H&C 576.
[17] [1976] 1 W.L.R. 810.
[18] [1970] A.C. 282.

4. Contributory Negligence

The Statutory Provision

The Law Reform (Contributory Negligence) Act 1945, ("the Act") **4–01** provides:

> "S.1(1) Where any person suffers damage as the result partly of his own fault and partly of the fault of any other person or persons, a claim in respect of that damage shall not be defeated by reason of the fault of the person suffering the damage, but the damages recoverable in respect thereof shall be reduced to such extent as the court thinks just and equitable having regard to the claimant's share in the responsibility for the damage . . ."
>
> "Section 4 . . . fault means negligence, breach of statutory duty or other act or omission which gives rise to liability in tort or would, apart from this Act, give rise to the defence of contributory negligence".

The Background to the Statute

Prior to 1945, contributory negligence, if proved, provided a complete **4–02** defence to a claim. There was no general power in a court to divide responsibility. If a claimant had the "last opportunity" to avoid the consequences of the fault of another and by blameworthy act or omission failed to take that opportunity, he could not recover anything.[1]

The effect of the Act was to remove an obstacle in the way of a claimant: the Act did not create any right of action.[2] Section 4 of the 1945 Act provides that the act or omission constituting contributory negligence must be such fault on behalf of a claimant as would have given rise to a defence of contributory negligence before 1945. In practice, pre-1945 cases rarely have relevance to modern cases on contributory negligence.

The Nature of the Claimant's Failure

If a tortfeasor (T) alleges contributory negligence against a claimant (C), **4–03** he (T) does not have to show that C owed him (T) a duty of care. C's fault for purposes of contributory negligence amounts to his failure to look after his own interests.

---

[1] *Davies v. Mann* (1842) 10 M&W 546.
[2] *Drinkwater v. Kimber* [1952] 2 Q.B. 281 at 288.

The defence of contributory negligence is only available when the claimant's own negligence contributes to the damage of which he complains. Therefore, in those cases where the claimant would have sustained the same injury even if he had taken all reasonable care for his own safety (such as by wearing a seat belt) his damages will not be reduced.[3]

However, the defence applies both to those situations where the claimant's own fault contributes to the *extent* of his injuries (such as by not wearing a seat belt) and also where his own fault contributes to the *occurrence of the incident* which itself inflicts the injuries[4] (such as failing to heed a warning instruction). If a court makes such a finding of causative fault on the part of the claimant it will then make a finding of contributory negligence, but only to the extent that is "just and equitable" to do so.

In assessing the appropriate degree of fault on a claimant two considerations are of paramount importance, namely blameworthiness and causative potency. Making such assessments will depend on the facts of each case and will often involve a comparison with the act or omission of the alleged tortfeasor.[5]

The Availability of the Defence

4–04   Contributory negligence is only a defence to a claim which falls within the definition of fault, as set out in section 4 of the 1945 Act. Essentially, it is only available as a defence to tortious claims. However, if a claimant makes a claim in contract and alleges only duties which are the same as would arise in tort, *e.g.* an implied duty to take reasonable care, contributory negligence will be an available defence.[6] However, if the relevant breach of contract relates only to a strict contractual duty, the 1945 Act will be inapplicable. The Law Commission has recommended that the defence should be more widely available in claims for breach of contract.[7]

A claimant's damages may also be reduced if he is vicariously responsible for the failure of another person, *e.g.* a servant, to look after his (the claimant's) interests.

Similarly, statute may provide that damages may be reduced even if the claimant is not personally at fault. Examples are claims by dependants of a deceased person[8] or claims arising from pre-natal injury to babies[9] where damages may be reduced by reason of the fault of the deceased or the mother, respectively.

---

[3] *Froom v. Butcher* [1976] Q.B. 286; *Capps v. Miller* [1989] 2 All E.R. 333, CA.
[4] *Craze v. Meyer-Dunmore Battlers' Equipment Co.* [1936] 2 All E.R. 1150 at 1151.
[5] *Davies v. Swan Motor Co. Ltd* [1949] 2 K.B. 291.
[6] *Barclays Bank Ltd v. Fairclough Building Ltd* [1995] Q.B. 214: see also 76 B.L.R. 1; *Forskringaktieselskapet Vesta v. Bukher* [1989] A.C. 852.
[7] Law Commission Report No. 215.
[8] Fatal Accidents Act 1976, s.5.
[9] Congenital Disabilities (Civil Liability) Act 1976, s.1(2).

Where there are Multiple Defendants

If a claimant sues more than one tortfeasor, the issue of contributory 4–05
negligence requires the court to contrast the claimant's conduct with the
totality of the tortious conduct of all the tortfeasors, rather than with each
tortfeasor's fault to the extent that it contributed to the damage.[10] Section
1 also suggests that for the totality of multiple tortfeasors' tortious conduct
to be considered, they do not all have to be joined in the action by the
claimant. The relevant facts, however, have to be pleaded and proved. It
would be open to any tortfeasor joined in the action to issue Part 20
proceedings against other tortfeasors who were not already joined. Such a
tortfeasor would have a longer period of limitation in which to sue those
other tortfeasors than the claimant would have.[11]

The above consideration may be important particularly in relation to the
court's consideration of blameworthiness and causative potency. For a
claimant it may be important that seriously blameworthy conduct by a
particular tortfeasor is considered even if the particular tortfeasor is not
worth suing.

The Requirements of Pleading and Proof

If contributory negligence is to be asserted, the party alleging it should 4–06
always have in mind the following:

- the burden of specifically pleading it;
- the legal burden of proof; and
- the evidential burden of proof.

No matter how strong the allegation of contributory negligence, the
court cannot act upon any such allegation unless it is pleaded.[12]

Once contributory negligence is pleaded the legal burden of proof at trial
rests upon the person alleging it. It is up to that party to establish it by
direct evidence or inference from the facts of the case. This is so in relation
to both (a) fault and (b) the causative effect of that fault.[13]

However, the evidential burden of proof is often a very important
feature. Whilst a claimant against whom contributory negligence is alleged
does not have to prove a negative in order to rebut an allegation of
contributory negligence, a party alleging contributory negligence may (and

---

[10] *Fitzgerald v. Lane* [1989] A.C. 328, HL.
[11] Limitation Act 1980, s.10.
[12] *Fookes v. Slaytor* [1978] 1 W.L.R. 1292.
[13] *Flower v. Ebbw Vale Steel* [1936] A.C. 206 at 221; *Lewis v. Denye* [1939] 1 K.B. 540 at
554; *Heranger (Owners) v. SS Diamond (Owners)* [1939] A.C. 94.

frequently does) prove the same in cross-examination of the claimant or the claimant's witness.[14]

The Standard of Care

4–07   The standard of care in contributory negligence is judged by what is reasonable in the circumstances.[15] Contributory negligence does require foreseeability of harm to oneself from a particular type of behaviour and such a finding will be made whenever a claimant ought reasonably to have foreseen that if he did not act prudently he might suffer injury.[16]

The test of what amounts to reasonable care and whether or not it was exercised must be approached broadly.[17] The concept of reasonable care is objective and the claimant must take such care as is necessary to avoid those accidents which fall into the general class, as opposed to simply that particular accident.[18] It follows that, except in relation to the failure of a person with special training or skill, the evidence of an expert is unlikely to assist the court.

A reasonable claimant must also be prepared for the fact that others may not exercise reasonable skill and care in their conduct. In *Grant v. Sun Shipping Company*,[19] Lord Du Parcq stated: "A prudent man will guard against the possible negligence of others, when experience shows such negligence to be common."

However, as can be seen from the following examples, it is necessary for the claimant's conduct to be judged in the context of his work or the circumstances of the incident:

(a) Where a claimant has been thrown off his guard by the conduct of the defendant and reasonably induced into believing that he may work in safety, less care will be expected of him.[20]

(b) Where a claimant had no choice but to work in a particular manner and was not free to avoid danger, the court will be reluctant to make a finding of contributory negligence.[21]

(c) The courts have emphasised that not all errors will amount to contributory negligence. Therefore, a momentary lapse of concentration, such as would affect a prudent employee whilst at work,

---

[14] *Kerry v. Keighley Electrical Eng. Co.* [1940] 3 All E.R. 399 at 402.
[15] *AC Billings & Son v. Riden* [1958] A.C. 240; *Harrison v. MOD* [1993] C.L.Y. 3929.
[16] *Jones v. Livox Quarries* [1952] 2 Q.B. 608.
[17] *ibid.*
[18] *Samways v. Westgate Engineers* (1982) 106 S.J. 937.
[19] [1948] A.C. 549 at 567.
[20] *Glasscock v. London Tilbury & Southend Ry.* [1902] 18 T.L.R. 295.
[21] *Green v. Chelsea BC* [1954] 2 Q.B. 127; *AC Billings v. Riden* [1957] A.C. 240.

will rarely be regarded as contributory negligence.[22] Likewise, where a claimant carried out work in the manner which the defendant expected of him, there is unlikely to be a finding of contributory negligence even where there has been a lack of care for his own safety.[23]

(d) In those cases where the applicable regulations or other provisions were introduced with the specific purpose of preventing those accidents which occur by reason of an employee's inadvertence, the courts are reluctant to make findings of contributory negligence.[24]

(e) Where a claimant acts in contravention of the applicable regulations or health and safety guidance, but does so on the instruction of his supervisor or manager there is unlikely to be a finding of contributory negligence.[25] However, if the claimant was doing an act against the defendant's advice or in contravention of accepted practice, a high degree of contributory negligence will usually be found.[26]

The Objective Test—its Application Generally

The test as to whether or not a person is in breach of his duty to another   4–08
is objective; likewise the test for purposes of contributory negligence is objective.

Where the claimant has a physical or mental disability the test of "reasonable care for one's own safety" must be assessed by reference to the claimant's particular circumstances, infirmities, knowledge and capacity for understanding risk, etc.[27] The degree of care expected by a court from a person who has a serious injury or mobility difficulties will be different to the degree of care expected from an able-bodied person. Thus, the courts have held that a blind person is only required to take such care for his own safety as his infirmities enable him to do so.[28]

Likewise, in some cases a court will conclude that the claimant has a mental or intellectual disability which is so serious that the degree of care expected of him will only be that of which he is capable given his disadvantage. Whether a claimant is so disabled will be a matter for the circumstances of each case.[29]

---

[22] *Donovan v. Cammell Laird* [1949] 2 All E.R. 82; *Hopwood v. Rolls Royce* [1947] 176 LT 514.
[23] *General Cleaning Contractors v. Christmas* [1953] 2 All E.R. 1110.
[24] *Johns v. Martin Simms* [1983] 1 All E.R. 127 at 130; *Mullard v. Ben Line Steamers Limited* [1970] 1 W.L.R. 1414.
[25] *Laszczyk v. NCB* [1954] 1 W.L.R. 1426.
[26] *McMullen v. NCB* [1982] I.C.R. 148.
[27] *Paris v. Stepney BC* [1951] A.C. 367.
[28] *Haley v. London Electricity Board* [1965] A.C. 778 at 806, 809.
[29] See *Charlesworth & Percy on Negligence* (9th ed., 1997), para. 3–47.

However, for those persons who would not be classified as mentally or physically disabled by a court the "normal" objective test applies, irrespective of their varying degrees of intelligence dexterity.[30]

The Objective Test—its Application to Children

4–09   A finding of contributory negligence can be made by a court against a child claimant. As a matter of law there is no age below which a child is immune from a finding of contributory negligence. Instead, the courts have adopted a variation of the objective test. It is important to remember that behaviour which would amount to contributory negligence for an adult will not necessarily be so for a child. Instead, a court will ask whether the child claimant took reasonable care for his own safety by reference to the degree of care which may reasonably be expected of a child of that age.[31]

Whilst the age of a child will be an important factor in deciding the issue of contributory negligence it is not the only factor to be considered. Other factors include:

(a) the particular danger to which the child was exposed and the capacity of the child to appreciate the risk;

(b) the child's knowledge of the perils to which the defendant's negligence has exposed him;

(c) the child's intellectual level; and

(d) all the circumstances of the case.[32]

A child, however, may have special knowledge and this may be relevant to the issue of contributory negligence. In one case,[33] the knowledge of a nine-year-old child of the explosive qualities of petrol could (if proved) have given rise to a finding of contributory negligence. Likewise, where the child has been a victim in a road traffic accident and claims damages, inquiries will often be made by the defendant as to what road safety training the child had received. The law does, of course, recognise the propensity of children, even when trained, to have lapses of concentration or moments of impetuousness.[34]

However, it is the actions of the child, and not those of the parents, which will determine whether an allegation of contributory negligence is

---

[30] *Baxter v. Woolcombers* (1963) 107 S.J. 553.
[31] *Gough v. Thorne* [1966] 3 All E.R. 398; *Devine (A Minor) v. Northern Ireland Housing Executive* [1992] N.I. 74.
[32] *Galbraith's Curator ad litem v. Stewart (No. 2)* [1998] S.L.T. 1305; *Gough v. Thorne, op. cit.*; *Hughes v. Lord Advocate* [1963] A.C. 837.
[33] *Yachuk v. Oliver Bais Co.* [1949] A.C. 386.
[34] *ibid.*

established. For instance, in the case of a three-year-old child who was injured in a car accident whilst not wearing a seat belt, the courts have held that the child was too young to be expected to appreciate the risk of injury from such a failure and any negligence on the part of the parents could not be imputed to the child.[35]

A forensic difficulty facing those representing child claimant's injured when young is that any delay in bringing the case to court will inevitably mean that the child's awareness of dangers will have moved on rapidly since the date of the accident. The court, therefore, has to take itself back to imagine the child at the date of the accident and apply the standard expected of a child of that age.[36]

The Objective Test—its Application in Rescue or Emergency Situations

In determining whether a rescuer has taken all reasonable care for his 4–10 own safety, the court will pay particular attention to the risk of danger and the level of urgency which was required. The courts have frequently refused to make a finding of contributory negligence where a rescuer had to act in the "agony of the moment", even when it also accepted that with hindsight the injury sustained could have been avoided if he had acted differently.

The relevant test seems to be that, provided the rescuer acted reasonably in the context of the emergency situation or dilemma, his conduct will not be regarded as amounting to contributory negligence.[37] Such an assessment will depend upon all the circumstances of the case. However, despite the level of urgency and danger, the law still requires a rescuer to have taken care for his own safety.[38]

In the case of ambulance drivers and other persons in emergency services vehicles, the question of contributory negligence will be decided by reference to the nature of their employment and the unusual demands which were placed upon them (such as responding to an emergency call).[39]

The Just and Equitable Test—Blame

As has already been stated, the Act requires the court in cases of 4–11 contributory negligence to reduce an injured person's damages to such degree as is just and equitable. This involves consideration of the relative

---

[35] *Ducharme v. Davis* [1984] 1 W.L.R. 699.
[36] *Gough v. Thorne* [1966] 3 All E.R. 398 at 400.
[37] *Sayers v. Harlow UDC* [1958] 1 W.L.R. 623; *Brandon v. Ostborne, Garrett & Co.* [1924] 1 K.B. 548.
[38] *Langley v. Dray* [1998] P.I.Q.R. P314.
[39] *Griffin v. Mersey Regional Ambulance* [1998] P.I.Q.R. P34.

blameworthiness of the tortfeasor and the injured person, as well as the causative effect (or potency) of their respective failures.

The following are commonly cited examples of contributory negligece.

A finding of contributory negligence will be made in those cases where a claimant sustained injuries in a road traffic accident as a result of accepting a lift from a driver whom he knew to be intoxicated.[40] A finding of contributory negligence will be made even where the claimant's capacity to assess the reasonableness of his conduct has been impaired by his own intoxication, provided that he knew, or ought reasonably to have known, of the driver's intoxicated state.[41]

Likewise, a person who sustained injuries as a result of ignoring warning signs and climbing over a fence into an open-air swimming pool (which was closed to be public) was found contributory negligent.[42]

In a recent case, the House of Lords held that there can be a finding of contributory negligence against a person who commits suicide where the defendant has been negligent. An example of such a case would be suicide by a prison inmate. However, such a finding will only be made in the case of a person who was of sound mind at the time of the suicide and not in the case of a person who was classified by the prison authorities as being a suicide risk.[43]

A claimant who is a passenger in a car is, of course, expected to wear a seat belt. Likewise a motorcyclist is required to wear a crash helmet.[44] However, it is important to note that if the claimant's injuries would have been exactly the same had he been wearing a seat belt (*e.g.* burn injuries from a car crash) or a crash helmet[45] (*e.g.* a broken leg) the allegation of contributory negligence will not be made out.[46] There is, however, confusion at present as to whether those riding pedal cycles should be held contributory negligent for failing to wear a cycle helmet.[47]

Whilst the personal views of a claimant as to the health and safety benefits of taking such care (such as wearing a seat belt) are irrelevant[48] the courts do accept that there are some circumstances in which a claimant will not be expected to take such precautions. For instance, if the claimant suffers from a genuine medical condition which would have been aggravated by him wearing a seat belt or helmet,[49] he will not be expected to do

---

[40] *Owens v. Brimmell* [1971] Q.B. 859; *Donelan v. Donelan* [1993] P.I.Q.R. P205.
[41] *Pitts v. Hunt* [1991] 1 Q.B. 24; *Stilton v. Stilton & MIB* [1993] P.I.Q.R. P135.
[42] *Ratcliff v. G.R. McConell & W. Jons* [1999] P.I.Q.R. P170.
[43] *Reeves v. Commissioner of Police for the Metropolis* [1999] 3 W.L.R. 363, see Lord Jauncey at p. 375.
[44] *Copps v. Miller* [1989] 1 W.L.R. 839 at 848E.
[45] *O'Connell v. Jackson* [1972] 1 Q.B. 270.
[46] *Traynor v. Donovan* [1978] C.L.Y. 2612.
[47] *For a case which suggests that there is no such need, see Williams v. Ashley* (1999) S.J. Vol. 143, 1144.
[48] *Froom v. Butcher, op. cit.*
[49] *McKay v. Borthwick*, 1982 S.L.T. 265.

so and, similarly, members of the Sikh community are not required to wear crash helmets.

In some cases policy considerations will play a significant part in decisions regarding contributory negligence. For instance, where contributory negligence is alleged by an employer who is guilty of a breach of statutory duty, a court is likely to pay particular regard to the underlying purpose of the statutory provision. Often the purpose of such a provision will be to to protect employees against the consequences of their own inattention or excessive haste.[50]

Whilst considering the issue of contributory negligence, it is also important not to forget in some situations the accident and injuries will have been caused solely by the claimant's own acts or omissions. In those cases, the claimant will fail to recover any damages. Usually, in order to persuade a court that it is not liable for the accident, an employer will have to establish that it took all proper precautions, such as training the claimant and the provision of suitable equipment, etc.

A person against whom contributory negligence is alleged may himself have been under a statutory obligation to take some relevant precaution. The existence of such an obligation may be highly relevant to the question of whether a person is to be blamed for the accident and his injuries. The most obvious example of such an obligation is that of wearing a seat belt whilst a passenger in a car.[51]

Likewise in the industrial context, an employee may be under a duty to act or abstain from acting in a particular way. In this context, general obligations imposed by statute or regulations upon unskilled or semi-skilled employees are not usually particularly important. However, specific statutory obligations imposed upon persons of particular skill are important when considering blame.[52]

The Just and Equitable Test—Causation and Causative Potency

In many cases the fact of causation will present no problems for a court, **4–12** such as where a workman puts his hand into part of a moving machine. In such a case the issues will simply be the extent of his blame and the level of contributory negligence.

Outside the straightforward cases, the question of proof of causation must be addressed.[53] Seat belt cases again present a good example of the

---

[50] *Staveley Iron Co. Ltd v. Jones* [1956] A.C. 627 at 648.
[51] *Froom v. Butcher* [1976] 1 Q.B. 286 (which was decided before the need to wear seat belts was made compulsory by Parliament).
[52] *ICI Ltd v. Shatwell* [1965] A.C. 656 (shotfirer).
[53] *Owens v. Brimmell* [1977] Q.B. 859.

various issues to consider. It would be easy to assume that a person who is known not to have worn a seat-belt and who has suffered serious injury in a motor accident should, therefore, accept a deduction for contributory negligence. However, a checklist of factors reveals that such an assumption should not be made. These factors would include:

- what bodily movement does a seat belt normally restrain?
- what were the claimant's precise bodily injuries and would they have been prevented or reduced in extent if he had worn a seat belt?
- what were the movements of the vehicle in the accident?
- what were the claimant's movements likely to have been in relation to the vehicle's structure?
- was the passenger space reduced by any distortion of the vehicle body (which would have caused personal injury of a type that the seat belt, if worn, could not have prevented)?

These factors, essentially, relate to whether there was a link (and if so, to what extent) between the claimant's behaviour which is alleged to constitute contributory negligence and his injury.

Whilst there is no logical or scientific test which can be applied to the issue of causation it is clear that:

(a) the principles applicable to determine whether the claimant's own fault contributed to his injury are the same as those principles governing whether the defendant caused those injuries[54];

(b) it matters not whether the operative fault of the claimant occurred prior, or subsequent, to the wrongdoing of the defendant[55];

(c) common-sense principles should he used to judge cause and effect, on the facts of each case[56]; and

(d) causes which are too remote must be discarded.[57]

The Just and Equitable Test—the Decision

4–13   The decision as to the just and equitable apportionment of fault is not a process of precise arithmetic, nor that of simply adding together percentages. It requires a broad and common sense approach.[58]

---

[54] *Jones v. Livox Quarries, op. cit.*
[55] *The Volute* [1922] 1 A.C. 129.
[56] *Stapley v. Gypsum Mines* [1953] A.C. 663; *Marvin Sigurdson v. British Columbia Electric Rly Company* [1953] A.C. 291 at 299.
[57] *Stapley v. Gypsum Mines, ibid.* at 681.
[58] *Gregory v. Kelly* [1978] R.T.R. 426 at 431H.

The decision as to apportionment has been described as the exercise of "a discretion".[59] This, however, merely appears to be an indication that a trial judge (having found the relevant facts in relation to blameworthiness and causative potency) is likely to have a range of percentages within which he can properly make his finding. Experience of actual decisions indicates that the trial judge's decision is often based upon a feel for the particular case.

Against this background it is not surprising that, so long as the judge places his decision on fault somewhere within an arguable range, his decision will not be reversed on appeal. In general, if there is evidence capable of supporting the first instance decision, it will be upheld.[60] An appeal court will also take into account that, unlike the trial judge, it did not observe the claimant and the other witnesses give their evidence.

However, in the following instances the appeal court will interfere:

(a) if the first instance decision is "seriously wrong"[61];

(b) if the trial judge failed to consider a material factor or, alternatively, based his conclusion on an irrelevant matter;

(c) if there is a "wide difference of view" between the appeal court and the first instance court[62]; or

(d) if the decision is plainly "wrong in principle".[63]

The 1945 Act and its Application to Different Torts

In actions which are based on breach of statutory duty or nuisance, **4–14** contributory negligence is a defence.[64] It has also been held that contributory negligence can be a defence to a claim of trespass to the person or other torts involving intentional harm to the person.[65]

However, it should not be assumed that contributory negligence is available as a defence to all torts. It is doubtful whether it applies to a claim under *Rylands v. Fletcher*.[66] Although the assimilation of liability under *Rylands v. Fletcher* with nuisance[67] leaves the position here uncertain.

---

[59] *NCB v. England* (1854) A.C. 403 at 420.
[60] *King v. Smith* [1995] P.I.Q.R. P49 at P54.
[61] *Jennings v. Norman Collision (Contractors) Ltd* [1970] 1 All E.R. 1121 at 1127.
[62] *NCB v. England, op. cit.* at 420.
[63] *Liddell v. Middleton* [1996] P.I.Q.R. P36 at P41.
[64] *Caswell v. Powell Duffryn Associated Collieries Limited; Trevett v. Lee* [1955] 1 W.L.R. 113 at 122, respectively.
[65] *Barnes v. Nayer, The Times*, December 19, 1986, CA.
[66] (1868) L.R. 3 H.L. 330.
[67] *Cambridge Water Co. v. Eastern Counties Leather* [1994] 2 A.C. 264.

5. Expert Evidence: the Duties and Liabilities of an Expert

Introduction

Expert evidence is one of the areas of civil litigation most affected by the 5–01
Civil Procedure Rules 1998 (CPR)—indeed, it was one of Lord Woolf's avowed aims in devising a new procedural code that the numbers of experts involved in civil litigation should be reduced to those absolutely necessary to a given case, with a view to reducing both cost and time of litigation. The CPR also aim to ensure that experts have at the forefront of their minds their status as independent, objective voices, whose function is to report to the court and not to associate themselves too closely—at the risk of losing independence or objectivity—with any party to the litigation itself.

The Civil Procedure Rules

The rules relating to experts are set out in Part 35 of the CPR, 5–02
supplemented by a Practice Direction. This Part of the CPR starts with rule 35.1, which requires expert evidence to be restricted to that which is *"reasonably required"* to resolve the proceedings. This signals one of the key aims of the Part, which is to cut down the numbers of experts involved in any particular case. This aim is furthered by rule 35.4 which prevents any party from calling an expert or relying on an expert's report without the court's permission, and rule 35.7 which allows the court to direct that evidence on a particular issue is to be given by one expert only.

The *"single joint expert"* is a true innovation of the CPR. He is not a court-appointed expert, but is instructed by the parties jointly. Plainly, there are cases where the issues requiring expert assistance are narrow, and a single joint expert is appropriate; but there are others where the issues are of a degree of complexity which make it impractical to appoint a single joint expert (contrast three decisions: *Baron v. Lovell*[1] where a judge's direction that medical evidence as to the claimant's personal injuries should be given by the claimant's expert alone was upheld; *S (a minor) v. Birmingham Health Authority*,[2] where a district judge's restriction to a single joint expert was overturned as inappropriate at the early stages of a

---

[1] [2000] P.I.Q.R. P20.
[2] [1999] QBD (Curtis J.) (unreported).

complex clinical negligence case; and *Walker v. Daniels*[2a] where the parties had agreed to instruct a joint care expert in a high value claim, and the defendant then sought permission to adduce its own expert evidence.

Walker v. Daniels provides a template for the correct use of expert evidence in most cases as follows[2b]. The first step is the joint instruction of expert evidence on a particular issue (this may often also be the last step); if a party wishes to obtain further information, for reasons which are not fanciful, subject to the discretion of the court, they should be entitled to obtain that evidence; in modest cases it would be appropriate to put questions to the expert who has prepared a report; in more substantial cases, it would be appropriate to instruct a further report (or reports); lastly, a decision should then be taken, after a meeting of experts has taken place, as to what evidence should be called.

The CPR only extends to an expert *"who has been instructed to give or prepare evidence for the purpose of court proceedings"* (r. 35.2). This exposes what is a critical difference between the expert engaged to *advise* the parties at the early stages of litigation, and the expert engaged to *report* his views to the court. That distinction is recognised in the (at present draft) Code of Guidance of Experts.[3] It is envisaged that the draft Code of Guidance will in due course become a Practice Direction to Part 35.

Unless an expert's report is disclosed, it cannot, without the court's permission, be used at trial, nor can the expert be called (r. 35.3).

The Duties of an Expert

5–03   Only the role of the expert who reports to the court in the course of litigation (and is an *expert witness,* as opposed to the expert who *advises*) is circumscribed by the CPR. There may be some personal injury actions where different experts will fulfil each of the two roles; but the great likelihood in such actions is that the same expert, who joins the team at the pre-litigation stage as an adviser, will subsequently become the reporter and so will have to change his hat to comply with the CPR requirements. Thus, all experts will need to be acutely aware of their obligations as reporting experts even at the earlier stage that they are consulted, because the scope of those obligations will necessarily inform and guide the expert in the stance that he takes even in the pre-litigation advisory stage.

It has always been the position that an expert should be independent and objective. An expert's functions were described by Lord President Cooper in *Davie v. Edinburgh Magistrates*:[4]

[2a] [2000] unreported, Lord Woolf M.R., Latham L.J., CA.
[2b] *See* paras 1.27 to 1.33 of the judgment of Lord Woolf.
[3] Consultation document circulated by a working party, chaired by Sir Louis Blom-Cooper, which reports to the Vice-Chancellor. Published at (1999) 5 Clinical Risk, 168.
[4] 1953 S.C. 34.

"Their duty is to furnish the judge with the necessary scientific criteria for testing the accuracy of their conclusions, so as to enable the judge or jury to form their own independent judgment by the application of these criteria to the facts proved in evidence."

More recently, in the Commercial court, Cresswell J. in *The Ikarian Reefer*[5] provided what remains the authoritative statement on the duties and functions of an expert witness (expressly endorsed by Lord Woolf in his Final Report):[6]

"1. Expert evidence presented to the court should be and should be seen to be the independent product of the expert uninfluenced as to form or content by the exigencies of litigation.
2. An expert witness should provide independent assistance to the court by way of objective unbiased opinion in relation to matters within his expertise. An expert witness in the High Court should never assume the role of advocate.
3. An expert witness should state the facts or assumptions on which his opinion is based. He should not omit to consider material facts which detract from his concluded opinion.
4. An expert witness should make it clear when a particular question or issue falls outside his area of expertise.
5. If an expert opinion is not properly researched because he considers that insufficient data is available, then this must be stated with an indication that the opinion is no more than a provisional one.
6. If, after exchange of reports, an expert witness changes his view on a material matter . . . such change of view should be communicated to the other side without delay and when appropriate to the court.
7. Where expert evidence refers to photographs, plans, calculations . . . or other similar documents, these must be provided to the opposite party at the same time as the exchange of the reports."

Although Cresswell J.'s findings were successfully appealed in the Court of Appeal, Stuart-Smith L.J. spoke of his guidance on expert evidence in the following terms:

". . . the judge gave an admirable résumé of the duties and responsibilities of expert witnesses. We have no hesitation in endorsing it. We should, however, add one word of caution in relation to paragraph 4: that an expert should make it clear when a particular question or issue falls outside his expertise."[7]

In the ill-fated case of *Vernon v. Bosley*,[8] both the judge at first instance **5-04** and the Court of Appeal was highly critical of the expert psychiatric evidence that was given on both sides. The Court of Appeal made the following broad points[9]:

---

[5] [1993] 2 Lloyd's Rep. 68 at 81, and see also Laddie J. in *Cala Homes (South) Ltd v. Alfred McAlpine Homes East Ltd* [1995] F.S.R. 818.
[6] See Access to Justice, Section III, paras 25–29.
[7] [1995] 1 Lloyd's Rep. 455 at 496.
[8] [1994] P.I.Q.R. 337, CA.
[9] (1991) 1 Med. L.R. 214 at 219.

(a) True objectivity is hard to achieve in the field of psychiatry; a court appointed expert would be more helpful, but this is only possible if the parties agree.

(b) Using treating clinicians as experts makes it harder for them to be objective. It also denies the judge access to some documents (*e.g.* the letter of instruction) on the ground of privilege.

(c) Daily attendance at court can jeopardise detachment.

(d) It is likely to be easier for an expert holding current NHS appointments or a chair in medicine to maintain detachment than one whose principal professional activity is medico-legal work.

Notwithstanding such clear guidance from the Court of Appeal on the role of an expert, Lord Woolf recognised that some experts were prone to sacrifice true objectivity in favour of the pursuit of his client's interests, and there were complaints from experts that they were being put under pressure to do precisely that by lawyers and lay clients. The CPR have scotched that approach. The expert owes an overriding duty to the court (r. 35.3). That duty overrides any obligation to the person from whom the expert has received instructions or by whom he is paid (r. 35.3(a)).

The expert's evidence is to be given in a written report which must be addressed to the court, unless the court directs otherwise (r. 35.5 and para. 1.1 of the Practice Direction). His report must contain certain information set out at rule 35.10 read with paragraph 1.2 of the Practice Direction:

"1.2 An expert's report must:

(1) give details of the expert's qualifications,
(2) give details of any literature or other material which the expert has relied on in making the report,
(3) say who carried out any test or experiment which the expert has used for the report and whether or not the test or experiment has been carried out under the expert's supervision,
(4) give the qualifications of the person who carried out any such test or experiment, and
(5) where there is a range of opinion on the matters dealt with in the report—
    (i) summarise the range of opinion, and
    (ii) give reasons for his own opinion,
(6) contain a summary of the conclusions reached,
(7) contain a statement that the expert understands his duty to the court and has complied with that duty (Rule 35.10(2)), and
(8) contain a statement setting out the substance of all material instructions (whether written or oral). The statement should summarise the facts and instructions given to the expert which are material to the opinions expressed in the report or upon which those opinions are based. (r. 35.10(3))."

An expert's report, in common with a witness statement must be verified by a statement of truth which should, in the case of an expert's report, say:

"I believe that the facts I have stated in this report are true and that the opinions I have expressed are correct".

(Practice Direction, paras 1.3 and 1.4)

At the moment, there is no "*approved expert's protocol*" as referred to at   **5–05** paragraph 1.6 of the Practice Direction.[10]

The sanction for failure to comply with these and other requirements imposed by the court on the expert may be severe. In *Stevens v. Gullis and Pile (third party)*,[11] a defendant's expert, whose report did not comply with the CPR and who had failed to comply with various directions made by the court, was debarred from giving evidence with the consequence that judgment was entered for the claimant. The Master of the Rolls in that case commented that the witness had "*demonstrated by his conduct that he had no concept of the requirements placed upon an expert under the CPR*".

The expert instructed as a joint single expert under rules 35.7 and 35.8 is under the same obligations as any other expert. His role in many ways may be harder: to whom should he address questions concerning, for example, the factual basis of his report, or the legal standard to be applied? Presumably as the recipient of joint instructions, such questions should be addressed in the first instance to all the instructing solicitors, using the expert's right to seek guidance from the court (under r. 35.14) if doubt remains.

The norm is now for experts of the same discipline to be invited to discuss their views at an experts meeting, the purpose of which is to:

"(a) identify the issues in the proceedings; and
(b) where possible, reach agreement on an issue"

(r. 35.12(1))

Somewhat paradoxically, rule 35.12(2) goes on to allow the court to "*specify the issues which the experts must discuss*". The current practice is for the court to specify that the experts must, following a discussion, prepare a statement for the court showing those issues on which the experts agree, and those on which they disagree, with a summary of reasons for disagreeing. The meeting itself is "without prejudice". Although an agreement between the experts will not bind a party unless that party has expressly agreed to be bound by the agreement (r. 35.12(5)), it is hard to see how a party's case could not be damaged—probably

---

[10] There is a draft Code of Guidance for Experts prepared by a working party under the chairmanship of Sir Louis Blom-Cooper Q.C. (published at (1999) 5 Clinical Risk 168). That Code of Guidance is expected to become a Practice Direction in its own right, and not merely a protocol.
[11] [1999] B.L.R. 394.

irreparably—by its own expert agreeing an issue in a manner inconsistent with the case subsequently advanced by that party at trial.[12]

An expert may now be questioned by any other party to the litigation (and, if he is a single joint expert, by those instructing him) (r. 35.6). Any failure by the expert to answer those questions may lead to a disallowance of his costs, or worse, to the instructing party not being able to rely on his evidence at trial (r. 35.6(4)) and his answers are treated as part of his report (r. 35.6(3)).

Another clear message conveyed by the CPR is that experts are expected to make themselves available to meet the court's timetable, even if that means changing holiday plans or staggering court appearances in other cases (*Matthews v. Tarmac Bricks and Tiles Limited*.[13] Furthermore, experts are to produce reports within the short time scales imposed by the court: if an expert is too busy to meet a particular date, the court is unlikely to be sympathetic, and the solicitor must consider simply instructing an alternative expert (see *Rollinson v. Kimberley Clark Limited*[14]

The Liabilities of an Expert

5-06   Does the expert witness have immunity from proceedings if his opinion turns out to be wrong? Clearly, as with any professional man, an expert witness owes a duty of care or a contractual duty of a like nature to those who instruct him and also the court.[15] To this extent, negligence in the preparation and production of a report may well be actionable. This is the position of a barrister who had given advice which turned out to be negligent,[16] prior to the lifting of advocates' immunity in *Arthur J.S. Hall and Co. v. Simons*[16a].

This area has most recently and comprehensively been reviewed by the Court of Appeal in *Stanton v. Callaghan*,[17] a case involving alleged negligence against a surveyor in the preparation of a report following an expert's meeting, on the basis of which the claim was subsequently settled. Chadwick L.J. said:

"What, then, is the position in relation to expert reports? It seems to me that the following propositions are supported by authority binding in this court:

---

[12] The Clinical Disputes Forum has, by a working party chaired by Mr Roger Clements, published guidelines on experts' discussions in the context of clinical disputes (*Clinical Disputes Forum Newsletter* Issue no. 1, August 1999). Although geared specifically to clinical negligence cases, the guidelines are relevant to personal injury cases also, with suitable adjustments for straightforward cases.

[13] *The Times*, July 1, 1999.

[14] *The Times*, June 22, 1999.

[15] *Craigola Mertha Co. v. Swansea Corporation* [1928] 1 Ch. 31 at 38.

[16] *Saif Ali v. Sydney Mitchell & Co.* [1980] A.C. 198.

[16a] July 20, 2000, HL.

[17] [1999] 2 W.L.R. 745.

(i) an expert witness who gives evidence at a trial is immune from suit in respect of anything which he says in court, and that immunity will extend to the contents of the report which he adopts as, or incorporates in his evidence;

(ii) where an expert witness gives evidence at a trial the immunity which he would enjoy in respect of that evidence is not to be circumvented by a suit based on the report itself; and

(iii) immunity does not extend to protect an expert who has been retained to advise as to the merits of a party's claim in litigation from a suit by the party by whom he has been retained in respect of that advice, notwithstanding that it was in contemplation at the time when the advice was given that the expert would be a witness at the trial if that litigation were to proceed."

Those propositions were all based on case law reviewed by the court, and set out more fully in the judgment.[18] The new point before the Court of Appeal, on which there was no existing authority, was whether an expert is immune from suit by the party who has retained him in respect of the contents of a report which he has prepared for the purpose of exchange prior to trial, in circumstances where he does not in the event, give evidence at the trial, either because the trial doesn't take place or because he is not called as a witness. On that point, Chadwick L.J. said:

"It is of importance to the administration of justice, and to those members of the public who seek access to justice, that trials should take no longer than is necessary to do justice in the particular case, and that, to that end, time in court should not be taken up with the consideration of matters which are not truly an issue. It is in that context that experts are encouraged to identify, in advance of the trial, those parts of their evidence on which they are, and those on which they are not, in agreement. Provision for a joint statement, reflecting agreement after a meeting of experts has taken place, is made by Ord. 38, rule 38 [now CPR r. 35.12]. In my view, the public interest in facilitating full and frank discussion between experts before trial does require that each should be free to make proper concessions without fear that a departure from advice previously given to the party who has retained him will be seen as evidence of negligence. That, as it seems to me is an area in which public policy justifies immunity. The immunity is needed in order to avoid the tension between a desire to assist the court and fear of the consequences of the departure from previous advice."

There is one word of caution about *Stanton v. Callaghan*, which 5–07 otherwise would appear to draw the parameters of an expert's liability fairly clearly. In that case, the Court of Appeal drew on the position of lawyers (barristers and solicitors) involved in litigation in reaching its conclusions in relation to experts. There is an obvious comparison to be drawn between the ambit of a lawyer's immunity from suit with that of an

---

[18] See *Rondel v. Worsley* [1969] A.C. 191; *Evans v. London Hospital* [1981] 1 W.L.R. 184 at 191; *Marrinan v. Vibart* [1963] 1 Q.B. 234; and *Watson v. McEwan* [1905] A.C. 480. See also *Palmer v. Durnford Ford* [1992] 1 Q.B. 480.

expert. The House of Lords has reviewed the immunity of advocates from suit in *Arthur J.S. Hall and Co. v. Simons*[19]) and concluded that the general principles of tort law and professional negligence should apply in full to advocates. The majority considered that no immunity should apply to advocates conducting criminal proceedings. Lord Hoffmann referred to the decision of the Court of Appeal in *Stanton,* and rejected the analogy of the lawyer who owes a duty of care to the client and the expert witness whose only duty is to tell the truth to the court. His Lordships considered that any justification for the immunity of an expert would be as an example of the traditional witness immunity.[20]

Finally, the validity of any rule of immunity from suit must be considered afresh in light of the European Convention on Human Rights, to be incorporated into domestic law by the Human Rights Act 1998 with effect from October 2nd, 2000. Article 6 provides that:

> "In the determination of his civil rights and obligations . . . everyone is entitled to a fair and public hearing within a reasonable time by an independent and impartial tribunal established by law."

Any rule of immunity from suit for professionals potentially impacts on an individual's right to have his complaint against the professional determined. The European Court of Human Rights has acknowledged that there are valid public policy grounds for excluding access to the courts in certain cases, but has indicated that the domestic courts should be free to evaluate the public policy considerations for and against exclusion in any given case.[21].

The Duties of Those Instructing an Expert

5–08   Issues arise relating to the duties of those who instruct experts. The function of instructing an expert is primarily undertaken by the solicitor, but the final draft of an expert's report is frequently achieved in, or as a result of, a conference or consultation. For reasons perhaps of self-preservation while under cross-examination, the opinions in the final report ought to be the expert's rather than counsel's. This is particularly true in the light of the CPR and their emphasis on the overriding duty being to the court. But although Lord Wilberforce said in *Whitehouse v. Jordan*[22] that:

> "whilst some degree of consultation between experts and legal advisers is entirely proper, it is necessary that expert evidence presented to the court should be and

---

[19] July 20, 2000.
[20] See the 18th heading of his Lordship's speech.
[21] *Osman v. U.K.* [1999] B.H.R.C. 239.
[22] [1981] 1 W.L.R. 241.

should be seen to be the independent product of the expert, uninfluenced as to form or content by the exigencies of litigation;"

—there is little express guidance in the Code of Conduct for the Bar of England and Wales as to the extent to which it is either permissible or desirable for counsel to have had a hand in the drafting of the expert's report. What happens, not infrequently, is that an expert's preliminary view is modified, having heard or seen the client and having discussed the matter in conference. Suggestions may well be made, but the safest course will be to allow the expert to go away and draft his own amendments.

Particular care now needs to be taken by a solicitor or barrister who "suggests" amendments to an expert's report, not only because of the renewed emphasis in the CPR on the expert's role as an independent reporter to the court, but also and more specifically, given the effect of rule 35(10)(b), dealt with below under *Confidentiality and Privilege*.

What of the expert's report which, while on the face of it, is favourable to the defendant's case, is accompanied by a letter to the solicitor which identifies serious weaknesses in the defence or a potentially fruitful line of cross-examination which might cause embarrassment to the expert? In *Kenning v. Eve Construction*,[23] Michael Wright Q.C. (sitting as a Deputy High Court Judge) had to deal with an interlocutory application relating to the accidental disclosure of a covering letter which identified possible (but as yet unpleaded) negligent causes for an accident. He held that he had:

> ". . . come to the conclusion that where . . . the effect of these two documents taken together is that the expert witness is in fact saying effectively: 'On the matters contained in the Statement of Claim it may be that the defendant had a complete answer but there are these other two matters which are not pleaded, but in respect of which I think the defendant is in very grave difficulty', then it seems to me that the solicitor who instructs him only complies with the requirement of Order 25, rule 8(1)(b) [automatic directions under old rules for disclosure of expert evidence] if the whole of the expert's opinion is disclosed because only if the whole of the opinion is disclosed, has the substance of his evidence been communicated to the other parties."

The CPR do not expressly deal with such a situation. In practice, experts continue to submit reports for disclosure under cover of a letter which gives their "real" views on the merits of the case—and that practice is a good one in that it ensures that each party has a proper appreciation of the strength of its case, which will often allow negotiations with a view to settlement to take place. But the spirit of the CPR is plainly that the expert should state in his report any particular feature which he considers to be significant, whether or not that feature arises on the case as it is pleaded or not. The point has yet to be tested before the courts, in light of the new rules.

---

[23] [1989] 1 W.L.R. 1189.

Finally, those instructing an expert are at liberty to put questions to the other side's expert or a single joint expert (r. 35.6). Rule 35.6(2)(c) states that the purpose of such questions must be for the purposes of clarifying the report only, and the costs of asking those questions and having them answered is in the first place borne by the questioning party (para. 4.3 of the Practice Direction). A copy of the questions is to be sent to the other parties to the litigation (para. 4.2 of the Practice Direction).

The Different Types of Experts in Personal Injury Cases

5–09   In personal injury litigation, two different types of expert may need to be commissioned.

Medical Expert Evidence

Since injury and its consequences are part of every action, expert medical evidence will be required to establish the nature of the injury and the prognosis for the future. Paragraph 4.3 of the Practice Direction to Part 16 states:

> "Where the claimant is relying on the evidence of a medical practitioner the claimant must attach to or serve with his particulars of claim a report from the medical practitioner about the personal injuries which he alleges in his claim."

The report must be "about the personal injuries". This is plainly a requirement to provide evidence as to the present condition and prognosis rather than legal causation of the injury. At its simplest, this will involve a description of the original injury or injuries and their natural consequences. However, the requirement to provide medical evidence is not mandatory and there may be cases of trivial injury where no medical evidence is necessary if some other evidence, *e.g.* photographs, exists.

Problems may, and often do, arise where there is a real issue as to whether the injuries complained of at trial are the true consequence of the accident, or are the result of some pre-existing condition, *"functional overlay/psychogenic illness"* or, more rarely, feigned.

The simple injury is easy to deal with; the more complicated requires a higher level of expert assistance. Insurers may have their own *"favourite"* experts, but they are unlikely to be the leaders in the medical field. In the current climate it is important to obtain proper experts from the particular medical specialty concerned. Purely as an example, in a *"whiplash"* case or a lifting injury, the parties will need evidence from a practising orthopaedic or neurosurgeon and a neurologist, not a *"medico-legal specialist"*. It may be necessary to obtain a Magnetic Resonance Imaging (MRI) scan and have a neuro-radiologist to interpret it. At a more basic forensic level, it may be necessary to have a video to compare the symptoms complained of in Harley Street with life in the real world!

In the very complicated case, particularly in the medical negligence field, there is a growing tendency to engage a "lead" expert who is willing to coordinate a team to deal with the different aspects of liability, causation and injury. The advantage of this approach is that the reports produced are likely to "dovetail" rather than conflict with each other and the case will be the more coherent as a consequence.

Non-medical Expert Evidence

It is impossible to predict in general terms the situations which may give **5–10** rise to a need for non-medical expert evidence. Specialists are available in road traffic accident reconstructions, although doubts have been expressed by the courts about their worth. There are also firms or companies which specialise in industrial accidents and building-site injuries. If they have a fault, it is a universal one of failing to distance themselves from their client's case. Their reports almost invariably proceed upon the following basis: "The plaintiff was . . . when the defendant/the unguarded machine cut his arm off/the scaffolding gave way," without allowing for the complete opposite version of the facts being presented by the other side. For an expert's evidence to be credible and helpful to the court, the expert must reflect upon the contentions being advanced by both sides—it may be that the expert will decide that the defendant is still negligent even on its own version of the facts.

Permission is now required to produce any expert's report or to call any expert to give evidence at trial (r. 35.4). Generally, the courts have demonstrated a reluctance to involve experts save where necessary. Accident reconstruction experts, health and safety experts, employment experts, and many other sub-specialisms which had emerged under the old regime may not be accepted nowadays, except where it can be shown that the evidence of such people will be valuable to the judge and the expense of their involvement can be justified. If permission is not given to rely on expert evidence, the cost of any advice or report already obtained from that expert will generally be irrecoverable from the other side, even if the case succeeds. This requires solicitors to think very carefully before instructing experts in anything but the most obvious disciplines; and it can work against the claimant, who may be discouraged from pursuing legitimate lines of enquiry for fear that the costs will not be recoverable, if the line does not in the end prove fruitful.

Confidentiality and Privilege

Confidentiality, or perhaps more accurately privilege, presents a problem **5–11** of considerable practical importance. Until disclosed, one party's expert report is privileged from disclosure to any other party. That does not stop the expert being called as a witness for another party, if he is not being called by the party who commissioned the report; but the original report itself remains privileged from disclosure.

What of the factual statements, letters or documents upon which the expert has relied in reaching his conclusion? It is often the case that an expert engaged by one or other party unwittingly discloses the existence of a statement which he has seen but upon which the commissioning party does not intend to rely.

There is at present conflicting authority on whether that document is privileged or not. *Booth v. Warrington Health Authority*[24] was a medical negligence case in which midwives gave statements which were disclosed to an expert consultant obstetrician who referred to them in his report. The report was disclosed to the other side. Tucker J. held that, in the absence of some unequivocal act of waiver, the incorporation of part of the witnesses' statement into an expert's report was not sufficient to amount to a waiver of privilege. *Booth v. Warrington* was based on a long line of authority and academic comment, which tended to protect one party's right of privilege save in cases where a waiver of privilege had quite clearly taken place.

Clough v. Tameside and Glossop Health Authority[25] was also a medical negligence case. The defendants had disclosed an expert's report which referred to an earlier statement from the doctor involved in the treatment of the claimant in the case. Bracewell J. reviewed the authorities, including *Booth v. Warrington*, and concluded that privilege in the doctor's statement had been waived. She said:

"For my part, I can appreciate a clear distinction between material supplied to an expert by an instructing solicitor as part of the background documentation in the case upon which an expert opinion is sought, and on the other hand, communications between solicitor and expert which fall outside that category. In the first instance, I am persuaded that the privilege is waived."

She went on:

"It is only by proper and full disclosure to all parties, that an expert's opinion can be tested in court, in order to ascertain whether all appropriate information was supplied and how the expert dealt with it. It is not for one party to keep their cards face down on the table so that the other party does not know the full extent of information supplied. Fairness dictates that a party should not be forced to meet a case pleaded or an expert opinion on the basis of documents he cannot see. Although civil litigation is adversarial, it is not permissible to withhold relevant information, or to delete or amend the contents of a report before disclosure, as was submitted by counsel for the defendants to be the practice of some firms of solicitors."

---

[24] [1992] P.I.Q.R. P137.
[25] [1998] 1 W.L.R. 1478.

Bracewell J.'s decision ends with express reference to Lord Woolf's report, Access to Justice. The decision has considerable ramifications, both for the solicitor in determining the documents which should be sent to the expert in the first place, and for the conduct of the litigation generally: where an expert refers, even by passing mention, to a document which has not been disclosed, if Bracewell J. is correct (and it must be likely that her approach would be endorsed by a higher court if it had to determine which of the two authorities on the point was correct), that document becomes discoverable.

This decision has dramatic practical consequences for practitioners, 5–12 particularly when combined with certain provisions of the CPR, most notably the enigmatic rule 35.10, which states as follows:

"(3) The expert's report must state the substance of all material instructions, whether written or oral, on the basis of which the report was written.
(4) Instructions referred to in paragraph (3) shall not be privileged against disclosure but the court will not, in relation to those instructions—
    (a) order disclosure of any specific document; or
    (b) permit any questioning in court, other than by the party who instructed the expert,
unless it is satisfied that there are reasonable grounds to consider the statement of instructions given under paragraph (3) to be inaccurate or incomplete."

As to what are "*material instructions*", paragraph 1.2(8) of the Practice Direction tells us that:

"the statement should summarise the facts and instructions given to the expert which are material to the opinions expressed in the report or upon which those opinions are based."

There are two categories of documents which fall to be considered in light of rule 35.10: first, instructions from solicitors; and second, documents enclosed with those instructions (such as medical reports and witness statements). As to the first type of document, solicitors instructions, the rule applies both to written and oral instructions. The solicitor must, therefore, be careful only to give instructions which can, both in substance and in detail, be disclosed without embarrassment. Does the obligation extend to instructions given at the *advisory* stage? The rule catches all instructions which are "*material*" to the opinion expressed or upon which those opinions are based, which could of course include instructions given at the advisory stage. One pragmatic solution is for a solicitor to provide a comprehensive letter of "*re-instruction*" at the stage when the expert is to prepare a report for disclosure, which letter the expert can then summarise.

The instructions themselves will only become discloseable where the court is satisfied that there are reasonable grounds to consider that the expert's summarising statement is inaccurate or incomplete. Thus, it will only be on rare occasions that the opposing party will seek an order for disclosure of the instructions themselves or the right to cross-examine about them. (Note in passing that the right to cross-examine about instructions is not apparently limited to cross-examination of the expert whose report is in question, but could extend to any other witness as well). But there is a point of real principle at stake here: instructions to an expert are undoubtedly within the head of legal professional privilege as a matter of law, and the CPR is merely a procedural code which does not affect substantive legal rights. At least one High Court judge has refused to allow the CPR to encroach on substantive legal rights, by holding that rule 48.7(3) of the CPR—which purports to permit disclosure of privileged documents in the context of wasted costs orders—was *ultra vires* and unenforceable (Toulson J. in *General Mediterranean Holdings SA v. Patel*).[26]

5–13   The other type of documents affected by rule 35.10 are those documents sent to an expert along with the solicitor's instructions, such as witness statements or reports from other experts. It follows from the terms of rule 35.10(3) that any such documents must be referred to by the expert if they form the basis of the report. The terms of rule 35.10(3) allow for an element of subjective judgment on the part of the expert, in that it is up to the expert to assess which of those documents do, in his view, form the basis of his report. (But note that this subjectivity in selecting what documents are referred to is wholly inconsistent with Bracewell J.'s view as expressed in *Clough v. Tameside and Glossop Health Authority*: it is part of the reasoning for that decision that *all* the background documents seen by the expert should be disclosed, not least so that the opposing party can consider whether the expert has wrongly discounted some evidence which was before him, or has assumed an incorrect significance for a particular piece of material).[27] Assuming, however, that the expert has based his views on certain documents sent to him—whether seen at an advisory or reporting stage—he must refer to them. The other side can then call to see that document relying on *Clough v. Tameside and Glossop Health Authority*.

It is self-evident that this process may well inhibit a party having a full and frank discussion with his or her own expert. For example, it is surely dangerous to show an expert who is likely to report in due course an adverse report from another expert, as this may lead to the discovery of the adverse report in due course; by the same token, if earlier drafts of witness statements are referred to these also may become discoverable. In the end, it may even be that a party simply cannot risk using the same expert who has been involved at the advisory stage, to report to the court for fear that documents which that expert has seen will become discoverable. In such a

---

[26] [2000] 1 W.L.R. 272.
[27] *ibid.* at 1484 G–H.

case (and one can only hope it will be the exceptional case) that party may be obliged to instruct an entirely different expert to report. Such practical complexity and duplication of expense is hardly consistent with the spirit of the new rules and cannot surely have been intended, if indeed it was foreseen, by the Rules Committee. The recent case of *Jenkins v. Grocutt and Hoyte*[28] emphasises the dilemma parties, in particular defendants, have in this respect. In that case Hale J. held that where it is clear than any party has adopted a selective approach to the evidence of the experts consulted, it must be open to the court to take than into account in considering what weight to attach to the opinions of those experts whose evidence is adduced.

---

[28] [2000] P.I.Q.R. Q17.

6. Recovering Damages for Psychiatric Injuries

Introduction

This is a topic within the law of tort in which there has been 6–01 considerable recent development, and therefore inevitably debate and controversy. Medicine and the law are questioning the distinction traditionally drawn between physical and psychiatric injury and where the law of tort is being asked to impose a duty situation on an ever-widening range of factual circumstances.

Claims for psychiatric injury can arise in any number of ways, in any number of places involving any number of claimants. They can arise on the road; at the factory; from going to a funeral; from going to a football match. There is even an American case involving a claimant finding out she had not after all won third prize in a state lottery!

It is well established that where a claimant suffers a physical injury and also develops a recognisable psychiatric illness as a result of the event that caused that physical injury damages are to be awarded in respect of such illness and, apart from the usual evidential and causation hurdles, no particular difficulties arise. It is in respect of claims for psychiatric illness alone that difficulties have arisen.

The present Lord Chief Justice, Lord Bingham, has said (in the Foreword to N. J. Mullany and P. R. Handford, *Tort Liability for Psychiatric Damage*, (1993), p. vii) that liability for psychiatric illness is:

> "one of the most vexed and tantalising topics in the modern law of tort. For what kinds of mental damage will a claim lie? And in what circumstances? These deceptively simple questions have lead to a welter of authority in a number of different jurisdictions. Underlying the cases has been the judges' concern that unless the limits of liability are tightly drawn the courts will be inundated with a flood of claims by plaintiffs ever more distant from the scene of the original mishap. So fine distinctions have been drawn and strict lines of demarcation established."

The law is at present exclusively by judicial precedent, of which there is a great deal, including important Commonwealth cases. However, the House of Lords has considered the law relating to liability for negligently inflicted "nervous shock" on five occasions, all within the last 100 years and all but one of those cases has been heard within the last 15 years. At present, it can safely be said that all the important principles on the law in this area are contained within those authorities, namely, *Bourhill v. Young*,[1]

---

[1] [1943] A.C. 92.

McLoughlin v. O'Brian,[2] *Alcock v. Chief Constable of South Yorkshire Police*,[3] *Page v. Smith*[4] and *Frost v. Chief Constable of South Yorkshire Police* [1998].[5]

The law on this topic is controversial. Lord Hoffmann observed in the *Frost* case, that the search for some unifying principle was called off in *Alcock*.[6] Also in *Frost,* Lord Steyn referred to the need for limitations to be imposed on the class of claimants entitled to recover, the imperfect justice that inevitably results and to some of the relevant policy considerations in this area of the law.[7]

The dissenting speech of Lord Goff in *Frost* represents a powerful view contrary to the majority and a strong critique of the leading speech of Lord Lloyd in *Page.* A lack of judicial unanimity is a particular feature of this corner of the law. There is also controversy in the academic world. Mullany and Handford, in their scholarly treatise, *Tort Liability for Psychiatric Damage* (1993), advocate abolition of the special rules limiting recovery for damages for psychiatric harm. The contrary view that there should be no recovery in tort for pure psychiatric injury is cogently expressed by Dr J. Stapleton in her paper "In Restraint of Tort" where she describes the law relating to liability for psychiatric illness as:

"the area where the silliest rules now exist and where criticism is almost universal."

Reform by legislation is proposed by the Law Commission.

A Recognisable Psychiatric Illness

6–02   The term "nervous shock," dating as it does from Victorian authorities, is now medically and legally discredited. In *Hinz v. Berry*,[8] Lord Denning used the alternative phrase "recognisable psychiatric injury" and the Law Commission also adopted that phrase.[9]

Lord Bridge said in *McLoughlin*[10]:

"The first hurdle which a plaintiff claiming damages of the kind in question must surmount is to establish that he is suffering, not merely grief, distress or any other normal emotion, but a positive psychiatric illness."

---

[2] [1983] 1 A.C. 410.
[3] [1992] 1 A.C. 310.
[4] [1996] 1 A.C. 155.
[5] [1998] 3 W.L.R. 1509.
[6] *op. cit.* at 1557D.
[7] *op. cit.* at 1539C, 1543D–1544F, 1457C–F.
[8] [1970] 2 Q.B. 40.
[9] Law Commission Paper No. 249, *Liability for Psychiatric Illness.*
[10] *op. cit.* at 431H.

Lord Steyn usefully analysed this distinction and its basis in *Frost*.[11]

Any "recognisable psychiatric illness" will suffice, but expert medical evidence will generally be required to establish that the claimant has suffered such a condition.

The Test of Reasonable Foreseeability

In the normal way of a negligence action foresight of harm must be 6–03 established. The nature of the harm that must be foreseen depends upon whether the claimant is a primary or secondary victim.

Primary Victims

In *Alcock*,[12] Lord Oliver said of cases in which damages are claimed for 6–04 recognisable psychiatric injury:

"Broadly they divide into two categories, that is to say, those cases in which the injured plaintiff was involved, either mediately or immediately, as a participant, and those in which the plaintiff was no more than the passive and unwilling witness of injury caused to others."

Lord Lloyd, in *Page*,[13] said that, in all claims relating to recognisable psychiatric injury, it is essential to make this distinction between primary and secondary victims. This issue must be considered at the outset so as to determine whether the three main requirements of such claims have been fulfilled (see below).

Whether or not a claimant is a primary or secondary victim is dependent upon the facts of the relevant incident. If, in that incident the claimant is, or reasonably believes that he (or she) is within the range of foreseeable physical injury, then he or she is a primary victim. If he is not or does not believe himself to be within the range of foreseeable injury but suffers injury as a result of the sight or perception of the death, injury or imperilment of another, then he is a secondary victim.

Page establishes that a primary victim may recover damages for a recognisable psychiatric illness suffered in circumstances where the defendant should reasonably have foreseen that his or her conduct might cause the claimant physical or psychiatric injury, whether or not the foreseeable physical injury does in fact occur. Where the claimant is not actually in danger, but because of the sudden or unexpected nature of events,

---

[11] *op. cit.* at 1539D.
[12] *op. cit.* at 407D–E.
[13] *op. cit.* at 197E.

reasonably believes that he or she is and the defendant should reasonably have foreseen that a person of ordinary fortitude in the claimant's position would have done so, the claimant is also a primary victim and can recover for psychiatric injury in the absence of physical injury (*McFarlane v. EE Caledonia Ltd*).[14]

Secondary Victims

6–05   A secondary victim is a person who suffers a reasonably foreseeable, recognisable psychiatric illness, as a result of another person's death, injury or imperilment. In short, the secondary victim is the unwilling witness who is shocked by events that physically endanger others; he or she is not himself or herself physically endangered.

In the Consultation Paper, "Liability for Psychiatric Illness", that preceded the Law Commission report, the Commission said[15]:

> "once such secondary victims were entitled to claim, the law inevitably had to face up to the difficulty of where to draw the line which demarcates those secondary victims who can claim from those who cannot. It is this central problem that continues to bedevil the law . . .".

It is now clear that in secondary victim cases a single unifying test for liability of foreseeability of recognisable psychiatric injury is not the present law. A secondary victim cannot recover damages for negligence unless he or she can satisfy three main requirements:

(a) that he or she had a close tie of love and affection with the person killed, injured or imperilled;

(b) that he or she was close to the "accident" in time and space;

(c) that he or she directly perceived the "accident" rather than, for example, hearing about it from a third person.

See *McLoughlin*,[16] *Alcock*[17] and *Frost*.[18]
These three requirements are now considered in turn.

A Close Tie of Love and Affection

6–06   A claimant must establish a close tie of love and affection to the immediate victim. Such a tie may be present in family relationships or those of close friendship, but the closeness of the tie must be proved in

---

[14] [1994] 2 All E.R. 1.
[15] Law Commission, No. 137, para. 2.13.
[16] *op. cit.* Lord Wilberforce at 418A–419B and 422A–422H.
[17] *op. cit.* Lord Ackner at 402G–H and Lord Jauncey at 419H–420C.
[18] *op. cit.* Lord Steyn at 1543C–G and Lord Hoffmann at 1548W–1552B.

each case by the claimant, although it may be rebuttably presumed in the case of a spouse, parent or child and possibly fiancé(e) (see *Alcock*[19]).

That such a tie is a prerequisite to liability is rooted in the concepts of proximity and reasonable foreseeability, which are central to the issue of liability in negligence. Proximity within the neighbourhood principle is the more likely to be established where a close tie of love and affection with the person killed, injured or imperilled is established. Further, the threshold of foreseeability is likely to be crossed in the case of those who have a close tie of love and affection with the person killed, injured or imperilled whereas customary phlegm or fortitude in the ordinary person is likely so to place the threshold of foreseeability that the tortfeasor in breach of duty to a primary victim owes no duty of care to a secondary victim (see *Bourhill*[20] and *Frost*[21]).

Physical and Temporal Proximity

To recover for recognisable psychiatric injury as a secondary victim a **6–07** claimant must be close to the accident in time and space. This requirement has been extended to include cases where the claimant perceives the immediate aftermath of an accident.

What constitutes the immediate aftermath is a matter of some difficulty. In *Alcock,* Lord Jauncey made plain that he thought it unwise to essay a definition of what constituted the immediate aftermath. However, in that same case, Lord Ackner[22] made clear that it should be narrowly construed.

Notwithstanding the warning of Lord Jauncey, the following pointers may assist in the determination of what constitutes the "immediate aftermath":

(a) The immediate aftermath is always spoken of as the aftermath of the event; this is to be distinguished from the aftermath of the emergency created by the event.

(b) Whilst there is no set time limit as to how much time may pass following the accident for the immediate aftermath itself to have passed, the period of two hours allowed in *McLoughlin* probably marks the outer limit of the aftermath doctrine. In *Alcock,* three of their Lordships understood the time in *McLoughlin* to have been one hour!

(c) Another way of assessing whether the immediate aftermath has passed is to determine what stage after the accident itself has been

---

[19] *op. cit.* Lord Keith at 397C–E, Lord Ackner at 402H–404G and Lord Jauncey at 422C–H.
[20] *op. cit.* Lord Porter at 117.
[21] *op. cit.* Lord Griffiths at 1512G–H.
[22] *op. cit.* at 400H–401A.

reached- for example, are the emergency services present; is some form of order being restored?

(d) A distinction should be drawn between the shock of the news—that is not to be compensated—and the shock of the experience of the primary event.

(e) It should be established what (if anything) the secondary victim saw of the primary victim and in what condition the latter was then found to be.

In the Court of Appeal decision of *Tranmore v. T. E. Scuddder Limited*[23] there has in effect been a restatement that the "immediate aftermath" doctrine is to be narrowly construed. The plaintiff's son was killed in an accident on a demolition site caused by the negligence of the defendant employer. The plaintiff arrived at the site two hours later and was told that his son was trapped in a collapsed building. After a further two hours, he was informed that his son was dead. He did not see his son's body on site, but did see something of the rubble or machinery under which his son had been buried without knowing where, in fact, he was located. He suffered psychiatric injury as a result of his experience and brought an action against the defendant.

The Court of Appeal unanimously dismissed the plaintiff's appeal, in respect of which the issue was whether there existed the proximity in time and space necessary to make the plaintiff a person to whom the defendant owed a duty of care. To differing degrees, each of the five factors identified in (a)–(e) appears to have influenced the court. In particular, the plaintiff did not go to the site for two hours after the accident had happened, and even during the brief period when he was in the collapsed building, his son was buried in rubble two floors above him. No part of his son's body was seen until he visited the mortuary 24 hours later. Throughout his presence at the scene the emergency services were in attendance. Taken together, such factors were decisive.

The Means of Perception

6–08   The shock must come through the sight or hearing of the event or its immediate aftermath. The question whether communication via a simultaneous broadcast would be sufficient to ground recovery was left open by Lord Wilberforce in *McLoughlin*.[24] However, in *Alcock* the House ruled that watching what was broadcast live of Hillsborough on the television did not equate to being within sight or hearing of the disaster.

A psychiatric illness induced by mere knowledge of a distressing fact (concerning the fate of a primary victim) is not compensable. Perception by the claimant of the distressing event is essential: (*Alcock*[25]).

---

[23] Transcript, April 28, 1998, CA.
[24] *op. cit.* at 422H–423B.
[25] *op. cit.* Lord Keith at 398C and Lord Ackner at 401B.

Involuntary Participant

The "involuntary participant" was identified as a category by Lord **6–09**
Oliver. In particular, he analysed in *Alcock*[26] the cases as falling into two
separate categories: those of participants and witnesses.

The authority taken as establishing the former category is the decision of
Donovan J. in *Dooley v. Cammel Laird & Co. Ltd*, but this is a very special
case[27].

Mr Dooley, a crane driver, was the unwitting hand who caused the
accident—a load fell into the hold of a ship. In the event, there was no
injury to the men below, but nothing turned on that. Rather, it was held
that "nervous shock" was a reasonably foreseeable consequence of witnessing an accident to another as it was proved that the claimant had been put
in the position of thinking that he was about to be or had been the
involuntary cause of another's death or injury. The phrase "unwilling
participant" is used as synonymous with the "involuntary cause of . . ."

In describing this category, Lord Oliver also spoke of the claimant as
being "mediately" involved. The use of the word "mediately" does not
cover cases of participation in the aftermath. Rather, "mediately" means to
form a connecting link or transitional stage, to act as an intermediary. For
example, it covers the situation where a workman gives a scaffolding pole
to a colleague that he then raises and hits an electricity wire whereby he is
electrocuted (see *Young v. Charles Church (Southern) Ltd.*[28]).

Two other cases are sometimes taken as more recent applications of the
proposition illustrated by *Dooley*. In the first case, *Galt v. British Railways
Board*,[29] the plaintiff train driver rounded a bend and saw two men on the
track and thought they had been killed. He suffered a myocardial
infarction. It is perhaps to be doubted, therefore, whether this was a case
involving psychiatric injury at all. In the second case, *Wigg v. British
Railways Board*,[30] a railway guard negligently gave the plaintiff train driver
a signal to start the train, leading to the death of another. The plaintiff got
out to help. He was in fact treated as a rescuer.

Before turning to rescuers, it should be noted that in *Dooley*, the case
against the employer (the second defendant) succeeded under the relevant
regulations. The case was not, therefore, authority for the proposition that
an employee is in any special position where the tortfeasor is his employer
(see below). Lord Oliver did not say that liability arose because the
employer was in breach of its duty of care at common law qua employer.

---

[26] *ibid.* at 407D.
[27] [1951] 1 Lloyd's Rep. 271; Lord Jauncey at 420F.
[28] Transcript, April 24, 1997, CA; also reported at (1998) 39 B.M.L.R. 146.
[29] (1983) 133 N.L.J. 870.
[30] *The Times*, February 4, 1986.

Rescuers

6–10   Rescue cases are also regarded as being in a special category. However, the category of rescuer is established in the law of negligence generally, not just when considering liability for recognisable psychiatric illness. If a rescuer, the claimant is not concerned with arguments of contributory negligence, *novus actus interveniens* or *volenti non fit injuria*.[31]

The question arose in *Frost* whether rescuers were in a special category to whom a duty of care is owed in relation to psychiatric injury. In the Court of Appeal,[32] Henry L.J. argued in favour of a broad definition of a rescuer saying:

> "that public policy favours a wide rather than a narrow definition, to ensure that those brave and unselfish enough to go to the help of their fellow men will be properly compensated if they suffer damage as a result."

Rose L.J. set the criteria for determination of the question of whether a person who suffered psychiatric injury should recover as a rescuer where otherwise they did not fulfil the secondary victim criteria by reference to a number of factors, namely:

> "the character and extent of the initial incident caused by the tortfeasor; whether that incident has finished or is continuing; whether there is any danger, continuing or otherwise, to the victim or to the plaintiff; the character of the claimant's conduct, in itself and in relation to the victim; and how proximate, in time and place, the plaintiff's conduct is to the incident."[33]

In the House of Lords the majority favoured a narrow definition of a rescuer and confirmed that, in claims for psychiatric damage, central to the concept of rescue is the notion of extricating someone from a situation of danger (see *Wagner v. International Railway Company*[34]). Accordingly, to recover under the rescue principle a claimant must prove that he or she is:

(a) exposed to danger; and

(b) engaged in a rescue as defined by law.

6–11   Being exposed to danger includes those who are primary victims, as for example in *Baker v. Hopkins*.[35] Lord Oliver clearly had such cases in mind when he dealt with rescuers in *Alcock*[36] and *McLoughlin* in the Court of Appeal.[37]

---

[31] *McLoughlin, op. cit. per* Lord Wilberforce; *cf. Frost, op. cit.* Lord Hoffmann at 1555F.
[32] [1997] 3 W.L.R. 1194 at 1220D.
[33] *ibid.* at 1203G.
[34] [1921] 232 N.Y. 176, Cardozo J. at 180.
[35] [1959] 1 W.L.R. 966.
[36] *op. cit.* at 408B–D; Lord Jauncey at 421A–C.
[37] [1981] 1 Q.B., CA *per* Griffiths L.J. at 623A.

Rescue then is to be defined by reference to peril. Once the primary victim is removed from the place where he or she is in peril or the peril has passed matters have moved to a more remote stage. What is done for treatment of the primary victim where he or she is alive goes to the fact of injury. If the victim is dead, activities such as standing by the bodies in the mortuary and the setting up of the mortuary go to the fact of death as distinct from the circumstances in which it came about.

The law as now enunciated may be compared with the decision identified by Lord Wilberforce as establishing the category of "rescuer" in this field, namely the decision of Waller J. (as he then was) in *Chadwick v. British Railways Board*.[38] Mr Chadwick had worked through the night tending to those injured in the Lewisham train disaster; that had involved him going into the carriages where the dead and injured were trapped.

Some had interpreted *Chadwick*[39] as being a case where the claimant was held entitled to recover because of the horror of the whole event; similarly in *Frost*.[40] Others had interpreted that authority on the basis that liability was founded on the risk of personal injury to which the plaintiff submitted himself (see *McLoughlin*[41] and *McFarlane*.[42]

The majority of the House of Lords in *Frost* preferred the latter interpretation. As Lord Hoffmann put it:

"there is no authority which decides that a rescuer is in any special position in relation to liability for psychiatric injury".[43]

The speech of Lord Steyn affords particular guidance. He said:

"[*Chadwick*] is not authority for the proposition that a person who never exposed himself to any personal danger and never thought that he was in personal danger can recover pure psychiatric injury as a rescuer. In order to recover compensation for pure psychiatric harm as rescuer it is not necessary to establish that his psychiatric condition was *caused* by the perception of personal danger. And Waller J. rightly so held. But in order to contain the concept of rescuer in reasonable bounds for the purposes of the recovery of compensation for pure psychiatric harm the Plaintiff must at least satisfy the threshold requirement that he objectively exposed himself to danger or reasonably believed that he was doing so".[43a]

It should also be noted that at the Court of Appeal stage of *Frost* there **6–12** was also heard the case of *Duncan v. British Coal Corporation*.[44] In that

---

[38] [1967] 1 W.L.R. 912.
[39] *ibid. per* Waller J. at 918A–B.
[40] *op. cit. per* Rose L.J. at 1202H–1203A.
[41] *op. cit. per* Griffiths L.J. at 622H, CA.
[42] *per* Stuart-Smith L.J. at 10F.
[43] at 1555F.
[43a] at 1546H–1547D.
[44] [1997] 1 All E.R.

case, it was held that a mining supervisor who gave mouth-to-mouth resuscitation to a colleague fatally injured in a mining accident for over two hours was not a rescuer because he had arrived some four minutes after the relevant accident.

The decision in *Duncan v. British Coal Corporation*, and in particular Rose L.J.[45] reflects, therefore, a restrictive view; similarly the decision in *McFarlane*. They emphasise that temporal and physical proximity is required where a victim is said to have functioned as a rescuer.

The latter decision also emphasises that a "function" test may usefully be applied when determining whether a given claimant is a rescuer. In *McFarlane*, merely handling some blankets was not enough to warrant the conclusion that the claimant was a rescuer; as Lord Griffiths put it in *Frost*:

"trivial or peripheral assistance will not be sufficient."[46]

As to the position of the professional rescuer, provided he or she is a rescuer as defined above, it is settled by *Frost* that such a rescuer is in no better or worse position than the volunteer rescuer. In short, as with physical injury, there is no "fireman's rule" regarding liability for psychiatric illness.

Employees

6–13   It was argued in *Frost* that although the claimants lacked a relationship with the primary victims of the disaster, they did have a relationship analogous to that of employment with the defendants. Technically, a police officer is a constable not "employed" by the police authority, but it was conceded in *Frost* at trial that the relationship of the chief constable with his officers was analogous to that of an employer to his employees with the concomitant rights and duties.

The argument, that found favour with the majority in the Court of Appeal, was that by reason of that quasi employment relationship, the claimants did not need to fulfil the three main requirements that a secondary victim claimant must ordinarily fulfil to recover, and, particularly relevant in the *Frost* case, the criterion of a close tie of love and affection with the person killed, injured or imperilled. It was contended that the relationship put them in a different and altogether easier position when considering the question of duty to that of spectators at the match even though what they saw and did at the match may have been the same. They were owed a duty of care as claimants who were directly involved in the incident caused by their employers' negligence which resulted in the injury or imperilment of another.

---

[45] at 554A.
[46] at 1514F.

This argument had earlier been made in the Scottish case of *Robertson v. Forth Road Bridge*.[47] Lord Hope's rejection of this argument[48] in the Inner House of the Court of Session was rejected by the Court of Appeal in *Frost* but accepted by the House of Lords.

As Lord Hoffmann put it, the argument really assumed what it needed to prove. He said:

> "The liability of an employer to his employees for negligence, either direct or vicarious, is not a separate tort with its own rules. It is an aspect of the general law of negligence. The relationship of employer and employee establishes the employee as a person to whom the employer owes a duty of care. But this tells one nothing about the circumstances in which he will be liable for a particular type of injury. For this one must look to the general law concerning the type of injury which has been suffered."[49]

He then considered whether the employment relationship should be a reason for allowing an employee to recover damages for psychiatric injury in circumstances in which he would otherwise be a secondary victim and not satisfy the *Alcock* control mechanisms asking the rhetorical question:

> "Why should the policemen, simply by virtue of the employment analogy and irrespective of what they actually did be treated different [sic] from first-aid workers or ambulance men?"

He concluded that, in line with authority, it would not be fair to permit recovery on such grounds.[50]

It is now clearly established that the existence of the relationship of employment does not dispose of the need to satisfy the criteria the law has laid down that must be met in secondary victim cases.

Bystanders

Whether a mere bystander (that is a person who witnesses the death, **6–14** injury, or imperilment of the immediate victim, but has no close tie of love and affection with him or her) may in any circumstances recover damages for psychiatric injury is not certain (see *McLoughlin*[51] and *Alcock*[52]).

That an accident may be sufficiently catastrophic that without more a duty of care is owed to witnesses of that accident is not (yet) the law. Three of their Lordships in *Alcock* touched on this issue: Lord Keith

---

[47] 1995 S.C. 364.
[48] *ibid.* at 370D–374B.
[49] *ibid.* at 1552E–H.
[50] *Alcock, op. cit.* at 1552H–1554G.
[51] *op. cit.* Lord Wilberforce at 422C–D.
[52] *op. cit.* Lord Ackner at 403E and Lord Oliver at 416C.

described such a case as "difficult" but did not rule it out if the circumstances of the catastrophe were "particularly horrific"[53]; Lord Ackner would not rule it out and gave an example of a petrol tanker careering out of control into a school in session and bursting into flames[54]; and Lord Oliver would not exclude it, speaking of "circumstances of such horror as would be likely to traumatise even the most phlegmatic bystander".[55]

Notwithstanding the events at Hillsborough and their scale, it was not suggested in *Alcock* that what occurred there was a sufficiently or particularly horrific disaster for that alone to entitle the claimants to recover.[56]

This issue arose in *McFarlane*. It would be difficult to imagine circumstances more horrific than the destruction by an oil fire storm of the Piper Alpha oil rig out of which event that case arose. Stuart-Smith L.J. expressed clear misgivings about the courts involving themselves in assessing degrees of horror as reactions to such events are entirely subjective. Accordingly he concluded:

> "In my judgment both as a matter of principle and policy the court should not extend the duty to those who are mere bystanders or witnesses of horrific events."[57]

Miscellaneous

6–15   To recover damages for recognisable psychiatric damage as a secondary victim the damage must be proved to have been shock induced (see *Alcock*[58]).

It is probably the law that the psychiatric illness grounding the claim must not result from the death, injury, or imperilment of the defendant him or herself (see *Alcock*[59]).

The Law Commission Consultation Paper (No. 137), "Liability for Psychiatric Illness," usefully poses a number of questions which as yet remain unanswered on the authorities. For example, in cases of simultaneous television, there is the instance given by Nolan L.J. in the Court of Appeal of a publicity seeking organisation arranging for the simultaneous broadcast of a balloon trip made by a number of children. Whilst filming and transmitting pictures of the event the cameras show the balloon suddenly burst into flames.[60]

---

[53] at 397E.
[54] at 403E.
[55] at 416B–C.
[56] see 392F, 393E, 398C and 399A.
[57] at 14E.
[58] *op. cit.* Lord Ackner at 400F and 401F.
[59] *ibid.* Lord Oliver at 418D–E.
[60] at para. 2.38.

Proposals for Reform

In *McLoughlin* Lord Scarman called for legislation in this area of the **6–16** law.[61]

The Law Commission, in their report, has recommended legislative reform designed to remove what it considers to be some unwarranted restrictions that presently apply in relation to liability for negligently inflicted psychiatric illness. It has recommended the *removal* of certain preconditions to liability in secondary victim cases:

(a) That the illness must be "shock" induced;

(b) That the illness must not result from the death, injury, or imperilment of the defendant him or herself.

(c) That the claimant must be close to the accident in time and space.

(d) That he or she directly perceived the accident rather than, for example, hearing about it from a third person.

The Law Commission recommended the *retention* of the rule that a secondary victim must have had a close tie of love and affection with the person killed, injured or imperilled.

---

[61] *op. cit.* at 413C.

7. Employer's Liability

The "Six-Pack"

The "Six-Pack" of Health and Safety Regulations (so called because all 7–01
six came into force on January 1, 1993) consists of the:

- Management of Health and Safety at Work Regulations 1992[1] ("the Management Regulations").
- Health and Safety (Display Screen Equipment) Regulations 1992[2] (the "Display Screen Equipment Regulations").
- Manual Handling Operations Regulations 1992.[3]
- Provision and Use of Work Equipment Regulations 1992[4] ("PUWER"). This has now been revoked and re-enacted, with additions and amendments, as the Provision and Use of Work Equipment Regulations 1998.[5]
- Personal Protective Equipment at Work Regulations 1992[6] ("the PPE Regulations").
- Workplace (Health, Safety and Welfare) Regulations 1992[7] ("the Workplace Regulations").

Since then, the following regulations cover the same or associated ground:

- Construction (Health, Safety and Welfare) Regulations 1996[8] ("the Construction Regulations", replacing the Construction (General Provisions) Regulations 1961,[9] the Construction (Working Places) Regulations 1966,[10] and the Construction (Health and Welfare) Regulations.[11])

---

[1] S.I. 1992 No. 2051. The original regulations have been amended to add protection for new and expectant mothers at work (by the Management of Health and Safety at Work (Amendment) Regulations 1994 (S.I. 1994 No. 2865), and for young persons, *i.e.* those under 18 years of age (by the Health and Safety (Young Persons) Regulations 1997 (S.I. 1997 No. 135).
[2] S.I. 1992 No. 2792.
[3] S.I. 1992 No. 2793.
[4] S.I. 1992 No. 2932.
[5] S.I. 1998 No. 2306.
[6] S.I. 1992 No. 2966.
[7] S.I. 1992 No. 3004. The provisions have been supplemented to include the provisions of the Workplace Directive (89/654/E.C.) in relation to fire precautions by the Fire Precautions (Workplace) Regulations 1997 (S.I. 1997 No. 1840).
[8] S.I. 1996 No. 1592.
[9] S.I. 1961 No. 1580.
[10] S.I. 1966 No. 94.
[11] S.I. 1966 No. 95.

- Working Time Regulations 1998.[12]
- Lifting Operations and Lifting Equipment Regulations 1998 ("LOLER").[13]

What the "Six-Pack" Does

7–02
- Replaces a piecemeal, industry-by-industry, approach to regulations with one general to all work and all workplaces.
- Replaces familiar protective legislation, both primary legislation (*e.g.* most provisions of the Factories Act 1961, and of the Office, Shops and Railway Premises Act 1963) and secondary legislation (*e.g.* the Protection of Eyes Regulations 1974).
- Each set of regulations gives effect in domestic law to a European Directive.[14]
- Encodes a standard *approach* to the protection of health and safety, rather than detailed provisions which are individual to specific tasks in specific situations.

Origin in European Directives

Principal Consequences

7–03   There are two consequences of the European origin of the six-pack of domestic regulations: (a) as to the interpretation of the domestic regulations, and (b) the possible direct effect of the Directives.

7–04   *(a) Interpretation.* The applicable principle is now well-established: ". . . it is for a United Kingdom court to construe domestic legislation in any field covered by a Community Directive so as to accord with the interpretation of the Directive as laid down by the European Court of Justice, if that can be done without distorting the meaning of the domestic legislation" (*Duke v. GEC Reliance Systems Ltd.*[15]) The ECJ itself has emphasised[16] that the courts must utilise "the full extent of their discretion" in interpreting and applying domestic provisions in conformity with Community law.

---

[12] S.I. 1998 No. 1833, implementing Council Directive 93/104/E.C. This has been amended, so as to be less specific in its record-keeping requirements, and, it seems, to confer an arguably wider latitude as to when it may be said that a worker is working unmeasured hours, or hours that cannot be pre-determined, by the Working Time Amendment Regulations 1999.

[13] S.I. 1998 No. 2307, repealing, *inter alia*, ss.22, 23 and 25–27 of the Factories Act 1961.

[14] They implement Council Directives 89/391/E.C. (the "Framework" Directive) (MHSWR); 89/654/E.C. (Workplace); 89/655/E.C. (PUWER); 89/656/E.C. (PPE); 90/267/E.C. (Manual Handling), and 90/270/E.C. (Display Screen).

[15] [1988] I.C.R. 339 at 352G, per Lord Templeman. See also Lord Keith in *Webb v. Emo Air Cargo Ltd* [1993] I.C.R. 175.

[16] In *Coloroll Pension Trustees Ltd v. Russell* [1995] I.C.R. 179 at para. 29 judgment.

(b) Direct Effect. Health and safety Directives are said to have vertical, not 7–05
horizontal, direct effect. This means that they may be directly enforced by
an individual against a state authority, but not against a fellow private
citizen or company.[17]

"State authority" has a wide scope. It extends not only to the executive
or the legislature, but also to the civil administration of the State (such as a
local authority). Not only that, a health authority is an emanation of the
State (*Marshall v. Southampton and South West Hampshire Area Health
Authority (Teaching)*.[18] British Gas[19] has been held to be an emanation of
the State, as has South West Water[20]—though not, it seems, Rolls-Royce.[21]
The test whether a given body is a State authority as expressed by the
House of Lords in *Foster v. British Gas*.[22] is a two-fold one—the organisation said to be an emanation of the State must (1) be made responsible,
pursuant to a measure adopted by the State, for providing a public service
under the control of the state, and (2) have for that purpose special powers
beyond those which result from the normal rules applicable in relations
between individuals.[23] However, it is arguable that this is too narrow a test,
since the ECJ has since then in *Kampelmann v. Landschaftsverband
Westfalen-Lippe*[24] stated the applicable test as satisfied if *either* part of the
two-fold requirement is satisfied.

Practical Effect of Direct Effect

Accordingly, any public authority (*e.g.* local authority, health authority, 7–06
most, but not all, schools), and any privatised utility which retains special
powers beyond the normal in order to provide a public service is subject not
only to the 1992 six-pack Regulations, but also to European Directives relating
to health and safety, and any body which satisfies one of the tests may be so
subject. Where a Directive goes beyond, or departs from the regulations, a
claimant may rely upon the Directive itself,[25] provided that the requirements
of the Directive are clear, unconditional and sufficiently precise.

Where a Directive is not Implemented

Where both a regulation cannot be interpreted to accord with the 7–07
Directive, and the defendant is not a State authority, an injured person still
may have a remedy. However, this is against the State itself (the action is

---

[17] In this latter case, enforcement is indirect only (*i.e.* by the interpretation route, if possible).
[18] [1986] Q.B. 401, ECJ.
[19] *Foster v. British Gas* [1991] Q.B. 405, ECJ.
[20] *Griffin v. South West Water Services* [1995] I.R.L.R. 15.
[21] *Doughty v. Rolls-Royce* [1992] I.C.R. 538.
[22] [1991] 2 A.C. 306.
[23] [1991] 2 A.C. 306 at 313, *per* Lord Templeman. *Doughty v. Rolls-Royce* [1992] I.C.R. 538,
CA, has confirmed that both these requirements are necessary.
[24] Cases C–253/96 to 258/96, reported at [1998] I.R.L.R. 333, ECJ, at para. 46 of the
judgment.
[25] The wording is to be found in the *Encyclopedia of Health and Safety*, (Sweet & Maxwell),
or in Redgrave. *N.B.* beware the frequently open-natured text of the European Directives,
which may promise more than can actually be delivered.

brought against the Attorney-General[26]), for failing in its duty properly to implement the Directive concerned in domestic law. Three conditions must be met where a Directive gives a wide discretion to a Member State: (1) the rule of law infringed must be intended to confer rights on individuals; (2) the breach must be sufficiently serious; and (3) there must be a direct causal link between the breach of the obligation resting on the State and the damage sustained by the injured party (*Brasserie du Pecheur SA v. Federal Republic of Germany; R. v. Secretary of State for Transport, ex parte Factortame Ltd and ors.,*[27] ECJ). Where the Directive gives a limited margin of discretion to the Member State, these conditions appear unnecessary.[28]

Codes of Practice and Guidance

Guidance: the Usual Approach

7–08   The legislative approach in the United Kingdom is to reduce primary legislative text to its bare essentials. Traditional English wisdom is that Statute and Regulations alone are compulsory, and that Guidance published alongside the Regulations is advisory only, entitled perhaps to respect but not to slavish obedience.[29]

Approved Codes of Practice (ACOPs)

7–09   The Health and Safety at Work etc. Act 1974 provides for such a split between primary regulation and required practice, but creates also a hybrid between "regulation" and "guidance". Codes of Practice may be formally *approved* by the Health and Safety Commission (these are known by the acronym ACOP). These are intended to provide for detailed and flexible reaction to recent developments in Health and Safety. The HSWA 1974, s.16 provides, in respect of criminal proceedings, that if the prosecution prove a failure to observe any provision of an ACOP which appears relevant to any matter which is necessary to prove to establish a contraven-

---

[26] Limitation does not begin to run until the Directive is properly implemented: *Emmott v. Minister for Social Welfare* [1991] I.R.L.R. 387, ECJ.

[27] [1996] Q.B. 404 at 499, para. 51 judgment.

[28] *ibid.* at 498, paras 45, 46 judgment. An example is where a Directive requires a Member State to take "all measures necessary" to achieve a particular result, yet the domestic legislation fails to do so (see para. 46, judgment). Where a Directive is *incorrectly* transposed, it is unclear whether the conditions apply where the discretion of the Member State is limited: see *R. v. Her Majesty's Treasury ex p. British Telecommunications plc* [1996] Q.B. 615 at 655A–D.

[29] Such guidance may, however, fix an employer with constructive knowledge of risks, *e.g.* HSE Guidance Note MS10 relating to "Beat Conditions, Tenosynovitis" dealing with the particular health risks of frequent and repeated movements of the forearm, hand and wrist.

tion of a requirement or prohibition in the regulations, then the contravention is to be taken as proved "unless the court is satisfied that the requirement or prohibition was in respect of that matter complied with otherwise than by way of observance of that provision of the Code".

(i) Limitations. Section 16 applies (a) to criminal proceedings, and (b) in respect of an ACOP only. However, if observance of an ACOP is necessary to avoid criminal liability (unless the protection aimed at by the regulation is conferred in some other way which is at least equally satisfactory) a civil court is highly likely to regard the provisions of an ACOP as being equally compelling in an action for damages.[30] Accordingly, it should be pleaded if a plaintiff intends to rely on it.

(ii) Future change. The (HSE)[31] has been seeking a change in the law such that a person owing a duty will be taken to have satisfied the law on the specific issues addressed by the ACOP if he or she complies with the provisions of that ACOP. This is likely to impact on common law as well as statutory liability: if a person is complying with regulations in the way he or she conducts his operations, why should the law hold him or her negligent in so doing?

Checking the relevant Code is thus very important for both claimant and defendant. Beware, the full text is not in every textbook.[32]

ACOPS and Guidance in the Six-Pack

Codes Applicable

- Codes of Guidance (note, *not* ACOPs, but guidance pure and simple) 7–10 exist for the:

  Display Screen Equipment Regulations,
  Manual Handling Operations Regulations,
  PUWER,[33]
  PPE Regulations.

---

[30] There is also a good "European" reason for this—many of the provisions in the Directives are assigned by domestic law to ACOPs rather than to the Regulations themselves (*e.g.* the ACOP attached to the Workplace Regulations).

[31] *The Role and Status of ACOPs—a statement by HSE*, available from HSE Information Centre, published spring 1996.

[32] It is in the *Encyclopedia of Health and Safety at Work*, but not in the body of the text of Redgrave. *Halsbury Statutes*, Vol. 20 contains the central provisions only.

[33] Although the guidance relates to the 1992 Regulations, these have been revoked by the 1998 Regulations. However, those Regulations provide essentially the same as before, and the guidance thus remains valid.

- There is both an ACOP and "mere" guidance attached to the Workplace Regulations.[34]
- An ACOP is attached to the Management Regulations.

Form of "Mere" Guidance

7–11   It is an open question whether the presence of both ACOP and "mere" guidance in relation to the Workplace Regulations dilutes the force of the latter. The better view is that it does not do so because (a) it has been possible to make ACOPs since the 1974 Act, yet this has not prevented civil courts giving weight to "mere" guidance, and (b) where authoritative guidance is given, the reasonable prudent employer must be expected to pay careful heed to it.

Regulation Under the Six-Pack

General Issues

7–12   Liability depends upon:
- WHO is covered by the regulations;
- WHAT is covered;
- WHERE it is covered; and
- WHEN it is covered.

These are not as obvious as one might expect.

When there is Liability

7–13   As to WHEN, all regulations were in full effect from January 1, 1997—with the exception of amendments made recently to some of them.[35] However, some regulations have full effect and others have partial effect at differing dates before that date. Until that time, the pre-existing law (*e.g.* the Factories Act 1961) continues to apply. See below for the dates in respect of each set of regulations.

What is Covered and Where?

7–14   Essentially, all *work* is covered, including that on offshore installations and in territorial waters, but not on board ships. Many a workplace and much display screen equipment is not covered (see below).

---

[34] The provisions of the Code and the ACOP are interleaved with each other.
[35] Notably the revocation of the PUWER Regulations 1992, and their replacement by PUWER 1998, with effect from December 5, 1998. The scope of PUWER is broadly the same (so far as the 1992 Regulations went), but adds further provisions.

Who is Covered?

Throughout the regulations, there are some specific provisions for the 7–15
self-employed, others for employers and those in control of work. Sometimes those in charge of premises where work is carried out are regulated.
However, there is a potential problem as to those protected. The regulations are made under the HSWA 1974, ss.52 and 53 of which define
"work" as "work as an employee or self-employed person". "Worker"
thus might seem to cover both categories, but the Directives apply to
"workers", who are defined as "any person employed",[36] and thus may be
confined to employees. In some situations, therefore, where a regulation is
not specific as to those whom it is intended to protect, an employer may be
able to argue that only employees are covered.

The Management Regulations

Overview

The Management Regulations generalise and rationalise the approach to 7–16
preventative health and safety. This is perhaps nowhere better illustrated
than in regulation 4(1) which provides:

> "Every employer shall make and give effect to such arrangements as are
> appropriate . . . for the effective planning, organisation, control, monitoring and
> review of the preventive and protective measures."

The "preventive and protective measures" are those which have been
identified by the employer in consequence of the risk assessment which he
is obliged to carry out under regulation 3.
Thus, the pattern is:

(a) a pre-planning stage: assess the risk, to identify appropriate preventive and protective measures; then he must:
(b) plan;
(c) organise;
(d) control the work in the light of those measures; and
(e) monitor and review their effectiveness.

---

[36] Council Directive 89/391 (the "Framework Directive"), Art. 3(a). The difficult question is
whether a contract of employment means something different in a European context as
compared to a domestic one. The Court of Appeal is shortly to hear employment appeals
which may clarify this. The concept of "employment relationship" appears in many
Directives relating to employment, and is wide enough to cover officers such as chairmen of
Tribunals: *Percival-Price and others v. Department of Economic Development* [2000] IRLR
380, NICA.

The order in which health and safety measures are placed, prevention first (*i.e.* prevent a danger arising at all, perhaps by job or plant design) and protection second (both mechanical, as by guarding, and personal, as by personal protective equipment), is adopted throughout the six-pack. Its influence goes far further, however. It informs the common law of employer's liability.[37]

Is there Liability for Breach?

7–17   Breach of a duty specifically imposed by the Management Regulations does NOT confer a right of action in civil proceedings.[38] It follows that neither does contravention of the ACOP. However: (i) failure to follow a provision will (it is suggested) be relevant to the issues of negligence/breach of statutory duty otherwise arising; (ii) where the defendant is a public authority, the Directive will apply—and Community law demands that there be an effective sanction for any breach.[39] Given that the purpose of the legislation is to protect employees, it is arguable that for domestic law to provide for criminal penalties alone is not an effective sanction.

Content of the Regulations

7–18   The Regulations principally require:

- appropriate health surveillance;
- the appointment of competent persons to help an employer with health and safety arrangements;
- procedures for serious danger;
- the informing of employees as to risks to their health and safety;
- the provision of adequate health and safety training;
- co-operation with other employers sharing the same workplace; and

---

[37] Take dermatitis or destructive stress at work—how do you establish the approach an employer should, and the courts will, take to it? The answer is: (1) assess whether the job involves particular exposure to, say, dangerous oils or to stresses and strains (this will involve considering the degree of risk shown, *e.g.* by the HSE publication on *Stress at Work*); (2) take preventive measures, by trying to design machinery so that it does not spew out oil, and design unnecessary stresses out of the job or prevent them arising, *e.g.* avoid making the last redundancy; be careful with profit-related pay; ensure that time is used efficiently rather than counter-productively; (3) take protective measures *e.g.* rubber gloves, stress management training or an EAP; (4) provide for immediate protective measures if the oil does get on the skin (washing facilities, emollient creams) or the stressful event is suffered (stress counselling), but always in the context of; (5) advice and information (telling the employee why rubber gloves are needed; how certain conflicts at work are to be resolved, *e.g.* by prioritising); and (6) monitoring the results (to ensure that the advice is heeded, is sufficient, etc.,) and reviewing the measures if it is not.

[38] reg. 15.

[39] *Marshall v. Southampton and South-West Hampshire Area Health Authority (No. 2)* [1994] 1 A.C. 530. There may arguably thus be civil liability *under the Directive* where there is none provided for *under the Regulations*.

- they impose a duty *on employees* to use machinery, equipment, etc., in accordance with the training and instruction given to them. Defendants should plead clearly any allegation that the claimant has breached this duty.

Points to Note

Risk assessments required of an employer by the Management Regu- 7–19 lations need to be recorded where he has more than five employees.[40] Claimants should obtain, and defendants should give, discovery of them.

Display Screen Equipment Regulations

When in Force?

January 1, 1993, but workstations already in service on that date were 7–20 not covered until January 1, 1997.

What is Covered?

Workstations involving VDUs and peripherals, but not portables, *e.g.* laptops. They are covered only if in "prolonged use" (undefined), and display screens on board a means of transport are not covered.

Where?

Anywhere that the VDU/workstation is used for work. Workers' homes are covered if homework is done.

Who is Protected?

A person who *habitually* uses display screen equipment as a *significant* part of his *normal* work, whether self-employed or an employee.[41] The words in italics are undefined.

Who is Regulated?

Employers.

---

[40] reg. 4(2).
[41] *e.g.* news sub-editors, air traffic controllers, secretaries, possibly airline check-in clerks, and some receptionists.

Content of the Regulations

7–21   An employer must:

- assess the risks, and reduce them to the lowest level practicable;
- plan for breaks in the pattern of work;
- provide free eye tests;
- give health and safety training and information; and
- ensure that a workstation meets detailed requirements in a Schedule, on such as absence of glare, flexible and adjustable arrangement of seats, work surfaces, and keyboards; adjustable chairs; sufficient suitable lighting; suitable software; operator posture, etc.

Points to Note

7–22
- Two useful diagrams of layout and operator posture accompany the schedule.
- Annex B to the Guidance records that work related upper limb disorders are liable to be caused by a combination of factors, including prolonged static posture of the back, neck and head, awkward positioning of the hands and wrists (*e.g.* because of inappropriate work height), high workloads and tight deadlines. This "requires a risk reduction strategy which embraces proper equipment, furniture, training, job design and work planning."

Manual Handling Regulations

When in Force?

7–23   January 1, 1993.

What is Covered?

Any "manual handling operation" (defined to include transporting, supporting, lifting, putting down, pushing, pulling, carrying or moving a load by hand or bodily force). A load includes a person or animal.

Where?

Anywhere at work, except on board ship.

Who is Protected?

An employee (a self-employed person must protect himself in the same way).

Who is Regulated?

Employers (and the self-employed in respect of themselves). Employees must make full and proper use of any system of work provided by their employer to reduce the risk of injury.

Content

The kernel of the Regulations is in regulation 4, which reflects the **7–24** approach of the Management Regulations (see above) in setting out a hierarchy of measures. An employer must (by regulation 4(1)):

(a) *so far as is reasonably practicable* avoid the need for manual handling operations (*e.g.* by mechanisation);

(b) where this is not not reasonably practicable,

   (i) he must assess the operations,
   (ii) take appropriate steps to reduce the risk of injury to his employees from those operations to the lowest level reasonably practicable, and
   (iii) provide his employees with general indications and, where reasonably practicable, precise information on the weight of each load and the heaviest side where the centre of gravity is not positioned centrally.

Points to Note

- There are diagrams in the Code of Guidance which provide **7–25** guidelines for the weights which may be raised and lowered safely. They are worth studying as they demonstrate how much more can be lifted/carried at waist height than elsewhere, and how much more close to the body than far away. Lifting, bending, repeating the task and being a woman all go to increase the risk significantly.
- The Regulations use the phrase "as far as reasonably practicable". The Directive[42] requires the employer to take "appropriate measures," although it envisages there are occasions when this may be impossible.[43] Reasonable practicability normally involves balancing financial considerations against that which may be done in the light of present knowledge and perceived risk. There may be room for the Directive to have interpretative effect here, or even direct effect against a State authority.

---

[42] Art. 3.
[43] Art. 3(2).

- The Directive requires instruction and training in methods of handling. This may often be vital.[44] Yet the Regulations do not implement this requirement in terms. Where the Directive is not directly effective, there is room to argue that the employer who fails to provide such instruction/training is nonetheless culpable, at least at common law, by virtue of other provisions (the Management Regulations, reg. 8, and HSWA 1974, s.2, though there is no cause of action created by breach of either). The Guidance Note (not an ACOP) does mention training, and the Regulations talk of an obligation to take "appropriate steps" to reduce the risk of injury.

Cases

In *Hawkes v. London Borough of Southwark*[45] a carpenter was employed single-handedly to manoeuvre a door up a staircase to a third-floor flat. In the course of doing so, part of the door caught against the wall of the stairwell, and knocked him off balance. The trial judge found there was a risk of injury, thus requiring the employer[46] to make an assessment of the risk. He did not do so. The judge held that if this had been done, the claimant's supervisor would, nonetheless, still have authorised him to do the work on his own, and dismissed the claim. Allowing the appeal, the Court of Appeal held that any suitable and sufficient risk assessment would have discovered that there was a risk. There was, accordingly, a duty to reduce that risk to the lowest level reasonably practicable,[47] which the employer could have done by providing a second man for the task. Further, the onus of showing that the taking of an appropriate step is not reasonably practicable lies on a defendant, and this also the defendant had failed to do.

Provision and Use of Work Equipment Regulations

When in Force?

7–26   January 1, 1993, but work equipment "first provided for use" before then is not covered by most provisions until January 1, 1997. Instead, the Factories Act 1961, ss.12–17, 19 continue to apply. The 1998 Regulations replaced the 1992 Regulations with effect from December 5, 1998.

What is Covered?

All work equipment, including machinery, appliances, apparatus, and tools, *e.g.* a tractor, lawn-mower, ladder, portable drill, and butcher's

---

[44] *e.g.* in a "nurse's lifting" case.
[45] As yet unreported: Case 97/0501/2, judgment February 19, 1998, CA, (Henry, Aldous L.JJ. Sir Christopher Staughton).
[46] Pursuant to reg. 4(1)(b)(i).
[47] reg. 4(1)(b)(ii).

knife, are all covered, *as is display screen equipment*. The 1998 Regulations additionally cover mobile work equipment such as fork-lift trucks, and many power presses.

Where?

At work, anywhere except on board ship (but including offshore installations).

Who is Protected?

Employees and the self-employed.

Who is Regulated?

The 1992 Regulations applied to employers, the self-employed in respect of themselves, anyone who has control[48] to any extent of non-domestic premises made available to persons as a place of work (in respect of work equipment used therein, and to the extent he has control), and the occupier of a factory within the meaning of the Factories Act 1961. The 1998 Regulations apply to employers, the self-employed, and a person who has to any extent control of work equipment (who is liable to the extent of that control).[49]

Content

PUWER replaces many piecemeal provisions relating to different indus- 7–27 tries and processes. Both general duties and duties specific to particular equipment are imposed.

There are general duties:

- to take into account working conditions and risks when selecting equipment;
- to ensure that equipment is suitable for the use that will be made of it, and is properly maintained; and
- to provide adequate information, instruction and training.

Specific requirements cover:

- protection from dangerous parts;

---

[48] In connection with the carrying on by him of a trade, business or other undertaking, whether for profit or not.
[49] reg. 3(3) 1998 Regulations.

- maintenance operations;
- parts and materials at high or very low temperatures;
- control systems and controls;
- isolation from power sources;
- stability of equipment;
- lighting; and
- warnings and markings.

The 1998 Regulations in addition cover:

- mobile work equipment such as fork-lift trucks;
- drive shafts; and
- (many) power presses.[50]

The most important regulation in practice is likely to be regulation 11, which requires a hierarchy of protection from dangerous parts of machinery (replacing the Factories Act 1961, s.14). Measures must be taken which are "effective: (a) to prevent access to any dangerous part of machinery or to any rotating stock-bar; or (b) to stop the movement of any dangerous part of machinery or rotating stock-bar before any part of a person enters a danger zone."

These measures are (by para. (2)):

"(a) the provision of fixed guards enclosing every part of a dangerous part or rotating stock-bar where and to the extent that it is practicable to do so, but where or to the extent that it is not, then
 (b) the provision of other guards or protection devices where and to the extent that it is practicable to do so, but where or to the extent that it is not, then
 (c) the provision of jigs, holders, push sticks or similar protection appliances used in connection with the machinery where and to the extent that it is practicable to do so, but where or to the extent that it is not, then
 (d) the provision of information, instruction, training and supervision."

There are minimum standards that guards and protection devices must satisfy.

Points to Note

7–28
- Work equipment was not subject to PUWER 92 until January 1, 1997 if it was "first provided for use in the premises or undertaking" before January 1, 1993.[51] The Guidance Note, para. 34 (not an ACOP), says that this refers to the date on which it is first supplied in the premises or undertaking, and does not mean the same as "first

---

[50] Thus implementing Council Directive 95/63/EC (O.J. L335, 30.12.95, p. 28).
[51] reg. 1(3).

brought into use", giving an example of equipment delivered into store before January 1, 1993, though not put to use till after. Although this may reflect a Court of Appeal decision on earlier law ("provided for use" was held in *Norris v. Syndic Manufacturing Co.*[52] to precede "bringing into use"), it may well be misleading—that case cannot be binding authority as to the meaning of 1992 Regulations inspired by a European Directive. The Directive uses the phrase "made available to workers".[53] The purpose of the Directive, hence that of PUWER, is to increase health and safety protection. Adopting the approach of paragraph 34 would have the contrary effect. Further, the Display Screen Equipment Regulations translate a similar phrase as "first put into service", which is clearer than that in PUWER.

- Similar problems occur with, *e.g.* "maintaining in an efficient state" (regulation 6 of PUWER 92, regulation 5 of PUWER 98). Efficient for what purpose? (The suggested answer is—for protecting health and safety).

- Amongst potentially the most important differences between the wording of the regulations and that of the Directives is the use in the English regulations of the "so far as practicable" test. This wording does not feature in the European Directives, though it is possible that there may be an equivalent.[54]

Personal Protective Equipment Regulations

When in Force?

January 1, 1993. 7–29

What is Covered?

Equipment intended to be worn or held by a person at work which protects him against a risk or risks to his health and safety. This includes accessories or additions designed for that purpose, and includes clothing designed to protect against the weather.[55]

"Ordinary working clothes which do not specifically protect the health and safety of the wearer" are NOT included, nor is equipment for playing competitive sports, nor equipment used for protection whilst travelling by road such as crash helmets and leathers.[56]

---

[52] [1952] 2 Q.B. 135 at 144, CA.
[53] Art. 3(1).
[54] See, *e.g.* Art. 3(1), and compare with Art. 3(2) of 89/655 (Equipment). The latter appears to envisage that work equipment may be used even though it does present some risk to the health of the worker using it.
[55] reg. 1(1).
[56] reg 3(2).

Where?

7–30 Anywhere at work, except on board ship, but including work within territorial waters and on offshore installations.

Who is Protected?

Every employee, and every self-employed person must provide himself with suitable protective equipment.[57]

Who is Regulated?

Employers, and the self-employed in respect of themselves.

Content

7–31 The Regulations impose duties on employers to:

- provide suitable personal protective equipment[58];
- ensure compatibility with other such equipment[59];
- assess the suitability of the equipment, and keep this assessment under review[60];
- maintain and replace protective equipment[61];
- provide information, instruction and training[62]; and
- ensure proper use.[63]

They also impose duties on an employee to:

- use such equipment in accordance with any training and instructions given to him[64];
- return it after use to the accommodation provided for it[65]; and
- report any loss or defect.[66]

Points to Note

7–32
- The effective Regulations, except that requiring equipment to be compatible with other such equipment, do not apply where there are more specific requirements under regulations relating to specific dangerous substances and processes.[67]

---

[57] reg. 4(1).
[58] reg. 4.
[59] reg. 5.
[60] reg. 6.
[61] reg. 7.
[62] reg. 9.
[63] reg. 10(1).
[64] reg. 10(2).
[65] reg. 11.
[66] reg. 11.
[67] *e.g.* the Control of Lead at Work Regulations 1980, the Ionising Radiations Regulations 1985, the Control of Asbestos at Work Regulations 1987, the Control of Substances Hazardous to Health Regulations 1988 ("COSHH"), the Noise at Work Regulations 1989 and the Construction (Head Protection) Regulations 1989.

- A risk assessment under the Management Regulations should be carried out, in order to identify the risks and what equipment is suitable to control or minimise them.
- The Protection of Eyes Regulations 1974[68] have been repealed by the Personal Protective Equipment at Work Regulations.[69] The 1992 Regulations are very generalised when compared with the specifics that were once required by the 1974 Regulations. There is an obvious danger that a judge might decide that a process, though once recognised by the 1974 Regulations as giving rise to a risk of injury, does not any more give rise to a sufficient risk for the 1992 Regulations to apply, or for liability to be established at common law. However, room for this approach is limited by Annex III of the Protective Equipment Directive,[70] which lists types of protective equipment and the processes where it may be required. Amongst them (following this example through) is that of protective goggles, face shields or screens for use in welding, grinding or separating, caulking or chiselling, drop forging, etc. Where such work is being performed, an employer should be aware that Community Law perceives a risk of injury against which it is necessary to guard by at least one of the means suggested: and accordingly, domestic law should recognise the same risk.

The Workplace Regulations

When in Force?

January 1, 1993, but workplaces in use as such before that date were not **7–33** covered until January 1, 1996, unless they had been modified, extended or converted after January 1, 1993. Until then the law applicable to factories under the Factories Act 1961, especially sections 28 and 29, and to offices, shops and railway premises under the Offices, Shops and Railway Premises Act 1963 continued to apply.

What precisely is a qualifying modification, extension or conversion may be uncertain—see below.

What is Covered?

Non-domestic premises used as a place of work[71] and accessible places **7–34** therein, together with access corridors, lobbies, stairs, roads, etc.,[72] but *not* on or in a ship, a construction site, nor agricultural or forestry workplaces

---

[68] S.I. 1974 No. 1681.
[69] S.I. 1992 No. 2966.
[70] 656/89 [1989] O.J. L393/18.
[71] But note that the Directive, Art. 2, includes domestic premises. Homework may thus be caught by European law, but not by domestic regulation.
[72] reg. 2(1)(b).

away from the undertaking's main buildings.[73] Offshore installations for mineral extraction are *not* covered.

Who is Covered?

7–35   Certainly employees. Probably (but arguably not) anyone else within the workplace. The hesitation arises because the Regulations apply to workplaces, rather than people, but provide (by regulation 4(1)) that an employer is under a duty in respect of "any workplace . . . which is under his control and *where any of his employees* work . . .". Yet the overall objective is the promotion of health and safety, and the Factories Act 1961, which these Regulations largely replace, covered those working who were not the employees of the factory occupier.

Who is Regulated?

7–36   Employees, and every person who "has, to any extent, control of a workplace . . ." in connection with a "trade, business or other undertaking (whether for profit or not)" so far as matters are within his control.

Use of the word "other" may suggest an *eiusdem generis* construction. It may thus be arguable whether this covers such as a health trust, a hospital, a school, a charity, or a sportsground.[74]

A second problem arises from this definition. What is the liability of an unincorporated association for work done by an employee of "the association"? Regulation 4(2)(1) refers to a "person" who has control. Can such an association be a "person", or, if not, how is it to be made liable?[75]

Content

7–37   The Regulations impose duties in respect of:

- the maintenance of the workplace, and devices and systems therein[76];
- temperature (indoors)[77];

---

[73] Except for requirements as to sanitary conveniences, washing facilities and drinking water, which apply "so far as is reasonably practicable".

[74] It is suggested that it does—for in the Directive the expression is "undertaking or establishment". A wide definition is given to "undertaking" in other areas of European law where the protection of employees is concerned, *e.g.* in relation to the Acquired Rights Directive (77/187/EC) [1977] O.J. L61/26. Here the purpose is the protection of employees wherever they may work, except domestically, and defining "other undertaking" as part of a restrictive class analogous to "trade and business" would be potentially antagonistic to this.

[75] Thus, cases such as *Robertson v. Ridley* [1989] 1 W.L.R. 872 relating to the liability of committee members of an unincorporated association may require reconsideration in this context.

[76] reg. 6.

[77] reg. 7.

- lighting[78];
- cleanliness and waste materials[79];
- room dimensions and space[80];
- workstations and seating[81];
- the condition of floor and traffic routes[82];
- falls or falling objects[83];
- windows (and their cleaning), doors, skylights, ventilators[84];
- organisation of traffic routes[85];
- doors and gates[86];
- escalators and moving walkways[87];
- sanitary conveniences[88];
- washing facilities[89];
- drinking water[90];
- accommodation for clothing and facilities for changing[91]; and
- rest and meals facilities.[92]

Of greatest practical importance amongst these are those which replace 7–38
the Factories Act 1961, ss.28 and 29. These are:

(a) Regulation 5 ("(1) the workplace and the equipment, devices and
    systems to which this regulation applies shall be maintained (includ-
    ing cleaned as appropriate) in an *efficient* state, in *efficient* working
    order and in good repair.

(b) Where appropriate, the *equipment, devices and systems* to which
    this regulation applies shall be subject to a *suitable* system of
    maintenance.")

(c) Regulation 12 "(1) Every floor in a workplace and the surface of
    every *traffic route* in a workplace shall be of such construction that
    the floor or surface of the traffic route is *suitable* for the purpose for
    which it is used.

(d) Without prejudice to the generality of paragraph (1), the require-
    ments in that paragraph shall include requirements that—

---

[78] reg. 8.
[79] reg. 9.
[80] reg. 10.
[81] reg. 11.
[82] reg. 12.
[83] reg. 13.
[84] regs 14–16.
[85] reg. 17.
[86] reg. 18.
[87] reg. 19.
[88] reg. 20.
[89] reg. 21.
[90] reg. 22.
[91] regs 23 and 24.
[92] reg. 25.

      (i) the floor, or surface of the traffic route, shall have no hole or slope, or be uneven or slippery so as, in each case, to expose any person to a risk to his health or safety;

     (ii) every such floor shall have effective means of drainage where necessary.

(e) So far as is *reasonably practicable*, every floor in a workplace and the surface of every traffic route in a workplace shall be kept free of obstructions and from *any article or substance* which may cause a person to *slip, trip or fall*;".

The construction of the floor must be *suitable*. This is not a lower standard than "sound", and it clearly has a wider application, relating to the expected use.

For holes, slopes, unevenness and slipperiness, so far as the construction of the floor is concerned, the standard is whether they expose a person to the risk of injury.

For holes there is no breach where adequate measures have been taken to prevent a person falling in the hole.

In assessing the risk to health and safety of slopes account must be taken of any handrail provided.

Keeping the floor free of obstructions, articles and substances which may cause persons to slip, trip or fall is subject to a requirement of *reasonable practicability*.

Points to Note

7–39   Various provisions are made by the Directive which are not by the Regulations, in particular:

(a) In the Directive[93] "technical maintenance" of the workplace and of equipment and devices therein is required of every employer. There is no obvious counterpart in the Workplace Regulations 1992.

(b) Annex 1 to the Workplace Directive lays down as a "minimum" that "buildings which house workplaces must have a structure and solidity appropriate to the nature of their use". There is no obvious counterpart in the Workplace Regulations 1992.

(c) The same applies to loading ramps (Workplace Directive, Annex 1, para. 14.3) which must, as far as possible, be safe enough to prevent workers falling off them, and to the requirement of the Directive that there be first-aid rooms in undertakings large enough (para. 19).

(d) PUWER and the Workplace Regulations both fall short of the requirement in the Annex to Directive 89/655 (Use of Work

---

[93] Art. 6 of Directive 89/654 [1989] O.J. L393/1 (Workplaces).

Equipment Directive)[94] as to the necessity for workers to have safe means of access to, and the ability to remain safely in, all the areas necessary for production, adjustment and maintenance operations.[95]

For the period between January 1, 1993 and January 1, 1996, modifications, extensions and conversions were subject to the Regulations *if complete.*[96] Problems may arise—what of the factory extension which, though not completed at January 1, 1993, was nonetheless in use as a workplace at that time? The reference to "completion" does not occur in the Directive. Moreover, the modification, extension or conversion must be started after December 31, 1992 if the Regulations are to be held to have applied to it before January 1, 1996. What if the foundation stone had been laid, but no more work had been done for six months? Has the modification, etc., been started?

Claims for slipping on snow and ice at the factory gate have gone both 7–40 ways under the Factories Act 1961.[97] In commenting on regulation 12(2)(a) (above), the ACOP (note. this *is* an ACOP) provides two apparently contradictory paragraphs: 93, which says "surfaces . . . which are likely to get wet . . . should be of a type which does not become unduly slippery . . . Floors . . . should be . . . kept free from slippery substances . . ." on the one hand and paragraph 96 on the other, which provides: "Arrangements should be made to minimise risks from snow and ice. This may . . ." (note that word) ". . . involve gritting, snow clearing and closure of some routes, particularly outside stairs, ladders and walkways on roofs . . ."

There is no equivalent to section 63 of the Factories Act (eliminating dangerous fumes).[98] Escape from fumes caused by smokers is not specifically provided for, except that rest areas must be available for the use of non-smokers. Yet any risk assessment nowadays must surely take account of the risks at the workplace of one person's smoke injuring another.

The Construction (Health, Safety and Welfare) Regulations

When in Force?

From September 2, 1996.   7–41

What is Covered and Where?

"Construction work" (including building work or repair, renovation, redecoration, maintenance and some specialised cleaning processes; site

---

[94] [1989] O.J. L393/13.
[95] *cf.* Factories Act 1961, s.29.
[96] reg. 2(2).
[97] *Thomas v. Bristol Aeroplanes* [1954] 1 W.L.R. 694, CA (icy surface on Monday morning in winter: P. lost); *cf., Woodward v. Renold Ltd* [1980] I.C.R. 387 (whole of icy car park should have been gritted) and *Gitsham v. Pearce* [1992] P.I.Q.R. P57, CA (employer must provide a system to neutralise falling snow or forming ice).
[98] But see the COSHH Regulations 1988 and their amendments since.

preparation; demolition; and the installation of the main supply and telecommunications services) is covered—but a construction site "set aside for purposes other than construction work" is not covered.

Who is Covered?

Both employees, and the self-employed, at work.

Who is Regulated?

Employers, and anyone who controls the way in which construction work is carried out (insofar as the duties relate to matters within his control).

Content of the Regulations

7–42   The Regulations replace the earlier Construction (General Provisions) Regulations 1961, Construction (Working Places) Regulations, 1966, and the Construction (Health, Safety and Welfare) Regulations, 1966. They cover:

- falls and falling objects;
- fragile materials;
- stability of structures;
- demolition and dismantling;
- explosives;
- cofferdams and caissons;
- the prevention of drowning;
- traffic routes;
- doors and gates;
- vehicles;
- fire risks;
- emergency procedures;
- welfare facilities;
- fresh air;
- temperature and weather protection;
- lighting;
- plant and equipment;
- training and inspection.

Points to Note

7–43   There are specific and detailed provisions[99] setting out requirements to which guard-rails, working platforms, personal suspension equipment, ladders, the means of arresting falls and welfare facilities should conform.

---

[99] In Schedules to the Regulations.

Working Time Regulations[1]

When in Force?

From October 1, 1998. 7–44

What is Covered?

Work by an employee or worker under a contract whereby he under-takes to do or perform personally any work or services for another party to the contract whose status is not that of client or customer of any profession of business undertaking carried on by the worker. However, there are a number of excluded areas of work, especially domestic service, sea-fishing, transport, other work at sea, doctors in training, and the uniformed services where the demands of the job inevitably conflict with provisions of the Regulations, and what is known as "unmeasured working time."[2]

Who is Covered?

Broadly speaking, those performing work as defined above.

Who is Regulated?

Employers (*i.e.* those with whom a worker, as defined above, contract). Note that many of the provisions are not mandatory, as under PUWER, etc., but are drafted as entitlements which the worker may elect to take.

Content

- Except where the worker has agreed beforehand in writing, the 7–45 employer must take "all reasonable steps" to ensure that he works no more than an average of 48 hours per week, averaged over a 17-week period (or, if he has worked for less, the period since he began to work).[3]

---

[1] Amended—with doubtful effect—by the Working Time (Amendment) Regulations 1999. The effect is doubtful because it merely replicates the wording of the original Directive, and, thus, should mean no difference in practice from that which the 1998 unamended regulations provided. At the time of writing a challenge to the Regulations has been intimated by some trades unions.

[2] This covers those who can decide their hours for themselves, such as managing executives or others with autonomous decision-making powers, family workers, and workers officiating at religious ceremonies. It is otherwise undefined. The 1999 Regulations appear to have watered down the impact of the Regulations in this area, but the extent to which they have done so remains debatable.

[3] reg. 4. There are record-keeping requirements, which are made less specific by the 1999 amendments, which provide a cross-check.

- A night worker[4] may not work more than an average of 8 hours in 24, averaged over a 17-week period.[5]
- An adult worker is entitled to a minimum of 11 hours consecutive rest in each 24-hour period; a young worker to a minimum of 12 hours.[6]
- An adult worker is entitled to an uninterrupted rest period of no less than 24 hours in each seven-day period, additional to the 11 consecutive hours of daily rest.[7]
- Where daily work time is more than six hours, the adult worker is entitled to a work-break which, in the absence of agreement, is to be not less than 20 minutes. Where a young worker's working time is over 4.5 hours, he is entitled to a break of no less than 30 minutes.[8]
- Annual leave of four weeks paid holiday must be provided in any leave year beginning after November 23, 1999.[9]
- Where the pattern of work may put an employee at risk—*e.g.* because it is at a predetermined work-rate or is monotonous—there must be "adequate rest breaks."[10]

Points to Note

7–46   The importance may be to set a standard of normal working hours beyond which the employer may have to justify that it is reasonable to ask an employee to work. Because the Regulations are expressly health and safety regulations, it may be assumed that there is some risk—dependent on the activity—from working longer hours in general than 48 per week.

However, the hours of work beyond the statutory figures may be exeeded by a number of agreements, in respect of which there are complicated provisions beyond the scope of this text. Moreover, the entitlement to refuse to work in excess of the weekly hours limit is part of the worker's contract of employment, such that he may refuse to work the excess hours, and cannot be compelled to do so, nor subject to discipline or disadvantage for refusing: *Barbour v. R.J.B. Mining (U.K.) Ltd.*[11]

Lifting Operations Regulations

When in Force?

7–47   December 5, 1998.

---

[4] Someone who works during night-time, *i.e.* between 11 p.m. and 6 a.m., unless otherwise agreed: but no such agreement may prevent the hours 12 midnight–5 a.m. being night-time.
[5] reg. 6.
[6] reg. 10.
[7] reg. 11.
[8] reg. 12.
[9] reg. 13.
[10] reg. 8.
[11] [1999] I.C.R. 679, Gage J.

What is Covered?

Lifting equipment provided for use *or used*[12] by an employee at work.

Where?

Anywhere in Great Britain, and those places outside Great Britain to which the HSWA 1974, ss.1–59 and 80–2 apply,[13] but there is limited application to ships' work equipment.[14]

Who is Regulated

Employers, self-employed persons in respect of lifting equipment they use at work, and any person who has to any extent control[15] of (i) lifting equipment, (ii) a person at work who uses *or* supervises *or* manages the use of lifting equipment, *or* (iii) the way in which lifting equipment is used.

Contents of the Regulations

The Regulations provide: 7–48
- for the strength and stability of lifting equipment;
- that lifting equipment for persons is (so far as reasonably practicable) such as to prevent them being crushed, trapped, or struck and such as to prevent falls;
- that lifting equipment be positioned so as to reduce any risk of loads striking a person, drifting, falling freely, or being released unintentionally;
- that falls down shafts are prevented by suitable devices;
- that lifting machinery is clearly marked with a safe working load;
- that lifting operations are properly and competently planned, appropriately supervised and carried out in a safe manner;
- that lifting equipment is thoroughly examined before use, and where it is exposed to conditions in which it may deteriorate is examined every six months (if used to lift people) or every 12 months (for other lifting equipment).

Points to Note

- Records have to be kept of E.C. declarations of conformity relating   7–49
  to the equipment. These should be available on disclosure.

---

[12] *Cf.* The provisions of PUWER, which relate only to equipment provided for work.
[13] As provided by the Health and Safety at Work etc. Act 1974 (Application outside Great Britain) Order 1995, S.I. 1995 No. 263.
[14] For this, see regs. 3(6) to 3(10).
[15] He is liable to the extent of his control: reg. 3.

- If equipment is borrowed by one employer from another it may not be used unless it is accompanied by "physical evidence that the last thorough examination required" by the Regulations has been carried out. This phrase is pregnant with possibilities.
- The information to be contained in a report of a thorough examination is scheduled (in detail) to the Regulations.
- The Factories Act 1961, ss.22, 23, 25–7, and the Mines and Quarries Act 1954, s.85, are repealed and the Construction (Lifting Operations) Regulations 1961 are revoked by the Regulations.

Procedural Implications of the Six-Pack

Principal Implications

7–50
- Pleadings should contain reference to the Directive where appropriate, and to the relevant paragraph of any ACOP.
- Breaches of the Management Regulations may amount to negligence, though insufficient to found civil liability on their own. They may also defeat an argument otherwise open to a defendant—where an employer should have made a risk assessment, but has in fact failed to do so, he will be treated as though he had not only carried out that risk assessment, but had caried it out thoroughly and properly.[16] Any argument to the effect that the risk assessment would not, if fact, have shown the risk or the need for any particular action will be rejected if that means that the assessment would be less than thorough and proper.[17]
- Defendants should plead any competing interpretation of the Regulations or Directive. They should continue to plead to practicability or reasonable practicability as previously.
- Defendants should consider any breach by an employee of the duties imposed on him, either by way of defence or (more likely) contribution.
- Disclosure should include risk assessments.
- Documents will be generated in making health and safety arrangements, providing information and making arrangements for training, and prescribing procedures for dealing with dangerous procedures.
- Maintenance in an efficient state may be difficult to establish without proper records.
- If in doubt as to the applicability of the Regulations when considering an accident occurring in the transitional time periods, both the "old" law and the Regulations should be pleaded.

---

[16] *Hawkes v. London Borough of Southwark,* (unreported) February 19, 1998, CA, *per* Henry L.J.
[17] *ibid.*

- Experts may be cross-examined against the information provided or suggested by the Codes of Guidance. Consultation with major employers occurred in the process of making the Directives (in 1989, so far as the six-pack is concerned), so that knowledge of the essentials should be established in any employer large enough to have a dedicated human resource department.

8. The European Dimension to Personal Injury Practice

Introduction

The aim of this chapter is to provide an introduction to the laws of the   8–01
European Union which have a direct impact on personal injury practice,
and a summary of the constitutional principles which apply in the English
courts when European law is sought to be invoked. There then follows a
brief treatment of the relevant European legislation which may apply in
relation to foreign accidents. Finally, and with the prospect of the
incorporation of the European Convention on Human Rights and Fundamental Freedoms into English law by means of the Human Rights Act
1998, there is a summary of the relevant jurisprudence under Article 6(1)
of the Convention on the right to a fair trial.

The Ambit of European Law

The Scope of European Law

Personal injury practice and European law intersect in three principal   8–02
areas: product liability and product safety; health and safety at work; and
accidents in other E.U. Member-State jurisdictions. The Treaty of Rome of
1957 set out to establish a common market, and to that end sought to
establish four freedoms, namely the free movement of capital, goods,
services and persons. Product standardisation and harmonisation is inte-
grally linked to the achievement of the free movement of goods, incorporating the need for the protection of consumers at the same time.[1]
Equally, with the increased free movement of individual tourists, the E.U.
has intervened to set minimum rules on motor insurance in relation to road
traffic accidents which occur in E.U. countries[2] and concerning package
holidays.[3] As a consequence of the amendments introduced by the Single
European Act of 1986, the E.U. has been granted express competence to
legislate to improve health and safety standards in the working
environment.[4]

---

[1] See Art. 30 E.C. Treaty (Consolidated Version, incorporating the Amsterdam Treaty
amendments) (formerly Art. 36), also Arts 152 and 153 (formerly Arts 129 and 129a).
[2] See Directives 72/166, O.J. 1972 L103/1; 84/5, O.J. 1984 L8/17; and 90/232, O.J. 1990
L129/33.
[3] Directive 90/314, O.J. 1990 L158/59.
[4] Previously Art. 118a E.C. Treaty, now see Arts 136 and 137 for the reformulated legal basis
under the E.C. Treaty. Mention should also be made of the separate competence in health
and safety matters under the Treaty establishing the European Atomic Energy Community
in the field of nuclear energy: see Directive 96/269/Euratom O.J. 1996 L159/1.

European legislation, in the form of Directives, covers such areas of interest as the protection of workers from risks related to the exposure to chemical, physical and biological agents at work,[5] major accident hazards of certain industrial activities,[6] protection of workers from exposure to metallic lead and its ionic compounds at work,[7] protection of workers from the risks related to exposure to asbestos at work,[8] protection of workers from the risks related to exposure to noise at work,[9] measures to encourage improvements in safety and health of workers at work (the framework Directive),[10] minimum safety and health requirements for the workplace,[11] minimum safety and health requirements for use of work equipment by workers at work,[12] minimum safety and health requirements for use by workers of personal protective equipment at the workplace,[13] minimum safety and health requirements for manual handling of loads where there is a risk particularly of back injury to workers,[14] minimum safety and health requirements for work with display screen equipment,[15] protection of workers from risks related to exposure to carcinogens at work,[16] minimum safety and health requirements at temporary or mobile construction sites,[17] the minimum requirements for the provision of safety signs at work,[18] improving safety and health protection of workers involved in mineral extraction,[19] minimum safety and health requirements for work on board fishing vessels,[20] on the protection of young people at work,[21] liability for defective products,[22] the safety of toys[23] and on general product safety.[24]

The United Kingdom does in general implement into domestic law in an appropriate manner its European obligations. However, it is often difficult

---

[5] Directive 80/1107, O.J. 1980 L197/12; Directive 88/364, O.J. 1988 L179/44; Directive 90/679, O.J. 1990 L268/71, amended by Directive 93/88, O.J. 1993 L268/71; Directive 98/24, O.J. 1998 L131/11; also Commission Directive 96/94, O.J. 1996 L338/86.

[6] Directive 82/501, O.J. 1982 L230/1, amended by Directive 87/216, O.J. 1987 L85/36; see also Directive 96/82, O.J. 1986 L10/13.

[7] Directive 82/605, O.J. 1982 L247/12.

[8] Directive 83/477, O.J. 1983 L263/25, as amended by Directive 91/382, O.J. 1991 L206/16. See also *Redgrave's Health and Safety*, 3rd ed., by J. Hendy Q.C. and M. Ford, para. 7.1303.

[9] Directive 86/188, O.J. 1986 L137/28. See *Redgrave*, para. 7.4603.

[10] Directive 89/391, O.J. 1989 L183/1, *Redgrave*, para. 3.1403; see also Directive 91/383, O.J. 1991 L206/19, concerning workers with a fixed duration or temporary employment relationship, *Redgrave*, para. 3.1425.

[11] Directive 89/654, O.J. 1989 L393/1, *Redgrave*, para. 8.503.

[12] Directive 89/655, O.J. 1989 L393/13, *Redgrave*, para. 5.1027.

[13] Directive 89/656, O.J. 1989 L393/18, *Redgrave*, para. 5.1044.

[14] Directive 90/269, O.J. 1990 L156/9, *Redgrave*, para. 6.503.

[15] Directive 90/270, O.J. 1990 L156/14, *Redgrave*, para. 5.2203.

[16] Directive 90/394, O.J. 1990 L196/1, *Redgrave*, para. 7.603.

[17] Directive 92/57, O.J. 1992 L245/6, *Redgrave*, para. 10.602.

[18] Directive 92/58, O.J. 1992 L245/23.

[19] Directive 92/91, O.J. 1992 L348/9; Directive 92/104, O.J. 1992 L404/10.

[20] Directive 93/103, O.J. 1993 L307/1.

[21] Directive 94/33, O.J. 1994 L216/12, *Redgrave*, para. 4.503.

[22] Directive 85/374, O.J. 1985 L210/29.

[23] Directive 88/378, O.J. 1988 L187/1.

[24] Directive 92/59, O.J. 1992 L228/24.

to know that a particular piece of legislation has been passed in order to comply with an obligation under E.U. law, from the title or provisions of the Act or statutory instrument concerned. The most clear indication that a national rule or regulation has been passed as a result of European law arises from a reference in the enabling power to the European Communities Act 1972, and/or in the explanatory note in a statutory instrument. One notable exception to this rule is the express reference in the Consumer Protection Act 1987, s.1(1), to the product liability Directive.[25]

It is important to understand the underlying rationale behind E.U. legislation, not only in order to recognise when there may be a European issue, but also because the purpose of the legislation may in fact incorporate more than one Treaty objective. At the heart of much E.U. legislation is the fundamental principle of establishing an internal market without national barriers to trade.

The Sources of European Union Law

The Treaty of Rome of 1957 has been amended by various Treaties of **8–03** Accession of new member states, the Single European Act, the Treaty of Maastricht and now the Treaty of Amsterdam. The legal competence of the E.U. has expanded over time, however, the new Treaty rights and legal bases have largely been programmatic or permissive in nature and have not granted significant rights to the individual. It is in secondary legislation that most concrete rights and obligations are to be found. In the context of personal injury rights and obligations, the most important legislative tool is the Directive.

Directives are essentially binding E.U. agreements which require the member states to introduce into domestic law legislation which implements the agreed standards set out in the Directive on or before a particular deadline set in the Directive.[26] Directives, therefore, require implementation, and are not, accordingly, the intended principal source of rights and/ or remedies for the individual. If a Directive has been correctly implemented, then the individual will rely on national rules and regulations, to be interpreted in the light of the general principles of European law as established by the European Court of Justice. Where there has been a failure correctly to implement a Directive into national law, then, in certain circumstances, an individual may rely upon the provisions of the Directive without reference to national law (known as "direct effect"). Finally, in very limited circumstances, an individual may sue for damages for failure properly to implement a Directive.

---

[25] See further Case C–300/95, referred to below, para. 8–09.
[26] See Art. 249(3) E.C. Treaty (formerly Art. 189(3)).

Rights and Remedies under E.U. Law[27]

2.1 Interpretation

8-04   Although the legislative text of any Directive is drafted in English, it is necessary to recall that the text of the Directive will also have been translated into the other official languages of the European Union. Since no linguistic text takes precedence over any other, it is important not to interpret the meaning of the text in accordance with English canons of interpretation. The European style of interpretation is rather more relaxed, and seeks out the broad purpose without reference to fine and precise analysis of the particular word. Thus, a word which is tolerably clear in English may have a different meaning when taking into consideration the need for uniform interpretation of E.U. law by reference to all of the E.U. languages, and in the light of the legislative intent and context of the measure in question.[28]

The English courts have recognised the duty upon the national judge to interpret national implementing legislation in a purposive manner in the light of a European obligation, in circumstances which may depart from a strict or literal interpretation, where it is possible so to do.[29] This may include, for example, the insertion of extra words in a statutory instrument. However, there is a limit to the lengths to which the national courts will apply such interpretative flexibility, and they will not go so far as to distort the meaning of words in a national measure.[30] The duty to apply a purposive interpretation to national legislation to give effect to a European obligation contained in a Directive covers both national legislation passed in order to implement the European law in question as well as pre-existing legislation passed without reference to Europe.[31]

Direct Effect

8-05   The question of direct effect will, generally, only arise where there has been a failure by the member state properly to implement all the obligations contained in a Directive, in circumstances where it is not possible for a national court to interpret any national measure in a purposive manner to comply with European law. Where there has been a

---

[27] See G. Barling Q.C. and M. Brearley eds., *Practitioners' Handbook of E.C. Law*, Trenton Publishing, 1998; M. Brearley and M. Hoskins, 2nd ed., *Remedies in E.C. Law*, Sweet & Maxwell, 1998.

[28] See Lord Diplock in *R. v. Henn and Darby* [1981] A.C. 850 at 906; *R. v. International Stock Exchange ex parte Else Ltd* [1993] Q.B. 534, at 545D–F (Sir Thomas Bingham M.R.).

[29] Case 106/89, *Marleasing* [1990] E.C.R. I–4135; [1992] 1 C.M.L.R. 305; *Litster v. Forth Dry Dock & Engineering Co. Ltd* [1990] 1 A.C. 546.

[30] *Duke v. GEC Reliance Ltd* [1988] A.C. 618.

[31] *Webb v. Emo Air Cargo Ltd* [1993] I.C.R. 175 at 186–7.

total or partial failure of implementation, or a wrongful implementation of a Directive, an individual may rely directly on any provision of the Directive which is sufficiently clear, precise and unconditional and which is capable of conferring on the individual a particular right. Where Directives are concerned, the time for implementation laid down in the Directive must also have expired.

Directly effective rights and obligations may only be enforced by an individual against an organ or "emanation of the State". That is to say, directly effective rights may be applied "vertically" but not horizontally. If a Directive has not been properly transposed into national law, a Directive cannot be used to impose on another private individual an obligation which the State has failed to incorporate into its domestic legal order.[32] The rationale behind the doctrine of vertical direct effect of Directives is a form of estoppel, namely that the State in all its manifestations may not take advantage of its own wrong for the failure to transpose all the provisions of a Directive into national law after the expiry of the due date for implementation.[33]

An "emanation of the State" is a term of art defined by the European Court of Justice. In Case C–188/89, *Foster v. British Gas Plc*,[34] the European Court held that "a body, whatever its legal form, which has been made responsible, pursuant to a measure adopted by the State, for providing a public service under the control of the State, and has for that purpose special powers beyond those which result from the normal rules applicable in relations between individuals" is a body against which the directly effective provisions of a Directive may be enforced.

The jurisprudence of the European Court has also been applied to tax **8–06** authorities,[35] police authorities,[36] health authorities,[37] and local or regional authorities.[38] The English courts have held an emanation of the State to include British Gas prior to privatisation,[39] the governing body of a voluntary-aided school,[40] and a water undertaker,[41] (but not a private company wholly owned by the State[42]).

The fact that the particular emanation of the State against whom an individual may wish to enforce a particular directly effective right had no responsibility for the implementation of the Directive, and was not

---

[32] Case C–91/92, *Faccini Dori v. Recreb* [1994] E.C.R. I–3325.
[33] Case 152/84, *Marshall v. Southampton and South West Hampshire AHA* [1986] E.C.R. 723, [1986] Q.B. 401.
[34] [1990] E.C.R. I–3313, [1991] Q.B. 405.
[35] Case 8/81, *Becker* [1982] E.C.R. 53, [1982] 1 C.M.L.R. 499.
[36] Case 222/84, *Johnston* [1986] E.C.R. 1651, [1987] Q.B. 129.
[37] *Marshall, op. cit.*
[38] Case 103/88, *Costanzo v. Comune di Milano* [1989] E.C.R. 1839, [1990] 3 C.M.L.R. 239.
[39] [1991] 2 A.C. 306.
[40] *National Union of Teachers v. St Mary's Church of England Junior School* [1997] I.R.L.R. 242.
[41] *Griffin v. South West Water Services Ltd* [1995] I.R.L.R. 15.
[42] *Rolls-Royce v. Doughty* [1987] I.C.R. 932.

therefore in any sense to blame, cannot exculpate that body from applying the provisions of the Directive. This may most readily be seen in the context of employment law where state bodies have been obliged to comply with rights granted under European discrimination law which obligations did not apply to the private sector until correct implementation.[43]

One particular difficulty has appeared in the application of the doctrine of direct effect, as a result of the findings of the European Court of Justice in the case of *Francovich*.[44] In that case, Italy had completely failed to bring into effect national laws establishing a guarantee fund responsible for the payment of a minimum level of protection for employees in relation to claims outstanding against an employer at the time of the insolvency of the employer. The European Court held that the provisions of the relevant Directive were sufficiently clear, precise and unconditional to grant directly effective rights insofar as the identity of the persons entitled to the guarantee were concerned and the content of the guarantee. However, the European Court also held that since Italy had a discretion when implementing the directive as to the nature and identity of the fund, which may or may not be a wholly publicly funded body, the individual applicants could not enforce any directly effective rights as against the State.[45] The *Francovich* case was subsequently applied by the European Court in the Spanish case of *Wagner Miret*.[46]

The European case law was followed and applied by the Court of Appeal in *Mighell v. Reading and the Motor Insurers Bureau*.[47] Schiemann L.J., with whose judgment Swinton-Thomas L.J. agreed, held that the Second Directive on Motor Insurance (84/5/EEC) did not have direct effect since there was a discretion provided to the Government when seeking to fulfil its obligations to implement the Directive whether by using the MIB or in some other way. Hobhouse L.J. preferred to hold that the MIB was a private law body and could not constitute an emanation of the State.

Effective Remedies

8–07   Whilst a Member State does not possess any particular discretion when implementing the substantive obligations contained in a Directive, the form and method of implementation are left open for the member state to choose. The discretion of the Member State as to how to implement the provisions of a Directive is only circumscribed to a limited extent. In principle, the question of what remedy shall be applicable is a question for

---

[43] *Marshall, op. cit.*
[44] Joined Cases C–6/90 and C–9/90, [1991] E.C.R. I–5357, [1993] 2 C.M.L.R. 66.
[45] At paras 10–27, see pages 5407–5413 and 109–113 respectively.
[46] Case C–334/92, [1993] E.C.R. I–6911, [1995] 2 C.M.L.R. 49.
[47] [1999] P.I.Q.R. P101.

the procedural autonomy of each member state, subject to two qualifications prescribed by the European Court of Justice. First, any remedy provided to implement a directly effective European right shall be no less generous than any equivalent national remedy (the principle of non-discrimination)[48]; and secondly, no condition attaching to a remedy should be framed so as to render it extremely difficult or virtually impossible in practice for an individual to obtain an effective remedy.[49]

Litigation in this area of interest to the personal injury lawyer has concerned limitation periods (both in terms of non-discrimination and effectiveness),[50] and ceilings on compensation/denial of entitlement to interest.[51]

Liability of the State for Failure to Implement a Directive

The *Francovich* case[52] is better known for the landmark ruling of the   8–08 European Court of Justice that a Member State may be liable in damages for a failure properly to implement a Directive into national law, which failure has caused the claimant loss and damage. This is really a longstop remedy if all else fails. The European Court has held that the principles governing the entitlement to damages for a failure of a member state to comply with its obligations under European law are identical to the principles governing the non-contractual liability of the institutions of the European Union.[53] In summary, it is necessary to prove a sufficiently serious breach of a rule of European law. Where Directives are concerned, a failure to adopt the provisions into national law in due time will constitute a sufficiently serious breach.[54] The rule in question must be intended to confer rights on individuals, and, of course, there must be a direct causative link between the breach and any damage suffered.

---

[48] First articulated in Case 33/76, *Rewe* [1976] E.C.R. 1989. For an English example, see *Fitzgerald v. Williams* [1996] 2 All E.R. 171.

[49] Case 199/82, *San Giorgio* [1983] E.C.R. 3595, applied in Case C–213/89, *R v. Secretary of State for Transport ex parte Factortame Ltd* [1990] E.C.R. I–2433, [1990] 3 C.M.L.R. 375, and Joined Cases C–46/93 and 48/93, *Brasserie du Pecheur v. Germany* and *R v. Secretary of State for Transport ex parte Factortame Ltd* [1996] E.C.R. I–1029, [1996] Q.B. 404.

[50] For a most recent authority, see Case C–231/96, *EDIS* [1999] 2 C.M.L.R. 995.

[51] See Case 271/91, *Marshall v. Southampton AHA (No. 2)* [1993] E.C.R. I–4367; [1994] Q.B. 126; also for a recent authority, Joined Cases C–279–281/96, *Ansaldo Energia* [1999] 2 C.M.L.R. 776.

[52] Joined Cases C–6/90 and C–9/90, [1991] E.C.R. I–5357, [1993] 2 C.M.L.R. 66.

[53] Joined Cases C–46/93 and 48/93, *Brasserie du Pecheur v. Germany* and *R v. Secretary of State for Transport ex parte Factortame Ltd* [1996] E.C.R. I–1029, [1996] Q.B. 404. See the jurisprudence under the former Art. 215(2) E.C. Treaty, now Article 288(2).

[54] Joined Cases 178, 179, 188–190/94, *Dillenkoffer and others v. Germany* [1996] E.C.R. I–4845, [1996] 3 C.M.L.R. 469.

European Court of Justice Caselaw on Health and Safety and Product Liability

8–09   There is scant jurisprudence from the European Court on the interpretation and application of either the health and safety Directives or the product liability Directive. However, two cases have involved the United Kingdom. Case C–84/94, *United Kingdom v. E.U. Council*[55] concerned a challenge to the working time Directive which it was argued had been adopted without due regard to the powers of the E.C. Treaty. Directive 93/104[56] concerning the organisation of working time had been adopted under Article 118a of the E.C. Treaty, the legal basis for the adoption of the health and safety directives. The European Court held that[57]:

> "There is nothing in the wording of Article 118a to indicate that the concepts of "working environment", "safety" and "health" as used in that provision should, in the absence of other indications, be interpreted restrictively, and not as embracing all factors, physical or otherwise, capable of affecting the health and safety of the worker in his environment, including in particular certain aspects of the organisation of working time. On the contrary, the words "especially in the working environment" militate in favour of a broad interpretation of the powers which Article 118a confers upon the Council for the protection of the health and safety of workers. Moreover, such an interpretation of the words "safety" and "health" derives support in particular from the preamble to the Constitution of the World Health Organisation to which all the Member States belong. Health is there defined as a state of complete physical, mental and social well-being that does not consist only in the absence of illness and infirmity."

Whereas the precise wording of the legal basis under the E.C. Treaty has been reformulated as a consequence of the consolidation effected by the Treaty of Amsterdam,[58] nevertheless it is clear that the scope of protection under the E.C. Treaty is a broad one, and therefore the interpretation of any secondary legislation should also apply a broad purposive construction.

8–10   Case C–300/95, *Commission v. United Kingdom*,[59] concerned infraction proceedings brought by the E.C. Commission for failure adequately to implement Article 7(e) of the product liability Directive[60] into national law. Article 7(e) provides producers with a defence if the state of scientific and technical knowledge at the time the product was put into circulation was not such as to enable the existence of the defect in the product to have been discovered. The Commission contended that section 4(1)(e) of the Consumer Protection Act 1987 effectively weakened the strict liability

---

[55] [1996] E.C.R. I–5755; [1996] 3 C.M.L.R. 671.
[56] O.J. 1993 L307/18.
[57] At 5800 and 710–1 respectively, para. 15.
[58] See Arts 136 and 137 for the reformulated legal basis, also Art. 152.
[59] [1997] E.C.R. I–2649; [1997] 3 C.M.L.R. 923.
[60] Directive 85/374, O.J. 1985 L210/29.

regime as set out by the Directive. The European Court dismissed the Commission's application.

The European Court held[61] that the defence set out in Article 7(e) is not directed at the practices and safety standards in use in the industrial sector in which the producer is operating, "but, unreservedly, at the state of scientific and technical knowledge, including the most advanced level of such knowledge, at the time when the product in question was put into circulation." Such an objective state of knowledge referred not to that which the producer knew or could have been apprised, but was that knowledge of which the producer is presumed to have been informed. The knowledge must have been accessible at the time when the product was put into circulation.[62] In assessing whether the Directive had been correctly implemented by the United Kingdom, the European Court paid particular note to the fact that section 1(1) of the Act made express reference to the Directive. The European Court considered that there was nothing in the material produced to the Court to suggest that the courts in the United Kingdom would not interpret section 4(1)(e) in the light of the wording of the Directive.[63]

Implementation of the Health and Safety Directives

Despite the fact that many of the domestic provisions implementing the new European standards came into force in 1993, there has been scant consideration by the English courts of the new regime, and whether the implementing regulations accurately transpose into national law the obligations contained in the "six-pack" Directives.[64]   **8–11**

The Management of Health and Safety at Work Regulations 1992 exclude civil liability by virtue of Regulation 15. This may be contrary to the principle of non-discrimination and/or effectiveness, in the light of the fact that the other implementing regulations permit civil liability. The debate is muddied by the fact that the Health and Safety at Work etc Act 1974 does provide for criminal liability. However, breach of criminal law can found a civil cause of action, and in that regard it is unclear whether claimants are in fact prejudiced.

More importantly, Article 6(1) and (2) of the framework Directive does specify a positive duty on employers to prevent occupational risks. There

---

[61] At 2670 and 940 respectively, paras 26–29.

[62] It would appear to be accepted by the European Court that the precise meaning of Art. 7(e) on this point is unclear, since the Court considers that it may be necessary for national courts to refer further questions of interpretation under Article 177 E.C. Treaty (now Art. 234). *Cf.* the opinion of A.G. Tesauro at paras 21–24.

[63] At 2672 and 941 respectively, para. 38.

[64] For a detailed analysis of the conformity of the domestic regulations with the Directives, see I. Smith, C. Goddard and N. Randall, *Health and Safety—The New Legal Framework*, Butterworths, 1993, and see also the commentary in *Redgrave*.

has not been any express implementation into national law of these provisions. The duty to take preventive and protective measures under the 1992 Regulations depends upon the employer carrying out a risk assessment and identifying such risks, breach of which as noted does not provide a civil remedy.

A second significant divergence concerns the repeated use of the familiar phrase "so far as reasonably practicable". This formulation found frequently in English legislation is alien to European law. European standards are largely prescriptive. It does not grant a residual discretion by reference to economic or other considerations of a commercial, non-safety nature. Where there is no qualifying wording in the European legislation, it is submitted that claimants may rely on the Directives against emanations of the State.

Foreign accidents

8–12   Two areas are covered in this section, namely jurisdictional rules under the Brussels Convention (and associated instruments), and particular rules in relation to package holidays which avoid the need to apply foreign or conflicts of laws.

The Brussels Convention

8–13   The first question which applies in any transnational litigation for an English advocate is whether the English courts have jurisdiction.[65] The Brussels Convention provides harmonised rules on jurisdiction and judgments across the European Union[66] including the EFTA states.[67] The purpose behind the Convention regime is to prevent multiplicity of litigation in different contracting states, and the risk of conflicting judgments. The rules under the Convention are mandatory. Accordingly, questions of *forum conveniens* do not apply when deciding which is the appropriate forum as between competing contracting states.

The starting point under the Brussels Convention is the domicile (not nationality) of the defendant. Article 2 states, "Subject to the provisions of this Convention, persons domiciled in a Contracting State shall, whatever their nationality, be sued in the courts of that State." Domicile is defined in the Civil Jurisdiction and Judgments Act 1982 at section 41[68] in relation to

---

[65] The preliminary question as to whether there is a more profitable forum than the United Kingdom will not frequently arise, since perhaps with the exception of Ireland, English levels of damages are generally towards the top of the European league table.

[66] Belgium, Denmark, France, Germany, Greece, Ireland, Italy, Luxembourg, Netherlands, Portugal, Spain and United Kingdom are parties to the Brussels Convention.

[67] Austria, Finland, Iceland, Norway, Sweden and Switzerland are parties to the Lugano Convention (which mirrors to all intents and purposes the Brussels Convention).

[68] Section 41 provides that an individual is domiciled in the United Kingdom if he is resident in the United Kingdom and the nature and circumstances of his residence indicate that he has a substantial connection with the United Kingdom. Where an individual has been resident in the United Kingdom for three months or more, it is presumed that he fulfills the requirement of substantial connection, unless the contrary is proved (s.41(6)).

individuals, and at section 42 for corporations and associations. Apart from the general rule encapsulated in Article 2, there are further special rules of jurisdiction which permit claimants a choice of forum in defined circumstances. In limited circumstances, in particular concerning actions in relation to land, the normal and special rules of jurisdiction are ousted by rules of exclusive jurisdiction.[69]

Article 5(1) governs any claim which is connected with "matters relating to contract". If a claim may be based on concurrent causes of action, say contract and tort, then for the purposes of jurisdiction, Article 5(1) applies[70] and not Article 5(3). Under Article 5(1), the English courts will have jurisdiction if England is the place of performance of the obligation in question, the breach of which gives rise to the claim for personal injury. Where an employee works in more than one Contracting State, it is necessary to establish the place where the employee mainly or habitually performs his obligations for his employer, that is the location of the effective centre of his working activities.[71]

Article 5(3) provides in relation to tort that contracting states have 8–14 jurisdiction where the harmful event occurred. Tort has been defined by the European Court as being "all actions which seek to establish the liability of the defendant and which are not relating to contract within the meaning of Article 5(1)."[72] The place where the harmful event occurred may be the place where the damage occurred or the place where the event giving rise to the damage occurred. In *Bier v. Mines de Potasse d'Alsace*[73] there was a release of polluting chemicals from a French factory into the river Rhine. Damage was suffered by Dutch market gardeners in the Netherlands. The European Court of Justice held that it was permissible to bring proceedings in either France or the Netherlands in accordance with Article 5(3). The fact that an injured claimant continues to suffer loss in the United Kingdom, due to say loss of earnings, as a result of injury or an accident suffered in another contracting state does not found jurisdiction in the English courts.[74]

By Article 5(4) of the Convention, a person domiciled in a contracting state may be sued in another contracting state for damages where the act giving rise to the claim is also the subject of criminal proceedings in the

---

[69] See Art. 16(1) which specifies the courts of the State where the land is located. In Case C–280/90, *Hacker* [1992] I.L.Pr. 515, the European Court of Justice held that a short term contract for a holiday home did not fall within the ambit of Art. 16(1). Different considerations may apply to timeshare arrangements, for example.

[70] See the definition of tort under Art. 5(3) below and Case 189/87, *Kalfelis v. Schroder* [1988] E.C.R. 5565.

[71] See Case 133/81, *Ivenel v. Schwab* [1982] E.C.R. 1891; Case 266/85, *Shenavai v. Kreischer* [1987] E.C.R. 239, and Case C–383/95, *Rutten v. Cross Medical Ltd* [1997] I.L.Pr. 199.

[72] See Case 189/87, *Kalfelis v. Schroder* [1988] E.C.R. 5565.

[73] Case 21/76, [1978] Q.B. 708.

[74] See Case C–220/88, *Dumez* [1990] E.C.R. I–49; Case C–364/93, *Marinari v. Lloyds Bank* [1996] Q.B. 217.

court seised of the criminal proceedings, to the extent that that court has jurisdiction under its own law to entertain such proceedings.

Finally, Article 6(1) permits a foreign domiciled defendant to be joined in proceedings where there is an English defendant. This will be particularly appropriate where there is a risk of conflicting decisions or findings of fact, in relation to connected disputes. This may be the most useful means of securing English jurisdiction over foreign European-based defendants under the Brussels Convention. However, the English courts will be astute to protect a foreign defendant who has been joined to an English domiciled defendant merely to obtain jurisdiction where there is no realistic bona fide claim in a connected cause of action against the English defendant.

Article 21 of the Convention states that where proceedings involving the same cause of action and between the same parties are brought in the courts of different contracting states, any court other than the court first seised shall of its own motion stay its proceedings until such time as the jurisdiction of the court first seised is established. Where the jurisdiction of the court first seised has been established, any other court must decline jurisdiction in favour of the court first seised. Article 22 grants a power to courts seised in related actions to stay proceedings pending the outcome of the litigation pending in the court first seised.

Where there has been a judgment in a court of a Contracting State, Article 26 permits such judgment to be recognised in the English courts. This allows claimants to rely upon issue estoppel and cause of action estoppel without having to relitigate facts and matters which have already been decided by a court of competent jurisdiction.

Package Holidays

8–15   Directive 90/314[75] is one of the few examples of European legislation which grants European citizens substantive rights when they travel abroad. The Directive has been implemented into English law by the Package Travel, Package Holidays and Package Tours Regulations 1992.[76] The importance of the Directive is that it removes the need for injured claimants to sue foreign defendants under foreign law in foreign jurisdictions. The Directive and implementing regulations impose a liability on package tour organisers for any failure to perform the obligations under the contract.[77] Thus, it is normally the case that the company who organises or sells a package holiday will have an English domicile, and the applicable law will be English law.[78]

---

[75] O.J. 1990 L158/19.
[76] 1992 S.I. No. 3288. See D. Grant and S. Mason, *Holiday Law*, 2nd ed., Sweet & Maxwell, 1998.
[77] reg. 15(1) and (2). In this author's opinion, the cause of action under reg. 15 is not contractual but for breach of statutory duty, although there may also be a parallel cause of action in contract: *cf.* reg. 15(6).
[78] Therefore, English law of limitation will also apply.

The Directive and Regulations only apply to package holidays, that is the pre-arranged combination of two out of three components, namely transport; accommodation; and tourist services not ancillary to transport or accommodation and accounting for a significant proportion of the package; sold at an inclusive price as a service, where the service covers a period of more than 24 hours or includes overnight accommodation.[79] There is a limited defence available where any injury is solely attributable to the consumer, or a third party unconnected with the provision of the services contracted for where any failure to perform the obligation under the contract is unforeseeable or unavoidable, or occurs in circumstances of *force majeure*.[80]

Human Rights: the Right to a Fair Trial[81]

The Treaty Right

Article 6(1) states: 8–16

"In the determination of his civil rights and obligations or of any criminal charge against him, everyone is entitled to a fair and public hearing within a reasonable time by an independent and impartial tribunal established by law. Judgment shall be pronounced publicly but the press and public may be excluded from all or part of the trial in the interest of morals, public order, or national security in a democratic society, where the interests of juveniles or the protection of the private life of the parties so require, or to the extent strictly necessary in the opinion of the court in special circumstances where publicity would prejudice the interests of justice."

The express rights to (i) a fair hearing, (ii) a public hearing, (iii) a hearing within a reasonable time, (iv) a hearing by an independent and impartial tribunal, and (v) the promulgation of a publicly declared judgment, have been supplemented by further rights by virtue of the caselaw of the European Court of Human Rights.

The Scope of Article 6(1): Substance Versus Procedure; Immunities

The European Court of Human Rights has held that the right to a fair   8–17 trial holds a "prominent place" within the Convention system and that "there can be no justification for interpreting Article 6(1) of the Conven-

---

[79] reg. 2(1).
[80] reg. 15(2).
[81] See for example D.J. Harris, M. O'Boyle and C. Warbrick, *Law of the European Convention on Human Rights*, Butterworths, 1995.

tion restrictively."[82] Personal injury litigation clearly falls within the scope of the Article in relation to the determination of civil rights and obligations, both as to the determination of liability and quantum. However, the Commission has held that compensation claims from a public fund do not fall within Article 6.[83] Article 6 is not concerned with ancillary proceedings not involving the determination of rights or obligations. Accordingly, disputes concerning interim relief, enforcement of judgments, or leave to appeal fall outside the right to a fair trial.

The principal starting point concerning Article 6(1) is that the right to a fair trial does not involve an assessment of the merits of any case. Therefore, a substantive rule which does not provide an individual with a right to bring a claim falls outside the scope of Article 6.[84] On the other hand, where a person is prevented from bringing a claim by virtue of a procedural rule, then Article 6(1) may apply. This distinction may be easier to conceive in theory than apply in practice.

In *Powell and Rayner v. United Kingdom*,[85] the Commission held that the lack of a cause of action for trespass and nuisance in relation to aircraft overflight and noise did not raise any issues under Article 6(1). In the light of the decision of the Commission on admissibility, the Court declined to entertain the complaint under Article 6. This may be contrasted with *Osman v. United Kingdom*[86] where the European Court of Human Rights did consider that the rule providing the police with immunity of suit against negligence claims was contrary to the Convention. In *Osman*, the United Kingdom accepted that the rule articulated in *Hill v. Chief Constable of West Yorkshire*[87] did not automatically prevent from the outset an action in negligence against the police, but rather allowed the domestic courts to make a considered assessment as to whether a particular case fell within or outside the immunity. On that basis, the European Court of Human Rights held that the applicants were entitled to pray in aid Article 6(1). Further, on the merits, the European Court considered that the effect of the ruling of the Court of Appeal automatically excluding access to a court was disproportionate, given the facts of the case and the nature of the allegations made against the police.

The effect of the judgment of the European Court of Human Rights was considered in the recent case of *Barrett v. Enfield LBC*.[88] Lord Browne-Wilkinson (with whom Lords Nolan and Steyn agreed) in a short but cogent speech dissected the logic of the *Osman* judgment, which he found

---

[82] *Moreira de Azevedo v. Portugal* (A/189) (1991) 13 E.H.R.R. 721, para. 66.
[83] *Berler v. Germany No. 12624/87*, 62 D.R. 207 (1989); *B v. Netherlands No. 11098/84*, 43 D.R. 198 (1985); *Nordh v. Sweden No. 14225/88*, 69 D.R. 223 (1990).
[84] *H v. Belgium* (A/127–B) (1988) E.H.R.R. 339, para. 40.
[85] (1990) 12 E.H.R.R. 288 (Commission Opinion), 355 (Court Judgment).
[86] (1998) 5 B.H.R.C. 293; [1998] H.R.C.D. 966; *The Times*, November 5, 1998.
[87] [1989] A.C. 53.
[88] [1999] 3 W.L.R. 79; [1999] 3 All E.R. 193.

"extremely difficult to understand". In fact their Lordships ruled in the *Barrett* case that there could in principle be a common law duty of care owed to a child taken into care by a local authority. However, Lord Browne-Wilkinson stated further:

"[in] view of the decision in *Osman's* case it is now difficult to foretell what would be the result in the present case if we were to uphold the striking out order. . . . In the present very unsatisfactory state of affairs, and bearing in mind that under the Human Rights Act 1998 art 6 will shortly become part of English law, in such cases as these it is difficult to say that it is a clear and obvious case calling for a striking out."[89]

Effective Access to a Court; Legal Aid

The first case in which the European Court of Human Rights articulated **8–18** a right of effective access to a court (both in law and in fact) was *Golder v. United Kingdom*.[90] This case concerned the rights of a prisoner to obtain access to a solicitor for the purpose of instituting libel proceedings. In principle, the applicant could obtain access to the High Court to institute proceedings, however, in fact this right was restricted by the refusal of the prison authorities to permit him access to legal advice. The European Court of Human Rights held that what was to be guaranteed was effective access to a court which had been denied to the applicant.

A case of greater significance for personal injury practitioners in the light of the proposed withdrawal of legal aid is *Airey v. Ireland*.[91] The applicant challenged the refusal to grant her legal aid in order to seek a decree of judicial separation from her husband. The European Court of Human Rights held that the possibility for the applicant to appear in person did not provide her with an effective right of access to a court. The Court recognised that it was not incumbent upon the state to provide legal aid for every dispute relating to a civil right. Nevertheless, the Court continued:

"Article 6(1) may sometimes compel the State to provide for the assistance of a lawyer where such assistance proves indispensable for an effective access to court either because legal representation is rendered compulsory . . . or by reason of the complexity of the procedure or of the case."

Stewart-Brady v. United Kingdom[92] illustrates a case where the right to legal aid was refused. There, the Commission rejected a claim arising from a refusal to grant legal aid for an appeal against the striking out of an action on the grounds that there were no reasonable prospects of success and the costs were disproportionate to the amount claimed.

---

[89] At 85 and 199–200 respectively.
[90] (1975) 1 E.H.R.R. 524.
[91] (1979) 2 E.H.R.R. 305.
[92] (1997) 24 E.H.R.R. CD 38.

Margin of Appreciation and Proportionality

8–19   Another English case which came before the European Court of Human Rights on the question of effective access to a court was *Fayed v. United Kingdom*.[93] The question of effective access arose in the context of proposed libel proceedings and the defence of qualified privilege of government inspectors in relation to allegations of fraud made in a report on the conduct of a company. The Court held that "the right of access to the courts secured by Article 6(1) is not absolute, but may be subject to limitations" which may vary in time and place according to the needs and resources of the community and of individuals. The Court continued by stating that "the Contracting States enjoy a certain margin of appreciation, but the final decision as to observance of the Convention's requirements rests with the Court. It must be satisfied that the limitations applied do not restrict or reduce the access left to the individual in such a way or to such an extent that the very essence of the right is impaired." Any limitation "will not be compatible with Article 6(1) if it does not pursue a legitimate aim and if there is not a reasonable relationship of proportionality between the means employed and the aim sought to be achieved." The task of the Court was to strike "a fair balance between the demands of the general interests of the community and the requirements of the protection of the individual's fundamental rights."

Ashingdane v. United Kingdom,[94] concerned a mental patient who sought to challenge his continued detention in a secure mental hospital under the Mental Health Act 1959. One of the preconditions to bringing proceedings against the Secretary of State was the need for leave, which could only be granted by the High Court on "substantial grounds". The European Court held that the restriction had a legitimate aim and was proportionate.

Time limits have also been the subject of challenge in Strasbourg. *Stubbings v. United Kingdom*,[95] which concerned an unsuccessful challenge to the time limit of six years from age 18 years in relation to personal injury claims for childhood sexual abuse, indicates the width of the discretion left to the State. This may be compared with *Perez de Rada Cavanilles v. Spain*,[96] where the European Court of Human Rights overturned the application of a very short time limit of three days governing the right to apply to set aside judgment.

Security for costs may also limit the right to access to a court. In *Tolstoy Miloslavsky v. United Kingdom*,[97] the European Court found no breach of Article 6 where the issue of security for costs arose in relation to an appeal

---

[93] (1990) 18 E.H.R.R. 393.
[94] (1985) 7 E.H.R.R. 528.
[95] (1997) 23 E.H.R.R. 213.
[96] [1998] H.R.C.D. 981.
[97] (1995) 20 E.H.R.R. 442.

to the Court of Appeal, whereas, in relation to first instance proceedings in *Ait-Mouhoub v. France*,[98] the European Court of Human Rights did intervene. In the latter case, the applicant, who had no resources, had applied for legal aid and had not received a reply from the legal aid office. The French court set as an amount of security the sum of 80,000 French francs. The European Court held that this was in breach of the applicant's rights under Article 6(1).

Equality of Arms

In the light of the new duty introduced by Part 1 of the Civil Procedure **8–20** Rules, it is pertinent to note that the concept of equality of arms is also present in the Strasbourg jurisprudence under Article 6(1). Thus, the European Court has held that "equality of arms" implies that each party must be afforded a reasonable opportunity to present his case—including his evidence—under conditions that do not place him at a substantial disadvantage *vis-à-vis* his opponent."[99] This extends to equal access to facilities.[1]

Delay

One of the express rights under Article 6(1) concerns the right to a **8–21** hearing within a reasonable time. The European Court of Human Rights will naturally assess the complexity of the case when coming to a conclusion. The case of *Robins v. United Kingdom*[2] is instructive as to the length of delay which may be considered unacceptable in normal, uncomplicated matters. The case concerned an appeal on costs which was considered to be a relatively straightforward matter. Delays of ten months (caused by the mistaken belief of the Legal Aid Board that the applicants had separated) and 16 months (due to inaction by the Civil Appeals Office) were found to be unreasonable and constituted a breach of Article 6(1).

---

[98] [1998] H.R.C.D. 976.
[99] *Dombo Beheer v. Netherlands*, (A/274) (1994) E.H.R.R. 213, para. 33.
[1] *Schuler-Zgraggen v. Switzerland* (A/263) (1993) 16 E.H.R.R. 405.
[2] (1998) 26 E.H.R.R. 527.

Section 2

DAMAGES

9. General Damages

The first part of this chapter deals with the general principles applying to the assessment, and the second part with the effect of the Court of Appeal's decision in the case of *Heil v. Rankin*.[1]

Introduction

Damages for non-pecuniary loss, or general damages, are awarded to a claimant for the pain, suffering and loss of amenity caused by physical or mental injury. In theory, "pain", "suffering" and "loss of amenity" are separate elements, but in practice "pain and suffering" is a term of art. Such damages are conventional sums, and in assessing them the court will have regard to the overall seriousness of the claimant's loss of amenity, rather than to each individual symptom.

The English system for the assessment of general damages runs on a tariff, and the ultimate source of the tariff is the courts. The courts' decisions are to be found in a number of well-known sources,[2] and these decisions have been collated into a set of guidelines (see *Judicial Studies Board*, below, para. 9–02). Perhaps the starting-point for a study of the tariff should be the maximum damages to be awarded for the worst of injuries: in theory, all other injuries should file themselves in order of severity behind such awards.

The cases of maximum severity present special problems of management and quantum, which are dealt with elsewhere in this volume. The victim will have suffered quadriplegia, paraplegia, hemiplegia[3] or very severe brain damage with a consequent total dependency on others and a requirement of constant care. He may be in pain, and may have insight into his condition. Advances in medical science have led to an increase in such "total wreck" claims during recent years.

The upper limit for general damages for pain suffering and loss of amenity has now substantially passed the six figure barrier. Awards of general damages overall, and for such cases in particular, have progressively risen over the last decade—a range of £110,000 to £150,000 for very severe brain damage. In the worst cases the claimant will have a degree of insight into his condition (which increases the "suffering"):

9–01

---

[1] [2000] P.I.Q.R. Q187.

[2] *e.g.* Kemp & Kemp (Sweet & Maxwell); *Butterworths Personal Injury Law Service*; *Personal Injury and Quantum Reports*; *Current Law* (monthly parts and annual volumes); *Halsbury's Annual Abridgement*.

[3] Quadriplegia = paralysis of all four limbs, otherwise known as tetraplegia. Paraplegia = paralysis of the lower limbs. Hemiplegia = paralysis of one side of the body.

"There may be some ability to follow basic commands, recovery of eye opening and return of sleep and waking patterns and postural reflex movement. There will be little, if any, evidence of meaningful response to environment, little or no language function, double incontinence and the need for full-time nursing care. The level of the award within the bracket will be affected by—

    (i) the degree of insight;
    (ii) life expectancy;
    (iii) the extent of the physical limitation.

The top of the bracket will be appropriate only where there is significant effect on the senses.

Where there is a persistent vegetative state and/or death occurs very soon after the injuries were suffered and there has been on awareness by the injured person of his or her condition the award will be solely for loss of amenity and will fall substantially below the bracket."

As an example of an award at the very top of the range, see *Janardan v. East Berkshire Health Authority*[4] in which McCullough J. awarded the claimant general damages of £115,000 for devastating injuries, compounded by the fact that his intelligence, understanding and other mental faculties were all normal. This award (made in May 1990) would be worth £151,500 at today's rates. Another example is *Brightman v. Johnson*,[5] in which Tudor Price J. awarded the claimant in £95,000 for equally terrible injuries: this award (in December 1985) would be worth £164,000 today.

Judicial Studies Board Guidelines

9–02   In 1992, the Judicial Studies Board published for the first time its *Guidelines for the Assessment of General Damages in Personal Injury Cases*. "It proved" (said the Rt Hon. Sir Thomas Bingham M.R. in his introduction to the second edition) "a runaway success". It is now in its fourth edition, published in 1998. Whether because it filled a gap, or because it simplified and mechanised the quantification of general damages for the commoner injuries, which hitherto had been conducted via a trawl of reported cases, is not stated. The Judicial Studies Board had been seeking a way of standardising awards of general damages:

"... whilst no two cases are ever precisely the same, justice requires that there be consistency between awards. The solution to this dilemma has lain in using the amount of damages awarded in reported cases as guidelines or markers and seeking to slot the particular case into the framework thus provided. That is easier stated than done, because reports of the framework cases are scattered over a variety of publications and not all the awards appear, from the sometimes brief reports, to be consistent with one another."

---

[4] (1990) Kemp & Kemp, para. A4–001.
[5] *The Times*, December 16, 1985.

There is no indication in the Guidelines as to what these elusive "framework cases" might be. There is clearly no intention that for those injuries covered by the Guidelines they should reflect what is already happening in the Courts. In their introduction to the 1996 edition the Editors said:

> "The purpose of this guide is not to preach but rather to reflect the approach adopted by those who assess damages."

This leads one in a circle. Lawyers are used to taking their law from the Court of Appeal, but only a minute fraction of cases go to the Court of Appeal on general damages. Lord Woolf says:

> "Especially in the case of appellate judges, it is important that they are kept up to date as to the value of the most common categories of awards. It is so easy for an appellate judge to lose touch with the current tariff . . ."

What is the status of the Judicial Studies Board Guidelines? The general 9–03 (but unjustified) feeling amongst practitioners is that (with the exception of one or two categories) the damages are on the low side. This feeling may be based on a misunderstanding of the Guidelines' function. It might be said that they show one the damages for the *platonic injury—i.e.* for the basic injury, stripped of many of the surrounding circumstances that will enhance an award. Take, for example, a case in which the claimant has suffered the total loss of one eye. The range of damages in the Guidelines is quite tight: £26,000 to £30,000, with the note that "the level of the award within the bracket will depend on age and cosmetic defect". If the claimant can satisfy the court that in his case the loss of an eye has had graver consequences than usual. See, for example, *Re Campbell*,[6] in which the 25-year-old female claimant suffered severe alkaline burns to both eyes, leading to the loss of sight in one eye and permanent cosmetic deformity. In the light of *all* the surrounding circumstances[7] she was awarded £30,000, which is worth £35,750 at today's rates. (For more detail, see *Individual Factors*, below.)

---

[6] Kemp & Kemp, D 2–024.

[7] The applicant was in hospital for ten days and subsequently had one major and various minor operations. Despite this extensive treatment she lost the sight in her right eye with no prospect of restoration. She was left permanently cosmetically deformed. She underwent a significant change in temperament, manifested in panic attacks, loss of confidence, sleeplessness and depression. The applicant, who had been developing a career in drawing and design, was dismissed from her job at the time of the attack and various subsequent jobs due to her unsightly appearance. Her prospects of employment in her chosen career were extremely limited. Her loss of sight and the onset of constant headaches had restricted her social activities, and she gave up participation in squash, tennis and horse training. Due to her limited lifestyle the applicant became extremely depressed. This and the pain she had suffered caused the applicant to have a stressful pregnancy. Her disability was permanent and the side effects were continuing.

9–04   The intention of the Guidelines was to provide a snapshot of what courts were awarding for common categories of injuries. Clearly, the Guidelines cannot exclude reliance on reported authorities. In *Wright v. British Railways Board*,[8] Lord Diplock said:

> "Non-economic loss constitutes a major item in the damages. Such loss is not susceptible of *measurement* in money. Any figure at which the assessor of damages arrives cannot be other than artificial and, if the aim is that justice meted out to all litigants should be even-handed instead of depending on idiosyncrasies of the assessor, whether jury or judge, the figure must be 'basically a conventional figure derived from experience and awards in comparable cases'."[9]
>
> My lords, given the inescapably artificial and conventional nature of the assessment of damages for non-economic loss in personal injury actions and of treating such assessment as a debt bearing interest from the date of service of the writ, it is an important function of the Court of Appeal to lay down guidelines both as to the quantum of damages appropriate to compensate for various types of commonly occurring injuries and as to the rates of 'interest' from time to time appropriate to be given in respect of non-economic loss and of the various kinds of economic loss. The purpose of such guidelines is that they should be simple and easy to apply though broad enough to permit allowances to be made for special features of individual cases which make the deprivation caused to the particular claimant by the non-economic loss greater or less than in the general run of cases involving injuries of the same kind. Guidelines laid down by an appellate court are addressed directly to judges who try personal injury actions; but confidence that trial judges will apply them means that all those who are engaged in settling out of court the many thousands of claims that never reach the stage of litigation at all or, if they do, do not proceed as far as trial, will know very broadly speaking what the claim is likely to be worth if 100 per cent. liability is established.
>
> The Court of Appeal, with its considerable case-load of appeals in personal injury actions and the relatively recent experience of many of its members in trying such cases themselves, is, generally speaking, the tribunal best qualified to set the guidelines for judges currently trying such actions, particularly as respects non-economic loss . . .
>
> A guideline as to quantum of conventional damages or conventional interest thereon is not a rule of law nor is it a rule of practice. It sets no binding precedent; it can be varied as circumstances change or experience shows that it does not assist in the achievement of even-handed justice or makes trials more lengthy or expensive or settlements more difficult to reach. But though guidelines should be altered if circumstances relevant to the particular guideline change, too frequent alteration deprives them of their usefulness in providing a reasonable degree of predictability in the litigious process and so facilitating settlement of claims without going to trial.
>
> As regards assessment of damages for non-economic loss in personal injury cases, the Court of Appeal creates the guidelines as to the appropriate conven-

---

[8] [1983] A.C. 773.
[9] *Wright v. British Railways Board* [1983] A.C. 773 at 777.

tional figure by increasing or reducing awards of damages made by judges in individual cases for various common kinds of injuries. Thus, so-called 'brackets' are established, broad enough to make allowance for circumstances which make the deprivation suffered by an individual plaintiff in consequence of the particular kind of injury greater or less than in the general run of cases, yet clear enough to reduce the unpredictability of what is likely to be the most important factor in arriving at settlement of claims. 'Brackets' may call for alteration not only to take account of inflation, for which they ought automatically to be raised, but also it may be to take account of advances in medical science which may make particular kinds of injuries less disabling or advances in medical knowledge which may disclose hitherto unsuspected long-term effects of some kinds of injuries or industrial diseases."[10]

The Guidelines do not pretend to be exhaustive either of all categories of injury, or of all injuries within the categories with which it does deal. As Lord Woolf M.R. says in his introduction to the 1996 edition, "Usually it will be the starting off point rather than the last word on the appropriate award in any particular case."

In *Arafa v. Potter*,[11] the Court of Appeal, speaking very much *de haut en bas*, said of the Guidelines:

"We have been referred to the guidelines of the Judicial Studies Board. They are not in themselves law; they form a slim and handy volume which anyone can slip into their briefcases on their way to the county court or travelling on circuit. But the law is to be found elsewhere in rather greater bulk. In this Court we ought to look to the sources rather than the summary produced by the Judicial Studies Board."

This passage seems to have been over-used in the next two years, because in his October 1996 introduction to the Guidelines, Lord Woolf M.R. said:

"I am aware of the dicta of one member of the Court of Appeal in the case of *Arafa v. Potter*. If the dicta was [sic] intended to suggest that the Court of Appeal should not regard this book as a source from which an approximate figure for damages can be obtained, I profoundly disagree. The other member of the Court in fact referred to this book in the course of his judgment as a check as to what the correct bracket of damages should be. He was entitled to do so. Unless Court of Appeal judges as well as judges at first instance have regard to the guidelines continued in this book, its purpose will be defeated. As in the past so in the future it should be used not only because it is convenient to do so, but because due to the way in which it is compiled and because of its extensive use, it is the most reliable tool which up to now has been made available to courts up and down the land as to what is the correct range of damages for common classes of injuries."

---

[10] Lord Diplock in *Wright v. British Railways Board* [1983] A.C. 773 at 784–785.
[11] [1994] P.I.Q.R. Q73, *per* Staughton L.J. It should be noted, however, that Wall J., sitting in the Court of Appeal in the same case, confessed to "having looked at the comparable cases in Kemp & Kemp and *Current Law*, and having checked them against the Judicial Studies Board Guidelines." He found no discrepancies between these three sources.

9–05   One comment of Lord Woolf's is not clear, however. He says that the Guidelines:

> ". . . will help judges to determine whether the attitude to damages which the parties are adopting is reasonable. This will be important in determining issues as to costs."

Wall J., sitting in the Court of Appeal in the same case, confessed to "having looked at the comparable cases in *Kemp and Kemp* and *Current Law,* and having checked them against the Judicial Studies Board Guidelines." He found no discrepancies between these three sources.

Although the CPR encourage early settlement by the making of realistic offers and counter-offers, it is hard to see how a claimant who has fairly beaten a payment into court could be penalised as to costs, and a judge who has just made such an award is unlikely to be impressed by a defendant who tries to point out that the award *should* have been within the Guidelines.

Increasing the Tariff

9–06   In recent years there has been a drift upwards in real terms in general damages for a number of injuries. Sometimes the drift has been a lurch. In the course of the appeal in *Heil,* the Court of Appeal heard evidence from an actuary who had compared the rise in general damages chronicled by the Judicial Studies Board Guidelines with rises in the Retail Price Index [RPI] and the National Average Earnings Index [NAE] between 1991 and 1998. During that period the RPI rose 22 per cent and the NAE rose 31 per cent. Meanwhile, the Judicial Studies Board Guidelines showed the following increases in general damages:

Vibration white finger—serious	228%
Vibration white finger—minor	213%
Mesothelioma	50%
Minor head injury	50%
Fracture of index finger	46%
Severe psychiatric damage	43%
Severe back injury	40%
Minor neck injury	40%
Below knee amputation of one leg	38%
Partial hearing loss	38%
Above knee amputation of one leg	33%
Minor brain damage	33%
Simple fracture of nose	33%
Quadriplegia	30%
Very severe brain damage	30%

Minor back injury	30%
Paraplegia	29%
Very severe ankle injury	28%
Complete loss of sight in one eye	25%
Moderate back injury	23%
Moderate neck injury	20%
Significant female facial scarring	16%

This was partly special pleading on the part of the defendants in *Heil*. It is   **9–07**
interesting to note that general damages for the gravest injury—
paraplegia— was in line with the RPI and the NAE: after all, injuries for
such injuries mark the upper limit of general damages, and therefore define
the tariff. The extraordinary increase in damages for VWF can be
accounted for by the fact that in 1991 there had been few awards for the
condition, and its seriousness was not fully appreciated. (Compare this, for
example, with the increase in awards of damages for rape over the 15 years
that have passed since the *Meah* cases. The increase in such awards was due
to the changing perception of the seriousness of the offence—and possibly
in part to the public outcry at the difference between the award to Mr
Meah for his injuries, and to the victims for his rapes: see *Griffiths v.
Williams* below.) The dramatic rise in the number of claims for damages
for mesothelioma—an asbestos-related disease that causes one of the most
terrible of deaths probably accounted for the 50 per cent increase for this
injury, and in increased appreciation amongst doctors and lawyers of the
nature of head injuries probably contributed to a similar increase.

The Retail Price Index

In *Wright v. British Railways Board*[12] The House of Lords made it clear   **9–08**
that it was the duty of the judge to assess general damages in the "money
of the day" as at the date of trial and not in the values which obtained at
the date of the injury. When increasing old awards in line with inflation,
the Retail Price Index is used. This is only one of a number of indices,
however: the House Price Index shows the effect of inflation on most
people's most valuable asset, and the Average Earnings Index demonstrates
that the rate of wage inflation is not the same as inflation generally (see
Increasing the Tariff above). As "the average accident trial should not be
coverted into a graduate seminar on economic forecasting[13]", it may suffice
to note that until the Court of Appeal's decision in *Heil,* a top-of-the-range
award of general damages was very approximately ten times the average
national wage, and twice the value of the average house[14]—proportions
which had not changed significantly for decades.

---

[12] [1983] 2 A.C. 773.
[13] *Doca v. Marina Mercante Nicaraguense S.A.* 634 F2d at 39.
[14] Taken from the Halifax Building Society's new mortgage figures.

The Retail Price Index is published widely: it can be found in Kemp & Kemp, Butterworths Personal Injury Litigation Service, and the financial pages of most newspapers. Current Law publishes each month the current index figure. To calculate the present value of an earlier award, multiply the award by the current index figure, and then divide it by the index figure for the month in which the award was originally made—*e.g.*

> In October 1980 a claimant was awarded £4,000 for a soft-tissue injury to the cervical spine. The RPI for that month stood at 68.92. To find the value of the award as at July 2000, when the RPI stood at 156.1:
>
> $$[156.1 \times £4,000] \div 68.92 = £9,060$$

Development

9–09   Lord Woolf in his introduction to the Guidelines, and Lord Diplock in *Wright*, both stress that guidelines are of most help in the commoner categories of injuries. Less common injuries pose their own problems, but even these must be fitted somewhere into the range of conventional damages. A one-off type of injury, and a new field of awards, shows this in practice. *Meah v. McCreamer*[15] was the unique case, and damages for rape the relatively new field.

Christopher Meah was aged 28 when in August 1978 a car in which he was a passenger left the road at speed and collided with a tree. He was a young man with a criminal record described by the judge as "by no means a record which indicates serious or grave criminal offences . . . one would not have regarded the plaintiff as being someone who had a record which indicated that he was committed to serious crime at the time of his accident". In the accident he suffered fractures of the right clavicle and both ankles, and a number of minor abrasions. He made a good recovery from these injuries, with the only long-term sequela being a tendency to degenerative changes in the left ankle. His main injury, however, was a closed head injury, with frontal lobe damage. As a result of his head injury he was unconscious for some weeks. After his discharge from hospital he started to become aggressive and violent, and carried out three vicious sexual assaults.

(a)   He subjected Mrs S to a two-hour sexual attack, stopping short of rape, at the end of which he stabbed her several times, causing two superficial wounds which needed a total of eight stitches. Four years later she was still suffering grave psychological hardship, and was expected never to lead a normal life.

---

[15] [1985] 1 All E.R. 367.

(b) He forced Mrs W at knifepoint to perform oral sex. Four years later she still suffered psychological disturbance.

(c) He raped Mrs D at knifepoint, tied her up with wire, and then stabbed her five times in the chest. She had made great efforts to lead a normal life after this, but she was still withdrawn and shy four years later: there was, nevertheless, hope of further improvement

At the date of the civil trial, Christopher Meah was serving three life **9–10** sentences for rape. Woolf J. (as he then was) found that his personality change had been caused by his injuries. The judge asked each of the doctors giving evidence when (if they were advising the parole board) they would say that it would be safe to release him. The answers indicated a minimum of 15 years, but that it might never be safe to release him. He suffered from no mental illness: as a result of the accident he now had a different personality, which meant that he would have to spend much (if not all) of his life behind bars. There was nothing he could do to help himself; there was nothing doctors could do for him. He had full insight into his condition. In judgment, Woolf J. said:

> "Neither of the very experienced counsel who appeared before me were able to provide any case to give me guidance as to what was the appropriate head[16] of damages. . . . Looking at the matter in the best way that I can, bearing in mind the sort of compensation which is provided by the courts in the case of the worst type of injury (I am here thinking of people who suffer from injuries that cause them to be mere vegetables), [and] bearing in mind the sort of compensation that is provided in cases where people are wrongly imprisoned, though I emphasise that with regard to those cases there is usually compensation for loss of employment as well and that factor plays a part in the amount which is given as compensation, I think the appropriate sum to award by way of general damages is a sum of £60,000."[17]

This award is worth £104,500 at today's rates. At a later hearing, Mrs D **9–11** and Mrs W brought claims for damages for assault against Meah.[18] At that time, the Criminal Injuries Compensation Board's tariff award for rape was £2,750, and Mrs D had in fact been awarded £3,600. Woolf J. said that despite the terrible circumstances in which the two claimants were injured:

> "it is important that the court bears in mind that the award in this case must bear a proper relationship to the awards which the court makes in more conventional personal injury cases."

He awarded Mrs D £10,250 (£18,000 today) and Mrs W £6,750 (£11,500 today). At a later date, Master Topley assessed Mrs S's damages[19]

---

[16] Presumably this should read "level".
[17] p. 383.
[18] *W v. Meah; D v. Meah* [1986] 1 All ER 935.
[19] *S v. Meah* [1986] C.L.Y. 1050.

at £12,500 (£22,000 today), saying that although the claim was analogous to Mrs D's, "if he had decided those cases, he would have awarded higher general damages".

9–12   Comparison of Mr Meah's awards with those of his victims raised a storm of protest. At that time awards of damages to victims of rape were virtually unheard. There is now a separate section in Kemp & Kemp dealing with sexual abuse. In November 1995 the Court of Appeal considered the awards in the *Meah* cases in *Griffiths v. Williams*,[20] a case in which the defendant appealed unsuccessfully against an award of general damages of £50,000 for rape. Lord Justice Rose referred to the words of Woolf J. quoted above:

> "In his lordship's judgment, the circumstances and consequences of rape placed it in a quite different category from personal injury cases in general. Attitudes to rape had changed in the decade since *W v. Meah*. The penalties passed by the criminal courts had increased and rape within marriage had become a criminal offence. It was possible that his lordship would not have awarded the plaintiff £50,000 damages, but it was impossible to say that such an award was out of all proportion to what was appropriate."

(It should be noted that this was the award of a jury.)

Individual Factors

9–13   The Statement of Case must give the claimant's age and a brief description of his injuries: it is not sufficient simply to refer to medical evidence. Each element of the injury should be pleaded: where an orthopaedic injury has caused post-traumatic stress disorder and may lead to degenerative osteoarthritic changes, each of these three elements should be raised in the pleading.

Pain and Suffering

9–14   The phrase is a term of art, although the elements are separable. Pain is a part of most injuries, but a claimant will be compensated even where he suffers pain and no other injury, *e.g.*, in anaesthetic awareness cases. Again, there may be suffering without pain—see *Moore v. Ministry of Defence*,[21] in which a claimant developed asymptomatic pleural plaques as a result of his exposure to asbestos. He had suffered immediate anxiety upon learning of the changes in his lungs, because he had had friends who had died of asbestos-related diseases, and had read newspaper reports of dockyard

---

[20] *The Times,* November 25, 1996.
[21] *ibid.* F 2–045/2.

workers dying such deaths. He was awarded £2,800 in November 1990 (worth £3,600 today).

The courts can make substantial awards for pain and suffering, even where the claimant survives for only a relatively short period. An example is *Gabriel v. Nuclear Electric plc.*[22] The claimant was aged 55 at the date of trial, which took place in March 1995, five months after mesothelioma was diagnosed. At the date of the trial he had only nine months to live, and in that time he would suffer "more pain than almost any other malignant disease". He had a fearful burden to bear and bore it with enormous courage. He was awarded general damages of £40,000, which is worth £45,000 today.

Loss of Amenity

Loss of amenity can exist without pain or suffering in cases of uncon- **9–15** sciousness, and in theory general damages can be awarded wherever the injured person is unconscious between the time of the injury and the time of death (but see *Fear of Impending Death*, below). Where the deceased did not die immediately, general damages are assessed in the same way as in any other personal injury case. In coma cases, or cases of persistent vegetative state, damages at the very top of the tariff will not be awarded, because the element of pain and suffering is not present:

> "An unconscious person will be spared pain and suffering and will not experience the moral anguish which may result from knowledge of what has in life been lost or from knowledge that life has been shortened. The fact of unconsciousness is therefore relevant in respect of and will eliminate those heads or elements of damage which can only exist by being felt or thought or experienced. The fact of unconsciousness does not, however, eliminate the actuality of the deprivation of the ordinary experiences and amenities of life which may be the inevitable result of some physical injury."[23]

There are a number of reported cases, but following the Court of **9–16** Appeal's guidance in *Housecroft v. Burnett*[24] the pre-1985 authorities are not reliable. See, however:

(a) *Kerby v. Redbridge Health Authority*[25] (February 1992), in which Ognall J. awarded general damages of £750 [worth £900 today] for a newborn child who lived in a coma for three days before dying.

(b) In *Cooke & Rippin v. Prushki*,[26] the deceased suffered diffuse brain injury and tetraplegia in a car accident. Although he was able to sit

---

[22] *ibid.* F 2–017/2.
[23] See Lord Morris of Borth-y-Gest in *West v. Shephard* [1964] A. C. 326 at 349.
[24] [1986] 1 All ER 332.
[25] Kemp & Kemp, M 6–014.
[26] *ibid.* A2–011.

up out of bed for short periods, he never fully regained consciousness, and died three months later. General damages of £9,000 were
awarded in October 1992, worth £10,700 today.

(c) In *Andrews v. Freeborough*,[27] the claimant remained deeply unconscious for almost a year before dying of injuries she sustained in a
car crash. So far as it was possible to say, she did not suffer at all.
Damages of £2,000 were awarded in November 1965 (worth
£23,000 today).

(d) In *Doleman v. Deakin*,[28] the deceased was unconscious for a period
of six weeks up to his death. An award of £1,500 (worth £2,250
today) was upheld by the Court of Appeal in January 1990.

Pre-existing Condition

9–17   In the majority of personal injury cases, the claimant's previous state of
health is irrelevant to the assessment of general damages: there will,
nevertheless, be cases in which a claimant is already ill, or suffering from
injury, at the time of the accident. In clinical negligence claims (with the
exception of those concerning the birth of handicapped children) one is
almost invariably obliged to take a pre-existing condition into account. In a
simple case—for example, mis-diagnosis as malignant of a benign tumour,
leading to excision and adjuvant therapy over a prolonged period—the pre-
existing condition may not affect general damages greatly. In a more
complicated case, *e.g.* the late diagnosis of a malignant tumour, there may
well be disagreement about whether the claimant has suffered any significant injury at all.[29]

In *Mustard v. Morris*[30] the claimant was a diabetic suffering from an
arterial insufficiency leading to increasing pain in the right leg. As a result
of the defendant's negligence he lost his left leg above the knee. The
defendant argued that the claimant was already seriously unfit at the time
of the incident, and that the damages for an impaired claimant should be
higher than those for a healthy one. The Court of Appeal described this
submission as misconceived, saying:

"An argument to the contrary might well be made. To impose upon a man who,
though natural causes, has been made ill to a certain extent, very grave injuries such

---

[27] *ibid.* L5–026.
[28] *ibid.* L5–027.
[29] For example, the prognosis of melanoma of the skin is related to the absolute thickness of
the tumour when it is removed. If the melanoma is less than 0.75 mm thick there is a 98
per cent chance of cure, but there comes a stage in thickness (c.5 mm) when the patient's
chance of survival is virtually hopeless (less than 5 per cent).
[30] Formerly in Kemp & Kemp, I 2–106, 604, now referred to only in the Law Commission's
Consultation Paper No. 140, *Damages for Personal Injury: Non-Pecuniary Loss* at para.
2.32, n. 127.

as were sustained in this plaintiff and which reduce his capacity to bear natural ill health, is in my judgment more likely to increase than reduce damages."[31]

Clinical negligence cases raise a number of problems not usually found in conventional personal injury claims. For example, the claimant's presenting condition may have been aggravated, either through the natural process of the disease, or as a direct result of the negligence, but it will be necessary to consider the extent to which medical science could have helped the patient in any event. There may have been a number of breaches of duty—for example, a road traffic accident, followed by negligence on the part of the casualty officer treating the claimant, and these separate causes of action may have different causative effects. **9–18**

It is very common in medical negligence cases to find negligence which has resulted in an unnecessary operation, or a delayed period of convalescence, but no separate long-term injury. If that is the extent of the claimant's injuries, he is entitled to an award, but it cannot be substantial. (The author often suggests to solicitors that in such circumstances they seek a sum—say £5,000—that will pay for a good holiday for the claimant and his family.)

There are two possible ways of dealing with the compromised claimant, the "loss of chance" basis, and the "balance of probabilities" basis.

If the defendant's negligence has made a *material contribution* to his injury, the defendant is liable: see *Bonnington Castings v. Wardlaw*.[32] This must, however, be qualified in cases of clinical negligence: see *Hotson v. East Berkshire Health Authority*.[33] In that case, the judge found that the defendant had been negligent, and the claimant had been injured, but there was only a 25 per cent chance that the negligence had actually caused the injury. The House of Lords held that on these facts the claimant would on balance of probabilities have suffered the injury even if the defendant had not been negligent: his findings effectively amounted to a finding of fact that the fall had been the sole cause of the condition. It should be noted that this was an all-or-nothing case: causation could not be split. Although Lord Mackay declined to lay it down as a rule that a claimant could *never* succeed in proving loss of a chance in a medical negligence case, Lord Ackner said that the debate on the loss of a chance could not arise where there had been a positive finding that before the duty arose the damage complained of had already been sustained or had become inevitable.

Effectively, therefore, a claimant cannot seek to quantify damages on a "loss of chance" basis in medical negligence cases, though it is still open to him to do so in solicitors' negligence cases.

---

[31] Watkins L.J. (The author recently had an extreme case of a young autistic girl who was blind and deaf: her only known sources of pleasure were tactile, and in particular she appeared to derive particular pleasure from smearing herself with her own excrement. As a result of the defendant's negligence the lower part of her body was permanently scarred, interfering even with this limited degree of amenity. How should the conventional damages for such scarring be adjusted in such a case?).

[32] [1956] A.C. 613.

[33] [1987] 3 W.L.R. 232.

On the other hand, the courts are well used to assessing simple risks—that a claimant will suffer degenerative changes in an injured joint, or that he will develop post-traumatic epilepsy. In assessing damages, courts will sometimes apply what amount to discounts, *e.g.*, for the future risk of epilepsy. The chance of particular losses that flow from an injury can also be quantified.[34]

Acceleration

9–19   Care is needed where the claimant's injury has accelerated a pre-existing condition, whether or not that condition was causing symptoms at the date of the injury. Reported cases commonly state that the accident "accelerated the onset of symptoms from a previous wrist injury by some three years", or "accelerated active symptoms in the lumbar spine, not present before, by about five years". The starting-point for calculating such damages is generally taken to be the injury itself, first quantified as though it were permanent, and then discounted to reflect the shorter period of pain and suffering for which the defendant himself was responsible.

Multiple injuries

9–20   The courts are concerned with the overall level of disability caused by the claimant's injuries, and will not usually make a separate award in respect of each injury. This can lead either to a rounding-up or a rounding-down. It is clear that the closer to the top of the tariff, the less difference further handicap makes to the award. For example, in *Francis v. Porch*,[35] the claimant suffered paraplegia, severe brain injury and complete blindness. The Judicial Studies Board Guidelines suggest a figure of £105,000 for complete blindness alone, and for paraplegia £9,000 to £110,000. The Court approved a settlement of her claim for general damages in the sum of £137,500.[36]

At a lower level, the Court of Appeal gave guidance in the case of *Durau v. Evans*[37]:

"To a limited extent, in a case where there are multiple injuries, the figures in the Judicial Studies Board table can help but I accept Mr Murphy's criticism of them that, where one has a multiplicity of injuries, it is necessary to take an overall

---

[34] See too the case of *Anderson v. Davis* [1993] P.I.Q.R. Q87, in which Rodger Bell Q.C. sitting as a deputy High Court judge held that the claimant had a 66 per cent chance of promotion, and therefore awarded 66 per cent of the loss of earnings flowing from not being promoted.

[35] Kemp & Kemp, A 5–001.

[36] Would it have been any different if she had not been blind. Suppose she had been blinded in a later, separate, accident? Would she have been entitled to a tariff award for such an injury? Presumably so.

[37] [1996] P.I.Q.R. Q18.

view. The off-setting process may mean it is not possible to derive a great deal of benefit from that particular source. One then looks to see if anything can be gained from looking at a comparable award, if one is to be found, in another case. Even that may not prove to be a particularly fruitful source of inquiry. It may be necessary, if it be possible, to select what may be the most serious head of injury to see if a comparable award can be found in relation to that and, if so, build on it to allow for the other heads of injury which have been sustained by the plaintiff in the instant case."

Sometimes it is not difficult to grasp the overall effect of injuries. Where, **9–21** for example, both legs have been injured, one looks at the effect on mobility; if an arm and a leg are injured, the total effect on independence and the ability to work may provide clear parallels with other cases. What is not so straightforward is the cumulative effect of two entirely unrelated injuries—a shortened leg and an increased risk of developing epilepsy, for example, or a whiplash injury and a facial scar. The only practical advice is to adopt the Court of Appeal's approach, and start with the more serious injury, taking a step back after alighting on a figure, to see whether the award reflects the overall gravity of the injuries.

Fear of Impending Death

In *Hicks v. Chief Constable of the South Yorkshire Police*,[38] the Court of **9–22** Appeal refused to award damages to the estates of three of the victims of the Hillsborough football stadium disaster, saying that the evidence of pain suffered by the victims in the few seconds between the onset of asphyxia, and the knowledge and fear of impending death, could not be distinguished from the deaths themselves:

"In the case of the Hillsborough disaster, as the situation worsened, many many hundreds of people in pens 3 and 4, I have no doubt, suffered acute feelings of fear and horror without sustaining either physical injury or psychiatric injury. Such persons will have spent some 30 minutes of acute mental anguish but no more. No action lies in respect thereof. Others, although they survived, will have suffered injuries. If those injuries resulted in pain and suffering that pain and suffering including fear for future consequences constitutes a recoverable head of damage, but the preceding mental anguish not caused by injury does not thereby become compensatable. In the case of death, the estate can recover for pain and suffering including if it be the case awareness of shortened expectation of life caused by the injuries which led to death and, if such is the case, pain and suffering caused by other injuries which have nothing whatever to do with death. . .

There remains in my judgment for consideration only such pain as may have occurred in the few seconds between the onset of asphyxia and unconsciousness

---

[38] [1992] P.I.Q.R. P63.

and the knowledge and fear of impending death which may have occurred in those few seconds. It is in my view possible to infer that both would probably have been suffered to some extent by all three deceased, but can damages be awarded? If so, such damages could in my view only amount to a small nominal conventional sum. In my view, however, when unconsciousness and death occur in such a short period after the injury which causes death no damages are recoverable. The last few moments of mental agony and pain are in reality part of the death itself for which no action lies under the 1934 Act."[39]

Loss of Expectation of Life

9–23   General damages are not awarded to compensate for a shortened life,[40] though they may be awarded where the claimant's knowledge that his life has been shortened causes particular distress. Administration of Justice Act 1982, s.1(1)(b):

> "If the injured person's life has been reduced by the injuries, the court, in assessing damages in respect of pain and suffering caused by the injuries, shall take account of any suffering caused or likely to be caused to him by awareness that his expectation of life has been so reduced."

In *Hicks v. Chief Constable of the South Yorkshire Police*,[41] Lord Justice Parker said: "In [asbestosis] cases apprehension for the future is an allowable head but this comes from knowledge that the injury suffered will or may lead to death in the future". (See *Whittaker (deceased) v. BBA Group*[42] for an example of such an award.)

Sex

9–24   In most claims the sex of the claimant will be irrelevant, though in cases of scarring (especially facial scarring) women are commonly awarded significantly higher damages than men. In younger women, the possible effect of hip, pelvic, and low back injuries on childbirth and child care should also be considered. For no easily-discernible reason, the loss of marriage prospects[43] is thought to be a greater blow to a woman than to a man.

Age

9–25   Age is relatively unimportant to damages for loss of amenity, though damages for pain and suffering may be higher if the claimant is young: a fit and active woman in her early 20s who suffers a permanent back injury

---

[39] Parker L.J. at P66, 67.
[40] Administration of Justice Act 1982, s.1(1)(a).
[41] [1992] P.I.Q.R. P63, 67.
[42] Kemp & Kemp, F 2–018/7.
[43] Or, presumably, loss of the prospect of cohabitation (more or less permanent) with a member of either sex.

will be awarded more than a woman in her 40s. Damages for the very old may be slightly lower: see *Laycock v. Morrison*,[44] in which a 79-year old claimant was awarded general damages worth £9,000 for loss of the senses of taste and smell, and compare this with *Patel v. Merton and Bailey*,[45] in which the award for a similar injury was worth £16,000 at today's rates, and the Judicial Studies Board Guidelines which suggest a figure of £18,250.

Means of the Claimant

It is irrelevant that an award will mean more or less to a claimant 9–26 (because of his wealth[46]) or nothing at all (because he is in a persistent vegetative state).

Claimant's Previous Lifestyle

There are numerous reported authorities in which sportsmen have been 9–27 awarded higher damages than the tariff would suggest, to take account of their prowess:

> "If there is loss of amenity apart from the obvious and normal loss inherent in the deprivation of the limb—if, for instance, the plaintiff's main interest in life was some sport or hobby from which he will in future be debarred, that too increases the assessment."[47]

The claimant in *Middleton v. South Yorkshire Transport Executive*[48] was a teacher of physical education, who greatly enjoyed sports. She suffered a fracture of the left femur and a paralysed left arm: the trial judge awarded her £37,500 (worth £62,000 today), identifying £7,500 of that figure (£12,500 today) as being in respect of her reduced ability to take part in the sporting activities she both taught and had previously enjoyed. It is clear from the report that this £7,500 did not overlap with either her claim for lost earnings or her *Smith v. Manchester Corporation* award.

Circumstances of the Accident

These may be relevant for a number of reasons: the accident may be 9–28 painful, or terrifying; the circumstances might cause psychological or psychiatric harm; it might be more difficult for the claimant to adjust to the injury because it was inflicted suddenly. In cases of medical negligence, the

---

[44] Kemp & Kemp, D 4–019.
[45] *ibid.* D 4–017.
[46] *Wise v. Kaye* [1962] 1 Q.B. 638.
[47] *West v. Shephard* [1965] A. C 326 at 365.
[48] Kemp & Kemp, H 3–051.

circumstances are less likely to be traumatic in themselves, however serious the actual injury.

Loss of congenial employment

9–29   "It is now well recognised that [loss of congenial employment] is a separate head of damage",[49] although a court may reflect it in an increased award of general damages. These damages are available when a claimant has to give up a job of which he was particularly fond. For example, in *Hale v. London Underground Ltd*[50] the claimant, who was 39 at the date of the accident and 46 at trial, had to give up being an active fireman, a job which had provided him with great satisfaction. He had taken a job as a fire prevention officer, which he did not enjoy as much, and he missed his old work. The judge bore in mind the claimant's age, and the fact that he might in the future find a job that provided greater satisfaction, and awarded £5,000. This appears to be more or less the tariff for awards under this head.

A claim for damages for loss of congenial employment must be specifically pleaded. The claimant must establish that he has suffered "a real loss . . . not mitigated by any enjoyment from his present work".

Loss of Leisure

9–30   Damages for loss of leisure may be claimed when a claimant has to work longer hours to earn the same income, though the court is more likely to take account of the loss of leisure in the global award of general damages. *Tindale v. Dowsett Engineering Construction Ltd*[51] was a case in which the judge made a separate award (worth £3,350 today) under this head to a claimant who worked ten hours a week longer for two years in order to earn the same income.[52] In pleading such a claim particulars should give the nature of the work, the number of extra hours worked, and when they were worked—evenings, weekends, instead of a holiday, etc.

Loss of Enjoyment of Holiday

If a claimant's holiday is interrupted by an accident, or he misses his annual holiday, moderate damages can be awarded, although again these may simply be included in the global general damages[53] (as in *Ichard v.*

---

[49] Otton J. in *Hale v. London Underground Ltd* [1993] P.I.Q.R. Q30.
[50] [1993] P.I.Q.R. Q30.
[51] Unreported, Mustill J., December 2, 1980.
[52] See also *Hearnshaw v. English Steel Corporation Ltd* [1971] 11 K.I.R. 306.
[53] These damages are not assessed on the same basis as those awarded in contractual "holiday disputes".

Frangoulis,[54] where the court held that the loss of a holiday was something to be taken into account, not as a separate item of damage, but in estimating general damages for an injury. For an example of a separate award see *Bush v. Philip (No. 2)*.[55] The claimant, aged 15 at the date of the accident and 17 at the date of trial, was involved in a road traffic accident at the start of a cycling holiday. He was taken to hospital but not detained, and as a result he missed the first week of his holiday. Damages worth £500 at current rates were awarded.

Note

The court need not make a separate award for each of the above factors (*e.g.*, the circumstances of the accident, loss of congenial employment, loss of leisure, loss of enjoyment of holiday), if it takes them into account in the global award for general damages—but if it does make a global award, it should spell out the elements for which the claimant is being compensated.

Checklist

At the end of the chapter is set out a checklist of the matters considered above. It is not exhaustive; nor (conversely) will it all apply to any but the most unfortunate of claimants.

Appeals Against Awards of General Damages

In *Clarke v. South Yorkshire Transport Ltd*,[56] the Court of Appeal 9–31 summarised its functions and limitations on hearing appeals against awards of general damages. After quoting with approval Lord Justice Kennedy's remarks in *Durau v. Evans* (see *Multiple Injuries* above), Lord Justice Mantell went on to say[57]:

> "I would add that in my judgment an appeal court should always be slow to interfere with the trial judge's assessment, even though it may seem that such assessment falls outside the Judicial Studies Board Guidelines, or is out of kilter with other roughly comparable cases. After all, the trial judge will have seen the plaintiff and, sometimes, as in this, have had the advantage of visiting the plaintiff's home and seeing film of her getting about both in the home and outside. The trial judge will have been in the best position to make a judgment as to the effect upon the plaintiff's life of the injuries and the consequent disabilities."

Heil v. Rankin

In its Report "Damages for Personal Injury: Non-Pecuniary Loss", the Law Commission recommended that awards of general damages should be

---

[54] [1977] 1 W.L.R. 556.
[55] [1989] C.L.Y. 1065.
[56] [1998] P.I.Q.R. Q104.
[57] At Q107.

increased. This recommendation was directed to both the Court of Appeal and the House of Lords. On March 23, 2000 the Court of Appeal delivered its judgment in *Heil v. Rankin,* a series of conjoined appeals which considered whether to increase general damages in a range of cases.

The Court of Appeal accepted its responsibility for keeping guidelines up to date, by reference to the dictum of Lord Diplock we recognise that there are issues of principle as to damages for personal injuries for which the House of Lords would be a more appropriate final arbiter than the Court of Appeal.

Despite submissions to the contrary, the Court of Appeal decided that it was the appropriate forum to consider the Law Commission's recommendations. The Defendants argued unsuccessfully that this was a matter best left to Parliament (whose lack of experience in such matters was held to be no greater disadvantage in this field than in any other). The legal principles on which the Court of Appeal relied were not in dispute—and in particular, the liability of a Defendant to provide "full compensation". They took into account changes in the RPI, while acknowledging that—

> "the changes which take place in society are not confined to changes in the RPI. Other changes in society can result in a level of damages which was previously acceptable no longer providing fair, reasonable and just compensation, taking into account the interests of the claimants, the defendants and society as a whole. For this reason, it is clearly desirable for the courts at appropriate intervals to review the level of damages so as to consider whether what was previously acceptable remains appropriate."

Their Lordships took a number of factors into account. Although invited to disregard the means of those who would actually be making the compensation payments (usually insurers) they said that—

> "Awards must be proportionate and take into account the consequences of increases in the awards of damages on defendants as a group and society as a whole. The considerations are ones which the Court cannot ignore. They are the background against which the fair, reasonable and just figure has to be determined."

In other words, the effects on society, as well as the opinions of society, were relevant considerations (as they must be, since there is no objective standard by which any award of general damages could be justified). The Court had been supplied with material which established the following:

1. After public consultation, four central messages came through

    (a) Damages for non-pecuniary loss for serious personal injury are too low;

    (b) There was no clear consensus on what the level of damages for non-pecuniary loss should be;

    (c) The views of society as a whole should influence the level of damages for non-pecuniary loss in personal injury cases; and

    (d) There must be clear information as to the relevance, if any, of other components of a damages award.

2. At least 75 per cent of the public thought that damages for non-pecuniary loss for very serious injuries were too low;

3. At least 50 per cent considered that *all* awards of general damages were too low;

4. Around 50 per cent though that damages for "minor" or "trivial" injuries were not too low.

5. About 12 per cent of those consulted took the view that damages for "trivial" injuries were too high.

The Court of Appeal were—

". . . of the opinion that a modest increase is required to bring some awards up to the standard, on which both sides are agreed, namely to a sum which is fair, reasonable and just.

"We are satisfied that it is in the case of the most catastrophic injuries that the awards are most in need of adjustment and that the scale of adjustment which is required reduces as the level of existing awards decreases. At the highest level, we see a need for awards to be increased by in the region of one third. We see no need for an increase in awards which are at present below £10,000. It is our view that between those awards at the higheset level, which require an upwards adjustment of one third, and those awards where no adjustment is required, the extent of the adjustment should taper downwards, as illustrated by our decisions on the individual appeals which are before us."

They proceeded to consider the eight individual cases before then: these are set out in Appendix 3. (Mr Heil himself, whose appeal was dismissed because his award was below £10,000, was left to derive what comfort he could from having made history.)

Making *Heil v. Rankin* work in practice

In *Heil* the Court of Appeal increased the level of general damages for claims worth over £10,000. The increase is tapered. At the top end, an award of general damages of £150,000 or more is increased by one-third in real terms; the uplift tapers down to zero at £10,000.

It is possible to set out the awards to the six successful claimants in *Heil* on a graph, and then plot a line through them, but this pseudo-scientific approach would be misleading because the Court of Appeal itself said that its increases were "approximate". The Court produced a graph showing the tapered increase. Their Lordships said that its rather smudged graph was provided to show "very approximately" the scale of the increase. Putting a straight-edge along the top line of the graph (the "uplifted" line) shows the line to be a shallow curve. In discussion after judgment was given, their Lordships said that they had not intended to lay down a mathematical formula.

What has happened, however, is that a formula is the only way in which the uplift can be calculated accurately.

To find the present-day value of a pre-*Heil* award, one must go through three stages: (i) the award must be updated to March 23, 2000 using the Retail Price Index; (ii) if the award was worth more than £10,000 on that day, the *Heil* formula must then be applied; and (iii) the Retail Price Index must be applied again to update award from March 23, 2000 to the present day.

The formula works like this:

1. The increase tapers from zero at £10,000 to one-third at £150,000.

2. The one-third increase therefore has to be spread between awards of £10,000 and £150,000—a range of £140,000.

3. We need to know by how many 1,140,0000ths of one-third to increase the award.

4. If the pre-*Heil* value of an award is £A, *Heil* increased it according to this formula:

$$£A + [\frac{(A-10,000)}{420,000} \times £A]$$

The part in square brackets is the uplift.

To take an example:

1. On January 26, 1988, McNeill J. awarded the Claimant in *Chan v. Chan* general damages of £75,000.

2. Updating £75,000 to March 23, 2000 in line with the Retail Price Index gives £120,800.

3. Subtract £10,000 from £120,800, and divide it by 420,000. This gives $^{110,800}/_{420,000}$ = 0.26. This is the percentage uplift.

4. Applying this uplift to the original award gives [0.26 × £120,800] = £31,400.

5. On March 23, 2000 the award in *Chan v. Chan* was therefore worth [£120,800 + £31,400] = £152,200.

6. Updating £152,200 from March 23, 2000 to the date of writing, by means of the Retail Price Index, gives £154,000.

On the following page is a table converting pre-*Heil* awards to post-*Heil* awards—again, as at March 23, 2000.

What the Court of Appeal did in *Heil v. Rankin*

Case	Injury	Original	Uplifted	Increase
Warren & **Annable**	Devasting brain damage	£135,000	£175,000	29¹/₂%
Ramsey	Moderately severe brain injury	£110,000	£138,000	25¹/₂%
Kent	Modern brain damage	£80,000	£95,000	19%
Rees	Death from mesothelioma	£45,000	£50,000	11%
Schofield	Death from mesothelioma	£40,000	£44,000	10%
Heil	Post-traumatic stress disorder	£6,000	*No change*	
Connelly	Whiplash	£3,000	£4,000	n/a

Note: Connelly's award was increased from £3,000 to £4,000 because it was too low, but being below £10,000 was not increased further.

To convert old awards of general damages into post-*Heil awards*

Old	New	Old	New	Old	New	Old	New	Old	New
0–10,000	No change	39,000	41,692	68,000	77,390	97,000	117,092	126,000	160,800
11,000	11,026	40,000	42,857	69,000	78,692	98,000	118,533	127,000	162,379
12,000	12,057	41,000	44,026	70,000	79,999	99,000	119,978	128,000	163,962
13,000	13,092	42,000	45,199	71,000	81,311	100,000	121,428	129,000	165,549
14,000	14,133	43,000	46,378	72,000	82,628	101,000	122,883	130,000	167,143
15,000	15,178	44,000	47,561	73,000	83,950	102,000	124,342	131,000	168,740
16,000	16,228	45,000	48,749	74,000	85,276	103,000	125,807	132,000	170,343
17,000	17,283	46,000	49,942	75,000	86,607	104,000	127,276	133,000	171,950
18,000	18,342	47,000	51,140	76,000	87,942	105,000	128,745	134,000	173,562
19,000	19,407	48,000	52,342	77,000	89,283	106,000	130,229	135,000	175,179
20,000	20,476	49,000	53,549	78,000	90,629	107,000	131,712	136,000	176,800
21,000	21,549	50,000	54,761	79,000	91,979	108,000	133,200	137,000	178,426
22,000	22,628	51,000	55,978	80,000	93,333	109,000	134,693	138,000	180,057
23,000	23,711	52,000	57,200	81,000	94,693	110,000	136,190	139,000	181,692
24,000	24,799	53,000	58,426	82,000	96,057	111,000	137,693	140,000	183,333
25,000	25,892	54,000	59,657	83,000	97,426	112,000	139,200	141,000	184,978
26,000	26,990	55,000	60,892	84,000	98,800	113,000	140,712	142,000	186,628
27,000	28,092	56,000	62,133	85,000	100,179	114,000	142,229	143,000	186,283
28,000	29,199	57,000	63,378	86,000	101,562	115,000	143,750	144,000	189,942
29,000	30,311	58,000	64,628	87,000	102,945	116,000	142,276	145,000	191,607

Old	New	Old	New	Old	New	Old	New	Old	New
30,000	31,428	59,000	65,883	88,000	104,343	117,000	146,807	146,000	193,276
31,000	32,550	60,000	67,142	89,000	105,740	118,000	148,343	147,000	194,949
32,000	33,676	61,000	68,407	90,000	107,142	119,000	149,883	148,000	196,628
33,000	34,807	62,000	69,676	91,000	108,549	120,000	151,428	149,000	198,311
34,000	35,942	63,000	70,949	92,000	109,961	121,000	152,979	150,000	200,000
35,000	37,083	64,000	72,228	93,000	111,378	122,000	154,533	> 150,000	Add –
36,000	38,228	65,000	73,511	94,000	112,800	123,000	156,093		
37,000	39,378	66,000	74,799	95,000	114,226	124,000	157,657	© Simon Levene	
38,000	40,533	67,000	76,092	96,000	115,657	125,000	159,226	September 2000	

Checklist for General Damages

This list cannot pretend to be exhaustive, but it should spur a client to **9–32** think of ways in which he has been affected by his injuries, which would not necessarily occur to his legal advisers. Except where they are obvious, the effects will need to be supported by medical evidence. The claimant's solicitors should take care to cover all the significant effects of the injuries in the claimant's witness statement.

(a) **The Injuries**
   The Claimant should deal with the injuries, the process of recovery, and the existing state of disability.

(b) **Pain**
   (i) Is it continuous or intermittent?
   (ii) How severe is it?
   (iii) How disabling is it?
   (iv) What treatment (if any) helps (*e.g.* painkillers, an orthopaedic mattress, TENS machine)?

(c) **Suffering**
   (i) Fear
   (ii) Worry
   (iii) Embarrassment
   (iv) Distress at awareness of accelerated death
   (v) Distress at the effect of the injury on the Claimant's family

(d) **Loss of amenity**
   (i) *Mobility*
   Climbing ladders

Climbing stairs
Getting out of bed
Getting—
  into and out of chairs
  into and out of the bath
  on and off the lavatory
Kneeling
Running
Sitting
Sleep (turning over in bed)
Squatting
Standing
Walking on uneven ground
Walking on a slope
Walking—distance

(ii) *Personal hygiene*
Grooming
Dressing
Bathing
Showering

(iii) *Housework*
Cleaning windows
Cooking
Dusting
Gardening
Hoovering
Ironing
Painting and decorating
Putting objects into cupboards or on high shelves
Shopping
Washing up
Washing floors
Washing
Other DIY tasks

(iv) *Other personal functions*
Sexual dysfunction
Lifting children

(e) **Work**

(i) Inability to work at all
(ii) Restricted ability to work—shorter hours, or different work, or both.
(iii) Able to work with the help of special equipment
(iv) Loss of enjoyment of work
(v) Loss of holiday

(vi) More hours' work to earn the same pay

(f) **Support for other heads of claim—e.g.**

(i) Care: help with activities listed in this checklist.
(ii) Housing
(iii) Aids and appliances
(iv) Help with shopping
(v) Greater reliance on motorised transport, or on public transport
(vi) Medical treatment

(g) **Sports and hobbies**
Cannot get out on trips, visits to the cinema, family visits, holidays, etc. Active hobbies such as swimming, cycling, aerobics, etc.
Did the claimant perform sports at a high level?
Other hobbies

10. Multipliers for Future Loss and Expenditure

Multipliers are used to calculate all future loss, for example loss of **10–01** earnings or benefits in kind. They are used to compensate for future expenditure, for example medical expenses, care costs, housing costs, transport costs and loss of services. They are also used in the calculation of pension loss.

The objective of any award of damages in personal injuries litigation is to achieve as nearly as possible full compensation for the claimant for the injury sustained.[1] To achieve that objective the court seeks to award such sum as is notionally required to be laid out in the purchase of an annuity which will provide an annual amount equivalent to the loss for the whole period of the loss: *per* Lord Oliver in *Hodgson v. Trapp*.[2] The basis of the calculation is an assumed annuity. The court makes an assumption about how the award will be invested.[3] Lord Fraser of Tullybelton in *Cookson v. Knowles* put it thus:

> "The assumed annuity will be made up partly of income on the principal sum awarded, and partly of capital obtained by gradual encroachment of the principal. The income element will be at its largest at the beginning of the period and will tend to decline, while the capital element will tend to increase until the principal is exhausted."

In the past the multipliers which were generally adopted in practice were **10–02** based on the assumption that the principal sum of damages would earn 4.5 per cent as a rate of return. Falling interest rates and severe shifts in the value of stocks and shares led to that being questioned. The House of Lords in *Wells v. Wells, Thomas v. Brighton Health Authority* and *Page v.*

---

[1] *Livingstone v. Rawyards Coal Company* [1980] 5 A.C. 25 p.25 at 39 *per* Blackburne J., quoted with approval by Lord Scarman in *Lin Poh Choo v. Camden Health Authority* [1980] A.C. 174 at 187, and also in *Pickett v. British Rail Engineering* [1978] 3 W.L.R. 955 at 979.

[2] [1989] A.C. 804. "Essentially what the court has to do is to calculate as best it can the sum of money which will on the one hand be adequate, by its capital and income, to provide annually for the injured person a sum equivalent to his estimated annual loss over the whole of the period during which that loss is likely to continue, but which, on the other hand, will not, at the end of that period, leave him in a better financial position than he would have been apart from the accident. Hence the conventional approach is to assess the amount notionally required to be laid out in the purchase of an annuity which will provide the annual amount needed for the whole period of loss." *per* Lord Oliver at 826E–F.

[3] [1979] A.C. 556 at 576G. How the award is invested is in fact irrelevant: Lord Lloyd of Berwick in *Wells* [1998] 3 W.L.R. 329 at 342: "how the plaintiff, or the majority of plaintiffs, in fact invest their money is irrelevant."

Sheerness Steel Plc[4] transformed the position. These were three appeals where each of the plaintiffs had been seriously injured and each case involved a substantial future loss claim. In the Court of Appeal[5] it was held that a discount rate of 4–5 per cent should be assumed and that a plaintiff could be expected to invest his or her damages prudently. Thus was born the concept of the prudent investor.

This concept of "the prudent investor" came from Lord Fraser of Tullybelton in *Cookson v. Knowles.* [6] He put it thus:

"The proper measure of the award . . . is a sum which, prudently invested, would provide her with an annual equity in amount to the support that she has probably lost through the death of her husband, during the period that she would probably have been supported by him."[7]

10–03   However, the exercise was and is a notional one as is apparent from a later passage in the judgment:

"I have referred to the 'assumed' annuity because of course the widow may not choose to apply her award in the way I have mentioned; it is for her to decide and she may invest it so as to make a profit or she may squander it but the defendant's liability should be calculated on the basis of an assumed annuity."[8]

In assessing the damages to be awarded in personal injury litigation no account has ever been taken of inflation. This was, formerly, on the basis that in times of high inflation the rate of interest that can be earned by prudent investment in fixed interest securities tends to be high as investors seek to protect their capital and also to obtain a positive rate of interest (after having allowed for the rate of inflation).[9] Today it is because the claimant is assumed to invest in index linked government stock, which retain their true value irrespective of the ravages of inflation.

Traditionally, actuarial tables were distrusted by the courts:

"The assessment of damages is not and never can be an exact science. There are too many imponderables. For this reason, the courts have been traditionally mistrustful of reliance on actuarial tables as the primary basis of calculation, approving their use only as a check on assessments arrived at by the familiar conventional methods."[10]

10–04   In 1984, the Inter-Professional Working Party of Actuaries and Lawyers reported[11] and produced actuarial tables for use in personal injury and fatal

---

[4] [1998] 3 W.L.R. 329.
[5] (1997) P.I.Q.R. Q1.
[6] [1979] A.C. 556.
[7] *ibid.*, at 576G.
[8] Page 577D.
[9] See Lord Fraser of Tullybelton in *Cookson v. Knowles* at 577A–B and Lord Diplock in *Mallett v. McMonagle* [1970] A.C. 166 at 176C–D.
[10] Lord Bridge of Harwich in *Hunt v. Severs* [1994] 2 A.C. 350 at 365E.
[11] Known as the "Ogden Working Party", after its Chairman Sir Michael Ogden Q.C. The tables are known as "The Ogden Tables".

accident cases. Those tables took account of mortality amongst the population but did not provide for contingencies other than mortality. The result was that the courts had to guess as to what might be an appropriate allowance for such contingencies.[12] In November 1993, the same Working Party produced a second edition which did take account of those contingencies. The current edition is the fourth, published in 2000.[13] The Working Party, in all four reports, urged the adoption of multipliers calculated upon the basis of presumed investment in index-linked government stocks (ILGS). ILGS had the advantage, from the claimant's point of view, that the capital sum was protected against inflation and the money invested produced a modest rate of return. In September 1994, the Law Commission[14] recommended that a practice of discounting for the accelerated receipt of payment by reference to returns on ILGS should be adopted. The Law Commission's reasoning was that ILGS constituted "the best evidence of the real return on any investment where the risk element is minimal, because they take account of inflation, rather than attempt to predict it as conventional investments do".

For that reason the Law Commission recommended that there should be legislative provision requiring courts when determining the return to be expected from investment of the sum awarded for damages for personal injuries to take account of the net return on ILGS. The Commission also recommended that the ILGS rate should be used unless the parties, by evidence, demonstrated that some other rate of return was more appropriate in any individual case. The Law Commission drafted a Damages Bill to give effect to its recommendations.

On March 23, 1995, the Minister for the Lord Chancellor's Department **10–05** in the House of Commons welcomed the report and said that it was the Government's intention to implement the Law Commission's recommendations. Those recommendations related not just to multipliers but also, *inter alia*, to structured settlements and the admissibility of the tables produced by the Inter-Professional Working Party of Actuaries and Lawyers (the Ogden Tables). Section 10 of the Civil Evidence Act 1995 implemented the latter recommendation, rendering the actuarial tables admissible in evidence.

Section 10 of the Civil Evidence Act 1995

"Admissibility and proof of Ogden Tables **10–06**

(i) The actuarial tables (together with explanatory notes) for use in personal injury and fatal accident cases issued from time to time by the Government

---

[12] Usually the risk of unemployment, injury at work, geographical and economic cycle factors.
[13] The third edition was published in 1998.
[14] Law Com. N. 224.

Actuaries Department are admissible in evidence for the purpose of assessing, in an action for personal injury, the sum to be awarded as general damages for future pecuniary loss.

(ii) They may be provided by the production of a copy published by Her Majesty's Stationery Office.

(iii) For the purposes of this section—

(a) 'Personal injury' includes any disease and any impairment of a person's physical or mental condition; and

(b) 'Action for personal injury' includes an action brought by virtue of the Law Reform (Miscellaneous Provisions) Act 1934 or the Fatal Accidents Act 1976."

Section 10 of the Civil Evidence Act 1995, five years later, is still not in force.

10–07 In the event, the Damages Act of 1996 is different from the Bill proposed by the Law Commission. Section 1 of the Damages Act 1996 provides:

"(1) In determining the return to be expected from the investments of a sum awarded as damages for future pecuniary loss in an action for personal injury the court shall, subject to and in accordance with rules of court made for the purposes of this section, take into account such rate of return (if any) as may from time to time be prescribed by an order made by the Lord Chancellor.

(2) Subsection (1) above shall not however prevent the court taking a different rate of return into account if any party to the proceedings shows that it is more appropriate in the case in question.

(3) An order under subsection (1) above may prescribe different rates of return for different classes of case.

(4) Before making an order under sub-section (1) above the Lord Chancellor shall consult the Government Actuary and the Treasury; and any order under that subsection shall be made by statutory instrument subject to annulment in pursuance of a resolution of either House of Parliament.

(5) In the application of this section to Scotland for references to the Lord Chancellor there shall be substituted references to the Secretary of State."

That section also has not yet been implemented and no rate of return has been prescribed by the Lord Chancellor. In March 2000, the Lord Chancellor issued a consultation paper entitled "The Discount Rate and Alternatives to Lump Sum Payments." In that document he canvassed the idea that a claimant can be expected to invest in a mixed portfolio of equities and gilts, including ILGS. Such an approach was rejected by the House of Lords in *Wells* and would result in lower awards through the selection of a higher multiplier. Such a reversal of a House of Lords decision may well need primary legislation and, in any event, may be open to challenge on the basis of an infringement of the European Convention on Human Rights and Fundamental Freedoms.[15,16] This Chapter is written on the basis of what the law is now.

---

[15] Now incorporated into domestic law by the Human Rights Act 1998.

[16] Where the rate is set by a minister in a government which is itself a litigant in the courts and the consultation document (para. 22) refers to the cost to the NHS, there may be a perceived conflict of interest.

When both sections become operative the multiplier to be selected to **10–08** compensate for future loss and expenditure will be determined by looking at the appropriate Ogden Table, choosing the discount rate set by the Lord Chancellor[17] and then choosing the multiplier appropriate to the age of the claimant at the date of trial. That "basic" multiplier should then be adjusted, in a loss of earnings claim, to reflect "other contingencies" such as the level of economic activity, unemployment, regional variations and the nature of the claimant's job. The explanatory notes, which accompany the tables, set out a method by which this can be done. It is, now, the usual method employed to adjust a multiplier for contingencies other than mortality. The previous practice of the judge adjusting the figures to take account of these factors resulted in substantial reductions which were unjustified and unfair. Lord Lloyd in *Wells* said:

> "The purpose of the award is to put the plaintiff in the same position, financially, as if he had not been injured. The sums should be calculated as accurately as possible, making just allowance, where this is appropriate, for contingencies. But once the calculation is done, there is no justification for imposing an artificial cap on the multiplier. There is no room for a judicial scaling down."[18]

Later he said, in relation to a multiplier for a proven life expectancy: **10–09**

> "Was it correct for the judge in the Court of Appeal to reduce the arithmetical multiplier, and therefore, in effect, override the expectation of life agreed by the doctors? Mr Owen submitted that there could be no rational basis for applying a further discount for 'contingencies' since the doctors had already taken account of all the contingencies that might affect the plaintiff, such as the increased risk of accident, chest infection and so on. The only reason given by the judge was that the courts tended to reduce multipliers by about 20 per cent. The Court of Appeal took the same line."

Lord Lloyd was referring to the practice which, up to then, was widespread of imposing a "judicial discount". Lord Lloyd said[19]:

> "There is no purpose in the courts making as accurate a prediction as they can of the plaintiff's future needs if the resulting sum is arbitrarily reduced for no better reason than the prediction might be wrong. A prediction remains a prediction. Contingencies should be taken into account where they work in one direction, but not where they cancel out. There is no more logic or justice in reducing the whole life multiplier by 15 or 20 per cent on an agreed expectation of life than there would be in increasing it by the same amount."

There is still a role for discounting the basic multiplier in loss of earnings claims. That was specifically recognised in the House of Lords[20]:

---

[17] Unless another rate is "more appropriate": section 1(2) of the Damages Act 1996.
[18] *See* page 332.
[19] at 346.
[20] at 346.

"Mr Havers conceded there is room for a judicial discount when calculating the loss of future earnings, when contingencies may indeed affect the result."

10–10   Before *Wells* and without section 10 of the Civil Evidence Act 1995 being in force the use of the Ogden Tables was confined to a check upon the multiplier chosen by the judge. Since *Wells, Thomas and Page* the Tables are the starting point and Lord Lloyd said:

> "I do not suggest that the judge should be a slave to the tables. There may well be special factors in particular cases. But the tables should now be regarded as a starting point, rather than a check. A judge should be slow to depart from the relevant actuarial multiplier on impressionistic grounds, or by reference to 'a spread of multipliers in comparable cases' especially when the multipliers were fixed before actuarial tables were widely used."

10–11   The explanatory notes to the Third Edition of the Ogden Tables set out the method to be employed in adjusting the basic multiplier. The House of Lords in *Wells* expressed the view that "the views of the Working Party the Law Commission and the author of Kemp & Kemp, The Quantum of Damages in favour of an investment in ILGS are entitled to great weight."[21]

The Fourth Edition of the Ogden Tables contains 38 tables. The Fourth Edition was the result of a recommendation of the Law Commission.[22] Tables 1 to 18 are based on mortality rates experienced in England and Wales in the three year period from 1990 to 1992. The actuaries who were members of the Working Party considered that failure to have regard to reasonable projected improvements in mortality rates would, inevitably, result in claimants receiving awards of damages which were lower than they ought to be. Taking account of increased mortality the Government Actuary, with whom all the actuaries on the Working Party agreed, produced tables 19 to 36 based upon mortality rates projected to 1998. The Working Party recommended that the court should use Tables 19 to 36 rather than Tables 1 to 18. This was the approach adopted by Mr David Foskett Q.C. sitting as a Deputy High Court Judge in *Worrall v. Powergen PLC*.[23] It is now the universal approach of the courts.

10–12   Until section 1 of the Damages Act 1996 and section 10 of the Civil Evidence Act 1995 come into force the multiplier should be chosen as follows:

(a)   To calculate loss of earnings for a 34-year-old man who would, had it not been for his injuries, have retired at age 65. Select Table 13.[24]

---

[21] at 342.
[22] Paragraph 7.14 of report No. 263 (Claims for Wrongful Death) recommended that the working party should consider how the tables should be used or amended to produce accurate assessments of damages in fatal accident cases.
[23] *The Times*, February 10, 1999.
[24] Kemp & Kemp, *The Quantum of Damages*, Vol. 1, para. 8–053.

From the 3 per cent discount rate table the appropriate multiplier is given as 19.71

(b) That is the "basic" multiplier. It has to be further discounted to take account of the risk, faced by that particular claimant, of unemployment or injury. The more risky his pre-accident job the higher should be the discount to reflect the possibility that he may not have been able to work throughout the entire period because of an accident at work. Conversely, if he lived and worked in an area of high economic activity the discount for the risk of future unemployment should not be very great. The mathematical formula whereby these contingencies can be calculated is in the Ogden Tables "Explanatory Notes".

(c) *An example:*
Basic multiplier: 19.71

    (i) Deduction for economic activity in the economy as a whole: assume similar economic activity to the 1980s and 1990s: reduce by 0.96
    (ii) Living in the South East, increase by 0.01
    (iii) Working in a job with a high risk of injury, reduce by 0.02.
    (iv) Final multiplier: $19.71 \times 0.96 = 18.9216 + 0.01 = 18.9316 - 0.02 = 18.9116$.

(d) Where the loss or expenditure will continue for the entire lifetime of the claimant, for example, care costs, the process is easier. For a 34-year-old woman, Table 12 of the Ogden Tables produces a multiplier at 3% of 25.51. Even though the Ogden Tables were prepared having taken account of population mortality, the whole life loss multiplier may have to be discounted further where there is evidence to suggest that the particular claimant may have a higher than average risk of an early death. If there is no such evidence then the appropriate multiplier is 25.51. The calculation is more straightforward. The "basic multiplier" is usually the appropriate final figure.

(e) Where the claimant's life expectancy can be established by evidence or agreed it will be appropriate to choose the multiplier appropriate to a fixed period.[25] Thus, an injured claimant with an agreed life expectancy of 15 years, using a 3 per cent real rate of return will be awarded a multiplier of 12.1.

In selecting the multiplier not all expenditure will attract a full life **10–13** multiplier from Tables 1, 2, 11 and 12. A claim for DIY or gardening does

---

[25] Kemp & Kemp, para. 8–055.

not end when the Claimant reaches 60 or 65. However, as he or she gets older it is unlikely that he/she would have continued to perform his or her own DIY and may well have, in old age, paid someone else to do it (or more likely, not do it at all), had the accident not occurred. That loss is irrecoverable. The claimant would, in any event, have had to incur that expenditure whether or not the accident happened. The court will thus select an appropriate multiplier from the Tables and further discount it to take account of the fact that it will not extend over the whole of the claimant's loss but will probably extend beyond normal retirement age. A sensible way to select this multiplier is to decide at what age that would occur and subtract the claimant's present age from that chosen age and then select a multiplier from Table 22 (Fixed periods).

Where the period of loss is likely to be short the multiplier will not be mathematically much less than the actual period for which the claimant has to be compensated. For example, a woman aged 55 at trial who would have retired from secure employment at age 60 will achieve an award of 4.59 before any deductions for contingencies other than mortality. The multiplier is always chosen to run from the date of trial. All loss before that date is special damage and is compensated as such. Where the expenditure has actually been incurred or the obligation to reimburse a person has arisen, interest on special damage will be appropriate.

10–14   In calculating the compensation to be awarded to the claimant for future expenditure account should be taken of the possibility that the cost of, for example, medical care may arise in the future. This is generally done by splitting the period into two or more phases. Evidence should be called as to the likely cost of various services in the future. For example, it is generally recognised that the cost of medical and other care rises faster than inflation. The court, having heard evidence, may be prepared to alter the multiplicand for the future. If, for example, a claimant was likely, within a ten-year period, to have been promoted and hence achieved higher earnings the court may be willing to split the multiplier and the multiplicand. The lower multiplicand will be multiplied by one part of the multiplier and the higher multiplicand by the balance. For example, a 24-year-old man, at the time of trial, in secure employment before injury, in a prosperous part of the country, who would have achieved higher earnings by the age of 34 would achieve a multiplier for loss of earnings, overall, of 23.17 from Table 13. Although he was in secure employment, the possibility of losing such employment through, for example injury, cannot be ruled out. That may result in 23.17 being reduced to 21 or 22, if the "judicial discount" approach is used. The court would probably apply a multiplier of 5/6 to the first period of loss and the balance to the remainder.

The same principles apply where it has been established, by evidence, that other losses and expenditure will escalate in the future. For example, it may be provable by evidence that the claimant will need a more intensive care regime at some point in the future which costs considerably more than the regime in place at trial.

The loss of pension calculation is dealt with elsewhere in this book. However, the multipliers to be selected for pension loss are set out at Tables 7–10, and 17–20 of the Ogden Tables. The same principles apply as in relation to the calculation of future loss and expenditure.

The items of future loss and expenditure are, of course, peculiar to the   **10–15** individual case. However, as a general guide the following should be considered:

(a) loss of earnings;

(b) loss of benefits in kind, *e.g.* car, health insurance, life insurance;

(c) the claimant's promotion prospects/prospects for achieving higher levels of earning;

(d) the prospects of the claimant facing unemployment through an economic downturn;

(e) the area the claimant lives in and its past and likely future level of economic activity;

(f) medical expenses likely to be incurred by the claimant in the future;

(g) the care regime the claimant is likely to need in the future (*e.g.* will that regime remain constant, will it diminish or increase in size and therefore cost?);

(h) the housing needs of the claimant, now and in the future?

(i) transport costs now and for the future as well as the past;

(j) pension loss incurred by the claimant?;

(k) the need for professional advice on the management of the damages and/or the claimant's future care?

The multiplier for future housing costs

Housing costs are dealt with slightly differently. Where the claimant has   **10–16** to purchase a property because of his special needs, brought about by the injury, the problem is how to value the cost involved as against the benefit of having a capital asset in the form of the new accommodation. The approach to be adopted was set out in *Roberts v. Johnstone*.[26] The Court of Appeal regarded the purchase of a residential property as the equivalent of

---

[26] [1989] Q.B. 878, CA.

the purchase of an investment secured against the risk of inflation. The Court of Appeal considered 2 per cent an appropriate rate of return on the net extra capital expenditure rather than higher net percentage rate which would be payable by the claimant on a mortgage of the property. In *Thomas v. Brighton Health Authority*[27] the House of Lords held that the same rate as is selected for the future losses should apply to these costs. This is consistent with the approach of assuming a risk free investment strategy, investment in ILGS. The Court of Appeal and House of Lords confirmed the *Roberts v. Johnstone* formula, albeit varying the rate. The judicial committee adopted the description of *Roberts* as "a satisfactory and elegant solution".[28] The court is, here compensating for ". . . the income which the capital would have earned over the period of the award after the deduction of tax"[29]

The damages for this loss are assessed by selecting a multiplier produced by a rate of 3 per cent of the net capital cost of the accommodation and applying that to the multiplicand in the same way as any other annual expense continuing for the rest of the claimant's life. In each individual case the calculation will vary depending upon the claimant's circumstances and the nature of the new accommodation. Some expenditure may not result in any capital benefit. For example, usually the cost of ramps and other modifications to enable a paralysed claimant to get about the house will reduce the capital value of the house. Another purchaser will want to remove those and thus will pay less for the property. The cost of installing ramps and the like should be regarded as special damages and recovered in full.

10–17   Where, at the time of the accident, the claimant already had a property the cost of that must be taken into account. For example:

- sale price of previous property £60,000;
- purchase price of new property £100,000;
- Cost of adaptions for the claimant's disability, *e.g.* lower-level fittings, widened doors, ramps £10,000.

If the modifications in fact reduce the value of the new property on the open market to £95,000 that has to be factored into the calculation. The claimant has a capital asset now worth £95,000 from which should be subtracted the value of the previous capital asset: £60,000. He recovers the £10,000 by way of special damages. He thus has to be compensated for his £35,000 being tied up in this accommodation. Three per cent of £35,000 is £1050. That is the multiplicand to which should be applied the appropriate multiplier (the ILGS rate, currently 3 per cent).

---

[27] [1998] 3 W.L.R. 329, HL.
[28] *op. cit. per* Lord Lloyd at 347.
[29] *ibid.* at 348.

What Rate of Return should be assumed?

It must not be assumed that the rate of return of 3 per cent is "set in **10–18** stone". The claimant must be compensated on the basis that he or she will invest their damages in a risk free fashion so as to produce a steady stream of income which, together with the gradual erosion of capital over the years will, at the end of the period, leave the fund exhausted. The House of Lords in *Wells* decided that such an investment strategy was best achieved by assuming that the claimant would invest in index-linked government stock. However, the rate of return obtainable on index-linked government stock varies from time to time. Since *Wells* was decided in the House of Lords in May of 1998, the rate of return has been consistently falling. Recently it has begun to rise again. When the Lord Chancellor exercises his powers under the Damages Act 1996 the rate so chosen will be the norm unless the parties can, by evidence, show that some other rate may be appropriate. This might, for example, be the case if the rate set by the Lord Chancellor had not altered so as to reflect market conditions and a higher or lower rate was in fact being paid on index-linked government stock. In such a case the parties would, by evidence, argue the point out and the court would then choose what the appropriate rate should be.

To determine the rate on any particular date reference should be made to the *Financial Times* for that day in the section headed "FTSE Actuaries Government Securities UK Indices" (abbreviated to "Fixed Interest Indices" in the contents list). The appropriate figure will be found in the section marked "Index-linked", within the subsection on yields under the column for that day in question with the group of columns headed "Inflation 5%" and in the line "Over 5 years".

The House of Lords in *Wells* set a "guideline" rate of 3 per cent net of **10–19** tax to be expected as a return on ILGS. That was the prevailing rate at the time of the decision. Since then the rate has fallen consistently. It has recently begun to rise again. This led to a number of challenges to 3 per cent as the appropriate rate of return to be assumed. In *Warren v. Northern General Hospital Trust*[30] the Court of Appeal held that since the Lords in *Wells* had said that the guideline of 3 per cent should last until the Lord Chancellor set a rate under the Damages Act 1996, the Court of Appeal would not adjust the guideline rate. Prior to the hearing the LCD had issued its consultation paper on what the rate should be. In *Wells*, Lord Hope of Craighead thought that the rate "should now be more closely related to the return to be expected from investment in ILGS"[31] and that rate should last "for the time being". He recognised that "adjustments may have to be made to that rate in the light of significant changes in the yield

---

[30] Unreported, Court of Appeal, April 4, 2000, QBENF 2000/0100/A2, *per* Stuart-Smith, Mummery and Tuckey L.JJ.
[31] at 359H.

on ILGS in the future".[32] Lord Clyde thought that the 3 per cent rate should last "for the immediate future, pending a reconsideration of the problem by the Lord Chancellor".[33] He did not regard the 3 per cent rate as "set in stone".[34] Lord Hutton thought that the 3 per cent rate should last until the Lord Chancellor set a different rate or there was a "very considerable change in economic circumstances".[35] Lord Lloyd of Berwick thought that the rate should be set by taking the rate over ". . . a period of month's rather than on a particular day".[36] He favoured taking the average over one year.[37] Lord Steyn thought that the rate should be 3 per cent which he derived from the net average rate of return on ILGS over the past three years".[38] He suggested that "only a marked change in economic circumstances should entitle any party to re-open the debate in advance of a decision by the Lord Chancellor".[39] The Judicial Committee held, by a majority, that the period over which the rate should be assessed was three years.

10–20   The 3 per cent rate set by the House of Lords in *Wells* was net of tax. In that case the Judicial Committee did, nevertheless, recognise that for higher awards a lower rate of return might well be appropriate. Their reasoning was that in a higher award producing a higher income stream the effects of taxation would be greater (since tax is regressive the higher the income the greater the percentage charged as tax) and therefore the net sum available to the claimant will be less. To counter that, a lower rate of return should then be assumed.

Lord Lloyd:

"There is something to be said for a bracket, since it allows some flexibility in exceptional cases, as where, for example, the impact of higher tax would result in substantial under-compensation. Thus on an award of £2 million the higher rate tax payable on the first half of a 20-year period would alone amount to nearly £75,000."

Lord Steyn:

"The rate of 3 per cent takes into account tax at standard rate. But counsel for the plaintiffs argued that the rate should be lowered for individuals subject to higher rates of tax. The position is that index-linked government securities are free of capital gains tax if held for more than a year—but the income is taxable. For my part I am content that the position regarding higher tax rates should

---

[32] at 360D.
[33] at 364B.
[34] at 364D.
[35] at 370H.
[36] at 343H.
[37] at 344B.
[38] at 355F.
[39] at 355F.

remain as Lord Oliver of Alymerton in *Hodgson v. Trapp*[40] described it, viz. that in such exceptional cases plaintiffs would be free to place their arguments for a lower rate before the court."

Lord Hope:

"The impact of higher rate tax on particular awards in exceptional cases should be dealt with in the manner prescribed by Lord Oliver of Alymerton in *Hodgson v. Trapp*."[41]

Lord Clyde:

"Of course in particular cases where the incidents of income tax can be shown to be out of the normal range for one reason or another an appropriate adjustment may be made."

Lord Hutton:

"I would make no alteration in the discount rate for higher rates of tax save that, as Lord Oliver stated—it would be open to Plaintiffs in very exceptional cases to contend that a higher multiplier should be taken."

In *Warren v. Northern General Hospital Trust*, the Court of Appeal refused to apply a lower rate of return to cater for the effects of higher taxation on an award of £3.1 million, of which future loss was £2.5 million. Their reasoning was that the effect of taxation, on the evidence, in that particular case, were not "exceptional".

The Ogden Working Party on April 26, 1999 recommended that courts should select a multiplier by assuming a 2 per cent net rate of return on index-linked government stock. This was because the Working Party felt that the rate of return had fallen. In *Barry v. Ablerex Construction Ltd*[42] Latham J. took the view that a fall of one full percentage point in the net rate of return was sufficient change in economic circumstances to justify departing from 3 per cent and assessing damages on the basis of an assumed 2 per cent rate of return, certainty being provided for in the choice of index (ILGS). That case was not considered by the Court of Appeal in *Warren*.

Finally, in selecting a multiplier a court is not concerned with how the damages will in fact be invested. Lord Lloyd, with whom the other Lords of Appeal agreed, described that as "irrelevant".

---

[40] [1989] A.C. 807 at 835D.
[41] *ibid.*
[42] Unreported, March 22, 2000.

11. Loss of Earnings and Earning Capacity

The Law

Principles

- The legal principle central to this area of damages is the principle **11–01** which underpins all compensatory claims—the Plaintiff should be placed, so far as possible, in the same position he or she would have been in if he or she had not sustained the wrong.[1]
- The claim may include profit as well as income.[2]
- The awards addressed in this chapter have been made for very many years. Until 1970, it was customary to award a single lump sum in personal injury cases, not distinguishing between heads of damage. As late as 1967, it was thought wrong to make itemised awards.[3] The modern practice followed the decision of the Court of Appeal and is now a requirement.[4] Part 16.4.2 of the Civil Procedure Rules (CPR) requires the claimant to serve a schedule of past and future losses with the Particulars of Claim for many years.
- Damages for loss of earnings or earning capacity are awarded without regard to how they will be applied or "spent".[5]
- The award must be reduced for the "cost of earning". The ordinary costs of living—"domestic expenses"—which the plaintiff would have defrayed from earnings if uninjured, must not creep into any care cost award. Observance of those principles will avoid the duplication of compensation.[6]

Evidence—Experts

The use of experts in this field requires careful planning by solicitors and **11–02** counsel. Part 35.1 of the CPR restricts expert evidence to that "which is reasonably required to resolve the proceedings". Cases vary from those

---

[1] *Livingstone v. Rawyards Coal Co.* (1880) 5 App. Cas. 25 at 39.
[2] See *Bellingham v. Dhillon* [1973] Q.B. 304.
[3] See *Watson v. Powles* [1968] 1 Q.B. 596.
[4] *Jefford v. Gee* [1970] 2 Q.B. 130.
[5] See *Lim v. Camden Health Authority* [1980] A.C. 174 and the speech of *Lord Scarman* at 190–192.
[6] See *Lim v. Camden Health Authority, op. cit.*

where experts are redundant to those where substantial number of experts are justified. Courts will not just "rubber-stamp" expert evidence and may, as alternatives to allowing the evidence, either refuse permission or insist on both parties jointly instructing an expert. Some courts have used "joint instructions" to force the defendant to accept the claimant's report if it already exists at the CMC.

Principles Concerning Experts

11–03   • Avoid experts who are or appear to be too partial—they are unlikely to be persuasive.

• Ensure that all experts are well briefed, have all of the material which may help them, including medical and other expert reports if appropriate, and are encouraged to ask questions before they report, if there are matters which are unclear.

• Ensure that the claimant's proof which goes to the expert is full and realistic. Any plans for career development or expressed hopes of promotion, must be realistic, consistent with the other features of the plaintiff's life and, if possible, have some independent support in evidence.

• Remind the expert that it is his or her duty to help the court and that this duty overrides any obligation to the party instructing. Keep in mind the *Ikarian Reefer* guidelines as to the proper role of the expert.[7] If appropriate, remind the expert of the guidelines in instructions or conference. The expert must be reminded that their report must conform with the requirements of CPR 35.10.

• Ensure that reports of experts prepared for exchange address the contents of the disclosed witness statements and are consistent with the other experts' reports to be exchanged

• Counsel or solicitor advocates who intend to call an expert at trial should review an expert's report before it is exchanged. They should *always* have the opportunity to see the expert in conference before a contested hearing.

Do we instruct an expert?

11–04   In the case of an employee who has a long stable employment record with one employer, and where the future claim is based on a continuation of that employment, it is very difficult to see how an expert can be justified.

Even in less straightforward cases, the court will accept the New Earnings Survey as giving a sensible idea of income levels, and, of course,

---

[7] See *National Justice Compania Naviera SA v. Prudential Assurance Co. Ltd (Ikarian Reefer)* [1993] 2 Lloyd's Rep. 68.

actual evidence of job advertisements, both as to availability of work and levels of pay. It seems likely that, as the court exercises its discretion to limit expert evidence, such elementary material will be left to the solicitor rather than an employment expert.

Where any of the following apply, an expert may be of real assistance in mounting or limiting a claim:

- The claimant was a child, or in the course of education, training or re-training
- The claimant was unemployed at the time of the injury.
- The claimant was a young employee whose career would be likely to develop and change.
- The claimant was a professional, a high flyer or high earner, or in a very specialised occupation.
- The claimant was disabled or otherwise limited in working capacity before the index injury.

What Sort of Expert?

There are a large number of general employment expert witnesses, who **11–05** can deal well with most employee cases. However, the legal team should always consider whether the case requires specialist knowledge, *e.g.* for a particular highly specialised employment market. The case of an injured money broker (or personal injury solicitor) cannot be adequately dealt with by a general employment expert alone, and may be better handled by a City broker, specialist recruiter or lawyer expert alone. Forensic track record is important, but less important than real knowledge.

Briefing the Expert

The importance of briefing the expert is emphasised above. The expert **11–06** must see:

- all relevant employment details, including a personnel file where one exists;
- educational details and papers;
- family details where predictions are to be made about a child;
- any medical, psychological or other expert reports which bear on working capacity;
- full details of personal and family plans, relocations, and any other detail which might affect the claimant's employment *either* uninjured *or* injured

The expert must be asked in the initial report to comment widely on the material supplied and to make recommendations which are realistic, rather than overly optimistic or destructive.

Accountants

11–07   Here, in addition to the choice between "generalist" employment expert and a more specialist witness, lawyers must consider retaining a forensic accountant. The cost can often be very high, and a stringent cost/benefit analysis should be made. Accountants should be asked to address the issues where their expertise is really needed, rather than to report the case generally. Accountants are not needed to add up figures provided by the evidence. They are appropriate to value a business, predict future performance of a professional practice, or assess the net annual income which a claimant would actually have achieved.

When instructing an accountant expert:

- ensure the accountant is forensically experienced—ask for previous copy reports;
- do not instruct an accountant who has been involved with the client—they may be open to attack on previous accounts, and cannot be seen as independent;
- obtain (1) a clear quotation of time rates and an outline estimate of overall cost *before* papers are delivered and (2) a revised estimate of cost *after* initial papers have been delivered;
- ensure the accountant is directed specifically to the necessary questions;
- ensure the accountant has all relevant papers from the beginning;
- ensure the accountant has all the specific or local knowledge required, *e.g.* as to desirability of business site, any special business climate, any special local market
- ensure the accountant is properly instructed as to any relevant point of law, *e.g.* the latest developments on multipliers, the return to be assumed on money invested by a successful claimant

Experts: Defendant's Experts

General Principles

11–08   In view of the court's power to limit expert evidence, the defendant is placed in a difficult position. The court may:

- exclude expert evidence;
- insist on a report obtained by the claimant be considered a joint report (which may lead to injustice if the expert is partial);
- allow joint instruction of an expert;
- permit both sides to obtain expert evidence with sequential disclosure with Schedule and Counter-Schedule;

- permit both sides and allow simultaneous exchange of experts' reports.

A decision may have to be made by the defendants as to whether to instruct an expert, in relation to loss of earnings, without knowing whether the claimant intends to, or what the court will eventually allow.

Some Defendants however, having seen that the claimant has such an expert, feel compelled to seek leave to serve their own late report. It is not always necessary to have an expert because the other side has; frequently the areas of generalisation or assumption without factual basis are apparent in the claimant's report and it is perfectly possible to test these in cross-examination without instructing an expert.

A half-way house can be achieved by sending the claimant's report to an expert of the same discipline and asking him, rather than writing a formal report, simply to provide some "bullet points" for cross-examination. These "bullet points" can be put to the claimant's expert in the form of written questions prior to trial in accordance with the provisions of CPR Part 35.6.

In the event that a decision is made to seek a full report, all the general comments above relating to experts apply to the defendants as much as to the claimants.

Particular Problems for Defendants

The defendant expert is frequently in a weaker position than the claimant's since he does not have the advantage of direct access to a co-operative claimant from the outset. Leave for the defendant's expert to interview the claimant should be sought; if it is refused, as it sometimes is, an order should be sought staying the action until such a time as the claimant consents. For extra information, serve a questionnaire drafted by the expert; or if there are difficulties obtaining an answer to that, serve Interrogatories. **11–09**

Other Questions of Evidence

Comparators

The comparator employee can very helpful in quantifying a claim, and in lending focus to an expert's report. The choice of comparator must be made carefully, and as early as possible. The claimant will often know best who should be chosen, but care must be taken to ensure the suggestion is realistic. **11–10**

In all cases the comparator should be asked to consent to their records being used. It can be appropriate and is legitimate to "anonymise" comparators, but this must be agreed early to minimise the risks of a lapse of anonymity.

Documents

11–11   When acting for a claimant, make an early request to preserve the employment and pay records of the claimant *and* potential comparators. Defendant employers are of course well placed to choose comparators and preserve records.

Past Loss of Earnings

The Basic Principles

11–12
- The claimant is entitled to the *net* earnings he or she has lost between the date of the accident and the date of trial.
- The basic guide to the appropriate figures is the amount he or she was earning at the time he ceased work.
- If the period immediately prior to ceasing work is not representative, an average over a preceding period should be adopted.
- If he or she would have achieved promotion or other increase in pay, that must be established, quantified and awarded.

Past loss of earnings if employed

(a) The straightforward case

11–13   In the straightforward case of the claimant employed under Schedule E, obtain from his employer:

- details of the claimant's take-home pay for, say, 12 weeks before his or her injury. This may fluctuate, usually because of overtime, in which case take a weekly average. Multiply this by the number of weeks off work since the injury occurred.

(b) More complex cases

11–14   Complexities may arise which render the above approach inadequate:

- If the past loss of earnings spans a period of time longer than a few months, the claimant's position at the time of his or her injury will be an inadequate gauge of the earnings he or she has lost since these will have increased either simply because of inflation or because of promotion/change of circumstances of employer, etc. In this case a *comparator* must be found who has actually worked the period of past loss for which the claimant is claiming and whose career path shadows that which the claimant would have had.

- There may be aspects in the claimant's circumstances which had he or she been working would in any event have affected earnings; for instance, a reduction in working hours because of personal circumstances; time off because of ill health unrelated to that which is the subject of the claim.
- "Earnings" may consist of more than is included in the pay packet: bear in mind the impact or benefits such as travel season tickets, luncheon vouchers, clothing allowance, special rates for loans, medical insurance, etc. The way in which these are treated will vary depending on the nature of the benefit. In some cases, a period off work will not affect the value of the benefit to the claimant at all. Others may be lost as a result of the period off work. In the latter case, an attempt should be made to put a monetary net value on the benefit and add the sum arrived at into the overall weekly net loss.
- "Medical" arguments may play a part in deciding what the appropriate period of time is during which loss of earnings may be claimed. Check with the medical expert as to when it was reasonable for the claimant to return to work; this question may well be determined by the nature of the work, *e.g.* a claimant who has recovered reasonably may be expected to return to a desk job, but not to manual employment.

Past Loss of Earnings for the Self-employed

(a) The straightforward case
If a claimant is self-employed, past of loss of earnings are likely to be less **11–15** easily calculated then when he or she is employed, even in the relatively straightforward case. However, the basic approach to the quantification of past net loss of earnings is to calculate them on the basis of accounts for the previous, say, three years. Remember that the net profit figure in the accounts will be net of business expenses, but *not* net of personal taxation and national insurance which must be calculated and deducted separately.

(b) Complexities
- Remember that business expenses deducted may in fact include **11–16** elements of benefit to the self-employed (*e.g.* use of office as home, phone bills, items such as car/travel and entertainment expenses) so that the true loss to the claimant is greater than the profit figure in the accounts.
- The accounts may be inaccurate either (as is particularly so in the case of the one man band) through inefficiency of book-keeping or because of deliberate ploys, *e.g.* a decision not to reflect cash payments into the business.

(c) Evidence required

11–17
- In addition to accounts, as referred to above, all revenue documents including income tax assessments and returns and any correspondence between the claimant/his or her accountant/the Inland Revenue.
- Comparison between accounts and documents prepared for the revenue may show up discrepancies. In the ultimate assessment, the claimant who has sought to reduce his or her earnings for the purposes of his or her tax calculations will not receive much sympathy from the court if he or she then seeks to inflate them for the purposes of the damages claim.
- The input of an accountant (ideally with expertise relating to businesses in that particular field) may well be required when assessing past and future loss for the self-employed—on this, see para. 11–03 on expert evidence.
- In cases where the future of a profession or business must be predicted, consider obtaining an independent outside knowledgeable witness to give evidence and to help the accountant

Future Loss

Employees

11–18
- The computation of future earnings for an employee is merely a continuation of the approach adopted in respect of past losses, but adopting a multiplier/multiplicand. The use of a comparator to build the case for past losses will provide the platform for future losses: What are the prospects for the comparator? How do they assist in regard to the claimant?
- Many categories must be considered in the future loss estimation. They may relate to the employee (wealth, probabilities of promotion, reasons for early retirement), the employer (expanding market, outdated product with financial difficulties, imminent takeover) or the general situation in the claimant's locality (low wage rates, with unemployment, new factory being built).
- Contingencies may affect the multiplicand or the multiplier. If a specific event can be predicted (promotion/redundancy) then it is usually better to alter the multiplicand and apply split multipliers to different periods. If the contingencies are less certain, then adjustment to the multiplier is usually more appropriate.
- In cases of female employees it should be remembered that multipliers are generally lower, to reflect earlier retirement and a greater tendency to work part-time or stop work for periods to deal with the demands of a family.

The self-employed

The prediction of future loss for the self-employed is often very **11–19** complex. Whether the injured party was a shop-owner or a plumber, an independent professional or a major businessman, the essence is to predict the future prospects of a business.

An accurate historical picture is the starting point. The need for full instructions and information is vital, and for realistic predictions and instructions from a claimant client. Usually, the most important documents will be the accounts. A judgment must be made about how many years accounts should be used for the case. A minimum of three years before the injury should suffice, where they exist.

Other documents which may be of use (which should be preserved by claimants and may be requested by defendants) are:

- credit card and bank accounts relevant to the business;
- all VAT records;
- customer lists;
- job offers;
- order books, including orders unfulfilled as a result of the injury.

Drafting the Schedule or Counter-Schedule

Schedule

Pleadings are dealt with generally in Chapter 26. It is helpful to consider **11–20** briefly how best to settle this part of a schedule of loss.

- Provide a short synopsis of the case on loss of earnings in the preamble to the Schedule or text in the appropriate section of the schedule.
- Identify in the Schedule the parts of the claimant's witness statement or any other factual evidence which are important to this head of claim.
- Ensure a clear division between historic loss of earnings and future loss of earnings. It will be a rare case when they appear together, rather than in the historic loss and future loss sections of the Schedule.
- Ensure that any evidential or legal assumptions upon which the figures are based are made explicit *before* the figures are given.
- If possible, design the layout of the Schedule so that it becomes the judge's working document—this may mean leaving space for the defendant's figures and the judge's conclusions to be filled in, like a Scott Schedule.
- Always ensure that the full calculations are clearly laid out, whether in the main Schedule, an appendix to the Schedule or in an appended accountant's report.

- Always ensure that there is a short summary of the figures in this head of claim at the end of this section of the Schedule.

The Counter-Schedule

11–21
- Part 16.14.2 required the defendant to attach to the defence a Counter-Schedule stating which items are agreed, disputed or where the defendant has no knowledge. Where the figures are disputed, the defendant must supply alternative figures where appropriate.
- Most of the comments made above in relation to the drafting of the Schedule apply equally to the drafting of the Counter-Schedule.
- If the claimant has not followed the suggestion above in relation to format, incorporate a synopsis of the claimant's case at the beginning of the section.
- Make a clear distinction between your criticisms of the claimant's claim and your case on behalf of the defendant: if the case is at all complex it is easiest to divide the Counter-Schedule response into three sections: "The claimant's case"; "The defendant's comments on the claimant's case"; and "The defendant's case".
- Make it clear precisely which figures you are contesting and which you are conceding.

Example

The Claimant's case

11–22   The claimant claims £X in respect of loss of earnings for the period (date) to (date).

The Defendant's Comments on the Claimant's Case

(a) The claimant has claimed for the whole period for which he was out of work although on a balance of probabilities he would in any event have been forced to give up his job by (date) because of the osteoarthritis from which he suffers and which is not attributable to the defendant's negligence.

(b) The claimant has failed to deduct National Insurance payments from his weekly earnings.

(c) The claimant's arithmetical calculation is in any event incorrect; £X × Y weeks in fact = £.

The Defendant's Case

- Taking into account the facts pleaded in (a)–(c) above, the defendant concedes past loss of earnings of £   p.w. ×   weeks. Total conceded: £ .

Handicap in the Labour Market

The Basic Principle

The award[8] is intended to cover the situation which arises when the **11–23** claimant has a disability which renders him at a disadvantage in the labour market either because he is employed at the time of trial and he is vulnerable to losing the job he has and/or if he does lose it he will be at a disadvantage, when competing with able-bodied applicants, in finding another job; or because he is unemployed at the time of trial and because of his disadvantage in the labour market cannot find a job. Such disadvantages are conventionally compensated by a lump sum payment (see *computation* at para. 11–28).

The Relationship with Other Earnings Claims

The award can be made to a claimant in addition to a future loss of **11–24** earnings claim or in substitution for it. It should not be confused with loss of amenity—*i.e.* it is *not* to compensate for loss of job satisfaction because of inability to perform so well, or disappointment because of type of employment closed to him because of the disability: those aspects are covered by the award for pain, suffering and loss of amenity.

Where the Claimant is in Employment at Trial

Even if a claimant is holding down a job effectively at trial, he may be at **11–25** a disadvantage in that job if, for example, he has to take time off because of sickness, or the need for medical treatment; or if he becomes tired quicker and is thus less available for overtime than fellow employees, or if he has to have some physical tasks performed for him. He may be the first to be considered if the need for redundancies arises.

Where the Claimant is Unemployed at Trial

The fact of unemployment at trial may itself be evidence of the **11–26** claimant's loss of advantage on the labour market—if he lost his job because of his injuries and has been unable to find another. Even if he has

---

[8] Otherwise known as *Smith v. Manchester* award (after *Smith v. Manchester Corporation*: [1974] 17 K.I.R. 17).

had no job for a substantial period of time and/or for a time predating the injury, his injury may be the "last straw" affecting his efforts to find employment.

Evidence Required

11–27   Note that a claim for damages for handicap in the labour market should be pleaded.[9]

At trial:

- When the claimant is in employment there must be a real (as opposed to a speculative or fanciful) risk that he will at some time in the future lose his job.
- This entails adducing evidence of the nature of the business and its prospects and of the nature of the claimant's particular circumstances—his qualifications, the length of his employment, his record (which may entail disclosure of his personnel file) and if possible the future intentions of his employers. Caution should be exercised since enquiries may put ideas as to future redundancies into an employer's head![10]
- If the risk of loss of the present employment is considered real, the court must consider the claimant's chances of obtaining alternative employment. This depends again on the claimant's particular circumstances, which must include his versatility and also the employment market applicable to his skills in his area.
- When the claimant is unemployed, the court must investigate the duration and circumstances of this; if he has lost his job because of his disability and is, therefore, claiming future loss of earnings, this does not necessarily preclude a claim under the present head as well; the best "proof" of a vulnerability in the labour market may be unemployment at trial. It is essential that the claimant proves realistic attempts to find employment and the reasons for his lack of success.

Computation

11–28   A lump sum is awarded, discounted in the normal way for accelerated receipt. Assessment is so speculative that the multiplier/multiplicand approach is not appropriate.[11]

---

[9] See RSC, Ord. 18, r. 32.

[10] see *Moeliker v. A. Reyrolle & Co. Ltd* [1977] 1 W.L.R. 132) for an analysis as to what constitutes a real risk.

[11] see for instance Scarman L.J.'s specific rejection of this approach in *Smith v. Manchester* itself.

No rule of thumb applies; only study of the individual authorities really provides a "feel".[12]

Courts can award significant sums: in *Foster v. Tyne & Wear*,[13] the court awarded £35,000. If updated in line with RPI, the present-day value is nearly £60,000.

Loss of Congenial Employment

Where the claimant has had to give up a job which gave particular **11–29** satisfaction, the courts will make a separate award for "the joy of a craftsman". This award has been criticised by the Law Society and the Law Commission (Damages for Personal Injury: Non Pecuniary Loss, Law Com. No. 257 para. 3.20) but has been described by the Court of Appeal as "well recognised [as] . . . a separate head of damage" (*Hale v. London Buses*[14].

Awards are usually a few thousand pounds.

---

[12] See for example *Forey v. London Buses Ltd* [1992] 1 P.I.Q.R. P48; *Foster v. Tyne & Wear County Council* [1986] 1 All E.R. 567; *Moeliker v. A. Reyrolle & Co. Ltd* [1977] 1 W.L.R. 132.

[13] *ibid.*

[14] [1993] P.I.Q.R. P30.

12. Loss of Pension

The Conventional Approach

Wider Principles

- Pension loss is a head of future pecuniary loss like any other and not **12–01** an esoteric subject outside the routine assessment of damages.
- The much and unfairly criticised leading case of *Auty v. National Coal Board*[1] embodied no abstruse method but only the then conventional approach.
- As the conventional approach has shifted following *Wells v. Wells*[2] so must the assessment of pension loss, away from the old method in *Auty*, into line with the present application of the conventional approach.

Conventional Approach in Practice following Wells v. Wells

- Assesses damages for personal injuries net of tax.[3] **12–02**
- Takes no account of future inflation, setting the multiplicand at date of trial and ignoring the particular avenues of investment open to an individual claimant.[4]
- Adopts a rate of discount to be set in the future by the Lord Chancellor and at the time of writing taken to be 3 per cent p.a.[5]
- No longer makes "judicial" discounts, using the Ogden Tables now as a starting point rather than a check, being slow to depart from the relevant actuarial multiplier on impessionistic grounds or previously decided multipliers,[6] and where there is agreed life expectancy an arithmetical multiplier is to be taken over that life expectancy.[7]
- Refuses to make pseudo-findings of "future fact" on the balance of probabilities, but reflects future chances by assessing the damages

---

[1] [1985] 1 W.L.R. 784; [1985] 1 All E.R. 930, CA.
[2] [1998] 3 W.L.R. 329, HL.
[3] *British Transport Commission v. Gourley* [1956] A.C. 185, HL.
[4] *Mallett v. McMonagle* [1970] A.C. 166 at 175B–176D, HL (N.I.). *Lim Poh Choo v. Camden and Islington Area Health Authority* [1980] A.C. 174 at 193B–194B, HL; upheld on this point in *Wells v. Wells* [1998] 3 W.L.R. 319, *per* Lord Lloyd at 334A, Lord Steyn at 353C and Lord Clyde at 361E.
[5] *Wells v. Wells* [1998] 3 W.L.R. 329, HL, *per* Lord Lloyd at 344A; but see discussion elsewhere in this book on discount rates generally.
[6] *Wells v. Wells, supra, per* Lord Lloyd at 347D–E.
[7] *Wells v. Wells, supra, per* Lord Lloyd at 345H–347F.

based upon an "assumption" which aims at doing justice in monetary terms balancing the favourable and adverse contingencies.[8] Sometimes the "assumption" itself balances all the contingencies in which case an arithmetical multiplier can be used on the basis of that assumption but more often the assumption is taken as the nearest convenient starting point and then varied further for contingencies.

- Involves "doing one's very best",[9] "making the best use of such tools to assist the process as are available"[10] and "now that detailed calculations and tables founded on a reasonably reliable basis are available, taking full advantage of them".[11]

Conventional Approach—Binding on Pensions?

12–03   Given the cornerstones of the conventional approach, recent first instance decisions before *Wells* based on *Auty* as binding authority were clearly correct.[12] The wider ratio of those cases, that the conventional approach applies to pension loss, remains intact following *Wells*. Encouragement to obtain a quotation on the financial markets to make good the loss and to proffer it as the measure of damage should be ignored.[13] One might as well suggest that nursing care beginning at some future date to run until the end of a claimant's life[14] be valued by reference to the cost of a deferred annuity; or, without any change in the logic, the cost of immediate nursing care to a simple annuity; or loss of earnings. . . . All of which is not the law as it stands. Further, it defies logic to assess a one off lump sum payment by reference to the sum required to generate an annuity without power in the court to impose an award of future periodical payments or even to enforce the purchase of the annuity after the case.

A Modern but Nevertheless "Conventional" Approach

12–04   The concept of using the Ogden Tables as a universally adopted basis for the calculation of future recurring losses and expenses over any future tracts of time commended itself to the House of Lords in *Wells*.[15] Indeed,

---

[8] *Mallett v. McMonagle* [1970] A.C. 166 at 173F, 174D and 176E–F, HL (N.I.); *Wells v. Wells* [1997] 3 W.L.R. 329 at 356F–357A.

[9] *Wells v. Wells, op. cit., per* Lord Lloyd at 332H–333A and Lord Clyde at 361A.

[10] *ibid., per* Lord Hope at 357E.

[11] *ibid., per* Lord Clyde at 3464C.

[12] *Page v. Sheerness Steel Company* [1996] P.I.Q.R. Q26 at Q38, Dyson J. and *Longden v. British Coal Corporation* [1995] P.I.Q.R. Q48 at Q50, CA noting Douglas Brown J.'s unchallenged decision on that score.

[13] It is one thing to attempt to refer to ILGS and past real rates of return in fixing the discount rate in *Wells* and quite another to adduce specific evidence of actual investment opportunity for an individual claimant as if itself the measure of loss.

[14] An exact analogy for a future loss of pension claim and the same method can be used in such cases.

[15] *op. cit., per* Lord Clyde at 364B–C.

the House of Lords used the Ogden Tables in relation to pensions to solve the question of how much discount should be given from an already paid ill-health retirement lump sum including commuted payments in *Longden v. British Coal Corporation*.[16] While the first edition of the Ogden Tables had just been published at the time of *Auty*, it had not gained the widespread acceptance which took over a decade in coming, and the judges in *Auty* did their best, perhaps with misunderstandings as to the nature of actuarial evidence, using the English Life Tables based upon Past Expectation of Life and the Bacon and Woodrow Arithmetical Discount Tables. It should go without saying in the light of the adjustments to the conventional approach enunciated so clearly in *Wells* that the time has come to move on from *Auty*, using the Ogden Tables "to do one's very best".[17]

Overview of Types of Pension Claims

There are two broad types of claim.   12–05

- *Type 1*: where the claimant is young without an established working history; where the position is insecure; or where there are major uncertainties. In such cases, the best one can do is to evaluate a notional claim using the Ogden Pension Tables as at the date of compulsory retirement which can then only be discounted dramatically with a broad brush given the flavour of the case.

- *Type 2*: where the claimant is in long-term secure employment with a good quality pension scheme and where there are multiple options for voluntary early retirement, ill-health retirement and death in service benefits. In these cases, if one is to do one's best following *Wells*, a more subtle approach is required with an appreciation of the monetary effects of early/ill-health retirement or death in service if proper compensation is to be made.

The Basic Ogden Multipliers

There is now widespread familiarity with the concept of earnings   12–06 multipliers and life multipliers which are applied to a current multiplicand to generate a lump sum providing a steady stream of income for the period up to the assumed date of retirement or death, with the fund extinguished at that point. A pensions multiplier is a multiplier to be applied again to a present multiplicand to provide a stream of payments from the assumed

---

[16] [1998] A.C. 653 and see n. 17.
[17] See n. 9, but this must be subject to practicalities, *e.g.* taking into account all the minute changes in tax reliefs and State pension entitlements at different ages will render calculations so unwieldy, difficult and tedious that, in the context of necessarily imperfect assumptions, the exercise is not worth the attempt. See the worked example below.

date of retirement until the assumed date of death. It already includes an actuarial discount for the chance of early death over the whole period and an arithmetical discount from the date of expected retirement to the date of calculation.

Solution to Type 1 Cases Using the Ogden Tables

Worked Example Using Basic Ogden Pensions Multipliers

12–07   Male, 23, in service for two years prior to road accident when lost a leg, compulsory retirement age at 65, and now unfit for work. Pension would have been based on the formula (very common):

Length of service (maximum 40 years) × 1/80 × final year's pensionable pay.

On ill-health retirement, length of service enhanced by five years or to 15 years, whichever is the greater (again a common type of term).

Pensionable pay £10,000 p.a.

Pension if retired at 65

40 years × 1/80 × £10,000 = £5,000 p.a.
say net[18]   £4,840 p.a.

Pension now payable

15 years × 1/80 × £10,000 = £1,875 p.a.
say net   £1,840 p.a.
Annual loss   £3,000

Multiplier (Ogden Table 17
at age 23 at 3% p.a. discount)
Capitalised annual loss   × 3.4
(before discount for eventualities)   £10,200

The discount after such a basic calculation will vary depending on the nature of the job and the likelihood of a sustained career. A policeman or fireman with two years' service is much more likely to have a long-term career than a private soldier (even if he hopes for promotion) where average length of service for raw recruits is as low as three years.

---

[18] See Type 2 worked example below for detailed tax calculations. Exactitude in a Type 1 claim is in any event impossible.

Solution to Type 2 Cases Using the Ogden Tables

Type 2 cases are those where there is a strong likelihood of a sustained **12–08**
career.

Now   Retirement   Death

| --- |

                    Period of life multiplier

| ----------------------------- |

     Period of earnings multiplier

                                   | --------------------------- |

                                   Period of pensions multiplier

The Multiplier

If one refers to the linear diagram of multipliers above the following **12–09**
relationship becomes apparent:

> Earnings Multiplier + Pensions Multiplier = Life Multiplier

If one does not presently accept the relationship it is evident from the
Ogden Tables themselves. At any given age, whether the retirement is at 60
or 65, the sum of the earnings multiplier and the pensions multiplier is the
life multiplier. In fact, we do not really need the Ogden Pensions Tables at
all so long as we have the Life and Earnings Tables.

The relationship can be rearranged to yield a simple but powerful
formula in the calculation of pension loss.

> Life Multiplier − Earnings Multiplier = Pensions Multiplier

The Ogden Tables already take into account mortality so that contingency is satisfied if the Tables are used as the starting points for the life
and earnings multipliers. Unless there is medical evidence to the contrary
or the claimant has a hazardous lifestyle, there is no justification following
Wells for tinkering with the life multiplier. The major contingency on the
earnings multiplier is the age of retirement. If, when deciding the earnings
multiplier the judge considers only the contingencies as to *age* at retirement
(leaving contingencies as to *wage*, *e.g.* promotion, etc., for consideration
when setting the earnings multiplicand—more logical after all), whatever
the process of balancing the contingencies from the basic Ogden earnings
multiplier, those very same contingencies are automatically taken into
account in the case of a claimant with long-term secure employment if the
pensions multiplier uses the actual earnings and life multipliers assessed on
other heads of loss. A "tailored" pensions multiplier can be reached by

simply taking the earnings multiplier in the case away from the life multiplier in the case.

The Multiplicand

12–10   The formula will establish the best starting point for the multiplier, but if the claimant retires at a date other than the one contended for, the multiplicand will be affected because of the different length of service. The potential problem can easily be solved. If the judge in setting the earnings multiplier and using the Ogden Tables articulates the "assumption" as to age at retirement, we will know in turn the correct assumption as to the length of service in order to fix the multiplicand under a final salary scheme. Even if the assumption is not specifically articulated, it can be worked out from the earnings multiplier how it translates into *age* at assumed retirement. For example, if the multiplier is set at 16 for a 40-year-old man (when 17.09 was the starting point for retirement at 65 from Ogden Table 13), the multiplier in itself takes into account the contingencies, good and bad, in relation to age at retirement so use Ogden Table 22 (multipliers for pecuniary loss for terms certain) to read off the number of years for which that multiplier is appropriate. A multiplier of 16 equates with an assumption of loss over about 21.75 years looking at Table 22, or retirement at 61.75 years for a man aged 40. If one has taken the precaution of obtaining the formula to apply to any given final salary scheme, the correct multiplicand will be a simple matter of calculation.

Further Adjustment

12–11   It would be a mistake to think that there will be no scope for adjustment on the facts of each case after the above method has been followed; but it is the best starting point. The various contingencies might not have been compartmentalised between multiplier and multiplicand quite as clearly as hoped. If the judge provides for the prospects of promotion by enhancing the multiplier rather than the multiplicand everything will be thrown out of line. As already discussed, the job may not involve long-term secure employment. The quality of the pension scheme may be poor so that there is no entitlement to early retirement/ill-health pension before the date of compulsory retirement. In all those circumstances, one can revert to using the Ogden Pensions Tables, but remembering that much greater adjustment for contingencies will be needed with a broad brush. However, if the judge is invited to articulate the relevant assumptions when deciding the loss of earnings claim, and the actual life and earnings multipliers are used to form the pensions multiplier, there will be a much more accurate preliminary assessment of the true pension loss.[19]

---

[19] See the worked example below.

The Evidential Framework

Much of the evidence going to the assumptions required for pension loss **12–12** calculation is assembled in relation to the heads of loss other than pension. Nevertheless, the following matters are relevant and can be stored on a standard draft for ease of completion and to ensure a methodical approach:

- claimant's age at date of calculation;
- claimant's life multiplier at date of calculation (using the Ogden Tables for Projected Mortality as a starting point,[20] only to be adjusted in the light of cogent evidence, when that evidence may give a life expectancy and an arithmetical multiplier from Table 22 should then be used);
- claimant's age at the "assumption" for retirement if the accident had not occurred;
- the "assumption" as to job title/position at retirement and hence as to "pensionable pay");
- claimant's attitude to any possible commutation of periodical payments to a tax-free lump sum;
- spouse's age;
- spouse's life multiplier (using similar considerations as for the claimant's life multiplier).

The pension fund trustees should then be invited to answer a questionnaire (which can again be stored as a standard draft) and to provide the main terms of the scheme which are usually within an explanatory booklet for employees. Questions include:

(a) What is the formula for pension entitlement under the final salary scheme?

(b) What constitutes "pensionable pay" under the scheme as distinct from overall earnings?

(c) What entitlement is there to a lump sum?

(d) If the lump sum is a commutation of entitlement to periodical payments, how is it calculated and with what effect upon annual pension?

(e) When did the claimant's pensionable service commence?

(f) Have there been any "pensions holidays" in respect of the claimant's service?

---

[20] *Worrall v. Powergen plc* [1999] P.I.Q.R. Q103.

(g) What are the provisions for:

    (i) voluntary early retirement?
    (i) ill-health early retirement?
    (iii) any payments under the pension scheme on redundancy?
    (iv) preservation of pension on voluntary resignation?
    (v) benefits on death in service or otherwise?
    (i) Widow's pension?

(h) In the case of a claimant who has already retired, what is the current value of the actual entitlement to pension and, if a commuted lump sum has been paid, when and how much?

The trustees should then be invited to show a worked example based upon the present day value of the assumptions contended for, so as to make clear how the calculation is to be done in the event of alternative assumptions requiring calculation at a later date.

Answers to the above questions coupled with the explanatory booklet should be more than sufficient in most cases. The problem with calculating pension loss is, and always has been, not so much a difficulty in carrying out the arithmetic once the correct evidence has been obtained, but in making sure that there is a sufficient breadth of evidence so that when the assumptions upon which the damages are to be awarded are articulated by the judge the figures are easily available and converted. If there is any difficulty in understanding the information from the pensions trustees then, at a relatively late stage, just prior to trial, when the issues between the parties are delineated, the trustees can be invited to fill in a questionnaire which can be tailored to meet the competing contentions of the parties and the possible middle ground.

Additional Receipt of Pension/Incapacity Pension

12–13   In many cases, a plaintiff will be able to exercise an early or ill-health retirement option following an accident and obtain periodical payments and/or a lump sum prior to normal retirement. The House of Lords' decision in *Parry v. Cleaver*[21] is the leading authority and the following propositions from it are sound:

- Additional receipts of pension are not to be deducted from other heads of loss.[22]
- After the date of normal retirement, credit must be given for any payments under the scheme. Whether labelled as "retirement" or "incapacity/injury", the pensions are of one and the same kind.[23]

---

[21] [1970] A.C. 1, HL.
[22] *ibid., per* Lord Reid at 20G–21A.
[23] *loc. cit.*

- No credit is to be given for periodical payments prior to the date of normal retirement, not even from the later pension loss claim itself.[24]

The first two propositions have never been challenged, nor were they in the recent case of *Longden v. British Coal Corporation*.[25] However, while the third proposition was clearly the ratio of *Parry v. Cleaver*, it arose essentially from the monetary result of the case as against any detailed discussion of the issues involved. It was challenged in *Longden*, but upheld. *Parry v. Cleaver* did not involve the commutation of periodical payments to a lump sum. In *Longden*, the House of Lords decided that:

> Where the lump sum is a commutation of periodical payments, that proportion of it which represents the period after normal retirement should be deducted.[26]

This is only logical bearing in mind the diagram set out above. We can again apply our formula, but rearranged:

> Deductible Proportion of Lump Sum = [Life Multiplier − Earnings Multiplier] ÷ Life Multiplier

Strictly, the multipliers are to be taken from the Ogden Tables *as at the date when the lump sum was actually paid not at trial*, but using the "assumptions" found or contended for in the trial to fix the end point of the earnings multiplier to ensure internal consistency and that the same contingencies are taken into account in the same fashion.

Longden was narrowly decided on the facts because the lump sum was a commutation. The whole tenor of *Longden* suggests that if the lump sum is not a commutation but paid compulsorily under the scheme, there should be no deduction of any part.[27]

Miscellaneous

Widow's Pension

The method used in *Auty* can be adapted for use with our more modern **12–14** tools.

The widow's pension is usually exprssed as a proportion of the claimant's entitlement—often $1/2$ or $2/3$. Adding on to the claimant's pension multiplier the extent to which the wife's life multiplier exceeds the claimant's life multiplier *but reduced by the proportion of the widow's entitlement*, produces a combined pensions multiplier for the couple.[28]

---

[24] See n. 25.
[25] [1998] A.C. 653, HL.
[26] *ibid.* at 672D–F.
[27] No decided case on the point, which may yet be litigated.
[28] See the worked example below.

Alternative Occupational Pension

12–15   It was conceded in *Auty* that where the claimant is able to obtain alternative pensionable work, the value of the additional pension should be offset. The eventualities of the alternative position are likely to be very different from those of the original. If so, it is not possible simply to subtract the alternative pension from the figures in the original calculation. Rather, a quick calculation in reverse gives the credit to be allowed, discounted back to date of trial, and then in turn adjusted for eventualities if necessary. Often the claimant is unemployed at trial, but with some residual earning capacity. The chance of obtaining alternative pensionable employment should be taken into account in the overall adjustment for eventualities, but there will usually be little or no chance of an injured claimant obtaining work with entitlement to a much-coveted *final salary* pension.[29]

Tax Allowances and Reliefs

12–16   As in any personal injuries action the damages must be computed net of tax. It should be remembered that age allowances are higher than the standard personal allowance and there are substantially increased married couples' allowances for those over the age of 65. At the relatively low levels of most pension loss calculations there will be little or no tax.

Age Allowances

	2000/2001
Single person	
aged 65–74	£5,790
aged 75 and over	£6,050
Married couple's allowance	Now largely abolished
Age allowance reduced by ½ of income over normal until personal relief is reached	£17,000

State Retirement Pension

Single person (non-contributory)	£40.40 per week or £2,100.80 p.a.

Personal Pension Plans

12–17   There can be no claim for losses under personal pension plans, which are

---

[29] *cf.* money purchase/personal pensions.

"money purchase" schemes, converted into an annuity with the option of a tax free lump sum at the date of retirement. There is no formula for fixing the value of the pension, but rather only speculation on the performance of the fund against inflation. More importantly, it is not remuneration for work done in the form of an insurance following *Parry v. Cleaver*. Rather it is easily distinguished as an investment by the individual, and only arguably in the form of insurance, of remuneration already received. The claimant should simply receive the loss of earnings before contributions into the fund. The loss of tax relief is a quite separate matter and, if properly proved, can be incorporated into the loss of earnings claim.

Hybrid Personal/Employer-Funded Schemes

Such schemes are "money purchase" or personal pension plans but **12–18** linked to an employer, perhaps instigated by and with contributions from him. Again there is no identifiable formula for fixing the value of the pension, which depends upon the performance of the fund. Similarly, the scheme is essentially an investment of remuneration albeit "at source". The only sensible solution is to calculate the claimant's loss of earnings before deduction of contributions (but taking into account tax relief) and to value the employer's contributions as current benefits in kind. If the scheme is categorised as an "investment" as against an "insurance" within the spirit of *Parry v. Cleaver*, there is no conflict with *Dews v. National Coal Board*,[30] which can in any event be distinguished as dealing with a classical final salary scheme.

Average Life Expectancy Short of Retirement

Unless medical evidence practically rules out survival beyond normal **12–19** retirement age, the chance that the claimant may survive is an eventuality which calls for compensation under the conventional approach. The medical evidence should address the longest realistic life expectancy and a calculation carried out to that date but then heavily discounted against the flavour of the medical evidence for its improbability.

Death-in-Service Benefits

Quite apart from the pension payments under a final salary scheme, **12–20** although unrelated to pension and to be paid prior to normal retirement, there are often death-in-service benefits. These have nothing to do with a claim for pension itself but certainly stand to offset any temptation to discount further for the risk of mortality. In fact, if the Ogden Tables are

---

[30] [1988] A.C. 1, HL.

used as the starting point and mortality is thereby taken into account, the loss of death-in-service benefit is a separate loss that stands to be compensated and was in fact compensated in *Auty*. Those not entitled to death-in-service benefits have to provide for themselves by purchasing "term life assurance" at the cost of a regular premium. Death-in-service benefits, therefore, amount to a benefit in kind which can be added on to the loss of earnings claim, as the "term life assurance" is for the term of the wage loss.[31] Some evidence will be required as to the size of the benefit in kind, *i.e.* the sort of premium that would be required each year to produce the lump sum envisaged under the scheme in the event of death.

Worked Type 2 Example

Basic Facts

12–21   Male aged 40, married, previously worked as an established company accountant in industry (basic pay plus contractual overtime: £25,000 p.a. gross) but now, following brain injury, capable only of low grade clerical work (basic pay with no available overtime: £10,000 p.a. gross) with the same company, a secure and sympathetic employer. The claimant is very likely to have remained as an employed company accountant and is now likely to remain with the company as a clerk. No impairment of life expectancy. Unconnected constitutional condition was/is likely to become increasingly troublesome and may force retirement between 55 and 65.

The Pension Trustees' Questionnaire

Question	*Answer*
(a) What is the formula for pension entitlement under the final salary scheme?	Pension = length of service (years subject to an overall maximum of 40 years) × $\frac{1}{80}$ × final year's pensionable pay.
(b) What constitutes "pensionable pay" under the scheme as distinct from overall earnings?	Basic pay and contractual overtime pay only without reference to bonus payments and additional voluntary overtime.
(c) What entitlement is there to a lump sum?	3 × final year's pensionable pay tax free on top of the annual entitlement.

---

[31] Some schemes also provide for a lump sum on death in early retirement and multipliers longer than the earnings muliplier may be appropriate.

(d) If the lump sum is a commutation of entitlements to periodical payments, how is it calculated and with what effect upon annual pension?

Not applicable.

(b) When did the claimant's pensionable service commence?

Aged 22$\frac{1}{2}$.

(f) Have there been any "pensions holidays" in respect of the claimant's service?

None.

(g) What are the provisions for:
  (i) Voluntary early retirement?

At 55 without penalty (subject to the company's approval which has never yet been known to be withheld).

  (ii) Ill-health early retirement?

At any age without penalty (but with the approval of the company medical officer) with an ill-health enhancement of 5 years additional service on top of actual years service or up to 20 years total service, whichever is the higher.

  (iii) Payments under the scheme on redundancy?

Not applicable.

  (iv) Preservation of pension on voluntary resignation?

Pension preserved with previous employer; or value transferable to new employer's final salary scheme; or value transferable into a personal pension plan.

  (v) Benefits on death in service or otherwise

2 × final year's pensionable pay.

  (vi) Widow's pension?

Not applicable.

(h) In the case of a claimant who has already retired, what is the current value of the actual entitlement to pension and, if a commuted lump sum has been paid, when and how much?

Not applicable.

Claimant's Schedule

12–22 Claimant's age   40

Claimant's life multiplier: 22.66 (Ogden Table 11)

Earnings multiplier: 16.5 (carried forward from future loss of earnings claim where based on Ogden Table 13 for retirement at 65: 17.09, but discounted for the chance of early retirement based on general contingencies and the constitutional condition).

Pensions multiplier: $22.66 - 16.5 = 6.16$

Assumption for age at retirement based on earnings multiplier of 16.5:   62.5 (Ogden Table 22: 22.5 years hence)

Length of service: $62.5 - 22.5 = 40$ years

Loss of annual pension at 62.5

Annual pension as company accountant: 40 years $\times$ $^1/_{80}$ $\times$ £25,000 = £12,500.00

Less tax on top slice of income[32]:

Company pension	£12,500
State retirement pension	
(£40.40 × 52 weeks)	£2,100.80
	£14,600.80 p.a.
less personal/age allowance	−£5,790
taxable income	£8,810.80

tax on first £1,520 @ 10%   −£152.00

tax on balance (£7.90) @ 22%   −£1,603.98

total tax liability   +£1,755.90

Net value of company pension   £10,744.02

Say   **£10,750.00**

Annual pension as clerk   40 years $\times$ $^1/_{80}$ $\times$ £10,000 = £5,000.00

Less tax on top slice of income

Company pension:	£5,000
State Retirement Pension	
(£40.40 × 52 weeks)	£2,100.80
	£7,100.80 p.a.
less personal/age allowance	−£5,740.00

---

[32] Assuming age allowances and entitlement to State retirement pension strictly only available at age 65 throughout the period given the closeness to that age and ignoring increased allowances at 75.

Loss of Pension

taxable income	£1,310.80	
tax on first £1,520 @ 10%	−£131.00	
total tax liability		−£131.00
Net value of company pension		**£4,869.00**

Net pension as an accountant	£10,750.00	
less		
Net pension as a clerk	−£4,869.00	
Net annual loss	£5,831.00	
Pensions multiplier	× 6.16	
Capital annual loss		**£35,919**

Loss of lump sum at the assumed age of 62.5

As a company accountant:	3 × £25,000 =	£75,000
less as a clerk	3 × £10,000 =	−£30,000
Loss at 62.5		£45.000
Discount over 22.5 years to age 40 (Table 21)	× 0.5145	
		£23,152.50
Total loss of pension claim		£59,071.50

Say, after adjustment for contingencies such as company
catastrophe, "Maxwell" pension fraud, etc.   **£55,000.00**

Defendants's Schedule

Claimant's age:	40	**12–23**
Life multiplier:	22.66 (Ogden Table 11)	
Earnings multiplier:	13.5 (Based on Ogden Table 15 for retirement at 60 − 14.75, but discounted further for the chance of ill-health or voluntary early retirement[33]	
Pensions multiplier:	22.66 − 13.5 = 9.16	
Assumption for age at retirement based on earnings multiplier of 13.5:	57.5 (Ogden Table 22: 17.5 years hence)	
Length of service:	57.5 − 22.5 = 35 years	

Loss of annual pensions at 57.5

Annual pension as company accountant:	35 years × $\frac{1}{80}$ × £25,000 = £10.937.50 p.a. gross

---

[33] Strictly, given the five-year enhancement of service in the event of ill-health retirement, the earnings multiplier should be adjusted for the pensions claim; but such exactitude is impractical and better taken into account at the end with a broad brush.

Less tax (detailed calculation omitted, but   £9,500.00
see above schedule for method[34]) net:

Annual pension as clerk: 35 years × ¹/₈₀ × £10,000
                                                  = £4.375 p.a. gross

Less tax, say, net: −£4,300.00

Net annual loss: £5,200.00
Pensions multiplier   × 9.16
Capitalised annual loss   £47,320.00

Loss of lump sum at 57.5

As a company accountant: 3 × £25,000 =   £75,000
less as a clerk   3 × £10,000 =   −£30,000

Loss at 57.5   £45,000

Discount over 17.5 years to age 40
(Ogden Table 21)   × 0.596

loss of lump sum   £26,820,00

Combined total annual and lump sum loss   £74,140.00

Say, adjusting for the chance of company catastrophe,
ill-health retirement enhancement, etc.   £70,000.00[35]

Agreed Schedule Following Findings by Judge

12–24 Claimant's age: 40
Life multiplier: 22.66
Earnings multiplier: 15 (Articulated as an assumption
                                         doing justice to both parties giving
                                         retirement at about 60).
Pensions multiplier: 22.66 − 15 = 7.66
Length of service to about 60:   37.5 years

Loss of annual pension at 60

Annual pension as company accountant: 37.5 years × ¹/₈₀ × £25,000
                                         = £11.718.75 p.a. gross

Less tax say: £10,250.00
Annual pension as clerk: 37.5 years × ¹/₈₀ × £10,000
                                         = £4.687.50 p.a. gross

Less tax, say: −£4,500.00

---

[34] Where, as here, there is a substantial period before 65, so that there will be 7¹/₂ years at
higher taxation because of lower personal allowances, but without the entitlement to State
retirement pension to take into account, it is strictly correct to work out the loss in the two
periods and split the multiplier. In practice, it is "swings and roundabouts".

[35] It can be seen that although the defendant will save on the loss of earnings claim by arguing
for early retirement, in a case such as this the claimant can recover some of that saving
through an increased pension claim.

Loss of Pension

Net annual loss at 60:	£5,750.00
Pensions multiplier	× 7.66
Capitalised annual loss	£44,045.00

Loss of lump sum at 60

As a company accountant:	3 × £25,000 =	£75,000
less as a clerk	3 × £10,000 =	−£30,000
Loss at 60		£45,000

Discount over 20 years to age 40 (Ogden Table 21)	× 0.5537	
Loss of lump sum		£24,916.50
Combined total annual and lump sum loss		£68,961.50
Say, adjusting for the chance of company catastrophe, etc.		£65,000.00

Schedule Incorporating Widow's Pension on Above Figures

Wife aged:	35	
Wife's life multiplier:	15.26 (Ogden Table 12)	
Widow's entitlement:	½	
Annual Loss (carried forward from above)		£5,750.00

Multiplier on account of claimant

Life multiplier	22.66	
less earnings multiplier	− 15	
		7.66

Multiplier on account of widow after claimant's death

Widow's life multiplier (25.26)		
Minus claimant's life multiplier (22.66)	2.6	
Widow's entitlement	× 50%[36]	
	+ 1.3	
Overall multiplier for the couple		× 8.96
Total (subject to adjustment)		£51.520.00

Loss of Death-in-Service Benefits

As an accountant	2 × £25,000	£50,000
less as a clerk	2 × £10,000	£20,000
Loss of term life assurance during period of service to the value of		£30,000

[36] In a pension scheme where the lump sum is a commutation, unlike this example, the widow's proportion is usually expressed as a fraction of the claimant's pre-commutation entitlement. In those circumstances the widow's entitlement should be adjusted upwards as a true proportion of the post-commutation multiplicand.

Claimant's Schedule

Loss of benefit in kind of term life
assurance of £30,000 between the ages of
40–62.5
equivalent to an annual premium of   £100 p.a.
earnings multiplier of 62.5   × 16.5
Total   £1,650

Defendant's Schedule

Loss of benefit in kind of term life
assurance of £30,000 between the ages of
40–57.5
equivalent to an annual premium of   £100 p.a.
earnings multiplier of 57.5   × 13.5
Total   £1,350

Compromise Schedule

Loss of benefit in kind of term life
assurance of £30,000 between the ages of
40–60
equivalent to an annual premium of   £100 p.a.
earnings multiplier of 60   × 15
Total   £1,500

13. Damages for Care

Care is usually the largest head of damage in claims for damages for **13–01** serious personal injuries. Reduction in the provision of publicly-funded care has encouraged privately-funded care which has led to considerable growth in the numbers of private carers, with increasing specialisation in different types of care.

Judicial input has been relatively small. This is hardly surprising. Cases have to be decided on evidence. Parties usually rely on care experts who invariably agree that care is needed and adopt an approach of valuing care by costing it by reference to commercial hourly rates. This approach has tacitly been accepted by the courts leaving only issues of type of care appropriate, hours of care necessary, hourly rate, and multiplier to be decided. Decisions on principle are few.

The need for care is not reserved to serious cases.[1] It may exist in any case where as a result of injury or disease a claimant needs care, medical or nursing, over and above that which he would normally require. Care may be provided professionally or by family or friends. Entitlement to damages to pay for necessary and reasonable expenditure on care is obviously just. However, the principle upon which awards for care are made is of uncertain validity. The historical development of this head of claim is not one of logical progression but one of the Common Law struggling to do justice in the face of logic. The leading cases are

(a) *Donnelly v. Joyce*[2];

(b) *Housecroft v. Burnett*[3]; and

(c) *Hunt v. Severs*.[4]

Historical Background

The need for care is part of the claim for loss of amenity. The cost of **13–02** paid care has been recoverable for many years but gratuitous care by family or friends raises different issues. The early view was that there could be no recovery for gratuitous care. A claimant had to prove his loss, mitigate his

---

[1] But see observations of Dillon L.J. in *Mills v. British Rail Engineering Limited* (see below at para 13–10).
[2] [1974] Q.B. 454.
[3] [1986] 1 All E.R. 332.
[4] [1994] 2 A.C. 350.

loss and give credit for benefits received (apart from the established exceptions of financial benevolence and insurance moneys): a claimant who received gratuitous care either suffered no loss under that head, or had mitigated that loss or had to give credit for gratuitous care as a benefit. Thus, family care provided gratuitously went uncompensated.

In *Roach v. Yates*[5], gratuitous care was compensated, but in *Schneider v. Eisovitch*[6] Paull J. held that before there could be recovery it had to be shown not only that the sums were necessary and reasonable but that the claimant undertook to pay the sum awarded to the provider. It became the practice for claimants to enter into commercial agreements with family carers thus removing the gratuitous element: see *e.g. Haggar v. de Placido*.[7]

It was this unseemly state of affairs that greeted the Court of Appeal in *Cunningham v. Harrison*[8] and *Donnelly v. Joyce*,[9] decisions by different divisions of the Court of Appeal on successive days. In *Cunningham*, the claimant had made an agreement to pay: Lord Denning M.R. said this should not be necessary and that the claimant husband should hold the award for care on trust and pay it to his caring wife. In *Donnelly*, Megaw L.J. set out to correct the unseemliness by holding that the claimant's loss was not the expenditure of money to buy the care but *the existence of the need for the care*, thus rendering irrelevant whether or not the care had to be paid for.

In the context of the provision of care few would quarrel with the result. The reasoning in *Donnelly* was reiterated in *Housecroft*.[10] But the importance of *Housecroft* rests on the guidelines given by O'Connor L.J., on how the award should be calculated.

Hunt v. Severs[11] decided that no claim could be made for care provided by the tortfeasor.

The Present Law

13–03   The following principles may be deduced from the decisions in *Donnelly*, *Housecroft* and *Hunt v. Severs*:

(a) Care whether paid for by a claimant or provided gratuitously is a recoverable head of damage.

(b) Where professional care has properly been employed, the costs if reasonable may be recovered.

---

[5] [1938] 3 K.B. 256.
[6] [1960] 2 Q.B. 430.
[7] [1972] 1 W.L.R. 716.
[8] [1973] Q.B. 942.
[9] [1974] Q.B. 454.
[10] [1986] 1 All E.R. 332.
[11] [1994] 2 A.C. 350

(c) The basis of a claimant's claim for gratuitous care is his need for care: it is the need for care that constitutes the loss.

(d) Where care has been provided gratuitously, *e.g.* by family or friends, then:

    (i) where the relative has reasonably given up work in order to care he or she should not be the worse off as a result;

    (ii) the ceiling would be the commercial rate;

    (iii) the award should enable a claimant to make reasonable recompense for the care provided.

(e) Who provides the care is a relevant, or at least not an irrelevant consideration:

    (i) where care is provided by the NHS a claimant has no claim;

    (ii) where gratuitous care is provided by the tortfeasor a claimant has no claim.

(f) The claimant holds the sums awarded for gratuitous care on trust for the carer(s).

The Basis of the Claim

The Claimant's Need for Care

In *Donnelly*,[12] Megaw L.J. said at pp. 461–462:   13–04

"We do not agree with the proposition inherent in counsel for the defendant's submission, that the plaintiff's claim, in circumstances such as the present, is properly to be regarded as being, to use his phrase, 'in relation to someone else's loss', merely because someone else has provided to, or for the benefit of, the plaintiff—the injured person—the money, or the services to be valued as money, to provide for needs of the plaintiff directly caused by the defendant's wrongdoing. The loss is the plaintiff's loss. The question from what source the plaintiff's needs have been met, the question who has paid the money or given the services, the question whether or not the plaintiff is or is not under a legal or moral liability to repay, are, so far as the defendant and his liability are concerned, all irrelevant. The plaintiff's loss, to take this present case, is not the expenditure of money to buy the special boots or to pay for the nursing attention. His loss is the existence of the need for those special boots or for those nursing services, the value of which for purposes of damages—for the purpose of the ascertainment of the amount of his loss—is the proper and reasonable cost of supplying those needs. That, in our judgment, is the key to the problem. So far as the defendant is concerned, the loss is not someone else's loss. It is the plaintiff's loss."

---

[12] [1974] Q.B. 454.

This reasoning has not gone without criticism. It has been rejected in Scotland and the Scottish Law Commission in their report, *Damages for Personal Injuries*[13] criticised *Donnelly* rejecting the argument that the loss was the claimant's stating:

"The loss is in fact sustained by the person rendering the services, a point vividly illustrated in cases where he has lost earnings in the course of rendering those services. We suggest, therefore, that it is wrong in principle, in cases where services have been rendered gratuitously by another to an injured person, to regard the latter as having in fact suffered a net loss."

The Commission recommended legislation to attend to the problem and in Scotland section 8 of Part II of the Administration of Justice Act 1992 now allows such a claim unless it is agreed or contemplated that no payment should be made.

13–05   In Australia, the reasoning has been rejected in a number of states: for references see the speech of Lord Bridge in *Hunt v Severs*.[14] In rejecting the proposition that the source from which the claimant's needs had been met was irrelevant stated[15]:

" . . . I do not find this reasoning (*i.e. Donnelly*) convincing. I accept the basis of the plaintiff's claim for damages *may* [emphasis added] consist in his need for services but I cannot accept that the question from what source that need has been met is irrelevant".

Hardly, when coupled with his views on the Australian authorities, a strong endorsement for the reasoning in *Donnelly*.

The *Donnelly* reasoning has not been confined to care in personal injury actions. In *McAll v. Brooks*[16] it was applied to enable a claimant whose motor car had been damaged in an accident to recover the cost of hire paid under agreement by a third party. The claimant's loss was held to be the need for the use of a motor car, the Court of Appeal considering itself bound by *Donnelly*.

In *Giles v. Thompson* 1994,[17] the House of Lords considered the point in the context of replacement vehicles finding on the facts that the claimant could recover but Lord Mustill added:

"In the light of this conclusion I find it unnecessary to discuss the question, by no means easy, what the position would have been if the use of a substitute car really had been free: as, for example, if it had been lent by a kindly friend. To do so would require a reconciliation of cases such as *Harlow and Jones Ltd v. Panex*

---

[13] Law Commission, Paper No. 51 (1978).
[14] [1994] 2 A.C. 350 at 364H–365D.
[15] *ibid.* at 361E.
[16] [1984] R.T.R. 99.
[17] [1994] 1 A.C. 142.

(International) Ltd [1967] 2 Lloyd's Rep. 509, *Donnelly v. Joyce* [1974] Q.B. 454, *McAll* [1984] R.T.R. 99 and *Cosemar SA v. Marimarna Shipping Co. Ltd* [1990] 2 Lloyd's Rep. 323. This question, which is of much general importance, is in my view far better left for decision when it actually arises . . ."

The question did arise in *Diamond v. Lovell* [2000] 2 W.L.R. 1121, a case concerning the free provision of a replacement motor car whilst the claimant's motor car underwent repair. Although the claimant had "hired" the replacement vehicle he had done so under an agreement which did not comply with the Consumer Credit Act and was therefore unenforceable against him so that, in effect, the replacement vehicle was provided gratuitously. The House of Lords, upheld the Court of Appeal's decision that the cost of the hire was not recoverable from the Defendant since the claimant had suffered no loss and overruled *McAll*. The House did not, however, overrule *Donnelly* and got nowhere near reconciling the conflicting cases. The facts of *Dimond* are, of course, far removed from the facts of *Donnelly* and *Diamond* is probably best seen as a case confined to claims for the cost of "free" replacement motor vehicles where policy considerations differ considerably from the field of gratuitous care. Thus the issue ruled on in *Donnelly* namely how one defines loss, whether in terms of expenditure or need for expenditure remains unresolved by the House of Lords. Since no one queries the merit of providing compensation for those who have provided care gratuitously, legislation as in section 8 of the Administration of Justice Act 1992 may provide the solution.

The Relevance of Who Provides the Care

Care Provided by the NHS

Section 2(4) of the Law Reform (Personal Injuries) Act 1948 as amended provides: 13–06

> "In an action for damages for personal injuries . . . there shall be disregarded, in determining the reasonableness of any expenses, the possibility of avoiding those expenses or part of them by taking advantage of facilities available under the National Health Service Act 1977 . . ."

The subsection prevents a defendant arguing that a claimant is being unreasonable in employing private medical care where such care is available to him under the NHS. It does not enable a claimant using or intending to use NHS facilities to recover the costs of medical care. This was made clear by Slade J. in *Harris v. Brights Asphalt Contractors* when he said[18]:

---

[18] [1953] Q.B. 617 at 635.

"I do not understand section 2(4) to enact that a plaintiff shall be deemed to be entitled to recover expenses which he will never incur."

This view was adopted by Lord Scarman in *Lim Po Choo v. Camden and Islington Area Health Authority*[19] and O'Connor L.J. in *Housecroft*[20] stated that the reason why a nil assessment is made when the claimant is looked after by the NHS is because no expense will be incurred. And see Lord Bridge in *Hunt v. Severs*.[21]

Care Provided by the Tortfeasor

13–07   In *Hunt v. Severs* an attempt was made to take *Donnelly* to its logical conclusion. If it was the claimant's need for care that fell to be compensated and the source of the care was irrelevant, the fact that the carer was the tortfeasor was also irrelevant. The Court of Appeal[22] accepted this argument rejecting the defendant's argument (or rather that of his insurers!) that damages being compensatory a claimant was entitled to either the value or the performance of the services but not both since both would mean double recovery. Sir Thomas Bingham M.R. giving the judgment at p. 831 described such services as "adventitious benefits" in the same category as services rendered voluntarily by a third party, charitable gifts or insurance payments stating that for considerations of public policy they should not be regarded as diminishing the claimant's loss.

The House of Lords held that the source from which the claimant's needs were met was not always irrelevant, that dicta to the contrary in *Donnelly* were wrong, that damages being compensatory a claimant should recover no more and no less than he has lost and that public policy could not justify any requirement that a tortfeasor should compensate a claimant twice over for the same loss. Thus, there was no recovery for care provided by the tortfeasor.

13–08   Lord Bridge at p. 361E after stating he did not find the reasoning in *Donnelly* convincing (see above at para. 13–05) observed:

" . . . I cannot accept that the question from what source that need has been met is irrelevant. If an injured plaintiff is treated in hospital as a private patient he is entitled to recover the cost of that treatment. But if he receives free treatment under the National Health Service, his need has been met without cost to him and he cannot claim the cost of the treatment from the tortfeasor. So it cannot, I think, be right to say that in all cases the plaintiff's loss is 'for the purposes of damages . . . the proper and reasonable cost of supplying (his) needs'".

He further observed that the absurdity of the argument that a claimant could recover the cost of the tortfeasor's care was brought home when the

---

[19] [1980] A.C. 174 at 187E–188D.
[20] *op. cit.* at 342j.
[21] *op. cit.* at 361E.
[22] [1993] Q.B. 454.

tortfeasor was not insured when, if the cost of his care were recoverable then he would have to pay for his own services.

Kemp & Kemp[23] has suggested that the resolution of the difficulty posed by *Hunt v. Severs* is a return to pre-*Donnelly* days, *i.e.*, the claimant should enter into a bona fide agreement with the tortfeasor for the provision of care. But difficulty may arise in establishing the bona fides or reasonableness of such an agreement. In *Housecroft*, O'Connor L.J. said[24]:

> " . . . I am very anxious that there should be no resurrection of the practice of plaintiffs making contractual agreements with relatives to pay for what are in fact gratuitous services rendered out of love. Now that it is established that an award can be made in the absence of such an agreement, I would regard an agreement made for the purposes of trying to increase the award as a sham."

Of course, these words were uttered before the decision in *Hunt v. Severs*. A related point is whether a tortfeasor, insured for third party liability but deprived of a claim for care via a claimant, can claim an indemnity from his insurer for the value of care he has provided.

The Evaluation of Gratuitous Care

The Approach in Housecroft

In *Housecroft*, O'Connor L.J. said[25]:   13–09

> "Where the needs of an injured plaintiff are and will be supplied by a relative or friend out of love or affection (and in cases of little children where the provider is under a parental duty) freely and without regard to monetary reward, how should the court assess the 'proper and reasonable cost'? There are two extreme solutions: (i) assess the full commercial rate for supplying the needs by employing someone to do what the relative does; (ii) assess the cost at nil, just as it is assessed at nil where the plaintiff is cared for under the national health scheme . . . the reason why a nil assessment is made where the plaintiff is to be looked after under the national health service is because no expense will be incurred in supplying the needs . . . It follows that in assessing the 'proper and reasonable cost of supplying the needs' each case must be considered on its own facts, but it is not to be assessed regardless of whether it will be incurred."

And [26]:

> "Once it is understood that this an element in the award to the plaintiff to provide for the reasonable and proper care of the plaintiff and that a capital sum

---

[23] Kemp & Kemp, *The Quantum of Damages*, para. 5–028/4.
[24] *op. cit*. at 343C.
[25] *ibid*. at 342h.
[26] *ibid*. at 343d.

is to be available for that purpose, the court should look at it as a whole and consider whether, on the facts of the case, it is sufficient to enable the plaintiff, among other things, to make reasonable recompense to the relative. So in cases where the relative has given up gainful employment to look after the plaintiff, I would regard it as natural that the plaintiff would not wish the relative to be the loser and the court would award sufficient to enable the plaintiff to achieve that result. The ceiling would be the commercial rate. In cases like the present I would look at the award of £108,550, remembering that there is in that sum a sum of £39,000 over and above the sum required to provide the expected outgoings, and ask: is this sufficient to provide for the plaintiff's needs, including enabling her to make some monetary acknowledgement of her appreciation of all that her mother does for her? I would also ask: is it sufficient for this plaintiff should her mother fall by the wayside and be unable to give as she gives now? . . .

The court is recognising that part of the reasonable and proper cost of providing for the plaintiff's needs is to enable her to make a present, or series of presents, to her mother. Neither of the extreme solutions is right. The assessment will be somewhere in between, depending on the facts of the case."

13–10   O'Connor L.J. appears to have had in mind modest awards—"some monetary acknowledgement", "a present, or series of presents", and the need to look at the award as a whole in cases where the relative has not given up paid employment to care. In *Mills v. British Rail Engineering Ltd,*[27] Dillon L.J. observed[28]:

"The basis, as explained by O'Connor L.J. in his judgment in *Housecroft v. Burnett*, is that the court will make an award to enable the sufferer or his estate to make reasonable recompense to the relative who has cared so devotedly. So it must be indeed only be in a very serious case that an award is justified—where, as here, there is no question of the carer having lost wages of her or his own to look after the patient."

However, modest awards have not been typical, courts have not looked at the award for care in the context of the award for loss of amenity as a whole and have not limited awards only to very serious cases.

In practice the following principles are frequently by consent applied:

(a) Where commercial care has properly been engaged the costs are recoverable in full. (It is difficult to show unreasonableness).

(b) Where family/friends have provided care the hours spent caring are assessed and the appropriate rate applied. Evidence of hours spent, rate applicable and the consequent calculations is invariably provided by nursing experts.

---

[27] [1992] P.I.Q.R. Q130.
[28] *ibid.* at 137.

(c) However, the rates nursing experts employ are commercial rates on which the professional carer will likely have to pay income tax, National Insurance and other costs associated with employment so the calculated figures are usually discounted to allow for these factors and the fact that the care is gratuitous.

The Appropriate Discount to the Commercial rate

Conventionally, discounts have varied from 25 per cent to 33.3 per cent. **13–11** In *Fitzgerald v. Ford*,[29] Stuart-Smith L.J. deducted 25 per cent pointing out[30]:

"£109,397 is the gross cost of employing a carer. Obviously that is not the relevant figure. It should be the net cost, which, after a reduction of 25 per cent for tax and national insurance comes to about £82,000."

For small sums a small deduction may be inappropriate.

Although the above approach is adopted every day there is no decision which has explored whether or not this is the correct approach. In *Housecroft*, Kilner Brown J., at first instance thought the commercial cost of care as the only yardstick by which to measure the cost of family care and that the trial judge had to have the assistance of costed figures for the appropriate type of assistance. On appeal, O'Connor L.J. observed[31]:

"Very often we find rates being agreed and, as is shown by the approach of the judge in the present case, regard is had to what it would cost to buy the services in the open market, but it is scaled down."

Given that the approach adopted by the judge at first instance in *Housecroft* was to take as his starting point commercial rates and that O'Connor L.J. was obviously aware of the practice of starting with commercial rates and then "scaling down", it is surprising that he did not adopt this as the correct approach. Instead, he concentrated on reasonable recompense as the criterion of assessment.

In *Daly v. General Steam Navigation Ltd*, Ormrod L.J. said[32]:

". . . in trying to assess what is fair compensation in an internal family situation, it is not necessarily at all reliable to have regard to market values of housekeepers or other comparable people. It introduces a wildly artificial concept if one resorts to that and talks about compensating the husband in this case at the rate of a daily woman at so many hours a week. It simply does not represent reality at all."

---

[29] [1996] P.I.Q.R. Q72.
[30] *ibid.* at 78.
[31] *op cit.* at 343b.
[32] [1981] 1 W.L.R. 120 at 130.

Despite such observations and O'Connor L.J.'s reasoning, parties and judges have continued to follow the approach of starting with the commercial cost and then reducing by a process of reasoned discounting for income tax, etc. Certainly, few judges have discounted to the stage of providing sufficient merely for "a present or series of presents".

13–12 Although discounts have varied conventionally from 25 per cent to 30 per cent, the time may have come to look more closely at this aspect. These percentages stem from the days when deductions for income tax and National Insurance were looked at broadly in such percentages. Over the years income tax has reduced and NI has increased a little. More significantly, tables are now readily available to calculate the incidence of income tax and NI. See, for example, the very helpful Table G1, "Net equivalents to a range of gross annual income figures" published in the *1998 Facts and Figures.*[32a] From Table G1, the net as a percentage of gross can be calculated as follows for the tax year 1988/1989:

Gross income	Net income	Net as % of gross
£5,000.00	£4,776.00	95.52%
£6,000.00	£5,555.55	92.58%
£10,000.00	£8,235.00	82.35%
£15,000.00	£11,585.00	77.23%

These figures show that the percentage deductions for income tax and NI vary considerably with the annual gross figure. Looking solely at income tax and NI on small awards, deductions of 25 per cent to 33 per cent are excessive: less than 5 per cent would be appropriate on £5,000.00. Of course, the gratuitous element must be remembered. Recently, in *Burns v. Davies*,[33] O'Connell J. said:

" . . . the discount arises partly because that person pays no income tax and does not suffer any other deductions on the sum awarded but also because the care is provided out of love and affection and in the convenience of the family home where commercial considerations are not so relevant. It is clear that individual cases depend on individual facts, and such a discount is not compulsory."

Then after pointing out that the mother had provided care in very difficult circumstances, at great cost to herself although she had not had to give up work, that there had been no uplift claimed for unsocial hours and that there was some substance in the suggestion that she had done work equivalent to two nurses he continued:

[32a] See *PNBA Facts and Figures 2000* (Sweet & Maxwell) for 1999/2000 and 2000/2001 figures.
[33] (Unreported): judgment at August 7, 1998.

"The task of the court . . . is to assess a fair valuation of the care provided. Given the features which I have mentioned, in my judgement the appropriate discount which should be applied to the figure of past care is a discount of 20 per cent. I take this figure, which is lower than the conventional 33 per cent or 25 per cent, bearing in mind first the high quality of the care provided and second the basic rate of tax applicable at the present time."

It is submitted that the appropriate discount should depend on the facts of each case, that the income tax and NI deductions appropriate to the sums claimed, and, possibly in relation to the position of the carer(s) should be considered together with the quality of care provided and the circumstances in which it is provided. There can be no justification in making a notional deduction for income tax and NI where none is payable nor any adequate justification for deducting say a standard 25 per cent across the board. At the same time, those caring gratuitously are not doing in a commercial context so that, assuming the initial commercial approach is appropriate, some deduction for the gratuitous or non-commercial component in the figures is appropriate.

Awarding More than the Loss of Earnings

In *Hogg v. Doyle*[34], Turner J. assessed a wife's care at 1.5 times her net **13–13** income as a nurse on the basis that she was doing work (24 hour care of a tetraplegic) the equivalent of at least two paid carers. He was upheld on appeal. But in *Fitzgerald v. Ford 1996*,[35] the Court of Appeal allowed an appeal against the trial judge's valuation of care based on 1.5 times loss of the carer's earnings, Stuart-Smith L.J. stating at p. 77:

" . . . there is no principle involved in *Hogg v. Doyle*. It is a case on its own facts. In particular, there is no principle that, simply because a member of the family gives up full-time paid work where they probably work eight hours a day for five days a week, when they become a full-time carer being available to help if need be throughout the 24 hours, they should be paid at the rate of 1.5 of their earnings, or, indeed, any more than their loss of earnings. In many cases, the actual nursing or physical assistance may only take a few hours distributed throughout the day or night. For the rest of the time it will be spent in preparation and cooking of meals, shopping, laundry, jobs concerned with the maintenance of the house, all of which have to be done for the carer and any other members of the family in any case. In addition time will be spent on going out on visits or acts of companionship, conversation or mutual occupation".

---

[34] (Unreported): Kemp & Kemp, *The Quantum of Damages*, para. A–006/1.
[35] [1996] P.I.Q.R. Q72.

No Recovery for Carer's Loss of Earnings as well as Care

13–14   Where a carer gives up work to care then the claimant cannot recover the loss of income as well as the value of care. No one can do two jobs at once. See *Fish v. Woolcock*.[36]

Who has title to the award?

13–15   In *Cunningham*, Lord Denning M.R. said a claimant held the award on trust for the carer. In *Housecroft*, O'Connor L.J.[37] considered this *obiter* and thought it inconsistent with *Donnelly*—the loss was the claimant's loss. In *Hunt v. Severs*, Lord Bridge[38] adopted Lord Denning's view.

There are difficulties in the concept of a trust in this context. What happens when the carer(s) change and more significantly when the need for care changes, diminishes or increases. If gratuitous care has to replace professional care are damages awarded for care still held on trust for the professional carers? The introduction of a trust in this context might create as many problems as it seeks to solve and is yet another illustration of the unsatisfactoriness of the present position of gratuitous care in law.

Interest on Care

13–16   Past care attracts interest as special damage: *Roberts v. Johnstone*.[39]

Practical Considerations

13–17   Future care is calculated on *the multiplier/multiplicand approach* based on life expectancy. Where there is no reduction in life expectancy then reference to the Ogden Tables will produce the appropriate multiplier for the claimant's age. Where life expectancy is agreed or decided by the judge as a fixed period then an arithmetic the multiplier is appropriate.[40]

Split multipliers are appropriate where the need for care will change. The need for care will almost certainly increase towards the end of life. But it may also increase earlier on events such as pregnancy and with the need to care for children.

Medical evidence on life expectancy is essential if a reduction or increase in normal life expectancy is to be argued. Lord Bridge's view in *Hunt v. Severs*[41] that life expectancy is not exclusively a medical question and that

---

[36] (1994) 5 Med. L.R. 230.
[37] *op. cit.* at 343d.
[38] *op. cit.* at 363C.
[39] [1987] Q.B. 878.
[40] See *Wells v. Wells* [1998] 3 W.L.R. 329, HL.
[41] *op. cit.* at 365G.

even where doctors agreed life expectancy some discount for "life's manifold contingencies" was appropriate was not followed by the House of Lords in *Wells v. Wells*. On the other hand, the approach of Stuart-Smith L.J. in *Fitzgerald v. Ford*,[42] who suggested that because of the uncertainties involved in the exercise the court should take the mean period or "50 per cent chance figure" between the competing periods contended for. *Wells v. Wells* makes clear that the actuarial figures should be the starting point and only departed from where evidence justifies it.

In assessing the value of gratuitous care bear in mind that *the carer may **13–18** not be able to continue to care*. See O'Connor L.J. in *Housecroft* at p. 342h ("Is it sufficient for this plaintiff should her mother fall by the wayside").

In cases involving tetraplegia, paraplegia and serious brain damage, there is no substitute for *early advice*. Not only will this assist in overall valuation of the claim, but it can be of inestimable value to a claimant: where a care claim is inevitable it is only sensible, if this can be achieved, for interim payments to be obtained to set up any necessary regime and go some way to taking the burden of caring from the family who might otherwise not cope satisfactorily. Interim payments are ultimately a matter for the discretion of the court but a court is not likely to reject such a request where reasonably made. In *Cambell v. Mylchreest*,[43] the claimant sought an interim payment expressly to set up a regime of part home care for a severely injured claimant cared for in a home. The defendants resisted payment on the basis that to make such an award would interfere with the "level playing field" which ought to exist between the parties. The Court of Appeal held the request reasonable. From a defendant's point of view, an early assessment not only assists in valuation, so necessary for the insurers' reserve, but enables a defendant to have some reasoned input into suggestions for care.

Different types of case will dictate different approaches to care. For example:

(a) In a typical case of a broken leg or arm most claimants do not think of claiming for care. Yet, almost inevitably, someone has to provide support and care and may lose income as a result. In such cases, no report ought to be necessary to value of care, which can be done by reference to any loss of income and/or the British Nursing Association rates for carers set out in *Facts and Figures*, unless the defendant is resisting the claim.

(b) In serious spinal injury cases the level of lesion is often crucial to the level of care needed. Here a report is essential. In such cases, it used to be the case that care was evaluated by a nursing expert and an

---

[42] [1996] P.I.Q.R. at 80.
[43] [1999] P.I.Q.R. Q17, CA.

occupational therapist dealt with aids, equipment and therapies. Nowadays, save in exceptional cases where the care requirement is exceptional, one expert will usually cover both.

(c) Brain damage cases form a separate category. Frequently, the brain damaged victim who can live in the community needs not care as much as supervision, which sometimes needs to be constant or near constant. A new class of carer, a trained companion, variously called an enabler, support worker, coach or the like, has emerged. Again a report is essential, but it is important that it is obtained from someone who understands the problems that brain damage can cause. Sometimes an assessment with attendance at a specialist hospital/unit to evaluate needs is appropriate.

(d) *Case managers*, whose expertise lies in organising and implementing systems of care, have become an established feature and awards are made for them. They have more relevance in brain damage than spinal injury cases but each case will depend on its facts. Good ones are in short supply and in some parts of the country the species is rare.

(e) Care reports frequently cost on the basis of two or more carers, it being said that in practice a system of two or more alternating carers is more practical and more reliable. In more demanding cases this is frequently so. With the introduction of restrictions on working hours the live-in housekeeper willing to be on call for 24 hours a day will probably become a thing of the past.

(f) Resident carers need to be housed and even daytime carers need space. It is, therefore, sensible in serious cases to ensure that an expert architect and care expert (and other experts with related expertise) discuss the options before any decisions are made. Too frequently, claimants needing care move home only to realise too late that the new home is unsuitable. Where both care and housing are required, a concerted approach is essential.

(g) Too frequently, care reports are updated only at the last minute and/or the initial recommendation for care has either not been implemented or has been varied with no revised costings available. Care experts are always too busy. Make sure that the up-to-date situation is appraised well before trial.

(h) Past care is usually appropriate for a Part 36 offer. Future care is more difficult; nevertheless, in many cases a Part 36 offer will be appropriate.

Recoupment of Care Costs by Health Authorities and Local Authorities

Care not funded privately is funded usually by a health authority or a **13–20** local authority. The decision of the Court of Appeal in *Avon County Council v. Hooper and Another*[44] that a local authority was entitled to recover the costs of residential care provided for an injured child has prompted concern amongst insurers on whether they will be called upon to pay for care which hitherto has been provided for the most part free of charge. Claimants have expressed concerns over whether they may have a liability to reimburse such authorities for care provided and whether they should seek indemnity against from tortfeasors in respect of such sums. For reasons which follow, it is crucial to discover who has funded the care and if both the health and local authority, in what proportions and under what statutory provisions.

Provision of Care by the National Health Service

The Secretary of State, who acts by health authorities, is responsible for **13–21** arranging and funding a range of services to meet the needs of people who require continuing physical or mental health care. The obligation to provide these services (hospital and other accommodation and facilities for, *inter alia*, care and after care) is now contained in sections 1 and 2 of the National Health Service Act 1977, as amended. Under section 23, the Secretary of State may arrange for such services to be provided by third parties, *e.g.* private nursing homes.

Provision of services under the National Health Service is, in the main, free.

Section 1 (2) of the Act provides:

> "The services so provided shall be free of charge except in so far as the making and recovery of charges is expressly provided for by or under any enactment, whenever passed."

Medical prescriptions, dental treatment and the provision of spectacles are examples of services for which charges may be made. There is no general provision enabling a health authority to recover for accommodation, treatment and residential care as such. However, sections 63 to 65 inclusive enable charges to be made in very limited circumstances: for accommodation not needed on medical grounds (s.63); to charge part of the costs of maintenance where resident patients are in remunerative employment (s.64); and for private patients (s.65).

---

[44] [1996] 1 W.L.R. 1605; [1997] 25 B.M.L.R. 26.

These sections do not authorise the Secretary of State to charge for NHS services provided pursuant to his duty whether under section 1 or section 23. To do so would be an abdication of responsibilities under section 1 and *ultra vires*: this is the implication of the decision in *Secretary of State for Social Security and the Chief Adjudication Officer v. Percival White*[45] where an attempt to deduct State benefits from cost of care in a private nursing home ("a hospital" within section 2) contracted under section 23 was held *ultra vires*. Section 122 states that charges under section 63 may, without prejudice to any other method of recovery, be recovered summarily as a civil debt:

(a) The Secretary of State for Health could exclude some nursing services from those provided by the NHS. Such services could then be provided as a social or care service rather than a health service.

(b) The nursing services, which could properly be left to social services to provide, were confined to those ancillary to accommodation being provided by social services.

(c) The Secretary of State could decide not to provide those services even though it meant the person receiving them would be liable to have to pay for them.

(d) Not all nursing services provided by social services to those in their care were social services.

Provision of Care by Social Services

13–22   Social services legislation, sometimes contained in NHS Acts, makes provision for community social services, many of which are made necessary by poor health. The duty or power to provide such services is vested in local authorities. One such power is contained in paragraph 2, Schedule 8 to the 1977 Act, which enables a local social services authority, with the Secretary of State's approval, to make arrangements for the prevention of illness and for the care and after care of persons suffering or who have been suffering from illness, in particular by the provision of residential accommodation. The power extends to the care of persons suffering from mental disorder who are received into guardianship under Part II or III of the Mental Health Act 1983.

Whereas, with very limited exceptions, the Secretary of State cannot recover the cost of NHS services provided pursuant to his duties, local authorities have rights of recovery under section 17 of the Health and Social Services and Social Security Adjudications Act 1983.

Section 17 provides:

---

[45] [1993] 17 B.M.L.R. 68.

"(1) Subject to subsection (3) below, an authority providing a service to which this section applies may recover such charge (if any) for it as they consider reasonable.

(2) This section applies to services provided under the following enactments: (The provisions listed include welfare arrangements for the blind and infirm, welfare of old people, services provided under Schedule 8 (which include care and aftercare) and meals and recreation for old people.

(3) If a person—

    (a) avails himself of a service to which this section applies and

    (b) satisfies the authority providing the service that his means are insufficient for it to be reasonably practicable for him to pay for the service the amount which he would otherwise be obliged to pay for it, the authority shall not require him to pay more for it than it appears to them that it is reasonably practicable for him to pay."

Health authorities and local authorities liaise on the provision of care and health authorities sometimes contribute to the cost of care provided both by local authorities and other bodies to whom the provision of NHS services has been delegated under section 23 of the Act. The line between care which has to be provided by health authorities and that which is provided by local authorities is a blurred one. Essentially, health authorities are responsible for "nursing" care and local authorities for "social" care. The former is usually provided in a hospital or specialist home and is free, and the latter in a residential home and is means tested. A recent example of the interaction/blurring of "nursing" and "social" care can be seen in *R v. North and East Devon Health Authority ex parte Coughlan*.[46]

In *ex parte Coughlan*, a patient, who had been rendered tetraplegic in a road traffic accident, had been assured by her health authority that she had a home for life at Mardon House, a purpose-built facility for the severely disabled. The health authority decided to close Mardon House and transfer her care to the local authority. The Court of Appeal, on judicial review, quashed the decision to close the home, in doing so considering the respective responsibilities of health authorities and local authorities on the provision of care. The Court decided that a health authority could transfer to a local authority responsibility for care the health authority had provided where that care could properly be described as social care, with the consequence that the local authority could then charge for that care. On the other hand, the fact that a local authority provides care did not mean that that care was necessarily to be classed as "social" care. Each case had to be considered on its own facts.

The case is a reminder of the need to ensure the security for the future of a claimant whose care is provided by a health authority. The authority should be asked to provide an assurance that they will continue to provide the care and will not transfer responsibility for it to the local authority. In default of such assurances the cost of care should be claimed.

---

[46] *The Times*, July 20, 1999.

The Decision in Avon C.C. v. Hooper[47]

13–23   In *Avon*, a child born in 1978 was brain damaged at birth as a result of negligence for which a health authority was liable. The child was cared for by the local authority in a Cheshire home from 1981 until his death in 1991. The child's claim had been the subject of an action against the health authority and the agreed settlement had included the cost of future care and an indemnity to the child's estate for any sums the claimant (*i.e.* the local authority) might *lawfully* recover from the estate for care from 1981 to November 1989. The local authority was held entitled to recover from the deceased child's estate the costs of care provided to the child but recovery was limited to the six-year period preceding the issue of the writ in 1991.

The case decided that a local authority could recover charges under section 17 retrospectively provided:

(a) the local authority acted reasonably (Hobhouse L.J. said that it was implicit in the section that the local authority had to act reasonably);

(b) the charge was reasonable; and

(c) the defendant had the means to pay.

No question arose of recovery for future loss and it would seem implicit in *Avon* that the indemnity was regarded as part of the child's means. The case is concerned solely with the right of recovery under section 17. It does not deal with obligations of the respective authorities *qua authorities* to fund care. It just happened to be that the health authority was the tortfeasor.

Defences to Claims under Section 17

13–24   Claims made by a local authority under section 17 are subject to the six-year limitation period: hence the limited recovery in *Avon*. Such claims would also seem to be subject to other defences, such as waiver and estoppel, so that if a local authority with full knowledge of the facts had made clear that a service was to be free and the service had been accepted on that basis it is doubtful whether they could recover their outlay.

Who is Liable to Pay under Section 17

13–25   The right under section 17 is to require "him", *i.e.* the person availing himself of the service, to pay: see the wording of section 17(3). It seems that the only person to whom these words can fairly be applied is the

---

[47] [1996] 1 W.L.R. 1605; [1997] 25 B.M.L.R. 26.

patient, and the section, in the absence of agreement, therefore gives no direct right of recovery against anyone else, *e.g.* a tortfeasor. That was said to have been the advice given to Avon C.C. in *Avon*.

The "Means" to Pay

If the claimant has no money whether he will have the means will likely 13–26
depend on the outcome of his action. The mere existence of a right of action is unlikely to constitute "means" within the section. An admission of liability out of court is doubtful. Even a judgment may not provide the means unless it were perfectly clear on the facts that it would be satisfied. The decided cases on "means" are all on its use in other statutes, but the meaning accorded is usually restrictive. For example, a judgment debtor's means do not include voluntary gifts from a brother. For the purposes of maintenance in matrimonial proceedings "means" has been held to mean "what he is in fact getting or can fairly be assumed to be likely to get".

Another point that arises is whether in examining the claimant's means for the purposes of a claim for the cost of care under section 17, a court would look at the totality of the award (as is done in matrimonial cases where an award for pain and suffering becomes part of a spouse's means) or merely that part awarded for care. If the totality, then the award for pain and suffering, even if not heads committed to other needs, could be regarded as "means". If it is permissible to look only at the award for care then it is necessary to decide what sums are recoverable for care and here some very nice points may arise.

Section 17 and the Funding of Future Care

The position as regards future care is different. A health authority has a *duty* to provide NHS care free and may charge for accommodation only in the limited circumstances set out in sections 63 to 65. A local authority by contrast has only the *power* to provide care and when it exercises that power can charge under section 17. A local authority could decide not to fund care and leave it to the claimant to sue for the costs of care. Should a claimant be held contributorily negligent, it may decide to make up the shortfall. A claimant facing an uncertain future over care charges would be better advised to make it part of his claim for damages rather than attempt to obtain a declaration that he is entitled to be indemnified against future care costs charged by a local authority.

Under section 2(4) of the Law Reform (Personal Injuries) Act 1948, as amended, the availability of services under the NHS Act 1977 is to be disregarded (see *The Relevance of Who Provides the Care*, above). No such provision exists with regard to services provided by social services and which are outside the provisions caught by the 1977 Act. In such circumstances one has to fall back on the common law rules of mitigation and reasonableness. Whether a claimant will, or should, rely on State provided services outside the 1977 Act would depend, subject to it raising a point of law, on the facts of each case.

This is a difficult, developing field where, as already observed, the demarcation of responsibilities between health authorities and local authorities is blurred in practice, where local authorities' practices differ and where local authorities are still cutting their teeth on section 17. It is a field where significant developments can be expected in the next few years as authorities fight more and more amongst themselves over funding.

Claims for Care in Fatal Cases

The Present Law

13–27   When parents die, children have to be cared for. Sometimes nannies are employed, sometimes the surviving parent or, not uncommonly, grandparents take over. The child, who was dependent on its deceased parent(s) for care has lost that dependency. How should that loss be calculated?

At common law the answer would be straightforward: assess the amount of loss of care, value it, then bring into the reckoning the value of any benefits resulting from the death. The essential decision to be made would be whether the substitute care resulted from the death, in which case it is to be brought into account, or whether it resulted from the decision of the substitute carer, motivated by generosity or otherwise, to undertake the care. In *Hay v. Hughes*,[48] surrogate care provided by a grandmother was held not to be a benefit resulting from the death but the result of generous action on her part so that it did not have to be brought into account, leaving the surviving children entitled to recover for care.

But the position is complicated by the Fatal Accidents Act 1976 as substituted by section 3(1) of the Administration of Justice Act 1982. The original section 4 of the 1976 Act provided:

"In assessing damages in respect of a person's death in an action under this act, there shall not be taken into account any insurance money, benefit, pension or gratuity which has been or will or may be paid as a result of the death."

Section 4 as substituted provides:

"In assessing damages in respect of a person's death in an action under this act, benefits which have accrued or will or may accrue to any person from his estate *or otherwise* [author's italics] as a result of his death shall be disregarded."

---

[48] [1975] Q.B. 790.

In the original section 4 of the 1976 Act (which replaced section 2(1) of the Fatal Accidents Act 1959 that in turn had replaced section 2(5) of the Law Reform (Personal Injuries) Act 1948), the word "benefit" is sandwiched in the phrase "insurance money, benefit, pension or gratuity" and it is not difficult to see it as being intended to cover financial benefits. The substituted section 4 refers simply to "benefits". How then should one deal with the benefit of substitute care provided following death? Should it be regarded as replacing the loss in whole or part, so that there is no loss or only a partial loss to claim? Or is replacement care a benefit to be disregarded under section 4? There have been three decisions of the Court of Appeal on the point: *Stanley v. Saddique*,[49] *Hayden v. Hayden*[50] and *R v. CICB ex parte K (Minors) and Others*.[51] *Stanley v. Saddique* and *Hayden v. Hayden* were not easy to reconcile; *ex parte K* has come down on the side of *Stanley v. Saddique*.

In *Stanley v. Saddique*, the Court of Appeal held that "benefit" in section 4 should be construed broadly: it was not restricted to pecuniary benefit but included benefit accruing to a claimant as a result of his absorption into a new family unit. Purchas L.J. at p. 467B thought decisions based on whether the benefit resulted from the death or from generosity were divided by "a thin and very artificial line" and accepted that Parliament must have intended to widen the scope of benefits to be deducted in what had become a field where common law rules of damages had largely been replaced over the years by artificial concepts. Therefore, the replacement care, which in *Saddique* was argued to be an improvement on the original care, was to be disregarded.

In *Hayden v. Hayden*, the majority in the Court of Appeal held that each case of dependency had to be decided on its own facts and that whether substitute care was a "benefit resulting from the death" was itself a question of fact. *Stanley v. Saddique* was regarded as a decision on its own facts.

In *Hayden*, a mother was killed in a collision caused by her husband's negligence. The husband defendant gave up work to care for their dependant child. At p. 999H, Sir David Croom-Johnson concluded on the evidence that:

> "No reasonable judge or jury would regard the defendant, in doing what he did, as doing other than discharge his parental duties, many of which he had been carrying out in any event and would be expected to continue to do so."

and, that the continuing services of the father were not a benefit to be disregarded in any event.

---

[49] [1992] Q.B.1; [1991] 2 W.L.R. 459.
[50] [1992] 1 W.L.R. 986.
[51] [1999] 2 W.L.R. 948.

Parker L.J. observed at p. 1000H:

" . . . in cases in which it is shown that the services of the father are in every respect as good as, or even better than the services previously provided by the mother it is, again on the face of it difficult to see that the child has suffered a recoverable loss. He will or she will of course have been deprived of the mother's love and affection but it is not and could not be suggested that this sounds in damages."

And at p. 1004H:

"In my judgment before one gets to section 4 it must first be established what injury has been suffered by the child. What it has prima facie lost, is the services provided by the mother but the fact that they were provided by the mother is irrelevant. If *in fact* those services were replaced without interval of time up to date of trial by as good or better services it is in my view at least open to a judge or jury to conclude that the child has lost nothing up to that date. But if the replacement services can be discontinued it is of course exposed to the risk that such services may be discontinued and that risk must be quantified."

In *ex parte K*, Brooke L.J. and Rougier J. came down on the side of *Stanley v. Saddique*. Brooke L.J. considered *Stanley v. Saddique* could not properly be regarded as a decision on its own facts (as it had been considered in *Hayden*) and noted that two of the three judges in *Hayden* (McCowan L.J. who dissented and Sir David Croom-Johnson) considered the Court bound by *Stanley v. Saddique*. He regarded *Hayden* as a decision based on its own facts.

Whilst it is clear that authority favours *Stanley v. Saddique* rather than *Hayden*, the position is far from satisfactory and resolution of the problem must rest with the House of Lords. The point is important and has a run on effect on section 3(3) of the 1976 Act.

Section 3(3) provides that remarriage or prospects of remarriage of a widow are to be disregarded in assessing damages payable to her in respect of the death of her husband. Section 3(3) is silent on the position of widowers and children. Remarriage and prospects of remarriage remain relevant considerations when assessing the loss of dependancies by widowers and children. Where a widow remarries, is the care provided by the stepfather a "benefit" within section 4 following *Stanley v. Saddique* or does it result from remarriage not death following *Hayden v. Hayden*? In *Watson v. Willmott*,[52] which preceded *Stanley v. Saddique*, Garland J. held that an infant's dependency on his mother for non-pecuniary benefits ended when he was adopted and his adoptive mother provided similar services, and that his pecuniary dependency on his natural father was reduced by the value of the dependency provided by the adoptive father.

---

[52] [1991] Q.B. 140.

Evaluating the Care of Children in Fatal Cases

In *Hay v. Hughes*,[53] the cost of employing a nanny was taken as the yardstick for evaluating care of children. *Spittle v. Bunney*[54] refined the approach on valuation of such care by stating a diminishing multiplicand was appropriate to allow for the fact that as a dependent child grew older, less care would be required. This approach remains valid where a nanny will be employed. But it is inappropriate where no nanny will be employed (see Sir David Croom-Johnson in *Hayden v. Hayden*.[55] In such cases it is submitted there is no reason why the approach in *Housecroft* should not be followed but with the following qualification.

The courts have recognised that there is something extra about the quality of a mother's care. This was stressed by Tasker Watkins J. in *Regan v. Williamson*. when he said[56]:

"I am . . . of the view that the word "services" has been too narrrowly construed. It should at least, include an acknowledgement that a wife and mother does not work to set hours and, still less, to rule. She is in constant attendance save . . . when at work. During those hours she may well give the children instruction on essential matters to do with their upbringing and, possibly, with such things as their homework. This sort of attention seems to be as much of a service, and probably more value to them than the other kinds of service conventionally so regarded."

Making allowance for these extra services he increased his valuation of services from £12.50 per week to £20 per week. In *Topp v. London Country Bus (South West) Ltd*,[57] 1992 P.I.Q.R. P206 in addition to an award for loss of a deceased mother's household services, awards were made for loss to the daughter of her mother's care and advice and for loss to the husband of his wife's individual care and attention: the claims had been accepted in principle by the defendants.

Thus, even if *Hayden v. Hayden* were ultimately to prevail, provided the mother was a good mother some award would appear appropriate for those services which only a mother can give, even though the quality of the replacement care is highly satisfactory.

---

[53] [1975] Q.B. 790.
[54] [1998] 1 W.L.R. 847.
[55] *op cit*. at 998B.
[56] [1976] 1 W.L.R. 305 at 309.
[57] [1992] P.I.Q.R. P206.

14. Valuing Aids and Equipment Costs

Introduction

Claims for the future cost of aids and equipment are essentially ancillary **14-01** to other heads of claim—in particular the claim for care where the regime recommended may well depend on the availability of aids and equipment to support it. To a lesser extent the need for aids and equipment will arise out of the need for alternative housing. There could be a problem about whether it should be categorised as part of the housing claim or as a separate claim for equipment: this may matter if in the quantification of future loss the aids and equipment are costed as part of the housing claim, pursuant to *Roberts v. Johnstone*,[1] or separately as "wasting assets" given an annual value which will then be multiplied by the appropriate multiplier. Because of the overlap with care and housing, the case for aids and equipment will normally depend on the same experts to support it as those parts of the claim and as a result the need for special aids or equipment is usually dealt with initially by the expert care reports. Thus, the evidence in support of the claim for aids and equipment will be subject to the same rules as apply to other expert evidence under the Civil Procedure Rules, Part 35.

Historically, separate consideration of a need for special equipment over and above general damages for pain, suffering and loss of amenity and the general figure for care costs is mainly a development of the last 15 years or so. This is illustrated by the judgment of O'Connor L.J. in *Housecroft v. Burnett*.[2] At p. 337 he set out the heads of damage awarded in a case called *Fowler v. Grace*[3] and compared them with the heads as awarded by the judge in Housecroft which he had set out at p. 334. In *Fowler* there were five heads:

(a) pain, suffering and loss of amenity;

(b) future nursing care;

(c) adaptation of house;

(d) special damage; and

(e) loss of expectation of life.

---

[1] [1989] Q.B. 878; The applicable interest rates for this calculation are to be determined in accordance with the principles of *Wells v. Wells* [1999] A.C. 345.
[2] [1986] 1 All E.R. 332.
[3] (1970) 114 S.J. 193.

14–02   It is not apparent whether the special damage included past expenditure
on any aids or equipment, however, in *Housecroft* the number had grown
to 11. In addition to those five there were:

(f) future motoring expenses, *i.e.* provision for outdoor mobility;

(g) a miscellany of future expenses: holidays, heat, services of a
gardener;

(h) provision of therapeutic equipment, telephone, future medical
expenses;

(i) future physiotherapy;

(j) past care; and

(k) future loss of earnings.

It will readily be understood that since 1986 these categories have
multiplied further, for example in relation to educational needs and the
provision of computer equipment in serious cases. O'Connor L.J. was
making the point that the figures in the two cases for pain, suffering and
loss of amenity were not comparable because the earlier figure had
included in it damages to cover the items listed as (f) to (i). As far as this
section of the Handbook is concerned, the significance of this is that
amongst those items in effect transferred from the pain, suffering and loss
of amenity damages to economically quantifiable heads were items (f) and
(h), which relate to aids and equipment. The process of the quantification
of individual items which can be assessed on an economic basis and so
effectively shifted from the category of general damages for pain, suffering
and loss of amenity has continued since 1986, though how much further it
will go is open to debate.

An important factor in these developments is the emergence of ever
more sophisticated equipment to assist handicapped people to combat their
disabilities and enable them to live a more normal life. However, the
overriding question in determining the liability of the defendant to fund
any aids or equipment claimed remains: is the equipment reasonably
necessary for the claimant and is the expense not unreasonably disproportionate to the anticipated benefit it will bring? As far as the overall
quantification of damages is concerned, these developments can work in
both directions, that is technological changes can have the effect of
equipping a claimant, for example, to earn a living who otherwise would
not have been able to and so reducing the total claim. Indeed, there are
many ways in which the provision of new aids and equipment, sensibly
assessed, will have an impact on the overall damages and may reduce as
well as increase them.

14–03   The final point to note by way of introduction is that there are very few
decisions directly on what aids and equipment may be included in the

claim. This is because they are almost inevitably subsidiary to other parts of the claim, are related very specifically to the individual needs of the claimant and are frequently agreed between the care experts. Thus, there are rarely issues of principle involved in these questions or the proper way to approach quantification which do not arise in other parts of the claim, *e.g.* the appropriate multiplier for future equipment needs arising from the care regime will normally be the same as that for the care itself.[4] Usually the need for aids or equipment occurs in the most serious cases, brain damage and paraplegia, but it can arise where there are less serious injuries as well.

It must not be forgotten that by the time of trial some aids and equipment will probably have already been purchased. The criteria for establishing that the cost of any such items is recoverable is the same as for future need, that is it must be shown that the item was reasonably necessary for the plaintiff as a result of the plaintiff's injuries. Of course, the cost in such a case can been established by what. has actually been spent.

Classification of Aids and Equipment

Ancillary to Care Needs

Most care reports nowadays will include advice on the aids and **14–04** equipment which are either necessary for the claimant or would be useful in helping in the claimant's future care. In the most serious cases many of the items suggested will be fundamental to the proper care of the claimant. Activities which may be included embrace, for example, the bodily functions, toileting, feeding, sleeping, bathing and washing and dressing. The range of aids is almost limitless, a random (and small) selection from a care report includes: a nursing bed, a special wash basin and taps, an adjustable bath chair, other leisure chairs, a toilet seat, non-spill mugs, grip extensions to facilitate dexterity, as well as more mundane objects such as extra sponges and towels.

To Help Mobility

The most obvious examples of aids to mobility are wheelchairs. In the **14–05** less serious cases there may be disputes about the need for a wheelchair and it is common for the parties not to agree on how many wheelchairs are needed, whether for getting about out of doors as well as inside, whether electric as well as manual or whether a folding as well as a rigid wheelchair

---

[4] See generally *Wells v. Wells*, [1999] A.C. 345.

is needed. But aids to help mobility include other things as well, from crutches and walking frames to stair hoists and bath rails to help the claimant get in and out of the bath. Fundamentally, aids to mobility will be justifiable for two reasons:

(a) first to increase the claimant's ability to live or carry on the normal range of human activities as independently as possible;

(b) second to ease or even relieve the burden of care.

To that extent, aids may enable the need for carers to be limited if not reduced. Included under this head also may be such things as adaptations to kitchen equipment or layout to enable the injured claimant to use it without assistance. For example, a paraplegic in a wheelchair will not be able to reach kitchen surfaces but the reconstruction of the kitchen and/or the provision of special equipment may enable him or her to do so. Thus, included in the concept of mobility is the idea of improving independent living by assisting the claimant to move about inside or outside and carry out normal household or domestic operations. On this aspect it is now commonplace for claims to include individual alarm systems, so that the injured person is safe as well as independent, and mobile phones are frequently advised by care experts, often in respect of transport needs so the injured claimant can get help if it is needed in an emergency.

To Supplement Mental Abilities—Education and Work

14–06   It is obvious that with children as claimants an important aspect of their needs will be the provision of anything which may help with education and learning. With the rapid development of computer technology the means of helping the disabled child, or indeed adult, to learn or to use and develop any intellectual skills are vast. One only has to think of Professor Stephen Hawking to realise the scope of help that may be available. In fact, the computer technology which enables the very seriously injured to work and communicate is becoming more widely available and is commonly provided for injured claimants. It is not necessary to go to that level of sophistication to find computerised assistance for either brain-damaged or severely physically-injured people, particularly children. For example, there are simple computer systems to enable a brain-damaged child to communicate as well as more complex ones designed to help with learning. Computer systems can empower adults to develop skills or manual dexterity which may even enable them to earn a living, so affecting other parts of the claim. Once again the range of possibilities is enormous and constantly changing. Aids and equipment to help mental development or activity are not confined to computers though they are the most obvious and dramatic in their possibilities.

Transport

Probably the first and in many ways the most obvious instance of aids **14–07** and equipment being treated as a separate head of damage is transport, not in relation to the use of public transport or conveyance by family or carers, but in terms of the provision of a vehicle. There are several aspects to this. Nowadays it is a fact that most people drive and own or have access to a car. It follows that most claimants, if they had not been injured, would have owned a car anyway which would probably have been paid for out of future earnings. What will be compensated therefore is not the whole cost of a vehicle but any extra transport needs or costs arising from the injuries. These commonly include three aspects:

(a) A specially adapted vehicle may be needed, *e.g.* if the claimant has lost an arm special controls will be needed or where a claimant is wheelchair-bound a specific type of vehicle will be essential which can accommodate the wheelchair either as the driver's seat or separately.

(b) A seriously-injured claimant is much more vulnerable if the car breaks down and so experts will normally advise that the car is changed more frequently than an uninjured person would need to do, while the mobile phone can provide an additional safety feature.

(c) By reason of the injury the plaintiff may need to use the car more and then there will be a claim for extra mileage based on that need.

The way in which car claims are to be costed has been considered in two recent cases in the Court of Appeal, *Woodrup v. Nicol*[5] and *Goldfinch v. Scannell*[6] which are considered further below.

Pure Amenity

Probably the most difficult types of claim to make are those which may **14–08** be called "pure amenity" claims. That is to say they are not founded in either care needs or specific and generally accepted needs of every day living. There may be a pure amenity element in transport claims which it appears has not, so far, been argued as something which should exclude them from separate compensation. However, with other types of aids or equipment the court's approach is that something which is not needed for care reasons or ordinary living will probably be treated as something to be paid for (if the claimant wishes) out of the general damages for loss of amenity.

---

[5] [1993] P.I.Q.R. Q.104.
[6] [1993] P.I.Q.R. Q.143.

This approach of the court is exemplified by the Court of Appeal decision in *Cassel v. Riverside Health Authority*[7] in which they reversed that part of the decision of Rose J, allowing a claim for £32,000 in an action by a paraplegic boy for a small swimming pool. Rose J., having asked the question: "Is such an additional claim allowable at all, or is it catered for by the loss of amenity award?" and after reviewing an earlier case in which Alliott J., had refused to allow a swimming pool, said, at p. Q12:

> "The evidence before me is that, for Hugo, swimming is not merely an alternative form of therapy or a source of enjoyment, but his principal source of relaxation and pleasure. It is the one thing he is able to do himself. Bearing in mind the difficulties of supervision in a public pool, it is in my judgment reasonable that he should have a suitably modest private pool and that he should not have to bear the cost of this from his loss of amenity award."

Thus, Rose J. founded his award on the proposition that this was a specific amenity item which should be allowed as a separate economically quantifiable head, he did not found his decision on the grounds of medical or therapeutic need. However, the Court of Appeal allowed the appeal in respect of this item on the basis that therapeutic need was not established by the evidence. Thus, Ralph Gibson L.J. said, at p. Q181:

> "I do not base that conclusion" (*i.e.* that the pool should not be allowed) upon any concept of what should or should not be provided out of the damages for loss of amenity but on the ground that there was no basis in the evidence for awarding this sum as an expense made necessary by the increased cost of caring for the plaintiff in his injured state."

Having regard to the fact that the judge had decided on the basis that it ought to be a separate item not funded from the amenity award, it is hard to see the logic of his statement that his conclusion was not based on "what should or should not be provided out of the damages for loss of amenity", and it does not give any guidance on whether any and, if so, what kind of "pure amenity" items will be separately valued. The other two members of the Court were more clear cut, thus, Farquharson L.J. said: "No doctor was called to say that swimming was an essential therapy for the injury Hugo sustained". Purchas L.J. said that the claim: ". . . was not supported by the medical evidence . . ." and "the provision of a swimming pool is more properly considered as an element in the damages for loss of amenity, etc". Interestingly, in the unreported case of *Willett v. North Bedfordshire Health Authority*,[8] where the proposal on behalf of the claimant that a house should be bought which happened to have a swimming pool,

---

[7] [1992] P.I.Q.R. Q168.
[8] November 13, 1992, see Kemp & Kemp, 5–042/1.

Hobhouse J. held that as the house was a reasonable choice for the claimant's needs there should be no reduction for the added value attributable to the pool although there was no therapeutic need for it.

Probably the conclusion to be drawn from this is that claims which are pure amenity claims unrelated to medical or therapeutic need will not be allowed.

Evidence

Changing Future Needs of Claimant—Children's Cases and Adult Cases

In any case of serious permanent injury, particularly, but not only, **14–09** serious brain damage and paraplegia cases, to compensate the claimant properly the claimant's future needs must be assessed so that the compensation will cover not only his or her current needs but also his or her future needs. This is, of course, a familiar requirement when assessing care but it is also important for appraising need for aids and appliances. It is particularly difficult with injured children who have not established any pattern of life before the injury. Educational needs will only last until adulthood, educational toys to be used after the age of 19 were disallowed in *Cassel,* but thereafter there may still be mental or intellectual needs which require attention. Housing needs will change radically as a child grows up and consideration has to be given to what equipment will be necessary as a result of the injuries for independent living. Forecasts have to be made of the progress of the condition and any impact they may have on the need, both to diminish or increase aids and equipment requirements.

At the other end of life the need for aids and equipment as the claimant grows older will also change. Travel and transport may reduce but equipment support around the home, including indoor mobility, may increase. The relevant experts have to address these issues.

The preparation and presentation of evidence on these issues as on others will of course be governed by the provisions of Part 32 of the Civil Procedure Rules.

Need for Support from Medical Evidence

Just as it is essential that any care claims made are firmly founded on the **14–10** medical evidence so the ancillary matters relating to aids and equipment in the last resort have to be justified by the medical evidence. The care experts will have to liaise closely with the medical experts, particularly any rehabilitation expert on issues relating to equipment just as those relating to the amount and type of care, so that their recommendations are firmly founded on medical or therapeutic necessity. In the same way, if the defendants challenge the claimant's reports they should do so on the basis of their medical evidence.

Care and Other Experts

In the usual care report the expert will deal with the aids and equipment needed for the claimant and the care regime which is proposed. This report will be the foundation of the claim for aids and equipment. The items proposed will also be costed, this involves the capital cost of each item, its life, the replacement costs, any maintenance costs. It is common for the report on aids and equipment to be supported by leaflets, advertising material or other documentary evidence about the equipment being recommended. The report will also deal with the care provision up to date and this will include any aids or equipment already obtained. The need for these should be explained and their costings supported by appropriate documents.

With some specialist types of equipment the care expert may not be able to give the necessary evidence alone in which case the report will have to be supported by appropriate experts with the particular relevant knowledge. An expert in educational computers may be needed, for example, or when specialist furniture or such things as stair hoists are suggested the relevant specialist with knowledge of the available options will be desirable. It is, however, always worth remembering that the expense proposed must be proportionate to the need and the anticipated benefit. This is something which experts who are committed to a specific product, whether as manufacturers, suppliers or otherwise can overlook in their enthusiasm for it.

When vehicle costs are being considered, the court will usually accept AA statistics for such things as annual depreciation of different makes of car and annual running costs.

Family and Friends

14–11   Just as with all aspects of a claim on behalf of a seriously injured claimant, the claimant's case will be strengthened by corroborative evidence from family. This is particularly important with a child's claim because the parents, when dealing specifically with the problem that an item of equipment is designed to deal with, can explain the problem and how the equipment proposed can help. If the equipment in question has already been bought, or if it has been obtained on hire, then this kind of evidence can be particularly helpful and indeed if a claim is being made for equipment already obtained the family will have to deal with it in evidence both in respect of its use and its cost. Also where the claimant has some equipment but of the wrong type, *e.g.* a heavy manual wheelchair for a child, parental evidence of what is wrong with it and how a different type would improve things and why it is needed can be very important.

Availability from Public Sources

Some items of equipment are available from the National Health Service, **14–12** *e.g.* types of wheelchair. Two questions will then arise:

- Will it remain available for as long as it is required by the claimant?
- Is the quality the best, or at least satisfactory?
- Evidence on this aspect will be needed from the claimant's family as well as, probably, the care expert. It may also be necessary to obtain evidence of what the future prospects are likely to be for the public service with regard to the specific matter.

Valuation of Claims for Aids and Equipment

The conventional way of costing items of aids and equipment for a claim involves six stages:

(a) establish the initial capital cost of the item;

(b) establish how long it is likely to last, *i.e.* the life of the item;

(c) what the capital cost of replacement will be;

(d) what the maintenance or running costs are likely to be;

(e) using those figures the annual cost can then be calculated; and

(f) once that has been done the annual figure will be multiplied by the appropriate multiplier, which may be the whole life multiplier or a shorter multiplier determined with how long the particular item will be needed. The appropriate multiplier can then be calculated in accordance with the established rules. Thus, different multipliers may have to be used for different items, *e.g.* for items of equipment that will not be needed for the whole of the claimant's future or not until some date in the future.

Thus, there may well be complex calculations to be made because different items will have different expected lives and in many cases the periods during which the various items of equipment will be used will vary, for instance as to when they start or when they are expected to finish. The question of the calculation of cost of future travel or car expenses has been considered in two recent cases in the Court of Appeal: *Woodrup v. Nicoll*[9]

---

[9] [1993] P.I.Q.R. Q104.

and *Goldfinch v. Scannell*.[10] In *Woodrup*, the finding was that the claimant needed a suitable car which required adaptations, that he would have bought a car anyway, that because of his injuries, (he was a paraplegic) he would do a much greater mileage than he would have done if uninjured and that because of that and the essential need for reliability the car would be changed more frequently than had he not been injured. The leading judgment was given by Russell L.J. who first said that a motor car, unlike a house, was a "wasting asset" so that:

"What the court has to do . . . is to achieve a capital figure which if properly invested will finance the plaintiff in the purchase of a motor car that will have to be replaced from time to time with a new motor vehicle . . . This requires the court to know the value of the new car . . . and a notional trade-in value of the car at the end of every period during which the car deteriorates."

In that case also there had to be a deduction for the sums which would have been spent on a car had there been no accident. The Court of Appeal, although confirming the award based on the capital expenditure, reduced the award in respect of extra mileage because they took a lifetime view of the claimant and said the volume of extra mileage would decline as he got older, something the judge had not considered.

In *Goldfinch,* a similar calculation was carried out, the approach being accurately set out in the headnote which reads:

"The judge's approach to damages for extra traveling costs was appropriate. On the findings that it would be appropriate for the plaintiff to have a new vehicle of her own, and that it was likely that she would have had a car in any event, probably a second-hand car, it was appropriate to award damages reflecting the difference in capital depreciation between a new and a second-hand car and apply the multiplier for future loss to a multiplicand based on a proportion of the annual capital depreciation of a suitable vehicle derived from Automobile Association statistics."

This method of calculation is clearly to be applied to future transport costs, but it also gives an indication of how future loss arising from the need for aids and equipment may be calculated and so is of more general importance.

---

[10] [1993] P.I.Q.R. Q143.

15. Housing

Heads of Claim

There are three principal heads of claim:

(a) *Adaption of existing accommodation.* Where existing accommodation can be adapted to meet the reasonably necessary requirements of the claimant, then the cost can be recovered as an item of special damage, subject to allowance for any betterment or diminution in value of the property.

(b) *New accommodation.* Where existing accommodation is inadequate and there is a net capital cost in purchasing accommodation, then under the *Roberts v. Johnstone* formula, the claimant is entitled to recover 3 per cent of the net capital expended, representing the lost interest on the forced investment, and any associated ancillary costs.[1] This may not reflect the true loss to the plaintiff always as will be seen below.

(c) *Increased running costs.* In both (a) and (b) there may be a claim for the increased running costs of the home. These are claimed on a traditional multiplier multiplicand basis.

Adaption of Existing Accommodation

When are Adaptions Reasonably Necessary?

Recovery for adaptions to the claimant's home will only be recoverable if they are reasonably necessary and are not merely to replace lost amenity that will be covered by an award of general damages for loss of amenity. Therefore, the claimant who is wheelchair-bound following an accident and cannot use existing accommodation without having all the doors widened will recover for such costs. The claimant who spends money having raised flower beds built in the garden for therapeutic reasons, risks not recovering such expenditure on the basis that it is a claim for loss of amenity.[2] Such a claim could be justified if the claimant were a keen

---

[1] *Roberts v. Johnstone* [1989] Q.B. 878, CA; *Wells v. Wells* [1999] 1 A.C. 345.

[2] An example of where this common claim for wheelchair-bound plaintiffs was disallowed is *Brown v. Merton Health Authority (Teaching)*, Q.B.D., (unreported), noted in Kemp & Kemp, *The Quantum of Damages*, (Release 67), para. 5–041.

gardener before the accident and in order to garden from a wheelchair raised flower beds were necessary. Similarly, the Court of Appeal in *Cassell v. Riverside Health Authority* may have allowed the claim for a swimming pool if there had been evidence that it was necessary to care for the claimant.[3] There was only evidence that it was the best means for Hugo Cassell to get exercise and enjoyment. It was disallowed on this basis.

It is always a question of fact and degree as to the dividing line between necessity and amenity. The evidence relating to proposed adaptions must always be scrutinised and presented by reference to the criterion of reasonable necessity.

Betterment of the Property

15–03   It is axiomatic that the cost of a particular adaption will not be recoverable if its function is to improve the property, rather than meet the claimant's changed requirements as a result of injury. However, there are many adaptions to accommodation that have both consequences. For instance, a conservatory added to the property may be necessary for the wheelchair-bound claimant because the medical evidence demonstrates that much more time will be spent in doors and there is a need to provide some sheltered access to the garden environment. Equally, a conservatory built on to an existing property in an appropriate context may add value to the property.

In the event of betterment, a deduction must be made from the claim for the value of betterment.[4] In the converse situation, the loss of value of the property should be added to the claim for the cost of adaptions.

Local Authority Grants

15–04   A disabled facilities grant from the local housing authority may be available to fund the adaption of accommodation.[5] The grant is mandatory for certain types of adaptions (such as the provision of access to and from the house and within the house to the claimant's bedroom).[6] Beyond this it is discretionary.[7] A house renovation grant may be obtained if the property requires renovation in order for the local housing authority to provide disabled facilities grant. However, this may be dealt with by a discretionary

---

[3] [1992] P.I.Q.R. Q168 at Q181.
[4] A working example is provided by *Almond v. Leeds Western Health Authority* (1990) 1 Med. L.R. 370 at 373.
[5] Circular No. 17/96, Private Sector Renewal: A Strategic Approach, issued by the Department of Environment, Chapter 7 and Annex I.
[6] Section 23(1) of the Housing Grants, Construction and Regeneration Act 1996 and Circular No. 17/96, Annex I, paras 14–30.
[7] Section 23(2) of of the Housing Grants, Construction and Regeneration Act 1996 and Circular No. 17/96, Annex I, paras 31–36.

disabled facilities grant,[8] which is cash-limited. The maximum amount of mandatory grant that can be given is £20,000, but the amount of discretionary grant is not cash-limited.[9]

It should be noted that disabled facilities grant aid is means tested.[10] This means that it will not be usually available to a claimant after settlement. However, it is common for claimants in the absence of an interim payment to apply for a disabled facilities grant to fund essential works. It should be borne in mind that the local housing authority can impose a condition requiring the claimant to take reasonable steps to pursue his or her claim for damages and to reapy the grant out of the proceeds of the claim. If a condition is imposed upon the grant, then the claimant comes under a duty to repay the local housing authority, subject to a discretion vested in the local housing authority to waive a claim or accept a lesser amount.[11] Where the local social services department has provided top-up assistance for equipment, such as hoists and the like, such financial assistance should be included in the claim.[12] Any settlement should provide an indemnity against the risk of recoupment, where recoupment is a possibility and there has not been specific provision for that item.

New Accommodation

The Problem of Valuation

A difficulty is posed where the injured claimant is forced to purchase **15–05** new and more expensive housing, namely to value the increased cost, while taking account of the enhanced capital asset, which the claimant's estate will retain. It is settled law that an award cannot be made for the whole of the cost of the new home because the claimant still has the capital asset.[13] However, this asset will not be realised while the claimant lives in it. Further, given that awards are made on the assumed basis that the claimant will only move once (about which see below at para. 15–10), any award is predicated upon the assumption that the enhanced value will only be realised at death.

One measure of loss is to calculate the additional expense to the claimant of the additional capital expenditure, *e.g.* mortgage interest on

---

[8] Circular No. 17/96, Annex F, para. 44.
[9] Section 33 of the Housing Grants, Construction and Regeneration Act 1996 and Circular No. 17/96, Annex I, para. 10.
[10] Circular No. 17/96, Annex J2.
[11] Section 51 of the Housing Grants, Construction and Regeneration Act 1996 and Circular No. 17/96, Annex F, paras 65–68.
[12] Section 2(1)(e) of the Chronically Sick and Disabled Persons Act 1970; Circular No. 17/96, Annex I, paras 2–6; section 17 of the Health and Social Services and Social Security Adjudications Act 1983; *Avon County Council v. Hooper and another* [1997] 1 W.L.R. 1605.
[13] *George v. Pinnock* [1973] 1 W.L.R. 118 at 124H–125H, CA.

that sum.[14] This used to be the approach, but was found to be inappropriate in *Roberts v. Johnstone*.[15]

An alternative is to calculate the loss of investment income on the additional capital expenditure. This is the elegant solution provided by *Roberts v. Johnstone*.

The Solution

15–06   In *Roberts v. Johnstone*, the Court of Appeal held:

> ". . . [T]hat where the capital asset in respect of which the cost is incurred consists of house property, inflation and risk element are secured by the rising value of such property particularly in desirable residential areas, and thus the rate of 2 per cent would appear to be more appropriate than that of 7 per cent or 9.1 per cent which represents the actual cost of a mortgage loan for such a property.
>
> We are reinforced in this view by the fact that in reality in this case that the purchase was financed by a capital sum paid on account on behalf of the defendants by way of interim payments, and thus it may be appropriate to consider the annual cost in terms of lost income and investment, since the sum expended on the house would not be available to produce income. A tax-free yield of 2 per cent in risk-free investment would not be a wholly unacceptable one"[16]

It was held by the House of Lords in *Wells v. Wells* that the rate of 2 per cent was not appropriate. The correct rate is that used for the calculation of multipliers for future loss, namely the net rate of return on index-linked government stock ["ILGS"]. The House of Lords in *Wells* decided then that the appropriate rate of return to take was 3 per cent.[17] However, currently the net rate of return on ILGS hovers around 2 per cent and at the time of going to press the Lord Chancellor has not set a rate under the Damages Act 1996 which would have been taken into account in a *Roberts v. Johnstone* calculation.[18] In *Warren v. Northern General Hospital NHS Trust*, the Court of Appeal decided that the appropriate rate of return to take remained 3 per cent, until the Lord Chancellor has set a rate.[19] It should be noted that it is not open to argue that the rate applied should be greater than 3 per cent on the basis that property prices will not keep pace with inflation.[20]

---

[14] *George, ibid.* at 123B-F; *Chapman v. Lidstone*, (unreported) December, 1982, Kemp & Kemp, *The Quantum of Damages*, (Release 59), para. A3-006 referred to in *Johntone*, *op. cit.* at 891F-H.

[15] *op. cit.* at 891HF–893A.

[16] *per* Stocker L.J. at 892F–893A.

[17] *Wells v. Wells* [1999] 1 A.C. 345 at 380F–381.

[18] See section 1(1) of the Damages Act 1996.

[19] [2000] Lloyd's Rep. Med. 234.

[20] *Thomas v. Brighton HA* [1996] P.I.Q.R. Q44 at Q55–6 (first instance, subsequently reported as *Wells v. Wells*). See also *Welch v. Albright and Wilson*, [1993] (unreported), Q.B.D., Birmingham, where Kay J. refused to vary the *Roberts v. Johnstone* formula because of the recent slump in house prices.

Test of Reasonable Necessity

As with all such claims it is necessary to show that the move to special   15–07
accommodation is reasonably necessary. This means that:

"it is for the plaintiff to satisfy the judge on the balance of probabilities that the
move is appropriate and necessary in the light of the injuries and disabilities
sustained".[21]

Application of the Formula

Generally, the claimant is entitled to recover as follows:

(a) The cost of the new property less the market value of the property
    sold at the rate of 3 per cent for the period of the life multiplier.
    This loss should be subtracted from the cost of the new property
    where the value of the new property is diminished by the works of
    adaption.

(b) The costs of adapting the new accommodation are recoverable as
    items of special damage. Where such work enhances the value of the
    property, such added value should be subtracted from the claim for
    costs thrown away.[22] Where such work diminishes the value of the
    property, then the diminution in value should be added to the claim
    for costs thrown away.

There is first instance authority to suggest that where the works of
adaption enhance the capital value, those works are not recoverable as
special damage in full, but only as an item subject to the *Roberts v.
Johnstone* formula. In *Willett v. North Bedfordshire Health Authority*,
Hobhouse J. (as he was then) treated the provision of a bedroom for a
second carer as a capital payment as subject to the formula and not
recoverable as a cost thrown away.[23] However, this is not consistent with
the general approach set out above. Further, it potentially significantly
undervalues a claimant's claim since the cost thrown away is immediately
incurred while the enhanced value of the property is only realisable on sale.

Fennell J. was persuaded in *Almond v. Leeds Health Authority* to award a   15–08
further head of loss, namely the value of the betterment caused by the
works recovered at the rate of 2 [would now be 3] per cent per annum

---

[21] *Almond v. Leeds Western HA* [1990] 1 Med L.R. 370 at 373 *per* Fennell J. An example of
  where the evidence did not met that test is *Maylen v. Morris*, CA, January 21, 1988,
  (unreported) where the medical and accommodation experts gave equivocal support for the
  claim for new accommodation for a paraplegic.
[22] *Roberts v. Johnstone, op. cit.* at 893C–G.
[23] [1993] P.I.Q.R. Q166 at Q172–3.

under the *Roberts v. Johnstone* formula, which he had deducted from the costs thrown away claim.[24] This is justifiable, if there has been no addition to the claim for the net capital cost of the accommodation to reflect the added value of the property.

In *Wells v. Wells*, the Court of Appeal confirmed that where new accommodation has been purchased before trial and mortgage interest payments made the claim for such past costs, as well as future costs, is subject to the *Roberts v. Johnstone* formula and consequently interest payments to date of trial are not recoverable as such.[25] This finding was not appealed to the House of Lords.

There should be no deduction from the claimant's claim where any element of betterment is not due to factors related to the claimant's need. Hence, in *Willett*, one coincidental advantage of the property purchased was that it had a swimming pool. Hobhouse J. refused to discount the award under the *Roberts v. Johnstone* formula to reflect the value of the unnecessary pool, since he found that the price paid was within the purchase price bracket for properties which it was reasonable to purchase.[26]

Deductions from the Roberts v. Johnstone claim

15–09 Where the claimant is not an owner occupier, credit must be given for any move that the plaintiff would have made but for the accident. A typical example would be the young tetraplegic who is living at home and now requires an adapted bungalow and who, but for the accident, would have bought a starter home at some point.[27] The housing expert should be instructed to provide a valuation of an appropriate starter home which can then be deducted from the capital cost of the new accommodation in such cases. The life multiplier may have to be split to take into account when a starter home and any subsequent homes would have been bought.

Similarly, where the claimant would otherwise have married and have made contributions to the capital cost of the matrimonial home, the pro-rated cost should be deducted from the capital cost of the new accommodation.[28]

Credit should be given for the housing expenses that would have been incurred by the claimant where the claimant is a child and the parents

---

[24] *op. cit.* at 373.

[25] *Wells v. Wells* [1997] 1 W.L.R. 652, CA.

[26] *op. cit.* at Q173–4.

[27] See *Biesheuvel v. Birrell* [1999] P.I.Q.R. Q40 at Q72 where Eady J. accepted discounts on a staged basis on the assumption that for his injury the claimant would have "traded up" over time.

[28] *Goldfinch v. Scannell* (March 26, 1992 (unreported), Q.B.D. Latham Q.C. sitting as a deputy High Court judge); *Lamey v. Wirrall Health Authority* [1993] Q.B.D. (unreported), Morland J., Kemp & Kemp (Release 67) at A4–120.

purchase the new accommodation.[29] There is an argument that in such circumstances the parents should be entitled to recover the full capital cost since there is no financial windfall to the claimant's estate. However, in *Thomas v. Brighton Health Authority*, although the argument was raised by Collins J., neither party pursued the point before him or on appeal.[30]

In the converse situation no deduction should be made where the child claimant purchases the property and the parents save rent thereby.[31]

More than One Move

If the circumstances arise and a further move is justified on the evidence **15–10** the cost can be recovered.[32] However, it should be noted that while most people will move several times in their life, no claim is usually put forward for future moves. It is assumed that the claimant once having purchased special accommodation will remain there for life. Consequently, the claim should envisage all likely future events, such as increased number of carers or children with an appropriate credit for accelerated receipt, although this will always be subject to challenge on the ground of remoteness of damage.[33]

Ancillary Costs

Typically, a claimant's claim will include the following costs: VAT **15–11** element on works, architect/surveyor design and supervision fees, quantity surveyor fees, structural engineer fees, local authority fees (these may be waived by some authorities), legal fees, estate agent's commission, removal costs, surveyor fees and mortgage valuer fees. Some of these costs (local authority fees, legal fees and the like) will be open to attack by the defendant on the basis that they would have been incurred in any event. The riposte may be that they would have been less for the purchase of another property, such as stamp duty and conveyancing charges.

Running Costs

In most cases, the move to specially adapted accommodation will involve **15–12** increased running costs that can be annualised and claimed as an item of future loss on the usual basis.

---

[29] *Cummings v. Clark* [1991] (unreported), Q.B.D., Judge J. (as he then was).
[30] *op. cit.* at Q55.
[31] *Thompson v. South Tees Area Health Authority* (April 10, 1990 (unreported), Q.B.D., Middlesbrough, French J.)
[32] *Almond, op. cit.* at 373; *Lay v. South West Surrey Health Authority* [1989] CA (unreported).
[33] In *Biesheuvel v. Birrell*, see n.26 above at Q72. Eady J. accepted a proposal for future accommodation which would be large enough to house a family in the event that the claimant had one without any apparant discount for accelerated receipt or for the fact that the claim was necessarily a contingent one.

Maintenance Costs

15–13   This covers all those maintenance activities that the claimant formerly did and cannot now do. Potentially, there is an overlap with any claim for DIY and gardening now done by others. Accordingly, defendants should scrutinise such claims for overlap. There will also be claims for maintenance of special equipment, such as closomat toilets, hoists and the like. These should be separately itemised. Again, there is a potential overlap with any claim for aids and equipment.

Council Tax

15–14   Any special features provided for the claimant which enhance the value of the property will be disregarded for the purposes of banding a property for council tax purposes. There will normally be a claim for increased council tax as result of living in a property in a higher valuation band, even allowing for the reduced council tax paid by the disabled.[34]

Utility Bills

15–15   The claim for increased utility bills should allow for the nature of the disability and its consequences. For instance, a tetraplegic will normally find it necessary to heat the house to a higher temperature than the able-bodied and will be in the home for more of the time. Further, a larger house with carers will cost more to run in terms of all utility bills, including the telephone.

Insurance

15–16   Building and contents insurance will also be increased if the property is larger and there is valuable special equipment in the house.

Evidence

15–17   The evidencing of accommodation claims will involve participation not only from an accommodation expert, but will also involve participation from the lead medical, care, and aids and equipment expert if cogent evidence is to be put before the court. The sensible time to ensure that the necessary expert interplay has occurred, on the claimant's side, is in

---

[34] See the Council Tax (Regulations for Disabilities) Regulations 1992 (S.I. 1992 No. 554) and the Council Tax (Additional Provisions for Discount Disregards) Regulations 1992 (S.I. 1992 No. 552).

conference before drafting a schedule of loss and certainly before any accommodation scheme is put into place. On the defendant's side, if a sustained assault on the claimant's claim is to be mounted, an effective expert alliance needs to be forged in conference before the Counter-Schedule is drafted.

Often, it is necessary for a claimant to invest in new accommodation before trial for tactical and practical reasons. This is particularly so where the care regime advocated on behalf of the claimant cannot be put into place without new accommodation and it is desired to test out such a regime by either or both parties. Further, there may be a tension between where the claimant and his or her family wish to live and where the most economical accommodation can be found.[35] In such circumstances, it is important for the claimant to recognise that the capital cost of any new accommodation will have to come out of the claimant's general fund. This is because compensation is only for the loss of investment income and not the initial capital cost. Therefore, the claim must be carefully examined to ensure that the proper evidential basis for the claim is there before a scheme is put into place. Such a scheme may have profound implications for other parts of the claimant's claim and will deplete the capital fund.

Accommodation Expert

There are several different disciplines that will need to be covered. It is **15–18** not always possible to embrace all the necessary areas within one expert report, although it would be unusual to seek to call more than one expert or be given permission to call more than one expert. An estate agent or chartered surveyor in general practice will usually be the most sensible person to instruct as to the identification and acquisition of property rather than an architect. Valuation calls for different skills and local knowledge of the area may be invaluable. Most importantly, the accommodation expert must be a specialist architect or chartered building surveyor experienced in the construction of schemes for the disabled. It is striking how often solicitors instruct experts without such first hand experience who then assess a scheme by reference to an out of date body of literature. The assessment of the increased running costs of adapted accommodation is best dealt with by a chartered building surveyor. The appropriate course is to agree joint instruction of a local estate agent or chartered surveyor to deal with the question of valuation evidence. Whether the principal accommodation expert can be made the subject of joint instructions must depend on the extent to which any accommodation scheme is likely to be controversial and a matter of disputed opinion.

---

[35] In *Biesheuvel v. Birrell*, see n. 26 above at Q74. Eady J. was persuaded to award the capital cost of more expensive accommodation under the *Roberts v. Johnstone* formula local to where the claimant's family and friends were, even though adequate and cheaper accommodation could have provided elsewhere.

Without any accommodation expert evidence, the court will take a broad brush approach, provided the medical evidence is in place.[36] Similarly, it is not adequate to rely on a "catch all" rehabilitation expert, unless there is only a very small claim for minor adaptions to a property.[37]

The expert should be asked to consider any list of properties produced by an estate agent critically to assess suitability and value (which is not necessarily the asking price). The other relevant experts must support any adaption scheme. Further, the nature of the scheme must be addressed to the needs and wishes of the individual claimant. There is no point including in a claim a piece of equipment or adaption that the claimant will never make use of.

15–19   Conversely, from the defendant's perspective it should be recognised that claimants do not always fall into neat categories of need. For instance, it may be wrong to assume that a head injured claimant does not require a conservatory whereas a tetraplegic would.[38] To this end, the defendant expert should be instructed as a matter of routine to visit the claimant at home. This way the expert's report can spell out the necessary understanding of the claimant's real, as opposed to theoretical, accommodation needs by reference to the literature and the other reports in the case. Without this, where a separate expert is instructed by the defendant, he or she is vulnerable to telling cross-examination.

The costing of works should be the result of a tendering process (where the works are contemplated before trial). Careful selection of the best tender may not necessarily result in the cheapest tender being accepted. Often the costs incurred by a claimant are challenged by reference to the *Quarterly Review of Building Tender Prices* produced by the Building Cost Information Service of the Royal Institution of Chartered Surveyors (BCIS). However, this may be quite misleading as BCIS does not provide costings for this type of scheme. A challenge is best mounted through a close examination of all the tender and contract documentation if the works have already been carried out or an actual costing.

An interim payment based on an estimate obtained by the defendant may be appropriate where there is agreement about the scope of the works to be done and the defendant suspects that the claimant could do the works on a cheaper basis, and will do so, rather than for the cost claimed in the schedule. This would prevent the claimant from pocketing the difference. A tied interim payment can be used to real effect in this context particularly where it is connected to the claim for future care.

---

[36] See, for example, *Welch*, above at n. 20.

[37] See for example *Welsh v. Robson Road Haulage Limited* (Court of Appeal, May 17, 1995, (unreported).

[38] Examples of head-injured plaintiffs recovering such items where the defendants have contested the need: *Page v. Sheerness Steel plc* [1996] P.I.Q.R. Q26 at Q42–3, upheld on this point by the Court of Appeal in *Wells, op. cit.*; *Walsh v. Allessio* [1996] (unreported), Q.B.D., Manchester, Gage J.

Medical evidence

For the claimant's claim to stand up at trial there must be cogent medical **15–20** evidence from the lead medical expert that the claimant requires rehousing or adaptions to the home. There are a number of claims that have failed or been substantially reduced because the accommodation expert has proposed and sometimes implemented a scheme that the medical experts think is overelaborate or can only be justified in 20 or 30 years time. Not only should the medical expert support the principle of an accommodation scheme, the detail needs to be supported. Expensive individual items, such as an environmental control system, will need underpinning based on actual need. Similarly, from the defendant's perspective, it may prove easy to eliminate individual items that have no medical basis (such as, a Closomat toilet for a claimant who is independent in using the toilet). Such an exercise will also have implications for a claim for aids and equipment.

Care implications

Participation from the care experts on both sides will often be crucial in **15–21** determining the extent of any accommodation claim. It is essential to explore what the implications are for the accommodation requirements of the claimant in a case where paid care is going to be required for the claimant. For instance, a seriously head-injured claimant who lives with his or her family but requires round the clock care at home from two resident carers is plainly going to have to provide appropriate accommodation for the carers.

Care experts will differ in their views about what accommodation requirements are necessary to attract and retain carers of quality. The minimum requirements are usually their own separate bed/sitting room with separate washing, toilet and cooking facilities. In *Tricker v. Hoban*, it was observed by the judge:

"The evidence on this [type of accommodation] is simply that the carers will require space. The carers will inevitably be around probably most of the time, even though they are not directly involved in the care. The one thing that governs the case entirely is the quality of the carers that are going to be obtained and employed and to stint upon the space that is made available to them is, in my judgment, going to militate against getting the right sort of person."[39]

If the argument that there should be residential care is weak and this is the foundation for the claim for new accommodation, then the claim may fail.[40] Therefore, it is critically important in such cases for both sides to

---

[39] *Tricker v. Hoban* [1994] Q.B.D. (unreported), Wolton Q.C. sitting as a deputy High Court judge.
[40] See, for example, *Welch*, above at n. 20.

closely examine the justification for new accommodation. This will be particularly important for a claimant who proposes to spend money on new accommodation before trial.

Where the care regime will change in due course requiring more accommodation, it is important that this is factored into the claim for future accommodation. For instance, a young tetraplegic may be quite capable of managing without resident care in the early years, but may require such care in the future. From the claimant's perspective, it will be important to present a united front between medical, care and accommodation experts that this future need should be met now. From the defendant's point of view, a challenge should be focused on persuading the court that this is just a medical possibility not a probability and to either oppose the claim completely or to insist upon a discount. In any event, a discount for accelerated receipt should be insisted upon for that part of the scheme dictated by future care requirements many years into the future. Again, this requires effective interplay between the accommodation, medical and care experts to decide what the risk is, when it would come about, if at all, and what the accommodation consequences would be, if it did so.

16. Recoupment of Damages

Introduction

The Social Security (Recovery of Benefits) Act 1997 completely changed   16–01
the law relating to recoupment and deduction of benefits from personal
injury damages. It came into effect on October 6, 1997. Under the old law,
if the accident occurred before January 1, 1989, half of the specified
benefits received by the claimant after the accident were deducted by the
defendant from the damages paid pursuant to the Law Reform [Personal
Injuries] Act 1948. If the benefits were not listed in the 1948 statute then
they were deducted in full: see *Hodgson v. Trapp*.[1] The defendant paid less
damages because he was allowed to deduct the benefits or a proportion
thereof which the claimant had received from the damages paid. Further,
the taxpayer had paid benefits to the claimant when, had the accident had
not occurred, nothing would have been paid out. One half of the specified
benefits were deducted, but only from the claim for loss of earnings and
not from damages for pain and suffering.

The old system [as amended] continued in force before October 6, 1997
where either (a) the compensation payment amounted to less than £2500:
a "small payment" or (b) the accident occurred before January 1, 1989. In
the case of small payments, the practice in most cases was to ignore the old
system altogether. The Social Security Act 1989 gave birth to the Compensation Recovery Unit (CRU). This was then consolidated and amended by
the *Social Security Administration Act 1992*. For the first time in personal
injury law "relevant benefits" which were paid to claimants were recouped
by the Government from compensation paid to the claimant. The benefits
were collected by the CRU.

There were many problems. Unemployed claimants, the elderly or ill,
who were receiving state benefits before the accident and were not in
work, had part or all of their damages for personal injury eaten up by the
CRU recoupment. A partial solution which developed was to claim
damages for loss of non-recoupable benefits. If before the accident the
claimant was available for work and fit, he was entitled to claim (non-
recoupable) benefits because he could find no work. After his accident
when he became unfit to work, as part of his special damage claim, he
claimed those benefits which he would otherwise have been paid had the
accident not happened. The claim for lost non-recoupable benefits was a
novel head of damage. In *Hassall v. Secretary of State for Social Security*,[2]

---

[1] [1988] 3 All E.R. 870.
[2] [1955] 3 All E.R. 909.

the Court of Appeal expressly approved of that new head of damage, suggested by counsel[3] for the claimant, and after that case the insurance industry generally accepted the new head of damage.

16–02 In a subsequent case, *Neale v. Bingle*,[4] the Court of Appeal confirmed this new head of damage was correct in law. There were other difficulties. Payments into court caused problems if no mention was made in the notice of whether the sums paid was net or gross. In *Houghton v. British Coal*,[5] the defendant made a payment into court of £15,800, having deducted £9,200 of benefits certified as recoupable from the gross offer of £25,000. They provided a notice of payment-in to the claimant, stating the payment-in was £25,000 but not stating whether this was net or gross. The claimant misinterpreted this as meaning that £25,000 was actually in court, so taking into account the sums due to be recouped he assumed that the total offer was £34,200. The claimant accepted the offer, then realised the mistake and sought to set the agreement aside. The Court of Appeal considered that claimants should assume that payments-in were made net of relevant benefits and forced the claimant to accept the £25,000 despite the mistake. The Court accepted that the RSC, Form 23, was ambiguous and recommended clarification of the difference between the gross and net payments in.

Another difficulty related to the small payments exemption of £2,500 which was being used in many cases to avoid large CRU clawbacks thereby depriving the Government of recoupment and no doubt causing some consternation. Cases settled for £2,500 when the actual value was far higher. Some settlements occurred after trials had started. Large claims settled for a small payments because both parties saved money. On June 21, 1995, after the decision in the *Hassall* case, the House of Commons Social Security Committee provided it's 4th report on the CRU. It had taken evidence from many interested bodies. They concluded (see paras 65–77) that:

> "the Government have passed too great a burden to the individual . . . some of the cases which we have encountered we believe are revolting to the ordinary man's sense of justice. In our view the present system operates in a way which is . . . contrary to public policy . . . we cannot accept that the general taxpayer should be reimbursed out of damages awarded for an individual's pain and suffering . . . or future loss of earnings . . . by allowing recovery from total settlement rather than simply from loss of earnings, we believe that injured parties have been most unfairly treated."

This led directly to the 1997 Act.

---

[3] Gary Burrell O.C.
[4] *The Times*, July 24, 1997, CA.
[5] *The Times*, February 13, 1997, CA.

The Social Security (Recoupment of Benefits) Act 1997[6]

Main Provisions

The main provisions of the 1997 Act include: 16–03

(a) Damages for pain, suffering and loss of amenity are ringfenced.

(b) Damages for future loss (all future loss including earnings, care costs and mobility) are ringfenced, effectively the same under the 1992 Act;

(c) the 1997 Act is completely retrospective.

(d) The burden of paying benefits is wholly transferred from the claimant's damages to the defendant's purse.

(e) The defendant is allowed to set off benefits against the compensation paid but only on a limited basis, namely:

(i) only like for like benefits are deductible; and
(ii) benefits are only deductible against past loss.

(f) The small payments exemption is abolished, although there is provision for such an exemption to be implemented in the future.

(g) Whatever compensation is paid to the claimant, the defendant is obliged to pay to the Compensation Recovery Unit *all* of the relevant benefits paid to the claimant during the relevant period.

(h) There is no provision dealing with contributory negligence. Thus, insurers still have to pay to the CRU the full amount of benefit and claimants suffer deduction of benefits in full against relevant heads of loss.

Implementation

The 1997 Act received Royal Assent on March 19, 1997. It came into 16–04 force on October 6, 1997.

Recoupment

Section 1 of the 1997 Act applies CRU recoupment to compensation 16–05 payments made:

---

[6] Hereafter referred to as the 1997 Act; also see the Social Security (Recovery of Benefits) Regulations 1997 (S.I. 1997 No: 2205) hereafter referred to as the 1997 Regulations.

"in consequence of any accident, injury or disease suffered" . . . "by or on behalf of any person who is . . . liable . . . in respect of the accident . . ."[7]

It includes payments by the Motor Insurance Bureau.[8]

Excluded Payments

16–06 Schedule 1 to the 1997 Act[9] excludes the following from CRU recoupment:

(f) small payments [no small payment limit has been set by the regulations so this can be ignored at present];

(g) payments under section 135 of the Powers of Criminal Courts Act 1973;

(h) payments out of trust property where the defendant/compensator owns no more than 50 per cent of the trust or some other trusts;[10]

(i) payment by insurers under the Insurance Companies Act 1982 under a contract of insurance entered before the accident or before the claimant first claimed benefits;

(j) any redundancy payment taken into account in the assessment of damages;

(k) costs;

(l) Fatal Accident Act payments;

(m) payments under the Vaccine Damages Payments Act 1979;

(n) CICB and CICA awards;

(o) NCB coal pneumoconiosis scheme payments;

(p) deafness payments where the loss is less than 50dB in either ear;

(q) any contractual sick pay;

(r) any payment under the NHS (Injury Benefits) Regulations 1995 or under the Secretary of State's scheme established on April 24, 1992.

Although the Government indicated that all excluded payments under the 1992 scheme would also be excluded under the 1997 scheme the following have not yet been so excluded: damages for insurance policy

---

[7] See s. 1(1) and (2).
[8] See s. 1(2).
[9] and regulation 2 of the 1997 Regulations.
[10] See Sched. 1, ss. 4 and 5.

excess; damage to motor vehicles; replacement of property; reimbursement of private medical expenses.

Which Accidents?

The 1997 Act covers all accidents. It is fully retrospective. The pre-January 1989 cases are covered. 16–07

Relevant Period

Benefits are recouped over a period of five years from the accident (beginning the day after the injury) or until the compensation payment settling the case is made. For disease cases, the five-year period starts on the date of the first claim for benefits.[11] As before, it is the date of payment of compensation not the date of agreeing the settlement which triggers the cap on recoupable benefits. 16–08

Certificates

The defendant or compensator must apply for a certificate before making a payment to the claimant[12]: 16–09

(a) The information which the compensator must give to the CRU in the application is set out in section 23 of the 1997 Act and regulations 3 and 7 of the 1997 Regulations. This includes the claimant's date of birth, full name and address, national insurance number, the date of the alleged accident, the nature of the disease or injury and the claimant's employment details in employers liability cases.

(b) The CRU is bound under this section to acknowledge the application,[13] and issue a certificate within four weeks [or earlier if the regulations so require: they do not at present]. The four-week period starts when the application for the certificate is received.

(c) The claimant has no right to apply for a certificate. However, when the CRU issues a certificate to the defendant it must also issue one to the claimant.[14] The defendant must also provide one when making a payment in.

---

[11] See s. 3.
[12] See s. 4(1).
[13] They say they will do so within seven days of receipt.
[14] See s. 5(5).

(d) The compensator can apply from time to time for fresh certificates and the CRU can issue these from time to time;

(e) section 5 of the 1997 Act sets out the required contents of CRU certificates—they are much as before.

(f) the parties may require details of the calculations made by the CRU.[15]

Insurer's Liability

16–09a   The defendant or his insurer, whoever the compensator is, becomes liable to pay the CRU once a compensation payment is made to the victim.[16] Payment must be made within 14 days so long as a certificate has been issued. Any payment including an interim payment will trigger recoupment. If the compensator has applied properly for a certificate and received an acknowledgment in writing, and yet within the appropriate time (4 weeks) the CRU has not issued a certificate, then compensation may be paid free of the CRU recoupment liability and no section 8 deduction is allowed.[17]

Enforcement

16–10   If the compensator fails to apply for a certificate or to pay the CRU, then the DSS may demand payment from the compensator and then sue in the county court and enforce. CRU certificates are conclusive evidence that the sums are due.[18]

The Section 8 Deduction

16–11   The compensator may reduce the compensation which he pays to the victim under section 8 of the 1997 Act. The reduction is allowed only against damages paid for three heads of loss:

- past loss of earnings;
- past care costs;
- past mobility costs.

In each case "past" means compensation within the relevant period: i.e. to the date of payment of the full compensation of five years, whichever is

---

[15] See s. 5(6).
[16] See s. 6.
[17] See s. 21.
[18] See s. 7(6).

shorter. Only certain listed benefits may be set off against each head. They are set out in Schedule 2 to the 1997 Act. This is "like for like" setting off. The table is set out as follows;

(1) *Head of compensation*	(2) *Benefit*
1. Compensation for earnings lost during the relevant period	Disability working allowance Disablement pension payable under section 103 of the 1992 Act Incapacity benefit Income support Invalidity pension and allowance Jobseeker's allowance Severe disablement allowance Sickness benefit Statutory sick pay Unemployability supplement Unemployment benefit
2. Compensation for cost of care incurred during the relevant period	Attendance allowance Care component of disability living allowance Disablement pension increase payable under section 104 or 105 of the 1992 Act
3. Compensation for loss of mobility during the relevant period	Mobility allowance Mobility component of disability living allowance

The effect of the like for like deduction regime is to ringfence that part of any award which relates to pain suffering and loss of amenity. Similarly, all other heads of loss are ringfenced against deduction on anything other than a like for like basis. For example:

Head of Loss	*Amount*	*Amount of relevant benefit*	*Net*
PSLA	5,000	NIL	5,000
Earnings	10,000	8,000	2,000
Care	6,000	9,000	NIL
Mobility	2,000	3,000	NIL
TOTALS	23,000	20,000	7,000

Of the total benefits paid (£20,000) only £16,000 has been set off against the total award. The balance of £4,000 (£3,000 care and £1,000 mobility) cannot be set off against loss of earnings or pain, suffering and loss of amenity. To that extent each head of loss is ringfenced against deduction save on a like for like basis. The compensator may give a statement to the claimant showing that he has been paid off if the section 8 deduction reduces the claim under any one head to NIL.[19]

Breakdowns of the Section 8 Deduction

16–12   There is no requirement in the 1997 Act that the compensator has to provide the claimant with the calculations of the deduction. The information which the compensator has to give to the claimant after a section 8 deduction has been calculated and a payment into court made, is minimal. The compensator has to inform the claimant of the fact that a deduction has been made and of the "date for payment" used in making the deduction calculation.[20] However the new CPR in effect require a breakdown. See below.

What Heads of Damage are Excluded?

Loss of Convivial Employment and Smith v. Manchester Claims[21]

16–13   These are excluded from the recoupment provisions. The former because it is a head of general damage and the latter because it is a head of future loss.

Pension Loss

This is excluded from recoupment, because it represents future loss of income.

Gratuitous Care

It is arguable that gratuitous care is excluded from the recoupment provisions because it is not: "Compensation for cost of care incurred during the relevant period" per Schedule 2. Ever since *Daly v. General Steam Navigation*[22] a claim for damages for the estimated value of unpaid care provided by a spouse has been regarded as general damages and

---

[19] See s. 8(2)(6).
[20] See s. 9.
[21] After *Smith v. Manchester Corporation* [1974] K.I.R 17.
[22] [1981] 1 W.L.R. 120.

technically read not really be pleaded in the schedule of special damages (although it always is in practice). So it probably should not be subject to recoupment, but the CRU may well have a different view (see below).

DIY and Gardening

It is likewise arguable that DIY or gardening done by a spouse unpaid for the injured spouse attracts an award of general damages and is thus excluded. Alternatively, as damages under these heads are held by the claimant on trust for the person who did the work they should be excluded.

Travel to and from Hospital for Visits

The cost of relatives travel to and from hospital probably does not come within "Compensation for loss of mobility": see for instance *Walker v. Mullen*[23]

Schedule 2

In relation to Schedule 2, it is of some considerable assistance that in **16–14** January 1999 the CRU published some guidance on which damages were considered (by them) to be within the heads specified by Schedule 2. This states as follows;

> "Since the introduction of the new scheme the CRU has been approached by various organisations seeking guidance on which of the many potential heads of damages in a compensation settlement fall within the scope . . . {of the Schedule} . . . Although the CRU has no wish or need to become involved in negotiations leading to the settlement of compensation claims and/or deductions from compensation payments, we must respond wherever possible to requests for guidance. Following discussion with representatives of both compensators and claimants a list of the types of damages which may or may not fall within the scope of Schedule 2 follows . . . It is stressed that the list is not definitive nor does it purport to be an interpretation of the law. It is for general guidance only and should be treated as such . . ."

Damages which may Fall Within Schedule 2

- Loss of earnings; loss of past earnings.   **16–15**
- Cost of care; nursing care and attendance inc holiday/respite care; inability to cook.

---

[23] *The Times*, January 19, 1984.

- Loss of mobility; travel to hospital for treatment. Additional costs of travel including vehicle/powered wheelchair/adaptations to transport/taxi fares (where paid as a result of injury or disease)/ increased cost of car/additional travel for holiday.

Damages Not Within Schedule 2

Pain and suffering. Loss of future earnings. Loss of future care. Loss of future mobility. Loss of expectation of life and bereavement. Loss of amenities of life. Loss of society. Loss of leisure. Loss of specific enjoyment. Loss of deprivation of privacy. Loss of marriage prospects. Breakdown of marriage. Second home on breakdown of marriage. Loss of carrying out DIY. Loss of housekeeping capacity. Handicap on the labour market (*Smith v. Manchester*[24]). Loss of congenial employment. Loss of benefits associated with claimant's work. Loss of use of motor car. Hospital visits other than for treatment. Medical expenses not included in cost of respite or nursing care and attendance. Special appliances except as mentioned in loss of mobility. Special diet. Special accommodation. Paid help, *e.g.* gardener/ cleaner. Guide dog. Court of Protection fees. Actuarial advice and related matters. Investment/management advice. Loss of financial interest. Loss of pension rights.

This is an eclectic list featuring (on one view) some interesting heads of damages, but it does serve to provide very helpful and much needed guidance for practitioners. It remains to be seen whether it will be supplemented and updated but this would no doubt be logical and appreciated by the profession. It is worth noting that incapacity benefit becomes taxable after 28 weeks and it should, therefore, be possible to reclaim the lost tax as special damage. Benefits are of course recovered gross and no account is taken of the fact that some benefits may be subject to taxation. Further, where it possible for another member of the household to claim the same entitlement to the same amount of benefit as the injured person would receive, then it may well be appropriate for the claimant not to claim income support so as to avoid recovery of benefit.

Reviewing Certificates

16–16   The rules governing reviews under the new law are broadly the same as those under the old law. Any party may apply for a review at any time. The basis of an application for review is:

> "the certificate . . . was issued in ignorance of, or was based on a mistake as to a material fact or that a mistake has occurred in its preparation."[25]

---

[24] [1974] K.I.R. 17.
[25] See s. 10.

On review, the certificate may be varied up or down. This is a change from the old law which only allowed reduction on review. If the certificate is reviewed down, then the effect for the parties is a refund. It will only be reviewed upwards if the DSS considers that the person who applied for the certificate gave the DSS "incorrect or insufficient information". The CRU has issued guidance notes which suggest that variations upwards will only occur where the claimant has supplied fraudulent information, but the Act allows for upwards variations where the insurer has made errors in providing information to the CRU.

Appealing Certificates

Appeals can only be brought after the compensation has been paid and **16–17** the CRU recoupment satisfied in full.[26] Provisional damages awards also trigger the right to appeal. Any party can appeal. The grounds of appeal are:

> "any amount, rate or period specified in the certificate is incorrect . . . or listed benefits which have been paid otherwise than in respect of the accident . . . in question have been brought into account."[27]

The procedure for appeals is set out in the Social Security (Recovery of Benefits) (Appeals) Regulations 1997. There is an approved form to be filled in, certain details have to be provided, a summary of the arguments supporting the appeal must be provided. No appeal may be made under section 11 until the claim giving rise to the compensation payment has been finally disposed of and the liability under so has been discharged. The appeal must be entered not more than three months after the compensator has paid the CRU, or after the certificate was reviewed, or a settlement whereby an earlier payment is treated as the final compensation payment. There is limited scope for appealing out of time in strict circumstances. The appeal hearings are held in public. Representation is allowed. There are rules to govern adjournment. The tribunal decides in the normal way and gives reasons in writing. No costs are awarded. The Medical Appeal Tribunal will decide medical issues concerning the amount of benefits and whether they are attributable to the accident.[28] The Tribunal is also given wider jurisdiction to decide the level of benefits and the period. And it is bound to take into account any decision of the court on the same or a similar issue concerning the injury.[29] An appeal from the Medical Appeal Tribunal on a point of law lies to the Social Security Commissioner.[30]

---

[26] See s. 11.
[27] See s. 11(1).
[28] See s. 12.
[29] See s. 12(3).
[30] See s. 13.

Refunds and Variations of Certificates

16–18   Once the appeal or review has taken place, if the certificate has been varied the CRU can either claim excess benefits from the compensator or refund the excess paid to the compensator.[31] If the CRU makes a refund to the compensator, then the compensator is bound to recalculate the section 8 deduction and pass the extra sums on to the claimant.[32]

Judgments

16–19   To help in calculating the section 8 deduction, where a case goes to full trial and judgment is given, section 15 of the 1997 Act requires the judge to specify the sums awarded for each head of damage listed in Schedule 2, namely past loss of earnings, past care and past mobility. No such requirement is imposed if the order is by consent. However, section 17 makes it very clear that recoupment by the CRU is to be ignored by the courts when assessing damages. So judges will not be required to make section 8 calculations. They will have to consider the section 8 calculation once costs are put in issue on Part 36 payments. Section 15 of the Act provides:

>   (1) This section applies where a court makes an order for a compensation payment to be made in any case, unless the order is made with the consent of the injured person and the person by whom the payment is to be made.

>   (2) The court must, in the case of each head of compensation listed in column 1 of Schedule 2 to which any of the compensation payment is attributable, specify in the order the amount of compensation payment which is attributable to that head. See the recent case of *Mitchell v. Laing* (*The Times*, January 28, 1998) The court must specify the amount of compensation payment attributed to each head of damages during the five-year post-accident period even if the court order date is less than five years post-accident. The compensators had to deduct those benefits paid or due to be paid up to the date of payment of the sum actually awarded.

Part 36 Payments

16–20   Section 16 of the 1997 Act and regulation 8 of the 1997 Regulations govern the law as to payments into court in personal injury cases. These sections have now been supplemented by the provisions of the Civil

---

[31] See s. 14 and reg. 11.
[32] See reg. 11(5).

Procedure Rules 1998 which came into force on April 26, 1999. Rule 36.23 CPR relates to the deduction of benefits in Part 36 payments. The rules make important changes to the position on payments into court and benefits paid.

By Rule 36.23(2)

"A defendant to a money claim may make an offer to settle the claim which will **16–21** have the consequences set out in this Part, without making a Part 36 payment if—

   (a) at the time he makes the offer he has applied for, but not received, a certificate of recoverable benefit; and
   (b) he makes a Part 36 payment not more than seven days after he receives the certificate."

By Rule 36.23(3)

"A Part 36 payment notice must state— **16–22**

   (a) the amount of gross compensation;
   (b) the name and amount of any benefit by which that gross amount is reduced in accordance with section 8 and Schedule 2 of the 1997 Act; and
   (c) that the sum paid in is the net amount after deduction of the amount of benefit."

By Rule 36.23(4)

"For the purposes of rule 36.20, a claimant fails to better a Part 36 payment if he **16–23** fails to obtain judgment for more than the gross sum specified in the Part 36 payment notice."

By Rule 36.23(5)

"Where— **16–24**

   (a) a Part 36 payment has been made; and
   (b) application is made for the money in court to be paid out, the court may treat the money in court as being reduced by the sum equivalent to any further recoverable benefits paid to the claimant since the date of payment into court and may direct payment out accordingly."

Para. 10.1 of Practice Direction 36 (1/PD/36)

This paragraph specifically relates to Part 36 payments and recovery of **16–25** benefits. It states;

"10.1 Where a defendant makes a Part 36 payment in respect of a claim for a sum or part of a sum:

(1) which falls under the heads of damage set out in column 1 of Schedule 2 of the Social Security (Recovery of Benefits) act 1997 in respect of recoverable benefits received by the claimant as set out in column 2 of that Schedule, and

(2) where the defendant is liable to pay recoverable benefits to the Secretary of State the defendant should obtain from the Secretary of State a certificate of recoverable benefits and file the certificate with the Part 36 payment notice.

10.2   If a defendant wishes to offer to settle a claim where he has applied for but not yet received a certificate of recoverable benefits, he may, provided that he makes a Part 36 payment not more than seven days after he has received the certificate, make a Part 36 offer which will have the costs and other consequences set out in rules 36.13 and 36.20.

10.3 The Part 36 payment notice should state in addition to the requirements set out in rule 36.6(2):

(1) the total amount represented by the Part 36 payment (the gross compensation);

(2) that the defendant has reduced this sum by £.........., in accordance with section 8 of and Schedule 2 to the Social Security (Recovery of Benefits) 1997, which was calculated as follows:
Name of Benefit............... Amount...............
and,

(3) that the amount paid in, being the sum of £.......... is the net amount after the deduction of the amount of benefit.

10.4   On acceptance of a Part 36 payment to which this paragraph relates, a claimant will receive the sum in court which will be net of the recoverable benefit.

10.5   In establishing at trial whether a claimant has bettered or obtained a judgment more advantageous than a Part 36 payment to which this paragraph relates, the court will base its decision on the gross sum specified in the Part 36 payment notice.

11.1   Where a party on whom a Part 36 offer, a Part 36 payment notice or a notice of acceptance is to be served is legally represented, the Part 36 offer, Part 36 payment notice and notice of acceptance must be served on the legal representative.

11.2   In a claim arising out of an accident involving a motor vehicle on a road or in a public place:

(1) where damages claimed include a sum for hospital expenses and

(2) the defendant or his insurer pays that sum to the hospital under section 157 of the Road Traffic Act 1988, the defendant must give notice of that payment to the court and all other parties to the proceedings.

11.3   Money paid into court:

(1) as a part 36 payment which is not accepted by the claimant or

(2) under a court order,
will be placed in a basic account . . . for interest to accrue.

11.4   Where money referred to in paragraph 12.3 . . .is paid in in respect of a child or patient it will be placed in a special investment account for interest to accrue . . ."

The basic point is that the defendant will pay a sum into court which is **16–26**
net of the section 8 deduction, but the claimant now has to know what the
gross offer is and has to be told in effect how the section 8 deduction has
been calculated as the name and amount of benefit is to be specified—
contrary to the position prior to the introduction of the Civil Procedure
Rules. It is also now the gross sum of damages which matters in relation to
ascertaining whether the payment in has been beaten. There should,
therefore, be no argument on whether, for example, some benefits should
in fact have been deducted. Problems are envisaged where a defendant
makes a Part 36 payment in, but makes an incorrect deduction under
section 8. Is the claimant to be forced to accept a net sum which is too low
just because the gross offer is correct? In *Bajwa v. British Airways*,[33] the
Court of Appeal held that a payment in made under the old law but not
adjusted after the new law came into force was to be looked at gross rather
than net and awarded costs accordingly. In addition, if there is a delayed
application to take sums paid in, it is now possible for the court to deduct
the claimant's further benefits obtained from date of payment in. The
making of a payment into court "shall be treated for the purposes of the
1997 Act as the making of a compensation payment"[34] and "a current
certificate of recoverable benefits shall be lodged with the payment".[35] The
effect of regulation 8(1)(a) and the Civil Procedure Rules as above, is that
the deductible benefits *must* be withheld from the payment in. However,
the obligation on the part of defendants to pay benefits to the CRU does
not arise until "the person making the payment into court has been
notified that the whole or *any part* of the payment into court has been paid
out of court to or for the relevant party." This is sufficiently wide to cover
interim payments paid out of monies in court.

Complex Cases

Section 18 of the 1997 Act and regulation 9 of the 1997 Regulations **16–27**
govern CRU repayment in complex cases or structured settlements. In
summary, where partial recoupment has already occurred after a interim
payment, that is taken into account when calculating the final recoupment.
The 1997 Act also deals with payment by various defendants to one
claimant. The usual practice is for the defendants to agree the apportionment of the CRU recoupment. Section 19 empowers the Secretary of State
to make regulations allowing the DSS to apportion the CRU recoupment,
but no such regulations have been made and it may be left to the insurance
industry to continue their apportionment agreements.

---

[33] [1999] P.I.Q.R. Q152.
[34] See reg. 8(1)(a).
[35] See reg. 8(1)(b).

Structured Settlements

16–28 Regulation 10 states as follows:

"10.—(1) This regulation applies where—

(a) in final settlement of an injured person's claim, an agreement is entered into—

(i) for the making of periodical payments (whether of an income or capital nature); or
(ii) for the making of such payments and lump sum payments; and

(b) apart from the provisions of this regulation, those payments would fall to be treated for the purposes of the 1997 Act as compensation payments.

(2) Where this regulation applies, the provisions of the 1997 Act and these Regulations shall be modified in the following way—

(a) the compensator in question shall be taken to have made on that day a single compensation payment;
(b) the relevant period in the case of the compensator in question shall be taken to end (if it has not done so already) on the day of settlement;
(c) payments under the agreement referred to in paragraph (1)(a) shall be taken not to be compensation payments;
(d) paragraphs (5) and (7) of regulation 11 shall not apply.

(3) Where any further payment falls to be made to or in respect of the injured person otherwise than under the agreement in question, paragraph (2) shall be disregarded for the purpose of determining the end of the relevant period in relation to that further payment.

(4) In any case where—

(a) the person making the periodical payments ('the secondary party') does so in pursuance of arrangements entered into with another ('the primary party') (as in a case where the primary party purchases an annuity for the injured person from the secondary party), and
(b) apart from those arrangements, the primary party would have been regarded as the compensator,

then for the purposes of the 1997 Act, the primary party shall be regarded as the compensator and the secondary party shall not be so regarded.

(5) In this regulation 'the day of settlement' means—

(a) if the agreement referred to in paragraph (1)(a) is approved by a court, the day on which that approval is given; and
(b) in any other case, the day on which the agreement is entered into."

16–29 Regulation 10(2)(a) and (b) trigger the fact of a compensation payment being made on the day of settlement. Thus, insurers are liable for payment of the CRU come what may. Can they deduct it from the "settlement" sums in some way? Regulation 10(2)(c) makes that part of the structure relating to future periodical payments and lump sums not subject to deduction. What about the lump sums "rainy day" contingency sums payable on or shortly after settlement which is part of the structure?

Regulation 10(1)(a) specifically includes the making of lump sum payments which are to "be taken not to be compensation payments". But do they refer only to future payments under the structure? Why should an up-front lump sum be exempt if based largely on past loss? It may be that the practical answer is for defendants not to agree to a structure unless they can set off the benefits they have to pay in any event against the contingency fund. Regulation 10(3) envisages the possibility of a number of compensators being involved.

Apportioning the Section 8 Deduction

Problems may arise when parties are attempting to settle personal injury **16–30** cases because defendants will be minded to attempt to minimise general damages and maximise special damage against which the section 8 deduction bites, whereas claimants will seek to do the opposite.

Contributory Negligence

There is a strain on both the claimant and the defendant. Consider the **16–31** following facts:

> Assume that the claimants's claim is worth £50,000 and liability is in dispute. The CRU benefits stand at £30,000. At trial the claimant is found to have contributed 75 per cent by his own negligence. The claimant will, therefore, recover only £12,500 and special damages will probably be wiped out perhaps leaving the claimant with generals of say £3,000. But the defendant will have to repay the whole £30,000 to the CRU.

No appeal or review will affect this liability. It is not a medical issue. However, the wording of section 1(2) of the 1997 Act makes it clear that the trigger for recoupment, namely payment of compensation, is intended to cover payments where the defendant is only partly liable for the injury or accident.

Interest

Interest is awarded on damages pursuant to the Supreme Court Act **16–32** 1981, s. 35A or the County Courts Act 1984, s. 69 and in accordance with the principles set out in *Jefford v. Gee*.[36] When the old law was introduced,

---

[36] [1970] Q.B. 130.

section 81(5) of the 1992 Act provided expressly that recoupment of benefits would be disregarded in the assessment of damages by the court. Did this mean that when calculating interest the benefits received by the claimant were to be disregarded? It probably did because Parliament considered in necessary to insert section 103 into the 1992 Act, which stated that in assessing interest on damages benefits should first be deducted. The 1997 Act contains a similar provision to the old section 81(5) which is set out in section 17. However, section 103 of the 1992 Act was repealed and no equivalent provision has replaced it. There is now the decision of the House of Lords in *Wisely v. John Fulton (Plumbers) Ltd*,[37] where it was held that, in personal injury actions, claimants do not have to give credit for deductible benefits received when calculating interest on past loss. The scheme of the 1997 Act was held to lead to the conclusion that benefits received by the claimant should be disregarded from the assessment of interest as well as the assessment of damages and the claimant was entitled to be awarded interest upon the special damages in respect of which judgment was given, including the sum of benefits, which the defendant must eventually pay over to the DSS. The House of Lords dismissed the defendant's appeals stating that the claimant who received such benefits (which would be repayable to the DSS) was entitled to recover interest on all his damages for past loss of earnings.[38]

Persons under a Disability—Approval of Settlement

16–33   The Act is silent on the point of approval of awards to patients and infants. However, the reference to the "consent of the injured person" must indicate capacity on the part of the injured person to give consent. Where the injured person is incapable of giving consent the section 15(1) exception will not apply and the obligation to apportion will apply. Thus, it is to be expected that judges will want to know the effect of any benefit deductions upon any proposed settlement that requires the approval of the court.

The Causation Problem

16–34   The claimant purports to value his claim at £50,000. It is (say) a chronic pain case. The claimant has a number of experts (orthopaedic/psychiatric etc.) Not all are wholly supportive of causation. The defendants have their own expert evidence which limits causation to a few years only. They may also have video evidence and/or enquiry agent evidence throwing some

---

[37] [2000] 2 All E.R. 545.
[38] 1998 S.L.T. 1026.

doubt or some considerable doubt on the claimant's alleged incapacity. The defendants value the case at £15,000. The CRU sum is £40,000 which covers a period of five years. The defendants' medical evidence puts the causation period at three years. All the CRU is deductible from past loss of earnings, care or mobility. The defendants pay in the ringfenced amount of general damages re PSLA of £10,000. The claimant knows he has been videoed and watched, decides his claim for loss of earnings was tenuous in any event and his experts are too "lukewarm" for a fight. He takes the £10,000 paid in and costs. The defendants are then stuck with a CRU sum to pay of £40,000 when it should really only be £24,000, on their evidence (*i.e.* three years at benefits of £8,000 p.a.). The defendants require a refund of £16,000.

There is no decision of the court to use in a subsequent Medical Appeal Tribunal hearing under section 12(3) of the Act. One possible solution is to appeal the certificate to the MAT. It might be appropriate to opt for a non-oral hearing to keep the costs down, sending in a fully reasoned application together with the relevant medical reports and any affidavit evidence from an enquiry agent plus a copy of the video and the doctor's comments on it. An oral hearing may be required by the chairman, but no costs will be recouped.

In practice, it is unlikely the CRU will seek to recover benefit already paid to the claimant, except possibly in the clearest possible case of a fraudulent claim. It is unlikely, therefore, that there will be any contest on the medical evidence so expensive live expert medical evidence should be obviated in most cases. One could also of course pray in aid the fact that the payment in was accepted. Another solution might be to act early and request a review of the certificate under section 10. This section may just "stretch" to cover a "mistake" on causation. Medical reports will need to be sent, as well as any other relevant evidence (enquiry agent statement/video). The problem here is that the CRU may well ask the claimant for his views and in the event of a dispute (particularly on the expert medical evidence) may well not carry out any review and alter the certificate. There is, however, no reason why a review cannot be requested, followed by an appeal after a payment-in is accepted or after a trial if necessary. Consider the following:

> Claimant is unemployed before accident. It is now four years after **16–35** the accident. The CRU is £20,000 (£5,000 per year). Claimant suffered a whiplash injury. Claimant's doctor says five years acceleration (say £6,000). Defendant's doctor says 18 months acceleration (say £2,500). Proposal—joint approach to the CRU for a "review" on the basis of 18 months acceleration. Result—if successful CRU reduces to £7,500. Trade off—insurers save £12,500 and agree to pay £8,000 generals to claimant. Benefit to claimant—£2,000 more than his case is worth. Benefit to insurers—avoids having to pay £26,000 and limits outlay to £8,000 + £7,500 = £15,500.

Regulations made to date are:

- the Social Security (Recovery of Benefit) Regulations 1997 (S.I. 1997 No. 2205);
- the Social Security (Recovery of Benefits) (Appeals) Regulations 1997 (S.I. 1997 No. 2237);
- the Social Security (Recovery of Benefits) Act 1997 (Commencement) Order 1997 (S.I. 1997 No. 2).

17. The Mentally Incapable Claimant and The Court of Protection: Procedure, Practice and Damages

Introduction

Any claimant who by reason of mental disorder is incapable of managing **17–01** and administering his affairs must have a litigation friend to conduct the action in which he claims damages for personal injury and consequential loss. In all cases of serious brain injury, careful consideration must be given to the capacity of the claimant and where appropriate the action begun in the name of the litigation friend.

Moreover, where a claimant, due to mental disorder, is incapable of managing his property and financial affairs, and has assets that need to be administered, the Court of Protection, being an office of the Supreme Court, is empowered to manage those assets. The Court of Protection charges fees for its services of management and administration. These fees, past and future, may be recovered as part of the damages claimed on behalf of the injured claimant. In addition, there are ancillary and related expenses that are likely to be incurred and these too may be recovered as damages.

The lawyers acting on behalf of a claimant who is in fact mentally incapable have no discretion as to whether or not the Court of Protection should be involved. Notification and submission to the jurisdiction is mandatory once there are assets or the probable likelihood of assets to be managed on behalf of the claimant. Any interim payment will be regarded as an asset for this purpose.

The Court of Protection deals with the elderly who are disabled by the mental infirmities of old age, with patients who are suffering from mainstream mental illness, with the mentally handicapped, and with claimants who have sustained from serious brain damage and have been awarded damages for personal injuries. The last category is the concern of this Chapter.

The Master of the Court of Protection himself deals with the cases of major awards arising from personal injury and clinical negligence claims. Any party who is aggrieved by a decision which was made otherwise than at an attended hearing may apply to the Court within eight days to have it reviewed. On hearing the application, the Court may either confirm or revoke its previous decision or make any other order that it thinks fit. Any party who is aggrieved at an order or decision made at a hearing or review may appeal to a nominated judge of the High Court, Chancery Division, within 14 days.[1]

The Court appoints a receiver to have day-to-day control and responsibility for the sums that are released for the benefit of the claimant.

The relevant statutory and procedural framework is provided by the Mental Health Act 1983, the Court of Protection Rules 1994, the Court of Protection (Amendment) Rules 1999 and the Civil Procedure Rules 1999 ("CPR") Part 21.

Claimants Subject to the Jurisdiction of the Court of Protection

17–02   The purpose of the Court of Protection[2] is to protect and administer the property and affairs of any person who is incapable, by reason of mental disorder, of managing and administering his property and affairs.[3] Any person whom the Master of the Court of Protection is satisfied, after having considered medical evidence, is so incapable should be described as a patient. Thereupon the Court of Protection assumes responsibility for such a person.

A claimant who is mentally incapable must conduct his action by a litigation friend and will be described as a patient in the statement of case. However, the Court of Protection will not normally become involved until there are actual assets to be managed or the real likelihood of assets to be managed. The trigger point for such involvement is not defined in either the Court of Protection Rules 1994 or in the CPR. In practice an application to the Court of Protection for the appointment of a receiver and the assumption of responsibility should be made once there is a substantial interim payment (in excess of £20,000 in aggregate) or the prospect of a substantial final award (*e.g.* where liability has been admitted and the action is proceeding on damages only).

Mental disorder means mental illness, arrested or incomplete development of mind, psychopathic disorder and any other disorder or disability or mind.[4]

The victims of catastrophic head injury and brain damage, having suffered unconsciousness, prolonged periods of rehabilitation and with continuing dementia or loss of cognitive functions, are likely to fall within the definition of patient.

---

[1] Court of Protection Rules 1994, rules 56 and 57.
[2] The Court of Protection and the Protection Division of the Public Trust Office are situated at Stewart House, 24, Kingsway, London WC2B 6JX. Telephone 020 7269 7000. LDX 37965 Kingsway. I am grateful to Master Denzil Lush, the Master of the Court of Protection, for his help with this Chapter.
[3] Mental Health Act 1983, ss. 93(2) and 94(2).
[4] Mental Health Act 1983, s. 1(2).

In the course of the preparation of the claimant's case, expert medical evidence on condition and likely prognosis will be obtained as a matter of routine from a neurologist or a neurosurgeon and/or a psychiatrist. One of these experts may be instructed to give an opinion on the claimant's mental capacity, but this is not mandatory. The requisite medical certificate (form CP3) is frequently signed by the patient's General Practitioner. However a registered medical practitioner must sign the form. A certificate from a clinical psychologist or similar expert is not acceptable.

The incapacity to manage and administer one's affairs is not defined by statute.

The actual wording of the Mental Health Act 1963 suggests that the test is probably subjective.[5] The question of the degree of incapacity of managing and administering a patient's property and financial affairs must be related to all the circumstances including the state in which the patient lives and the complexity and importance of the property and affairs which he has to manage and administer.[6]

In *Re MacGregor*,[7] Mr Justice Starke in Australia upheld the subjective **17–03** test and said:

> "The Act itself appears to me to lay down the test. It speaks of managing his affairs, not the ordinary routine affairs of man. The court under the Act is exercising its protective jurisdiction in respect of individuals, not a class of persons, albeit before the jurisdiction is exercised it must be shown that the person is an infirm person for the purpose of the Act."

A cerebrally injured claimant may have the capacity to handle small sums of money under supervision, *e.g.* buying goods at a supermarket. However the same person may very well require help in order to make decisions about his affairs and would be vulnerable to suggestions about expenditure. Such a person would be unable to manage a substantial award of compensatory damages given the size of the award and the need to make careful investment decisions. Provided that the test of mental incapacity is satisfied, in such a case the Court of Protection must be involved.

Before the Court of Protection will assume jurisdiction, a claimant who is a patient, as defined by the Mental Health Act 1983 and the CPR[8], must have assets that need to be managed and administered. If he has no capital

---

[5] Section 94(2) "... incapable, by reason of mental disorder, of managing and administering his property and affairs. CPR rule 21.1(2)(b) and the Practice Direction—Children and Patients which supplements CPR Part 21 at paragraph 1.1 each define "patient" as a person who by reason of mental disorder within the meaning of the Mental Health Act 1983 is incapable of managing and administering his **own** affairs (author's emphasis).

[6] Heywood & Massey: Court of Protection Practice 12th ed., 1991) at page 17; *Re CAF* (Mr Justice Willberforce, as he then was) March 23, 1962; the Court of Protection by Master Denzil Lush, *PI Major Claims Handling: Cost-Effective Case Management*, Goldrein, De Haas & Frankel (1999).

[7] [1985] V.R. 861; *cf. PY v. RJS* [1982] 2 N.S.W.L.R. 700, cited by Lush, *ibid*.

[8] CPR r. 21.1(2)(b).

and no income other than DSS benefits, the Court of Protection will not usually wish to become involved. In claims involving brain damaged claimants, there is normally no need to apply to the Court of Protection for the appointment of a receiver until either a substantial interim or a final award is about to be made.

17–04   However, save as ordered by the court[9] in which the action is heard, if the claimant is mentally incapacitated and falls within the definition of a patient, no one may deal with any capital or income on his behalf until a receiver has been appointed.[10] The litigation friend may not do so, nor may the instructed solicitor.[11]

The basic practice is clear. Where, in any action, money is recovered on behalf of or for the benefit of a patient or money paid into court is accepted on behalf of a patient, the money shall be dealt with in accordance with directions given by the court in which the action is heard and not otherwise.[12] The directions may provide that the money shall be paid wholly or partly into court and so invested. Where there is an urgent need for the purchase of special equipment or accommodation or similar, the court may order the use of the funds for such a purpose.[13] Unless the remaining sum of money is modest, the appropriate order is to transfer the balance to the Court of Protection with a direction that an application be made for the appointment of a receiver.

Where an interim payment is ordered in the course of on-going litigation, the court of record should be invited to give directions about the placement of the awarded sum. Moreover, where a voluntary interim payment to a patient is agreed between the parties the approval of the action court must first be obtained[14] and this approval hearing will give the court the opportunity to give directions about the placement of the interim award. Unless the interim payment is less than £20,000 and the action court gives an alternative direction, both ordered and voluntary interim awards trigger the involvement of the Court of Protection. An application should be made to the Court of Protection for the appointment of a receiver who will then have authority in respect of the interim payment.

---

[9] By CPR 21PD 8.2: the court may order that certain sums be paid direct to the litigation friend or his legal representative for the immediate benefit of the patient or for expenses incurred on his behalf.

[10] Where the sum to be administered is under £20,000, it may be retained in the action court and placed in the special investment account, invested by the investment managers of the Public Trust Office or otherwise invested as directed by the court: CPR 21PD 10 and 11. In any event, if the Court of Protection is not involved, such sum should be the subject of direction from the Master or district judge of the action court.

[11] *Leather v. Kirby* [1965] 1 W.L.R. 1489; *M v. Lester* [1966] 1 W.L.R. 134; and see Lush: The Court of Protection, *op. cit.*

[12] CPR rule 21.11.

[13] CPR 21 PD 8.2: the court may direct that the money be paid into the High Court for investment; and may direct that certain sums be paid direct to the patient, his litigation friend or his legal representative for the immediate benefit of the patient or for expenses incurred on his behalf.

[14] CPR 21 PD 1.7.

Proceedings on Behalf of a Patient: Litigation Friend

A patient, being a person under a disability, is obliged to conduct any 17–05
proceedings in the name of a litigation friend.[15] Any step in the action
taken before the patient has a litigation friend will have no effect, unless
the Court otherwise orders.[16] A person may act as a litigation friend
without order of the court if he is files a certificate of suitability.[17] A person
is suitable if he:

(a) states that he consents to act;

(b) states that he knows or believes the claimant is a patient;

(c) states the grounds of his belief and if his belief is based on medical
opinion, attaching any relevant document to the certificate;

(d) can fairly and competently conduct proceedings on behalf of the
patient;

(e) has no interest adverse to that of the patient; and

(f) undertakes to pay any costs which the patient may be ordered to
pay in relation to the proceedings, subject to any right he may have
to be repaid from the assets of the patient

(g) has signed the certificate of suitability in verification of its
contents.[18]

The person who is to act as the litigation friend must file the certificate
of suitability at the time when the claim is made, stating that he satisfies
each of the conditions of specified suitability.[19] The certificate must be
served on the person with whom the patient resides or in whose care the
patient is. The litigation friend must also file with the court a certificate of
service when he files the certificate of suitability.[20]

The court has power to change the litigation friend and to prevent a
person from acting further as the litigation friend.[21] An application for a
change of litigation friend must be supported by evidence. A new litigation
friend will not be appointed unless the court is satisfied that he complies

---

[15] CPR r. 21.2(1).
[16] CPR r. 21.3(4).
[17] CPR rr. 21.4 and 21.5.
[18] CPR r. 21.4(3); and 21PD 2.3.
[19] A person may be authorised by the Master of the Court of Protection under section
96(1)(h) of the Mental Health Act 1983 to conduct legal proceedings in the name of the
patient or on his behalf. Such a person will become the litigation friend by filing an official
copy of the order, or other document which constitutes his authorisation to act, at the time
when the claim is made.
[20] CPR r. 21.5 and rule 6.6.
[21] CPR r. 21.7.

with the conditions of suitability. The application may be made, for example, where the Court of Protection or the solicitors acting on behalf of the claimant believe that the litigation friend is no longer acting in the best interests of the patient claimant. This may occur when the litigation friend seeks to use, or indeed succeeds in using, an interim payment for his own benefit or advantage rather than for the benefit of the patient.

Approval of a Settlement on Behalf of a Patient

17–06   No compromise or settlement of the patient's claim for damages may be concluded without the prior approval of the court in which the claim was brought.[22] Without such approval, any agreement between the parties has no validity and neither side is obliged to consider the compromise as binding.[23]

The approval of the court must also be obtained before the making of a voluntary interim payment to a patient.[24]

An agreement for the settlement on a patient's claim may be reached before proceedings are begun. Approval by the High Court or County Court is required as if proceedings had been begun, but the application for approval should be brought in accordance with CPR Part 8, the Alternative Procedure for Claims.[25]

The Court of Protection expects to be informed of any proposed compromise of a personal injury or clinical negligence action prior to approval being sought from the court in which the action has been brought.[26] This is usually effected by correspondence rather than attendance and the Court will need to see the statements of case, the medical reports, other expert reports, the schedules which have been served on each side and counsel's opinion on quantum.

17–07   Where a compromise includes a structured settlement, the Court will also strictly need to see the documents particularised in the Practice Note (Structured Settlements: Court's Approval) [1992] 1 W.L.R. 328; 1 All E.R. 862, namely:

---

[22] CPR r. 21.10.

[23] *Dietz v. Lennig Chemicals* [1969] 1 A.C. 170; [1967] 2 All E.R. 282.

[24] CPR 21PD 1.7.

[25] CPR r. 21.10(2).

[26] This is the view of Master Lush in *PI Major Claims Handling: Cost Effective Management*, Goldrein, de Haas & Frenkel (1999): "Any proposed compromise ... must be approved by the Court of Protection prior to approval by the Queen's Bench Division or District Registry." No specific authority is given in support of the proposition. However, by section 96(1)(h) of the Mental Health Act 1983 the Master of the Court of Protection has the power to such directions as he thinks fit for the conduct of legal proceedings in the name of the patient. As a matter of practice the Court of Protection will assume responsibility for the approval of a proposed settlement. Certainly the Master expects to be consulted for the purpose of approval in all cases which involve a structured settlement.

(a) the statements of case (the pleadings);

(b) an opinion of counsel assessing the value of the claim on a conventional basis—unless a preliminary approval has already been given—and, if practical, the opinion of counsel on the proposed structured settlement;[27]

(c) a report of forensic accountants setting out the advantages and disadvantages, if any, of the structure bearing in mind the claimant's life expectation and the anticipated costs of future care;

(d) a draft of the proposed agreement as approved by the Inland Revenue[28] and by the Treasury where the defendant is a health authority;[29]

(e) sufficient material with which to satisfy the Court that enough capital is available free of the structure to meet anticipated future needs—for example, accommodation and transport;

(f) sufficient material with which to satisfy the Court that the structure is secure and backed by responsible insurers;

(g) evidence of other assets available to the claimant beyond the material award.[30]

The documents should be lodged with the Public Trust Office prior to **17–08** the court of action hearing in order to obtain the consent of the Court of Protection, if this consent has not previously been obtained. In practice, the court in which the action is heard does not now insist on all the documents being lodged where a comprehensive opinion from counsel has been provided and the advantages of a structured settlement are clear.

In any event, the requirement under item (f) is now largely otiose since the amendments made by the Finance Act 1966 to the Income and Corporation Taxes Act 1988 and the coming into force of the Damages Act 1996 on September 24, 1996. The claimant will be the policy-holder of the annuity[31] under the structured settlement agreement, and will therefore enjoy the security of the Policyholders Protection Act 1975. Moreover, by virtue of section 4 of the 362 Damages Act 1996 the protection under the 1975 Act is to be 100 per cent and not 90 per cent as before.

---

[27] These opinions are not disclosed to the defendant.

[28] The specific approval of the Inland Revenue for each and every agreement is not, as a matter of practice sought, provided the agreement follows the approved form.

[29] Present experience indicates that approval by the Treasury may take a prolonged period as a value for money report is prepared. It is, therefore, crucial that proper agreement is reached in respect of the continuing liability for the payment of interest from the defendant to the claimant.

[30] The other assets available to the claimant are usually confined to the continuing non-means-tested benefits. The means-tested benefits will terminate on the receipt of the compensation funds.

[31] Save in cases where the defendant, for example a health authority, self-funds the structure.

The intermediary who is instructed on behalf of the claimant will ensure that the life office that provides the annuity is an authorised insurance company within the meaning of the 1975 Act. The structured settlement report should contain confirmation of this fact.

The Transfer of Damages to the Court of Protection

17–09   The court in which the action is heard and the Court of Protection both have protective and supervisory functions in relation to any money recovered on behalf of a patient claimant. The action court will give approval for payment and then give directions for the placement of the funds. In the case of any substantial payment (over £30,000) the court will normally direct that the funds be transferred to the Court of Protection for the purpose of investment and management.[32] The practice is applicable as much to interim payments as to final awards. Under no circumstances should money recovered on behalf of a patient be managed or expended by either the litigation friend or the solicitors acting on behalf of the claimant.

Where the sum to be administered is over £30,000 the order approving the settlement or the interim payment should contain a direction to the litigation friend to apply to the Court of Protection for the appointment of a receiver, after which the fund will be transferred to the Court of Protection for investment and management.[33]

Where the sum to be administered is under £20,000 it may be retained in court and invested by being placed in the special investment account of the Courts Funds Office, or invested by the investment managers of the Public Trust Office or upon the specific direction of the court.[34]

Where the sum to be administered is between £20,000 and £30,000 the advice of the Master of the Court of Protection should be sought[35] prior to the application before the action court for approval and directions.

The damages awarded by way of interim payment or final compensation should be transferred to the Court of Protection with a form of order drafted pursuant to the Practice Note (Mental Health: Transfer of Damages) [1991] 1 W.L.R. 2; [1991] 1 All E.R. 436 issued on September 7, 1990.[36] The fund of damages will not be controlled by the litigation friend at any stage.

---

[32] CPR r. 21.11 and 21PD 8.1 and 11.1.
[33] CPR 21PD 11.2(1).
[34] CPR 21PD 11.2(2).
[35] CPR 21PD 11.2(3).
[36] The judgment should include a provision to the following effect: "That the defendant do within days pay the said sum of £   into court to be placed to and accumulated in a special account pending an application by the litigation friend to the Court of Protection for the appointment of a Receiver for the claimant and that on such appointment being made the said sum of £... together with any interest thereon [subject to a first charge under the Legal Aid Act 1988] be transferred to the Court of Protection to the credit of the claimant to be dealt with as the Court of Protection in its discretion shall think fit."

It is important to remember that any interim payment is subject to the **17–10** control of the court in which the action has been brought and is also subject to the control of the Court of Protection in the case of substantial payments. Neither the litigation friend nor the solicitors acting on behalf of the claimant are empowered simply to receive, control or even less to expend interim payments which have been paid either by order of the court or made voluntarily, without order. Unless the action court makes specific directions for the use of the interim payment or for investment in accordance with CPD 21PD 11, a receiver should be appointed by the Court of Protection and the funds transferred.

Where the claimant is both a patient and a child, and is likely to remain a patient as defined on reaching full age, the compensation will be administered as a patient's fund under CPR 21PD 11.2 and the Court of Protection will normally agree to assume jurisdiction.[37] It is in the claimant's best interests that a long-term regime of investment should be put in place at an early stage.[38]

In order that the Court Funds Office of the action court may release to the Court of Protection a damages fund which is subject to a legal aid charge,[39] the litigation friend or his legal representative should provide the relevant area office of the Legal Service Commission with an undertaking in respect of a sum to cover their costs. The area office will then advise the Court Funds Office in writing of that sum, enabling the Office to transfer the balance to the Court of Protection on receipt of a CFO form 200 payment schedule authorised by the court.[40] The amount reserved for costs will remain in the Special Account[41] to gain interest until the area office confirms that it can be released to the Court of Protection or to the Legal Services Commission, as the case may be.

The Appointment of the Receiver

The day-to-day financial affairs of the patient are controlled by a receiver **17–11** who is appointed by, and subject to the supervision of, the Court of Protection.

Historically, the Court has tended to appoint the litigation friend as receiver. This will generally be a member of the claimant's family. The Public Trustee may be appointed as receiver of last resort.

---

[37] CPR PD21 8.4.

[38] *Stringman v. McArdle* [1994] 1 W.L.R. 1653 (CA): a decision concerning an interim payment.

[39] Where a patient is Publically funded, the damages fund will be subject to a first charge (the statutory legal aid charge) and an order for the investment of the money of the patient's behalf must contain a direction to that effect: CPR 21PD 8.5.

[40] CPR PD11.4, 11.5, 11.6 and 11.7.

[41] The current rate of interest is 7 per cent, from August 1, 1999. The rate was previously 8 per cent.

A receiver is entitled to recover his reasonable out-of-pocket expenses, including postage, telephone calls and travelling expenses but is granted remuneration from the patient's funds only in exceptional circumstances, for example if he is a solicitor, accountant or other similar professional.

Before applying to become the receiver, the applicant should give notice of his intention to all the patient's relatives of a degree of relationship that is equal or nearer than the applicant or the proposed receiver.[42]

The following documents should be completed and returned to the Public Trust Office:

(a) two copies of the application (form CP1);

(b) the medical certificate (form CP3);

(c) the certificate of family and property (form CP5);

(d) a copy of the patient's will and other testamentary documents (if any);

(e) payment for the commencement fee (currently £100).

The Public Trust Office will generally take up a reference as to the suitability of the proposed receiver by sending a questionnaire (form CP8) to the referee named in the certificate of family and property.

17–12 Where an order is to be made appointing anyone other than the Public Trustee or the Official Solicitor as receiver, unless the Court otherwise orders, the receiver is required to give a security for the due performance of his duties.[43] The amount covered by the security bond is usually one and a half times the patient's annual income.

The receiver should open a receivership bank account that is then used for the receipt of income and the payment of expenditure. The receiver is required to deliver annual accounts of how the money received has been spent on behalf of the patient.[44] A receiver may prepare and submit his own accounts or he may instruct a solicitor, accountant or other professional (*e.g.* a case manager) to prepare them.

The receiver may purchase suitable accommodation on behalf of the patient, but only with the approval of the Court of Protection. This will be provided once the Court has had sight of a survey and valuation (and an architect's report where alterations are proposed), planning permission has been obtained for any alterations or extension, and evidence that there are sufficient funds for the purchase is available. Where the patient is an adult, the receiver will be authorised to sign the contract and transfer on behalf of the claimant. Where the patient is a child, the property must be

---

[42] CPR, r. 27.
[43] CPR, r. 58. The annual insurance premium will be a recoverable item.
[44] CPR, r. 63.

transferred to a minimum of two trustees who hold it on behalf of the claimant.

The Fees of the Court of Protection are Recoverable as a Head of Damage

A commencement fee is payable to the Court on any first application for **17–13** the appointment of a receiver and this may be recovered from the defendant as an item of past or prospective expense.

The claimant's fund of damages will be invested by the Public Trustee Office[45] on the advice of its investment managers. An investment policy is established for each patient. Where the fund is a sum in excess of £150,000 and the patient is likely to live longer that five years, the investment will usually be in a mixed portfolio of conventional and index-linked gilts, in UK ordinary shares and common investment funds (similar to unit trusts) with a cash balance being held in the Special Account. By rule 80(1) of the Court of Protection Rules 1994, an annual administration fee is payable for the investment and management service which is provided on behalf of the patient. The annual fee is calculated on the basis of a sliding scale.[46] This fee has a direct relationship to the clear annual income which has been earned from the investment of the compensation sum and which is at the disposal of the patient for his benefit each year.[47]

The past and future administration fees of the Court of Protection are recoverable against a defendant as a separate head of damages for pecuniary loss.[48]

The administration fees are claimed against the defendant as part of the damages to which the claimant is entitled, having been injured. They are not costs of the proceedings in the sense of the cost of providing the right to damages. Accordingly where a claimant is found to have been contrib-

---

[45] The Public Trustee Office is expected to be replaced by a Private agency in 2001.

[46] See Appendix 1, Court of Protection administration charges.

[47] CPR, r. 80(1): "An annual administration fee shall be payable in respect of the clear annual income at the disposal of the patient from the date of the issue of the first application for the appointment of a receiver or other originating process until the termination of the proceedings."

[48] The first decision on the point appears to have been by Edwin Jowett Q.C., sitting as a Deputy High Court Judge, as he then was, in *Duller v. South East Lincolnshire Engineers* [1981] C.L.Y. 585, May 2, 1980; the learned judge awarded damages for the future expenses of the Court of Protection, the claimant being unable to manage his own affairs, and the judge having himself directed the administration of the fund by the Court of Protection. The same judge gave a similar decision in *Futej v. Lewandowski* (1980) 124 S.J. 777. The Court of Appeal approved the principle in *Rialas v. Mitchell* (1984) 128 S.J. 704, *The Times*, July 17, 1984, Kemp & Kemp, A2–010, *per* O'Connor L.J.: "Finally, the defendant appealed against the £5,000 awarded for the fees of the Court of Protection in managing the damages fund. That was a loss which flowed directly from the plaintiff's injury and was recoverable from the defendant."

utorily negligent, the damages which represent the future administration fees will be subject to reduction as any other head of damage.[49]

The likely future administration fees cannot be precisely determined until the award of compensation has been made and from that sum have been deducted the past expenses and loss, including any gratuitous care, attributable to the claim. The final amount of the fund that is available for investment will only then be known, and at the end of the first year of investment, for the first time, the clear annual income can be estimated. However, in order to award an appropriate sum for the future expense, which is represented by the ongoing administration fees, the court in which the action is heard will have to make an early estimate of the likely fees that will be charged by the Court of Protection for the administration of the fund.

17–14 In order to calculate the likely clear annual income, the Court of Protection's current expected rate of return on capital invested first needs to be ascertained.[50] The likely rate of return is then applied to likely sum which is available for long term investment so that the annual investment income may be estimated. To such sum must be added the likely income or payments from any other source in order to produce the gross annual income.

The expression "clear annual income at the disposal of the patient" is not formally defined in the Court of Protection Rules 1994 and there is no judicial interpretation.

Generally speaking, the "clear income" can be calculated by deducting from the gross annual income to be received such payments that have to be made in order to earn the income.[51] In addition, certain receipts are deductible in order to calculate the clear income.

The most common deductions from the gross income are:

(a) social security benefits which do not attract income tax;

(b) capital sums received during the accounting year;

(c) premiums paid on the receiver's security bond;

(d) any income tax payments, but not capital gains tax;

---

[49] *Cassel v. Riverside Health Authority* [1992] P.I.Q.R. Q168, *per* Ralph Gibson L.J. at Q182: "I think it is clear that these costs do form part of the plaintiff's damages and are subject to the 10 per cent reduction."

[50] In practice, and for an obvious reason, the Court of Protection is reticent about estimating the likely future annual income. The stockbrokers employed by the Public Trustee have no special fast-track to the crystal ball of future investment. However, as a rule of thumb, the Court would expect to achieve a return at least equivalent to, or better than, the return from the Special Account of the Court Funds Office (currently 7 per cent gross as from August 1, 1999; previously 8 per cent).

[51] Heywood & Massey, *Court of Protection Practice* (12th ed., 1991) at page 85). A comprehensive list of deductible and non-deductible items for the calculation of the clear annual income is given at pp. 87–90.

(e) one half of any annuity payable;

(f) bank charges;

(g) refunds received;

(h) outgoings on a tenanted property;

(i) mortgage interest and interest on other charges on the patient's property;

(j) commissions and salaries to an agent for managing the patient's property;

(k) the salary of an agent of an unpaid receiver;

(l) solicitor's costs for preparing, lodging and passing receiver's accounts.

Where a structured settlement is eventually agreed between the parties, only one half of the periodical payments are treated as clear income for the purpose of calculating the administration fee.[52]

The following common items are not deductible:

(a) disablement or sickness benefits and attendance allowances;

(b) rents, rates, insurances and repairs of the house in which the patient resides;

(c) the wages of nurses or attendants employed for the provision of care to the patient;

(d) receiver's remuneration unless he definitely performs the duties of a land agent;

(e) costs of general management;

(f) the administration fee.

Once the clear annual income is estimated, this becomes the multiplicand for the judicial assessment of the future Court of Protection expenses.

The editors of Kemp & Kemp, *The Quantum of Damages*,[53] suggest that **17–15** the parties should make alternative realistic estimates of the likely award and that the Court of Protection be asked to assess the probable fees on the basis of each estimate in order to assess the relevant multiplicand. However, in practice, claims are generally settled and damages awarded on the estimates provided by the parties and without recourse to the Court of Protection.

---

[52] CPR r. 85(1).
[53] At 5–052.

In *Roberts v. Johnstone*,[54] Alliott J. adjourned the assessment of the future Court of Protection fees until after he had given judgment on all other heads of damage.

The amount of the annual administration fee varies as to whether the receiver is someone other than the Public Trustee or is the Public Trustee. If the Public Trustee is appointed, the Court of Protection administration fees will be substantially greater than if some other party, for example, a relative, friend or case manager, is appointed.[55]

It is now clearly established that the future expense of the administration fees constitutes a recoverable head of damage.[56] The appropriate award will be assessed on a multiplier-multiplicand basis. For a number of reasons the calculation is generally on the basis of broad estimation:

(a) A precisely accurate multiplicand cannot be calculated in advance of actual investment performance.

(b) The appropriate multiplier has been the subject of some judicial inconsistency.

(c) Finally, an allowance must be made for the fact that the investment fund will gradually decline in value with the draw down on the capital which is used for the continuing needs of the patient. In theory, the award of damages should reduce to a nil balance at death.

17–16   The judicial approach to the assessment of the correct multiplier has varied as this area of compensation has developed. In *Hodgson v. Trapp*,[57] the judge at first instance applied the full life multiplier to the annual fee multiplicand in order to produce an award of £11,900 (£850 × 14).

However, in the later decision of *Roberts v. Johnstone*,[58] Alliott J. refused to award the full sum as claimed, namely £2,100 (the multiplicand of the annual administration fees) × 16 (the full life multiplier applicable to the other heads of future expense). He held that the Court of Protection fees are based on the size of the fund which is being invested and that with the passage of time the capital would reduce as withdrawals were made from the fund. Consequently, the clear annual income at the disposal of the

---

[54] Kemp & Kemp, A4–007 at first instance; [1989] Q.B. 878, CA.
[55] CPR r. 78 and Appendix. For example, where the Public Trustee is not the receiver, the administration fee for a clear annual income of between £10,000 and £15,000 will be £800 per annum; for the same bracket of clear annual income where the Public Trustee is appointed the receiver, the administration fee will be £2,800 per annum.
[56] CPR 21PD 11.1: Fees are charged for the administration of funds by the Court of Protection and these should be provided for in any settlement.
[57] At first instance: Taylor J., 8 May 1987, Kemp & Kemp, A4–011 & A4–103; on appeal on different issues: [1989] A.C. 807; [1988] 3 All E.R. 870.
[58] At first instance: Alliott J., July 1986 (unreported), Kemp & Kemp, A-007; Court of Appeal: [1989] Q.B. 878.

patient would diminish. The judge adopted a broad brush approach and reduced the multiplier from 16 (used for other heads of future loss) to about 12, awarding the sum of £25,000 (being approximately £2,100 × 12). The claimant did not appeal against the decision on this issue.

In *Thames v. North West Surrey Health Authority*,[59] Tucker J. reduced the multiplier from 17 which was adopted for other life long expenses to 12.75 for the same reason as adopted by Alliott J. in *Roberts v. Johnstone*.

In *Cassel v. Riverside Health Authority*,[60] the multiplier was reduced from 18 (that was adopted for other heads of future expense) to 14 for the calculation of the award in respect of the future administration fees.

Despite the decision at first instance in *Hodgson v. Trapp*, the better view is that a reduction should be made from the full life multiplier which is applied to the multiplicand of the annual administration fees. The discount is logically justified because the capital sum gradually reduces with the passage of time, theoretically declining to a nil balance at death. As the fund becomes ever smaller, the annual clear income and the corresponding administration fee will reduce in amount.[61]

The adjustment of the award of damages for the future administration fees of the Court of Protection could be achieved by either a year on year estimation of the fees from a reducing fund or by a discount of the multiplier. In practice, the latter is adopted as a simpler and more practical solution to the problem

Further Recoverable Heads of Damage Arising from Receivership and the Court of Protection

In addition to the damages that represent the future fees to be levied by **17–17** the Court of Protection, the claimant patient may claim damages which actually arise from the fact of the receivership itself. This is a developing area of law and practice. If the receiver is a professional provider of services such as a solicitor or an accountant there will be future professional fees to be paid. If the receiver is a member of the family or a close friend, the patient will want to see such a person recompensed for his or her gratuitous services in the same way that a gratuitous carer is recompensed; in addition the gratuitous receiver may need to call on professional services to assist him in the process of receivership and fees for those services will then be incurred.

---

[59] January 11, 1990 (unreported); cited in *Cassel v. Riverside Health Authority* [1992] P.I.Q.R. Q1 and [1992] P.I.Q.R. Q168, CA.

[60] [1992] P.I.Q.R. Q1 and [1992] P.I.Q.R. Q168, CA.

[61] And see: Multipliers applicable to Court of Protection costs, *1999 Facts & Figures—Tables for the Calculation of Damages*, section H7. For example, if an award of £1,000,000 has been made using a 3 per cent full life multiplier of 8.5, it is appropriate to apply a reduced multiplier of 5.2 to the first year's Court fee in calculating the present day value of the fees over the full life period.

A Professional Receiver

17–18   Usually the receiver is a relative or close friend the patient. However, in some cases it will be appropriate to appoint as receiver the solicitor who has acted on behalf of the claimant throughout the litigation or an appropriate member of the same legal firm. The likely services of such a receiver will include regular meetings with the claimant and the family, distribution of income from the fund through a bank account, dealing with tax returns, commenting on investment advice obtained by the Court of Protection and preparing an annual account and report for the Court of Protection. The reasonable fees and expenses of such a professional receiver will be recoverable from the defendant in the action as a head of damage. They do not simply fall on the fund.

In *Cassel v. Riverside Health Authority*,[62] the trial judge allowed the sum of £2,650 per annum as the appropriate fee for employing the claimant's solicitor to undertake the tasks of a professional receiver. To this multiplicand, the full life multiplier of 18 was applied. No reduction to the multiplier in respect of the legal fees was made because there was no reason to believe that the receiver's responsibilities and activities would become any less over the years. There was no appeal against the award of the damages that represented the future fees of the professional receiver.[63]

A Non-Professional Gratuitous Receiver

17–19   Where a professional receiver is not appointed, but a member of the claimant's family or a friend takes on the role of the receiver of the claimant's affairs, that person must perform the various time-consuming administrative tasks demanded by the office during each accounting year. A claim for damages, analogous to that made for gratuitous family care, can be made for such services. The argument is that just as the claimant would want to recompense the unpaid family or friend carer, so would he want to recompense the otherwise unpaid organiser of his affairs.[64]

---

[62] *Sub nom. Cassel v. Hammersmith and Fulham Health Authority* [1992] P.I.Q.R. Q1 at Q17 and [1992] P.I.Q.R. Q168, CA. And also see *Futej v. Lewandowski* [1980] 124 S.J.777 *per* Edwin Jowitt Q.C. sitting as a Deputy High Court Judge, where the court awarded as part of the damages both the administration fees of the Court of Protection and professional fees of the Official Solicitor who had been appointed the receiver.

[63] Save that the award (£47,700) was reduced on appeal by 10 per cent in order to allow for the agreed settlement at 90 per cent. The damages as a whole were subject to the reduction of 10 per cent that had been agreed for the liability risks of litigation.

[64] In *Wells v. Wells* [1996] P.I.Q.R. Q62, the judge at first instance allowed a claim in respect of the time spent in the administration provided by Mrs Smith, the claimant's daughter and receiver, of the general management of her mother's affairs. At p. 68: ". . . it is right that I have already recognised her importance in the administration of her mother's care and the continuity that she provides and that interface, too, with the mother, the carers, the administration and, ultimately, the receiver." An allowance of £2,769 per annum was awarded. There was no appeal on this issue and the award was not disturbed.

The patient's claim needs to be carefully scheduled in order to ensure that there is no overlap or double recovery in relation to the gratuitous care and gratuitous receivership services.

Furthermore, if the gratuitous receiver is likely to obtain professional advice and assistance in order to carry out the role as receiver, an allowance for the likely cost of that assistance may also be claimed. In *Wells v. Wells*,[65] the Court of Appeal considered a claimant where in the future a number of different parties would be assisting in the management of her affairs in connection with the Court of Protection. Mrs Wells had suffered severe brain damage and, as a result, was unable to look after her own financial interests. In addition to an award of damages which included the expense of both the professional services of a case manager for the claimant's care and the administrative and accounting work of her daughter as the gratuitous receiver, the Court held that it was reasonable for the receiver to have the paid assistance of a solicitor in the management of the claimant's affairs and dealings with the Court of Protection. Hirst L.J. said[66]:

"But for the injury and award and the consequential need to involve the Court of Protection in the administration of her affairs, Mrs Wells would not need such sophisticated assistance. There is no justification for treating it as an impost on the sum considered necessary by the court to compensate her for what she has lost . . .

Here Mrs Wells' solicitor gave evidence to the judge as to the legal assistance and its cost likely to be required over the coming years, and as to the reasonableness and correspondence of the estimated costs with the taxed costs granted by the Court of Protection in other similar cases. We recognise that such costs are in addition to those payable in respect of case management and of some administrative assistance to be given by Mrs Wells' daughter as receiver. However, it does not seem to us that such additional costs for this legal input into the general management of such a large sum is unreasonable, given the solicitor's uncontradicted evidence; of the nature and need for the proposed services in this case; and of the practice of the Court of Protection to allow comparable sums by way of taxation where there in no professional receiver."

The claim was allowed and an award for legal fees made of £3,900 for the first year and £1,400 for the subsequent years.[67] Cogent evidence about

---

[65] [1997] P.I.Q.R. Q1, CA; [1997] 1 W.L.R. 652 (but not reported on this point).
[66] *ibid.* at Q40–41. The award was not disturbed by the House of Lords on appeal [1998] 3 W.L.R. 329; [1998] 3 All E.R. 481.
[67] *cf. Cunningham v. Camberwell Health Authority*, July 21, 1988, (unreported) Kemp & Kemp, A4–105, where Otton J. (as he then was) refused to make any award in respect of the claim for an extra sum to cover the likely fees of financial advisers in respect of income deriving from the fund and for the professional assistance in discharging the various bills and drawing up the annual accounts of the expenditure for presentation to the Court of Protection; from the brief facts recounted by the judge in his judgment, it does not appear

the likely professional fees is clearly needed in order to sustain this head of damage.

Of course, much may depend on the competence of the non-professional receiver and the nature and complications of a large fund income. However, where a professional receiver is appointed the reasonable future fee costs of such a receiver will be allowed either in the form of the increased administration fees of the Public Trustee pursuant to the Court of Protection Rules 1994 or in accordance with the decision in *Cassel v. Riverside Health Authority*.[68] By a parity of reasoning the expenses of a non-professional receiver who needs to turn to a solicitor for assistance in the yearly tasks of required administration should also be allowed.

The Costs of a Trust Created for the Benefit of the Patient

17–20   Where the claimant is both a patient and a child, the trial judge may approve the creation of a trust for his benefit. In *Bell v. Gateshead Area Health Authority*,[69] Alliott J. awarded £30,000 for the setting up and the future administration costs of a trust; no Court of Protection costs were involved.

Conclusion

The Court of Protection plays an essential role in safeguarding the claimant patient's actual and potential financial assets, including awards of both interim and final damages. However, there is some overlap with the control given to the court in which the action is heard under CPR Part 21 and therefore some duplication of procedure. Approval of a settlement by the action court is mandatory by reason of the explicit wording of the CPR Part 21. In practice, the Court of Protection also expects to be consulted

---

that the head of claim was argued either on the basis of a professional receiver or an unpaid family member whom the claimant would want to recompense for their time and trouble.

In *Hodgson v. Trapp*, unreported on this point at first instance, May 8, 1987, Kemp & Kemp, *The Quantum of Damages* A4–103, [reported on the issue of consortium at 1988 1 F.L.R. 69] the claimant had suffered very severe brain damage and her husband was appointed her receiver by the Court of Protection. At the trial, evidence was called to the effect that, as receiver, he should have the benefit of professional advice in his dealings with the Court of Protection. The trial judge awarded damages by way of a single sum to cover the cost of the initial advice and assistance of his solicitor who has handled his action and was familiar with the needs of his family, but refused to award damages for any periodical advice or assistance or acting as an intermediary between the receiver and the Court of Protection thereafter.

[68] *ibid.*

[69] October 22, 1986 (unreported), Kemp & Kemp, *The Quantum of Damages*, A4–013.

for approval and the Master of the Court is entitled to be consulted as a result of the supervisory role provided by section 96 of the Mental Health Act 1983 in relation to the conduct of legal proceedings in the name of a patient.

The costs which the patient claimant will incur in relation to the obligatory involvement of the Court of Protection are recoverable as separate heads of damage. The assessment of the future administration fees is generally based on a broad estimate of the likely cost. The ancillary cost and expenses of the receiver, both professional and non-professional, are recoverable, but cogent evidence of reasonable loss will be needed. Care is necessary to avoid duplication of claims.

Appendix 1: Court of Protection Fees[70]

(1)   Where the receiver is NOT the Public Trustee[71]

Commencement fee: £200

Annual administration fee:

clear annual income	fee
less than £1,000	£50
£1,001 – £2,000	£70
£2,001 – £3,000	£130
£3,001 – £5,000	£200
£5,001 – £7,000	£350
£7,001 –£10,000	£550
£10,000–£15,000	£800
exceeding £15,000	£800 plus 5% of the income exceeding £15,000

Transaction fee: £50[72]

(2)   Where the receiver is the Public Trustee[73]

Commencement fee: £250[74]

Annual administration fee:

---

[70] The administration fees of the Court of Protection are likely to be amended again in the near future but no details are available.

[71] Court of Protection Rules 1994, Appendix and Table 1; as amended by the Court of Protection (Amendment) Rule 1999.

[72] In a special case as defined in rule 81 of the Court of Protection Rules 1994, the transaction fee is 1/4 of the pecuniary consideration. No transaction fee is payable if the property is worth less than £50 and no such fee is to exceed £500.

[73] Court of Protection Rules 1994, Appendix and Table 2, as amended by the Court of Protection (Amendment) Rules 1999.

[74] Except where the patient's clear annual income is less than £1,000.

clear annual income	fee
less than £1,000	£100
£1,001 – £2,000	£250
£2,001 – £3,000	£525
£3,001 – £5,000	£800
£5,001 – £7,000	£1,300
£7,001 –£10,000	£1,800
£10,000–£15,000	£2,800
exceeding £15,000	£2,800 plus 5% of the income exceeding £15,000

Transaction fee: £50

Note:

Where a structured settlement is in place or a series of payments arise annually from an annuity, insurance bond or similar arrangement for the benefit of a patient only one half of the periodical payments are to be treated as clear income for the purpose of calculating the annual administration fee.

Appendix 2: Specimen Schedule of Heads of Damage

Future loss and damage

Court of Protection administration fees
(assuming invested fund of £1,000,000 at 4.5% return net of tax; and receiver NOT the Public Trustee)
£45,000 clear income = £1,750 annual administration fee
£1,750 × 10.5 (reduced multiplier)   18,375

Services of gratuitous (non-professional) receiver
2 hours a week × 52 × £8 (less 25% as non-commercial): £624
£624 × 16 (full life multiplier)   9,984

Professional assistance and advice provided to gratuitous receiver
£1,469 (being £1,250 + VAT) × 16 (full life multiplier)   23,504

                                                        Total   £57,638

Note

If the Public Trustee alone had been employed as the receiver the claim could be put at £4,600 [administration fee] × 10.5 = £48,300 and a defendant may argue that the claim should be limited to such sum on the basis of mitigation of loss. In fact, part of the enhanced administration fee charged where the Public Trustee is the receiver relates to the fact that there is an additional administrative burden. Where the clear annual income exceeds £10,000 per annum the additional fee charge is £2,000 in excess of the administration fee where the Public Trustee is not the receiver. On large awards the annual clear income will be maintained at a sum exceeding £10,000 per annum until shortly before the end of the period of loss and the liability for the enhanced fee will also be maintained. A significantly reduced multiplier should not be applied in cases where the Public Trustee is the receiver.

18. Interest

The successful claimant in an action for damages for personal injuries **18–01** has a right to interest on damages[1]: see section 35A of the Supreme Court Act 1981 and section 69 of the County Courts Act 1984. Recently, in *Davies v. Inman*,[2] Roch L.J. referred to "the *presumption* that interest is to be awarded on compensation arising from personal injuries."[3]

A claim for interest must be specifically pleaded whether it is claimed under section 35A of the Supreme Court Act 1981[4] or otherwise: "Particulars of claim must include—. . . if the claimant is seeking interest, a statement to that effect and the details set out in paragraph (2)." (Civil Procedure Rules 1999.[5])

Paragraph (2) sets out in detail the requirements which draftsmen of claimants' statements of case must take care to include, or to eliminate, (as the case may be;). Taking out some of the the bullet points, the requirements are as follows:

(a) The claimant must state whether he is claiming interest under the terms of a contract (hardly likely in a personal injuries case) or under an enactment (almost invariably section 35A of the Supreme Court act 1981 or section 69 of the County Courts Act 1984) "and if so *which*".

(b) If the claim for interest is upon some other basis, what that basis is.

(c) If the claim for interest is for a specified amount of money, the claimant must state:

   (i) the percentage rate at which interest is claimed;
   (ii) the date *from which* it is claimed;
   (iii) the date *to which* it is calculated[6];
   (iv) the total amount of interest claimed to the date of calculation; and
   (v) the daily rate at which interest accrues after that date.

Interest will not be awarded if it is not claimed. One of the obvious purposes behind the strictness of this rule is to enable defendants to make

---

[1] Exceeding £200.
[2] [1999] P.I.Q.R. Q26.
[3] At Q36: emphasis added.
[4] In the county court, section 69 of the County Courts Act 1984.
[5] CPR r. 16.4(1).
[6] Which must not be later than the date on which the claim form is issued.

an accurate assessment of the total value of a claim, to enable them to make a proper payment into court if they wish to do so.

Interest on Special Damages: Half-Rate or Full Rate?

18–02   In many, if not most, cases the claimant has nothing at all to lose by claiming interest *at full rate* from the date of the accrual of each item of loss until the date of judgment. It *may average out* at a figure which corresponds to half-rate if the loss is a continuous one from accident to trial, and there are no major items (*e.g.* some high-value personal possessions) which were lost completely in the accident. The averaging process results from some items in the total sum claimed as special damage being subject to years of interest, whilst others, such as the most recent week's loss of wages, will attract a negligible amount. The "half-rate" approach simply expresses this average in rough-and-ready arithmetical terms.[7]

The legal advisers who, without giving the matter real thought, expressly restrict a claimant's claim to a *maximum of half-rate*,[8] however, may be letting their client down badly. If the majority of his special damage claim occurred in, say, the three months after the accident, rather than continuously to trial, he is entitled to full-rate from the end of the three months. To do so may deprive the claimant of up to half the interest to which he is entitled and may give the defendants a corresponding benefit to which they are not entitled. An example of the arithmetical difference is set out below. Claimants' advisers would, thus, be wise to claim interest at full rate in any case where the loss is not a continuous one from accident to trial: see *Prokop v. DHSS*.[9]

In *Jefford v. Gee*,[10] Lord Denning M.R., giving the judgment of the court, said that:

> "In *all ordinary cases* we should have thought that it would be fair to award interest on the total sum of special damages from the date of the accident until the date of trial at half the [special account] rate . . ."[11]

It is quite clear from the judgment that the court was greatly influenced in that case by the continuing loss of wages. The claimant had not worked from the date of the accident to the date of trial. In dealing with this, Lord Denning said:

---

[7] In reality the arithmetic is done by cutting *the period* in half to allow for some items being long-accrued losses and some being very recent. Thus it is not in fact a calculation based on *half-rate*: it is based on full-rate *but* for half the period—which has an identical arithmetical result.

[8] By using a formula such as "the claimant claims interest at half the average special account rate on each and every item of loss and damage . . ."

[9] [1985] C.L.Y. 1037, CA.

[10] [1970] 2 Q.B. 13D.

[11] Emphasis added.

"*Loss of wages*. This occurred week by week. In principle, the interest should be calculated on each week's loss from that week to the date of trial. But that would mean too much detail. Alternatively, it would be possible to add up the loss every six months and allow interest on the total every six months until trial. That would seem fair, especially as the loss for the initial weeks might be for total incapacity, and afterwards only for partial incapacity, when he could do light work. More rough and ready, the total loss could be taken from accident to trial: and interest allowed only on half of it, or for half the time, or at half the rate."

In other words, in a case where loss is *continuing*, allowing half-rate, or only half the period, or half the loss, provides a short cut in the arithmetic for calculation of the interest upon the money in respect of which the claimant has been "kept out".

An example of a different, but not uncommon, situation is where the claimant has lost earnings, say, £1,000 per month for six months, and has then returned to work. He begins proceedings promptly. The defendants cause delays in the hearing of the claim so that the case is not heard until five-and-a-half years after the accident. The claimant has been kept out of his £6,000, as an accrued loss, for five years. In such circumstances if the average full special account rate were (for ease of illustration) 10 per cent, five years' interest would amount to 50 per cent, or £3,000. If the claimant is only allowed half-rate, he will lose £1,500, and the defendants will have profited by having had the use of the money to that extent by reason of their own delay.   18–03

In *Prokop v. DHSS*,[12] May L.J.[13] said that the half-rate approach referred to in *Jefford v. Gee* is:

"... only applicable to cases where the special damages comprise more or less regular periodical losses which are continuous from the date of the accident to the date of trial; these are more often than not lost earnings.

If there is any general view in any quarter that the interest on special damages is in any event to be calculated at half-rate, when the losses do not continue from accident to trial, then I think that this is wrong and should not hereafter be followed."

In *Dexter v. Courtaulds Ltd*,[14] the Court of Appeal affirmed the general principle of the half-rate approach for interest upon specials. Lawton L.J. referred to circumstances in which full-rate interest might be appropriate, citing a passage from an unreported decision of Forbes J. in *Dodd v. Rediffusion (West Midlands Ltd)*[15] in which he explained the half-rate principle as "a short cut in the mathematics". Kerr L.J. in argument in *Dexter* had said that when the claimant wishes to say that there are special

---

[12] *op. cit.*
[13] J. May Q.C. had appeared as *amicus curiae* in *Jefford v. Gee*.
[14] [1984] 1 W.L.R. 372.
[15] [1980] C.L.Y. 635.

circumstances which exclude the *Jefford v. Gee* principle, he should "say so".[16] Lawton L.J. expressly adopted this view in his judgment, and Fox L.J. agreed.

In calculating interest on damages a judge is free to depart from the *Jefford v. Gee* method if an actuarial method of calculation would produce a fairer and more accurate figure.[17]

When considering a respondent's notice on an appeal from a striking-out order on the ground of delay, the Court of Appeal has no jurisdiction to fetter the trial judge's discretion to reduce the rate or period of interest. Absent abuse of process, the Court of Appeal could not tamper with a claimant's pleaded case on interest.[18]

Delay

18–04   The basic rule or general principle is that a claimant who has been guilty of unjustifiable delay in bringing the case to trial should suffer disallowance of interest *at full rate*, in the absence of any reason special to the individual case entitling the judge to depart from the rule.[19] This rule, however, has in practice been modified significantly.

In *Read v. Harries*,[20] seven years elapsed between the relevant accident and the trial, and delays totalling over three years were caused by the claimant's failure to give her solicitors sufficient information to her solicitors to permit them to formulate her claim. Interest was allowed only to the date (three years earlier) at which the case would have been tried but for such delay:

> "Insurers ought to be entitled to close their books in respect of claims within a reasonable period of time; they are prejudiced if they have to keep alive an outstanding claim, which inevitably results in increased costs payable by them to their solicitors which are not recoverable from the claimant."[21]

In a commercial case it was held recently that where there had been substantial delay by the plaintiff in bringing an action to trial, the primary cause of the claimant being deprived of his money was his own conduct and, therefore, interest was to be reduced. Rather than disallow interest for any specific period, however, which led to complications as to the rates applicable to particular periods, the overall rate which should be applied to

---

[16] By raising the matter in (now) the statement of case, and giving reasons for departing from the half-rate rule.

[17] *Hobin v. Douglas (No. 1)* [1998] C.L.Y. 1431, *The Independent*, October 26, 1998, *per* Roch L.J.

[18] *Headford v. Bristol & District Health Authority* [1995] P.I.Q.R. P180.

[19] *Spittle v. Bunny* [1988] 3 All E.R. 1031.

[20] [1993] P.I.Q.R. Q25.

[21] *Read v. Harries [addendum]* [1993] P.I.Q.R. Q34.

the whole period should be reduced: see *Derby Resources AG v. Blue Corinth Marine Co. Ltd (The Athenian Harmony) (No. 2).*[22]

Where the claimant in a personal injuries case was a minor, and his next friend delayed bringing proceedings for 17 years, which the judge described as understandable in human terms, the delay was, nevertheless, so unjustifiable forensically as to result in interest on special damages being payable for only seven years. To have done otherwise would be to have placed a premium on delaying litigation: see *Nash v. Southmead Health Authority.*[23]

Interim Payments

Until an interim payment reduces the amount payable for special **18–05** damages a claimant is entitled to interest at half the special account rate on the full amount due, and thereafter to interest at that rate on the amount outstanding. Where an interim payment was made which exceeded the amount of special damages due on the date it is paid there was no reason why the balance should not be taken to have been paid in diminution of the compensation payable as general damages. Thereafter, the claimant would be entitled to interest at half the special account rate on special damages accruing between the date of payment of the interim payment and the date of trial and 2 per cent on the outstanding amount of general damages: see *Bristow v. Judd.*[24]

Relevance of Payments by Volunteers

In *Davies v. Inman,*[25] a claimant's employers voluntarily continued to **18–06** pay him sums equivalent to his wages during a period of absence from work following an accident caused by the negligence of an unconnected defendant (under an agreement that the allowance would be refunded by the claimant to the employers from any damages awarded against the defendant.) At trial, only 13 weeks of the total period of 60 weeks absence was found to have been attributable to the accident. The defendant argued that no interest should have been awarded in respect of the loss of earnings, since the employers had made good the claimant's losses, and thus he had not been "kept out of his money". The argument was rejected. The Court of Appeal held that the proper approach to interest in such a case was to consider the position of the volunteer-employers who made

---

[22] [1998] 2 Lloyd's Rep. 425 *per* Colman J.
[23] [1993] P.I.Q.R. Q156.
[24] [1993] P.I.Q.R. Q117.
[25] [1999] P.I.Q.R. Q26.

good loss by analogy, *e.g.* with volunteer-carers: the authorities (such as *Hunt v. Severs*,[26] considering *Donnelly v. Joyce*[27] establish that damages are awarded to a claimant to compensate for either the value of the services performed or the amount of money contributed. The employers had a legal right to recover the money from the claimant. They had lost the use of the money. If the claimant were to recover interest on it from the defendants, he would hold it on trust for the employers. There was "no question" in the light of the court's decision in *Roberts v. Johnstone*[28] but that an award of interest on damages which represent the value of voluntary care is a proper order. Moreover, there was a public interest to encourage volunteers.

Interest and Social Security Benefits

In *Wadey v. Surrey C.C.*,[29] £49,197 of an award of over £220,000 represented loss offset by state benefits paid to the claimant over a five year period. The sum of £49,197 was left out of account by the trial judge for the purpose of calculating interest on special damages. Allowing the claimant's appeal, the Court of Appeal held that the scheme of the Social Security Recovery of Benefits Act 1997 made it clear that not only should state benefits be disregarded from the assessment of damages but also from the assessment of interest.[30] The claimant was entitled to the award of interest upon the special damages in respect of which judgment was given including the sum of benefits which the defendants would eventually have to pay over to the DSS. The Court of Appeal were much influenced by the Scottish case of *Wisley v. John Fulton (Plumbers) Ltd*,[31] in which the Court of Session "had occasion to consider the exact same question which is now before this court . . ."[32]

Repayment of Interest Following Reduction of Award on Appeal

18–07   In *Goldfinch v. Scannell*,[33] the defendant appealed against quantum in a case involving a patient. The award of over £470,000 was reduced by some £82,000 on appeal. The defendant had not sought a stay because the

---

[26] [1994] P.I.Q.R. Q60, HL.
[27] [1974] Q.B. 454.
[28] [1989] 1 Q.B. 878.
[29] [1999] P.I.Q.R. Q128, CA.
[30] 1998 S.L.T. 1026.
[31] Contrast the earlier first-instance decision in *Web v. J. Bowbart & Co. Ltd* [1998] J.P.I.L. 324 where the claimant claimed interest (but only at half-rate) in respect of loss of earnings from the date of the accident to the date of trial. The court took the view that the purpose of the interest was to compensate the plaintiff for being kept out of his money. As he had received social security benefits in respect of part of his loss the court took the view that he could not be said to have suffered a loss of interest.
[32] *per* Otton L.J. at Q132.
[33] [1996] C.L.Y. 2124.

moncy was not be paid to the claimant personally, and it would not have been possible to have contended that the money might prove to be irrecoverable. The defendant claimed to be entitled to interest on the £82,000 for the period during which it was wrongly in the hands of the Court of Protection on behalf of the claimant. Ordering the claimant to return the interest, in addition to the £82,000, it was held, that the defendant had been justified in not applying for a stay, although if the sum had been paid to a personal claimant the outcome might have been different.

Interest on General Damages

In *Birkett v. Hayes*,[34] the Court of Appeal held that a rate of 2 per cent **18–08** per annum from the date of service of the writ to trial was appropriate for interest upon general damages for pain, suffering and loss of amenity. Much of the basic reasoning for this conclusion has been subject to radical revision in *Thomas v. Brighton Health Authority & Others* and *Wells v. Wells*.[35] More significantly, in *C. Burns v. Joseph C. Davies*,[36] Connell J. awarded 3 per cent interest on generals. A well-argued review of the problem is set out in a recent article by Andrew Buchan in the Journal of Personal Injury Litigation.[37] Although *Burns v. Davies* is mentioned only in an addendum, a thorough analysis is made of the basis for the 2 per cent rule, and the reasons for its suggested reform.

Pleading the Claim for Interest

The form which a claim for interest under the CPR *might* take is as **18–09** follows:

"Further the claimant claims interest upon such damages as may be awarded to her pursuant to the provisions of section 35A of the Supreme Court Act 1981 [OR: section 69 of the County Courts Act 1984.]

PARTICULARS OF INTEREST CLAIMED

(1) Interest is claimed upon damages under section 35A of the Supreme Court Act 1981 [or section 69 of the County Courts Act 1984]

---

[34] [1982] 1 W.L.R. 876 and see also *Wright v. British Railways Board* [1983] A.C. 773, HL. The history of the case law is lucidly and economically set out in Munkman, *Damages for Personal Injury & Death*, (9th ed.) at pp. 44–45 concluding with the author's memorably felicitous observation that ". . . in analysing this tangled case law one cannot help feeling like an archaeologist excavating successive layers of potsherds in the ruins of Jericho."

[35] [1998] P.I.Q.R. Q56, HL.

[36] (Unreported) August 7, 1998.

[37] "Is it time to review interest on General Damages at 2 per cent? Shouldn't it be 3 per cent?" [1998] J.P.I.L. 296.

(2) The amount of interest claimed upon special damages at the date hereof is [£1,000 *or as the case may be*]

(3) In respect of special damages:

(a) the percentage rate at which interest is claimed is the full special account rate of [x] per cent; *or [the average rate for full special account throughout the relevant period, namely [y] per cent]*

(b) the date from which it is claimed is the date of the accident set out above in paragraph 1, and continuing until the date of judgment herein;

(c) the date to which it is calculated is the date of issue of the claim form herein namely [date];

(d) the total amount of interest claimed to the date of calculation is [£2,000];

(e) the rate at which interest accrues after that date is [£2.50] per day.

(4) The amount of interest claimed upon general damages is [£300]

(5) In respect of general damages

(a) the percentage rate at which interest is claimed is [3] per cent;

(b) the date from which it is claimed is the date of the claim form herein [date] and continuing until the date of judgment;

(c) the date to which it is calculated is the date of issue of the claim form herein namely [date];

(d) the total amount of interest claimed to the date of calculation is [£300];

(e) the rate at which interest accrues after that date is [£0.30] per day.

AND the claimant claims:

(1) Damages.

(2) Interest, as set out above, pursuant to section 35A of the Supreme Court Act 1981 [OR: section 69 of the County Courts Act 1984.]"

19. Provisional Damages

The Law

The general rule in English law is that damages are assessed on a once **19–01** and for all basis. The availability of provisional damages provides an exception to that rule. Section 32A of the Supreme Court Act 1981 (inserted by the Administration of Justice Act 1982, section 6(1)) provides for an award of provisional damages to be made in certain defined circumstances. In essence, an award of provisional damages may be made in an action for personal injuries where:

"there is proved or admitted to be a chance that at some definite or indefinite time in the future the injured person will, as a result of the act or omission which gave rise to the cause of action, develop some serious disease or suffer some serious deterioration in his physical or mental condition."

Section 32A was inserted to remedy what was perceived to be a defect in the court's powers to award damages for personal injuries in cases where there was a known risk of a further development either by way of a new disease or a serious deterioration in the claimant's present physical condition: see *Hurditch v. Sheffield HA*[1].

An award of provisional damages involves a two stage process in the **19–02** assessment and award of damages for personal injury. First, an initial award of damages is made on the assumption that the injured person *will not* develop the disease or suffer the deterioration. Rule 41.2(2) of the Civil Procedure Rule (CPR) requires that the order of the court awarding these initial damages specifies the disease or type of deterioration. Thus, no award of provisional damages can be made unless it is possible to identify the disease or diseases which are envisaged as possible developments or the condition in respect of which serious deterioration might result[2]. At this stage, however, it is not necessary for there to be complete agreement between the parties, or their experts, on the prognosis and likely development of the specified disease or deterioration which may trigger the later award of damages. (See CPR rule 36.7 for the way in which a Part 36 payment notice must be worded and how a Part 36 payment will take effect where a claimant claims provisional damages.) If applicable, a further award of damages will be made if the person does develop the specified disease or suffer the deterioration within the specified time period.

---

[1] [1989] 2 W.L.R. 827, *per* Purchas L.J. at 829.
[2] *ibid*. at 839.

Questions relating to causation and attributability may be tried at the time when the further award of damages is being considered.[3] See also *O'Kennedy v. Harris*.[4]

19–03   CPR rule 41.2 makes it clear that the court has a discretion whether or not to make an award of provisional damages where the requirements of section 32A are satisfied. Further, the court has a discretion to make an award of provisional damages on such terms as it thinks just.

The obvious contrast is between an award of provisional damages in which the initial assessment of damages effectively ignores the possibility of future suffering or disease or deterioration, and a conventional award of damages in which the possibility of further deterioration in the claimant's condition is taken into account in either the assessment of general damages or in the choice of multiplier applied to future loss. One advantage of an award of provisional damages is thus that in making the award it is unnecessary for the court to attempt to assess/quantify the risk of the claimant developing a particular disease or of his condition deteriorating at some point in the future. However, if it is a probability that the disease or deterioration will happen, an award of provisional damages should not be made because the judge would be able to deal with the future potential complication or sequel and should do so in his award of damages (see Roch L.J. in *Curi v. Colina*.[5]

Award of Provisional Damages—the Circumstances

19–04   It is not possible to set out in any detail the precise circumstances in which an award of provisional damages will be made. Section 32A does not define the words "chance" or "serious". What is clear is that provisional damages should not be awarded in every case in which a court is called upon to assess a risk of further deterioration in the claimant's condition at some point in the future: see the judgment of Michael Davies in *Allott v. Central Electricity Generating Board*[6] cited in *Wilson v. Ministry of Defence*.[7] Roch L.J. in the Court of Appeal in *Curi v. Colina* set out his views as to when an award of provisional damages should be made as follows:

> "[Provisional damages] should be confined to those cases where to compensate for the condition for which there is a chance on the basis that it will occur would be unfair to the defendant and to leave the plaintiff without the opportunity to ask for further compensation should the condition, of which there is a chance, materialise would be unfair to the plaintiff."

---

[3] *ibid.* at 839.
[4] [1990] QBD (unreported) and P.D. 41.2.5.
[5] [1998] CA (unreported).
[6] December 19, 1988 (unreported).
[7] [1991] 1 All E.R. 638 at 644.

"Chance"

In *Wilson v. Ministry of Defence*, Scott Baker J. held that there are three **19–05** questions that have to be considered where a claimant has made an application for an award of provisional damages. First, is there a chance of further disease or deterioration? It was held that a chance is a term capable of covering a wide range of circumstances. To satisfy the requirements of section 32A, however, it must be "measurable rather than fanciful." (*Wilson v. Ministry of Defence*[8] *per* Scott Baker J. at 642 affirmed by Roch L.J. in *Curi v. Colina*). In *Patterson v. Ministry of Defence*[9] an order for provisional damages was made where there was a 2–3 per cent chance that the claimant would develop malignant mesothelioma. One factor which weighed with Simon Brown J. in *Patterson* was that "it would surely be the duty of the claimant, were he to seek life assurance, to disclose the existence of his condition; prudent insurers would surely require to be informed of it". In *O'Kennedy v. Harris*[10] Sir Gervase Sheldon sitting as a judge of the High Court, awarding provisional damages in respect of a small and diminishing risk of post-traumatic epilepsy, said:

> "if it amounts to a significant risk, the smaller it is and the shorter the period to be covered, the more important it may be for the claimant to keep open his or her right to seek further compensation if it were to materialise."

The proper interpretation to be given to "chance" was considered in *Mann v. Merton and Sutton Health Authority*.[11] In that case it was held that an award of provisional damages could be made specifying a disease notwithstanding that at the time of the award the claimant would not have succeeded in proving that the disease was caused by the negligent act or omission. It was held that there was:

> "a chance—small but real—not only of his contracting one or other of the cancers but of being able at a later stage, if a further application does ever have to be made, of satisfying that court that the condition was induced by his exposure to asbestos. I do not accept the submission that at this stage that link has to be firmly proved before those diseases are specified."

"Serious"

Secondly, is such disease or deterioration in the claimant's physical **19–06** condition of a kind which can properly be described as serious? In *Wilson*, it was held that what is serious is a question of fact in every case. Further,

---

[8] *ibid.* at 642.
[9] [1987] C.L.Y. 1194.
[10] [1990] QBD (unreported).
[11] [1988] QBD (unreported).

it is a question which depends in part upon the impact of the disease or deterioration on the particular claimant. Thus, the court must take into account both the degree of risk and the consequences of the risk in determining whether or not it is "serious" (see also the decision of the Outer House in *Robertson v. British Bakeries Ltd*[12]. To quote from Roch L.J. in *Curi v. Colina*

> "A disease or a deterioration could be serious because of the effect on the activities and capabilities of the injured party, or because of its effect on his or her life expectancy, or because of its effect on his or her financial position. If, as in this case, the natural progression of the condition will affect the plaintiff's earning capacity in the future so that compensation for that will be awarded, then that element will have to be disregarded by the judge when answering the question is the possible deterioration serious, unless the possible deterioration will accelerate by a significant period the loss or reduction in the plaintiff's earning capacity."

In *Wilson*, it was held that to qualify as serious, deterioration in the claimant's physical condition must be more than "ordinary". In *Patterson*, Simon Brown J. held that an award of provisional damages should only be made in cases where the disease or deterioration is:

> "reasonably clear cut and where there would be little room for later dispute whether or not the contemplated deterioration had actually occurred."

Where, instead, the deterioration the subject of the application for provisional damages is merely a progressive development of the claimant's current condition, or would have only a doubtful effect on the claimant's physical condition, an award of provisional damages should not be made. These views were adopted by Scott Baker J. in *Wilson* where he held that to satisfy the criteria in section 32A it was necessary for there to be some ascertainable deterioration or disease and not merely a continuing progression of a particular disease or physical condition. In his words:

> "the section [section 32A] envisages a clear and severable risk rather than a continuing deterioration".

Thus, it was not sufficient in *Wilson* for the claimant to show that the deterioration in his condition may or may not have continued to the extent of requiring surgery. Nor was it sufficient to show that the deterioration may have progressed to such a point that the claimant's employment or recreational activities may have been affected.

19–07 It is not appropriate to award provisional damages in cases where there is a general band within which a disease or condition may develop and the

---

[12] 1991 S.L.T. 434.

precise course of that development cannot be foreseen. Rather there must be some "clear cut event which, if it occurs, triggers an entitlement to further compensation" (see *Wilson v. Ministry of Defence per* Scott Baker J. at 644). Some precise threshold must be established which, if crossed, will entitle the claimant to an award of further damages. This can be illustrated by reference to the decision of Scott Baker J. in *Hennigan v. Jackson*[13] where he held that a real risk of deterioration of the claimant's back sufficient to case loss of or lighter employment was not an event which was appropriate to trigger an award of provisional damages. In his judgment the courts "are well used to quantifying a figure for risks of this kind."

Also of interest is the distinction drawn in *Wilson* between disease or deterioration on the one hand, and injury on the other hand. It is not sufficient to satisfy the criteria in section 32A merely to show that the claimant's physical condition is such that there is a risk of further injury at some point in the future if, for example, the claimant suffers an accident by reason of weakness resulting from the initial tortious event. The claimant in every case must establish that in his physical condition at the time at which his application for provisional damages is considered, there is a present chance of disease or deterioration which can properly be described as serious.

Discretion

Thirdly, the court must consider whether or not it should exercise its **19–08** discretion in the particular case (*Wilson v. Ministry of Defence per* Scott Baker J. at 641–642. At this stage of the enquiry the court must balance the possibility of doing justice by a once-and-for-all award of damages against the possibility of doing better justice by making an award of provisional damages (*Wilson v. Ministry of Defence per* Scott Baker J. at 645). Factors to be taken into account include, for example, the possibility that where the contemplated deterioration is in fact death, a claimant may be overcompensated in the initial award if he is awarded damages on the basis of an increased life expectancy. In *Molinari v. Ministry of Defence*,[14] Mr W. Crowther Q.C. (sitting as a Deputy High Court Judge) illustrated this point with the example of a young man, with no dependants who spent all his earnings on himself, who contracts a disease with a 50 per cent chance of death within a relatively short period. If provisional damages were awarded, he would be compensated for his full loss of earnings. If, however, he were to die, the deduction from his lost earnings of his living expenses during "the lost years" would offset them entirely, reducing his entitlement to damages for lost earnings entirely. Thus, the award of provisional damages would lead to overcompensation in the event of the

---

[13] [1990] QBD (unreported).
[14] [1994] P.I.Q.R.Q33.

identified deterioration in his physical condition. But there is no provision in section 32A for overcompensation to be remedied at the further award of damages. According to *Molinari*, in such a case a judge might properly refuse an award of provisional damages on the basis that the potential injustice to the defendants of such an award outweighed the potential injustice to the claimant of a traditional award. On the facts of *Molinari*, however, where the court awarded provisional damages to a claimant who suffered acute lymphoblastic leukaemia and had a risk of a relapse, it was held that there would be no such injustice since any overcompensation in terms of lost earnings resulting from an award of provisional damages would adequately be offset by the increased loss under other heads of damage.

In *Ivory v. Martens*,[15] a case concerning a small risk of further functional deficit, it was held that the court can take into account the fact that a risk is very slight in exercising the discretion whether or not to award provisional damages.

Fatal Accidents

19–09   Section 3 of the Damages Act 1996 (which came into force on 24 September 1996 and operates retrospectively) reversed the effect of *Middleton v. Elliott Turbo-Machinery*.[16] Section 3 applies where a person who has been awarded provisional damages dies as a result of the act or omission which gave rise to his cause of action.

The mechanism which section 3 of the Damages Act 1993 applies to fatal accident claims where there has been an earlier award of provisional damages is as follows:

(a) The award of provisional damages *shall not operate* as a bar to an action in respect of that person's death under the Fatal Accidents Act 1976 (the section appears to assume that this can include both an award of provisional damages and an award of further damages before his death).

(b) Such part of the damages already awarded (provisional and further) as was intended to compensate the deceased for pecuniary loss in the period which in fact was subsequent to his death shall be taken into account in assessing the amount of loss suffered by his dependants pursuant to the Fatal Accidents Act 1976.

(c) no award of further damages made in respect of that person after his death shall include any amount for loss of income in respect of any period after his death;

---

[15] [1998] QBD (unreported).
[16] *The Times*, September 29, 1990.

The Practice (see also CPR Part 41 and PD41)

- A claim for provisional damages must be specifically pleaded **19–10** together with the grounds for claiming provisional damages (CPR rule 16.4(1)(d) and PD 16.4.4. See also *Curi (Iane Branderburgo v. Colina (Louise Ignacia)*. The particulars of claim must specify the disease or type of deterioration in respect of which the application for further damages may be made (PD 16.4.4).

- An order for the award of provisional damages must specify the disease or type of deterioration in respect of which an application may be made at a further date and must specify the time period within which the application may be made. A different time period may be specified in respect of different diseases or type of deterioration specified in the order (CPR Part 41.2(2)).

- Upon giving judgment for provisional damage the court must direct what documents are to be filed and preserved as the case file in support of any application for further damages (PD 41.2.1). Such documents must be set out in a schedule to the judgment (PD 41.2.3). These documents must be preserved during the period specified as being the period during which a claim for further damages may be made (PD 41.3.1). Such documents will usually include judgment, statements of case, a transcript of the judge's oral judgment, all medical reports relied upon and a transcript of any parts of the claimant's own evidence which the judge considers necessary (PD 41.3.2).

- The period of time for claiming further damages may be extended on application (CPR Part 41.2(3)). More than one such application may be made. A medical report should be filed in support of such application (PD 41.3.5). Any order extending the time within which a claim for further damages may be made must be included in the case file (PD 41.3.4).

- All legal representatives should preserve their own case file (PD 41.3.6)

- An application to give effect to a consent order for provisional damages should be made in accordance with the usual rules for applications (PD 41.4.1). The order should comply with the provisions of PD 41.4.2.

- A consent order for provisional damages in respect of a child or a patient requires court approval (PD 41.4.1)

- Where provisional damages are part of the relief claimed it is not possible to enter judgment in default. Rather, if the defendant does not file an acknowledgement of service or a defence, the claimant should make an application in accordance with Part 23 for directions. It is then for the court to consider whether the claim is an appropriate one for an award of provisional damages and, if so, on what terms and the amount of immediate damages (PD 41.5)

- Part 36 payments may be made in relation to a claim for provisional damages (CPR Part 36.7). The Part 36 payment notice must specify whether or not the defendant is offering to agree to the making of an award for provisional damages. If so, the notice must also state that the sum paid into court is in satisfaction of the claim for damages on the assumption that the claimant will not develop the disease or suffer the deterioration specified in the notice and that the offer is subject to the condition that further damages may be claimed within a specified period. If the Part 36 payment is accepted, the claimant must within seven days apply to the court for an order for the award of provisional damages (CPR Part 36.7(5).

- Only one application for further damages may be made in respect of each disease or type of deterioration specified in the order (CPR Part 41.3(2)).

- No application for further damages may be made after the expiration of the time period (including any extension) (CPR Part 41.3(1)).

- Not less than 28 days written notice must be given to the defendant and, if it is known that the defendant is insured, his insurers if the claimant intends to apply for further damages (CPR Part 41.3).

- The rules about making interim payments apply to an application for further damages (CPR 41.3(6)).

20. Interim Payments

Introduction

Definition and Availability

An interim payment is a payment on account of any damages, debt or **20–01** other sum (excluding costs) which the defendant may be held liable to pay to or for the benefit of a claimant.[1] A claimant may make an application for an interim payment at any time after proceedings have been served on the defendant after the time provided for the acknowledgement of service has expired and before the full trial in respect of quantum.[2]

Overview of the Civil Procedure Rules on Interim Payments

Interim remedies, which include interim payments, are dealt with in Part **20–02** 25 of the Civil Procedure Rules (CPR) and the Practice Directions which accompany it. The new rules relating to interim payments preserve much of the old regime found in RSC Ord. 29, rr. 9–18. There are, however, a number of changes, the principle ones of which can be summarised as follows:

(a) Where there are two or more defendants to a claim, it is no longer necessary for the claimant to demonstrate that he will obtain judgment for substantial damages against the particular defendant from whom the interim payment is sought—it is enough for a claimant to show that he will succeed against at least one or other of them[3] (see below).

(b) It is no longer possible to apply for an interim payment against a defendant who it is believed has the means/resources to enable him to meet the order: qualifying defendants are now confined to insurers and public bodies (see below).

In theory, if the Woolf reforms achieve their aim of improving the speed and efficiency with which justice is dispensed, the number of applications for interim payments should reduce. However, in practice, it is suggested that they will still prove a valuable tool for claimants, particularly in multi-

---

[1] CPR 25.1 (1)(K).
[2] CPR 25.6(1).
[3] CPR 25.7(3).

track cases, who wish to gain a tactical advantage and/or who need to mitigate their financial losses swiftly. In such cases, other parts of the new procedural regime, such as the pre-action Protocols on disclosure and the rule obliging the defendant to serve a Counter-Schedule of special damages with his defence (admitting those losses not in dispute), can be used to good effect by claimant's advisers.

Circumstances Required

20–03   At the first stage the claimant must prove one of the following[4]:

(a) the defendant has admitted liability, or

(b) the claimant has obtained judgment, or

(c) if the action proceeded to trial, the claimant would obtain judgment for substantial damages against the defendant who is the respondent to the application, or, if there are two or more defendants, against at least one of them (provided they all comply with the criteria set out below).

Even if the claimant establishes one of the circumstances set out above, the court may only make an order if it appears that the defendant is:

(d) a person who is insured in respect of the claim, or whose liability will be met by an insurer under section 151 of the Road Traffic Act 1988; or

(e) an insurer concerned under the Motor Insurers Bureau agreement; or the MIB where it is acting itself; or

(f) a public body.[5]

The Requirements in Detail

If the Action Proceeded to Trial, the Claimant would Obtain Judgment

20–04   There are competing principles here. On the one hand, the court is reluctant to award an interim payment to a claimant who might spend the money, lose at trial and be unable to repay the defendant who had to pay the money in advance of trial. On the other hand, many injured claimants

---

[4] CPR 25.7(1) & (3).
[5] CPR 25.7(2).

lose their employment in consequence of the accident for which the defendant is ultimately held responsible; they are insufficiently supported by benefits or insurance income, so their standard of living is threatened, their homes may be at risk and general stress is increased. It is no part of the role of the court to keep an injured claimant from his money. Against this background the Courts have attempted to develop an appropriate standard for ascertaining whether an interim payment may properly be made.

In *Ricci Burns Limited v. Toole*,[6] a two-judge Court of Appeal considered whether it was inconsistent to award two defendants unconditional leave to defend at the same time as ordering one of them to make an interim payment to the claimant. It concluded that it was not. The distinction, according to Ralph Gibson L.J., was a fine one, but not so fine as to present a conceptual difficulty. Reasonable doubt as to the possibility of success of a defendant on some issue of fact on affidavit evidence would preclude summary judgment, even though the claimant would win if the evidence was unaltered at trial. Yet on the same material a court could be sufficiently confident of the claimant's success to order an interim payment since it was not necessary to exclude every possibility of failure before awarding an interim payment. The requirement was of proof to a high standard on the balance of probabilities and the burden was said to be towards the top end of the flexible scale of the civil burden of proof.[7]

This relatively liberal test was contrary to the view of a different, three **20–05** judge Court of Appeal propounded just three weeks earlier in *Shanning v. George Wimpey Limited*.[8]

A few months later another three judge Court of Appeal considered the issue and concluded that a court had no jurisdiction to make an order for an interim payment where a defendant had been given unconditional leave to defend: see *British & Commonwealth Holdings Plc v. Quadrex Holdings Inc.*[9] Browne-Wilkinson V.-C. (as he then was) said that the two previous cases could not be reconciled and that he preferred *Shanning*. He pointed out:

> "Order 29 . . . requires the Court, at the first stage, to be satisfied that the claimant *will* succeed and the burden is a high one; it is not enough that the Court thinks it likely that the claimant will succeed at trial. For myself, I find it an impossible concept that the same Court can be simultaneously 'satisfied' that the claimant *will* succeed at trial and at the same time consider that the defendant has an arguable defence sufficient to warrant unconditional leave to defend."[10]

---

[6] [1989] 1 W.L.R. 993; [1989] 3 All E.R. 478.
[7] [1989] 1 W.L.R. 993 at 1004; [1989] 3 All E.R. 478 at 485.
[8] [1989] 1 W.L.R. 981; [1988] 3 All E.R. 475.
[9] [1989] Q.B. 842.
[10] [1989] Q.B. 842 at 865II–866B.

He added that any distinction between the two concepts required a nicety of approach so fine that the requirements of certainty in the law would make it undesirable to recognise. However Browne-Wilkinson V.-C. went on to point out that in the present case there should only be *conditional* leave to defend—and that made a difference, a fortiori where the claimants were a commercial organisation and could repay if they did not succeed at trial. Thus, although this decision is memorable and strong, the passage relating to the incompatibility of unconditional leave to defend with an interim payment is strictly speaking *obiter dicta*.

20–06   The latest case to consider these issues is *Andrews v. Schooling*.[11] On the claimant's application for an interim payment the Master granted unconditional leave to defend and ordered an interim payment of £7,500. This was upheld on appeal by a Deputy High Court Judge to whose attention *Quadrex* was not drawn. On appeal Balcombe L.J. took a robust approach and referred to "sensible concessions" made by counsel for the claimant, namely that the decision in *Quadrex* is binding.[12] In effect the Court of Appeal had to determine the whole matter *de novo* and Balcombe L.J. with whom the other two members of the court agreed, said that the issue was:

> "Are we satisfied that the claimant will succeed at the trial ... and that the defence is so shadowy that the defendant should only be given condition leave to defend, the condition being an interim payment to the claimant?"[13]

The decision was that the Court of Appeal was so satisfied.

It follows from the above that it would take an extremely bold advocate to pursue the *Ricci Burns* approach that there can be unconditional leave to defend and an interim payment, because three separate Appeal Courts have all taken a different view. Nonetheless, the matter is not closed to all argument, since one of the contrary cases was decided before *Ricci Burns* and in the other two the matter was strictly *obiter* and/or the subject of a concession.

Judgment against at least one Defendant

As indicated above, the CPR alter the previous situation whereby a claimant had to demonstrate that he would succeed at trial against the particular defendant who was the subject of the interim payment application. This had long seemed unjust bearing in mind that claimants often felt obliged to join a second defendant to protect their position when faced with a defence in which another party was blamed for their injury and that the court always had the power to order one defendant to reimburse

---

[11] [1991] 3 All E.R. 723, CA.
[12] [1991] 3 All E.R. 723 at 726–772.
[13] *ibid*. at 727d.

another, once liability had been determined between them. Now all the claimant must show is that he will succeed against at least one of the defendants. Defendants are protected by the further requirement that such an application can only succeed if all the defendants fall into one of the prescribed categories (ie. insured, MIB or a public body).[14]

Orders for interim payments against several defendants in the same action which were available under the RSC (see *Schott Kem Limited v. Bentley & Others*,[15]) should still be possible in appropriate cases under the CPR.

Judgment for "Substantial Damages"

The claimant has to establish that he would, if the action proceeded to 20–07 trial, obtain judgment for substantial damages. It must be uncontroversial to say that what is substantial varies with the circumstances: a commercial matter is not to be compared with a personal injury action. There is no authority as to what constitutes substantial damages. In some cases it will be clear: a young, employed adult who suffers disastrous injuries so that he cannot work again will clearly, upon success, be entitled to substantial general damages, special damages and future loss. Other cases will be less clear: an older claimant, irregularly self-employed or with long periods of unemployment and having suffered an injury that interferes with only some kinds of employment or which has simply accelerated a pre-existing condition by a few years may fail to surmount this hurdle. The CPR do not limit the availability of interim payments to multi-track cases and therefore it is arguable that damages totalling £15,000 or less can be deemed to be "substantial" in appropriate cases.

The damages with which the court is concerned are those that will be awarded in a personal injury action at the end of the trial. Usually that will comprise general damages, special damage and future loss. It follows that the court will, on an interim payment application, be looking for evidence on these matters, as to which see further under the headings *Amount of Interim Payment* and *Mode of Application* below.

Defendant within a Permitted Category

The wording of CPR 25.7(2), as with its predecessor (RSC, Ord. 29, 20–08 r. 11(2)) is neutral. That is, it does not put the burden upon the claimant to show that the defendant falls within a permitted category: rather it leaves it open to the defendant to demonstrate that he is not or the court may simply decide that it is not satisfied. However, the claimant is obliged to provide the court with evidence in support of the application dealing with

---

[14] CPR 25.7(3).
[15] [1991] 1 Q.B. 61 *per* Neill L.J. at 74F.

"the reasons for believing that the conditions set out in rule 25.7 are satisfied".[16] This will probably come in the form of correspondence from the defendant's insurers or documentation disclosed whilst the parties pursued the pre-action Protocol.

Whilst the vast majority of personal injury actions are brought against insured defendants or public bodies, the removal of the right to seek an interim payment from an uninsured defendant demonstrably capable of satisfying an order may produce harsh results in a minority of cases. The CPR's use of the expression "public body" instead of "public authority" (RSC, Ord. 29, r. 11(2)(b)) is, presumably, designed to remove any lingering doubt as to whether organisations such as NHS Trusts can strictly be said to be "insured" or within the definition "public authority".

The CPR also differ from previous rules of Court in providing expressly that the MIB itself, as well as an insurer appointed by it to act, can be the subject of an order for an interim payment, thereby implementing the decision of the Court of Appeal in *Sharp v. Pereira*.[17]

Amount of Interim Payment

20–09   CPR 25.7 provides as follows:

> (4) The court must not order an interim payment of more than a reasonable proportion of the likely amount of the final judgment.
>
> (5) The court must take into account—
>
>   (a) contributory negligence; and
>   (b) any relevant set-off or counterclaim.

Thus, although the position remains that the court has a discretion, which must be exercised judicially, whether or not to make an order for an interim payment and as to the amount of such payment: the wording of RSC, Ord. 29, r. 11(1) has been altered to emphasise the court's obligation not to award too high a sum, by reference to the factory mentioned. It will always weigh in favour of an order are that there is no reason in equity or justice why a claimant should be kept out of his money. On the other hand, the Courts are concerned that a claimant may be dissatisfied if, when the final award is made, he receives little or nothing in addition to the interim payments which have already been received. The overriding objective set out in CPR 1.1 may also be relevant here, particularly the suggestion that, wherever possible, parties to litigation should be on an equal footing.

20–10   Does the claimant have to show that he *needs* an interim payment? Recent caselaw based on the provisions of RSC, Ord. 29 has suggested not

---

[16] PD 25, Interim Payments, para. 2.1(4).
[17] [1998] 4 All E.R. 145, CA.

(see *Stringman v. McCardle*[18]), although is has long been the practice for applicants to depose to their reasons for seeking an interim payment as a means of persuading the judge to exercise his or her discretion in their favour. The CPR themselves do not resolve this issue expressly. However, whilst there is no reference to need or hardship in the list of matters about which evidence should be provided in support of an application for an interim payment in para. 2.1 of the Practice Direction on Interim payments the claimant *is* required to provide evidence of "the item or matters in respect of which the interim payment is sought". Contrary to the decision in *Stringman*, therefore, it is to be assumed that the court will now be concerned with the purpose for which the money is sought, and inevitably therefore its necessity, when exercising its discretion. This provision is no doubt designed to discourage purely tactical applications for interim payments.

A working rule commonly encountered, for which there is no reported authority, is that interim payment awards are not usually made in respect of general damages and are unlikely to exceed two-thirds of the special damage accrued to the date of the order for payment. It is only exceptionally, where for example a claimant demonstrates that he plans to undergo an expensive operation or set up a care regime, that the amount awarded for an interim payment includes a sum in respect of future loss or expense. The purpose of the working rule is that it allows for a margin of error and that there will be no overpayment (with concomitant difficulties in recovery) if the claimant should die of unrelated causes or discontinue his action. An amount of approximately two thirds of special damages ought generally to be sufficient to alleviate hardship and thus to satisfy the interests of justice. It is not in the claimant's interest to receive too much bearing in mind that any overpayment will have to be repaid, with interest.[19]

A note of caution is necessary. When a defendant makes an interim payment, voluntarily or pursuant to a court order, the provisions of the Social Security Administration Act 1992, s. 81(2) apply. In other words, payment is to be made net of benefits recoverable by the Compensation Recovery Unit.[20]

Adjustment

CPR 25.8 provides for the court to make an order adjusting an interim 20–11 payment, whether such payment was made pursuant to an order of the court or voluntarily. There are three separate scenarios set out below.

---

[18] [1994] 1 W.L.R. 1653; [1994] P.I.Q.R. 230.
[19] CPR 25.8(5).
[20] PD, Interim Payments, para.4.

Repayment

20–12   The claimant may discontinue the action, lose on liability or recover less by way of damages than the amount received as an interim payment. In such circumstances, the court may order the claimant to repay all or part of the amount received (or the excess received) to the defendant. CPR 25.8(5) now puts it beyond question that the court may also order the claimant to pay interest on the amount to be repaid, from the date the interim payment was made. Although the rule states that in these circumstances interest "may" be awarded, the accompanying Practice Direction states that an order for interest on an overpayment "should" be made.[21]

Variation or Discharge

20–13   Where there is judgment in a particular sum for the claimant, that sum may be varied (*i.e.* reduced downwards), or discharged by the amount of any interim payment. The details must be recorded in the judgment and the final order for payment should set out the amount, if any, outstanding to the claimant, as well as specifying the amount(s) and date(s) of the interim payments.[22]

Payment as between Defendants

20–14   Finally, the court may at any time order one or more co-defendants to repay part or all of the amount of interim payment to the defendant who in fact made the payment if that defendant is entitled to and has claimed contribution, indemnity or some relief related to the claim. If the application for reimbursement is dealt with before the final disposal of the claim, the applicant must also show that the interim payment he seeks to be reimbursed in respect of was made in circumstances falling within the criteria for interim payments in CPR 26.7.[23]

Timing, Tactics and Mode of Application

Timing/Tactics

20–15   The issues really are when and what should be sought. It is appropriate to note at the outset that there is nothing to prevent more than one application for an interim payment being made, but the claimant's repre-

---

[21] PD, Interim Payments, para. 5.5.
[22] PD, Interim Payments, para. 5.2.
[23] CPR 25.8(3).

sentatives must be astute to avoid incurring unnecessary costs by repetitious applications in consequence of mistimed requests or the presentation of insufficient evidence. In the vast majority of personal injury actions, the injured claimant is very keen to obtain some money as soon as possible. However, this is not always the case: for example, generous sick pay and the absence of other expenses may mean that a claimant's preference would be for a larger lump sum at the end of litigation. The best advice is to follow the claimant's wishes, but to remember that unless you tell him he may not have heard of the possibility of an interim payment. One safe guiding principle is that the defendant should always be asked to make a voluntary payment and given reasonable time (one to two weeks) in which to agree to do so before an application is made to court.

If the defendant admits liability in the Defence, an application for an **20–16** interim payment may be combined with an application to enter judgment. This simplifies matters, because liability is disposed of. If liability is denied, the representative must assess both the law and the evidence in order to establish the prospects of success against the requirements described above. It will, for example, be sensible to amass a quantity of evidence, rather than to rely solely upon what the claimant says. The relative strengths of the parties' cases should now be capable of assessment at an early stage and claimant's solicitors should already have all their client's evidence on liability in their possession before proceedings are commenced. In a road traffic accident one will be concerned to have a Certificate of Conviction in respect of the defendant driver, to obtain the police report and to flesh out the statements of any witnesses who are identified. A clear plan of the scene will often assist at this stage. Sometimes further expert evidence will be needed, particularly in respect of injuries at work. Such evidence will be dependent upon inspection, will require the provision of a report and is likely to take longer to obtain. In essence, the claimant is seeking to show that his is a very strong case.

In practice, success often depends upon the degree of robustness exhibited by the Master or a District Judge before whom the application comes.

Mode of Application

Applications for interim payments, like all other interlocutory appli- **20–17** cations, should be made in accordance with the provisions of CPR Part 23. This must, however, be read in conjunction with CPR 25.6 which prescribes different time limits for interim payment applications, and therefore overrides Part 23 to this extent. The time limits are as follows:

- 14 days' notice of application required (evidence to be served with application);
- respondent's evidence in reply to be served seven days before the hearing;

- applicant's further evidence in reply to be served three days before the hearing.

The application must be supported by evidence and the quality and detail of such evidence is usually central to the success or otherwise of the application. Paragraph 2.1 of the Practice Direction lists the matters which must be dealt with by the claimant's evidence as follows:

(1) the sum of money sought by way of interim payment;

(2) the items or matters in respect of which the interim payment is sought;

(3) the sum of money for which final judgment is likely to be given;

(4) the reasons for believing that the conditions set out in rule 25.7 are satisfied;

(5) any other relevant matters;

(6) in claims for personal injuries, details of the special damages and past and future loss; and

(7) in a claim under the Fatal Accidents Act 1976, details of the person(s) on whose behalf the claim is made and the nature of the claim.

If these matters are dealt with in the claimant and/or his solicitor's statement clearly, thoroughly and in a logical (and where appropriate chronological) order, this will significantly increase the prospects of success. Those advising defendants should bear in mind that any evidence which challenges the claimant's assertions must be before the court if it is to receive due consideration and the time for preparing and serving the same will often be very tight indeed.

At the Hearing

20–18 The claimant goes first. If it becomes apparent that there is a serious dispute as to liability or quantum which was not previously predicted, an outright loss may be avoided by seeking an adjournment of the application to deal with what has unexpectedly arisen. Another alternative here is to seek to have the case reallocated to the fast track to ensure a speedy trial or an order made for a split trial.

Summary

20–19 In the right hands an application for an interim payment is a useful tool which may benefit the claimant enormously. Practical difficulties, in particular in respect of liability and the effect of the benefit recovery rules, must always be taken into account and will often mean that it is not in fact practicable to press for an interim payment through the court. It seems that purely tactical applications are unlikely to be favourably received. None-theless, it may be in the interests of both defendant and claimant and in the spirit of Woolf that a voluntary payment is made, so it is always worth asking.

21. Structured Settlements

Introduction

Conventionally, compensation for personal injury has been by way of a **21–01** lump sum. The lump sum includes (in more serious cases) compensation for future losses, such as earnings and care. The claimant must make his own arrangements to ensure that the lump sum is managed and invested to provide the necessary compensating stream of income. Theoretically, he could do so by the purchase of an annuity, but the annuity would be subject to the incidence of taxation (in relation to the income element).

Structured settlements now provide a vehicle whereby the compensation is payable (in whole or in part) by a series of periodical payments. These payments are (normally) secured by means of the purchase (by the insurer of the tortfeasor) of an annuity. Unlike an annuity purchased directly by the claimant the payments are free of income tax. At common law, this freedom from tax was attributable to the fact that the payments were deemed to be payment of a capital debt, by instalments. There is now a statutory basis for the tax exemption.

The payments may be fixed or (more usually) indexed; they may be for **21–02** a fixed period or for the life of the claimant. If indexed for life, the payments provide to the claimant a guaranteed tax-free income, increasing annually, for the rest of his life, without the need to worry about managing the lump sum. It should be noted, however, that there will normally be a lump sum, in addition to the periodical payments, to provide a contingency fund.

It will be apparent that this arrangement will be very attractive to many claimants, provided always that the level of periodical payments adequately compensates for that part of the lump sum foregone. In more serious cases, those acting for a claimant will need to give active consideration to the question whether a structured settlement is in the claimant's best interests.

However, there is a major limitation to the implementation of structured settlements, namely that they require the consent of both parties. The Law Commission has considered, but rejected (at least in the foreseeable future) the possibility of structures imposed by the court.[1]

---

[1] Law Commission Paper No. 224, *Structured Settlements and Interim and Provisional Damages.* However, in a recent consultation paper, "Damages; the Discount Rate and alternatives to lump sum payments" the Lord Chancellor has again raised the question of structured settlements, imposed by the courts; and the (even more radical) question of reviewable periodic payments imposed by the courts. At the date of going to press the Lord Chancellor's response to consultation is awaited; it is now considered premature to consider these issues futher in this chapter.

Genesis

Revenue Concession

21–03 Structured settlements achieved a tax-free status in the United States
(1979–80), and in Canada (1980), and subsequently blossomed in those
jurisdictions. As a result, the Inland Revenue was approached and entered
into discussion with the Association of British Insurers (ABI), culminating
in agreement in Summer 1987. A model agreement, drafted by the ABI was
approved by the Inland Revenue. Four different types of periodic payment
schedules were envisaged:

Basic Terms	–	fixed payments for a fixed period
Indexed Terms	–	indexed payments for a fixed period
Terms for life	–	fixed payments for life
Indexed Terms for Life	–	indexed payments for life

The last were likely to prove the most popular.

The rationale behind Inland Revenue approval was that the instalment
payment of damages remained capital, rather than income, and thus not
chargeable to income tax.[2]

By the model agreement, the claimant accepted, and the insurer (not the
tortfeasor) agreed to pay, a capital sum in full and final settlement, but the
settlement was to be discharged by payments, as scheduled. The periodical
payments were to be secured by the purchase, by the insurer, of an annuity,
in accordance with the schedule. To preserve the tax break, the insurer,
not the claimant, was to be beneficially entitled to the annuity. Thus, the
life office, from which the annuity was purchased, was required to pay the
annuity directly to the insurer, who would distribute to the claimant. This
arrangement introduced administrative and fiscal complications for the
insurer, initially discouraging some insurers from agreeing to structure.

Judicial Approval

21–04 Despite this concession by the Inland Revenue of tax-free status, the
legal profession was slow to execute structured settlements. It was not until
July 1989 that the first English structure was implemented in *Kelly v.
Dawes*.[3] By chance, this case involved a patient, and thus required the
approval of Potter J. In giving approval, the judge suggested guidelines as
to the material to be placed before the court:

---

[2] Based upon *Dott v. Brown* [1936] 1 All E.R. 543.
[3] July 14, 1989 (unreported), but cited in full in Kemp & Kemp, *The Quantum of Damages*
(Release 74), para. 6A–075.

(a) a detailed opinion of counsel as to value, on a conventional basis;

(b) a report by accountants or other financial experts as to the fiscal and investment advantages of the proposed structure;

(c) a draft of the form of agreement, with confirmation of Inland Revenue approval;

(d) confirmation of approval by the Court of Protection;

(e) material to satisfy the court that there were sufficient funds available outside the structure to satisfy capital needs; and

(f) material to satisfy the court that the agreement involved secure arrangements by responsible insurers.

(The necessities for Inland Revenue approval, and—to an extent— investigations into security, have probably been superseded by subsequent developments.)

Example

It is worth revisiting the facts of *Kelly v. Dawes*, as an illustration of the working of a structured settlement. The claimant had sustained cata- strophic head injuries resulting in a permanent vegetative state. By the date of trial she was cared for in a nursing home with annual fees of £20,000. After an initial wide divergence in medical opinion as to life expectancy, life expectancy was "agreed" at 20 years; the parents were extremely concerned as to the reliability of this assessment. Conventional lump sum damages were agreed at £427,500. **21–05**

The structured settlement approved by the judge provided for:

(a) £60,000 already paid by way of interim payment;

(b) £50,000 by way of further lump sum; and

(c) annual payments for the benefit of the claimant, commencing at £25,562 p.a., and index linked, payable for 10 years or life, whichever the longer.[4]

Item (c) was secured by the purchase by the insurers of an annuity at a cost of £300,000. It will be noted, therefore, that the insurers paid only £410,000, a saving of £17,500, representing a discount for their agreement to the structure. This discount was more than counterbalanced by the tax saving achieved by the claimant. Most importantly, the parents' misgivings as to life expectancy were overcome by the lifetime guarantee of periodical payments.

---

[4] The claimant still survives, and the payments, after 10 years, were £36,618 p.a.

Development

21–06   Since *Kelly v. Dawes*, there has been a significant growth in the use of structured settlements. Examples of their extension are:

(a) *Boobbyer* (January 1992) in which a structured settlement was utilised in a Fatal Accident Act case, for the first time.

(b) *Field* (October 1991) was the first structured settlement in a medical negligence case.

(c) *O'Toole* (August 1992), which was the initial example of a self-funded structure, *i.e.* instead of purchasing an annuity to fund the periodical payments, the defendant Health Authority itself met the periodical payments from its own resources. In *Field*, and the handful of previous medical negligence actions to be structured, funding had been by purchase of an annuity.

(d) *Mrs J.* (1995), a case in which a structured settlement was combined with a provisional damages agreement.

Practice and Procedure

21–07   Judicial enthusiasm for the concept of structured settlement has been expressed on several occasions. For example, in one case Latham J. is reported to have said:

> "May I say that, as far as the courts are concerned the advent of these structured settlements . . . has given infinitely greater confidence that we are in fact doing better justice at the end of the day to both sides, and I am very happy that more and more, when one comes to deal with settlements in such cases as this, it is the structured settlement which fortunately has been chosen by the parties in order to reflect the fact that it is usually, not inevitably, the most sensible and just solution".

In order to cope with the increasing numbers of applications for approval of structures, in the case of persons under a disability, complicated by the short duration of annuity quotations, a Practice Direction was issued in February 1992,[5] incorporating, *inter alia*, the guidelines suggested by Potter J. in *Kelly v. Dawes*.

The Court of Protection itself came under pressure as to the level of fees in structured settlement cases. The arguments to reduce the level were twofold: (a) that the Court of Protection was saved the costs of managing that part of the lump sum utilised for the purchase of structure, and (b)

---

[5] [1992] 1 W.L.R. 328.

that the periodical payments were capital in nature, and thus ought not to form part of the "clear annual income" for the calculation of fees. Ultimately, in August 1992, the Court of Protection announced an amendment to its Rules,[6] with the effect that only one half of the periodical payments was to be treated as income. Thus, fees were reduced to a significant extent.

Medical Negligence

In medical negligence cases, the Department of Health became generally 21–08 supportive of structured settlements, and indeed instigated the first self-funded structure. It should be noted, however, that a complex balancing exercise is undertaken by way of an "Options Appraisal" report. As described by the Law Commission[7]:

"If an annuity is to be purchased by the NHS, the options appraisal must show it as the most favoured option and it must meet Treasury guidelines for the cost of the Exchequer as a whole. The discount to the Health Authority and the fact that the [claimant] is less likely to run out of funds and to have to revert to relying on NHS care, are weighed against the loss of tax which would have accrued to the state from the tax on the income of a conventional award".

A similar analysis is required in the case of self-funded structures.

Problems

Despite the burgeoning success of structured settlements, problems 21–09 remained.

Judgments

A pre-condition of the tax break was that there was *agreement* as to the 21–10 antecedent debt, payable by instalments. Thus, if a judgment were obtained, the possibility of a structured settlement would be lost. In a contested quantum matter, one method of circumventing the problem might be to request the court to make findings of fact as to the value of heads of claim under RSC, Ord. 33, r. 3, instead of giving judgment.[8] Whether this is a practical proposition is another matter: where the parties proceed to trial, the necessary goodwill for a structure may no longer exist.

---

[6] Rule 82A, introduced by The Court of Protection (Amendment) Rules 1992 (S.I. 1992 No. 1899). Now Rule 85, Court of Protection Rules 1994.
[7] Law Commission Paper No. 224, para. 3.106.
[8] Suggested by Adrian Whitfield Q.C., "The basics and tactics of Structured Settlements" (1992) New L.J. 135. See now CPR 3.1(2).

Certainly, however, in cases where approval is required under CPR 21.10, the practice became established that the judge merely approved the notional lump sum award in principle, if necessary adjourning for further consideration of a structured settlement.

Finally, care needed to be taken where there had been a payment into court. Mere acceptance precluded a structure, and accordingly careful orders had to be drawn reflecting an agreement between the parties, and providing for disposition of the moneys in court.

Administrative/Fiscal

21–11   As indicated above, one of the major drawbacks to the success of structured settlements was the requirement for the life company (annuity provider) to pay to the insurer (annuity purchaser), rather than to the claimant direct. The consequence was that the insurer suffered a loss in cash flow, as well as incurring a continuing administrative burden. The former arose because the insurer received the payments net of tax from the life company, but had to pay the claimant the gross sum. Tax could only be reclaimed at the end of each year. Many insurers regarded these features as disincentives, and were thus reluctant to agree to structures. Alternatively, the alleged additional costs were used as a factor to increase the discount demanded from claimants as the price of agreeing to a structure.

Excluded Bodies

21–12   By reason of the fiscal procedures, *mutual insurers* were effectively debarred from structuring, because they could not write off the tax. Similar difficulties applied to *medical defence organisations*, although, since 1990 (and the introduction of NHS indemnity) their involvement has reduced to claims against general practitioners and doctors in private practice.

Other bodies such as the Criminal Injuries Compensation Board, and the Motor Insurers Bureau (MIB) could not engage in structured settlements. In each case, the payments which they make were considered to be *ex gratia* and, therefore, no antecedent debt could be established. However, the Inland Revenue was willing to approve structured settlements where the liability of the MIB, under the Uninsured Drivers Agreement, was to be met by the Domestic Regulations Insurer rather than the MIB itself.[9]

Security

21–13   Potter J. was concerned with the question of security in *Kelly v. Dawes*. Under the Policyholders Protection Act 1975, if the life company collapsed, there was protection to the insurer up to 90 per cent, so that most

---

[9] See below, para. 18–23, for a fuller discussion.

of the insurers' obligations to the claimant were guaranteed. However, if the insurer collapsed, the claimant had no protection under the 1975 Act because he was not a policyholder. Thus, a potential lack of security rose.

Guarantees

Some difficulties arose with self-funded structures, mainly involving **21–14** medical negligence cases, because of concern as to the long-term solvency of Health Authorities. "Comfort letters" were provided by NHS representatives which satisfied most of those acting for claimants, but doubts remained as to their legal efficacy.

Law Commission

Consultation

In 1992, the Law Commission published its Consultation Paper No. 125, **21–15** *Structured Settlements and Interim and Provisional Damages*. This paper addressed, *inter alia*, the problems identified above. Matters for consultation fell into two broad categories, rationalisation of the existing voluntary regime, and proposals for major reforms. The latter category included the possibilities of court-imposed structures, of subsequent judicial review of structures, and (most radically) of alteration of the existing tax regime to allow claimants directly to purchase their own annuities on a tax-free basis.

Report

On September 6, 1994, the Law Commission's recommendations were **21–16** finally published in their Report, *Structured Settlements and Interim and Provisional Damages*.[10] The proposals for major reforms were rejected. In particular, it considered it "too soon to legislate to give the courts the power to impose structured settlements". It cited difficulties over appeals, and assessment of discount, together with the fact that the process of development of structuring was incomplete. The main problem, it concluded, "is that structured settlements are creatures of negotiation and are born of agreement between the parties".[11] For the present, therefore, structured settlements will remain dependent upon the agreement of the parties.

Recommendations

However, the Commission made wide-ranging recommendations for **21–17** rationalisation.[12] In summary:

---

[10] Law Commission No. 224.
[11] *ibid.* at para. 3.51.
[12] *ibid.* at paras 6.5 and 6.6.

(a) Arrangements should be rationalised to enable life offices to make payments under annuities bought by defendants with personal injury damages free of tax direct to the claimant.

(b) Provision should be made for statutory structured settlements, subject to specified conditions.

(c) Claimants should be given protection under the Policyholders Protection Act 1975, and such protection should be increased from 90 to 100 per cent.

(d) The courts should have jurisdiction to make an order by consent that the parties settle an action by way of statutory structured settlement.

(e) The tax-free benefits of a statutory structured settlement, together with policyholders protection should extend to structures purchased by the MIB in respect of uninsured drivers.

21–18   In addition, although not the subject of formal recommendations, issues relating to the Criminal Injuries Compensation Board (CICB), and government guarantees of self-funded structures were addressed. The Commission supported the view that the CICB ought to be able to offer structures,[13] and considered that a legislative guarantee would provide valuable additional protection in the case of self-funded structures.[14]

With remarkable pace, the proposed reforms reached the statute book within two years of the Law Commission Report.

Recent Reforms

Direct Payments

21–19   By section 142 of the Finance Act 1995, two new sections were inserted into the Income and Corporation Taxes Act 1988. Section 329A introduced the scheme of statutory structured settlements envisaged by the Law Commission. Provided that the agreement qualified under the section, the payments were to be tax free. The effect was that payments could now be made directly to the claimant by the life company.

Section 329B accorded similar treatment where an annuity, which had been purchased under a common law structure, was subsequently assigned to the claimant. Thus, the benefits of the new statutory scheme could be obtained, in the case of pre-existing structures, by assignment.

---

[13] *ibid.* at para. 3.105.
[14] *ibid.* at para. 3.109.

Somewhat confusingly, these sections have already been repealed, but re- **21–20** enacted in refined form, by section 150 and Schedule 26 to the Finance Act 1996, which introduces into the Income and Corporation Taxes Act 1988, s.329AA. Since this section now forms the basis of tax exemption for structured settlements, it is reproduced below:

"329AA—(1) Where—

(a) an agreement is made settling a claim or action for damages for personal injury on terms whereby the damages are to consist wholly or partly of periodical payments; or

(b) a court awarding damages for personal injury makes an order incorporating such terms, the payments shall not for the purposes of income tax be regarded as the income of any of the persons mentioned in subsection (2) below and accordingly shall be paid without any deduction under section 348(1)(b) or 349(1).

(2) The persons referred to in subsection (1) above are—

(a) the person ("A") entitled to the damages under the agreement or order;

(b) any person who, whether in pursuance of the agreement or order or otherwise, receives the payments or any of them on behalf of A;

(c) any trustee who, whether in pursuance of the agreement or order or otherwise, receives the payments or any of them on trust for the benefit of A under a trust under which A is during his lifetime the sole beneficiary.

(3) The periodical payments referred to in subsection (1) above, or any of them, may, if the agreement or order mentioned in that subsection or a subsequent agreement so provides, consist of payments under one or more annuities purchased or provided for, or for the benefit of, A by the person by whom the payments would otherwise fall to be made.

(4) Sums paid to, or for the benefit of, A by a trustee or trustees shall not be regarded as his income for the purposes of income tax if made out of payments which by virtue of this section are not to be regarded for those purposes as income of the trustee or trustees".[15]

Furthermore, by section 329AA(7), "damages" includes an interim **21–21** payment.

As a consequence of these reforms, all the fiscal and administrative problems have been swept away by the new statutory scheme. There are now no disincentives to insurers to agreement to a structured settlement.

Criminal Injuries Compensation Board/Authority

A further provision (s.329C) was introduced into the Income and **21–22** Corporation Taxes Act 1988 by the Criminal Injuries Compensation Act 1995. The effect of this section was to exempt from income tax structured settlements made, whether under the new statutory Criminal Injuries Compensation Scheme, or under the previous non-statutory scheme.

---

[15] Subs. (5)–(8) not reproduced.

Section 329C was itself repealed by section 150 of the Finance Act 1996, which substitutes section 329AB(1) and (2) to similar effect.

The first such structure (*Boulding*) was implemented in 1996.

Motor Insurers Bureau

21–23   *(i) Uninsured Drivers Agreement.* By the Uninsured Drivers Agreement, dated December 21, 1988[15a], the MIB agreed with the Secretary of State for Transport effectively to underwrite judgments against uninsured motorists. Under the Domestic Regulations between the MIB and its members, if a policy of insurance exists, even though the tortfeasor is not insured by it, that insurer meets the MIB "obligation", without recourse. Otherwise, claims are handled by a nominated insurer who is reimbursed by the MIB.

As explained previously, with common law structured settlements the Inland Revenue conceded tax free status to structured settlements agreed by Domestic Regulations Insurers. However, the residual category of payment could not be structured.

Now, as a result of the new statutory scheme of structured settlements introduced by section 150 of the Finance Act 1996, structured settlements undertaken by the MIB, in its own right, are entitled to the tax break in the hands of the claimant.

The first MIB structure (Hadfield) was implemented in 1996

21–24   *(ii) Untraced Drivers Agreement.* The other area of involvement of the MIB is under the Untraced Drivers Agreement with the Secretary of State for the Environment, dated November 22, 1972[15b]. Payments under this Agreement are not covered by the statutory scheme. However, by section 329AB(3) of the Income and Corporation Taxes Act 1988 (introduced by section 150 of the Finance Act 1996):

> "(3) If it appears to the Treasury that any other scheme or arrangement, whether established by statute or otherwise, makes provision for the making of periodical payments by way of compensation for personal injury within the meaning of section 329AA, the Treasury may by order apply that section to those payments with such modifications as the Treasury consider necessary".

21–25   The intention of this subsection is to give the Treasury the power to extend the tax concessions to other schemes or arrangements, such as the Untraced Drivers Agreement. Negotiations are still underway with the Treasury to apply this provision to payments under the Untraced Drivers Agreement.

[15a] With effect from October 1, 1999, the governing Agreement is that dated August 13, 1999.

[15b] With effect from July 1, 1996, the governing Agreement is that dated June 14, 1996.

Whilst referring to section 329AB(3), an interesting possibility arises. Claims against solicitors for negligence, in connection with the handling of personal injury claims, are not themselves personal injury claims, and thus not subject to the statutory structured settlements scheme. It is understood, however, that the Treasury might be persuaded to include payments, in respect of such claims, under the powers given by section 329AB(3). This would certainly be a logical extension because there is no reason, in principle, why a claimant, who has lost his personal injury action by the negligence of his solicitor, should also lose the prospect of a statutory structured settlement. However, at present, the Solicitors Indemnity Fund, responsible for underwriting such claims, is believed to be unwilling to contemplate structured settlements in such circumstances.

Mutual Insurers

21–26 The effect of the new statutory structured settlement provisions is to remove any fiscal disadvantage which previously precluded mutual insurers from entering into structured settlements. The same applies to medical defence organisations, and indeed the first structure involving a medical defence organisation has been implemented.

Security

21–27 The recommendations of the Law Commission for the enhancement of protection for structured settlement annuitants have been given statutory force by sections 4 and 5 of the Damages Act 1996 (in force September 24, 1996). In brief, not only are claimants given the benefit of direct protection under the Policyholders Protection Act 1975, but also that protection is extended to the full amount, rather than merely 90 per cent. The provisions are retrospective in the sense that, although applying only to liquidations after the September 24, 1996, they cover structured settlement annuities, whenever purchased.

The extended protection is expressly stated to apply also to structured settlement annuities purchased by the MIB or a Domestic Regulations Insurer.

It is unclear how such protection would work in practice; there was a suggestion in a recent case, *In the matter of W (a patient)*,[16] that a claimant might nevertheless be disadvantaged:

"There is no experience of how such protection would work and it is possible that a lump sum will be provided by a new annuity which might give rise to a

---

[16] June 10, 1998 (unreported). This matter arose when the Master of the Court of Protection refused to authorise structured annuity policies provided by Windsor Life Assurance Company Limited, by reason of concern as to security. Pumfrey J. concluded that there was no substance to such concern, and that the company should be reconsidered as a provider of structured settlements.

reduction in the amount of funds being received by the annuitant. It has also been suggested that there are also potential tax problems in that such an annuity might not qualify for tax-free status as at present . . .”

However, Pumfrey J. did not seem to be impressed by the cogency of such potential problems:

"Upon the insolvency of the insurer, it seems to me that were the Policyholders Protection Board to exercise its discretion so as to make a payment of a lump sum in respect of any shortfall in benefits, then on the face of it that exercise of the Board's discretion might be open to challenge having regard to the statutory duty of the Board set out in section 11 of the Act, which is essentially to secure continuity of insurance. It is to be noted that the statutory duty of the Board extends to "securing that the Policyholder will receive [the full amount] of the value of any future benefit under his policy" and I have difficulty in seeing how this requirement could be met by the payment of a lump sum which was insufficient to purchase an equivalent further annuity".

Moreover, the Judge expressed assent to the conclusion of an expert actuary in the following terms:

"In the event of a company getting into difficulties the likelihood would be that the full amount of its structured settlement annuities would be secured with another company and in extremis if there were insufficient funds the Policyholders Protection Act would provide any additional funds required to achieve this".

Thus, there are substantial grounds for optimism that any perceived problem is theoretical, rather than real, although the question will remain untested, unless and until a life company fails.

Self-funded Structures

21–28 The previously described difficulties of guaranteeing self-funded structures in medical negligence actions were removed by section 1 of the National Health Service (Residual Liabilities) Act 1996 which provides:

"(1) If a National Health Service Trust, a Health Authority or a Special Health Authority ceases to exist, the Secretary of State must exercise his statutory powers to transfer property, rights and liabilities of the body so as to secure that all of its liabilities are dealt with.
(2) For the purposes of subsection (1), a liability is dealt with by being transferred to—

(a) the Secretary of State;
(b) a National Health Service Trust;
(c) a Health Authority; or
(d) a Special Health Authority".

Thus, the long-term security of self-funded structures, in medical negligence actions, is underwritten by the Secretary of State.

However, self-funded structures may also be undertaken by other government departments. In these cases, provision has now been made, by section 6 of the Damages Act 1996, for a Minister of the Crown to guarantee the payments under such a structure.

Court Orders

Although the Law Commission rejected the grant of judicial power to **21–29** order structured settlements, it did recommend that the courts should have power to make orders for structured settlements, by consent. This recommendation is now enacted by section 2 of the Damages Act 1996, which further extends the power to include interim payments.

Summary

In brief, each of the problems in relation to common law structured **21–30** settlements, addressed by the Law Commission, has now been overcome by legislative provision. The present position is that there are essentially no obstacles to structured settlements, in cases involving personal injury, save only for the requirement of consent of the parties.

Discount

Level of Discount: 1992

At the date of publication of the Law Commission Consultation Paper **21–31** No. 125, in 1992, it would appear that the size of discount ranged from 8 to 15 per cent, with an average of around 10 per cent.[17] It should be stressed that the discount applied only to that part of the notional lump sum award to be utilised for the purchase of the annuity (or, in the case of self-funded structures, that part of the notional lump sum foregone).

In the Consultation Paper, the Law Commission calculated that, for a standard rate taxpayer, the value of the tax break amounted to "only a little over 8 per cent of the value of the annuity".[18] The value of the tax break was certainly one of the major justifications, from the claimant's viewpoint, for the allowance of a discount. Thus, on the basis of the Law Commission calculation, it was suggested that the extent of discounts then being achieved was excessive. The Commission suggested that there must

---

[17] Consultation Paper No. 125, at para. 3.28.
[18] *ibid.* at para. 3.29.

be other factors "such as the strength of the case, the desire to settle it and the desire to achieve certainty of future payments".[19]

Level of Discount: 1994

21–32   In the Law Commission Report No. 224, the Commission acknowledged that its calculations of the value of the tax break were unrealistic.[20] In particular, the ABI presented actuarial calculations tending to show that much higher tax savings were being achieved. Nevertheless, by the date of the report (September 1994), the average discount was said to have fallen to 7.5 per cent.[21] Moreover, as a consequence of the rationalisation recommended by the Commission, and now implemented, another factor in the assessment of the level of discount was removed, namely the fiscal and administrative disadvantages previously suffered by insurers. Estimates of the cost of those disadvantages ranged from 2–4 per cent of the purchase price of the annuity. The Commission expected that claimants ought, therefore, to be able to insist on further reductions in the discounts.[22]

No recommendations were made for the control of discounts, but the Commission considered that, in making provision for courts to make consent orders for structures, they provided an opportunity for judicial observations as to reasonable levels of discounts. The Commission also suggested that the Law Society ought to prepare and maintain "guidelines on average discount levels and what they represent".[23]

Current position

21–33   In practice, the current position appears to be that insurers are no longer demanding discounts. However, increasingly, they are insisting that any costs of investigating and implementing a structure are met by the claimant. This constitutes discount in another guise, in the form of irrecoverable fees or commission. In the case of payment by commission, this "hidden" discount is effectively 2 per cent.

It needs to be recognised, however, that the question of discount (if any) is merely one aspect of the negotiating process. Many other factors may enter the equation. For example, if liability is in issue, the extent of the dispute may be bridged by securing an appropriate structure. The availability of a structure may tilt the balance in the negotiations where the parties' assessments on a conventional basis diverge, but a suitable structure

---

[19] *ibid.*
[20] Law Commission Paper No. 224, at para. 3.126.
[21] *ibid.* at para. 3.127.
[22] *ibid.* at para. 3.128.
[23] *ibid.* at para. 3.129.

for the claimant's needs may be purchased in the middle ground. A good example of the latter was the previous uncertainty as to the appropriate discount rate for the calculation of multipliers. The massive divergence created by this uncertainty was (in some cases) capable of resolution by the purchase of an annuity guaranteeing the necessary stream of income for the claimant's lifetime.

The negotiations in each case will depend on the facts and the needs of the claimant and, therefore, little further guidance can be offered here. In patient cases, however, it should be borne in mind that a discount, if given, will need justification to the Court of Protection, as well as approval of the court. It was not unknown for the Court of Protection to insist on a lower level of discount.

Disclosure of Purchase Price

There is one other feature which merits consideration in this context. **21–34** The vast majority of structured settlements proceed upon the basis of an initial calculation of the conventional value of the claim, before progressing to the question of an appropriate structure. However, there is another less common approach, namely the "bottom up" structure. Here, attention is directed primarily to obtaining a structure to meet the claimant's needs.

In cases involving patients, where approval is required, the question inevitably arises whether the court needs to know the price paid for the structure in order to give approval. In the case of *Braybrooke v. Parker*,[24] this issue arose before Morland J. The judge concluded that disclosure was not essential because the only question for determination was whether the claimant's interests were properly met by the structure proposed.

The Law Commission considered whether the defendant should be obliged to disclose the purchase price, but decided against any mandatory requirement.[25] The consequence is that there may be an element of silent discount in such cases. However, in practice, the claimant's legal adviser ought to be able to obtain a good general idea of the price of the structure by instigating (through financial advisers) an inquiry as to the market price. This was recognised by Morland J. in *Braybrooke v. Parker*.

Advantages/Disadvantages

Advantages

For the claimant, the obvious primary advantage is the *tax saving* **21–35** available. This saving is especially valuable in serious cases, where the stream of income generated by a lump sum award would be likely to attract higher rates of tax (currently a maximum of 40 per cent).

---

[24] October 22, 1991 (unreported): discussed in Law Commission Paper No. 224, at paras 3.139–3.140.
[25] Law Commission Paper No. 224, at para. 3.143.

Equally important for the claimant is the *certainty* provided. The payments can be guaranteed for life, and index-linked to retain their real value. This element of certainty is best illustrated, however, by those cases where there is a genuine and significant dispute as to life expectancy, often a major bone of contention in serious personal injury cases. By agreeing to a structure, the claimant no longer has to depend upon the opinion of medical experts, or the finding of the court. He can rest assured that the payments will continue, even if he outlives expectations. Ironically, the more pessimistic the predictions of life expectancy, the better the quotations that can be obtained. Whilst it is true that, if the claimant were to die earlier than expected, there would be no lump sum available for his estate, this is irrelevant if there are no dependents; and if there are dependents some provision may be made by means of a minimum guarantee period (although this will increase the cost of the structure). It is suggested that structures are eminently suitable for cases of dispute as to life expectancy.

21–36   Further, not only is a claimant protected from the risk of dissipation of the fund, but he is also saved the worry and costs of *administration* of a large lump sum (although there will be a contingency fund in most cases to administer). Although a matter of some debate (see *Anderson v. Davies*[26]), there is authority for the proposition that a claimant who is not under a disability is not entitled to claim as damages the costs of investing and managing the fund.[27] This controversy is circumvented in the case of a structured settlement, in that there will be no such costs in relation to the structured payments.

Finally, there is an element of *flexibility*, at the outset, in the construction of the structure. It is possible for structures to be tailored to meet individual needs. For instance, in the case of a child, it might be appropriate to provide for a larger income, to reflect lost earnings, when he reaches working age. Similar arrangements can be made to coincide with anticipated increases in costs of care, and it is possible to provide for a future large capital payment to purchase accommodation at a future stage. Of course, it will be necessary to make an accurate prediction of future needs at the time of arranging the structure.

21–37   For insurers, the main initial attraction of a structure was possibility (now largely illusory) of obtaining a *discount*. It is suggested that a more important benefit is that the possibility of a structure provides a useful tool in *negotiation*. As previously indicated, willingness to enter a structure may prove the vital link in bridging differences, and thus achieving a negotiated settlement. In cases of disputes as to *life expectancy*, there may also be an advantage to insurers. It might be thought that many judges, faced with a

---

[26] [1993] P.I.Q.R. Q87. See also the dicta of the Court of Appeal in *Wells v. Wells* [1997] P.I.Q.R. Q1 at Q40–41.

[27] *Francis v. Bostock*, November 8, 1985 (unreported), but cited in Kemp & Kemp, *The Quantum of Damages* (Release 69), para. A2–005.

substantial dispute as to life expectancy, will be reluctant to adopt the pessimistic view: the risk of a sympathetic, but over-optimistic, assessment is removed by agreeing to a structure. The life companies frequently take more note of pessimistic predictions than the courts.

A final avenue of advantage for insurers is the potential for arranging the structure with a life company within the same group, and thus gaining the benefit of the life business. Previously, this was impossible in the case of composite companies, but this difficulty is removed by the new section 329AA(3) of the Income and Corporation Taxes Act 1988.[28]

Disadvantages

It should not be thought that structures represent a perfect solution to the problems of personal injury litigation. There are drawbacks which need to be balanced in the equation. **21–38**

The flexibility referred to as an advantage is only initial, and is dependent upon the accuracy of the forecasts at that time. If the forecasts prove to be wrong then the structure is *inflexible*. To an extent, these risks can be met by the provision of an adequate supplementary lump sum, by way of contingency.

Just as a structure removes the worries and risks of investment and management, it also removes the prospect of *better returns* by favourable investment. Some claimants may prefer to take their own chance in the investment markets. Careful financial advice is required in each case as to the respective merits of a structure as opposed to conventional investment. However, over lengthy periods into the future, predictions become inevitably speculative.

It is often suggested that index-linking does not adequately provide for *care costs*, which historically rise in advance of inflation. Whilst this proposition may be valid, the problem is not exclusive to structures. On a conventional basis, damages are usually calculated with reference to the current costs of care, and thus if those costs are exceeded, in real terms, the conventional award will itself become inadequate.

For many claimants who decide against structures, the governing objections are often *loss of control* and especially of the opportunity to provide for the family after death. This is a legacy of the lump sum culture. Although claimants of full capacity have the right to choose, they need to be given careful advice. Certainly, in the case of patients, the availability of an estate after death, in the absence of true dependants, is unlikely to be a significant factor in the decision whether to structure.

Conclusion

On balance, in principle, in most cases the advantages outbalance the disadvantages, to a significant degree. However, in practice, the balance will naturally depend upon the level of periodical payments achievable for **21–39**

---

[28] Which uses the words "annuities purchased or *provided for*" (emphasis added).

the lump sum foregone. This will be a matter for financial advice in each case.

With interest rates at a historic low, quoted annuity rates often seem disappointing (especially in the case of unimpaired lives). In theory, this may not matter, in that the rates are reflected in the returns on index-linked government stocks, which themselves now affect the calculation of the multiplier[29]. In practice, however, a prudent financial adviser will need to consider whether taxed returns on conventional investments are likely to be more attractive in the long term. This is a matter for financial, rather than legal advice, and it is beyond the scope of this Chapter to comment further.

Costs

21–40   It is often suggested that structures may result in a saving in costs. This is unlikely to be the case in most instances. Evidence will need to be garnered in the normal fashion, and thereafter it will be necessary to value the case on a conventional basis. Indeed, if anything, there may be additional costs involved in obtaining and analysing quotations for the annuity.

However, there will be a saving in costs where the agreement to the structure results in a negotiated settlement where otherwise there would be a trial.

Intermediaries

Law Commission: Consultation

21–41   The role of the intermediary was raised for discussion in the Law Commission Consultation Paper No. 125. In summary form the questions posed were[30]:

(a) should intermediaries be able to act for both parties, and, where they do, do they in fact act for one or both;

(b) what views were held as to the extent of their duties;

(c) whether adequate protection was provided by the [claimant's] legal advisers who should supervise the settlement;

(d) whether, where the intermediary has acted without due care, the law of negligence provided adequate protection for the parties affected;

---

[29] *Wells v. Wells* [1998] 3 W.L.R. 329, HL.
[30] Summarised in Law Commission Paper No. 224, at para. 3.131.

(e) what views were held on payment by commission; and

(f) whether the position of the intermediary in structuring cases raised special problems not adequately addressed by the law of fiduciary duties and professional negligence, which should accordingly be dealt with in the context of a reform of structured settlements or whether its position in structuring was simply an aspect of wider issues concerning intermediaries and professional advisers.

Recommendations

Considerable concerns have been expressed about the role of intermedi- **21–42** aries, and the form of remuneration. However, the Law Commission, in its Report No. 224, finally judged that there should be no legislative interference.

(i) Role of Intermediaries. On the role of intermediaries the recommenda- **21–43** tion was merely to the effect that the relevant professional bodies consider whether their rules required amendment in the light of concerns about intermediaries acting for both parties.[31] Specifically favoured safeguards were:

(a) joint instructions;

(b) full information as to the risks of joint instructions and the basis of charges;

(c) independent advice to be sought by the claimant's solicitor on the intermediary's report; and

(d) costs to follow the event so that the claimant is not penalised in any way as she or he would be if the costs were paid out of the award.

(ii) Remuneration. The form of remuneration has become an "old **21–44** chestnut". The competing forms are payment by commission, and payment by hourly rate. The former is utilised by the major intermediary, which is believed to have undertaken up to 75 per cent of structures to date. The commission rate is 2 per cent of the structured sum, and therefore, in large cases, may represent a very significant sum in relation to the work undertaken. Moreover, it is an effective deduction from the notional lump sum, to the claimant's detriment. The *quid pro quo*, however, is that it is a contingent fee, so that no fee is due unless a structure is implemented. Thus, it permits preliminary investigations into the feasibility of a structure without costs penalty.

---

[31] Law Commission Paper No. 224, at para. 3.134.

Although a majority of consultees opposed payment by commission, neither the Law Society nor the General Council of the Bar were opposed to such means of payment. The Law Commission agreed with the view that payment by commission was "part of the process of flexible negotiation which is still evolving" to be controlled merely by market regulation. It considered that there was likely to be a continuing trend against payment by commission, and made no recommendations for reform.[32] It must be stated that there is little evidence of such trend to date.

A note of caution should be sounded to those who would prefer to engage intermediaries who charge on an hourly basis. Such fees are unlikely to be contingent, and accordingly claimant's advisers run the risk that the defendant will refuse to pay such fees, especially where no structure results. It is prudent, if possible, to seek the defendant's agreement before incurring such fees. In practice, insurers are likely to resist any such request.

Practical Aspects

Financial Report

21–45   An important prerequisite of agreement to a structured settlement by a claimant is a comparison of the returns from structured settlements to returns from invested conventional lump sums. As interest rates fall, the apparent attraction of available annuities diminishes. It is essential, therefore, to obtain a proper financial appraisal of the comparative returns.

With the leading firm of intermediaries, such an appraisal is automatically included, and forms part of the service provided for the commission. The appraisal inevitably makes various assumptions which are necessarily speculative over the long term. Moreover, inevitable questions arise as to the independence of any such appraisal, in the context of commission. The Court of Protection told the Law Commission that such comparisons "do not always give an accurate picture and tend to over-favour structures".[33]

Whatever the shortcomings of such a comparison, (from whatever source) a suitable report ought to be obtained in order for the claimant's legal advisers properly to tender informed advice. It is mandatory, of course, in cases involving patients.

Guarantee Period

21–46   A minimum guarantee period is normally written into quotations, so that, if the claimant dies within such period, the periodical payments continue to be made to his estate. The longer the guarantee period the

---

[32] Law Commission Paper No. 224, at para. 3.137.
[33] Law Commission Paper No. 224, at para. 3.30.

higher the quotation. Accordingly, it is usually sensible, especially if there are no dependants, to consider alternative annuities based upon lower (or nil) guarantee periods.

Costs

Before undertaking any inquiries into the advisability of a structure **21–47** (other than on a contingency fee basis), it is prudent to obtain confirmation from the defendant's insurers that they are willing, in principle, to consider this form of settlement.

Size

Although structured settlements typically involve large claims, there is no **21–48** reason, in principle, why they should not be utilised for smaller claims. There are examples of structures below the £100,000 level. Perhaps the most appropriate case would be that of an elderly person, with very limited life expectancy, which would produce a small multiplier, and thus a relatively low award. Correspondingly, an attractive annuity might well be available, with the comfort of having a lifetime guarantee.

Quotations

It must be appreciated that annuity quotations are short-lived, usually **21–49** available only for about 14 days. If a suitable quotation is obtained, speed is, therefore, of the essence. The Practice Direction[34] makes provision for speedy listing (in cases requiring approval) but it is prudent to have the necessary documents available as soon as possible. For example, it is sensible to have counsel's opinion on conventional value, at the earliest opportunity.

Uberrimae Fidei

An annuity contract is one involving the utmost good faith. Accordingly, **21–50** no relevant medical evidence (whether or not disclosed in the action) ought to be withheld by the party seeking the quotation, or indeed by any party.

Professional Negligence

In serious cases, at least, consideration needs to be given to the **21–51** possibility of a favourable structure. Even if it is quickly dismissed as inappropriate, it ought to be on counsel's checklist, to avoid any subsequent allegation of professional negligence.

---

[34] [1992] 1 W.L.R. 328.

Conclusions

21–52   As a result of the deliberations of the Law Commission, and the remarkably speedy intervention of Parliament, there are now very few obstacles to the implementation of structured settlements. Disincentives to insurers have been eliminated. The only serious qualification is the need for consent of the parties.

The new statutory system of structured settlements provides a rationalised and effective scheme affording tax free periodical payments, index-linked, and guaranteed for life (or whatever is the appropriate period). Structured settlements afford security and certainty to claimants. Subject to appropriate financial advice in each individual case, they merit serious consideration in most large value personal injury cases. At present, however, quoted annuities tend to be discouraging.

22. Criminal Injuries Compensation

Introduction

State compensation has been available in Great Britain for victims of **22–01** crimes of violence since 1964. For claims made before April 1996, the assessment of compensation for successful applicants was based on common law damages. That link with common law damages was broken for claims made from April 1, 1996 when the Criminal Injuries Compensation Act 1995 placed criminal injury compensation on a statutory footing and introduced a tariff of awards. It also created a new body, the Criminal Injuries Compensation Authority (CICA), to administer it. When the tariff was devised, its awards were based on common law levels. However, a tariff which determines awards for 366 differing injuries according to the nature of the injury, necessarily provides a blunter and less sophisticated approach to compensation. Further, the level of tariff awards has now mostly, though not in all cases, fallen behind common law levels. The changes in 1996 made relatively few alterations to the rules determining eligibility to an award, so that case law relating to pre-1996 decisions is mostly still relevant.

The social basis of criminal injury compensation was expressed by a Home Office Minister in an adjournment debate held on January 19, 1999 after the introduction of the tariff. He said:

> "The State is not liable for injuries caused by the acts of others, but we are determined to continue to acknowledge in some way the public sense of responsibility for and sympathy with the blameless victim. Through the criminal injuries compensation scheme, the State provides a monetary award on behalf of the community . . . the scheme no longer seeks to provide finely judged compensation covering every head of damage that might be awarded in a successful civil suit. [It] represents some extra public recognition of the harm suffered by a blameless victim."

Sources of Information

The rules which determine when, how much and how compensation can **22–02** be paid are set out in a document known as the "scheme". The current scheme is the tariff, or 1996, scheme. It is made by the Home Secretary and has been approved by Parliament. It was last revised in April 1999. Also in 1999, the Home Office initiated a consultation on the operation and effect of the scheme. This is likely to lead to procedural and other changes, which will be set out in a revised scheme, but at the time of writing none have been announced. The tariff scheme differs from earlier schemes. Awards were formerly made by the Criminal Injuries Compensation Board (CICB) and were ex gratia. There have been five successive *ex gratia* schemes since 1964, the last being the 1990 scheme. Although the CICB was wound up on March 31, 2000, the 1990 scheme remains effective for about 5,000 claims made before April 1996 that have not yet been resolved. Most involve only the assessment of common law damages. Accordingly, paragraph references in this Chapter are to the tariff scheme.

Guides

22–03   The CICA publishes a guide to the operation of the scheme called a *Guide to the Criminal Injuries Compensation Scheme*. It explains the procedures for dealing with applications and sets out the criteria by which decisions are normally reached. It is not, however, a substitute for the scheme and does not cover every situation. It, too, was last revised in April 1999. The CICA publishes two other guides: a *Guide to Applicants for Loss of Earnings and Special Expenses*, and a *Guide to Applicants for Compensation in Fatal Cases*. They explain the relevant provisions of the scheme and set out worked examples of assessments.

Who Can Recover?

22–04   If the victim is alive, compensation may be paid to those who have sustained a criminal injury, and who satisfy the other rules in the scheme for eligibility. If the victim has died as a consequence of sustaining a criminal injury, and would otherwise be eligible, compensation in tariff claims may be paid to "qualifying claimants". They are defined in paragraph 38 of the scheme. The tariff scheme, generally, provides more generous compensation, and for a wider class of claimants, than do the Fatal Accidents Acts. In 1990 scheme cases, recovery follows Fatal Accidents Acts rules. The rules as to eligibility contain a number of absolute and discretionary bars to recovery (see below).

Criminal Injury

22–05   The principal definition of a "criminal injury" is an injury directly attributable to a crime of violence. Paragraph 8 of the scheme (which is not materially different from the wording of the 1990 scheme) defines a criminal injury. It means one or more personal injuries directly attributable to:

>   (a) a crime of violence (including arson, fire raising or an act of poisoning); or

(b) an offence of trespass on a railway; or

(c) the apprehension or attempted apprehension of an offender or a suspected offender, the prevention or attempted prevention of an offence, or the giving of help to any constable who is engaged in any such activity.

Most claims (97 per cent) are founded on crimes of violence, but sub-paragraphs (b) and (c) set out two other ways in which a criminal injury can be sustained. The claims they give rise to are often referred to as "railway suicide" and "law enforcement" claims.

The railway suicide provision is principally for the benefit of railway employees who either witnessed and were present when another person sustained physical or fatal injury, or were involved in the immediate aftermath (para. 9b of the scheme). This usually occurs following railway suicide attempts.

Police officers are the principal claimants under the law enforcement provision, though it also assists security guards, store detectives and on occasions members of the public. The offence referred to in this sub-paragraph is any offence (*e.g.* shoplifting, or theft from a car) and does not have to be a crime of violence. When a person involved in law enforcement activities, or in any activity directed to containing, limiting or remedying the consequences of a crime (*e.g.* firefighters, paramedics) is injured accidentally, compensation is not paid unless the person was taking an exceptional risk at the time (para. 12 of the scheme).

Crime of violence

A crime of violence is not defined in the scheme. In *R. v. CICB, ex p.* **22–06** *Warner*,[1] the Court of Appeal emphasised that what matters in deciding whether unlawful conduct amounts to a crime of violence is its nature and not its consequences. Lawton L.J. said

"... (the) submission that what matters is the nature of the crime, not its likely consequences, is well founded. It is for the Board to decide whether unlawful conduct because of its nature, not its consequence, amounts to a crime of violence. As Lord Widgery C.J. pointed out in *Clowes'* case, the meaning of crime of violence is very much a jury point. Most crimes of violence will involve the infliction or threat of force but some may not. I do not think it is prudent to attempt a definition of words of ordinary usage in English which the Board, as a fact finding body, have to apply to the case before them. They will recognise a crime of violence when they hear about it, even though as a matter of semantics it may be difficult to produce a definition which is not too narrow or so wide as

---

[1] [1987] Q.B. 74.

to produce absurd consequences, as in the case of the Road Traffic Act 1972 to which I have referred."

Thus, not every breach of criminal law is a crime of violence, even though its consequences may be indistinguishable from the effects of what is clearly a crime of violence. Breach of the Health and Safety Regulations, dangerous parking of a motor vehicle (Lawton L.J.'s example), or theft of an elderly person's possessions can lead to physical or psychological consequences similar to those of assaults, but the victims in such cases will not be within the scheme. On the other hand, assaults can be committed recklessly as well as with hostile intent. A pedestrian unintentionally knocked down and injured by a fleeing robber may, nevertheless, recover on the basis the robber was reckless as to the pedestrian's safety. Criminal damage can be a crime of violence as it can be committed intending to endanger life or being reckless as to whether the life of another would be thereby endangered: see *R. v. CICB, ex p. Clowes*.[2] As the law develops, current disputes centre on the circumstances when stalking or making telephone calls, or when indecent exposure, may amount to a crime of violence. Possible tests involve the intent of the perpetrator and whether the circumstances of the stalking, calls or exposure caused the victim to apprehend immediate personal violence: see *R. v. Ireland*[3] for discussion in context of criminal law.

Secondary Victims

22–07   The tariff scheme expressly recognises that persons who have not been the physical victim of a crime of violence but have themselves suffered mental injury because of the effects of the crime on the victim, can make a claim as secondary victims. The class of victims who may recover is limited by rules set out in paragraph 9 of the scheme, which substantially follow the principles of *McLoughlin v. O'Brian*.[4]

Absolute Bars to Eligibility

22–08   Compensation cannot be recovered in the following circumstances (listed in approximate frequency of occurrence):

(a) For an injury sustained outside Great Britain (para. 8 of the scheme). (Northern Ireland has its own scheme.) "Great Britain" is

---

[2] [1987] 3 All E.R. 854.
[3] [1998] A.C. 147.
[4] [1983] A.C. 410.

given an extended definition to include lighthouses off the British coast, installations on the continental shelf, the English part of the Channel Tunnel system, and British aircraft, hovercraft, and ships: see Notes 1 and 2 to the scheme for the complete definition.

(b) For a criminal injury sustained before August 1, 1964, which is the date the first scheme was introduced (para. 6).

(c) When the injury is attributable to the use of a vehicle, except when the vehicle was deliberately used to inflict or attempt to inflict injury (para. 11).

(d) For an injury sustained before October 1, 1979 and when the victim and assailant were living together at the time as members of the same family (para. 7b). Cohabitees living together as husband and wife are treated as members of the same family. There is no logic in this exclusion. Its existence depends on the date when eligibility to an award was extended to include offences occurring in the home, and the change was not made retrospective. The pre-1979 exclusion has survived since then. It still arises relatively frequently with adult applicants who claim they were abused when children, within the home. Whether they were living together with their assailant or abuser as a member of the same family is a question of fact, and the phrase member of the same family is to be given its ordinary sensible meaning. In *R. v. CICB, ex p. Staten*,[5] the parties were "living together" though the evidence given was that they slept apart and the wife neither cleaned nor cooked for her husband.

(e) Unless there is no likelihood that an assailant would benefit if an award were made (para. 15a). In the case of minors the likelihood can usually be circumvented by keeping the money on deposit until the child is of age. More acute problems arise when a woman continues to have occasional contact with the boyfriend who assaulted her, or when a severely disabled child is being cared for by a reformed parent who was party to the assault that maimed the child.

Discretionary Bars to Eligibility

The scheme is associated both with assisting blameless victims and with **22–09** encouraging the prosecution of violent crime. Paragraph 13 of the scheme contains five provisions which permit an award to be withheld or reduced when an applicant has fallen short of these requirements. They are dealt

---

[5] [1972] 1 All E.R. 1034.

with in some detail in paragraph 8 of the CICA Guide to the scheme. In summary an award may be withheld or reduced if:

(a) an applicant failed to take without delay all reasonable steps to inform the police or other appropriate body of the circumstances giving rise to the injury. If a crime is not reported, investigation cannot start, nor are the circumstances verified. However, a measure of delay is normally accepted in the case of young, elderly or incapacitated applicants;

(b) an applicant failed to cooperate with the police in bringing the assailant to justice;

(c) an applicant failed to give all reasonable assistance to the CICA in connection with the application. If an applicant does not keep in touch with the CICA nor responds to enquiries or letters it is difficult to assist;

(d) the conduct of the applicant before during or after the incident makes a full or any award inappropriate. It is provocative or reprehensible conduct, something which could fairly be called bad conduct or misconduct, which is taken into account and not merely conduct amounting to "contributory negligence": see *R. v. CICB, ex p. Ince*;[6]

(e) the applicant's character as shown by any unspent criminal convictions or by evidence available to a claims officer makes a full or any award inappropriate. The Authority has instituted a points system for assessing the degree to which an award should be reduced, and 10 points or over usually lead to an award being withheld. The details are set out in paragraphs 8–15 to 8–17 of the CICA Guide. It is irrelevant that the conviction has no bearing on the occurrence of the injury (*R. v. Thompstone*[7]); or that the convictions are subsequent to the injury (*R. v. Thomas*[8]).

There are additional provisions in paragraph 16 of the scheme setting out circumstances when an award should be withheld. This occurs when, at the time the injury was sustained, the victim and the assailant were living in the same household as members of the same family:

(i) unless the assailant has been prosecuted, except where there are good reasons why a prosecution has not been brought; or

(ii) if the violence is between adults in the family, unless the applicant and assailant have stopped living together and are unlikely to share the same household again.

---

[6] [1973] 3 All E.R. 808.
[7] [1984] 3 All E.R. 572.
[8] [1995] P.I.Q.R. P99.

Attributability

The scheme does not refer to causation, but instead provides compensa- **22–10** tion when the injury is *directly attributable* to a relevant event. *R. v. CICB ex p. Ince* (above) concerned a claim by a widow whose police officer husband had been killed whilst answering an emergency call in his police car. The Board had decided that his death was not directly attributable to the attempted prevention of an offence but to his own act of folly in crossing lights at red. In his judgment Lord Denning said:

> "In my opinion 'directly attributable' does not mean 'solely attributable'. It means directly attributable, in whole or in part, to the state of affairs as P.C. Ince assumed them to be. If the death of P.C. Ince was directly attributable to his answering the call for help, it does not cease to be attributable because he was negligent or foolish in crossing the lights. In such a case there are two causes: (i) the call for help; (ii) his negligence or foolishness. His widow can rely on the first, even though the second exists."

Attributability and Secondary Victims

The problem becomes more acute with secondary victims. Issues arise as **22–11** to whether or not the psychological condition on which the claim is based is directly attributable to events they were told about. In two recent decisions, judges have emphasised the importance of proximity between the event and the illness. In *R. v. CICB, ex p. K & Another,*[9] a mother and stepfather had claimed compensation for depression they had suffered following being told by their daughter that she had been indecently assaulted by her step-grandfather. Dyson J. did not interfere with the Board's decision that the injuries were not directly attributable to the assaults. He said that the word "directly" was intended to impose a restrictive limitation on the causation contemplated by the word "attributable", and held that proximity was relevant to the question whether the injury was directly, as opposed to indirectly, attributable to the crime. He said:

> " . . . the more remote from the crime in time and place the recounting of the experience, the more difficult it is to say that any psychiatric illness suffered as a result of being told about the crime is directly attributable to it . . . The closer in time and place the secondary victim is to the commission of the crime of violence, the more likely it is that any personal injury suffered by him or her as a result of being told about the crime will be directly attributable to it."

He rejected the argument that a finding of direct attributability must be made no matter how many links there are in the chain of causation, unless

---

[9] [1998] 1 W.L.R. 1458.

one of those links was an unusual event. The Court of Appeal refused leave to appeal.

In *The Petition of CW*, decided in Scotland in March 1999 and not so far reported, Lord Johnston commented on the words "directly attributable". He said they should not be fenced around with the cumbersome terminology that the common law used for the issue of causation, but should be given a simple common sense meaning, namely was there a direct link both in time and space between the criminal conduct and the injury to the claimant. He mentioned Dyson J.'s judgment in *ex parte K & Another*.

How Much Can You Recover?

22–12   The scheme identifies three general heads of compensation. The overall award is capped at £500,000 (paras 22 and 23 of the scheme).

(a)   There is a "standard amount of compensation" set out in a scale of 25 fixed levels of compensation in the tariff (paras 22 and 25). The lowest level is £1,000. Applicants whose injuries do not qualify for the minimum award do not receive a tariff award (para. 24). The highest level is £250,000, awarded for tetraplegia and for extremely serious permanent brain damage. Awards of the standard amount of compensation are "ring-fenced" in that they are not subject to deductions for benefits or insurance or pension payments received (paras 45 and 47).

(b)   There is an "additional amount" in respect of compensation for loss of earnings (para. 22b). Compensation for loss of earnings does not begin to be payable until 28 weeks after the commencement of an applicant's incapacity for work. Paragraphs 31–34 provide a code of rules for assessing the loss, including future loss. They largely follow the common law approach, and include a provision to permit the payment of a lump sum award for loss of earning capacity. However, there is a cap on the weekly amount which can be awarded, which is one-and-a-half times the gross average industrial earnings at the time of assessment. The treatment of deductions has its own rules (paras. 45–47). Loss of earnings claims are reduced for social security benefits, for pensions accruing as a result of the injury (*Parry v. Cleaver* does not apply), and for insurance payments; but there are exceptions for pensions accruing solely as a result of payments by the victim, and for insurance personally effected, paid for and maintained by the personal income of the victim.

(c)   There is "an additional amount" in respect of any "special expenses" incurred by the applicant. Paragraph 35 of the scheme identifies six heads of special expenses which can be claimed. In summary they are for:

(i) equipment relied on as a physical aid where the loss or damage was as a result of the injury (*e.g.* spectacles, or false teeth);

(ii) costs associated with NHS treatment for the injury (*e.g.* prescription and dental charges);

(iii) the cost of private health treatment where both the treatment and its cost are reasonable;

(iv) the reasonable cost of special equipment;

(v) the reasonable cost of adaptations to the applicant's accommodation;

(vi) the cost of care which is necessary as a direct consequence of the injury (and this can include the expense of unpaid care provided by a relative or friend).

None of these heads are recoverable unless the applicant has lost earnings or earning capacity for a longer period than 28 weeks. However, once the qualifying period has run, incurred expenses are recoverable from the date of injury. Future losses are recoverable. Full credit has to be given for social security benefits and, in the case of the last four items listed ((iii)–(vi)), for insurance receipts even when paid as a result of insurance personally effected by the applicant.

Multiple Injuries

An applicant receives the tariff award for the highest-rated description of injury 10 per cent of the tariff amount for the second highest-rated injury, 5 per cent of the tariff amount for the third highest-rated injury, and there is no award for any further injuries (para. 26 of the scheme). 22–13

Multipliers for Future Loss

In selecting a multiplier, paragraph 32 of the scheme refers to Note 3 and a summary table which illustrates the multipliers applicable to various periods of future loss to allow for the accelerated receipt of compensation. The table was prepared long before *Wells v. Wells* was decided in the House of Lords. Nevertheless, the multipliers for short periods are more favourable to applicants than currently available at common law. For longer periods there is a shortfall. The paragraph provides that in selecting a multiplier reference may be made to the Government Actuary's tables (the Ogden Tables) and that relevant factors and contingencies may be taken into account. 22–14

Fatal Claims

The scheme provides for a standard award of £10,000 to be paid to a single qualifying claimant, and £5,000 to each qualifying claimant if there is more than one. There is no limit on the number of qualifying claimants 22–15 who may receive a £5,000 award. The categories of qualifying claimants include not only spouses, but also the parents and children ("accepted" as well as "natural" and of any age) of the deceased victim (paras 38 and 39 of the scheme). Paragraphs 40 and 41 provide a code for assessing a dependency which largely follows that used in Fatal Accidents Acts claims, but the rules on deductions are more onerous (paras 45–47). For children there is an award of £2,500 a year to age 18 for loss of a parent's services when the child was dependent on the deceased victim for services, and there is provision for additional compensation if there are other losses (*e.g.* the cost of employing a housekeeper or nanny). Funeral expenses to an amount considered reasonable are payable for the benefit of the estate.

Making a Claim

22–16   An application for compensation has to be made on the form provided by the CICA. There is a two-year time limit for applying, but there is power to waive the time limit if it is reasonable and in the interests of justice to do so (para. 17 of the scheme). When a claim is received, the CICA makes enquiries of the police (or other appropriate authority) to help reach a decision on eligibility, and of the hospital and doctor the applicant has attended to reach a decision on the level of award. The decision is made by a civil servant (a "claims officer") working for the CICA. In most cases the decision is sent to the applicant within eight months of making the claim. If the applicant is dissatisfied, he can ask for the decision to be reviewed by the CICA. The review is carried out by a civil servant senior to the one who made the initial decision. If still dissatisfied, the applicant has 30 days in which to appeal to the Criminal Injuries Compensation Appeals Panel (CICAP). There is power to extend or waive the time limit.

Appeals

22–17   When there is no dispute as to the material facts or conclusions upon which the review decision was based, and a different decision could not have been made, an appeal can be dismissed on the papers (para. 70 of the scheme). The appellant is given the opportunity to make further representations or obtain further evidence before a decision to dismiss is made. About 10 per cent of appeals received are rejected on consideration of the papers. Otherwise, the appeal goes to an oral hearing. The CICAP aims to resolve an appeal within six months of receiving the notice of appeal, but that timetable depends substantially on the time taken by the CICA to prepare the case for hearing and on the cooperation of other parties, not least the applicant and his advisers.

Preparation before Hearing: CICA Case

When the CICA has collected the evidence it intends to use at the oral **22–18** hearing, it prepares a case summary. This identifies the issues raised. It also contains a list of witnesses who are to be invited to attend and a schedule of the documents to be used at the hearing. A copy is sent to the appellant. Once the CICA's documents have been agreed the appeal is ready to be listed. There are several matters to bear in mind.

(a) The list of witnesses may include a convicted or alleged assailant. In the interests of fairness such persons usually have to be invited to hearings involving eligibility issues. They rarely attend. If an assailant has indicated he wishes to attend, and the possibility of facing such a person is likely to cause the appellant distress, CICAP can, if given sufficient warning, make arrangements for the appellant and witness to be kept apart at the hearing.

(b) There is no onus on the CICA to go out and look for evidence in a case. It is for an appellant to produce the necessary evidence, though if eligibility is in issue the CICA will usually obtain evidence from the police. However, if the circumstances indicate that it is likely that evidence does exist which, if produced, might support the appellant's case, fairness dictates that it should be obtained before a decision is reached. *In R. v. CICB, ex p. A*,[10] a rehearing was ordered after a board had rejected an appellant's claim without sight of a report of a contemporaneous medical examination by a police doctor undertaken after her allegation of rape. If possible, such evidence should be obtained before the hearing so as to avoid an adjournment.

(c) Because of issues of confidentiality, copies of witness statements made to and provided by the police (other than the appellant's own statement) and any list of previous convictions may not be supplied in advance of the hearing. However, this procedure is currently subject to challenge by judicial review. The statements are at present made available on the day of the hearing and can be read before the hearing starts. If the statements contain material which the appellant wishes to challenge and an adjournment is necessary to do so, a Panel will reasonably consider any application for an adjournment.

(d) If eligibility is not in issue and the hearing is for assessment, the documents are likely to comprise only medical (or other expert) reports, possibly GP records, and the CICA's calculations of any financial loss.

---

[10] [1999] 2 W.L.R. 974, HL.

(e) The hearing is likely to be in a city near the location of the incident if eligibility is in issue, but at a hearings centre convenient for the appellant or his representatives if only assessment is involved.

(f) If there is an issue of eligibility as well as complex matters of assessment, the CICA may agree to a split hearing, deciding eligibility first.

Appellant's Case

22–19   An appellant or his advisers may wish to provide their own evidence. The CICAP Notes on Procedure, which are sent to all appellants, say that CICAP must be provided with a copy of any documentary evidence to be used at least 2 weeks before the hearing. If not provided in sufficient time there is a risk that the material will either not be admitted, or its late production may lead to an adjournment and wasted costs. The CICAP aims normally to resolve 8 cases in a hearings day, so forward reading is essential. The receipt of bulky or complex fresh documentation shortly before a hearing prejudices other appellants and makes the expeditious resolution of lists impossible.

Procedure at Hearing

22–20   There are rules in paragraphs 72–78 of the scheme, though some may be affected following the implementation of the Human Rights Act. There are several aspects to mention:

(a) The procedure at a hearing differs from that in a court. The hearing takes place in private, though the appellant is entitled to bring a friend or legal adviser to assist in presenting a case. It is held before two or three adjudicators (usually three) one of whom will almost certainly be legally qualified. Those not legally qualified may have experience in either the private or public sector. Some are medically qualified. Their CVs can be found in CICAP's annual report or on its website.

(b) The appeal is a hearing of the application afresh, and an award may be refused even if one had been offered initially: see *R. v. CICB, ex p. Lain.*[11]

(c) The burden of proof, which is on the balance of probabilities, is placed on the appellant, and it is for him to make out his case (para. 64 of the scheme).

---

[11] [1967] 2 Q.B. 864.

(d) The procedure at the hearing is not adversarial. It is by way of inquiry, and is as informal as is consistent with the proper determination of appeals.

(e) The inability to compel the attendance of witnesses has led to the provision in the scheme that adjudicators are not bound by rules of evidence which may prevent a court from admitting any document or other matter or statement in evidence. Accordingly, hearsay evidence is often admitted, on both sides, as is opinion evidence in appropriate cases. However, if the only evidence on a vital issue is offered by way of hearsay evidence, but the best evidence is available, a Panel is likely to allow an adjournment to enable it to be called and challenged: see *R. v. CICB, ex p. Cobb*.[12]

(f) The procedure to be followed for any particular appeal is a matter for the adjudicators hearing the appeal. It is common for the issues to be introduced by the chairman and then, if the issue is eligibility, for the appellant to be asked questions by the CICA's presenting officer. If the issue is assessment, it is likely that after the introduction the appellant or any representative will be invited to call any evidence that is required and asked how the case is put.

Medical Evidence

It is rare for medical witnesses to attend a hearing. Their evidence is **22–21** usually taken from reports. These should substantiate that the injury was sustained in the incident, describe the nature of the injury, and deal with its treatment and how long its effects lasted, or with its present effects, as well as with issues such as exacerbation of pre-existing conditions. There is seldom a need for a detailed report on prognosis such as is common in personal injury claims. The tariff generally does no more than distinguish between disabilities which are permanent or continuing and those in which there has been recovery.

There is a provision in the scheme (para. 56) enabling a case to be reopened when there has been such a material change in a victim's medical condition that injustice would occur if the original assessment of compensation were allowed to stand. Accordingly, a doctor does not have to provide a prognosis to deal with such a risk. Nor is there any need for provisional awards. The application form for compensation which an applicant signs contains the applicant's agreement to disclose all medical reports obtained or to be obtained on his behalf. As public funds are involved, the CICA and the CICAP do not expect selective disclosure, but

---

[12] [1995] P.I.Q.R. P90.

look to receive copies of all reports that have been obtained so that the full picture, warts and all, can be seen.

Financial Evidence

22–22   In all but the simplest claims the CICA will provide a calculation of the loss based on the material supplied to it. If an appellant does not agree with the figures and has reached a different figure, the issues between the two calculations should be identified so that the adjudicators may decide on them. If the claim is at all complex, the CICA would expect to see copies well in advance of the hearing of relevant P60s, final tax assessments and accounts, so that a fair calculation can be prepared.

The CICAP Decision

22–23   The decision will usually be given orally after a short adjournment immediately following the conclusion of the hearing. Short reasons will be given so that the appellant knows the factual basis on which the relevant conclusion has been arrived at, and what considerations had been taken into account. If the appeal involves a large assessment, the appellant can expect the panel to provide the factual basis for its conclusions and a concise statement of the means by which it arrived at the figure awarded.

Matters Ancillary to the Decision

22–24   There is no power for the CICA or CICAP to make awards of interest. Nor of costs, though the reasonable expenses of the appellant and of witnesses who attend to give evidence may be paid (para. 74 of the scheme). Interim awards can be made, either by the CICA (para. 53), by the panel on an adjournment of the hearing (para. 77), or informally pending hearing by the panel chairman by arrangement with the CICA. Structured settlements are available provided prior agreement has been reached with the CICA (para. 52). In minors' claims, awards can be, and often are, placed on deposit until majority is reached. If an applicant subsequently receives any other payment in respect of the same injury by way of criminal injury compensation from another fund, civil damages or compensation from a criminal court, the CICA requires repayment (paras 48 and 49).

Further Appeals

22–25   The decision of the CICAP is final and there is no appeal to the Secretary of State (paras 3 and 56 of the scheme). However, since awards were first made, the courts have exercised the power to supervise the CICB by way of judicial review (see *Lain* above), and there is now a body of reported case law (and many unreported decisions) on the operation of the CICB's schemes.

Section 3

PROCEDURE

23. Limitation

Policy and History

Since the Limitation Act 1623, which imposed a limitation period of six 23–01
years in respect of causes of action essentially concerned with simple
contract and tort, the legislature has recognised as a matter of policy that
there should be finality and certainty in litigation. The 1623 Act also
recognised that a fixed period of limitation could cause injustice and by
section 7 of the Act provided that time would not run against a claimant
who suffered under a disability. The six-year period in which to bring an
action based on simple contract or tort survived until the Law Reform
(Limitation of Actions, Etc.) Act 1954, when the period for instituting
proceedings with respect to personal injuries was reduced to three years.
The 1954 Act did, however, abolish the limitation period of one year, then
in force, in favour of public authorities as instituted by the Public
Authorities Protection Act 1893 and the Limitation Act 1939.

One effect of the 1954 Act was to aggravate the harshness of limitation 23–02
law when applied to imperceptible injury where time expired even before
the diagnosis of incipient disease was possible. Following criticism of these
hard cases,[1] the Limitation Act 1963 was enacted which introduced the
concept of "date of knowledge" which allowed a claimant to commence an
action after three years if it could be demonstrated that material facts of a
decisive character were outside his knowledge within the primary three
year period. The 1963 Act allowed a claim to be initiated with leave if
proceedings were started within 12 months of a claimant's date of
knowledge. This period was extended to three years by the Law Reform
(Miscellaneous Provisions) Act 1971.

The 1975 Limitation Act, following recommendations made by the 23–03
Inquiry Report on Limitations of Actions in Personal Injury Claims, Cmnd.
5630, (1974) invested the court for the first time with a discretion to
disapply the primary limitation period if in all the circumstances of a case it
was thought equitable to do so. The thinking behind the Committee was to
invest the court with a power to investigate actual hardship arising from
the operation of strict periods imposed both by the primary limitation
period and by the claimant's date of knowledge.

The Limitation Act 1980, in force on May 1, 1981, consolidated all
limitation legislation and now contains the total legislative code in respect
of personal injury actions. The Consumer Protection Act 1987, which

---

[1] *cf. Cartledge v. Jopling & Sons Limited* [1963] A.C. 758.

created a statutory cause of action for damages including those arising out of personal injury due to unsafe products, has caused a further amendment to the Limitation Act 1980, ss.14(1A) and 11A. Actions brought under the Act for damages arising out of the use of unsafe products may be brought within three years of the cause of action accruing or three years from the date when the claimant knew or could with reasonable diligence have discovered the existence of his cause of action. However, no such action under the Act may be brought after 10 years from when the product in question was last supplied.

The Primary Limitation Period

23–04   Section 11 of the Limitation Act 1980 imposes a primary limitation period of three years from the date of the accrual of the cause of action or three years from the date of knowledge of the person injured if later. In cases brought on behalf of an estate following the death of the injured person, the limitation period is three years from the date of death or three years from the date of the personal representative's knowledge, whichever is later (section 11(5)). In fatal cases brought on behalf of a dependant under the Fatal Accidents Act 1976, the dependants have three years to initiate an action from the date of death or three years from the date of knowledge of the person for whose benefit the action is brought, which-ever is later (section 12). Further, in fatal cases under the Fatal Accidents Act 1976 where the action is brought for the benefit of more than one person, the limitation period is to be applied separately to each of the dependants with respect to their dates of knowledge.

There is no long-stop provision for personal injury actions except those brought alleging a breach of the Consumer Protection Act 1987 which prohibits any claim brought after the expiry of 10 years (section 11A).

23–05   In tort, a cause of action accrues when damage which is more than minimal occurs (see *Cartledge v. Jopling*[2]; *Hopkins v. MacKenzie*).[3] Time stops running when proceedings are issued and not from when they are served. In calculating the period of limitation, the day upon which the cause of action arose is excluded (see *Marren v. Dawson Bentley & Co*).[4] If process cannot be issued because the court office is closed, as on a weekend or on a public holiday, the limitation period is effectively extended until the next date upon which the court is open for business (see *Pritam Kaur v. S. Russell & Sons Limited*).[5]

Time does not run for a minor until the age of 18 is reached and accordingly a minor has three years from the age of 18 to bring an action

---

[2] [1963] A.C. 758.
[3] (1995) 6 Med. L.R. 26.
[4] [1961] 2 Q.B. 135.
[5] [1973] Q.B. 336.

for personal injury (section 28(6)). Similarly, a person suffering from a mental disability within the meaning of the Mental Health Act 1983 and who is thereby incapable of managing and administering his property and affairs has three years to bring a claim after the cessation of the disability (section 28 and section 38(4)). There is, therefore, no limitation period in respect of a permanently brain-damaged claimant minor or adult who sues in respect of the incident which caused the brain damage. Such a person may have a claim brought in his name at any time including up to three years after his death. (See *Bull v. Devon Health Authority*[6-7] and *Headford v. Bristol and District Health Authority*.[8])

Negligence, Nuisance and Breach of Statutory Duty

Section 11 of the Limitation Act 1980 provides: 23–06

"11(1) This section applies to any action for damages for negligence, nuisance or breach of duty (whether the duty exists by virtue of a contract or of provision made by or under a statute or independently of any contract or any such provision) whether damages claimed by the claimant for the negligence, nuisance or breach of duty consist of or include damages in respect of personal injuries to the claimant or any other person".

Accordingly, the vast bulk of personal injury claims will fall within the 23–07
definition of negligence, nuisance or breach of duty. The major exception has been held by the House of Lords in *Stubbings v. Webb*[9] to be those personal injuries resulting from deliberate assaults including sexual assault and rape. The primary limitation period for such causes of action is six-years under section 2 of the Limitation Act 1980. This six-year period is not subject to a claimant's date of knowledge nor is the court invested with any discretion to disapply the period. This decision raises a significant issue as to what is the appropriate limitation period in that class of action brought against medical practitioners based upon an allegation of failing to obtain consent for treatment. In *Dobbie v. Medway Health Authority*,[10] the Master of the Rolls indicated that section 11 of the Limitation Act 1980 did not apply to actions in trespass for which no extension of time in law was permissible. It would appear, therefore, possible to have a claim with two causes of action, one alleging no consent for medical treatment based on trespass which would have a limitation period of six years and another based upon negligent treatment which would have a three-year period but subject to a date of knowledge provision and a possible extension under

---

[6-7] (1993) 4 Med. L.R. 117.
[8] (1995) 6 Med. L.R. 61.
[9] [1993] A.C. 498.
[10] [1994] 4 All E.R. 450.

section 33 of the Limitation Act 1980. It may be that in cases of so-called unintentional trespass the court may construe the cause of action as essentially being based in negligence and apply the provisions of section 11 (see *Letang v. Cooper*).[11]

"Consists of or Includes Damages in Respect of Personal Injuries to the Plaintiff or any Other Person"

23–08   Section 38 of the 1980 Act defines personal injuries to include: "Any disease and any impairment of a person's physical or mental condition and 'injury' and cognate expressions shall be construed accordingly". This definition will *not* include professional negligence actions against solicitors who fail to launch personal injury actions in time or who fail to prevent a claim being struck out for want of prosecution. (see Nicholls L.J. in *Howe v. David Brown Tractors (Retail) Limited*[12]; *Ackbar v. Green*[13]; and *McGahie v. Union of Shop Distributive and Allied Workers*.[14] However, if such a professional negligence action includes a claim for personal injury in the form of an anxiety and stress condition caused by the solicitor's failure to handle a claim properly then the professional negligence action will be a personal injury claim and will be subject to the provisions of Section 11 of the Limitation Act 1980.[15] A claimant may not be allowed to merely jettison the personal injury claim in an attempt to obtain a longer period of limitation under sections 2 or 5 of the 1980 Act.[16]

Similarly, a claimant cannot avoid the provisions of section 11 of the 1980 Act by putting forward a claim as an economic loss of a partnership, firm or company if in fact the true nature of the loss is a loss of income or profit arising out of a personal injury occasioned to a partner or director. In *Howe*, the Court of Appeal held that an attempt by the claimant to add his father and his firm to an action so as to claim for the whole of the firm's loss of profit arising from the claimaint's inability to work due to a personal injury, if such a claim existed as a matter of law at all, did not avoid the provisions of section 11 because the claim was for damages in respect of personal injuries to the claimant or to *any other person*.

23–09   A similar approach was taken by the Court of Appeal in *Walkin v. South Manchester Health Authority*[17] where it was held that a failed sterilisation resulting in an unplanned pregnancy was a claim based on personal injury

---

[11] [1965] 1 Q.B. 232.
[12] [1991] 4 All E.R. 30.
[13] [1975] Q.B. 582.
[14] [1966] S.L.T. 74.
[15] *Bennett v. Greenland Houchen & Company* [1998] P.N.L.R. 458.
[16] *Oates v. Harte Reade & Co.* [1999] P.I.Q.R. P120.
[17] [1995] 4 All E.R. 132.

even if the mother did not bring a claim for the impairment to her health which the pregnancy created or for the pain and suffering of the birth. In *Walkin*, the mother's claim was for the economic loss resulting from bringing up the unplanned child. The court held that the unwanted pregnancy was an impairment of the mother's physical condition within the definition of section 38 of the 1980 Limitation Act and damage was said to have occurred at the moment of conception. The court, therefore, would not allow the claimant to obtain the benefit of a six-year limitation period by simply jettisoning her own personal claim for personal injury. Different considerations might, however, apply to a failed vasectomy (see *Patterson v. Hobbs*[18], *Naylor v. Preston Area Health Authority*[19] and *Allen v. Bloomsbury Health Authority*.[20] In such cases, there obviously is no physical injury to the father when a claim is based upon the economic loss of bringing up a child as a result of a failed vasectomy. However, Auld L.J. doubted this proposition and expressed a view that he could see no reason why a failed vasectomy was not a personal injury because it related to damages in respect of injury not to the claimant but to "any other person", namely the "injury" to the mother. A failure to ascertain whether an unborn child had rubella and which, thereby, resulted in the birth of a disabled child may give rise to a personal injury cause of action on behalf of a mother on the basis that her continued pregnancy was a personal injury.[21] In *Anderton v. Clwyd*,[22] the Court of Appeal held that dyslexia was a constitutional condition and any failure to mitigate or reduce its consequence was not an injury.[23]

Date of Knowledge: Section 11(4), Section 14 of the Limitation Act 1980

Section 14(1) provides: 23–10

"In Sections 11 and 12 of this Act references to a person's date of knowledge are references to the date on which he first had knowledge of the following facts—

(a) that the injury in question was significant; and
(b) that the injury was attributable in whole or in part to the act or omission which is alleged to constitute negligence, nuisance or breach of duty; and
(c) the identity of the defendant; and
(d) if it is alleged that the act or omission was that of a person other than the defendant, the identity of that person and the additional facts supporting the bringing of an action against the defendant;

---

[18] *The Times*, November 11, 1985.
[19] [1987] 2 All E.R. 353.
[20] [1993] 1 All E.R. 651.
[21] *Das v. Ganju* [1999] Lloyd's Rep. Med. 198.
[22] [1999] E.L.R. 1.
[23] See also *Phelps v. Hillingdon London Borough Council* [1999] 1 W.L.R. 500.

and knowledge that any acts or omissions did or did not, as a matter of law, involve negligence, nuisance or breach of duty is irrelevant."

"The Date on which he First had Knowledge of the Following Facts . . ."

23–11   The limitation period does not begin to run against a claimant until he has knowledge that his injury was significant, was attributable to an act or omission on the part of the defendant whose identity he must know or, alternatively, he must know the identity of a person who is vicariously liable for the acts or omissions of the defendant. The leading authority on what constitutes knowledge is to be found in the product liability case of *Nash v. Eli Lilly & Co. and Others*.[24] This action concerned preliminary trials on limitation arising from reactions to the drug Opren such as skin sensitivity, abnormal hair growth and liver and kidney failure. Knowledge for the purposes of the section is now defined by the court as a condition of mind which imports a degree of certainty which might reasonably be regarded as sufficient to justify the claimant embarking upon the preliminaries to the making of a claim such as taking legal or other advice. Knowledge does not, therefore, mean knowing for certain and may amount to no more than a reasonably firmly held belief which would warrant a claimant taking steps to investigate the claim. Investigating whether the claimant had such a degree of certainty would involve the court looking at not only the intellectual capacity of the claimant to understand information but also considering, as a matter of fact, whether the claimant did comprehend the information obtained. The Court of Appeal in *Nash* also stipulated that time was not suspended or interrupted because an expert opinion contradicted the claimant's firmly held belief that the injury sustained was due to the defendant's act or omission. Providing that a claimant has a firm enough belief that the defendant's act or omission did in fact cause his injury, then time runs irrespective of what an expert says. Alternatively, if a claimant has a suspended belief but feels the need for confirmation of that belief by an expert, then time would not run until the expert's positive opinion was obtained. The Court of Appeal has reaffirmed the approach in *Nash* by emphasising that all a claimant had to know was the essence of the complaint not the full details required to plead a case and all the court had to inquire into was how far the claimant had knowledge in broad terms of the facts upon which the complaint was based (see *Whitfield v. North Durham Health Authority*[25]; *Gregory v. Ferro (GB) Limited*[26]; *Spargo v. North Essex District Health Authority*[27]; *O'Driscoll v.*

---

[24] [1993] 1 W.L.R. 782.
[25] (1995) 6 Med. L.R. 32.
[26] (1995) 6 Med. L.R. 321.
[27] [1997] P.I.Q.R. P235.

Dudley Health Authority[28]; *Roberts v. Winbow*[29]; *Irshad Ali v. Courtaulds Textiles Limited*.[30] In *Spargo* and in *Roberts,* the Court of Appeal has emphasised that the claimant's belief that injuries were caused by the tort in question may be without evidence or justification and might be irrational but this will not stop time running against the claimant as long as the belief is firmly held. The cases of *O'Driscoll* and *Irshad Ali* are examples of where the Court of Appeal has held that knowledge was not achieved until confirmation of the relationship between the injury and the tort had been made by expert evidence.

Significance: Section 14(1)(a)

"Significant" is defined by section 14(2) in the following terms: 23–12

"For the purposes of this section an injury is significant if the person whose date of knowledge is in question would reasonably have considered it sufficiently serious to justify his instituting proceedings for damages against a defendant who did not dispute liability and was able to satisfy a judgment".

This test makes even relatively trivial matters significant because it might well be worth suing over minor injuries if a defendant is able to pay damages and does not put liability in issue. The courts have emphasised that significance is to be determined by looking at the first injury and its manifestations not by looking at any subsequent deterioration (see *Miller v. London Electrical Manufacturing Company Limited*[31] and *Bristow v. Grout*).[32] In *Miller,* the claimant developed dermatitis in 1967 and needed some time off work but by 1971 the condition had deteriorated to eczema all over his body. The court held that his significant injury ran from the development of the dermatitis and not from the deterioration. There are, however, occasions when the court will consider whether it was reasonable that a claimant did delay because he did not consider the injury sufficiently serious. The test of reasonableness was said in *McCafferty v. Metropolitan Police Receiver*[33] to be both subjective and objective. The court can examine whether the particular claimant in question subjectively considered the injury sufficiently serious but must also look objectively as to whether he was acting reasonably if he did not regard it as sufficiently serious (see *Stephen v. Riverside Area Health Authority*.[34] However, in *Dobbie v. Medway Health Authority*,[35] the Master of the Rolls indicated that the

---

[28] [1998] Lloyd's Rep. Med. 210.
[29] [1999] P.I.Q.R. P77.
[30] [1999] 8 Lloyd's Rep. Med. 301.
[31] [1976] 2 Lloyd's Rep. 284.
[32] *The Times,* November 9, 1987.
[33] [1977] 1 W.L.R. 1073.
[34] (1990) 1 Med. L.R. 261.
[35] [1994] 4 All E.R. 450.

question of significance was to be directed solely to the quantum of the injury, namely whether he would reasonably have accepted it as a fact of life or not worth bothering about. In *Briggs v. Pitt-Payne and Liars*, the Court of Appeal emphasised that in assessing whether an injury caused by a drug regime was significant did not require a fine analysis of whether the side effects outweighed the beneficial effects of the drug. In *Roberts v. Winbow*, the court found that time ran against the claimant when he knew that a lesser part of his injuries from a drug regime, namely a Stevens Johnson Syndrome was caused by drugs he had been given although he did not know that a more significant injury namely a oesophageal stricture was also the result of the drugs. There are cases where the court has been willing to postpone the running of time where a claimant has adopted a wait and see attitude particularly in back cases where it might be reasonable to wait a little while to see if the back complaint was merely a strain or an ache and might soon settle (see *Devonport v. A.V. Wright (Builders) Limited*[36] and *Pacheco v. Brent and Harrow Area Health Authority*).[37]

"Attribution"

23–13 Section 14(1)(b) provides:

". . . that the injury was attributable in whole or in part to the act or omission which is alleged to constitute negligence, nuisance or breach of duty . . ."

The concept of attribution has generated a great deal of case law. In *Dobbie v. Medway Health Authority*, the Court of Appeal reviewed a number of leading authorities on attribution and came to conclusions which are likely to result in bringing forward a claimant's date of knowledge *closer* to the act or omission giving rise to the injury. Mrs Dobbie was admitted for a biopsy on a lump in her breast on the April 27, 1973 and the surgeon considering that the lump was pre-cancerous carried out a left mastectomy without microscopic examination and allegedly without the claimant's consent. On the May 14, 1973 it was found that the lump was in fact benign and the claimant was told this on the June 11, 1973. The claimant developed a significant psychiatric reaction to the loss of her breast but did not issue proceedings until 1989 following hearing about a similar case reported in a newspaper and on a local radio. The trial judge found that time ran against the claimant as soon as she was informed about the laboratory analysis of the lump and the Court of Appeal concurred with that view. The Court held first, that attribution meant "capable of being attributed to" and not caused by. Secondly, the Court

---

[36] LEXIS April 23, 1985.
[37] LEXIS April 17, 1984.

emphasised that the claimant did not need to know that the defendant's act or omission was capable of being attributed to fault because that was specifically excluded on the clear words of the statute indicating that knowledge that any act or omission as a matter of law involved negligence, nuisance or breach of duty was irrelevant. Thirdly, the Court confirmed that all that the claimant needed for knowledge was a broad understanding of the essence of the act or omission and confirmed the reasoning in *Nash v. Eli Lilly & Co.*[38] and *Broadley v. Guy Clapham & Co.*[39] Those authorities indicated that knowledge of detailed acts or omissions such as would be necessary to draft particulars of negligence were not required. The Court concluded that Mrs Dobbie knew within hours of the operation that she had suffered a significant injury, and knew from the beginning that the injury was capable of being attributed to an act or omission of the Health Authority. What she did not know was whether the act or omission was negligent or blameworthy but that knowledge of fault did not stop time beginning to run. (For recent cases which have followed *Dobbie*, see *Whitfield v. North Durham Health Authority*[40]; *Gregory v. Ferro (GB) Limited*[41]; *Brady v. Wirral Health Authority*[42]; *Spargo v. North Essex District Health Authority*[43]; *O'Driscoll v. Dudley Health Authority*[44]; *Roberts v. Winbow.*[45]

It remains, however, important to realise that attribution may be delayed **23–14** in cases where it is by no means clear whether the persisting problems a claimant has are extensions of a pre-existing condition or whether in fact there has been a medical mishap. In *Forbes v. Wandsworth Health Authority*,[46] the Court of Appeal held, in a medical negligence action, that there must be knowledge of some causative link between the treatment or lack of it and the claimant's condition. Mr Forbes was operated on in 1982 for a by-pass: the operation failed and a second operation was carried out the next day. That operation was unsuccessful and the claimant was told that he needed to have his leg amputated to prevent gangrene and this was done on the November 5, 1982. Subsequently, the claimant obtained a report in 1992 which alleged that the practitioners had been negligent not to perform the second operation sooner. The defendant contended that all that was needed was knowledge that there was a period of time between the first and second operations, that the second operation was not successful and as a result the claimant had his leg amputated. The Court of Appeal found, however, that the claimant did not know that the loss of his

---

[38] [1993] 4 All E.R. 383.
[39] [1994] 4 All E.R. 439.
[40] (1995) 6 Med. L.R. 32.
[41] (1995) 6 Med. L.R. 321.
[42] [1996] 6 C.L., CA.
[43] (1996) 7 Med. L.R. 219.
[44] [1998] Lloyd's Rep. Med. 210.
[45] [1999] P.I.Q.R. P77.
[46] [1996] 4 All E.R. 881.

leg was capable of being attributed to the act or omission of the defendant until the receipt of an opinion by a vascular surgeon. The Court held that in many medical negligence cases the claimant would not know that his injury was attributable to the omission of the defendant until he also learned that there had also been negligence. That, however, did not mean that there was no distinction between causation and negligence, the first being relevant to section 14 and the second irrelevant. A similar approach was taken in the case of *Smith (Michael John) v. West Lancashire Health Authority*.[47] Mr Smith injured his right hand on November 12, 1981 and attended hospital for emergency treatment where a diagnosis of an uncomplicated fracture to the ring finger was made. In January 1982, an operation was necessary as the conservative treatment had not worked. In 1989, Mr Smith was dismissed from his job as a labourer due to loss of function in the right hand. In 1991, an expert medical report said that there had been a failure in November 1981 to treat the finger properly, which had resulted in degenerative changes that now meant loss of function in the hand. The Court of Appeal held that the claimant did not have requisite knowledge on which to found his claim until 1991 because although he was aware that the first treatment had not worked that did not imbue him with a knowledge of an omission on the part of the treating physicians. (See also *Ostick v. Wandsworth Health Authority*[48]; *Hallam-Eames v. Merrett Syndicates*[49]; *Hind v. York*.[50]) In *Irshad Aliv v. Courtaulds Textiles Limited*,[51] the Court of Appeal allowed an appeal in a deafness case holding that the claimant did not know whether his deafness was due to the ageing process or to industrial noise until an expert informed him of that fact.

"Identity"

23–15   The final fact a claimant must know to establish his date of knowledge is the identity of the defendant or someone who may be vicariously liable for the defendant's acts or omissions. These provisions are designed to deal with cases where a claimant cannot ascertain immediately who was responsible for the injury such as in a road traffic accident where a driver might fail to stop, or where there might be a complex division of labour and division of responsibility on a building site and it is not clear which sub-contractor was responsible for a particular act of negligence. In addition, where a third party is blamed in a defence, the claimant may have an extended period of time to sue on the basis of not knowing before then

---

[47] [1995] P.I.Q.R. P514, CA.
[48] (1995) 6 Med. L.R. 338.
[49] [1995] 2 C.L. 304.
[50] [1998] P.I.Q.R. P235.
[51] [1999] 8 Lloyd's Rep. Med. 301.

that the third party was responsible (see *Davies v. Reed Stock & Company Limited*[52]; *Foster v. Mall Builders Limited*[53]; *Lead Bitter v. Hodge Finance Limited.*[54]

Similar problems can arise where the precise legal identity of a defendant is difficult to ascertain because of a complex corporate structure which might have connected companies with similar names. Time may not run until the claimant had knowledge of the actual name of his employer in such circumstances (see *Simpson v. Norwest Holst Southern Limited*[55]; *Eidi v. Service Dowell Schlumberger S.A.*[56]; *Stevens v. Nash Dredging and Reclamation Company Limited.*[57]

In *Nash v. Eli Lilly*,[58] the Court of Appeal indicated that a claimant might be fixed with constructive knowledge in respect of the names of different companies in a group structure as the law applicable to the operation of such corporations provides the true position of the individual members of the corporate structure.

"Constructive Knowledge"

Section 14(3) provides: 23–16

"For the purposes of this section a person's knowledge includes knowledge which he might reasonably have been expected to acquire—

(a) from facts observable or ascertainable by him; or
(b) from facts ascertainable by him with the help of medical or other appropriate expert advice which it is reasonable for him to seek;

but a person shall not be fixed under this sub-section with knowledge of a fact ascertainable only with the help of expert advice so long as he has taken all reasonable steps to obtain (and, where appropriate, to act on) that advice."

This important subsection may provide a good deal of protection to prospective defendants. A claimant is required to act reasonably in using information he has and in obtaining information which he could get to establish knowledge of the significance of his injury, to whom the injury might be attributed to and the identity of the defendants. When a court is examining a claimant's date of knowledge it will firstly inquire as to what the actual claimant's knowledge was and then, if necessary, ask what the claimant could reasonably have known if he had applied his mind to the matter and if he had sought assistance. It is for the claimant to establish

---

[52] LEXIS, July 26, 1984.
[53] LEXIS, March 17, 1983.
[54] [1982] 2 All E.R. 167.
[55] [1980] 1 W.L.R. 968.
[56] [1990] C.L.Y. 2961.
[57] LEXIS, July 27, 1982.
[58] [1993] 4 All E.R. 383.

that his actual date of knowledge is within time, but if a defendant contends for an earlier constructive date of knowledge then the onus is on the defendant to prove that.

23–17   The courts have held that what is reasonable will depend upon the subjective capabilities of a particular claimant but have also attempted to suggest that the test is also to a degree objective. (See *Davis v. City and Hackney Health Authority*.[59]) In *Nash v. Eli Lilly*[60] it was held:

> "The standard of reasonableness in connection with the observations and/or the effort to ascertain are therefore finally objective but must be qualified to take into consideration the provision and circumstances and character of the plaintiff . . . In considering whether or not the inquiry is, or is not, reasonable the situation, character and intelligence of the plaintiff must be relevant".

In *Davis*, the claimant was not fixed with an earlier date of knowledge on the basis that it was held to be reasonable for a child born with spasticity in 1963 to wait until he was 17 to ask his mother as to what caused his disabilities and thereafter to delay a further five years before consulting solicitors because his mother had not encouraged him to litigate. Alternatively, in the case of *Forbes v. Wandsworth Health Authority*,[61] the claimant was fixed with a constructive date of knowledge on the basis that it was held not reasonable for the claimant to have changed his mind about investigating the loss of his leg. The court accepted that it might be reasonable at one stage for a patient who was not cured to say that it was one of those things, but if after many years he changed his mind and sought advice the court would fix him with constructive knowledge. The court indicated that the claimant would be given a certain amount of time to overcome the shock, take stock of his disability and seek advice but this would have only taken approximately one year to 18 months. Roch L.J. gave a dissenting judgment on this interpretation of constructive knowledge indicating first, he found it difficult to reconcile how the test could be both objective and subjective simultaneously and secondly, that he thought it was unfortunate to impute a would-be claimant with an unconscious decision to do nothing and then require him to stand by that decision. However, *Jeffrey v. CMB Speciality Packaging (UK) Limited*,[62] the Court of Appeal found a claimant was not fixed with constructive knowledge concerning his development of tinnitus. The claimant was told by his consultant that a natural cause of the problem was being investigated and the Court of Appeal held that it would have been expecting the claimant to be unrealistically inquisitive to make further inquiries and to go behind the knowledge that his tinnitus might have a natural origin. (See

[59] (1991) 2 Med. L.R. 366.
[60] [1993] 4 All E.R. 383.
[61] [1996] 4 All E.R. 881.
[62] *Current Law* 1998, CA.

also *Saunders v. West Glamorgan HA*[63]; *Hind v. York*[64]; *Smith v. West Lancashire Health Authority*[65]; *James v. East Dorset Health Authority.*[66])

It appears that knowledge of facts which a claimant may have includes **23–18** knowledge which he might reasonably have been expected to acquire from facts ascertainable by him through the services of a solicitor. This was a view which Hidden J. came to at first instance in *Nash v. Eli Lilly*[67] and which the Court of Appeal partially endorsed. The Court of Appeal emphasised that the only relevance of a solicitor was in respect of factual information as the legal consequences were irrelevant for the section. The Court of Appeal further emphasised that it was for the defendant to establish not only that a solicitor, with whom the claimant might consult, would have the necessary knowledge, but also that it was reasonable to expect the claimant to consult him.

In *Hepworth v. Kerr,*[68] a claimant underwent an ear operation in 1979 and was rendered paraplegic. The hospital diagnosed this to be an hysterical reaction and the claimant discharged himself to the care of another hospital where a treating neurologist indicated the claimant had sustained a vascular lesion to the spinal cord which was unrelated to the operation on his ear. In 1987, the claimant went to solicitors and obtained an opinion that he had suffered a thrombosis due to the anaesthetic technique used during the operation on his ear. The court held that the claimant's date of knowledge ran from the date when he received that expert opinion and declined to fix him with an earlier constructive date of knowledge as contended for by the defendants. The defendants argued that the claimant or any solicitor he might have instructed should have questioned the neurologist's view and particularly queried whether the neurologist had the proper notes available to him upon which he could assess his opinion. The court found that approach as unreasonable. (See also *James v. East Dorset Health Authority*[69]; *Khan v. Ainslie*[70]; *Atkinson v. Oxfordshire Health Authority.*[71]

The tenor of recent authorities is towards fixing a claimant with both an earlier date of actual knowledge and an earlier date of constructive knowledge. This process has led to an increasing reliance on the provisions of section 33 of the Limitation Act 1980.

---

[63] *Current Law* 1998.
[64] [1998] P.I.Q.R. P235.
[65] [1995] P.I.Q.R. P514.
[66] [1999] M.L.C. 00129.
[67] (1991) 2 Med. L.R. 169 at 182.
[68] (1995) 6 Med. L.R. 135.
[69] [1999] M.L.C. 00129, CA.
[70] (1993) 4 Med. L.R. 319.
[71] (1993) 4 Med. L.R. 18.

Section 33 of the Limitation Act 1980: Discretion, Prejudice and "all the Circumstances of the Case"

23–19   The court has a power in personal injury actions to allow a statute-barred claim to proceed if it appears equitable having regard to the respective prejudices likely to be suffered by each party. The discretion within section 33 of the Limitation Act 1980 to disapply a period of limitation is entirely unfettered. In most personal injury actions there is no "out of time" long-stop beyond which a case is statutorily too stale and this includes those class of cases where the claimant has an unarguable claim over against negligent legal advisers. The major class of actions excluded from this section are those cases where a second writ has been issued because the first writ was never served or lawfully renewed, or where the first action was struck out for want of prosecution or was otherwise discontinued (*Walkley v. Precision Forgings Limited*[72]; *Whitfield v. North Durham Health Authority*).[73] Unless in such cases it can be established that the date of knowledge occurred within three years prior to the issue of the second writ, such cases will be statute-barred as the court has no power to apply the provisions of section 33 of the 1980 Act. The only possible exception would be those cases where the first action having been brought in time was discontinued due to misrepresentation or improper conduct on the part of the defendant (*per* Lord Diplock in *Walkley, Deerness v. John Keeble & Son (Brantham) Limited*)[74]; *Forward v. Hendricks*[75]; see also *Re Philip Powes Limited*[76]).

23–20   Where, however, an invalid writ has been issued such as against a company in compulsory liquidation the writ is wholly ineffective and if subsequent leave is given to issue proceedings then section 33 of the 1980 Act can apply (*Wilson v. Banner Scaffolding Limited*[77]; *Rose v. Express Welding Limited*[78]; *Re Workvale Limited No. 2*[79]; and *White v. Glass*[80]). In exercising its discretion the court looks at:

(a) the balance of prejudice to each party;

(b) the six specific factors contained in section 33(3); and

(c) "all the circumstances of the case" (section 33(3)).

There are very many cases involving the application of section 33 of the Limitation Act 1980 and they cannot be treated as precedents because of

---

[72] [1979] 2 All E.R. 548.
[73] (1995) 6 Med. L.R. 37.
[74] [1983] 2 Lloyd's Rep. 260.
[75] [1997] 2 All E.R. 395.
[76] [1997] 2 B.C.L.C. 481.
[77] *The Times*, June 22, 1982.
[78] LEXIS, January 21, 1986.
[79] [1992] 2 All E.R. 627.
[80] *The Times*, February 18, 1989.

the varied factual circumstances they give rise to and because judicial conceptions of discretion and equity vary. Certain principles, however, do arise and some of the following illustrations indicate the current judicial attitude to both questions of prejudice and discretion.

Prejudice

In *Hartley v. Birmingham District Council*,[81] Parker L.J. became one of **23–21** the first appellate judges to make some general observations on the nature of section 33 prejudice although like other appellate judges before him he refused to lay down guidelines. In *Hartley*, the claimant issued a writ only a matter of hours out of time but no section 33 discretion was granted at first instance notwithstanding the minimal delay. Parker L.J. held that in all or nearly all cases the prejudice in terms of refusing or allowing an action to proceed was equal and opposite because the stronger on liability the claimant's case was the greater the prejudice to him was if the claim was barred and the greater the prejudice would be to a defendant if the limitation period was disapplied. Alternatively, the weaker the claimant's case was the less the claimant would be prejudiced by being shut out because his claim was likely to fail and equally the defendants would suffer less prejudice in that they would be more able to defeat a weak case. This line of reasoning led the court to express the view that the most important question concerning prejudice was evidential prejudice as specified in section 33(3)(b) which dealt with the effect of the delay on the defendant's ability to defend the case on its merits. The court went on to state that if it was legitimate to consider, as it was, whether a claimant had a claim over against his solicitors, it was also legitimate to consider whether the defendant was insured. The court expressed the opinion that suing one's previous solicitors always created prejudice because the original wrong-doer may know very little about the weaknesses of the claimant's case particularly on quantum whereas the previous solicitor could well be appraised of them. Further, the court indicated that if the delay resulted in a windfall defence only and did not seriously affect the evidence then the power within section 33 would generally be exercised in the claimant's favour.

Approximately a year later, a differently constituted Court of Appeal remarked in *Nash v. Eli Lilly*[82] that Lord Justice Parker's remarks were not of universal application. In *Nash*, the Court emphasised that if a claimant's claim lacked merit then there might well be significant prejudice in allowing an action to proceed particularly where the claimant was legally aided and where a defendant would be put to great expense in defeating an unmeritorious claim. In those circumstances, the claimant was in a position

---

[81] [1992] 2 All E.R. 213.
[82] [1993] 4 All E.R. 344.

to extract a nuisance value settlement. Such considerations are likely to be more relevant to high cost complex pharmaceutical or product liability actions. In *Nash*, several claimants were denied section 33 dispensations primarily on the weakness of their case on the merits (*e.g. Eastern, O'Hara and Jenkins*). In *Kelly v. Bastible*,[83] the Court of Appeal held that whereas *Hartley* could permit a claim under the 1980 Limitation Act, s.33, where a short delay occurred which did not effect the defence and where there had been early notification of the claim it did not preclude insurers from relying on any evidential points which demonstrated prejudice. The proper approach in such a case should be to consider the insurer and the insured as forming a composite whole when considering prejudice.

23-22   In *Donovan v. Gwentoys Limited*,[84] the House of Lords determined that prejudice which occurred before the expiry of the limitation period was a relevant matter for the Court to consider in deciding whether to grant a section 33 dispensation. The date of a letter before action in this context can be an important matter. In *Donovan*, the defendants were not put on notice as to the nature of the claimant's claim until over five years from the date of her accident. The claimant, being a minor, had an extended period of limitation but even so issued proceedings five and a half months outside her primary limitation period.

Economic prejudice arising out of changes in the payment of damages in medical negligence actions which arose due to restructuring of the National Health Service with effect from the January 1, 1990 might also constitute prejudice within a section 33 application. In *Whitfield v. North Durham Health Authority*,[85] the trial judge accepted that if the claim had been prosecuted in time damages would have been met by Medical Defence Organisations, but because the claim was brought late the Health Authority would need to fund any claim with respect to damages below £300,000. The trial judge took the view that any patients who might have to wait for treatment because a claimant was awarded damages would be probably willing to do so. The Court of Appeal reversed the trial judge's exercise of his discretion in allowing the case to proceed and found that an assumption of altruism on the part of patients who may be kept waiting longer for the treatment was something which was too speculative for the judge to properly consider.

In *Dobbie v. Medway Health Authority*,[86] the claimant's case was not allowed to proceed following a 16-year delay on a number of grounds including one that the surgeon and hospital would be prejudiced by having the action hanging over them indefinitely. In the Court of Appeal, Beldam L.J. remarked that he could not see how Damoclean sword type prejudice

---

[83] [1997] 8 Med. L.R. 15.
[84] [1990] 1 All E.R. 1018.
[85] (1995) 6 Med. L.R. 32.
[86] [1994] P.I.Q.R. P353.

could apply to a doctor who did not know that any action was being contemplated against him. The fact that a defendant has had a number of claims brought against him in the past for example concerning industrial deafness which have been settled or compromised does not mean that a defendant may not be prejudiced by the delay in any particular case (*Price v. United Engineering Steels Limited*,[87] *Barrand v. British Cellophane plc*,[88] disapproving *Buck v. English Electric Company Limited.*[89]

Discretion

Section 33(3) provides: 23–23

> "In acting under this section the court shall have regard to all the circumstances of the case and in particular to:
>
> (a) the length of, and reasons for, the delay on the part of the claimant;
> (b) the extent to which having regard to the delay the evidence adduced or likely to be adduced by the claimant or the defendant is or is likely to be less cogent than if the action had been brought within the time allowed by section 11 . . . or as the case may be by section 12;
> (c) the conduct of the defendant after the cause of action arose, including the extent (if any) to which he responded to requests reasonably made by the claimant for information or inspection for the purpose of ascertaining facts which were or might be relevant to the claimant's cause of action against the defendant;
> (d) the duration of any disability of the claimant arising after the date of the accrual of the cause of action;
> (e) the extent to which the claimant acted promptly and reasonably once he knew whether or not the act or omission of the defendant, to which the injury was attributable, might be capable at that time of giving rise to an action for damages;
> (f) the steps, if any, taken by the claimant to obtain medical, legal or other expert advice and the nature of any such advice he may have received."

The six factors contained within section 33 are exemplary only, and not   23–24
exclusive, and cannot be analysed in isolation of each other. Trial judges tend, however, to look at each factor in turn in exercising their discretion. In *Nash v. Eli Lilly*[90], the Court of Appeal indicated that it would be very slow to interfere with the exercise of discretion under this section but would do so where a judge either took into account factors which he should have ignored or ignored factors which he should have taken into account. The Court expressed the view that, provided that it was relevant, the judge may take into account a factor not specifically listed in the sub-paragraphs of section 33(3), but alternatively, if it was established that he

---

[87] [1998] P.I.Q.R. P407.
[88] *The Times*, February 16, 1995.
[89] [1997] 1 W.L.R. 806.
[90] [1993] 4 All E.R. 383.

failed to take into account any of the matters mentioned in section 33(3) which were relevant to the carrying out of the balancing exercise, then his judgment would be susceptible to attack. A powerful illustration of intervention by the Court of Appeal with the exercise of discretion is found in the case of *Whitfield v. North Durham Health Authority*.[91] In analysing the judge's exercise of his discretion, the Court of Appeal said first, that the judge ought to have taken into account that it was by mere oversight that the practitioner sued was excluded from the first writ which had been issued and accordingly it was relevant to consider whether the claimant should have such a windfall advantage from the incompetence of her own first solicitors. Secondly, the Court indicated that the judge gave way to speculation concerning Crown indemnity as discussed above. Thirdly, the Court felt that the claimant could not be separated from her advisers and any delay by the legal advisers was a relevant matter in considering the defendant's prejudice. Fourthly, the Court indicated that the trial judge had given insufficient weight to the prejudicial effect of a doctor having to rely on his powers of recollection with the increasing passage of time. Waite L.J. in *Whitfield* said this:

> "The outcome of the balancing exercise under Section 33 is not to be determined on comparative scales of hardship (though hardship can never be irrelevant in a jurisdiction where all circumstances are to be taken into account). The overriding question is one of equity: Would it be equitable for the action to be allowed to proceed on the balance of prejudice weighed with due regard to all the circumstances and specific facts mentioned in the section? In determining such a question there can be no severance of the Plaintiff's conduct from that of her advisers."

(See also *Brady v. Wirral Health Authority*[92]; *Skitt v. Khan and Wakefield Health Authority*[93]; *Farthing v. North East Essex Health Authority*.[94])

Section 33(3)(a): "The length of and reasons for the delay on the part of the plaintiff"

23–25   The delay here refers to delay since the expiry of the limitation period. Cases of extreme delay of over 20 years have been allowed to proceed but, principally, when they involve the contraction of insidious diseases due to exposure to substances arising out of allegations of negligence concerning a system of work rather than from a specific injury in a particular accident. (*See Buck v. English Electric*[94a]; *McLaren v. Harland & Wolf Limited*[95]).

---

[91] (1995) 6 Med. L.R. 32.
[92] Judgment, June 25, 1996, CCRTF 90/1502/C.
[93] (1997) 8 Med. L.R. 165.
[94] (1998) 9 Med. L.R. 38.
[94a] [1977] 1 W.L.R. 806.
[95] 1991 S.L.T. 85.

Generally speaking, however, the shorter the delay the more likely the court is to allow an action to proceed. In *Hendy v. Milton Keynes Health Authority*[96]; a nine-day delay which gave rise to no evidential prejudice was excused by the court in respect of an action for damages arising out of injury sustained during a hysterectomy. Even when there has been extensive delay and prejudice the court on occasions does allow a claim to proceed. In *Doughty v. North Staffordshire Health Authority*,[97] an action was brought some 25 years after the removal of a port wine stain on the claimant's face and some 13 years after the claimant's date of knowledge. The judge found the delay was due to discouraging advice and problems with legal aid. The action was allowed to proceed notwithstanding the fact that the treating surgeon had had a stroke and was unable to testify (see also *Kidd v. Grampian Health Board*[98]; *Baig v. City and Hackney Health Authority*[99]). The court is obviously influenced by what is an acceptable reason for the delay and the claimant's prospects are enhanced if there is no direct criticism of the claimant himself as occurred in *McCafferty v. Metropolitan Police District Receiver*[1] where a policeman had delayed in bringing an action because of a combination of his liking his job, feeling insecure with respect to his tenure and his desire to preserve good relations with his employer. Similarly, cases where a claimant's injury has suffered a severe exacerbation are likely to be looked upon favourably. In *Das v. Ganju*,[2] inaccurate and misleading advice given by lawyers was held not to be a fault attibutable to the claimant and in the absence of substantial prejudice to the defendants a claim was allowed to proceed in respect of the birth of a child suffering from rubella syndrome. In *Skitt v. Khan*,[3] the relative poverty of a claimant during his lifetime was held not to be a good enough reason for a failure to obtain a medical report. In *Coad v. Cornwall and Isle of Scilly Health Authority*,[4] the Court of Appeal held that in considering the length of, and reasons for, the delay the test was a subjective one and ignorance of legal rights was a factor to be considered.

Section 33(3)(b): "The extent to which having regard to the delay the evidence adduced or likely to be adduced by the plaintiff or the defendant is or is likely to be less cogent than if the action had been brought within the time allowed by section 11"

Again the delay referred to in this sub-paragraph is delay since the expiry **23–26** of the limitation period and was considered in *Hartley v. Birmingham District Council*[5] to be the most significant matter in the exercise of the

---

[96] (1992) 3 Med. L.R. 114.
[97] (1992) 3 Med. L.R. 81.
[98] (1994) 5 Med. L.R. 251.
[99] (1994) 5 Med. L.R. 221.
[1] [1997] 2 All E.R. 750.
[2] [1999] Lloyd's Rep. Med. 198.
[3] (1997) 8 Med. L.R. 165.
[4] [1997] 1 W.L.R. 189.
[5] [1992] 2 All E.R. 213.

court's discretion. Few cases are likely to be allowed to proceed where the defendants establish significant evidential prejudice such as the death of a witness or the destruction of written or other evidence. (See *Bater v. Newbold*[6]; *Wilding v. Lambeth, Southwark and Lewisham Area Health Authority*[7]; and *Pilmore v. Northern Trawlers Limited.*[8]) Accordingly, those medical negligence actions primarily based upon expert opinion where the written clinical and nursing notes have been preserved are more likely to be allowed to proceed if time barred than those which raise issues concerning consent and warning as to risks which will turn upon oral recollection. In *Baig v. City and Hackney Health Authority*,[9] the trial judge refused to allow a statute-barred action to proceed partly on the basis that it would not be possible to have valuable recollections of the warnings given with respect to an operation performed some 17 years earlier. (See also *Gregory v. Ferro (G.B.) Limited*[10]; *Brady v. Wirral Health Authority*[11]; *Whitfield v. North Durham Health Authority*[12]; *Roberts v. Winbow*[13]; *Coad v. Cornwall*[14]; *Briody v. St. Helens and Knowsley Area Health Authority.*[15])

Section 33(3)(c): "The conduct of the defendant after the cause of action arose including the extent (if any) to which he responded to requests reasonably made by the plaintiff for information or inspection for the purposes of ascertaining facts which were or might be relevant to the plaintiff's cause of action"

23–27   Refusals by potential defendants, insurers or solicitors to deal with a claim quickly or at all will not stop time running against a claimant. However, if such activity can be shown to have slowed down the progress of the claim such behaviour might be relevant for the exercise of the court's discretion. In *Atkinson v. Oxfordshire Health Authority*,[16] the court held that had it been required to exercise its discretion under section 33 it would have done so in the claimant's favour because a large part of the delay was a failure by the defendant to tell the claimant's mother precisely what had happened during an operation to evacuate a tumour on the claimant which had resulted in injury to him. A similar approach was adopted by the court in *Scuriaga v. Powell*[17] where the claimant was told

---

[6] LEXIS, July 30, 1991.
[7] LEXIS, May 10, 1982.
[8] [1986] 1 Lloyd's Rep. 552.
[9] (1994) 5 Med. L.R. 221.
[10] (1995) 6 Med. L.R. 320.
[11] Judgment, June 25, 1996 CCRTF 90/1502/C.
[12] (1995) 6 Med. L.R. 32.
[13] [1999] P.I.Q.R. P77.
[14] [1997] 1 W.L.R. 189.
[15] [1999] Lloyd's Rep. Med. 185.
[16] (1993) 4 Med. L.R. 18.
[17] (1979) 123 S.J. 406.

that a failed abortion was due to a structural defect in her rather than a practitioner's own negligence. In *Marshall v. Martin*,[18] the Court of Appeal held that the defendant's conduct need not be discreditable or unsatisfactory and the fact that the defendant had made an interim payment would be relevant in considering how that operated on the claimant's mind in respect of a belief that the case was likely to be settled.

Section 33(3)(d): "The duration of any disability of the plaintiff arising after the date of the accrual of the cause of action"

Disability here refers to unsoundness of mind pursuant to the definition **23–28** contained in section 38(2) of the Limitation Act 1980 as the only other form of disability namely infancy cannot arise after the accrual of a cause of action. Dicta which treated disability within the meaning of this subsection as a physical disability (*Bater v. Newbold*[19]; *Pilmore v. Northern Trawlers Limited*[20] are probably wrong, see the Court of Appeal's decision in *Yates v. Thakeham Tiles Limited*[21]; *Thomas v. Plaistow*.[22] Such physical disability not amounting to disability within the meaning of Section 38(2) of the Limitation Act 1980 is, however, frequently relevant when considering the reasons for the delay in section 33(3)(a) and in considering all the circumstances of the case).

Section 33(3)(e): "The extent to which the plaintiff acted promptly and reasonably once he knew whether or not the act or omission of the defendant, to which the injury was attributable, might be capable at that time as giving rise to an action for damages"

One of the major reasons for recommending a discretionary power to **23–29** disapply the limitation period was to mitigate the effect that ignorance of the law should not stop time running against a claimant. Once, however, a claimant has personal knowledge that he has a cause of action upon which he can sue the court will inquire into how expeditiously the action was progressed before the issue of proceedings. The claimant will be fixed with the action and behaviour of his lawyers as well as himself (*Thompson v. Brown*[23]). In *Doughty v. North Staffordshire Health Authority*,[24] the court was willing to excuse the delay of the claimant's lawyers and exonerated the claimant from any personal blame in respect of failing to insist her lawyers prosecuted the claim more quickly. In *Davis v. Jacobs and Camden*

---

[18] LEXIS, June 10, 1987.
[19] LEXIS, July 30, 1991.
[20] [1986] 1 Lloyd's Rep. 552.
[21] [1995] P.I.Q.R. P135.
[22] [1995] P.I.Q.R. P135.
[23] [1981] 2 All E.R. 296.
[24] (1992) 3 Med. L.R. 81.

and Islington Health Authority,[25] the Court of Appeal was of the view that in construing section 33(3)(*e*) that it was concerned only with the conduct of the claimant (at p. 86, column 2). This would appear to run contrary to the speech of Lord Diplock in *Thompson v. Brown.* In *Obembe v. City and Hackney Health Authority,*[26] parents sued in 1988 for alleged malpractice occurring at the birth of their son in 1979. They included a claim for damages in respect of themselves which was statute-barred and the court rejected the contention put forward that because they had 21 years to sue in respect of their son that was a reasonable excuse for not bringing their own action earlier.

Section 33(3)(f); "The steps if any taken by the plaintiff to obtain medical, legal or other advice and the nature of any such advice he may have received"

23–30   Negative legal or medical advice is frequently a problem for claimants and can delay the prosecution of an action because of difficulties over negligence or causation. In some legal aid cases it can lead to the discharge of the certificate. (See *Bentley v. Bristol and Western Health Authority*[27]; *Halford v Brooks*[28]; *Das v. Ganju.*[29])

The wording of the sub-paragraph indicates that it is relevant for the Court to consider what the advice was. In *Jones v. G.D. Searle & Co. Limited,*[30] the defendants wanted to know what previous legal advice had been given in a case where it was claimed new developments in science had made previous advice, which was negative, out-dated. The defendants sought leave to administer an interrogatory to ascertain this but the claimant said that that would amount to waiving legal professional privilege. The Court of Appeal found that as a consequence of giving the answer to the interrogatory which limited itself to seeking to know whether the previous advice was negative or not it did not follow that Counsel's Opinions were liable to discovery. In *Tatlock v. G.P. Worsley & Co. Limited,*[31] the defendants sought disclosure of the contents of an allegedly negative medical report together with correspondence with medical experts which meant that a claim was not proceeded with earlier than it was. The Court of Appeal held that section 33(3)(f) did not override the rules of legal professional privilege save in the restricted sense of requiring a Plaintiff to indicate the nature of the advice only. As a matter of tactics and evidence the claimant might need to waive privilege if he was to rely effectively on the contents of the documents in issue.

---

[25] [1999] Lloyd's Rep. Med. 72.
[26] LEXIS, June 9, 1989.
[27] (1991) 2 Med. L.R. 359.
[28] [1991] 1 W.L.R. 428.
[29] [1999] Lloyd's Rep. Med. 198.
[30] [1978] 3 All E.R. 654.
[31] LEXIS, June 22, 1989.

"All the circumstances of the case"

As indicated in *Donovan v. Gwentoys Limited*,[32] the House of Lords **23–31** stipulated that although Section 33(3)(a) and (b) required the court to look at the delay after the expiry of the limitation period the injunction to look at all the circumstances of the case allowed the court to consider what prejudice had occurred within the primary limitation period. The court is also likely to consider the strength of the claimant's case, the likely size of the award, the strength of the defendant's case on the merits, whether a claimant is legally aided or not, whether a defendant is insured, whether there is an alternative remedy such as a good claim over against the claimant's solicitors or perhaps the possibility of a judgment being satisfied by the Motor Insurers' Bureau.

Procedure

A District Judge or a Master in addition to a Judge is empowered to **23–32** exercise discretion under section 33 of the Limitation Act 1980 pursuant to RSC, Ord. 32, r. 9A. However, in the county court a district judge did not have the jurisdiction to hear section 33 applications unless the claim did not exceed £5,000 (*Hughes v. Jones*).[33] That was because the determination of a section 33 issue was a final rather than an interlocutory matter and a county court district judge had no jurisdiction to make a final determination in claims over £5,000. The Court of Appeal, in *Dale v. British Coal Corporation*,[34] stipulated that whether a section 33 takes place at an interlocutory hearing or as a preliminary hearing before the main trial of the action the judge's determination is final and no leave is required to appeal. The onus of persuading the court to disapply the primary limitation period lies on the claimant (*Thompson v. Brown Construction (Ebbw Vale) Limited*.[35]

Practitioners are divided as to whether the proper pleading practice is for a claimant to particularise the facts and circumstances which he tends to rely on in seeking to persuade the court to disapply section 11 by exercising section 33 in his favour in the Particulars or Statement of Claim, or whether it should be pleaded to in a Reply following the defendant taking the defence in the Defence. In that limitation is not a bar to a case but is a defence it would seem that there is no need to anticipate the defence but it might be preferable to wait and see if the defendant takes the point (see *Ogunsanya v. Lambeth Area Health Authority*).[36]

---

[32] [1990] 1 All E.R. 1018.
[33] *The Times*, July 18, 1996, CA.
[34] [1992] 1 W.L.R. 964.
[35] [1981] 1 W.L.R. 744.
[36] LEXIS, July 3, 1985. See also Chapter 20, *Pleadings*.

Special Time Limits

23–33   Section 39 of the 1980 Limitation Act provides a saving for those period of limitation prescribed in other statutes:

> "This Act shall not apply to any action or arbitration for which a period of limitation is prescribed by or under any other enactment (whether passed before or after the passing of this Act) . . ."

Accordingly, practitioners should be alert to the different time limits imposed by many statutes governing transport such as the Maritime Conventions Act 1911 (two-year limitation period), the Merchant Shipping Act 1979 (two-year limitation period), the Carriage by Air Act 1961 (two-year limitation period), the International Transport Convention Act 1983 (three-year period but a five-year long-stop), the Carriage of Passengers by Road Act 1974 (three-year period but with a long-stop of five years), the Consumer Protection Act 1987 (three-year period but with a 10-year long-stop), the Nuclear Installations Act 1965 (30 or 20-year long-stops depending on the circumstances). Similarly, the Foreign Limitation Periods Act 1984 may impose a different period of limitation with respect to a tort committed overseas but litigated in England.

24. The Civil Procedure Rules 1998

Introduction

Part 1 Rule 1.1 of the Civil Procedure Rules (the CPR) provides that: **24–01** *These rules are a new procedural code with the overriding objective of enabling the court to deal with cases justly.* This Chapter looks in general terms at the CPR and a few of the significant changes; it does not set out to provide a rule-by-rule analysis and it presupposes that the reader will obtain and study the various components of the new code.

There is one code for the High Court, the county courts, and the Court of Appeal, but within this provision is made for specialist jurisdictions. The actual rules (now collected together in *Parts* rather then "Orders") are supplemented by *Practice Directions* (PD) which form an integral part of the code. Forms are prescribed. *Protocols* are to be laid down setting out those steps which parties should take to seek information from and to provide information to each other about a prospective claim. At the moment two have been approved for personal injury claims and clinical disputes (broadly, but not exclusively, medical negligence). However, it is clearly envisaged that a significant number will be approved in the near future. Some provisions of the RSC and the CCR remain in force. As a crude simplification: if there is no Part which covers a particular procedure, it is probable that the Schedules will have retained the previous rules. However, this will not be permanent. The Rules Committee intend in due course to recast the remaining provisions into the CPR. Finally, although there is one code, there are still significant variations within the system and many of the forums now have their own Guides which are essential reading. The Queen's Bench Guide has not yet been published, but it is promised.

The CPR follow the policies enunciated in the "Access to Justice" Reports. It is of interest that the Final Report recognised that the CPR will not deal with all possible situations. It certainly provides a detailed framework in which litigation is to be carried out, but there remains a flexibility which is intended to allow courts to act in accordance with the "overriding objective". It is also intended that those involved in the litigation, whether as parties, witnesses, experts or lawyers should behave in the spirit of the overriding objective and that this is radically different to the way litigation was conducted under the RSC and the CCR.

The CPR have applied to all proceedings issued after April 26, 1999. The transitional arrangements are in Part 51, PD 51.19 provides that proceedings which have not been before a judge by April 25, 2000 shall be stayed. There are limited exceptions including of particular relevance to personal injury practitioners, cases "where there is no issue on liability but the proceedings have been adjourned by court order to determine the prognosis". Whilst there is a right to apply for a stay to be lifted, it remains very much in doubt whether such applications will succeed other than in exceptional circumstances.

The Tracks

24–02   A central feature of case management is the allocation of cases to a "track":

(a) *Small Claims Track:* normal track where financial value is not more than £5,000, unless—in personal injuries the financial value is not more than £5,000 and the damages for personal injuries are not more than £1,000.

(b) *Fast Track:* cases which are not small claims, which have a financial value of not more than £15,000 and only if the court considers:

    (i) the trial is likely to last no longer than one day;
    (ii) oral expert evidence will be limited to one expert per party in any expert field and to expert evidence in two expert fields.

(c) *Multi-Track:* not Small Claims and not Fast Track cases.

(d) *Value*: the actual amount in dispute (excluding interest, costs and contributory negligence; any potential counterclaim or set-off and any Compensation Recovery Unit (CRU) deduction).

Protocols

24–03   The pre-action Protocols are an essential part of the new code. The personal injuries Protocol is primarily designed for cases involving with a value of less than £15,000 which are likely to be allocated to the Fast Track: *This is because time will be of the essence, after proceedings are issued, especially for the defendant, if cases are to be ready for trial within 30 weeks of allocation.*

The notes to the Personal Injury Protocol, however, make it plain that a "cards on the table" approach is equally appropriate to some higher value claims and the spirit of the Protocol, if not the letter, should be followed in multi-track type claims. What is required is early notification of a claim by the claimant's advisers using standard letters. There is then a three-month period for the defendant to investigate and respond to a claim before proceedings are issued. It is intended that defendants give early disclosure of documents. Categories of relevant documents are specified in the Protocol.

The Personal Injury Protocol encourages the joint selection of and access to experts. It promotes the practice of the claimant obtaining the medical report, disclosing it to the defendant who then asks questions and/or agrees and does not obtain his own report. This is consistent with the general approach to experts—their use is to be limited to what is strictly necessary and will be subject to close scrutiny and control by the court.

Compliance with Protocols is not voluntary. The CPR enable the courts to take into account compliance or non-compliance with an applicable Protocol when giving directions on the management of proceedings and when making orders for costs. A claimant may be deprived of interest or the defendant may be ordered to pay at a higher rate with the object of placing the innocent party in the same position as he would have been had the Protocol been complied with.

The implementation of the Protocols has coincided with the radical changes in the funding of this class of litigation. The abolition of legal aid and the pressure from the insurance companies' accountants mean that all those involved in personal injury litigation must be constantly cost conscious. Protocols can assist in this. Standard letters and responses should be stored in a word processor and programmes have been widely written to reduce to a minimum the time taken on any step.

Case Management

This is where the most fundamental changes involved with the new rules **24–04** begin. In all cases, following the filing of a defence the court will serve an "Allocation questionnaire" [N150] on each party. This is a multi-section document which initiates the court's case management and as such is essential reading! On receipt of the allocation questionnaires the court will either stay the case for a month to allow the parties to attempt settlement or will proceed with allocation. Primarily on the basis of the value of the claim, the case will be allocated to a track.

In the Fast Track and the Multi-Track cases, on allocation, the court will set up a case management timetable and fix a trial date or trial period. Part of this process is not unlike the obtaining of directions and the elements of the timetable will cover those areas generally familiar to practitioners: a timetable by reference to calendar dates; rules about disclosure of documents (formerly discovery) and provision for factual and expert evidence. The real difference is that the trial date or trial period is fixed at this very early stage and the court will actively manage the case to achieve a trial on that date/within that period.

At the allocation stage the parties may submit an agreed timetable and trial date/period for approval. To gain approval, those matters set out above must be properly covered. If the parties do not propose suitable directions, the court will impose its own and may hold a case management conference to enable the parties to be heard. Such a conference may be held at any time to review the steps taken; to ensure compliance with any directions already given; to give directions as to the future; and to ensure that all agreements which can be made, have been and are properly recorded.

Subsequently, a "listing questionnaire" will be sent out to ascertain all the necessary arrangements for trial (evidence, particularly expert evidence; timetable and time estimate; preparation of trial bundles). The time for returning this is set at the time of the fixing of the trial date/period.

It will no longer be enough for the parties to conduct their case at "their pace": the court will set the pace through the rules and the Practice Direction. This is not to say that the views of the parties will not be taken into account especially if they have already reached a sensible agreement. However, by the (eventual) use of IT and by monitoring, courts intend to ensure that all cases are disposed of within the time scale they set. At present the computer systems necessary for this task have not become available.

The court will also be involved in setting the agenda. Part 1, rule 1.4 sets out a list of what a court will do in actively managing cases. Twelve examples are given of how the conduct of litigation can be undertaken in accordance with the overriding objective of that Part. The court actively ensure that issues are identified and narrowed so that the parties concentrate on the key issues and how best to resolve them.

The Trial Date

24–05   The underlying ethos of case management is that the trial date should be fixed early and not changed. The sanctity of the trial date is to be preserved even in situations when the parties are not in breach of directions and have apparently strong reasons for an adjournment. Dealing with a case justly, in accordance with the overriding objective, requires *allocating to it an appropriate share of the court's resources, whilst taking into account the need to allocate resources to other cases*. This will mean in practice that a court, when dealing with an application to adjourn a trial date, will take into account the knock on effect on all other cases. The result is that only in exceptional circumstances will a trial date be altered.

The failure of the other side to comply with the case management timetable will certainly not justify adjourning the trial. Both Fast Track and Multi-Track Practice Directions have the same provisions for what happens when there has been a failure to comply with case management directions. Both provide (PD 28.5.1.and PD 29.7.1): "the court will not allow a failure to comply with directions to lead to the postponement of the trial unless the circumstances of the case are exceptional." In both PDs the sections end: "Litigants and lawyers must be in no doubt that the court will regard the postponement of a trial as an order of last resort."

This is probably the most crucial change to litigation as we have known it. So far, timetables have had beginnings but not ends. Even automatic directions provisions such as CCR, Ord. 17, r. 11 have been operated in practice so that where the claimant had a genuine reason as to why the case should not be set down within the time limits of that rule, it did not have to be. RSC, Ord. 25, r. 8 (automatic directions in personal injury actions) applied even less rigidly with the time limit for setting down in 8(1)(e) generally observed in the breach. If the earlier part of either timetables slipped, setting down did not occur until it had been made up.

The same approach cannot work if there is a period certain determined at the beginning of a case. If the trial date is fixed, the case will have to be prepared by that date. The consequence is that all litigators will be required to adopt rigorous methods: the days when cases could drag on for years with time limits disregarded without any real sanction are over. No longer are time limits simply targets to be aimed for.

Sanctions

The final sanction for failing to comply with case management directions **24–06** is that Statements of Case will be struck out and judgment without trial will be given if appropriate. Before that stage is reached, there is a wide range of options open to the court in the event of non-compliance. However, it is worth noting that the implementation of sanctions is intended to be done in a manner that enables the case to come on for trial on the day or within the period previously set. This means that the court will assess what steps each party should take to prepare the case for trial, direct that those steps are taken in the shortest possible time and impose a sanction for non-compliance. Such a sanction might, for example, deprive a party of the right to raise or contest an issue or to rely on evidence to which the direction relates. Alternatively, if one or more issues can be made ready for trial at the time fixed but others cannot, the court can direct that the trial will proceed on the issues which are then ready and make suitable costs orders. Finally, if the case has to be adjourned it will be for the shortest time possible.

What has Happened in Practice (since April 26, 1999)?

The recent decision of the Court of Appeal in *Baron v. Lovell*[1] is a good **24–07** example of the underlying principles in practice. In a fairly small claim arising out of a road traffic accident, a circuit judge of the modern school

---

[1] [2000] P.I.Q.R. P20.

refused the defendant permission to call the doctor he had instructed and limited the medical evidence overall to the written reports of the claimant's expert. The defendant appealed. In dismissing the appeal, Brooke L.J. enunciated many of the sentiments that courts now adopt:

(a) A fairly small claim has to be dealt with in a way proportionate to the amount of money involved. The issues were not complex and the case was not important, except to the claimant. The judge had to ensure that the case was dealt with expediously and fairly. One day of the court's time was an appropriate share of the court's resources.

(b) As the defendant had not complied with automatic directions as to expert evidence, he was at the mercy of the court.

(c) The case ought to have been settled at the pre-trial review, if the experts' reports and updated witness statements had been served in good time in advance. The court may make it obligatory for a party to attend accompanied by the person who has responsibility for making the decisions. Do not (as here) use a local agent unfamiliar with the case and without the necessary authority.

Case Management Conferences

24–08   There is no doubt that significant tactical advantages can be gained by those who attend Case Management Conferences (CMCs). This is a new skill that has had to be developed and it is one which is well worth cultivating. Perhaps the most important factor to bear in mind is that the advocate must have assimilated the detail but the judge cannot be expected to have done so before the CMC, nor to be particularly interested in doing so at the CMC. What is important for him is to be given a "thumb-nail sketch" of the case and the outstanding issues. There is a requirement in PD 29.5.7 for a case summary to be prepared—*to assist the court to understand and deal with the issues before it*. It should not normally exceed 500 words in length and that is not much. Just as the preparation of skeleton arguments is a skill that had to be mastered, so the skilful preparation of a case summary must be mastered and can be used to advantage. If the other side can be made to appear unreasonable, tardy or disorganised, the judge will be more likely to make orders which place them under pressure.

Summary Procedures

24–09   One of the matters which is specifically to be raised at a CMC is summary disposal of the claim. This can be done formally. Part 3, rule 3.4 allows the court to strike out a Statement of Case if it discloses no reasonable ground for bringing or defending the claim, because it is an abuse of process or otherwise likely to obstruct the just disposal of the proceedings, or if there has been a failure to comply with a rule, Practice Direction or court order.

Part 24 sets out a procedure for seeking summary judgment loosely based on RSC, Ord. 14, but with certain significant changes. So far as the substance of the procedure is concerned:

(a) The court may give summary judgment on the application of either the claimant or the defendant or of its own motion.

(b) The test to be applied by the court is whether the court considers that the claimant or defendant has a real prospect of success on the claim/issue/defence and /or there is no other reason why the case or issue should not go to trial.

In *Swain v. Hillman and Gay*,[2] the Court of Appeal held that *no real prospects of being successful or succeeding* speak for themselves. The court must decide whether there is *realistic* as opposed to a *fanciful* prospect of success.

It should also be noted that there are less formal ways of disposing of the claim. The judge is entitled to invite concessions at the CMC; and cases are now settling at this door rather than at the trial court's door. The well-prepared advocate can take advantage of such opportunities.

---

[2] [2000] P.I.Q.R. P51.

25. Pleadings

Introduction

Since July 1, 1991, the county court has had jurisdiction to hear and **25–01** determine any personal injury action.[1] The High Court only has original jurisdiction where the damages which the claimant reasonably expects to recover exceed £50,000.[2] This remains true under the Civil Procedure Rules 1998 (CPR).[3] For all practical purposes therefore, the county court has become and will remain the most important court for the determination of all personal injury actions.[4]

The procedural and administrative conduct of personal injury litigation in common with all actions in the High Court and county court is now governed by the Civil Procedure Rules 1998. These rules are profoundly unclear as to the philosophy of pleading, such that unless or until established experience of the court's approach to the application of the new rules or appellate court authority established to the contrary, litigants who fail to comply with the literal letter of the rules do so at their peril, and their representatives at the peril of their professional indemnity insurers. It has been suggested that until the contrary is established by precedent a wholly different approach is required to pleading than that which prevailed in the past. That fear may have been allayed to some degree by the decision in *McPhilemy v. Times Newspapers Limited*[5] in which Lord Woolf M.R. in deprecating the previous practice of comprehensively particularised defamation pleadings, suggested that under the CPR the need for extensive pleadings including particulars should be reduced and he added:

> "What is important is that the pleadings should make clear the general nature of the case of the pleader. This is true both under the old rules and the new rules . . . No more than a concise statement of . . . facts is required."[6]

On reflection, the author now subscribes to the view, therefore, that a less literal and more flexible approach may be adopted to pleading in personal injury litigation than he previously feared.

---

[1] County Courts Act 1984, s.75.
[2] *ibid.* s.76.
[3] CPR PD, Part 7, para. 2.2.
[4] The Chief Executive of the Court Service, on behalf of the Parliamentary Secretary to the Lord Chancellor's Department, in a written reply dated June 24, 1997 to a parliamentary question asked by Andrew Dismore MP, estimated that in 1996 1,543 writs and originating summonses were issued in the High Court for personal injury actions while in the same year 253,500 summonses were issued in the county court.
[5] [1999] 3 All E.R. 775.
[6] Page 793 b–c—the underlining is the author's, the italicised emphasis is of the Judge.

Pre-action

25–02   The Civil Procedure Rules enable the court to take into account compliance or non-compliance, *inter alia*, with relevant pre-action applicable protocols both when giving directions for the management of proceedings[7] and when making Orders for costs.[8] The pre-action Protocol for Personal Injury Claims must, therefore, be complied with. Although primarily designed for road traffic, tripping and slipping, and accident at work cases likely to be allocated to the fast track,[9] the philosophy is advocated as equally appropriate to higher value claims so that the spirit of the Protocol should still be followed in multi track claims.[10] While the author accepts this principle in accident cases, disease and product liability cases may not suit precise adoption of the Protocol because of the need to obtain expert evidence in order to determine whether there is a claim fit to be intimated in the first place.

Proposed claimants should intimate claims promptly, and proposed defendants have up to a maximum of three months and 21 days, claim and response to be detailed. Whereas it is provided that letters of claim and response are not intended to have the same status as Statements of Case in pleadings such that "it would not be consistent with the spirit of the Protocol for a party to 'take a point'" when the "pleaded" case "is presented slightly differently" than in the letter of claim or response,[11] it is the author's belief that such points will continue to be taken on the alleged basis that one is entitled to enquire in order to investigate whether the change of position was intended to mislead the other party, for which purpose the taking of the point is permitted.[12] In the author's submission, great care therefore should be taken to ensure as close an approximation as possible between the letter of claim and response, on the one hand, and the Particulars of Claim or Defence when subsequently served, on the other.

Issue

25–03   There is now one unified method of issuing proceedings for damages for personal injury, namely by Claim Form under CPR. Part 7. Proceedings including claims for damages in respect of personal injuries must not be started in the High Court unless the value of the claim is £50,000 or more.[13]

---

[7] CPR r. 3.1(4) and (5), and 3.9(e).
[8] CPR r. 44.3(5)(a) defining conduct relevant to the Court's discretion as to costs to include "conduct before, as well as during, the proceedings, and in particular the extent to which the parties followed any relevant pre-action protocol".
[9] Protocol, para. 2.3.
[10] Protocol, para. 2.4.
[11] Protocol, para. 2.9.
[12] Protocol, para. 2.9.
[13] CPR, PD to Part 7, para. 2.2 preserving for this purpose the High Court and County Courts Jurisdiction Order 1991 (S.I. 1991 No. 724).

Proceedings are started when the court issues a Claim Form, and issue for this purpose is on the date entered on the form by the court,[14] but for the purposes of any limitation legislation, where the Claim Form was received in the Court Office on a date earlier than the date on which it was issued by the court, the claim is "brought" on that earlier date on which it was received in the Court Office.[15]

The Claim Form initially is valid for service within four months after the date of issue[16] unless the Claim Form is to be served out of the jurisdiction in which case the period of validity is six months.[17] An innovation under the new Rules provides that where a Claim Form has been issued against a defendant but has not yet been served on him, the defendant may serve a Notice on the claimant requiring the claimant to serve the Claim Form or discontinue the claim within a specified period which must be not less than 14 days after service of the Notice,[18] and failure to comply with the notice entitles the Court on application to dismiss the claim or make any other Order it thinks just.[19] Practitioners, therefore, should beware against premature issue of proceedings unless there is a limitation or analogous reason requiring it. Particulars of Claim may, but need not, be contained in or served with the Claim Form, subject only to the requirement that they must be served on the defendant within 14 days after the service of the Claim Form,[20] with the overall limit that they must be served on the defendant no later than the latest time for serving the Claim Form.[21] A claimant may apply for an Order extending the period of validity of the Claim Form for service subject to requirements,[22] but the author submits that safe and prudent practice demands that where a claimant for any reason wishes to delay the action the proper and prudent course is to serve the Claim Form and to apply to the defendant and, ultimately, the court for an extension of time to serve the Particulars of Claim, rather than attempting to invoke the jurisdiction to extend the period of validity of the Claim Form.

The new procedure is more closely analogous to the old High Court procedure in that a generally endorsed Claim Form may be issued without filing Particulars of Claim or medical report or Schedule of Special Damage.

---

[14] CPR r. 7.2(2).
[15] CPR PD to Part 7A, para. 5.1.
[16] CPR r. 7.5(2).
[17] CPR r. 7.5(3).
[18] CPR r. 7.7(1) and (2).
[19] CPR r. 7.7(3).
[20] CPR r. 7.4(1).
[21] CPR r. 7.4(2).
[22] CPR r. 7.6.

Statement of Value

25–04   In actions in respect of personal injuries where the amount being claimed is unliquidated damages, the claimant must in the Claim Form:

(a) state whether he expects to recover not more than £5,000 or more than £5,000, but not more than £15,000 or more than £15,000[23]; and

(b) whether the amount he expects to recover as general damages for pain and suffering and loss of amenity is not more than £1,000 or more than £1,000.[24]

If the Claim Form is issued in the High Court, the Statement of Value must be to the effect that the claimant expects to recover £50,000 or more, if there is a claim for personal injuries.[25] For the purpose of calculating these threshold sums, the claimant must disregard interest, costs, the possibility of a finding of contributory negligence, any set-off or counterclaim on the part of the defendant, and any amount that may be payable to the Compensation Recovery Unit of the Department of Social Security under the Social Security (Recovery of Benefits) Act 1997.[26] Perhaps somewhat surprisingly, however, the Statement of Value does not limit the power of the court as to the amount awarded, which may therefore exceed the Statement of Value.[27] If the defendant disputes the claimant's Statement of Value, he must state why he disputes it and, if he is able, give his own Statement of Value of the claim.[28]

Statement of Case

25–05   Statement of Case is defined as a Claim Form or Particulars of Claim or Defence, or Part 20 Claim or Reply, or Further Information.[29] A Request for Further Information for this purpose, however, is not a Statement of Case. The point is relevant because all Statements of Case must be verified by a Statement of Truth[30] in prescribed form[31] signed either by the party or his Litigation Friend or his legal representative,[32] failing which it is liable to

---

[23] CPR r. 16.3(2).
[24] CPR r. 16.3(3).
[25] CPR r. 16.3(5)(c).
[26] CPR r. 16.3(6).
[27] CPR r. 16.3(7).
[28] CPR r. 16.5(6).
[29] CPR r. 2.2(1).
[30] CPR r. 22(1)(a).
[31] CPR PD to Part 22 para. 2.1.
[32] CPR PD to Part 22 para. 3.1.

be struck out[33] or it may attract an Order from the court that the document be verified.[34] It should be appreciated that subject to those proceedings being brought by the Attorney-General or with the permission of the court, proceedings for contempt of court may be brought against any person who makes or causes to be made a false statement in a document verified by a Statement of Truth without an honest belief in its truth.[35]

Particulars of Claim

The Particulars of Claim must include: 25–06

(a) "A concise statement of the facts on which the claimant relies".[36] Whereas on its face this requirement appears significantly wider than the old law (because under the old law the word "facts" was qualified by the word "material", thereby limiting what had to be pleaded, under the new rule the word is qualified by the wider requirement to plead "any" facts relied upon), in practice there may already have been a watering down of this requirement so that it is only necessary to plead the "nature" of a party's case so as to make the general nature of it clear and identify the issues, rather than having to engage in encyclopaedic particularisation of the evidence relied on[37];

(b) any claim to interest if made,[38] and if the claim is for a specified amount of money, such as past loss, the percentage rate at which interest is claimed, the date from which it is claimed, the date to which it is calculated, the total amount of interest claimed to the date of calculation, and the daily rate at which interest accrues after that date must be specified[39];

(c) any claim for aggravated or exemplary damages if made, including the grounds for claiming them[40];

---

[33] CPR r. 22.2(2).
[34] CPR r. 22.4(1).
[35] CPR r. 32.14.
[36] CPR r. 16.4(1)(a).
[37] *per* Lord Woolf M.R. in *McPhilemy v. Times Newspapers Limited* [1999] 3 All E.R. 775.
[38] CPR r. 16.4(1)(b).
[39] CPR r. 16.4(2)(b).
[40] CPR r. 16.4(10)(c).

(d) any claim for provisional damages and the grounds for claiming them[41];

(e) such other matters as are set out in the Practice Direction.[42]

The Particulars of Claim must contain the claimant's date of birth[43] and brief details of the claimant's personal injuries.[44] The claimant must attach to his Particulars of Claim a Schedule of Details of any past and future expenses and losses which he claims.[45]

25–07   Thus, the purpose of the Particulars of Claim is to put the defendant on notice of the case which he has to meet, and that includes as to damages. Somewhere in the pleading, therefore, there must be particularity as to the heads of claim to be sought. The writer conventionally adds pleas as to such heads of claim under the particulars of injury, although there is no rule so requiring. Examples are:

(a) disadvantage on the labour market[46];

(b) loss of congenial employment[47];

(c) loss of valuable pension rights[48];

(d) assistance with domestic chores and activities and nursing care and services from members of the family[49];

(e) inability to undertake the do it yourself activities, gardening, and motor maintenance activities[50];

---

[41] CPR r. 16.4(1)(d). See generally the Supreme Court Act 1981, s.32A; County Courts Act 1984, s.51; CPR Part 41 and CPR PD to Part 41 for the jurisdiction and procedure to be applied; see also *Hurditch v. Sheffield Health Authority* [1989] Q.B. 562; [1989] 2 All E.R. 869 CA; *Middleton v. Elliott Turbo-Machinery, The Times*, October 29, 1990, CA; *Willson v. Ministry of Defence* [1991] 1 All E.R. 638 for guidance as to the principles to be applied in deciding whether or not to make a provisional award. It is now specifically required that in a provisional damages claim the claimant must state in the Particulars of Claim that there is a chance that he will develop some serious disease or suffer some serious deterioration in his physical or mental condition and specify the type of disease or deterioration in respect of which an application may be made at a future date—CPR Part 16 PD, para. 4.4.

[42] CPR r. 16.4(1)(e).

[43] CPR PD to Part 16, para. 4.1(1). Note that under the old law the age of the plaintiff had to be pleaded but the date of birth did not, and under the new law the requirement is the opposite.

[44] CPR Part 16 PD, para. 4.1(2).

[45] CPR Part 16 PD, para. 4.2.

[46] See *Smith v. Manchester Corporation* [1974] 17 K.I.R 1; *Moeliker v. A Reyrolle and Company Limited* [1977] 1 All E.R. 9; *Foster v. Tyne and Wear County Council* [1986] 1 All E.R. 567.

[47] See *Hale v. London Underground Ltd* [1993] P.I.Q.R. Q30; *Morris v. Johnson Matthey and Company Limited* (1968) 112 S.J. 32; *Hearnshaw v. English Steel Corporation Limited* [1971] 11 K.I.R. 306.

[48] See generally *Auty v. National Coal Board* [1985] 1 All E.R. 930.

[49] See generally *Housecroft v. Burnett* [1986] 1 All E.R. 332.

[50] See generally the unreported decisions summarised in *Butterworth's Personal Injury Litigation Services* Division I, section H paragraphs [435] to [436].

(f) loss of income during the lost year[51];

(g) loss of social security benefits which the claimant would have continued to be entitled to and to receive[52];

(h) special accommodation needs by reason whereof the claimant will incur loss and damage[53],

(i) special accommodation needs, currently provided gratuitously by the local authority and/or social services department, for which provision the claimant will become and remain liable to pay commercially, after damages have been awarded[54];

(k) Court of Protection costs.[55]

As regards the interest to be pleaded, the High Court[56] and the county **25–08** court[57] have power to award interest on damages but can only do so if such a claim is pleaded,[58] even if only by amendment, and if no claim is pleaded, no interest can be awarded.[59] In personal injury actions, conventionally, interest if pleaded, will be awarded as, but only as, follows:

(a) on general damages for pain and suffering and loss of amenity at 3 per cent per annum from the date of service of proceedings[60];

(b) on past financial losses, including loss of dependency from date of death to date of trial in a claim under the Fatal Accidents Act 1976,

---

[51] See generally *Pickett v. British Railway Engineering Limited* [1980] A.C. 136, which continues to apply to cases of a surviving claimant, despite the provisions of the Administration of Justice Act 1982 restricting the availability of such claims after death; as to quantification, see generally *Harris v. Empress Motors Limited* [1983] 3 All E.R. 561 [1984] 1 W.L.R. 212, CA. Note: the restriction of lost years claims to cases of lost earnings—see *Phipps v. Brooks Dry Cleaning Service Ltd* [1996] P.I.Q.R. Q100.

[52] See *Hassall v. Secretary of State for Social Security* [1985] 3 All E.R. 909, which recognised the legitimacy of claiming benefits lost as a result of an accident when other benefits that are otherwise recoupable under the Social Security Administration Act 1992 (the statutory predecessor of the Social Security (Recovery of Benefits) Act 1997) have been substituted therefore, thereby avoiding the injustice of recoupable benefits eroding the award of general damages for pain and suffering and loss of amenity. It should be observed, however, that by virtue of both the common law duty to mitigate loss and the social security law obligation to accept work, it would be wrong to assume that those in receipt of benefits at the time of an accident can and should only claim loss of benefits in this way. Care should be taken to seek to present the case on the basis, if evidenced, that work would have been obtained by a defined date from which date damages for loss of earnings should be claimed conventionally, the *Hassall* (ante) claim then being: (a) advanced for the period from the date of accident to the date by which it is contended that employment would have been obtained; and (b) thereafter only as an alternative to the loss of earnings claim.

[53] See *Roberts v. Johnstone* [1989] Q.B. 878, CA.

[54] See *Avon County Council v. Hooper* [1997] 1 All E.R. 532, CA.

[55] See *Rialas v. Mitchell* (1984) 128 S.J. 704.

[56] CPR r. 16.4(1)(b).

[57] County Courts Act 1984, s.69(1).

[58] RSC, Ord. 18, r. 8(4).

[59] *Ward v. Chief Constable of Avon and Somerset* (1985) 129 S.J. 606, CA.

[60] *Burns v. Davies* [1998] QBD (unreported) as logically following from *Wells v. Wells* [1998] 3 All E.R. 481, HL.

at half the court special account rate from time to time prevailing (previously the short-term investment account rate) for the full period from the date of the accident to payment or trial, on the full amount claimed[61];

(c) on damages for bereavement under the Fatal Accidents Act 1975, s.1A, at the full court special account rate from the date of death.[62]

Any special circumstances to be prayed in aid as justifying a departure from the above principles, must be pleaded specifically,[63] whether that be the circumstances relied upon by a claimant or circumstances relied upon by a defendant. The circumstances thus far recognised by the courts are:

(a) where the loss has fully crystallised at or near the time that the cause of action accrued, so that the claimant has been deprived of the full amount for virtually the whole period, interest may be awarded at the full court special account rate[64];

(b) where there has been culpable delay by the claimant in the pursuit of the claim, the court may reduce the period for which interest is awarded or the amount of any interest awarded[65].

In fatal accident claims, the claimant in the Particulars of Claim must state that the claim is brought under the Fatal Accidents Act 1976, state the dependants on whose behalf the claim is made, state the date of birth of each dependant, and set out details of the nature of the dependency claim[66] and state if any claim is made for damages for bereavement.[67] If the claimant also brings a claim under the Law Reform (Miscellaneous Provisions) Act 1934, the nature thereof should be specified.[68]

25–09 The Practice Direction adds certain other specific pleading requirements relevant to personal injury litigation, namely:

(a) any conviction relied upon under Section 11 of the Civil Evidence Act 1968 must be pleaded[69] in which case the date of the convic-

---

[61] *Jefford v. Gee* [1972] 2 Q.B. 130; [1970] 1 All E.R. 1202; *Cookson v. Knowles* [1979] A.C. 556; [1978] 2 All E.R. 604, HL; *Dexter v. Courtaulds Limited* [1984] 1 W.L.R. 372.

[62] *Sharman v. Sheppard* [1989] 10 C.L. 98; *Khan v. Duncan* [1989] Q.B.D. Popplewell J. (unreported).

[63] See *Dexter v. Courtaulds Ltd* [1984] 1 All E.R. 70; [1984] 1 W.L.R. 372, CA.

[64] *Prokop v. DHSS* [1985] C.L.Y. 1037, CA.

[65] See *Birkett v. Hayes* [1982] 1 All E.R. 300; *Spittle v. Bunny* [1988] 3 All E.R. 1031; [1988] 1 W.L.R. 847, CA; *Corbett v. Barking, Havering and Brentwood Health Authority* [1991] 2 Q.B. 408; [1991] 1 All E.R. 498, CA.

[66] CPR Part 16 PD, para. 5.1.

[67] Implicit from CPR Part 16 PD, para. 5.2 which curiously simply gives permission to make a claim that statute has already provided for.

[68] Implicit from CPR Part 16 PD, para. 5.3.

[69] CPR Part 16 PD, para. 10.1(1).

tion, the Court where it is made, and the issue to which it relates must be pleaded;

(b) any allegation of fraud, illegality, misrepresentation, notice or knowledge of a fact, details of unsoundness of mind, and any facts relating to mitigation of loss or damage must be pleaded[70];

(c) where a claim is for a sum of money expressed in a foreign currency, that must be pleaded, with the reason for so claiming, the Stirling equivalent of the sum at the date of claim and the source of the exchange rate relied upon.[71]

The author submits that, either deficiently or curiously, these requirements are expressed only to apply to claimants, but this assumes that they were intended also to apply to defendants, although the only vehicle under which such a requirement could be imposed is that calling for a defendant to put forward a different version of events to that given by the claimant.[72]

There is a *discretion* on claimants in addition to refer to any point of law on which the claim is based[73] or name witnesses proposed to be called[74] or attach to or serve with the Particulars of Claim a copy of any document considered to be necessary to the claim including any expert's report[75] or inferentially therefore including any witness statement or document to be revealed by way of disclosure. There is no requirement as such on claimants to avail themselves of this facility.

The author submits that it remains the case that certain points will **25–10** always have to be pleaded in any Particulars of Claim, namely:

(a) those facts which give rise to a legal submission that a duty of care was owed by the defendant to the claimant whether at common law (*e.g.* the defendant employed the claimant) or pursuant to statute (*e.g.* the defendant was a highway authority responsible for the condition of a highway or otherwise the occupier of a factory);

(b) those facts which give rise to a legal submission that the defendant was in breach of that duty (*i.e.* the respects and circumstances in which it is alleged that he was negligent or in breach of statutory duty);

(c) those facts which complete the cause of action (*i.e.* the fact of damage, because no cause of action is complete without damage, but any damage which is not de minimis will suffice[76]);

---

[70] CPR Part 16 PD, para. 10.2.
[71] CPR Part 16 PD, para. 11.1.
[72] CPR Part 16.5(2)(b) as to which see para. 25–11 below.
[73] CPR Part 16 PD, para. 10.3(1).
[74] CPR Part 16 PD, para. 10.3(2).
[75] CPR Part 16 PD, para. 10.3(3).
[76] See *Cartledge v. E. Jopling & Sons Ltd* [1963] A.C. 758; [1963] 1 All E.R. 341, HL.

(d) those facts which connect the damage alleged to the breach of duty alleged (*i.e.* causation in the sense that the damage was caused or materially contributed to by the alleged breach[77] and foreseeability in the sense that the kind of harm alleged was foreseeable as possible in the event of a breach of duty as alleged[78]);

(e) those facts which by the rules have to be pleaded, if relied upon (*e.g.* a criminal conviction[79] and grounds for claiming aggravated or exemplary damages[80]);

(f) the principle *res ipsa loquitur* to the effect that the facts of the accident speak for themselves is a rule of evidence and strictly speaking not a matter which needs to be pleaded expressly[81] but the author submits it to be good practice frequently adopted for the intention to rely upon the maxim to be pleaded. However, retention of shorthand latinisms is now frowned upon.

The author submits that to this time-honoured list must now be added particulars of knowledge in appropriate cases.[82]

Defences

25–11   As a general rule the Defence must be filed within 14 days after service of the Particulars of Claim.[82a] No Defence need be filed where a Claim Form alone is served without Particulars of Claim. If the defendant is unable to file a Defence within 14 days after service of the Particulars of Claim, by filing an Acknowledgment of Service under Part 10, the time for service of the Defence is automatically extended to 28 days after service of the Particulars of Claim. Failure to file and serve a Defence or an Acknowledgment of Service in time entitles the claimant to obtain default judgment[83] unless the defendant has applied for summary judgment,[84] as long as not more than six months has expired since the end of the period for filing a Defence,[85] in which latter event the claim is automatically

---

[77] Material contribution suffices: see *Bonnington Castings Ltd v. Wardlaw* [1956] A.C. 613; [1956] 1 All E.R. 615, HL.
[78] See *The Wagon Mound* [1961] A.C. 388; [1961] 1 All E.R. 404 subject to the suggestion in *Page v. Smith* [1996] 1 A.C. 155; [1995] 2 All E.R. 736 that foresight of any physical or psychological injury is sufficient, which the author submits might now mean that it is not necessary to foresee the particular kind of personal injury as long as some form of personal injury was foreseeable.
[79] See the Civil Evidence Act 1968, s.11 and CPR Part 16 PD, para. 10.1.
[80] CCR, Ord. 6, r. 1B, RSC, Ord. 18, r. 8(3).
[81] *Bennett v. Chemical Construction (GB) Ltd* [1971] 1 W.L.R. 1571.
[82] CPR Part 16 PD, para. 10.2(5).
[82a] CPR r. 15.4(1)(a).
[83] CPR r. 12.3(2).
[84] CPR r. 12.3(3)(a).
[85] CPR r. 15.11(1)(b).

stayed. The form of judgment in personal injury cases will normally be for an amount to be decided by the court.[86]

In any Defence, the defendant must state which of the allegations in the Particulars of Claim he denies, which of the allegations he is unable to admit or deny but requires the claimant to prove, and which of the allegations he admits.[87] In the event of a denial, he must state the reasons for the denial, and put forward a different version of events from that given by the claimant, if he intends to advance that at trial.[88] In the absence of any authority or decided case on the point, the author submits that this latter requirement imports an obligation on the part of the defendant to plead any fraud or illegality, or notice or knowledge of any fact, or of any unsoundness of mind, or any facts relating to mitigation of loss or damage that may be relied upon.[89] If the defendant fails to deal with an allegation, he shall be deemed to admit it,[90] unless he has set out in his Defence the nature of the case in relation to the issue to which the allegation is relevant, in which case he shall be taken to require the allegation to be proved.[91] The defendant should deal with every allegation in the Particulars of Claim in accordance with the requirements of CPR r. 16.5(1) and (2).[92]

The Practice Direction specifically provides that the defendant must state **25–12** in his Defence whether he agrees or disputes, or neither agrees nor disputes, but has no knowledge of the matters contained in the medical report and give his reasons for dispute if any and must attach any medical report of his own on which he intends to rely[93] and must include or attach to the Defence a Counter-Schedule stating which of the items contained in the claimant's Schedule of Past and Future Expenses he agrees or disputes, or neither agrees nor disputes, supplying alternative figures "where appropriate"[94] and must "give details of the expiry of any relevant limitation period relied on".[95]

As for claimants, defendants are given a discretion without obligation to refer in the Defence to any point of law relied upon[96] or give the name of

---

[86] CPR r. 12.4(1)(b).
[87] CPR r. 16.5(1).
[88] CPR r. 16.5(2).
[89] Not specifically provided for in the Civil Procedure Rules except as against claimants under CPR Part 16 PD, para. 10.2.
[90] CPR r. 16.5(5).
[91] CPR r. 16.5(3)—it is not clear to the writer what the position would be if the defendant has no positive case relevant to the particular allegation but has pleaded a positive case in relation to other allegations. Will that suffice to put the claimant to proof or will the defendant be deemed to admit the allegation not specifically dealt with?
[92] CPR Part 16 PD, para. 12.2.
[93] CPR Part 16 PD, para. 14.1.
[94] CPR Part 16 PD, para. 14.2.
[95] CPR Part 16 PD, para. 16.1.
[96] CPR Part 16 PD, para. 16.3(1).

any witness proposed to be called[97] or attach or serve with the statement a copy of any document considered necessary including an expert's report.[98]

Thus, fundamental change has been effected to what is required of defendants by way of pleading. If, and to the extent that, a defendant wishes to assert a positive case that the accident occurred otherwise than as described by the claimant, or in circumstances other than those described by the claimant, he must so plead. If, and to the extent that, a defendant wishes to assert any positive defence, a positive pleading again is necessary. Examples are as follows:

(a) contributory negligence[99];

(b) *volenti non fit injuria*;

(c) act of stranger or act of third party;

(d) latent defect;

(e) limitation of action[1];

(f) the taking of all reasonable care, or any other statutory Defence, in denial of allegations of breach of statutory duty[2];

(g) set off[3];

(h) counterclaim.[4]

Failure to plead such Defences will be fatal to the defendant's prospect of being permitted to adduce evidence in support of such positive Defences.[5]

25–13 The generality of the principles suggests that any positive case which the defendant wishes to raise as regards quantum, must also be pleaded. The following are examples:

(a) unreasonable failure to mitigate loss;

(b) symptoms and disabilities caused or contributed to by the progression of a pre-existing degenerative condition of the claimant's lumbar spine;

---

[97] CPR Part 16 PD, para. 16.3(2).

[98] CPR Part 16 PD, para. 16.3(3).

[99] Contributory negligence must be pleaded and particularised—*Fookes v. Slaytor* [1979] 1 All E.R. 137.

[1] CPR Part 16 PD para. 16.1.

[2] See for example the Highways Act 1980, s.58, as an example of where a defendant is given a statutory Defence.

[3] Set-off must be specifically pleaded—CPR Part 16.6.

[4] This requires a Part 20 Claim—CPR Part 20.2(1)(a).

[5] It remains to be seen whether such failures will be dealt with by exercising power to strike out Defences under CPR Part 3.4 or by summary judgment under CPR Part 24, or by exercising powers to control evidence by excluding it in the absence of a pleaded case under CPR Part 32.1 or any combination of these three.

(c) the claim is fraudulent, because the claimant was not disabled to the extent alleged in the medical report, but rather, he was fit to engage on that date, and on dates thereafter, in heavy manual labour as a builder, which work he undertook.[6]

In addition, that injury was either not caused by the alleged accident, or alternatively, was not foreseeable, though not necessarily positive cases, ought to be pleaded specifically.

Admissions

Under the old rules where the defence admitted negligence and admitted 25–14 *some* damage, simply putting in issue the extent of the damage, then the plaintiff was entitled to interlocutory judgment for damages to be assessed. If, however, the defence, while admitting some negligence, denied any damage whatsoever, the plaintiff was not entitled to judgment because the cause of action was not admitted, because damage was a necessary ingredient to complete the cause of action. In the latter case, the action would proceed to a hearing in the ordinary way. Under the new rules the only[7] circumstances in which a claimant may seek damages on admissions in a personal injury action where the amount of money claimed is not specified, is if either the admission is to pay the whole of the claim[8] or where the admission of liability to pay only part of the claim, and the admission contains an offer of a sum in satisfaction.[9] Accordingly, it is no longer possible to obtain interlocutory judgment for damages to be assessed where breach of duty is admitted by the extent of damage is not. Such claims now must proceed to full trial, rather than to assessment of damages. The author submits that, as a consequence, the extended jurisdiction of the District Judge to hear assessments of damages[10] will not be available for the purpose of disposal of this class of case.

Under the old rules, a defendant making an open letter admission of liability was not allowed to resile from or withdraw that admission unless it could be done in the interests of justice to *both* parties.[11] If, however, the claimant acted in reliance on the admission and became prejudiced thereby

---

[6] The allegation that the claimant is a malingerer amounts to an allegation of fraud, which must always be specifically pleaded—see by implication CPR r. 16.5(2)(b) and CPR Part 16 PD, para. 10.2(1) and *Davy v. Garrett* (1878) 7 ChD 473 at 489; *Behn v. Bloom* (1911) 132 L.T.J. 87; *Smith v. Chadwick* (1884) 9 App.Cas. 187. See also *Cooper v. P&O Stena Line Limited*, *The Times*, February, 1999.

[7] CPR r. 14.1(3).

[8] Under CPR r. 14.6.

[9] Under CPR r. 14.7.

[10] Without financial limit: CPR PD 2B, para. 11.1(c).

[11] See *Bird v. Bird's Eye Walls Limited*, *The Times*, July 24, 1987; but see also *Gale v. Superdrug Stores Plc* [1996] P.I.Q.R. P330.

(for example by failing to obtain and preserve evidence that otherwise would have been available) an estoppel may have arisen which debarred the defendant from resiling from the admission. Under the new rules it is provided that "the court may allow a party to amend or withdraw an admission".[12] No guidance is given as to how this power should be exercised or in what circumstances other than that the general power to make such an order subject to conditions under case management powers would apply.[13] The author submits that the new rules do not amend or overturn the substantive law such that if an estoppel has arisen, that continues to be available to the claimant to debar the defendant from defending, in which case it may be necessary to plead the admission by way of Reply. The jurisdiction to allow amendment or withdrawal of admissions, it is submitted, therefore operates only where no estoppel arises, and may be a less narrow jurisdiction than the common law jurisdiction under the old rules.

Limitation of Action

25–15　　Limitation of action is a special case, both as regards to position of the claimant, and as regards the position of the defendant, from the point of view of pleading. The claimant need not, and the author submits, should not, engage in "anticipatory pleading" by addressing any limitation issue in his Particulars of Claim in the first instance. It has always been the case that a claimant may bring an action without the leave of the court, after the apparent expiry of the limitation period.[14] It is then for the defendant to take the limitation point, or not to do so, as he may choose. This seems to the author to accord with the Civil Procedure Rules, which provide that the defendant must give details of the expiry of any limitation period relied on.[15] Once the point is taken, however, the claimant has the burden of proving (and therefore pleading) relevant facts, either that the cause of action is not statute barred[16] or that it is equitable to allow the action to proceed.[17] The author submits that the former course can be taken without amending the Particulars of Claim, in that it can be taken by way of Reply. However, the latter course requires seeking relief from the court, and strictly speaking, that requires a prayer for relief, and ought to be sought

---

[12] CPR r. 14.1(5).

[13] CPR r. 13.1(3).

[14] *Per* Lord Cairns LC in *Dawkins v. Lord Penrhyn* (1878) 7 App. Cas. 51 at 59; *Dismore v. Milton* 1938 3 All E.R. 762, CA.

[15] CPR Part 16 PD, para. 16.1.

[16] For example, by proving a later date of knowledge within the Limitation Act 1980, ss.11(4)(b) and 14; or by prayer in aid a disability having delayed the running of time for the purposes of the Limitation Act 1980 within the meaning of s.28.

[17] Thereby invoking the equitable jurisdiction of the Court to disapply the provisions of s.11 under the Limitation Act 1980, s.33.

by way of amendment of the Particulars of Claim. Whomsoever alleges a positive case on limitation, whether that be the claimant, as to the date of knowledge, or the defendant, as to either the date of knowledge or in equity, must plead it, with proper particularity.

Pleadings Subsequent to the Defence

Implicitly, there remains a joinder of issue between claimant and **25–16** defendant upon the terms of the Defence in that a claimant who does not file a Reply to the Defence shall not be taken to admit matters raised in the Defence[18] and is taken to require any matter raised in the Defence which is not dealt with in a Reply be proved by the defendant.[19] The new Rules do not repeat the requirement under the old rules[20] that to defend a counterclaim, a Defence to the counterclaim must be served, but the author submits that it remains good practice to do so.

Examples of where a Reply is necessary are as follows:

(a) An allegation that disability delayed the running of time for the purposes of limitation, pursuant to the Limitation Act 1980, s.28.

(b) An allegation that the claimant's date of knowledge only arose within three years before the issue of the summons, pursuant to the Limitation Act 1980, s.11(4) (b);

(c) An allegation that the defendant is estopped from denying liability due to an admission he may have made.[21]

(d) Any special cases where an answer to the Defence can be provided—for example, in response to a Defence that injury was due to latent defect in equipment supplied by an employer, a claimant may still pray in aid the Employer's Liability (Defective Equipment) Act 1969, s.1.[22]

The new rules no longer provide for any pleading subsequent to a Reply, whether with or without leave.

---

[18] CPR r. 6.7(1).
[19] CPR r. 16.7(2).
[20] RSC, Ord. 18, r. 14(1).
[21] Estoppel must be pleaded specifically—*Coppinger v. Norton* [1902] 2 Ir. R. 241; in that it is a shield and not a sword, it cannot be pleaded as a cause of action, but only therefore by way of Reply; to found the estoppel, the claimant must show that he has materially changed his position detrimentally, in reliance on the representation, by for example not investigating or evidencing liability, witnesses having ceased to be traceable.
[22] By which the fault of any third party, like the manufacturer, is deemed to be attributable to the negligence of the employer.

Amendment

25–17   The power to amend a Statement of Case, either at any time before it has been served[23] or after service with the written consent of all other parties,[24] or otherwise only with the permission of the Court,[25] is subject to the new proviso that the court may, nonetheless, disallow the amendment,[26] either of its own motion or upon application after service of the Amended Statement of Case by any party.[27] The situations in which the court may disallow an amendment include, but may not be limited to, cases where the Statement of Case as amended discloses no reasonable grounds for bringing or defending the claim,[28] or where the court considers in the exercise of its case management powers that amendment will obstruct the just disposal of the proceedings,[29] or because a rule or Practice Direction has not been complied with,[30] or because a cause of action based on new facts has been included outside the relevant limitation period.[31] Accordingly, unless or until clear court guidance is given to the contrary, the author submits that one must assume that amendment will not be as readily available as it used to be under the old rules. It can no longer be safe to assume, as was the old law,[32] that amendment will be permitted unless the opposite party would suffer prejudice that was not remediable by adjournment and/or an Order for costs against the amending party.

In the particular context of personal injury litigation however, note must be made of the Limitation Act 1980, s.35, by which it is provided, in effect, that amendment to join a new party[33] or a new cause of action,[34] outside the limitation period, must not be allowed, unless either in respect of the addition of a new claim it arises out of the same facts or substantially the same facts as the claim already in existence,[35] or the joinder of a new party is in substitution for a party already named in the claim who has been joined by mistake and the claim cannot properly be carried on unless the new party is added or substituted,[36] or leave to proceed out of time is granted under the Limitation Act 1980, s.33. Strictly speaking, this might indicate that the proper course is the issue of fresh proceedings against the proposed second defendant, with an application under the Limitation Act

---

[23] CPR r. 17.1(1).
[24] CPR r. 17.1(2)(a).
[25] CPR r. 17.1(2)(b).
[26] CPR r. 17.2(1).
[27] CPR r. 17.2(2).
[28] CPR r. 3.4(2)(a).
[29] CPR r. 3.4(2)(b)—for example because it is made too close to trial.
[30] CPR r. 3.4(2)(c).
[31] CPR r. 17.4—see paragraph [34] below.
[32] See *Ketteman v. Hansel Properties Limited* [1987] A.C. 189.
[33] Now specifically provided for in CPR r. 19.4.
[34] Now specifically provided for in CPR r. 17.4.
[35] CPR r. 17.4(2).
[36] CPR r. 19.4(3).

1980, s.33, with a view to consolidation of the two actions, if such relief is granted[37] rather than by way of amendment. If, however, there is a "date of knowledge" issue, then amendment may be appropriate and power is now given to direct that the date of knowledge issue be determined at trial.[38] If the date of knowledge issue is not clearly balanced in favour of the claimant, the court may easily be persuaded to exercise its discretion to refuse, or on appeal, set aside, the amendment even if the effect is to deprive the claimant of an opportunity to pursue the cause of action sought to be raised by amendment.[39] A new defendant does not become a party to the proceedings until the Amended Claim Form has been served on him.[40]

Further Information

The belief expressed by Lord Woolf[41] that identification of documents   **25–18** on which reliance is placed, together with disclosure of witness statements combining to "reduce the need for particulars", is reflected in the abolition of the old entitlement to request particulars and entitlement to interrogate and the substitution of the combined entitlement to seek further information. A court may at any time order a party to clarify any matter[42] or give additional information in relation to any matter,[43] whether or not the request relates to matter contained in or referred to in a Statement of Case. Before making an Order there must have been a written Request served by the applicant party allowing the responding party reasonable time to respond.[44] There is, therefore, no restriction as to the timing of such requests or as to the subject matter thereof, but merely a requirement that requests must be made as far as possible in a single comprehensive document and not piecemeal.[45] The response requires the Statement of Truth.[46] While there is an entitlement to object to complying with a Request or therefore giving further information,[47] no guidance is given as to the grounds upon which, or circumstances in which, that may be justified other than that compliance would cause disproportionate expense would be a valid reason for refusal.[48]

---

[37] See *Kennett v. Brown* [1988] 2 All E.R. 600; [1988] 1 W.L.R. 582, CA; *Howe v. David Brown Tractors (Retail) Ltd* [1991] 4 All E.R. 30, CA.

[38] CPR r. 19.4(b).

[39] See *Marshall v. Gradon Construction* [1997] 4 All E.R. 880.

[40] CPR Part 19 PD, para. 3.3, correctly reflecting *Marshall v. Gradon Construction Limited* [1997] 4 All E.R. 880.

[41] *McPhilemy v. Times Newspapers Limited* [1999] 3 All E.R. 775 at 793.

[42] CPR r. 18.1(1)(a).

[43] CPR r. 18.1(1)(b).

[44] CPR Part 18 PD, para. 1.1.

[45] CPR Part 18 PD, para. 1.3.

[46] CPR Part 18 PD, para. 3.

[47] CPR Part 18 PD, para. 4.1(1).

[48] CPR Part 18 PD, para. 4.2(2).

Additional Claims

25–19   A counterclaim by a defendant against a claimant, or against a Claimant and some other person, or a claim by a defendant against any person whether or not already a party for a contribution or indemnity, is a Part 20 Claim. Counterclaim against the claimant may be commenced without permission, and claims for contribution or indemnity against existing defendants may be made simply by filing a notice and serving it. All other Part 20 claims require the permission of the court, the service of a Part 20 Claim Form, and, thereafter, adherence to the directions that the court makes, and compliance with the above rules as to pleadings.

26. Fast Track

This Chapter reviews those rules which have a particular impact upon **26–01**
the Personal Injury Fast Track.

The New Terminology

As soon as the rules come in it is best to become familiar with the new **26–02**
terminology whereby:

- plaintiffs become claimants;
- discovery becomes disclosure;
- pleadings (that is the Summons and the Particulars of Claim) become Statements of Case;
- Next Friends or Guardian Ad Litems become Litigation Friends;
- Summons becomes Claim Form.

The Overriding Objective

CPR 1.1 provides that the Civil Procedure Rules 1998 (CPR) are a new **26–03**
procedural code with the overriding objective of enabling the court to deal
with cases justly. CPR 1.1 (2) sets out a list of the matters that the court
has to, insofar as is practicable, take account of:

(a) ensuring that the parties are on an equal footing;

(b) saving expense;

(c) dealing in the case in ways in which are proportionate to:

    (i) the amount of money involved;
    (ii) to the importance of the case;
    (iii) to the complexity of the issues;
    (iv) to the financial position of each party;

(d) ensuring that the case is dealt with expeditiously and fairly;

(e) allotting to it an appropriate share of the court's resources, while taking into account the need to allot resources to other cases.

The Courts have shown, in their treatment of the CPR since April 1999
that this is the starting point for every application that they consider—they
are the new guidelines that practitioners must have uppermost in the
litigation process.

The changes to previously widely accepted principles can be far reaching. In *Elli Christofi v. Barclays Bank Plc*,[1] the Court of Appeal refused leave to amend pleadings resulting in the claimant's case being struck out. The decision was founded upon the overriding principle including, particularly, reference to saving expense and the importance of sharing the court's time appropriately. This would appear to be a departure from the widely accepted doctrine under the old rules that if another party could be compensated by costs for an amendment then it was likely to be allowed.

Further, in *Chilton v. Surrey County Council & Foakes*,[2] the claimant had mistakenly failed to file an amended Schedule of Special Damages that took the claim from being worth £5,000 to £400,000. The court found that the disclosed medical evidence clearly foreshadowed a large loss of earnings claim and that the defendants should have realised that the claimant had made a mistake by not making such a claim. The amendment was allowed, with time for the defendant to investigate the claim. The Court of Appeal also held that the parties were required to help the court to further the overriding objective. The parties should have cooperated so as to avoid satellite litigation.

The position has arisen, therefore, that no longer can the parties necessarily remain silent in the face of an opponent's error, but that they should cooperate to ensure that the matter is dealt with justly.

A full Court of Appeal reiterated the need for the parties to cooperate so that the litigation could be conducted justly and economically in *Adoko v. Hussein Jemal*.[3]

If courts continue to interpret the overriding objective to its teleological conclusion, then it may be that adversarial litigation will be slowly replaced by a system that is less confrontational and more inquisitive.

On considering an appeal as to a decision to strike out a claimant's case the Court of Appeal in *Biguzzi v. Rank Leisure Plc*,[4] held that the CPR were a new procedural code and that their whole purpose was that they were a new self-contained code that rendered earlier authorities irrelevant. This approach may be contrasted with a differently constituted Court of Appeal in *Breeze v. John Stacey & Sons Limited*,[5] who held that the principles to be applied in considering whether to prevent the use of privileged documents that had been disclosed in an exhibit to an affidavit in support of an application to strike out were the same as under cases decided in Discovery and that the CPR did not affect the position.

---

[1] June 28, 1999, Stuart-Smith and Chadwick L.JJ.
[2] June 24, 1999, Henry and Waller L.JJ.
[3] June 22, 1999, Buxton, May and Laws L.JJ.
[4] July 26, 1999, Woolf M.R, Brooke and Walker L.JJ.
[5] *The Times*, July 8, 1999, Peter Gibson Judge and Clark L.JJ.

The Protocols

The introduction of the pre-action protocols will mark the greatest 26–04 practical changes to the personal injury practitioner. On April 26, 1999, the Pre-action Protocol for Personal Injury Claims and the Pre-Action Protocol for the Resolution of Clinical Disputes came into force. The PI Protocol is particularly important in the Fast Track where compliance should be considered mandatory. The Code of Guidance for Experts is expected to be ready by the end of 1999 and it may be that the Lord Chancellor will also introduce a Road Traffic Accident Protocol that is used on a private basis between some insurers and solicitor members of MASS. Personal injury, medical negligence and perhaps, in the future, road traffic accident claims that are worth less than £15,000 may begin, finally, to have a cost proportionate to the amount of money that is claimed.

Background to the Protocols—the Court's Approach

The Personal Injury Protocol does not require from the practitioner 26–05 anything other than timeliness and an efficient system for processing claims. The Practice Direction provides that the objectives are to encourage early exchange of information, avoid litigation and support efficient litigation where it is unavoidable. If non-compliance has lead to litigation or costs unnecessarily, then sanctions include costs (they may be on an indemnity basis), lower or no rates of interest and or a rate of interest not exceeding 10 per cent above base rate.

The Personal Injury Protocol v. The Road Traffic Accident Protocol

The Road Traffic Accident Protocol was undergoing its second six- 26–06 month pilot stage when the Personal Injury Protocol was introduced. There is some tension between the two Protocols. The Personal Injury Protocol was intended by the members of its Working Party to apply to road traffic accidents. However, the Road Traffic Accident Protocol sets out a very much more detailed procedure to be followed by those who are injured in a road accident. Thus, on April 26, 1999, practitioners need only be concerned with the Personal Injury Protocol. Subsequently, should the Lord Chancellor's Department approve and implement the Road Traffic Accident Protocol, then practitioners should follow that Protocol in preference to the Personal Injury Protocol only in cases involving road traffic accident victims. The RTA Protocol represents best practice and there can be little harm if the practitioner follows the RTA practitioner in those areas where the Personal Injury Protocol is silent.

The Personal Injury Protocol

The Personal Injury Protocol consists of four main parts: 26–07

(a) specimen letters;

(b) disclosure of documents;

(c) schedules of damages;

(d) joint selection of, and instructions to, experts.

Specimen Letters

26–08 *The Letter of Claim.* A practitioner following best practice will already be fulfilling most of the requirements as to the specimen letters. The main purpose of the letter of claim is for sufficient information to be given by the claimant to the defendant so that the defendant can commence investigations and put a broad valuation on the risk.

The Letter of Claim Guide provides for the following:

(a) Claimant's full name, address, date of birth and National Insurance No.

(b) Claimant's clock or works No. (if applicable).

(c) Claimant's employer and name and address.

(d) Date of accident.

(e) Place of accident that is sufficiently detailed to establish location.

(f) A Request for the defendant to identity of insurers and warning:

    (i) that the insurers will need to see a copy of the letter as soon as possible;

    (ii) it may affect insurance cover if they do not send a copy of this letter to their insurers.

(g) A brief outline of the circumstances of the accident so that investigations can be started.

(h) A simple explanation as to why fault is alleged (regulations or statutory instruments).

(i) A brief outline of the claimant's injuries.

(j) Brief statement of occupation and dates of absence and approximate weekly income, if known.

(k) If the defendant is the employer, then the usual earning details should be requested.

(l) If a police report is to be obtained, the defendant should be informed and invited to contribute half the fee.

(m) If another defendant is involved then a copy of that letter should be attached with the name of the insurers and claim no.

(n) The claimant's solicitor should set out that the documents contained in the appropriate parts of the standard disclosure list are relevant to the action (as to standard disclosure lists see below). Disclosure as to these items are not required where the defendant admits liability.

(o) Invite defendant to send a copy to his insurers.

(p) A reply is expected within 21 days.

The Defendant's Letter. Defendants should be aware that they have a strict **26–09** time limit within which to investigate the claim and to admit or deny liability. Judges will not be sympathetic to the defendant who merely does not admit liability and gives no reasons. The Protocol intends to change the approach to litigation—positive reasons for denial of liability will have to be given. Failing to deal with correspondence, not asserting a positive case where liability is denied or filing a bare defence will be to invite costs sanction from the court.

The Scope of An Admission. The protocol suggests that defendants will have **26–10** to be careful when admitting liability in a claim worth less than £15,000 where other claimants allege that they have been injured in similar circumstances. If the defendant or a firm of insurers admits liability for one claim, then it is presumed to have admitted for all other claims up to £15,000. The presumption is rebuttable but, nevertheless, it is a trap that insurers and defendants should be wary of. Any admissions in respect of liability should be very carefully worded to apply only to the particular case in which an admission is intended.

The Defendants' Guide

(a) If there is no reply from the defendant or the insurer within 21 days **26–11** of the letter, then there is no sanction against the claimant for proceeding with the action.

(b) Defendant's insurers have a maximum of three months, inclusive of the 21 days, to investigate liability.

(c) If liability is denied, reasons have to be given.

(d) Where liability is admitted, the presumption is that the defendant will be bound by this admission for all claims of a value up to £15,000.

Disclosure of Documents

Where a defendant denies liability, documents which are clearly relevant **26–12** to the issues between the parties should be enclosed with the letter. The Protocol sets out that the relevant test is for:

"Documents in his possession which are clearly relevant to the issues between the parties, and which will be likely to be ordered to be disclosed by the court, either on an application for pre-action disclosure, or on disclosure during any proceedings"

If documents are disclosed after the action has been commenced that prompt the claimant to reconsider its case under liability and, perhaps, to discontinue, then a claimant may be able to avoid paying costs or even to recover its wasted costs in pursuing the claim from the defendant as a result of its breaches of the rules.

26–13 *Suggested Documents.* Annex B of the Personal Injury Protocol sets out non-exhaustive lists of documents that should be inserted by the claimant into its pre-action letter. Such lists should guide the defendant as to the type of documents that may be relevant. Defendants should note that it is *not* up to the claimant necessarily to notify them of documents that the claimant considers relevant—the primary duty of disclosure as to relevant documents rests with the defendant in whose possession most of the documents will exist.

Schedules of Damages

26–14 The claimant should note that the Protocol provides that a schedule should be provided along with supporting documents as soon as possible. It is the clear intention of the Protocol that this schedule is provided before the action is issued. There may be cases where, if a schedule, or at least an indication of the damages, is not provided to the defendant, costs sanctions may apply at a later time.

Joint Selection of, and instructions to, Experts

26–15 One of the greatest changes that the Fast Track personal injury practitioner will notice is in the removal of partial experts and the phasing out of oral evidence. The Protocol sets out the following procedure for the instruction of an expert:

(a) Before any prospective party instructs an expert, the other party must be given a list of the name or names of one or more experts in the relevant speciality whom they consider suitable.

(b) Within 14 days, the second party may indicate an objection to one or more such experts and the first party should then instruct a mutually acceptable expert.

(c) If the second party objects to all the listed experts, the parties may then instruct experts of their own choice.

(d) If the second party does not object to an expert nominated, they shall not be entitled to reply upon their own expert evidence within that particular speciality unless:

(i) the first party agrees;

(ii) the court so directs;

(iii) the first party's expert report has been amended and the first party is not prepared to disclose the original report.

Consequences of Unreasonable Rejection of An Expert

If proceedings are subsequently issued and agreement of experts was not **26–16** possible, then it is for the court to decide if either party has acted unreasonably. If the court takes the view that either a party put forward experts which it knew or should have known would not be suitable or if the second party rejected experts which it knew or should have known would be suitable, then costs sanctions such as the disallowance on taxation of the medical report will be applied. A party should have a good objective reason in rejecting an expert if it is to avoid penalty. It is to be expected, in the Fast Track at least, that the courts will move inexorably towards the single expert.

Medical Notes

It is for the claimant's solicitor to organise access to relevant medical **26–17** records. The claimant can no longer simply send the defendant an authority for disclosure and the defendant can no longer, as of right, seek to gain primary access to the notes themselves. Defendants should be cautious of any claimant seeking to assert privilege over any medical records that do not, in reality, merit such a status. It would be good practice for the defendants to ask the claimant's representatives to set out whether they have asserted privilege over any notes that have been provided.

Permission to Rely Upon An Expert

It is clear that, unless the second party objects to a nominated expert, he **26–18** may not rely on his own expert evidence unless there is agreement or a direction to that effect.

Amendments to Reports

If the first party has caused an amendment to appear on the report, the **26–19** original must be disclosed to the second party, otherwise the second party may be entitled to rely upon another report. In such circumstances, one can easily envisage the second party being able to apply for a costs sanction against the initial instructing party for causing him to instruct a further expert.

Exploiting The Rules

There is a real tactical advantage in being efficient and proposing to **26–20** instruct the first expert. The Protocol makes it clear by using the terminology of "the first party" and "the second party" that it is not necessarily the claimant's solicitor who can be the first and therefore the original instructing party. The Protocol envisages a situation whereby a defendant writes to the claimant setting out a list of nominated doctors who are then instructed. In this way the organised defendant could take the initiative from the tardy claimant. Therefore, the party for whom the practitioner is acting for should always be the first to nominate experts, thereby shifting the burden of rejection and potential unreasonable conduct to the other side.

Clarifying The Expert's Report

26–21   The Protocol provides that if either party has written questions on the report relevant to the issues then those questions should be sent via the first party solicitor and the expert should then despatch his replies to both parties separately. Practitioners should note that in the Fast Track it will be *unusual* for experts to give oral evidence. Further, CPR 35.6 only allows a party to put written questions to the expert once, within 28 days of the receipt of the report. Therefore, practitioners *must*:

> (a) consider a medical report quickly;
>
> (b) instruct one's own expert to comment on the report so that more information can be asked for—strict time limits have to be observed;
>
> (c) note that once litigation commences the scope for questions is narrowed.

The Protocol is more generous.

The Pre-action Protocol for The Resolution of Clinical Disputes

The Structure of the Protocol

26–22   The Protocol sets out seven good practice commitments for health-care providers and encourages patients and advisers to take a number of steps to ensure that the health-care provider is aware of their complaints. The protocol is divided into the following material parts:

> (a) obtaining the health records;
>
> (b) the letter of claim;
>
> (c) the defendant's response;
>
> (d) experts;
>
> (e) alternative approaches to settling disputes.

The Aim of the Protocol

The Protocol aims to encourage a climate of openness when something 26–23 has gone wrong. It provides general guidance and recommends a timed sequence of steps for patients and potential defendants. The Clinical Disputes Forum hope that it will lead, in the area of medical negligence, to a changing attitude between the claimants and health care providers in handling litigation. These objectives reflect concern that, historically in this area of litigation, above all others, claimants feel injustice, not only for the loss that they have suffered, but in the way in which they are treated by the health-care provider after the medical accident.

The Status of the Protocol

The Protocol states immediately that it is not a comprehensive code but 26–24 sets out a code of good practice which parties should follow. However, in the light of the Lord Chancellor's Foreword to the Protocol, it is likely to take on the status of mandatory practice for those approaching clinical disputes in the Fast Track.

Obtaining the Health-Care Records. The Protocol provides that the practi- 26–25 tioner should:

(a) provide sufficient information to alert the health-care provider where an adverse outcome has been serious; and

(b) be as specific as possible about the records which are required. Requests for copies of the patient's clinical records should be made using the standard forms that have been in use by both the Law Society and the Department of Health for some time and that are enclosed at Annex B of the Protocol.

Time Limit for Compliance

Most importantly, from a practical point of view, the copy records 26–26 should be provided within 40 days of the request. If the health-care provider has difficulty in complying with the request then it should state this quickly and set out the action that it is taking. The Protocol expects non-compliance with the 40-day limit to be rare. If the records are not provided within 40 days, then an Order for pre-action disclosure can be made to the court. In keeping with the carrot-and-stick approach of the Protocols, the court will have the power to impose costs sanctions for unreasonable delay in providing records. If records are required from a third party, then it is expected that the third party health-care provider will co-operate.

26–27 *The Letter of Claim.* Where the practitioner is seized of enough information to decide that there are grounds for a claim, then they should send, as soon as practicable, a letter of claim to the health-care provider.

26–28 The Letter of Claim Guide provides for the following:

(a) Claimant's name, address and date of birth.

(b) Dates of allegedly negligent treatment.

(c) Events giving rise to the claim including:

(i) outline of what happened; and
(ii) details of other relevant treatments.

(d) Main allegations of negligence and causal link with injuries (a brief outline or, in a more detailed and complex case a detailed list).

(e) Outline of the causal link between the allegations and the injuries.

(f) Client's condition and prognosis.

(g) Request for clinical records (Law Society form if appropriate):

(i) specify records required.

(h) State what other investigations have been carried out to date.

(i) Likely value of the claim.
(i) main heads of damage or in straightforward cases the details of loss.

(j) Optional enclosures:

(i) an offer to settle without supporting evidence;
(ii) suggestions for obtaining expert evidence (follow the recommendations in the Personal Injury Protocol);
(iii) suggestions for meetings, negotiations, discussion or mediation;
(iv) chronology;
(v) clinical records, request form and client's authorisation;
(vi) experts' reports;
(vii) schedules of loss and supporting evidence.

Status of the Letter of Claim

26–29 The letter of claim is not intended to have the same formal status as a pleading and sanctions will not, necessarily apply, if the Statement of Case is different from the letter of claim.

Issuing After the Letter of Claim

26–30 The Protocol sets out that proceedings should not be issued until after three months from the letter of claim unless there is a limitation problem and/or the patient's position needs to be protected by early issue.

Offers to Settle

The Protocol refers to the full Civil Procedure Rules 1995 and the fact **26–31**
that a claimant may wish to make an early offer to settle. If an offer to
settle is made, this should generally be supported by a medical report
which deals with the injuries, condition and prognosis, and by a Schedule
of Loss and supporting documentation. The level of detail is dependent
upon each case.

The Defendant's Response. The bare defence is dead. Any defendant who **26–32**
delays actions merely by denying the claimant's case without asserting a
positive case can expect to be penalised by the courts. The court will
expect the defendant to have a case if liability is not admitted. Defence
practitioners will be under heavy pressure to investigate fully a case within
a comparatively short period and to formulate a case that should be
advanced.

The Guide to the Defendant's Response

   (a) Acknowledge letter within 14 days.   **26–33**

   (b) Provide requested records and invoice for copying by the claimant
      and:

      (i) explain if records incomplete or extensive records are held;
      (ii) ask for further instructions; and
      (iii) request additional records from third parties.

   (c) Within three months, provide a reasoned answer:

      (i) if the claim is admitted, say so in clear terms;
      (ii) if part of the claim is admitted, the health-care provider should
         make clear which—

        • issues of breach of duty and/or causation are admitted;
          and
        • which are denied and why.

   (d) If the claim is denied, this should include specific comments of the
      allegations of negligence and:

      (i) if a synopsis or chronology of relevant events has been pro-
         vided and is disputed, the health-care provider's version of
         those events should be set out;
      (ii) where additional documents are relied upon such as internal
         protocols, copies should be provided;

(iii) if the patient has made an offer to settle, the health-care provider should respond to that offer in the response letter with reasons;

(iv) the provider may make its own offer to settle at this stage.

26–34 *Experts.* The Clinical Protocol deliberately avoids any prescriptive approach to medical experts. It provides that this matter should be left to the parties and their advisers. One can see that the Lord Chancellor's Department has accepted this approach in respect of clinical negligence but, where the value of the case is less than £15,000, it is hard to see that the costs would remain proportionate to the sum claimed.

Cost Effectiveness

26–35 It is in the area of Fast Track that cases involving clinical negligence are least likely to be cost-effective. Whereas more than 75 per cent of personal injury actions supported by the Legal Aid Board succeed, only about 25 per cent of medical negligence cases result in a recovery being make. If parties are allowed to continue to instruct partial experts, then costs will continue to dwarf the amount at stake in such cases. Should a fixed-costs regime be introduced then it is impossible to see how the parties could stay within the strict cost limits and still instruct partial experts—medical negligence, in the fast track, would disappear. A result of fixed fees may be that those who are involved in low-value cases, that are expensive and where costs are less proportionate, would be denied an effective remedy. The level of recoverable costs would be so low as to preclude a case being brought. This may allow medical negligence practitioners to argue forcefully that fixed costs should not apply to such cases and, indeed, that such rules are unlawful in the light of the incorporation of Article 6 of the European Convention on Human Rights into the Human Rights Act 1998.

26–36 *Alternative Disputes Resolution.* The Clinical Disputes Protocol concludes by noting that there are alternative approaches to settling disputes in the Clinical Forum such as the NHS Complaints Procedure, Mediation and Arbitration. It does not prescribe that the parties should take any steps.

Pre-action Disclosure and Inspection

26–37 Sections 52 and 53 of the County Courts Act and sections 33 and 34 of the Supreme Courts Act will continue to be in force once the new Civil Procedure Rules come into force. As before, these rules apply in respect of personal injury and death claims (although they have also been broadened).

The Application

26–38 CPR 31.16(3) requires that an applicant must show by evidence that:

(a) the applicant and respondent are likely to be parties to subsequent proceedings; and

(b) if proceedings had started, the respondent's duty, by way of standard disclosure, would extend to the documents sought;

(c) pre-action disclosure is desirable to dispose fairly of the anticipated proceedings or to assist dispute resolution without the need for proceedings or to save costs;

(c) it is clear per CPR 31.16(3)(c) that pre-action disclosure does not go beyond what one can obtain under standard disclosure.

Inspection

CPR 25.5(2) provides that an applicant must show by evidence: 26–39

(a) if practicable, by reference to any Statement of Case prepared in relation to the proceedings or anticipated proceedings;

(b) that the property is or may become the subject matter of such proceedings;

(c) that the property is relevant to the issues that will arise in relation to such proceedings.

The Tracks

Part 27—the Small Claims Track

Claims that have a financial value of not more than £5,000 (CPR 26–40
26.6(3)), except where per CPR 26.6(1)A it is a personal injury claim where the financial value of the claim is not more than £5,000 and the value of the claim for damages for personal injury is not more than £1,000, are allocated to the Small Claims Track. Whether or not the courts will continue to apply the rule but one only needs a reasonable prospect of achieving £1,000 or more is a moot point. The wording of the rules is merely that the value of the claim is not more than £1,000. It will be important for this uncertainty to be resolved as soon as possible.

Part 28—the Fast Track

Per CPR 26.6(4) claims with a financial value of not more than £15,000 26–41
and for which the Small Claims Track is not the normal track fall into the Fast Track. CPR 26.6(5) provides that the Fast Track is not the normal track for the following:

(a) where there will be oral expert evidence at trial in more than two expert fields;

(b) that the trial is likely to last for more than one day;

(c) that there will be more than one expert called by any party in any one field.

In the Fast Track, the trial date—30 weeks after the allocation notice—is considered inviolable save in exceptional circumstances.

Part 29—the Multi-Track

26–42   CPR 26.6(6) provides that claims for which the Small Claims Track or Fast Track is not the normal track will fall to be considered here. In the Practice Direction, it is stated that the hallmarks of the Multi-Track are the ability of the court to deal with cases of widely differing values and complexity, and the flexibility given to the court in the way it will manage cases in an appropriate way to its particular needs.

Starting the Action

The Claim Form Guide

26–43   The Claim Form must contain the following:

(a) A concise statement of the nature of the claim (CPR 16.2(1)(a)).

(b) Specify the remedy which the claimant seeks (CPR 16.2(1)(b)).

(c) If the Particulars of claim are not contained in or are not served with the Claim Form, the claimant must state on the Claim Form that particulars will follow (CPR 16.2(2)).

(d) The representative capacity of the claimant and his capacity must be stated; if the defendant is sued in a representative capacity his capacity must also be stated (CPR 16.2(3) and (4)).

(e) A statement of the value of the whole action as to whether it is worth (CPR 16.3(2)(:

   (i) not more than £5,000;
   (ii) more than £5,000 but not more than £15,000; or
   (iii) more than £15,000; or
   (iv) the claimant should state that he cannot say how much he expects to recover.

(f) In personal injuries the claimant must state whether the claim is worth (CPR 16.3(3)):

  (i) not more than £1,000; or
  (ii) more than £1,000.

In the rules the term "Claim Form" means, to all intents and purposes what used to be referred to as the "Summons". Remember to ignore interest, costs, contributory deductions, counterclaims and set offs when calculating the likely value of the action.

The Practice Direction

The Practice Direction provides that, if it is practicable, the full **26–44** particulars of the claim should be set out in the Claim Form. If the claimant does not include the Particulars of Claim in the Claim Form, they may be served separately, either at the same time as the Claim Form or within 14 days after service of the Claim Form provided that the service of the Particulars of Claim is not later than four months from the date of issue of the Claim Form. Therefore, the claimant must ensure that the Particulars of Claim are served within the four-month period of validity of the Claim Form.

The Particulars of Claim

Serious concerns have been expressed that this rule would require a **26–45** Claim Form as detailed as the claimant's statement. Alternatively, others have said that to meet the costs the new Particulars will be very short imprecise documents, where the person doing the drafting is selected more for his low cost than his skills. The rules provide (CPR 16.4(1)(a)) that the Particulars of Claim must only include a concise statement of the facts on which the claimant relies. The Particulars can refer to law and documents may be attached to it. No more than a concise statement of the claim is needed. Further, as will be seen below the defendant has to answer each allegation. If a short set of Particulars is drafted, an opportunity to force the defendant's hand is missed. The defendant might only then have to assert a case in respect of a few short matters and then take a claimant by surprise at exchange of witness statements. However, with a properly settled Particulars, the defendant would be hemmed in and either have to meet the pleading head on (which it would have to verify) or be forced to admit liability earlier than otherwise.

However, in *McPhilemy v. Times Newspapers Ltd*,[6] Lord Woolf said that no more than a concise statement of the facts on which a defendant relied

---

[6] *The Times*, May 26, 1999, Woolf M.R., Judge and May L. JJ.

was required—witness statements reduced the need for extensive pleadings.

The Guide to the Particulars of Claim

26–46 As before, interest should be pleaded and the particular statute referred to. Aggravated or exemplary damages and the grounds for claiming such should also be stated. In the annex to the Practice Direction, paragraph 2 sets out that Particulars of Claim must contain following:

(a) The claimant's date of birth.

(b) Brief details of the claimant's personal injuries.

(c) A Schedule of any past and future expenses and losses claimed.

(d) Where medical evidence is relied upon, a report from a medical practitioner about the personal injuries alleged must be attached.

(e) Provisional damages per section 32A of the Supreme Court Act 1981 must be specifically pleaded and:

(i) it is stated that there is a chance that at some future time the claimant will develop some serious disease or suffer some serious deterioration in his physical or mental condition; and

(ii) specify the disease or type of deterioration.

(f) In a fatal accidents claim the following must be stated:

(i) the action is brought under the Fatal Accidents Act 1976;

(ii) the dependants on whose behalf the claim is made;

(iii) the date of birth of each dependant.

(g) Statutory/contractual claim for interest.

Statement of Truth

26–47 As with all other actions issued by Claim Form a statement of truth has to be appended to the Statement of Case. Practitioners must note that if no statement of truth is attached then the defendant can apply to strike out the Particulars of Claim and, if the Particulars of Claim are not verified within the specified period, then the Particulars shall be struck out. A lawyer may verify a Statement of Case for a client but in doing so has to explain to the client that it is as if the client had signed it and would be liable thereunder.

Defending the Action

Time Limits

26–48 The rules provide that the Defence shall be filed 14 days after service of the Particulars of Claim or, by agreement this period may be extended by 28 days. If an extension is given, the defendant must notify the court in writing. It is clear from the rules that an extension of more than 28 days may not be agreed by the parties without reference to the court (normally per CPR 3.8(3)—the parties cannot even agree an extension between themselves without recourse to the court). This is a new development and parties cannot seek to oust the court's jurisdiction. Although the new rule might, at first glance, require parties to apply for unnecessary time extensions, the rule has to be seen in the context of the parties having fulfilled the pre-action protocols, which should mean that the defendant will have no difficulties in complying with the time limits.

The Contents of the Defence

In personal injury actions, like all other actions, the rules require from **26–49** the defendant the following:

(a) Specify which of the allegations in the Particulars of Claim are denied (CPR 16.5(1)(a)).

(b) If the defendant is to advance a positive case at trial that is different from the claimant's case, it must be stated (CPR 16.5(2)(b)).

(c) Specify which allegations the defendant is unable to admit or deny, but which he wishes the claimant to prove (CPR 16.5(1)(b)).

(d) Specify which allegations are admitted (CPR 16.5(1)(c)).

(e) A defendant who does not deal specifically with an allegation but sets out the case in relation to that issue shall not be taken to have admitted that allegation (CPR 16.5(3)).

(f) In respect of damage, a defendant is not taken to admit a claim unless a specific admission is filed (CPR 16.5(4)).

(g) Subject to the exceptions, the defendant will be taken to have admitted all other allegations that he has not dealt with (CPR 16.5(5)).

It is Defences that the reforms have most affected. Those acting for defendants must plead any case that will be advanced. For instance, a simple denial of a failure to provide a safe system of work is not enough under the rules. The defendant will now have to set out the particulars of the safe system that it set up and implemented.

Disputing the Valuation

If the defendant disputes the valuation of the claim by the claimant, he **26–50** must say why he disputes it and put his own valuation on the form (CPR 16.5(6)). This will be vital when it come to the Allocation stage.

Statement of Truth

26–51   The Defence must be verified in a similar manner to the Statement of Case and failure to do so carries the same sanctions (CPR 22.5(3))

The Medical Report

26–52   (a) The defendant should state whether:

        (i) he agrees;

        (ii) disputes; or

        (iii) neither agrees nor disputes, but has no knowledge of the matters contained in the medical report.

    (b) Where the medical report is disputed the defendant should give in his Defence his reasons for disputing it.

    (c) Where the defendant has obtained his own medical report it should be attached to his Defence.

The Schedule of Special Damages

26–53   (a) Where a Schedule of Damages has been served upon the defendant, the defendant should attach a Counter-Schedule and state which of those items he:

        (i) agrees;

        (ii) disputes; or

        (iii) neither agrees nor disputes, but has no knowledge of;

        (iv) where appropriate supply alternative figures of valuation.

Reply

26–54   In the same way as under the old rules, a claimant will be taken to join issue with those matters which are put forward in a Defence. However, a claimant can, and probably should in cases where a limitation Defence is taken, serve a Reply. However, no further pleadings are allowed without the leave of the court after the service of the Reply.

Allocation

26–55   The claimant is likely to wish either to move from the Small Claims Track to the Fast Track or from the Fast Track to the Multi-Track. The defendant will be keen to resist such moves.

On the filing of a defence, the court will serve an allocation questionnaire on each party unless the court dispenses with the need (CPR 26.3(1)).

A stay of one month may be ordered by agreement, request or on the order of the court so that the parties might consider settlement (CPR 26.4)

CPR 26.8 provides a list of factors which the court must have regard to when allocating to the appropriate track. These matters include the following:

(a) The financial value, if any of the claim:

    (i) disregarding amounts not in dispute;

    (ii) disregarding any claim for interest;

    (iii) disregarding costs;

    (iv) disregarding any contributory negligence;

    (v) in a case where two or more claimants have made claims against the same defendant using the same claim form and the claims are separate from each other, considering the claim of each claimant separately.

(b) The nature of the remedy sought.

(c) The likely complexity of the facts, law or evidence.

(d) The number of parties or likely parties.

(e) The value of any counterclaim or other Part 20 claim and the complexity of any matters relating to it.

(f) The amount of oral evidence which may be required.

(g) The importance of the claim to persons who are not parties to the proceedings.

(h) The views expressed by the parties.

    (i) The circumstances of the parties.

Cases can be subsequently reallocated and further information may be requested. The court does not have to hold an allocation hearing. It is important, therefore, when trying to escape into the next highest level or when trying to push another down a level to put full reasons in the questionnaire and also note that a hearing may be appropriate if the circumstances of the case demand it. If a party disagrees with allocation, then the remedy is either by way of application if there was no hearing and by way of appeal if there was a hearing. The Practice Direction makes it clear that the parties should cooperate in the questionnaires. If both the claimant and defendant do not file a questionnaire, the usual order provided for in the Practice Direction will be that the claim is struck out.

Allocation Factors of Particular Importance in the Fast Track

Paragraph 9 of the Practice Direction sets out those matters which are **26–56** particularly important when considering allocating a case to the Fast Track:

(a) The limits placed on disclosure.

(b) The extent to which expert evidence may be necessary.

(c) Whether the trial is likely to last more than one day (five hours)—this factor is not, however, conclusive of the decision and the court will take into account its powers to control evidence and cross examination when arriving at the time limit.

Fast Track Directions

26–57   When a case is allocated to the fast track, directions are given that include (CPR 28.2):

(a) Fixing the trial date to take place within a period not exceeding three weeks.

(b) The trial date or period will be specified in the allocation notice.

(c) The standard period between directions and trial is 30 weeks.

(d) Directions for the filing and service of further information to clarify the case.

(e) Standard disclosure.

(f) Service of witness statements and expert evidence by mutual and simultaneous exchange:

    (i) directions for a single expert unless there are good reasons;
    (ii) if more than one expert and they are not agreed then direct a discussion and preparation by the experts of a joint report as per Part 35.12(3).

(g) Expert evidence.

The court will jealously guard the trial dates and the Parties cannot, without the Court's permission vary the date for the return of the listing questionnaire, the trial (or the trial period) (CPR 28.4). In *Matthews v. Tarmac Bricks & Tiles Ltd*,[7] the Court of Appeal held that it was essential that the parties cooperated in organising a trial date. The old practice of finding a date to fit the convenience of the doctors was not acceptable. An expert had to be prepared to accommodate the court as far as practicable and, if a date was not practicable, reasons had to be given to the court.

The Practice Direction refers to the expectation of the court that the parties will cooperate. Hearings will, if possible, be avoided.

---

[7] *The Times*, July 1, 1999, Woolf M.R., Clarke and Mance L.JJ.

The Parties are encouraged to file agreed directions. To obtain the approval of the court they have to contain:

- the matters referred to above;
- a timetable by reference to calendar dates;
- a period or date for the trial not later than 30 weeks later than the date for directions;
- provision for disclosure which can limit disclosure to less than standard disclosure or disclose without list;
- provision for factual and expert evidence. In regard to Expert evidence the directions should set out the names of the experts and whether there is permission for oral evidence (this permission for oral evidence is only given where it is necessary in the interests of justice to do so);
- a trial timetable and estimate;
- the preparation of the bundle.

Any directions may contain timetables for amendments, Part 18 requests, Part 35.6 requests and the use of single experts. The Practice Direction has a useful Appendix that can be used as a template for directions.

The Listing Questionnaire

When the parties are sent a Notice of Allocation then, unless the court 26–58 considers that the case can be listed for trial without the need for a "listing questionnaire" one will be sent out. A hearing may be necessary if a questionnaire is not completed fully and returned in time. If a hearing is brought about by the default of a party, they can expect to pay the costs of that hearing. If no listing questionnaire is filed, the normal order will strike out the claim and any counterclaim. Once the questionnaires are filed, then the court fixes or confirms the date for trial (three weeks' notice will be given unless the circumstances are exceptional) and give any directions that are necessary such as a trial timetable.

A Typical Timetable

The Practice Direction sets out a typical case and parties would be well 26–59 advised to follow those limits if it is proposed to submit agreed Directions. The time is from the date of the allocation notice:

(a) Disclosure	4 weeks
(b) Exchange of witness statements	10 weeks
(c) Exchange of Experts' Reports	14 weeks
(d) Sending out of listing questionnaire	20 weeks

    (e) Filing of listing questionnaire   22 weeks

    (f) Trial   30 weeks

If directions are given that cannot be complied with or should not be, then application to the court must be made within 14 days of service of the Directions Notice. A court can be asked to reconsider directions or the route of appeal can also be followed.

Time is of the essence and the Court of Appeal has held in *Jones & Jones v. Wrekin District Council*[8] that the Court's approach to non-compliance with times limits would be much more vigorous under the CPR. The enforcement of time limits is tempered by *Cowland & Kendrick v. District Judge of the West London County Court*[9] where a solicitor breached the rules in relation to the production of a witness statement where the Court allowed an appeal so that the statement could be relied upon. Time limits were not targets, but the overriding principle was that justice had to be done and justice did not require the exclusion of this evidence which was uncontested.

Standard Disclosure

26–60   CPR 31.6 provides that standard disclosure requires a party to disclose only:

    (a) documents upon which he relies;

    (b) documents which:

        (i) adversely affect his own case;
        (ii) adversely affect another party's case;
        (iii) support another party's case;

    (c) documents required by a relevant Practice Direction to be disclosed;

    (d) a party's duty of disclosure extends only to documents which are or have been in his control.

This is the normal requirement for disclosure under the Fast Track.

The Duty of Search

26–61   CPR 31.7(1) provides that a party giving standard disclosure is under a duty to make a reasonable search for documents which must be disclosed. Factors relevant to whether or not a search is reasonable include per CPR 31.7(2) the following:

---

[8] July 9, 1999, Woolf M.R. and Walker L.J.
[9] July 20, 1999, Woolf M.R., Brooke and Walker L.JJ.

- the number of documents involved;
- the nature and complexity of the proceedings;
- the ease and expense of retrieval of any particular document;
- the significance of any document which is likely to be located during a search;
- if a party has not carried out a search for a category or class of document on the ground that to do so would be unreasonable that must be stated in the disclosure statement and must identify the class or category of document (CPR 31.7(3)).

The Disclosure Statement

Per CPR 31.7, paragraph 6. This is a statement which: 26–62

(a) sets out the extent of the search which was carried out to locate documents required to be disclosed;

(b) certifies that the party understands the duty to disclose documents;

(c) certifies to the best of the party's knowledge he has carried out that duty;

(d) where a party making a disclosure statement is a company or some such other body, the statement must identify the person making the statement and explain why that person is considered to be an appropriate person to make that statement (CPR 31.7(7));

(e) the parties may agree in writing to give disclosure without making a disclosure statement (CPR 31.7(8)(b));

(f) the duty of disclosure is a continuing one.

Miscellaneous Disclosure Points

(a) CPR 31.12 gives the court power to order disclosure, a search for 26–63 and the inspection of documents.

(b) Inspection does not have to be given by a party disclosing a document, if it considers that it would be disproportionate to the issues in the case to permit the inspection.

(c) Documents mentioned in a Statement of Case, witness statement, witness summary or affidavit are, per CPR 31.14, documents that may always be inspected whether or not disclosed in a list.

(d) Documents referred to in expert's report are always liable to inspection, save that CPR 35.10(4) provides that a court will not order disclosure of any specific document in relation to an expert's instructions unless there are reasonable grounds to consider that the statement of instructions included in the expert's report is inaccurate or incomplete.

(e) CPR 31.15 provides for notice to be given before inspection.

(f) If a party asserts a right to withhold inspection of a document, it must make a statement as to the fact that it is asserting the right to withhold inspection and the grounds on which the claim is made.

(g) CPR 31.20 provides that, where a document has been inadvertently disclosed and inspected, the document can only be used by the inspecting party with the court's permission.

(h) If a party fails to disclose a document or fails to permit inspection of it, then that party may not rely on that document without the court's permission (CPR 31.21).

(i) A court may make an Order particularly restricting the use of a document outside of the proceedings in which it is disclosed.

(j) Documents properly disclosed may not be used for other purposes unless it was referred to or read out in a public hearing, or the court gives its permission, or there is an agreement between the parties.

Taking the Initiative

26–64   It is clear that the Fast Track procedure will favour the organised litigator who has set up and implemented efficient systems to deal with litigation. The requirements of the Personal Injury Protocol and, certainly the Road Traffic Accident Protocol, will probably put the parties and, certainly should put the claimant, in a position in which to litigate speedily once proceedings have been issued. The party who has its evidence ready and has speedily prepared to deal with the issues that will arise in the course of proceedings will be put in a strong position by forcing the pace of the other party. Judges are likely to be much less sympathetic to parties who fail to meet deadlines. This will be particularly true where one party is in a position to meet the deadlines. Defendants and claimants would do well to prepare their witness statements before issue of proceedings in a standard Fast Track action. If the other party is not prepared, their statements or their case is likely to suffer, especially where the other party is forcing the pace.

Interlocutory Applications

26–65   The organised party in litigation can use interlocutory applications not only to force the less organised party to comply with the directions timeously, but also use them to gain a consistent costs advantage over the opposite party. This is not to suggest that applications should be used frivolously or on minor points. The court will not be impressed if a part fails to cooperate with an opponent and merely applies to the court at every opportunity. The emphasis of the Fast Track is that the trial date must not be moved. The parties should cooperate to ensure that this does not happen. Courts will encourage parties to use the sanction of the court by way of costs or by excluding evidence to encourage a defendant or claimant to comply with directions. A further advantage in having set out a detailed Claim Form and Particulars of Claim is that the Statement of Case can be used as a source of evidence at the trial itself.

A note of caution should be sounded. The practitioner will have to ensure that an application is reasonable. Correspondence attempting an attempted cooperative approach should be exhibited in any application. The Court of Appeal has already expressed dissatisfaction at unnecessary satellite litigation and a party will be penalised for it.

The Procedure for Making an Application

Unless an Order, rule or Practice Direction permits otherwise, CPR 23.3 **26–66** provides that a party must file an Application Notice at Court. Where the Notice has to be served, it must be served as soon as practicable after filing and, in any event, at least three days before the court is to deal with the application. Under CPR 23.7(4), where the applicant has failed to serve the Notice at least three days before the court, the court can deem that sufficient notice has been given for the circumstances of the case warranted.

Requirements of the Application Notice

The Notice must state what Order is sought and why it is sought. In **26–67** addition, the Notice can be verified by a Statement of Truth, if the applicant wishes to rely on the matters set out in the Notice as evidence (CPR 23.6). This can be a useful device to prevent having to swear a separate affidavit.

Default Judgment

It is important to remember that in a case where the claimant served the **26–68** Claim Form, the claimant has to file the Certificate of Service per CPR 6.14, or default judgment will not be entered. CPR 12.4–12.10 provide for restrictions on which procedural route to follow when entering judgment. For instance per CPR 12.10(a)(iii), default judgment cannot be entered in a claim against the Crown unless an application is made in order to obtain default judgment.

However, CPR 12.4(1)(b) still provides that one can enter default judgment by filing a form where a claim is for an amount of money to be decided by the court. Further, CPR12.8(1) provides that filing a request for default judgment against one defendant does not prevent the claimant from continuing against the others.

Setting Aside Default Judgment

26–69   As under the current rules where an irregular judgment must be set aside, the new rules provide that the court must set aside default judgment if a judgment was wrongly entered because any of the requirements for default judgment was not met. If the judgment is, in current terminology regular, then the court has a discretion to set aside or vary a judgment in default if the defendant has a real prospect of defending the claim, or if it appears to the court either that there is some good reason why the judgment should be set aside or varied or that the defendant should be allowed to defend the claim per CPR 13.3. Please note—and this will be useful for personal injury actions—a matter to which the court must have regard is whether the person seeking to set aside or vary the judgment made an application promptly per CPR 13.3(2).

Summary Judgment

26–70   Under CPR 24.2, a court can give judgment against a claimant or a defendant on *any issue* in the case or in respect of the whole claim without a trial, if it considers that the defendant has no real prospect of successfully defending the claim or issue, or if the claimant has no real prospect of succeeding on the claim or the issue in question. Judgment can be obtained by *either* side. Judgment may be given provided that there is no other reason why the case should go to trial. One should note per CPR 24.4(1) that the claimant cannot apply for summary judgment until the defendant in question has filed either an Acknowledgement of Service or a Defence, unless the court grants permission. Practitioners should be ready to use the wider scope of Part 24 to obtain judgments as to particular facts so that the issues can be narrowed or a tactical advantage gained.

Summary Judgment Procedure

26–71   The normal rule for services of Notices of Applications is varied in respect of summary judgments as follows:

(a) The Respondent must be given a period of at least 14 days' notice of the date fixed for the hearing.

(b) The Respondent must be given at least 14 days' notice of the issues which it is proposed that the court will decide.

(c) Evidence in support of the application must be filed at the same time and served at the same time as the Application Notice (CPR 23.7(2) and (3)).

(d) Any written evidence on behalf of the respondent to resist the application must be filed and served at least seven days before the hearing (CPR 24.5(1)).

(e) If the party applying for summary judgment wishes to rely on any written evidence in reply, it must be filed at least three days before the hearing (CPR 24.5(2)).

(f) One must remember that the court may give judgment on the whole of the claim or on any issue of the claim per CPR 24.2 and may give directions for the filing and service of a Defence and any other case management directions (CPR 24.6).

(g) As is the case under the present rules, the court may impose conditions when it makes any Order (CPR 3.1(3)).

Summary judgment is easier than it used to be. The rules provide both the claimant and the defendant with a powerful new tool to narrow the issues before trial and or force earlier settlements. Practitioners acting for either party should always examine their opponents Statements of Case to establish whether their client would be assisted by the disposal of some issues at an interlocutory stage.

Interim Payments

Per CPR 25.6(7), the Court may make an Order for an interim payment **26–72** only if:

(a) the defendant has admitted liability to pay a sum of money to the claimant (CPR 25.7(1)(a)); or

(b) the claimant has obtained judgment against a relevant defendant for damages or another sum of money apart from costs, to be assessed (CPR 25.7(1)(b); or

(c) the court is satisfied that, if the claim went to trial, the claimant would obtain judgment for a substantial amount of money, apart from costs, against the defendant from whom the interim payment is sought (CPR 25.7(1)(c)).

An application for an interim payment in personal injury work should contain the following:

- the amount of damages or sum of money which the application relates to;
- the reasons for the application;
- details of special damages and past and future loss of earnings;
- in a claim under the Fatal Accidents Act 1976, details of the persons on whose behalf the claim is made and the nature of the claim;

- documents in support of the application should be exhibited including, in personal injury claims, the medical reports.

Personal Injury Restrictions on Interim Payments

26–73   An interim payment order will only be made if:

(a) the defendant is insured in respect of the claim;

(b) the defendant is:

(i) the Road Traffic Insurer 1988;
(ii) an insurer acting under the Motor Insurers Bureau Agreement;
(iii) the defendant is a public body.

Deduction of Benefits

26–74   Where there is an application for an interim payment that does not go by consent and the application is one which includes damages which stand to be recouped by the Compensation Recovery Unit and which the defendant is liable to pay recoverable benefits upon, then the defendant should obtain a certificate of recoverable benefits and the Order should be reduced in accordance with that certificate.

Experts

26–75   Practitioners must remember that:

(a) experts' evidence to be restricted to what is reasonably necessary (CPR 35.1);

(b) no party can call an expert or rely on his evidence without the court's permission (CPR 35.4(1);

(c) where permission to rely upon an expert is sought he must identify:

(i) the expert's field; and
(ii) where practicable, the expert himself.

Practitioners must now be more aware of the specialists whom they instruct. If a psychologist is instructed where a client is suffering from a clinical depression and a psychiatrist should have been instructed, then it is very unlikely that one would be able to obtain the costs of both reports back on assessment of costs.

Oral Evidence

26–76   The normal position in the Fast Track is that experts will not give oral evidence. Therefore, it is of the first importance that practitioners use their opportunities, first under the Protocol to question and, secondly under Part

35.6. If an expert does not answer a proper question, the party relying upon the expert may be prevented from doing so or unable to recover the costs associated with the expert. Unless the other party agrees or the court allows, written questions may only be put once and within 28 days of service of the report.

The Experts' Meeting

Part 35.12 sets out the system for the experts' meeting. The Code of 26–77 Guidance, when completed, will also contain detailed provisions for agenda and times. The experts should identify the issues and, where possible, reach agreement. In the Fast Track, a statement should be prepared as to those issues on which they agree and as to those they do not and the reasons they do not agree.

In *Baron v. Lovell*,[10] the Court of Appeal held that a defendant, who had not kept to the trial timetable should not be allowed to rely upon his own medical expert. The experts were, in any event, close to each other and the defendant's breach of directions put him at the mercy of the court. The same Court, in the same sitting, refused to intervene with a Judge's order debarring the defendant from calling a crucial witness where that witness had failed to comply with the requirements of 35.12 (*Stevens v. Gullis*). The judgment is a warning to parties that they must ensure that their experts comply with directions. Further, in *Rollinson v. Kimberly Clark Ltd*,[11] Peter Gibson L.J. held that it was inappropriate to instruct an expert without regard to his availability where the trial was so near. If availability was a problem an alternative expert should be used.

Provisional Damages

If the defendant agrees to the payment of provisional damages, then the 26–78 payment notice must state the following per CPR 36.7(3):

(a) That the sum paid into court is in satisfaction of the claim for damages on the assumption that the further condition/deterioration will not take place.

(b) That the offer is subject to the condition that the claimant must make any claim for further damages within a limited period and that period is specified.

Costs: Reasonableness and Proportionality

Per CPR 44.5(3), the Court must have regard to: 26–79

---

[10] July 27, 1999, Woolf M.R., Brooke and Walker L.JJ.
[11] *The Times*, June 22, 1999.

(a) the conduct of all the parties including, in particular:

    (i) conduct before, as well as during, the proceedings; and

    (ii) the efforts made, if any, before and during the proceedings in order to try to resolve the dispute;

(b) the amount and value of any money or property involved;

(c) the importance of the matter to all the parties;

(d) the particular complexity of the matter or the difficulty or novelty of the questions raised;

(e) the skill, effort, specialised knowledge and responsibility involved;

(f) the time spent on the case;

(g) the place where and the circumstances in which work or any part of it was done.

Fast Track Costs

26–80   Practitioners first expected the Lord Chancellor's Department to introduce fixed costs for all Fast Track cases in April 1999. CPR 46.2(1) provides for a fee of £350 for cases up to £3,000, £500 up to £10,000 and £750 up to £15,000. In awarding costs to a claimant, the sum excludes contributory negligence deductions, interest and costs (CPR 46.3(3)(a)) and when awarding costs to a defendant, the figure is that specified in the claim for or, if not specified, then the maximum amount that the claimant could reasonably expect to recover (CPR 46.3(3)(b)). An additional £250 can be paid to a party's legal representative if it was necessary for him to attend to assist the advocate.

The standard practice is either for a summary assessment of costs or, if matters are delayed to a detailed assessment, then the court should, on a rough-and-ready basis, order an amount (less than the full amount) to be paid to the successful party on account (*Mars UK Ltd v. Teknowledge Ltd (No. 2)*).[12]

Ominously, pre-trial costs in Fast Track cases will be monitored in order to provide the data to inform the development of a fixed-costs regime. The personal injury practitioner must prepare systems and reduce costs to survive in this regime where, it might appear, further fixed fees will be introduced.

Appeal

26–81   An appeal lies to the circuit judge on a trial before a district judge unless the party consented to the order. The Notice of Appeal must be served within 14 days after the judgment or order was given or made. The judge's

---

[12] *The Times*, July 8, 1999, Jacob J.

power is limited to the exercise of his discretion—the original judgment has to be one in which no reasonable district judge could have exercised the court's discretion in the way it was done.

An appeal lies from the circuit judge as the trial judge to the Court of Appeal in the normal way. Permission is required.

Procedural Appeals

In terms of procedure, Woolf M.R. stated in *Baron v. Lovell*[13] that the **26–82** Court of Appeal would only interfere with a judge's discretion if he was plainly wrong. The Court of Appeal has also given a guide to appeals from cases that were decided under the old rules in *McPhilemy v. Times Newspapers Ltd.*[14] The Court will not interfere if it would not have done so under the old rules. However, if the Court does interfere with the appealed decision, then the CPR would be taken into account in relation to any future orders.

The Changing Rules

Amendments have been made to the rules on March 1, April 1, April 19, **26–83** May 26 and June 28, 1999. Unless the practitioner has a loose leaf copy of the rules with an updating service or visits the Lord Chancellor's website (*www.open.gov.uk/lcd/*), any copy of the rules is likely to be out of date. This can be very serious. For instance, the effect of the word "defendant" inserted into Part 36.20(1) as occurred on April 19, 1999 removed the risk that a claimant would be very likely to be penalised in costs should he fail to beat his own Part 36 offer. The new rule significantly reduces this risk. The rules as stated are correct as of July 12, 1999 and the authorities are correct as at July 27, 1999.

---

[13] *op. cit.* n. 10.
[14] *op. cit.* n. 6.

27. Striking Out

The High Court and The County Court

As with so many areas of civil proceedure, the Civil Procedure Rules 27–01
1998 (CPR) have effected wholesale changes. The rules are "a new and
self-contained entity",[1] which apply to county courts, the High Court and
the Civil Division of the Court of Appeal.[2] The starting point is the
overriding objective under CPR r. 1.1 and r. 1.4 which imposes a duty on
the court to manage cases. This duty is expressed in mandatory terms:
"(1) The Court *must* further the overriding objective by actively managing
cases". The list of matters which fall within this duty then follows at (PR.
r. 1.4(2) and includes: "(g) fixing timetables or otherwise controlling the
progress of the case", and "(1) giving directions to ensure that the trial of a
case proceeds quickly and efficiently".

Hence, one principal aim of the CPR is to seek to prevent any case from
going to sleep. If case management works as intended, then cases will be
actively promoted towards settlement or trial by the court. In that event, it
may be thought that applications to strike out of the sort initiated by a
party that formed much of the core material in this area previously will be
increasingly rare. It is, however, important to note that the inherent
powers of the court to strike out are preserved under by CPR r. 3.4(5),
which will be discussed further below.

Fundamental Principles

In place of the principles as set out by the House of Lords in *Birkett v.* 27–02
James,[3] the overriding objective provides the test by which the court must
interpret any rule[4]. No apologies, therefore, for setting out the overriding
objective here:

"CPR r. 1.1
(1) These rules are a new proceedural code with the overriding objective of
enabling the court to deal with cases justly.
(2) Dealing with a case justly includes, as far as is practicable,

   (a) ensuring that the parties are on an equal footing;

---

[1] See CPR r. 1.
[2] See CPR r. 2.1(1).
[3] [1978] A.C. 297; [1977] 3 W.L.R 38.
[4] CPR r. 1.2(b).

(b) saving expense;
(c) dealing with the case in ways which are proportionate—

    (i) to the amount of money involved;
    (ii) to the importance of the case;
    (iii) to the complexity of the issues; and
    (iv) to the financial position of each party;

(d) ensuring that it is dealt with expeditiously and fairly; and
(e) alloting to it an appropriate share of the court's resources, while taking into account the need to allot resources to other cases".

The points set out here are no more than issues to be considered in the context of dealing with a case "justly". Nowhere is the court specifically referred to the proposition that dealing with a case "justly" ought involve, in any circumstances other than the most exceptional, securing a hearing at which there is a disposal of the issues between the parties *on the merits*. However, this most basic principle is surely going to be the main consideration in applications to strike out.

Case Management Powers

27–03   It is probably reasonable to assume that the introduction of a duty on the court to manage cases actively carries with it an intention that the court will be less willing to excuse the conduct of those whose actions threaten to defeat the fulfilment of that duty and the overriding objective. It is this consideration, as much as any particular change in the substance of the rules as they relate to striking out, which is likely to have the most substantial effect in practice.

Practice Direction

27–04   The rules are supplemented by the Practice Direction—Striking Out A Statement Of Case at CPR Part 1, Practice Direction, para 3.4.

Glossary

27–05   Note that the meaning of "strike out" is the subject of guidance in the glossary to the rules which states that "Striking out means the court ordering written material to be deleted so that it may no longer be relied upon".

Specific Powers

27–06   ● CPR r. 3.1(3)(b). The court has a general power to specify the consequence of failure to comply with an order or condition in an order, which could include a provision for the action to be struck out in the event of non compliance. Note that under CPR r. 3.3 the court may exercise this and its other powers (unless constrained by some other rule or enactment) of its own initiative or upon application by a party; there are safeguards built in by virtue of CPR r. 3.3(5) and under the Practice Direction. Plainly, the burning question in this context is whether, in practice, the response of the court to the plea for mercy of a non-compliant litigant or legal representative will or will not be significantly different from the response that might have been anticipated prior to Woolf. Preliminary soundings, unsurprisingly, suggest that the exercise of discretion, wherever that is appropriate, and notwithstanding the touchstone of the overriding objective, is likely to be less predictable than formerly for some time to come.

- CPR r. 3.4. Power to strike out a statement of case. The court may strike out a Statement of Case or part thereof in the circumstances set out under CPR r. 3.4(2), the grounds being:

  (a) that the Statement of Case discloses no reasonable grounds for bringing or defending the claim;
  (b) that the Statement of Case is an abuse of the court's process or is otherwise likely to obstruct the just disposal of the proceedings; or
  (c) that there has been a failure to comply with a rule, Practice Direction or court order.

Whilst, these grounds seem in many ways to restate the traditional and familiar position as set out in RSC, Ord. 18, r. 19(1), it is right to treat the interpretation of them as a wholly new matter, not least because the resolution of whether or not a particular case comes within the relevant ground is an issue which must be decided by reference to the overriding objective and the practice direction.

The notes at CPR r. 3.4/3 state that the test at (a) above **27–07** "addresses two situations—

  1. Where the content of a statement of case is defective in that, even if every factual allegation contained in it were proved, the party whose statement of case it is cannot succeed; or
  2. Where the statement of case, no matter how complete and apparently correct it may be, will fail as a matter of law."

The Practice Direction at 1.4 gives examples of cases where the court may conclude that a statement of case falls within rule 3.4(2)(a).

However, the contents of paragraph 1.7 of the Practice Direction suggest that an application to strike out upon this ground might be made where "a party may believe he can show without a trial that an opponent's case has no real prospect of success on the facts, . . .". Since the terms of the rule at 3.4(2)(a) require an analysis of the Statement of Case, it is submitted that the notes and not paragraph 1.7 of the Practice Direction more accurately reflect the true position. It may be that there is some confusion here between the rules as they relate to striking out and those concerned with applications for summary judgment which can now be made on the merits—see CPR r.24.2.

The Practice Direction at 1.6 gives examples where a defence may be struck out, *e.g.* bare denial or allegations not giving rise to a claim in law.

Concerning rule 3.4(2)(b), the notes refer to previously decided cases which may assist in deciding whether any given situation may come within this rule. So it is suggested that where issue estoppel, unnecessary duplication of proceedings, or a collateral attack on an earlier decision of a competent court, is the challenge which a litigant wishes to raise, then an application to strike out may well be appropriate. Again the Practice Direction at 1.5 states that a claim may fall within rule 3.4(2)(b) where "it is vexatious, scurrilous or obviously ill-founded".

Lastly in this area, the court is invested with a specific power to strike out where there has been a failure to comply with a rule, practice direction or court order. Again, this power must be exercised in line with the overriding objective.

- CPR r. 3.4(5), paragraph (2) does not limit any other power of the court to strike out a Statement of Case. Hence the inherent powers of the court, insofar as they are not now incorporated specifically, are preserved. In reality, it is probably only in exceptional circumstances that it will be necessary to have recourse to this residual power.

The Discretion

27–08   As for the exercise of the discretionary power provided for by the use of the word "may" in the first sentence of CPR r. 3.4(2), again the overriding objective and the practice direction must be the points of reference.

Entering Judgment After Striking Out

27–09   Under CPR r. 3.5, a party may obtain judgment where there has been failure to comply with an order and the sanction expressed in the order is that the Statement of Case shall be struck out. CPR r. 3.5(2) sets out the circumstances in which this can be done.

Setting Aside

Under CPR r. 3.6, within 14 days of judgment being served upon him a 27–10
party against whom judgment has been entered under rule 3.5 may apply
to set the judgment aside. Judgment must be set aside if, at the time when
judgment was entered, the right to enter judgment had not arisen.
Otherwise, rule 3.9 (relief from sanctions) will apply.

Relief from Sanctions

Relief from any sanction imposed by a rule, Practice Direction or court 27–11
order will fall to be adjudicated by reference to the provisions of CPR
r. 3.9 and, of course, the overriding objective. The court is required to
consider all the circumstances including:

(a) the interests of the administration of justice;

(b) whether the application for relief has been made promptly;

(c) whether the failure to comply was intentional;

(d) whether there is a good explanation for the failure;

(e) the extent to which the party in default has complied with other
rules, practice directions court orders and any relevant pre-action
protocol;

(f) whether the failure to comply was caused by the party or his legal
representative;

(g) whether the trial date or the likely trial day can still be met if relief
is granted;

(h) the effect which the granting of relief would have on each party.

Any application must be supported by evidence (r. 3.9(2)).

Transitional Cases

In a transitional case, the old principles applying to striking out should 27–12
be applied subject to special recognition of the new rules in so far as they
affect the outcome.[5]

Starting a Second Claim

CPR r. 3.4(4) provides that the court may, upon application by the 27–13
defendant, stay a subsequent claim arising from substantially the same facts
as those in respect of which a statement of case has already been struck
out, and an order for costs remains unpaid.

---

[5] *Goodfellow v. Woolwich Building Society* N.L.D., April 28, 1999, full judgment awaited.

Automatic Striking Out

27–14   Under 1/PD/51, Practice Direction—Transitional Arrangements, paragraph 6(3) provides that where automatic directions have begun to apply before April 26, 1999 the provisions for automatic strike out under the old CCR Ord. 17, rule 11(9) will *not* apply. This means that the critical date for consideration of whether a county court case has been, or may have been, automatically struck out is, normally, to determine whether or not the 15-month timetable had started to run by January 26, 1998. It follows that the extensive case law that that built up concerning the automatic striking out provisions[6] will be relevant if cases still exist which have been or may have been automatically struck out prior to April 26, 1999, at least insofar as it is necessary to determine any issue of law or interpretation relating to the old rules, *e.g.* whether or not a particular case has or has not been automatically struck out. However, if there is no issue but that the case has been automatically struck out, then the application to reinstate it will fall to be considered by reference to the overriding objective (see Part 1, Practice Direction 51, para. 12). Some of the principles which were elucidated in cases such as *Rastin v. British Steel*[7] and *Williams v. Globe Coaches (a firm)*[8] are, however, reflected to a degree in the content of the CPR, and in that way the court may consider it helpful, to a degree, when dealing with an application to reinstate such a case to have some regard for the case law so recently developed on the topic.

Automatic Stay

27–15   Whilst not strictly a matter of "striking out", the concluding words of Practice Direction 51, para. 6(3), which refer the reader to paragraph 19, should not be ignored. Paragraph 19(1) provides that, subject to the exceptions set out under 19(3): "If any existing proceedings have not come before a judge, at a hearing or on paper, between the 26 April 1999 and 25 April 2000, those proceedings shall be stayed". Whilst sub-paragraph (2) makes provision for a party to apply for a stay so imposed to be lifted, it might be thought that the pospects of such an application in the world as governed by the CPR must be bleak.

---

[6] See *Bannister v. SGB plc* [1997] P.I.Q.R. P165 and associated case law.
[7] [1994] 1 W.L.R. 734.
[8] [1996] 1 W.L.R. 553.

28. Proceedings By and On Behalf of Children

Matters have been considerably simplified by the new Civil Procedure **28–01** Rules (CPR) and the Practice Directions attached thereto. The subject is largely dealt with in Part 21 of the CPR and its attendant Practice Direction.

A child means a person under 18.[1] Save where the court makes an order pursuant to rule 21.2(3), the child must have a Litigation Friend to conduct proceedings on his behalf.[2] The Litigation Friend, therefore, replaces the old Next Friend, as formerly provided for by RSC, Order 80 and CCR, Order 10 (who acted when the child was plaintiff/claimant) and the Guardian Ad Litem (where the child was a defendant).

No Litigation Friend

Rule 21.2(3) is new. It permits the court to allow a child to conduct **28–02** proceedings without a Litigation Friend. By rule 21.2(4):

"(4) An application for an order under paragraph (3)—
   (a) may be made by the child,
   (b) if the child already has a litigation friend must be made on notice to the litigation friend, and
   (c) if the child has no litigation friend may be made without notice."

However, even where the court has made an order permitting the child to conduct proceedings without a Litigation Friend "where it subsequently appears to the court that it is desirable for a Litigation Friend to conduct the proceedings on behalf of the child, the court may appoint a person to be the child's litigation friend".[3]

Paragraph 1.5 of the Practice Direction annexed to rule 21 provides that: "Where . . . (2) the child is conducting proceedings on his own behalf, the child should be referred to in the title as 'AB (a child)'."

Proceedings Against Children

Unless the court has made an order permitting the child to act on his **28–03** own behalf, then the provisions of rule 21:3 apply.

---

[1] CPR rule 21.1(2)(a).
[2] CPR rule 21.1(2).
[3] CPR rule 21.2(5).

Rule 21.3(2) provides as follows:

"(2) A person may not without the permission of the court:

(a) make an application against a child or before proceedings have started, or

(b) take any step in proceedings except—

(i) issuing and serving a claim for, or

(ii) applying for the appointment of a Litigation Friend under rule 21.6

. . .

(iv) any step taken before a child has a Litigation Friend shall be of no effect unless the court otherwise orders."

Discussion

28–04
- Rule 21.3 clearly applies to a Part 20 Claim against a child, including a claim by a defendant against any child for contribution or indemnity.
- Bearing in mind that this rule does permit the issuing and serving of a claim form, I am not quite sure how it fits in with Part 6.6(1) of the CPR. That sets out in table form the person on whom a document must be served if it is a document which would otherwise be served on a child. Under the heading "Type of Document", there is a reference to a Claim Form and the person to be served is specified as "one of the child's parents or guardians or if there is no parent or guardian, the person with whom the child resides or in whose care the child is". Presumably, if the would-be claimant has no idea who the child's parent or guardian is or with whom the child resides or in whose care the child is, it would be permissible to serve on the child himself. This might have some practical importance where, for example, a limitation period was about to run out.
- Rule 12.1 of the CPR provides that:

  "In these rules, default judgment means judgment without trial where a defendant (a) has failed to file an acknowledgment of service or (b) has failed to file a defence."

Where those conditions obtain, a claimant can normally enter a default judgment. However, this normal default procedure does not apply in respect of children. Where the claim is a claim against a child, "the claimant must make an application in accordance with Part 23".[4] An application for a default judgment against a child must be supported by evidence.[5] Paragraph 4.2 of the Part 12 Practice Direction provides that:

---

[4] CPR rule 12.10.

[5] CPR rule 12.10(3).

"On an application against a child . . .

(1) a litigation friend to act on behalf of the child . . . must be appointed by the court before judgment can be obtained, and
(2) the claimant must satisfy the court by evidence that he is entitled to the judgment claimed."

- Part 14 of the CPR deals with admissions. Rule 14.1(1) provides that:

"A party may admit the truth of the whole or any part of another party's case."

Further, by rule 14.1(4):

"Where the defendant makes an admission as mentioned in paragraph (3) the claimant has a right to enter judgment except where (a) the defendant is a child . . ."

This is then followed by a specific reference to rule 21.10, namely that:

"Where a claim is made by or on behalf of a child . . . or against a child . . . no settlement compromise or payment shall be valid so far as it relates to that person's claim, without the approval of the court."

Appointment of Litigation Friend without Court Order

This paragraph is concerned with the appointment of a Litigation Friend 28–05 without court order. If nobody has been appointed by the court then, rule 21.4(3) provides that a person may act as a litigation friend if he:

"(a) can fairly and competently conduct proceedings on behalf of the child; and
(b) has no interest adverse to that of the child; and
(c) (where the child is a claimant) undertakes to pay any costs which the child may be ordered to pay in relation to the proceedings, subject to any right he may have to be repaid from the assets of the child."

A person wishing to act as Litigation Friend must follow the procedure set out out in rule 21.5(1), namely that he must file a certificate of suitability stating that he satisfies the conditions specified in 21.4(3). If he is acting for a claimant, he must file the certificate of suitability at the time when the claim is made. If he is acting for a child defendant, he must file the certificate of suitability at the time when he first takes a step in the proceedings on behalf of that defendant child. In addition, he must serve the certificate of suitability on every person on whom, in accordance with rule 6.6, the Claim Form should be served. If he is acting for a child defendant, then pursuant to rule 6.1(4), when he files the certificate of service on behalf of the defendant he should likewise file the certificate of suitability (form N235). Further information in respect of the procedural aspects in and about becoming a Litigation Friend is set out in the Practice Direction. Paragraph 2, 3 of the Practice Direction provides that the person who wishes to act as Litigation Friend must file a certificate of suitability:

(a) stating that he consents to act;

(b) stating that he knows or believes that the claimant or defendant is a child;

(d) stating that he can fairly and competently conduct proceedings on behalf of the child and has no interest adverse to that of the child;

(e) where the child is a claimant, undertaking to pay any costs which the child may be ordered to pay in the proceedings subject to any right he may have to be repaid from the assets of the child; and

(f) which he has signed in verification of its contents.

By paragraph 2.4, the Litigation Friend must serve a certificate of suitability:

"(1) in the case of a child on one of the child's parents or guardians or if there is no parent or guardian on the person with whom the child resides or in whose care the child is."

And by paragraph 2.5:

"The litigation friend must file . . . the certificate of suitability together with a certificate of service of it—
(1) where the litigation friend is acting on behalf of a claimant, when the claim form is issued, and
(2) where the litigation friend is acting on behalf of a defendant, when he first takes a step in the action."

Appointment of Litigation Friend by Court Order

28–06   Rule 21.6 sets out the procedure by which a person may become a litigation friend by virtue of a court order. By 21.6(2): "An application for an order appointing a Litigation Friend may be made by (a) a person who wishes to be the litigation friend or (b) a party". Obviously, a person wishing to sue a child or who wishes to pursue a Part 20 Claim against a child will want a Litigation Friend appointed.
By 21.6(3):

"Where (a) a person makes a claim against a child; (b) the child has no Litigation Friend; (c) the court has not made an order that a child can act without a Litigation Friend, and (d) either (i) someone who is not entitled to be a Litigation Friend files a defence or (ii) the claimant wishes to take some step in the proceedings, the claimant must apply to the court for an order appointing a Litigation Friend."

The court has to be satisfied that the Litigation Friend satisfies the criteria set out in 21.4(3) (*supra*). The application for an order appointing a Litigation Friend must be supported by evidence. Paragraph 3.3 of the Practice Direction provides that the application notice must be served on one of the child's parents or guardians or, if there is no parent or guardian, on the person with whom the child resides or in whose care the child is. Paragraph 3.2 reiterates that the application must be made in accordance with Part 23 and be supported by evidence. In other words, following Rule 23.6 the application notice must state: (a) what order the applicant is seeking, and (b) briefly why the applicant is seeking the order.

According to paragraph 3.4 of Part 21 of the Practice Direction, the evidence in support of the application must satisfy the court that the proposed Litigation Friend (i) consents to act, (ii) can fairly and competently conduct proceedings on behalf of the child, (iii) has no interest adverse to that of the child, and (iv) where the child is a claimant, undertakes to pay any costs which the child may be ordered to pay in relation to the proceedings, subject to any right he may have to be repaid from the assets of the child.

It is to be noted that if the person seeking the appointment wishes to rely upon matters contained within the application notice itself, then the application has to be verified by a statement of truth. This is in accordance with Part 32.6(2) which provides that:

"At hearings other than the trial, a party may in support of his application rely upon the matters set out in . . . his application, if the statement or application is verified by a statement of truth."

Replacement of Litigation Friend by Court Order

By rule 21.7(1), the court may (a) direct that a person may not act as a **28–07** litigation friend, (b) terminate a litigation friend's appointment, (c) appoint a new litigation friend in substitution for an existing one. The application for an order under this paragraph must be supported by evidence (see discussion at para. 28–04).[6] In any event, the court may not appoint a litigation friend unless it is satisfied that the person appointed complies with the conditions specified in rule 21.4(3).[7] Paragraph 4 of the Practice Direction provides further limited information in respect of the appointment of a Litigation Friend and the prevention of a person acting as Litigation Friend. Paragraph 4.2 reiterates that the application must be supported by evidence. Further, if there is to be a new Litigation Friend in place of an existing Litigation Friend, the evidence will have to satisfy the

---

[6] CPR rule 21.7(2).
[7] See CPR rule 21.7(3).

court of the matters specified in paragraph 3.4 of the Practice Direction which has been set out above.

Discussion

28–08   There is nothing in rule 21.7(1) which gives a hint as to the circumstances in which the litigation friend's appointment may be terminated. Obviously, if a Litigation Friend dies or goes to prison or himself becomes a patient, it would be appropriate for a new Litigation Friend to be appointed. I would suggest that the bottom line should remain that, absent the type of circumstance referred to in the previous sentence, the test should be that the Litigation Friend should only be removed if he is not pursuing the best interests of the child. Allowing only for some possible updating of language, I can see no reason why that which was said by Lord Denning in *Re Taylor's Application*[8] should not apply. He said:

> "I take it to be clear that the father is prima facie the person entitled to be the next friend of his child so as to look after the interests of the child. He is the person entitled to consider his child's case on its own merits. He is not bound to consider the cases of others which may not be as strong as his child's. If he is to be removed, it should only be done if the proposed settlement is so clearly beneficial for his child that he is acting improperly in refusing it. . . . The burden is clearly on those who seek to remove a parent to show that he is not acting properly in the interests of his child as its next friend".

(This of course was said in the context of the thalidomide litigation where a particular parent did not desire to join in the general settlement of that litigation.)

Compromise

28–09   Both the rules of the Supreme Court and the County Court Rules made detailed provision (not always entirely clear) about the procedures to be adopted in and about the compromise of claims involving infants. The basic requirement of court approval continues pursuant to Part 21. By rule 21.10(1) where a claim is made (a) by or on behalf of a child or (b) against a child, no settlement compromise or payment and no acceptance of money paid into court shall be valid so far as it relates to the claim by, on behalf of or against the child without the approval of the court.

In respect of the compromise of actions made after proceedings have been commenced, Part 21 is somewhat silent as to the appropriate procedure by which that court approval is to be obtained. Obviously, if the

---

[8] [1972] 2 Q.B. 369.

case settles at trial, the old rules are likely to apply, namely that the approval will be given by the trial judge. However, if the case settles after proceedings have been commenced but before trial, presumably an application has to be made pursuant to Part 23 by way of an application notice.

One would assume that the requirements of the Part 21 Practice Direction, paragraph 6.2, will have to be complied with, namely that the application will have to include information including whether and to what extent the defendant admits liability, the age and occupation of the child, the Litigation Friend's approval of the proposed settlement or compromise, and the circumstances of the accident, any medical report, a schedule of special damages and future loss, police reports in a running-down case, and details of the result of any criminal prosecution. Presumably again, on the basis of paragraph 6.3, the application for the approval of the settlement or compromise should normally be heard by a Master or district judge.

Settlement of Claim Prior to Proceedings Being Brought

As with the old rules, provision is also made for the situation which 28–10 arises where a case is settled prior to proceedings being brought. Rule 21.10(2) provides as follows:

> "Where (a) before proceedings in which a claim is made by or on behalf of or against a child (whether alone or with any other person) are begun, an agreement is reached for settlement of the claim and (b) the sole purpose of proceedings on that claim is to obtain the approval of the court to a settlement or compromise of the claim, the claim must (i) be made using the procedure set out in Part 8 (alternative procedure for claims) and (ii) include a request for the court for approval of the settlement or compromise."

It is not proposed to set out in detail here what the Part 8 procedure involves. The requirement as to the contents of the appropriate Claim Form is set out in rule 8.2. Further, the Part 21 Practice Direction at paragraph 6 sets out further information in respect of settlement or compromise of claims by or on behalf of a child. By paragraph 6.1(3), the Part 8 procedure, in addition to including a request for approval of the settlement or compromise must, in addition to the details of the claim, set out the terms of the settlement or compromise or have attached to it a draft consent order in the appropriate practice form, namely N292. In addition, the application must be accompanied by the information required by paragraph 6.2 of the Practice Direction (see para. 28–09 above).

Costs on Settlement

Whether the case settles after proceedings are brought or prior to the 28–11 commencement of proceedings, Part 48.5 dealing with costs will apply. It applies to any proceedings where the claimant is a child and (a) money is ordered or agreed to be paid to or for the benefit of that child or (b) money is ordered to be paid by him or on his behalf. By rule 48.5(2), the general rule is that (a) the court must order a detailed assessment of the costs payable by any party who is a child to his solicitor and (b) on that (detailed assessment), the court must also assess any costs payable to that child (unless a default costs certificate has been issued).

Where the claimant is a child and the detailed assessment has taken place, the only amount payable by the child to its solicitor is the amount which the court certifies as payable. The court need not order detailed assessment of costs where in circumstances set out in the Costs Practice Direction obtain. This is dealt with in the Part 48 Practice Direction under the heading, "Costs Special Cases".

Under the heading, "Costs where money is payable by or to a child", it is provided by paragraph 1.2 that the court need not order the assessment of costs under rule 48.5(2), (a) where there is no need to do so to protect the interests of the child or (b) where another party has agreed to pay a specified sum in respect of the costs of the child and the solicitor acting for the child has waived the right to claim further costs, or where the court has decided the costs payable to the child by way of summary assessment and the solicitor acting for the child has waived the right to claim further costs or where an insurer is liable to discharge the costs which the child would otherwise be liable to pay to his solicitor and the court is satisfied that the insurer is financially able to discharge those costs.

Court Approval and the Fatal Accidents Act 1976

28–12   Part 21 itself is silent in respect of the Fatal Accidents Act 1976. However, the Practice Direction does deal with it. Paragraph 1.6 of the Practice Direction provides that:

> "An offer of settlement includes a proposal for a sum to be apportioned to a dependant child under the Fatal Accidents Act 1976".

By paragraph 7.3 of the Practice Direction it is provided that:

> "In order to approve an apportionment of money to a dependant child, the court will require the following information, namely (1) the matters set out in paragraphs 6.2(1) and 6.2(2) (to what extent the defendant admits liability and the age and occupation of the child) and (2) in respect of the deceased where the death was caused by an accident, the matters set out in 6.2(3)(a), (b), (c)."

(Note: This, in fact, should clearly be a reference to paragraph 6.2(4)). That information includes the circumstances of the accident, the medical reports and a schedule of any past and future expenses. Further, the extent and nature of the dependancy has to be set out.)

Discussion

I note that the Practice Direction does not say in terms that the 28–13 application must include the particulars of all dependants upon whose behalf the action has been brought (compare RSC, Ord. 18, r. 11(2)). However, I assume this remains the case. It is of some considerable importance because only one action lies in respect of the death which gives rise to the claim and it is vital that all persons with claims to be dependants are covered by the settlement—see Fatal Accidents Act 1976, s.2(3) which provides: "Not more than one action shall lie for and in respect of the same subject matter or complaint".

In *Avery v. London and North Eastern Railway Company*,[9] Lord McMillan said:

"The remedy given by the statute is to individuals, not to a class, but it still remains essential that one action only shall be brought and if any individual who has a claim is either not a plaintiff nor mentioned in the particulars as a person on whose behalf the action is brought, so much the worse for that individual. He cannot bring a second action against the wrongdoer."

In *Cooper v. Williams*,[10] Lord Denning said:

"I am satisfied that, if one of the dependants brings an action under the Fatal Accidents Acts (which is the only action which can be brought) it is the duty of that person (just as it is clearly the duty of an executor or administrator) to take all reasonable steps to see that all those dependants of the deceased person who desire to claim for their losses are informed of the action and named as persons on whose behalf it is brought."

In any event, it was always the law that in respect of claims under the Fatal Accidents Act 1976, a purported compromise in a case involving children was not valid without the approval of the court even though there was an adult dependant, for example, a widow who was *sui juris* and who would ordinarily be capable of validly compromising an action. In *Jeffrey v. Kent County Council*,[11] Paull J. said, at p. 157:

"The conclusion to which I have come is that when the administrator enters into an agreement with the defendant to take a lump sum to cover all the dependants that agreement is not a valid agreement unless (a) each of the dependants who is *sui juris* and desires to claim has approved thereof and (b) the court has sanctioned the agreement as being one for the benefit of each of the dependants who are infants. . . . Where however the administrator has with the approval of

---

[9] [1938] A.C. 606.
[10] [1963] 2 Q.B. 567.
[11] [1958] 3 All E.R. 155.

any dependant who is *sui juris* entered into an agreement with the defendant that the defendant should pay to that dependant (whom I shall call the settling dependant) a sum of money which is agreed to be sufficient as being proportionate to the injuries suffered by the settling dependant, then the settling dependant is bound by the agreement as he would be if he personally entered into such agreement, but the claim of the other dependants still remain to be settled by the court and the court in judging what is the proper amount to be paid to each of the remaining dependants does not take the sum paid to the settling dependant into account unless the amount so paid affects the loss which has been suffered by any of the other dependants. For instance, if a widow agrees to take a sum of money (not as part of a general lump sum settlement but individually) which the court considers is too small and which does not result in her having these resources behind her which she would otherwise have had for the bringing up of her infant children, the court in deciding the injury which has been suffered by the infant children by the loss of their father may give sums to such infants much larger than the sums which the court would have awarded had the widow received a proper capital sum. Clearly the ability of the widow to support the children in the future may be affected by the fact that she has too small a capital sum at her disposal and that would increase the loss suffered by the children by the death of their father."

28–14   Having said that, on the assumption that all relevant claims are validly in front of the court for the approval of the court and accepting that the court has to apportion the sum awarded between the various dependants, it is not possible to specify any detailed rules governing the apportionment beyond saying that in the ordinary case involving a widow and dependant children, the majority of the money is awarded to the widow. (The learned authors of Kemp & Kemp,[12] cite a passage from the 1959 report of the Committee on Funds in Court which is Cmnd. 818, to the effect that: "The present practice is to award the greater part of the total to the widow on the reasonable assumption that she will maintain the children as long as they are dependant and to award comparatively small sums to the children. Usually, though not always, a younger child is awarded more than an older child because the period of expected dependancy is greater.") It is, however, worth pointing out that the foregoing general rule may always be set aside in the particular circumstances of a particular case: see *R. v. Criminal Injuries Compensation Board ex parte Barratt*.[13]

How Money Recovered is Dealt With

28–15   As with the old Order 80 of the Rules of the Supreme Court, Part 21 also deals with the question of how money recovered by or on behalf of a child is to be dealt with. Rule 21.11(1) provides that: "Where in any

---

[12] *The Quantum of Damages* (4th ed.), Vol. 1, Chap. 23.
[13] [1994] P.I.Q.R. Q44.

proceedings (a) money is recovered by or on behalf of or for the benefit of a child or (b) money paid into court is accepted by or on behalf of a child, the money shall be dealt with in accordance with directions given by the court under this rule and not otherwise". Those directions may provide that the money shall be wholly or partly paid into court and invested or otherwise dealt with.[14]

The Practice Direction contains fairly detailed rules about these matters. Paragraph 8 is headed, "Control of money recovered by or on behalf of a child". By paragraph 8.2 the court (1) may direct the money to be paid into the High Court for investment, (2) may also direct that certain sums be paid direct to the child, his Litigation Friend or his legal representative for the immediate benefit of the child or for expenses incurred on his behalf, and (3) may direct that applications in respect of the investment of the money be transferred to a local district registry.

By paragraph 8.3 of the Practice Direction it is provided that:

"The Master or District Judge will consider the general aims to be achieved for the money in court (the fund) by investment and will give directions as to the type of investment. Where the child is legally aided the sum will be subject to a first charge under the Legal Aid Act 1988 (the Legal Aid Charge) and an order for the investment of money on the child's behalf must contain a direction to that effect".

Paragraph 10 of the Practice Direction is headed, "Investment on behalf of a child". Paragraph 10.1 provides that:

"At the hearing of the application for the approval of the agreement, the litigation friend or his legal representative should provide a CFO Form 320 (Request for Investment) for completion by the Master or District Judge".

By paragraph 10.2:

"On receipt of that form in the court funds' office, the investment managers of the Public Trust Office will make the appropriate investment".

Lastly, by paragraph 10.3: "Where an award of damages for a child is made at trial the trial judge may direct (1) the money to be paid into court and placed in the special investment account and (2) the litigation friend to make an application to the Master or District Judge for further investment directions."

It should be noted that by paragraph 10.4, if the money to be invested is very small, the court may order it to be paid direct to the Litigation Friend to be put into a building society account or similar for the child's use. In any event, if the money is invested in court, it must be paid out to the child when he reaches full age.[15]

---

[14] See CPR rule 21.11(2).
[15] See para. 10.5.

Where the Child is Also a Patient

28–16   The Practice Direction provides in paragraph 8.4 that: "Where a child is also a patient and likely to remain so on reaching full age, his fund shall be administered as a Patient's Fund". This of course will bring about the involvement of the Court of Protection. This assumes that a reference to a patient's fund in paragraph 8.4 brings in paragraph 11 of the Practice Direction.

By paragraph 11.2, where the sum to be administered is over £30,000, the order approving the settlement will contain a direction to the Litigation Friend to apply to the Court of Protection for the appointment of a Receiver, after which the fund will be transferred to the Court of Protection. If the sum to be administered is under £20,000, it may be retained in court and invested in the same way as the fund of a child. In respect of sums between £20,000 and £30,000 the advice of the Master of the Court of Protection should be sought. Applications for the appointment of a Receiver are governed by the Court of Protection Rules 1994. The application should normally be made by the "nearest relative" (who presumably will be the Litigation Friend) or a partner in a solicitors' firm dealing with the patient's affairs. Practice Form N292 is the appropriate form to be used for effecting the transfer of the fund to the Court of Protection. If the claimant is legally aided, the appropriate undertaking has to be given to the Legal Aid Board. The Legal Aid Board then communicate with the Court Funds Office and the Court Funds Office can transfer the money on a CFO Form 200.

When a Child Reaches Full Age

28–17   When a child who is not a patient reaches the age of 18, the appointment of the Litigation Friend ceases.[16] By Rule 21.9(4) it is provided that:

> "(4) The child . . . in respect of whom the appointment to act has ceased must serve notice on the other parties—
>
> (a) stating that the appointment of a litigation friend to act has ceased,
> (b) giving his address for service, and
> (c) stating whether or not he intends to carry on the proceedings."

It is important to note that if the child does not comply with the foregoing sub-paragraph within 28 days after the date on which the appointment of the Litigation Friend ceases, the court may on application

---

[16] CPR rule 21.9(1).

strike out any claim or defence brought by him.[17] It should also be noted that the liability of the Litigation Friend for costs continues until:

(a) the person in respect of whom his appointment to act has ceased serves the notice referred to in paragraph (4); or

(b) the Litigation Friend serves notice on the parties that his appointment to act has ceased.[18]

Paragraph 5 of the Practice Direction spells out the procedure where the need for a Litigation Friend has come to an end. In particular it is provided by paragraph 5.2 that:

"A child on reaching full age must serve on the other parties to the proceedings and file with the court a notice:

(1) stating that he has reached full age

(2) stating that his litigation friend's appointment has ceased

(3) giving an address for service

(4) stating whether or not he intends to carry on with or continue to defend the proceedings."

Lastly, it is provided by paragraph 5.3 that:

"If the notice states that the child intends to carry on with or continue to defend the proceedings, he shall subsequently be described in the proceedings as 'AB formerly a child but now of full age'."

---

[17] CPR rule 21.9(5).
[18] CPR rule 21.9(6).

29. Medical Examinations

Expert medical evidence is required in all personal injury claims, yet the **29–01** commissioning and content of those reports are often matters to which insufficient attention is paid.

The aim of this chapter is to consider the requirements for medical examination in personal injury claims, and in particular:

(a) the Purpose of a Medical Examination;

(b) the Commissioning of a Medical Report;

(c) the Structure of the Medical Report;

(d) the Requirement that a Party undergo Medical Examination;

(e) Disclosure and Admissibility of Medical Reports;

(f) The Impact of Woolf and the Civil Procedure Rules; and

(g) The Impact of the Human Rights Act 1998.

The Purpose of a Medical Examination

The function of a medical report and the maker is primarily to assist the **29–02** court and not the requisitioning party: considerable emphasis was placed upon this by Lord Woolf[1].

Principal Requirements

(a) A medical examination is required to be carried out to ascertain the nature and severity of a claimant's injuries, the prognosis, and any needs arising from the sequelae of the injury;

(b) Such examination should be carried out by someone with the relevant expertise who restricts the content of the report to matters within his expertise, save where it is necessary to consider the extent to which, if at all, the material injury affects other clinical assessments, *e.g.* a psychiatrist should not given an opinion upon orthopaedic matters but is entitled to comment upon the extent to which reported orthopaedic sequelae may have affected the psychological condition upon which the report has been sought.

---

[1] See the report of Lord Woolf: *Access to Justice*, s.III, chap. 13.5.

(c) The examination should be confined to medical matters and should not, for example, include observations as to the honesty or evasiveness of the person being examined unless these are based upon sound clinical findings, *e.g.* responses to tests and examination which are illogical or inconsistent with the alleged injury.

(d) Unless there are special reasons, it is preferable that this examination is not by any doctor who has treated the claimant and should be by a doctor who is in current clinical practice and not retired.

The Commissioning of a Medical Report

29–03   In the post-Woolf era, the instructions given to medical examiners when commissioning a report and thereafter in the preparation of a distillation of the issues remaining in dispute at trial, have assumed ever increasing importance. The significance of this development and change of emphasis cannot be understated. Recommendations concerning experts and their reports were set out at p. 156 onwards at the end of the Woolf Report[2], together with the draft rules. However, these have been considerably modified and the reforms encapsulated in the Civil Procedure Rules (CPR) are far less sweeping than those originally envisaged.[3] The procedural rules now governing experts and assessors are set out at Part 35 of the CPR and are discussed elsewhere[4]. The spirit of Woolf has nonetheless been retained:

> "13.3   "Under the new system, transparency of instructions to experts will be particularly important . . . it will be absolutely essential for the parties and the judge to know the basis on which the experts have been instructed"[5].

In January 1995, and in anticipation of these reforms, the Law Society issued a Code of Practice setting out specific guidelines for medico-legal reports in personal injury cases[6] in which emphasis was laid upon the importance of the clarification of medical issues *before* the case goes to court. This includes agreeing with the opposing party the exchange of comments with a view to resolving any points of difference and encouraging a discussion between the respective medical examiners[7]. If the dif-

---

[2] Lord Woolf, *Access to Justice*, s.III, Chap. 13.5.
[3] See the note at 35.10.5, *Civil Procedure 2000* Sweet & Maxwell.
[4] See Chapter. *Experts*.
[5] See generally discussion at *The Impact of Woolf and the Civil Procedure Rules* below.
[6] *Code of Practice for Medico-legal Reports in Personal Injury Cases*, The Law Society, January 1995. This report was prepared jointly by the Medico-legal Committee of the British Orthopaedic Association and the Civil Litigation Committee of the Law Society.
[7] Part 35.12 of the CPR, formerly RSC, Ord. 38, r. 38 and CCR, Ord. 20, r. 27. Part 35.12 provides that the statement must not only show areas of agreement and disagreement but a summary of the experts' reasons for disagreeing.

ferences remain incapable of resolution, it is suggested that a schedule or agenda be prepared setting out the unresolved medical issues for the use of the medical examiners and the court. These agenda are increasingly being settled by counsel.

These recommendations have largely been incorporated into CPR r. 35.12 and include provision that where the court directs a discussion between experts and gives specific directions under r.35(1), (2) and (3) concerning that discussion, compliance with those specific directions is a condition to be satisfied before the evidence of the experts may be admitted at trial. The discussion remains privileged (see para. 35.12.2) but the joint statement, though not binding on the parties, is not privileged: *Robin Ellis v. Malwright Ltd.* (1999)[8].

Experts themselves have also demanded greater regulation and maintenance of standards which it is hoped will see the demise of the biased and hostile expert[9]. In November 1996 the Expert Witness Institute was launched in response to the demands of experts and legal advisers, the objectives of which include "early resolution of disputes through fair and unbiased expert evidence." Their prosposals were finalised in July 2000 into "The Code of Guidance of Expert Evidence" which closely mirrors the requirements and criteria of CPR Part 35.12.

However, despite the removal of immunity from suit from members of the Bar, an expert who gives evidence at trial retains this immunity: *Stanton v. Callaghan*[10].

The Letter of Instruction

All requests for medical reports should be accompanied by a detailed 29–04
letter of instruction which should set out with clarity those issues upon which attention is likely to focus. In complex cases it is appropriate for this to be settled by counsel. The instructions should not be perfunctory but detailed and explicit and not stray beyond the expert's field of professional competence. This aspect is considered more fully in Chapter 4, above.

The Structure of a Medical Report

It is inappropriate and unethical for any party's advisers to write reports 29–05
or to tell the experts the views they are allowed to hold: *Robin Ellis Ltd. v. Malwright Ltd.*[11]

---

[8] (1999) B.L.R. 81, Const. L.J. 14, Judge Bowsher Q.C. See too, para. 35.12.1 *Civil Procedure,* The White Book Service, Sweet & Maxwell.
[9] see discussion below under *The Need for Objectivity* at 29–07.
[10] [1999] 2 W.L.R. 745, C.A.
[11] (1999) B.L.R. 81; 15 Const. L.J. 141, Judge Bowsher Q.C.

The structure of reports has assumed greater importance in the post-Woolf era[12], especially when only one expert is instructed[13]. The presentation of reports is considered in detail in the chapter on *Experts* but it is helpful if experts generally adopt the following format:

(a) cover page;

(b) history;

(c) present complaints;

(d) examination;

(e) investigations;

(f) specific issues;

(g) opinion and prognosis;

(h) summary.

(i) 'Woolf' declaration CPR Part 35.10(2); and

(j) the expert's *conculum vitae*.

In any event the report should comply with the requirements of any approved expert's protocol (Practice Direction (Experts and Assessors), paragraph 1.6.[14] The expert's overriding duty is to the court (CPR 35.3) and his report should be addressed to the court and not to the party instructing the expert.[15] This is an important change made by the CPR reinforcing the "management" role of the judiciary in the collation of evidence.[16] Recently, draft proposals on the structure of a medical report have been drawn up into a final form.[17]

Keeping to his "Brief"

29–06   Each expert should be aware of the parameters of his instructions and not stray beyond them. This is particularly important where the expert is examining on behalf of the opposing party.

---

[12] See CPR Part 35.10 Contents of Report.

[13] See Pt 35.8 CPR, "Instructions to a single joint expert".

[14] See para. 35.10.4 and para. 35PD–001 *Civil Procedure*, Vol. 1, The White Book Service 2000, Sweet & Maxwell.

[15] See para. 35.10.2, *Civil Procedure*, Vol. 1, The White Book Service 2000. See too Part 35.45 (second supplement to the 2000 edition) which provides that in multi-track cases, agreed directions on allocation should include provision for expert evidence; Practice Direction (The Multi-Track) paras. 4.7(1)(d) and 4.8(4) (para. 29PD–004 *civil procedure*, vol. 1, The White Book Service 2000, Sweet & Maxwell.

[16] See Pt 35, Practice Direction (Experts and Assessors, para. 11).

[17] See too the Academy of Experts "Guidelines for experts and those who instruct them" (http://www.academy-experts.org) which gives guidance on this and other CPR topics. The emphasis is upon the three "i's"—independence, integrity and impartiality. See too *CPR Rule 35—Problems for the experts (and those who instruct them)*, Michael Cohen, Chairman Emeritus of The Academy of Experts. *The Barrister* June 6, 2000.

Individual hobby-horses should be discouraged: a particular doctor may advocate surgical intervention where the treating doctor prefers a conservative approach. Unless such approach is viewed by the medical expert to be *Bolam*[18] unreasonable, it is inappropriate to criticise the claimant for following the advice of the treating physician.

By following this format, unnecessary duplication with other experts and confusing contradictions are likely to be avoided.

The Need for Objectivity

It is essential that the report is an independent and dispassionate clinical 29–07 review, and with this in mind, Lord Woolf canvassed the idea that personal injuries cases should be able to rely on one expert only who, in default of agreement between the parties, can be appointed by the court in its new case management role.[19] The difficulty with this approach in practice and why both the Law Society and the Bar greeted this proposal with considerable reservations, is that the requirement for objectivity is sometimes honoured in its breach rather than in its observance.

CPR Part 35.7 introduces the concept of the appointment by the Court of a single joint expert "where it appears to the court . . . that the issue falls within a substantially established area of knowledge and where it is not necessary for the court to sample a range of opinion. There is no presumption in favour of the appointment of a single joint expert.[20] The object is to do away with the calling of multiple experts where, given the nature of the issue of which the parties are at odds, that is not justified. This has the advantage of reducing costs and delays and of strengthening the impartial role of experts".

The concern over 'court experts' is avoided by the court not having a list of experts but, in the event of non-agreement between the parties, selects in some "other manner", such as by requesting one of the experts' professional bodies to make an appointment. CPR Part 35.8 concerns instructions to a joint single expert.

Where, however, a party is dissatisfied with the report of a single joint expert—and this is likely to arise quite often in personal injury cases—he can apply for permission to instruct another expert. In *Daniels v. Walker*[21]

---

[18] *Bolam v. Friern Hospital Management Committee* [1957] 2 All E.R. 118, HL.

[19] Lord Woolf in his interim report "*Access to Justice*", p. 185: "inappropriate use of experts to bolster cases [which] leads to additional cost and delay".

[20] See the emphasis upon this phrase by Mantell J. in *Oxley v. Penwarden* [2000] Medical Litigation Cases 0250. However, see para. 35.7.2 added in the second supplement to the 2000 Edition of *Civil Procedure*, The White Book Service, Sweet & Maxwell. In incorporating the provisions of Practice Direction (The Multi-Track), it is stated that the Court's "general approach will be to give directions for a single joint expert on any appropriate issue unless there is good reason not to do so." (para. 29PD–004). This would appear to reverse the original presumption stated in Part 35.7 and if fully implemented, could have serious implications in personal injury cases.

[21] [2000] 1 W.L.R. 1382, C.A.

it was held that provided the dissatisfied party's reasons were not fanciful, such permission may be given as to enable the party to make a decision as to whether or not there were aspects of the report of the single joint expert which might wish to challenge. It was expressly stated that such permission is more likely to be granted where a substantial sum is involved (on the princple of 'proportionality') and thus this concession is unlikely to be made freely available in modest personal injury cases.

The difficulty addressed by lawyers' reticence to use joint experts other than upon largely uncontentious matters of quantum, is that many experts seem to find difficulty in grasping the concept that although they are *retained* by one party or the other, their approach and conclusion must be truly independent. No report should be predicated on the basis that the author feels he must put the case on behalf of the party who has requested the report.[22] Partisanship is not only unprofessional but unhelpful: claimants are encouraged to believe that their case is stronger and thus is likely to attract higher damages than is in fact the case and insurers are encouraged to fight "losers", only to find at the court door that the expert has "cold feet". This leads to dissatisfaction on both sides, significantly increases costs and is against the present spirit of settlement and mediation.

Judges are increasingly willing to condemn biased expert evidence and in *The "Ikarian Reefer"*,[23] Cresswell J. set out a definitive statement of the duties and functions of an expert witness.

Thorpe L.J. commented on *The Ikarian Reefer* in *Vernon v. Bosley (No. 1)*[24]:

"The area of expertise in any case may be likened to a broad street with the plaintiff walking on one pavement and the defendant on the opposite one. Somehow, the expert must be ever mindful of the need to walk straight down the middle of the road and to resist the temptation to join the party from whom his instructions come on the pavement."

See also *Scott v. Bloomsbury Health Authority & Ors*[25] and *Parry v. N.W. Surrey Health Authority*[26]:

"I interpose to say that I found [the expert witness] to be more of an advocate at times . . . Also his evidence on the anatomical impossibility points was a firm indication that I could not treat his evidence as reliable. I do not wish nor do I need to say more."

---

[22] See *De Mssey* [1996] Med. L.R. where the claimant's expert was strongly criticised by Turner J. for "rubbishing" the defendant's expert.
[23] [1993] 2 Lloyds Rep. 68 at 81.
[24] [1997] 1 All E.R. 577 at 612, CA.
[25] [1990] 1 Med. L.R. 214.
[26] [1995] Clinical Risk and AVMA Journal, Vol. 1, p. 33.

The Requirement that a Party undergo Medical Examination

With the "front-loading" of case preparation which has occurred under 29–08 the CPR and Pre-Action Protocols, both parties tend to obtain their medico-legal evidence at an earlier stage of the litigation process than in the pre-Woolf regime and this is both encouraged and enforced by the Practice Directions for Multi-track and Fast Track cases.[27] Generally, however, the claimant is the first to obtain medico-legal evidence in order to comply with the requirements of CPR Part 16.4(e) and Practice Direction—Statements of Case, paragraph 4.3 (formerly RSC, Ord. 18, r. 12(1A)(a)). The number and frequency of reports will depend upon the severity and nature of the injuries, and also upon the extent to which the courts in the exercise of their case management powers are prepared to allow reports to be obtained or relied upon[28]. All reports should deal in as much detail as possible with the particular injuries and disabilities suffered by the claimant[29].

Difficulties rarely occur with consent where the claimant is being examined by his own expert or an expert jointly instructed by both parties, although occasionally a claimant will refuse to attend a particular doctor for a further examination. In these circumstances it is wise to seek an alternative expert both for the further report and for trial as all reports should be up-to-date when the case is heard. Similarly, in relatively straightforward cases where the prognosis is unlikely to be contentious, a defendant may be prepared and indeed be encouraged by the court to accept the claimant's medical evidence without recourse to a report from a specialist of his own choice.

The problem, however, arises when a claimant having issued proceedings in respect of personal injuries:

(a) refuses to undergo a medical examination by the doctor nominated by the defendant or the court; or

---

[27] See the *Access to Justice* Report recommending the development of pre-action protocols "to build on and increase the benefits of early but well informed settlement which genuinely satisfy both parties to dispute" See too CPR, Pt. 16.5 concerning the "Contents of Defence" and the accompanying Practice Direction, para. 13.1 dealing with personal injury claims. This provides that where the defendant disputes any part of the claimant's medical report, he should give in his defence his reasons for doing so (13.3(2)) and "where he has obtained his own medical report on which he intends to rely, attach it to his defence" (13.3(3)).

[28] "Expert evidence shall be restricted to that which is reasonably required to resolve the proceedings" (CPR, Pt. 35.1) and "no party may call an expert or put in evidence an expert's report without the court's permission" (CPR, Pf. (35.4) and that permission is limited to the expert or the field identified (CPR, Pf. 35.4(2) and (3)). See too the Court's power to direct that evidence is to be given by a single joint expert [Part 35.7] and provision for the instruction of joint single experts [Part 35.8].

[29] See "*The Structure of a Medical Report*", above.

(b) objects to medical tests or further investigations required by the defendant's doctor; or

(c) seeks to impose conditions on such examination, *e.g.* being accompanied by a friend or having his/her own doctor present.

Such reluctance is sometimes with just cause: doctors have been guilty of dismissive or abrupt behaviour or have used the examination as a means of extracting evidence far beyond the scope of the medical examination. Proposed investigations may be invasive, be considered unnecessary by the claimant's own medical expert and/or may carry an element of risk. Sometimes the objection is simply that the consulting room is geographically inconvenient, particularly where the claimant is significantly disabled.

Under the former Rules of the Supreme Court, there was specific provision for medical examination by the opposing party's medical expert: namely RSC, Ord. 25, r. 6(1):

" . . . It shall be the duty of the parties to the action and their advisers to give all such information . . . on any hearing of the summons (for directions) as the court may reasonably require . . .".

Supreme Court Practice 1999, Vol. 1, paragraph. 25/6/2 to RSC Ord. 25, r. 6 provided that:

"It is incumbent upon a claimant, who claims damages for personal injuries, to afford the defendant a reasonable opportunity to have him medically examined, and if he should decline to submit himself to a medical examination of a reasonable character which is reasonably required, the Court has power, under its inherent jurisdiction, to stay the action unless and until he does so",

and cited with approval the dicta in *Edmeades v. Thames Board Mills Ltd*[30] in which the general principle was laid down that if a claimant unreasonably refuses to submit to a medical examination on behalf of a defendant in circumstances which would prevent the just determination of the cause, the court will exercise its inherent jurisdiction to grant a stay in the proceedings until the claimant submits to such examination. This compared with the approach previously taken by the Court of Appeal in *Pickett v. Bristol Aeroplane Co. Ltd*[31] where it was held that a claimant could reasonably object to an examination by a particular doctor without having to give any reasons.

Until recently, there was no corresponding specific provision in the CPR to RSC Ord. 25, r.6(1). This has now been rectified to some extent by an amendment made in May 2000 to CPR Part 35. A new paragraph 35.2.3 in

---

[30] [1969] 2 Q.B. 67; [1969] 2 All E.R. 127, CA.
[31] Unreported; (1961 C.A. No. 114); Willmer and Donovan L.JJ.

the Second Cumulative Supplement to *Civil Procedure,* The White Book Service 2000 recites the current position with regard to examination of a claimant by a medical expert. This paragraph cites with approval *Edmeades*[32], *Lacey v. Harrison*[33] and *Lane v. Willis*[34] and gives examples where a stay has been granted by the Court in circumstances where a claimant has refused to submit to such examination. It confirms the previous position, namely that "if the proposed examination is unpleasant, painful or risky the court will be reluctant to order a stay unless the interests of justice imperatively require" citing *Aspinall v. Sterling Mansell*[35] and *Prescott v. Bulldog Tools*[36], both of which cases are discussed later in this chapter when considering *How is the test of reasonableness applied?*[37].

Whilst 'examination of claimant by medical expert' has belatedly been tacked on to Part 35 dealing with Experts and Assessors, the position remains that this inherent jurisdiction has been retained under the court's extensive general powers of case management set out at Part 3.1 of the CPR. These powers may be exercised on the court's own initiative or on an application (3.3) and include power to strike out all or part of a statement of case (3.4 and Practice Direction to 3.4).

Specifically, of Part 3.1 (2) of the CPR provides:

"(2) . . . the court may—

   (f) stay the whole or part of any proceedings either generally or until a specified date or event; . . .
   (m) take any step or make any other order for the purpose of managing the case and furthering the overriding objective;" and

and Part 3.1(3) of the CPR further provides:

(3) When the court makes an order, it may

   (a) make it subject to conditions . . .; and
   (b) specify the consequence of failure to comply with the order or a condition."

CPR (2)(c) Part 3.4 provides for strike out of a statement of case where there has been a failure to comply with a court order.

". . . if it appears to the court—

   (b) that the statement of case is an abuse of the court's process or is otherwise likely to obstruct the just disposal of the proceedings".

---

[32] *ibid.*
[33] *discussed later in this chapter**
[34] [1972] 1 W.L.R. 326, discussed later in this chapter under **Refusal to Undergo Medical Examination,** *Procedure* at 29–09.
[35] [1981] 3 All E.R. 866.
[36] [1981] 3 All E.R. 869.
[37] see 29–14 below.

It is a reasonable assumption that this latter provision would include that part of the claimant's case relating to his injury or an issue arising in respect of that injury where he has refused to submit to medical examination by the defendant's nominated expert.

Practice Direction 2.4 provides that the orders the judge may make under 3.4 include a stay (2.4(1)).

These general powers of case management are intended to enable the court to carry out its duty to *actively* manage cases (r. 1.4(1), so as to further the overriding objective (r. 1.1) and the list of powers is not intended to be exhaustive: see the guidance given in *Mortgage Corporation Ltd v. Sandoes*.[38] It is still early days within which to discern a clear pattern indicating any in the stance taken by the courts, in the exercise of their greater Case Management powers, where a party does refuse to undergo medical examination, and no new authorities are quoted in paragraph 35.2.3. However, it has been observed that:

> "when making an order requiring somebody to do something for the first time, the court may be less reluctant than it previously was to impose an express sanction in the event of non-compliance. Even if no express sanction is stated the court may later strike out all or part of a statement of case of a party who fails to comply with the order (see further r. 3.4)"[39].

There is nothing, therefore, in the CPR to suggest any radical departure from the approach adopted in *Edmeades*[40]. On the contrary CPR paragraph 35.2.3 indicates that the guidance in this case will continue to be followed subject to any impact the Human Rights Act may have upon the exercise of the court's discretion.[41]

Refusal to Undergo Medical Examination

General

29–09   *Edmeades* therefore remains authority for the proposition that refusal or imposition of conditions by a claimant is likely to provoke an application to stay the action until the claimant submits to examination.

The granting of a stay is in the discretion of the Master or District Judge and has been very broadly and diversely exercised.[42]

---

[38] [1996] T.L.R. 75, CA; *The Times*, December 27, 1995 *per* Lord Woolf.
[39] See *Civil Procedure*, Vol. 1, The White Book Service 2000, s.A, 3.1.3
[40] *ibid.*
[41] See below "*The Impact of the Human Rights Act*". However, this should be seen in the light of Lord Woolf's clear warning that "it would be highly undesirable if the consideration of [case management decisions] were made more complex by the injection into them of Art. 6 style arguments": see *Daniels v. Walker, The Times*, May 17, 2000, CA.
[42] See the wide range of powers conferred by CPR Part 3.1(z)(m) *ibid.*

Failure after the action has been stayed to submit himself for examination exposes the claimant to the risk of his claim being stayed or struck out.[43] See *Jassim v. Grand Metropolitan Information Services Ltd*[44] and *Lacey v. Harrison*.[45]

Procedure

Supreme Court Practice 1999, Vol. 1, paragraph 25/6/2 provided that: **29–10**

"Such an order ought only to be made when it is reasonable in the interests of justice, and the onus lies on the party applying for such a stay to show that he cannot properly prepare his case without the medical examination he is seeking".

This is entirely compatible with the "overriding objective" considered at Part 3.1 of the CPR and commented upon at paragraph 3.1.3, and is yet further support for the assumption that the court's approach to the exercise of its inherent discretion under the CPR will be broadly similar to that under the former Rules of the Supreme Court. "The ruling consideration is whether, by refusing a reasonable request for examination, the party is preventing the just determination of the claim" (CPR Part 35, comment at 35.2.3). See too *Lacey v. Harrison*.[46]

The test was laid down in *Lane v. Willis; Lane v. Beath (Executor of Estate of George William Willis)*[47] and is that of "reasonableness": the reasonableness of the claimant in refusing to be examined by a particular doctor, and the reasonableness of the defendant in insisting upon examination by a doctor unacceptable to the claimant. In the exercise of its discretion the court must balance:

(a) the claimant's rights not to have his/her personal liberty invaded; with

(b) not unfairly restricting the defendant's right to defend himself in the litigation as he and his advisers think fit, which includes the freedom to choose the witnesses that he will call.

"The principles upon which a court should, in aid of obtaining a medical examination of one of the parties to an action, act when deciding whether or not to take the somewhat strong course of staying the action if a medical examination is not afforded, are by now clear. An order for a medical examination of any party to an action has been well said to be 'an invasion of personal liberty'.

---

[43] *ibid.*, CPR Part 3.4(2)(c).
[44] January 18, 1999, CA unreported (referred to in paragraph 35.4.3 *ibid.*)
[45] The Times, April 22, 1992.
[46] *ibid.*
[47] [1972] 1 W.L.R. 326; [1972] 1 All E.R. 430, CA. (examination of plaintiff by named psychiatrist).

Accordingly, it should only be granted when it is reasonable in the interests of justice so to order. When the refusal of a medical examination is alleged to be unreasonable, the onus lies on the party who says it is unreasonable and who applies for the order to show, upon the particular facts of the case, that he is unable properly to prepare his claim (or defence) without that examination.[48]"

This passage was expressly approved by the Court of Appeal in *Smith v. Ealing, Hammersmith and Hounslow Health Authority*.[49]

In that case, the plaintiff, a transsexual male, alleged that negligent mandibular reconstruction surgery had left him with a blemished face which was particularly distressing as he dressed as and considered himself to be a woman. He did not specifically claim psychological injury but the defendants nevertheless applied for him to undergo medical examination by a psychiatrist of their choosing. This was to support their case that even had the surgery been successful the plaintiff would still have been embarrassed and disappointed—the Court of Appeal whilst acceding to the application for disclosure of the plaintiff's medical records, held that these would provide the defendants with sufficient material to prepare their case without the need for a psychiatrist's examination and the "inevitable invasion of personal liberty". This chimes very closely with the wording of Article 8 of the European Convention on Human Rights.

In determining the balance, the court must consider whether the proposed medical examination is:

(a) of a reasonable character? and

(b) "reasonably required"?

In *Lane*, the claimant was injured in a motor accident and claimed he had suffered bruising, nervous shock and a depressive anxiety. He was examined by the defendant's neurologist but thereafter the gravity of the neurological injury was enlarged upon in an amended statement of claim. The claimant submitted to two further examinations by the defendant's neurologist but refused to submit to a psychiatric examination. The Court of Appeal held that in view of the substantial difference between the injuries as originally pleaded and as pleaded in the amended statement of claim, the request for psychiatric examination was reasonable. Other examples include *Jackson v. Mirror Group Newspapers Ltd*[50] (stay ordered where issue of claimant's disfigurement arose in defamation claim), and *Baugh v. Delta Water Fittings Ltd*[51] (in the absence of any concrete basis for requiring an examination, a stay was refused in a Fatal Accidents Act claim brought by a widow).

---

[48] *per* Sachs L.J., p. 331.
[49] Unreported, May 1, 1997, Kennedy & Waite L.JJ. and McCullough J.
[50] The Times, March 29, 1994, CA.
[51] [1971] 1 W.L.R. 1295; [1971] 3 All E.R. 258.

The decisive factor, therefore, is the interests of justice—the "just determination" of a particular case: *per* Lord Denning M.R. in *Edmeades v. Thames Board Mills Ltd* and thus turns on the particular facts of each case, as does the "overriding objective" to achieve justice under the CPR. The onus lies on the party applying for such a stay to show that he cannot properly prepare his case withou the medical examinatin he is seeking. A stay should not be ordered if the party can show some substantial ground for this refusal, such as the particular medical expert is likely to conduct his examination or make his report unkindly or unfavourably (see *Starr v. National Coal Board.*[52] In an application for a stay, therefore, each party should file detailed witness statements deposing to the reasonableness of the request/refusal so that the court, fully informed, can properly exercise its discretion.

A practical solution, canvassed in *Starr,* and touched upon in the commentary to CPR Part 35.7[53], is to offer the claimant a choice of doctors.

Refusal by the Claimant to Undergo Examination

The defendant has the burden of establishing that the stay should be **29–11** imposed: *Starr v. National Coal Board.*[54] If a defendant puts forward the name of a particular doctor and can show that an examination by a doctor is necessary in the defendant's interest and that this particular doctor is apparently well qualified to examine the claimant, the claimant then has to give reasons for objecting to him. He must at least be able to show some substantial ground on which he or his legal advisers have formed the opinion that the doctor in question lacks the proper qualifications or is likely to conduct his examination and to make his reports unkindly or unfairly (*per* Cairns L.J. in *Starr*)[55]. Objections based on allegations of bias, however, should be approached with great care:

" . . . It is a very serious matter to say of any properly qualified and experienced doctor that it would not be reasonable for him to carry out a medical examination, unless the ground of objection is personal to the particular claimant. If, on the other hand, the objection is to the doctor's skill or his probity or his anticipated behaviour at the examination, then a finding adverse to him might constitute in effect a bar to his examining any other person for the purposes of litigation. That sort of possibility would act as a serious disincentive to any doctor minded to undertake that sort of work, and would militate against

---

[52] [1977] 1 W.L.R. 63; [1977] 1 W.L.R. 63; [1977] 1 All E.R. 243, CA., see below, *Refusal by the Claimant to Undergo Examination* at 29–11.
[53] see Second Cumulative Supplement to *Civil Procedure,* The White Book Service 2000, Sweet & Maxwell.
[54] [1977] 1 All E.R. 243 at 249, *per* Scarman L.J.
[55] *ibid.* at p. 256.

the candour and forthrightness in reporting which are so valuable to any judge who has the difficult task of evaluating medical evidence at the hearing" (*per* Geoffrey Lane L.J. in *Starr*).

Objection to a Particular Doctor

29–12   Despite the greater emphasis upon individual "rights" with the forth-coming implementation of the Human Rights Act, the courts in the future are likely to look less kindly upon a claimant's refusal to undergo examination by a particular doctor. There are a number of reasons for this, the principal one being the *nirvana* of the "overriding objective", the emphasis upon experts being appointed by and answerable to the court rather than to any particular party,[56] and the increasing desire of the masters and district judges to encourage/compel the appointment of joint experts even on liability and causation issues.[57] It may, nonetheless, be helpful to consider the approach in established case law.

In *Murphy v. Ford Motor Co. Ltd*,[58] the claimant refused to undergo a medical examination on the basis that the defendant's doctor was not independent as he only accepted instructions in medico-legal cases from insurance companies and that he was "unprofessional in his conduct in examining and reporting on claimants in the past". He was stated to be "an hostile examiner of claimants" and therefore the claimant argued it was unreasonable to expect him to be examined by that particular doctor. Cooke J. stayed the proceedings until the claimant submitted to medical examination by this doctor and this was upheld by the Court of Appeal:

"If the defendants in a personal injury case made out a reasonable case for the claimant to be medically examined by a doctor the claimant should accede to such request unless he has reasonable grounds for objecting to that particular doctor." (*per* Lord Denning, M.R.).

Seven years later, in a less rigid judicial climate, the Court of Appeal in *Starr v. National Coal Board*[59] was prepared to examine closely the claimant's allegations of bias, accepting the principle that objection could be made to examination by a hostile examiner and that such objection constituted "reasonable grounds":

"I certainly do not think that it is incumbent on a claimant in this situation to have to prove to the satisfaction of the court that the doctor had erred in the past ... All that has to be proved is that the claimant and his advisers were entertaining a reasonable apprehension that that might be so, and that those

---

[56] See generally the provisions of Pt 35 of the CPR.
[57] See observations of Lord Woolf in *Daniels v. Walker,* [2000] 1 W.L.R. 1382, CA.
[58] (1970) 114 S.J. 886, CA.
[59] *ibid.*

apprehensions, if realised, might make a 'just determination of the cause more difficult than it would be if another doctor conducted the examination'." (*per* Scarman L.J. at 251b in *Starr*).

In that case, the claimant failed to show bias on the evidence but the eprinciple upon which objection could reasonably be made was established. With increasing emphasis on objectivity, independence and expert witness protocols, and a readiness to criticise and expose bias (*Ikarian Reefer*[60]) claimants should not be reticent in lodging objections to notorious "professional" witnesses whose appointment diaries reflect a flourishing medico-legal practice rather than "hands-on" clinical duties.[61]

Refusal by the Claimant to Undergo Medical Tests

"Every human being of adult years and sound mind has a right to determine **29–13** what should be done with his body;" (*per* Cardozo J. in *Schloendorff v. Society of New York Hospital*[62]).

This "right" has been reinforced by the adoption of Article 8 of the European Convention on Human Rights into the Human Rights Act 1998.

Doctors are not normally permitted to carry out tests unless they are for therapeutic purposes in the course of investigation and treatment, and the General Medical Council and the Royal Colleges give specific guidance on this point, *e.g.* the Royal College of Radiologists deems it an act of professional misconduct to perform radiological examinations other than for clinical reasons. Yet frequently doctors require claimants to undergo tests and investigations purely for the purposes of preparing their reports: a worrying example of this is where brain-damaged claimants are required to undergo MRI scans to determine the nature and extent of the neurological injury and whether this is causally linked to the material insult. Such a scan requires complete stillness by the patient and therefore many of these claimants are given general anaesthetics—a highly invasive procedure— essentially for legal forensic purposes and not because of any intrinsic therapeutic benefit.

If, therefore, a claimant refuses to undergo a test which the defendant's doctor wishes to carry out, *e.g.* a lumbar spine X-ray, the defendant must apply for a stay of the proceedings until the request is complied with. A court must then balance the claimant's personal liberty against the defendant's right to defend the case. A number of factors will be taken into consideration, including:

   (a) the amount of pain or discomfort involved;

---

[60] [1993] 2 Lloyds Rep. 68.
[61] See too *Vernon v. Bosley (No. 1)* [1997] 1 All E.R 579, CA *per* Stuart-Smith L.J.
[62] 211 N.Y. 125; 105 N.E. 92 (N.Y., 1914) at 93–94.

(b) the risk of injury to health;

(c) whether similar tests have recently been carried out elsewhere and whether the films and results are available for inspection, *e.g.* X-rays, CT and MRI scans; and

(d) the extent to which the result of the test is likely to assist the court in the determination of the medical issues between the parties.

In view of the latter requirement, the appropriate time for such application is at a case management conference.

A claimant's advisors should therefore be alert to the precise nature and extent of the defendant's routine request for medical facilities to examine the claimant in that some doctors interpret unconditional facilities for examination to include the facility to carry out investigations such as taking X-rays. These facilities should not be granted by a claimant's advisors without an appropriate undertaking in respect of any damage caused by radiation: see generally *Aspinall v. Sterling Mansell*[63] and *Prescott v. Bulldog Tools*[64] as applied in *Sampson v. Boddy Timber. Ltd.*[65] where the defendant was required to given an undertaking in respect of frontal tomography.

How is the test of reasonableness applied?

29–14   A claimant is likely to succeed where his objection is that the medical examination will involve him in some element of risk or discomfort. In *Aspinall v. Sterling Mansell Ltd,*[66] the claimant allegedly suffered from industrial dermatitis. The defendant's doctor wished to carry out a patch test which carried a small but identifiable risk of the recurrence of this condition. The court held that by reason of that risk the claimant's objection was reasonable.

By way of contrast, in *Prescott v. Bulldog Tools,*[67] a case concerning industrial deafness, the defendant's doctors wished to carry out three tests on the claimant's ears to determine the aetiology and extent of the deafness. These tests comprised a water test, an X-ray of the inner ear and piercing of the ear drum with a very fine needle. The claimant's objections were principally that he had already been examined by the defendant's doctors on four occasions. The court held that both the defendant's requests and the claimant's refusal were reasonable but that with regard to the second and third of the proposed tests, which were both uncomfortable

---

[63] [1981] 3 All E.R. 866, CA.
[64] [1981] 3 All E.R. 869, CA.
[65] [1994] Q.B.D., *Leeds District Registry, District Judge Harrison*; (1995) P.M.I.L.L., Vol. 10, p. 77.
[66] *ibid.*
[67] *ibid.*

and invasive, the claimant's objection outweighed the reasonableness of the defendant's request, whereas with regard to the water test, the defendant's request carried the day.[68] In so doing Webster J. outlined a three-stage approach:

(i) was the request made by the defendant reasonable;

(ii) was the claimant's refusal reasonable; and

(iii) balancing on the one hand the defendant's need for further information, against the refusal of the plaintiff on the other, and the grounds which each had, what conclusion should the court reach?

This approach was adopted by Gage J. in *Hill v. West Lancashire Health Authority*.[69]

In *Laycock v. Lagoe*,[70] the Court of Appeal dismissed the defendant's appeal against a refusal to stay an action unless the claimant submitted to an MRI scan. The Court of Appeal, whilst pointing out that the case depended on its particular facts, took the opportunity to lay down principles of general application. They made reference to *Prescott*[71] and *Hill v. West London Health Authority*[72] but felt the test expounded in those cases could be reduced to two stages:

(i) Do the interests of justice require the test which the defendant proposes? If the answer is in the negative the enquiry need go no further. If, however the answer is in the affirmative, then

(ii) the court should go on to consider whether the party who opposes the test has put forward a substantial reason for the test not being undertaken; "a substantial reason being one that is not imaginary or illusory".

Kennedy L.J. said:

"In deciding the answer to that question, the court will inevitably take into account, on the one hand, the interests of justice in the result of the test and the extent to which the result may progress the action as a whole; on the other hand, the weight of the objection advanced by the party who declines to go ahead with the proposed procedure, and any assertion that the litigation will only be slightly advanced if the test is undertaken. But, if the claimant, for example, has a real objection, which he articulates, to the proposed test, then the balance will come down in his favour."

---

[68] See too *Hill v. West Lancashire Health Authority* (1996) P.M.I.L.L. (April) where the "balance of reasonableness" test was applied in an application for the infant claimant to undergo an MRI scan and the defendant's application was refused.

[69] (1996). P.M.I.L.L. 18.

[70] July 18, 1997, CA: Beldam & Kennedy L.JJ.

[71] *ibid.*

[72] *ibid.*

This test anticipated the courts' case management powers under the CPR and the rights of the parties' gainsaid by the European Convention on Human Rights (ECHR) as incorporated into the Human Rights Act 1998.

In *Wilson v. Fylde Borough Transport*[73], the plaintiff in a personal injury action refused to attend medical examination by a neurosurgeon appointed by the defence. It was held that the trial date would be vacated since a fair trial would not be possible if the defence could not produce evidence to counter that of the neurosurgeon appointed by the plaintiff.

Where, therefore, the objection is simpliciter to a reasonable request, a court is unlikely to deprive the defendant of the expert of his choice as this would amount to prevention of the just determination of the cause (*per* Webster J. in *Prescott v. Bulldog Tools Ltd*)[74]. This would also, arguably breach the defendant's right to a fair trial under Article 6 of the ECHR.[75] However, in *Daniels v. Walker*[76], Lord Woolf firmly sought to leave human rights issues outside the ambit of consideration of case management decisions, making it clear that they had no place in CPR determinations.[77]

The Law Commission has recommended structured settlements to become the norm.[78] Should this occur, provision would have to be made for claimants to submit to any medical examination required for the purposes of obtaining quotations for annuities from the financial markets. This raises all manner of spectres in terms of the claimants' right to privacy under Article 8 of the ECHR (see below).

Examination by a non-medical expert

29–15   The increasing scope and complexity of personal injury claims has resulted in an increase in the number of non-medical experts. The view currently held is that defendants are not entitled to facilities to have the claimant examined or interviewed by any non medical expert: *Larby v. Thurgood*[79] and *Lock v. Chief Constable of Leicestershire* and *Lock v.*

---

[73] Unreported. C.A. Kennedy L.J., June 22, 1998.

[74] See too *Selvanayagam v. University of the West Indies* [1983] W.L.R. 585 where it was held that part of the plaintiff's duty to take reasonable steps to mitigate his loss included submitting to a medical examination and/or submitting to medical treatment or accepting a reduced award.

[75] See "*Impact of the Human Rights Act*" below.

[76] [2000 1 W.L.R. 1382, CA.

[77] See the discussion below: "*The Impact of the Human Rights Act*". In *Daniels v. Walker* it was expressly held that a refusal by the court to permit a party dissatisfied with the report of a single joint expert to instruct another expert would not conflict with the Convention for the Protection of Human Rights and Fundamental Freedoms art. 6 (Human Rights Act 1998, Sched. 1) On the facts of the case, however, the defendant's appeal for subsequent permission to instruct his own occupational therapy expert, was allowed. (see discussion below under *Imposing Conditions* at 29–17).

[78] Report 152.

[79] [1993] I.C.R. 66 (refusal to allow the claimant to be interviewed by an employment expert).

Leicestershire Health Authority.[80] In *Lock*, the defendant Health Authority sought a stay until the claimant agreed to be examined by an occupational therapist. Such examination contemplated inspection of the claimant's living accommodation and interviewing the claimant as to how he was coping with his disability. His Honour Judge Bentley Q.C. was not prepared to allow the examination to go beyond inspection of the living accommodation:

> "He has already been examined by a plethora of medical experts who are competent (as the occupational therapist is not) to assess the extent of the plaintiff's disability. I see no purpose in a so called examination by someone who has no medical qualifications when there is already a number of medical reports prepared by medical men who have examined the plaintiff."

He described as "misconceived" the suggestion that the occupational therapist be allowed to question and interview the plaintiff making specific reference to the judgment and objections in *Larby*.

Comment

The decision in *Lock* extends the principle set out in *Larby* and **29–16** effectively bars examination and interview by any non-medical expert although, presumably, this will not extend to a psychologist? One questions, however, whether this will continue to be the attitude of the courts in the current climate of conciliation and arbitration, particularly given the emphasis upon "proportionality" and the requirement under the "overriding objective" to ensure the parties are placed on an equal footing.[81] Moreover, whilst it may be undesirable for a claimant to be questioned by an employment consultant, similar considerations do not necessarily apply to skilled therapists. Many experienced physicians in the treatment and rehabilitation of patients who have suffered catastrophic injuries acknowledge the specialised knowledge and skills of such therapists and accept that often they are better placed to *assess* the claimant's ability to cope with his disability within his home environment using the available aids and equipment, than is the doctor who *describes* the disability and the likely prognosis. Certainly, the multi-disciplinary approach in the care of such patients reflects the need for skills other than those of medical experts alone and it is difficult to see how a defendant expert can deploy such skills if he is deprived of the opportunity to question the claimant as to how he is coping within the confines of the disability.[82] If necessary, the presence of a

---

[80] (1996) A.P.I.L. Newsletter, Vol. 6, issue 6, p. 17; (1997) P.M.I.L.L. Vol. 13, p. 4.
[81] See *Civil Procedure*, Vol. 1, The White Book Service 2000, para. 1.3.6.
[82] See *Daniels v. Walker ibid.*, The joint expert was an occupational therapist reporting on the care of the claimant. The care issue would have substantial implications for the defendant's insurers: there could be hundreds of thousands of pounds involved. The defendant's appeal for subsequent permission to instruct his own expert in the same discipline as the jointly instructed single expert, was allowed.

representative of the claimant's solicitors should provide adequate protection from unreasonable or aggressive questioning.

Imposing Conditions

29–17 *(i) Attending with a Companion.* It may sometimes be legitimate for a claimant to be accompanied to a medical examination by the defendant's doctor: the examination may be sensitive, *e.g.* a gynaecological examination or the claimant may have suffered a head injury and be forgetful, and need a companion to her him and the doctor in providing a history and assisting on clinical details. Sometimes the requirement for a companion is a condition placed by the claimant upon an examination; in other circumstances, the court may require that the claimant be permitted to have a friend present, as a condition of granting a stay.

It is, however, a grey area where the companion is perceived by the doctor to be required to check up on him or to intercept perceived unfairness, *e.g.* trick questions or rigorous physical examination: see *Hall v. Avon Area Health Authority (Teaching).*[83] If therefore a claimant wishes a companion to attend, the doctor can object to this in principle or to the nominated companion, and a court before imposing such a condition, even if the request is reasonable, requires a good or substantial reason for it. Normally, however, a court will not restrict a claimant's right to be accompanied to a physical examination and it is well-recognised by doctors and lawyers alike that claimants suffering from brain injury should be accompanied to assist in the provision of coherent answers. Any claimant "under a disability" will not be expected to attend unaccompanied. The need for this and the claimant's vulnerability are self-evident.[84]

Problems often arise where claimants with psychiatric/psychological conditions, request a companion and are refused. In *Hall*, Stephenson L.J. observed that:

> "If the plaintiff was in a nervous state or confused by a serious head injury, or if the defendants' nominated doctor had a reputation for a fierce examining manner . . . it might be reasonable for her solicitors to insist, for her, on such a condition."

In *Whitehead v. Avon County Council*[85], an orthopaedic surgeon reporting to the defendant, described the claimant's "illness behaviour" and "gross psychological problem". He recommended she be seen by a

---

[83] [1980] 1 W.L.R. 481; [1980] 1 All E.R. 516, CA. The court held it was unreasonable for a claimant to have his own medical expert to be present to be able to testify to the inaccuracy of the other expert's report should this issue arise.

[84] See the observations of Buckley J. in *Shaw v. Skeet & Ors* [1996] 7 Med. L.R. 371 that it was entirely reasonable to have a parent present at an examination of an infant.

[85] *The Times*, May, 3 1995; (1996) P.M.I.L.L., Vol. 9, p. 19; Nourse, Millett and Otton L.JJ.

psychiatrist and the plaintiff, a psychiatric nurse, agreed on condition that she was accompanied by a friend who was herself a nurse and a qualified psychological. The defendants refused and obtained a stay. On appeal to the judge in chambers the plaintiff relied upon an affidavit from her psychiatrist who had examined her in the presence of this friend. The psychiatrist maintained this was a common and acceptable practice but the defendant's expert contended that this would impede and detract from the quality of his own examination, and that it was not in any case his practice to work in that way. The stay was upheld and the plaintiff appealed to the Court of Appeal.

In his judgment Otton L.J. reviewed the case law and set out guidelines. These are:

(a) There can be no objection in principle to a friend or relative being present, citing the example of a nervous plaintiff when it would be preferable to have some other person present (see *Hall*[86]).

(b) Nonetheless, the insistence of the defendants' experts on seeing the plaintiff alone was "in accordance with established clinical practice, albeit not universally followed."

(c) Where (as in the instant case) both the defendant and plaintiff are being "reasonable" in their respective request and refusal, the issue was to be determined by "the exercise of judicial discretion, in which all relevant factors should be weighed up and a balance struck between the interest of the parties".

(d) A court should be slow to restrict a defendant's choice of expert when he has "a sound reputation . . . and is not eccentric".

There is nothing in Part 35 of the CPR or the Expert Witness Protocols to suggest that these guidelines are other than sound.

(ii) Attending with another doctor present. Sometimes the nominated companion is the claimant's own doctor and defendants often consent to this. Otherwise the test is still as with a non-medical companion and remains a matter for the court's discretion: the claimant does not have an automatic right to have his own doctor present when being examined by the defendant's doctor, and the court requires a substantial reason for such a condition being imposed. In these circumstances, however, a court is less likely to view the defendant's objections as being reasonable. Often the sensible compromise is for the parties to agree to a joint examination where both parties' experts attend. This has the added advantage of enabling the respective experts to reach agreement or to identify those

---

[86] [1980] 1 W.L.R. 481; [1980] 1 All E.R. 516, CA.

issues on which they cannot agree, and is very much in keeping with the spirit of the CPR which allows and encourages joint instructions to a single expert and meetings between experts.[87]

Comment

29–18   A balance has to be achieved between the integrity of professional men and the fact that "rogue" experts do exist where a party's concerns as to their probity are valid. As Stephenson L.J. observed in *Hall:* "all professions have their blacksheep and good men have 'off days'".

On the other hand:

> "Courts of law, as well as parties to litigation and their solicitors, must give a Fellow of the Royal College of Surgeons, of high standing in his profession . . . credit for being fair and considerate in his treatment of those whom he examines on behalf of the other side and fair and accurate in his recording of such examination, and for needing no third party, whether medically qualified or not, to prevent him from misleading the court by inaccuracies or . . . to restrain him from confusing the party examined by unfair interrogation."

In the seven years which have passed since *The Ikarian Reefer*, the duty and function of the expert have been considerably refined. The "hired gun" became extinct quite some time ago and it is encouraging to note that with the implementation of specific guidelines and protocols, together with direct involvement of case management, "rogue" experts are becoming rarer. However, in order to survive, an objective clinician must still be able to demonstrate his expertise and demonstrate a basic understanding of the legal framework in which he is working. This was emphasised recently in *Stevens v. Gullis (Pile, third party)*[88] where in a building case, the Court of Appeal took the opportunity of reinforcing the Woolf definition of an acceptable expert (see the Woolf "declaration" discussed above.)

On the assumption that increasingly the courts will demand compliance by experts with expert witness protocols and the Woolf "declaration", it is likely to become harder rather than easier in the future to seek to impose conditions. The obvious check on such behaviour would be the rights of privacy of the party to be examined, as conferred by Article 8 of the ECHR. However, Lord Woolf has made it abundantly clear that such "rights" will not be allowed to interfere with decision-making under the CPR for the purpose of pursuing the "overriding objective" to achieve justice: see *Daniels*, above.

---

[87]See CPR, Pt. 35.8 (instructions to a single joint expert) and Pt. 35.12 (discussions between experts). Further, para 6. of the Draft Guidelines on Experts Discussions prepared by the Clinical Disputes Forum in July 1999, concluded that following a meeting the experts must all sign an agreed statement, and this provision has been incorporated into the final version published in July 2000.

[88] *The Times*, October 6, 1999.

Psychiatric Examination

A distinction appears to have been made in *Whitehead* between psychi-   29–19
atric and other medical examinations. The judge at first instance seemed to
accept that a court would be slow to prevent a claimant being accompanied
to a physical examination and the Court of Appeal appears to have
endorsed this. However Otton L.J. acknowledged that a psychiatric
examination was reliant upon answers from the patient rather than on
objective physical symptoms: "If he feels that a correct diagnosis can only
be made on the basis of answers free from outside observation, that is
reasonable."

It is arguable, therefore, that in that case, the rights and choice of the
individual were placed second to the defendant's rights to investigate the
claim. This means that a claimant is denied choice in two respects:

(a) he is unlikely to be permitted a say in who examines him and
     thereby his consent—essential in all other areas of medicine—is
     neither sought nor required.

(b) he is not allowed a companion in this uneasy situation even though
     in the event of any dispute as to what may have occurred during the
     course of the examination, the doctor's version will almost invaria-
     bly be preferred to his own. Despite the observations of Otton L.J.
     in *Whitehead*[89] this is particularly likely to be the case where the
     examiner is a psychiatrist; indeed a psychiatrist may appreciate the
     present of a third party for his own protection against any subse-
     quent unfounded accusation of unfairness or impropriety. There is,
     unusually, no authority as to what is the position where the medical
     examiner seeks to have a third party present to whom the claimant
     objects: normally this is a nurse but one imagines a court would
     uphold as unreasonable a condition that the defendant's solicitor be
     present!

The decision in *Whitehead*, confirming that the reasonableness of such a
condition is entirely one for the court's discretion, means this remains an
area of uncertainty which will be richly fertile ground for applications
where both sides remain intransigent. It might be considered a reasonable
assumption that such applications will increase now that the Human Rights
Act is in force. This, however, is the very sort of time and costs-absorbing
interlocutory procedure which Lord Woolf wishes to dispense with[90].
Nothing is said at paragraph 35.2.3 concerning the attachment of conditions to the submission to a medical examination at the request of the

---

[89] *The Times*, May 3, 1995.
[90] See his observations in *Daniels v. Walker, The Times*, May 17, 2000, CA.

opposing party, and, therefore, clear guidance on the entire issue of conditional medical examinations is still required.

Prior to the introduction of the CPR, and in anticipation of the Woolf proposals, the courts increasingly assumed greater control over proceedings, and it was not uncommon for a court in a desire to speed up the process or enable a fixed trial date to stand, to order that a claimant be examined by a particular doctor before a specified date even though it was not known whether or not the doctor was free before that date; or indeed even where the court had expressly been told that the doctor had no available appointments before that date. Such orders have now become the norm although one questions the enforceability of such an order upon the third party doctor. However, it must be conceded that when such orders are made, doctors do tend to find that their otherwise full schedule has developed a convenient gap.

If objection is lodged, a detailed witness statement should be sworn setting out why the claimant requires the companion and this should preferably be supported by a statement from another doctor—perhaps the general practitioner—as to the reasonableness of this request in the given circumstances.

Refusal by a Defendant

29–20   Although it is undoubtedly true that in many cases the claimant may be submitting to examination or tests against his own will, it must be borne in mind that he has the ultimate decision whether or not to continue the action. Contrast, however, the situation where in the absence of a counterclaim for personal injuries, a defendant is compelled to submit to medical examination.

This is a novel and unusual situation which was considered by the Court of Appeal in *Cosgrove v. Baker*.[91] This claim arose out of a road traffic accident where the defendant's motor car had suddenly crossed onto the wrong side of the road and struck the plaintiff's van. The defendant relied upon "inevitable accident" by reason of having without prior warning suffered a myocardial infarction (heart attack) leading him to lose consciousness and control of his car. Initially the defendant objected to any medical examination but before the Court of Appeal, on appeal from Milmo J. it was submitted that the defendant was prepared to undergo medical examination on condition that no questions should be asked during that examination which might relate to the issue of liability. The Court of Appeal affirmed Milmo J.'s decision that the defendant submit himself to medical examination within 28 days on the basis that it "is now the well-established rule that a court can order a party in a personal injury action to submit to a medical examination", *per* Roskill L.J.

---

[91] Unreported, December 14, (1979) C.A. 744; Roskill & Templeman L.JJ.; Kemp & Kemp, *The Quantum of Damages*, Vol. 1, paras 15–039 and 15–211.

It is submitted, however, that a distinction should be drawn between the circumstances in *Cosgrove* and those in *Lacey*. In *Cosgrove* the defendant's medical condition was crucial because unless he could show he had a heart attack, he would be held liable. In *Lacey* on the other hand, his medical condition went to his recollection of events not to the facts of the accident. The plaintiff was therefore seeking to pre-empt evidential findings by establishing that on medical grounds the defendant could not realistically be expected to have recall of the material events.

On this analysis, the approach of Judge Dobry must be suspect, particularly in the current judicial climate: to strike out a defence is a draconian act. Such a sanction should only be imposed if the failure to comply is intentional and contumelious: *Re Jo Kai Tea Holdings Ltd.*[92]

Refusal to submit to medical examination is *not* contumelious conduct. In *Lacey* this could equally have been dealt with by a request for information under Part 19 of the CPR and discovery of medical records relating to the defendant's injuries in the accident,[93] as well as an order for early exchange of witness statements. It would then be open to the plaintiff to satisfy the court that the defendant was negligent.

It is submitted, therefore, that inherent in this rule is the concept that the party in question has suffered injury in respect of which he is seeking to recover damages "in a personal injury action". It therefore should not apply to the determination of liability alone: the invasion of the defendant's liberty is self-apparent and somewhat akin to the investigation of the "fitness to plead" of an accused in criminal proceedings.

Adopting the balancing exercise of "reasonableness" (*Whitehead*),[94] it is difficult to see how in these circumstances the plaintiff's request could be considered to be more reasonable than the defendant's refusal, or that without such an examination a just determination of the issue of liability could not be achieved.

It may be that if, in *Cosgrove*, the concession to submit on terms had not been made in the Court of Appeal, Roskill L.J. would not have been able to state "I do not think that this case raises any questions of law".[95] This point is elegantly argued at 15-041 onwards in Volume 1 of Kemp & Kemp and will repay close attention. The essential point, made clearly by Denning M.R. and Widgery L.J. in *Edmeades*[96] is that a court has no power to order a party to submit to a medical examination but it can grant a stay "whenever it is 'just and reasonable' to do so . . . if the conduct of the

---

[92] [1992] 1 W.L.R. 1196.
[93] See *Smith v. Ealing, Hammersmith & Hounslow Health Authority*, Unreported, May 1, 1997, where the Court of Appeal adopted this approach but refused to impose a stay upon the plaintiff's refusal to undergo a medical examination by the defendant's expert (above).
[94] *The Times*, May 3, 1995.
[95] *ibid.* Kemp & Kemp, *The Quantum of Damages*, para. 15–049.
[96] [1969] 2 All E.R. 127, CA. where the Court of Appeal drew attention to several alternatives to strike out under Part 3.4.

claimant in refusing a reasonable request is such as to prevent the just determination of the cause". In such a situation a claimant still has a choice whereas in *Cosgrove* he was given none other than to be in contempt of a court order or to have his defence struck out for breach of a peremptory order, which are far more draconian sanctions than a stay. However, although the power to strike out is specifically set out in the case management powers of the CPR (Part 3.4(2)(c)), the courts have, as a rule, been reluctant to invoke this sanction in the present climate where the overriding objective is to achieve justice (see *Biguzzi v. Rank Leisure plc*[97] and *Walsh v. Misseldene*[98]). In *Purdy v. Cambran*[99] the Court of Appeal explained the relevance of the former authorities on striking out for delay or non-compliance with a court order, in the light of *Biguzzi v. Rank Leisure plc*[1] (see too *Chapple v. Williams*[2], *Woodward v. Finch*[3] and *Habib Bank Ltd v. Jaffer*[4]). However, in *Arrow Nominees Incorporated v. Blackledge*[5] the Court mused that if the failure to comply with Rule, Practice Direction or Court Order has not rendered a fair trial impossible (*pace* refusing to submit to a medical examination may not be considered on the facts to be fatal to the defendant's case) an Order striking out a case even for contumacious breach is likely to be a breach of Article 6 of the European Convention on Human Rights and Fundamental Freedoms (1953, Cmd 8969) as being a breach of the Respondent's (claimant's) right to a determination of his civil rights and obligations at a fair and public hearing within a reasonable time by an independent tribunal.

It is possible, therefore, that decisions such as in *Lacey v. Harrison*[6] (where the court struck out a defence to a personal injuries action unless the defendant agreed to undergo a medical examination to investigate whether he was capable of remembering the accident, where he was the only witness for his pleaded defence) are now only of historic interest, although it is quite conceivable that a stay would be imposed in such circumstances.

Disclosure and Admissibility of Medical Reports

Disclosure

29–21   No party may call an expert or put in evidence an expert's report without the court's permission (Part 35.4(1) of the CPR). In seeking this permission, the party must identify the field in which he wishes to rely

---

[97] [1994] 1 W.L.R. 1926; [1999] 4 All E.R. 934, CA.
[98] [2000] All E.R. (D) 26, CA.
[99] December 17, 1999, CA unrep.
[1] *ibid.,* [1999] 1 W.L.R. 1926, CA.
[2] December 8, 1999, CA. unrep.
[3] December 8, 1999, CA. unrep.
[4] The Times, April 5, 2000 CA.
[5] December 8, 1999, Ch.D.
[6] [1993] P.I.Q.R. p. 10, Judge Dobry Q.C. sitting as a judge of the QBD.

upon expert evidence (Part 35.4(2)(a)) and, where practicable, identify the expert in that field on whose evidence he wishes to rely (35.4(2)(b)). A party who fails to disclose an expert's report may not use the report at the trial or call the expert to give evidence orally unless the court gives permission[7].

The CPR do not impose on a party who has obtained the court's permission to call an expert or put in evidence an expert's report, a duty to disclose that report. Until disclosed, therefore, an expert report is privileged from disclosure to any other party but that does not prevent that party calling the expert as a witness. This applies even where the report has been obtained upon order of the court overruling a party's refusal to submit to examination consent or imposition of conditions. *Previous practice* demanded reciprocity in circumstances where the claimant was ordered to submit to medical examination by a doctor nominated by a defendant and a stay was granted on terms that the defendant should provide the claimant with a copy of a report of that examination, and that the claimant should provide the defendant with copies of the medical reports on which he intended to rely. In *Clarke v. Martlew*[8], the defendants contended that such a condition was unreasonable. However, Denning M.R. held that fairness required that, if a defendant required a claimant to be medically examined, any report obtained should be disclosed, and a condition of reciprocity was therefore attached to the stay.

This approach was applied by Bean J. in *McGinlay v. Burke*[9] who, whilst accepting that the plaintiff did not have to disclose *all* his reports, stated:

> " . . . the plaintiff must at least offer reciprocity. If his advisers require to see a copy of the defendant's medical report as a condition of a particular examination, they must be prepared to offer in exchange their own equivalent medical report upon which they propose to rely . . . there must be fairness between the parties."

It is this "fairness between the parties" which Lord Woolf seeks to enforce and it is no longer unusual for the letter of claim sent pursuant to the personal injury or other protocols, to be accompanied by all of the medical reports which the claimant has obtained and on which he intends to rely. This is particularly so where such letter contains a claimant's Part 36 offer. Nonetheless, neither Lord Woolf nor the CPR go so far as the reciprocity advocated by Lord Denning and Bean J. Indeed, in *Megarity v. D.J. Ryan & Sons Ltd*,[10] the Court of Appeal disapproved the *Clarke v. Martlew* line of authority which led to the position laid down in the RSC Ord. 38. rr. 36 *et seq*. prior to the implementation of the CPR in April 1999.

---

[7] CPR, Pt. 35.13.
[8] [1973] 1 Q.B. 58, CA.
[9] [1973] 1 W.L.R. 990.
[10] [1980] 2 All ER 832, CA.

The position was reviewed by the Court of Appeal in *Hookham v. Wiggins Teape*[11] where the claimant sought to argue that she should only be ordered to submit to a further medical examination if the defence were ordered to disclose the report obtained following that examination. The Court of Appeal held that the rules have to draw a careful balance between the need to disclose in advance experts' evidence on which a party intends to rely at trial and the importance of preserving legal or professional privilege in respect of evidence obtained by a party in the course of preparing for the trial but which he decides not to use. The imposition of the condition by the judge required the defendant to waive legal professional privilege and flew in the face of the rule that a party is only under an obligation to disclose those reports upon which it intends to rely at trial.

Interestingly, though, in a dissenting judgment, Butler-Sloss L.J. held that in certain circumstances a court may be entitled to order that an action be stayed until the claimant submits to a medical examination upon condition a copy of the report is supplied to the claimant. This is a dangerous precedent which may gain currency in the present Lupine procedural climate.

However, although the court's case management powers are far more extensive now in relation to expert reports, there is, as yet, no authority to suggest that the guidelines to the former RSC Ord. 38, r. 36 are being disregarded. On the contrary, the addition of paragraph 35.2.3. suggests that these guidelines remain entirely appropriate.

Present Practice does not demand reciprocity and thus it is not appropriate to impose any condition as to disclosure on the grant of an application by the defendant that the action be stayed until the claimant submits to a medical examination on behalf of the defendant. If thereafter the defendant wishes to rely upon that report, he will have to apply to the court for permission to do so. Disclosure will normally be mutual and simultaneous although sequential disclosure is increasingly being ordered where the reports relate to quantum issues only (see below).

The Requirement for Mutuality

29–22   The practice of sequential disclosure whereby the defendants' medical evidence could be prepared in full awareness of the manner in which the claimant pleaded his case, was ruled unacceptable in a series of decisions including *Naylor v. Preston Area Health Authority*[12]. Thereafter, the rule was for mutual and simultaneous exchange of reports on a fixed date, and this was expressly provided for in the Rules of the Supreme Court in the subsequent October 1, 1987 amendment to RSC Ord. 38.[13]

---

[11] [1995] P.I.Q.R. P392, CA.
[12] [1987] 1 W.L.R. 958; [1987] 2 All E.R. 353, CA.
[13] See *Supreme Court Practice 1988*.

The exercise of case management powers post CPR, however, has made considerable inroads into the principle established in *Naylor*. It is now common for masters and district judges to order sequential disclosure, particularly of quantum reports, requiring the claimant to disclose and append all of his quantum reports to the schedule of past and future loss. So wide-reaching are the powers on case management that there is little to gainsay this approach. In some cases it undoubtedly does result in the saving of costs and it is unlikely that in the present judicial claimant, an appeal on the "mutuality" point would succeed.[14] The overriding objective of "achieving justice" tends to give short shrift to any procedural niceties on the fairness of mutual exchange

This can, however, be turned to the parties' advantage if agreement can be reached as to joint instruction of a single expert on such issues as accommodation, employment, speech therapy and so on (see the facts of *Daniels* (above)). However, the practical result is that much of the clinical evidence, *e.g.* as to life expectancy is also ordered to be disclosed sequentially and, paradoxically, this tends to produce the very unfairness which the Court of Appeal sought to redress in *Naylor*.

The Position After Disclosure

It must be borne in mind that reports, once served, become part of the **29–23** statement of case and thus expose the party to a number of procedural tactics. The other side are entitled to inspect any document referred to in the report unless privilege can be pleaded. Similarly, if that document incorporates other documents by reference, these are prima facie disclosable even if they are considered to be highly confidential, *e.g.* a confidential internal memorandum concerning a patient.

---

[14] See Practice Direction—Appeal—Explanation and guidance on new provisions governing civil appeals in private law matters: *Tanfern Ltd v. Cameron-MacDonald* [2000] 2 All E.R. 801, CA, where it was held that under new provisions governing civil appeals in private law matters which came into effect on May 2, 2000, "an appeal court . . . will, as a general rule, only allow an appeal where the decision of the lower court was wrong, or where it was unjust because of a serious procedural or other irregularity. Moreover, the Court of Appeal will only hear a second appeal if it considers that such an appeal will raise an important point of principle or practice or that there is some other compelling reason to do so. Accordingly, the decision of the 'first instance judge in what used to be called an 'interlocutory appeal will assume a much greater importance than under the old procedure in which the judge in chambers' conducted a complete rehearing, with an entirely fresh discretion to exercise and the decision of the appeal court, whether a circuit judge or a High Court judge, is in most cases now likely to be final. Those changes will compel litigants and their advisers to pay even greater attention to the need to prepare their cases with appropriate care because they may now find it much more difficult to extricate themselves from the consequences of an ill-prepared case before a judge at first instance in a lower court", *per* Lord Woolf M.R., Peter Gibson and Brooke L.JJ. Note also that from May 2, 2000 appeals from the county court (other than in family proceedings) will mostly lie to the High Court rather than the Court of Appeal (Art. 3(1)) Access to Justice Act 1999 (Destination of Appeals) Order 2000 (S.I. 2000 No. 1071).

Procedure

29–24 This is governed by the CPR and has already been covered in earlier discussion in this Chapter.

The "achievement of justice" is the overriding objective and it has already been discussed how this has effectively relegated "mutuality" to the sidelines in terms of disclosure of quantum reports. In relation to the medical evidence on the substantive issues, however, where possible, it is sensible to invite the court to order mutual exchange as this prevents either side from merely preparing a negative critique of the other side's report. It is submitted that the overriding objective is unlikely to be achieved in a situation where one party can compel the disclosure of a report from an opposite party without *at the same time* disclosing his own expert evidence to that party or being precluded from calling such expert evidence at the trial. Indeed Part 16 (statements of case) makes specific provision for a party to disclose supporting medical evidence where his pleaded case differs from that of the opposing party.[15]

The only *exceptions* to this rule are:

(a) where legal professional privilege is waived;

(b) in Part 16.4, Practice Direction, paragraph 4.3 whereby in personal injury actions the claimant is now required to serve his medical evidence with his Particulars of Claim[16]; and

(c) where special circumstances render it proper and fair for there to be sequential disclosure, *e.g.* where the area of inquiry goes back many years and involves investigation of the claimant's various working conditions and the state of knowledge about the consequences of particular activities: see *Kirkup v. British Rail Engineering Ltd*[17].

But all of these are subject to the extensive case management powers under the CPR. The claimant should still therefore beware of the defendant applying for an examination *after* the time laid down for exchange of witness statements and expert reports. Applications for a stay in such circumstances should be strenuously resisted and are unlikely to succeed in the post-Woolf era of early investigations of claims and identification of the issues: see *Maloney v. Regan*[18] where six weeks before the hearing the defendant requested medical examination of the plaintiff, the late request being explained by a mistaken belief by the solicitor that the defendant's

---

[15] See Pt. 16.5(2)(b) and Practice Direction to Pt. 16, para. 13.1.
[16] Previously RSC, Ord. 18, r. 12(1A) and CCR, Ord. 6, r. 1(5)(a) and 1(b)(a) and (b).
[17] [1983] 1 W.L.R. 165; [1983] 3 All E.R. 147, CA.
[18] (1993) April 23, Central London C.C., District Judge Litchfield, P.M.I.L.L. Vol. [*complete*] p. 52.

insurers had arranged such examination some six months earlier. The plaintiff refused and upon the defendant's application to stay, it was argued that the report could be produced and served in good time for the hearing. The court ruled that the application was too late and although an appeal against this decision was lodged, the case was settled before this could be argued.

At the case management conference following the filing of the statement of case an order is likely to be made for the expert medical evidence of each party to be disclosed in the form of a written report which shall be agreed if possible (Part 35.5(1) of the CPR and the Personal Injury Protocol). If the claim is on the fast track, the court will not direct an expert to attend a hearing unless it is necessary to do so in the interests of justice. Part 35.1 imposes upon the court a duty to restrict expert evidence to "that which is reasonably required to resolve the proceedings" and Part 35.4 sets out the court's powers in this regard. These include reducing the incidence of inappropriate use of experts to bolster cases.[19]

The overriding objective, therefore, is fairness and what is perceived to be in the interests of justice: see *Mortgage Corporation Ltd v. Sandoes*[20] and *Hill v. William Tomkins Ltd*,[21] settlement and mediation being the ultimate goals, tempered by speedy processing of claims.

Evidential Status of Medical Reports

In *Bryant v. London Fire and Civil Defence Authority*[22] the claimant **29–25** fireman suffered soft tissue injuries when a fire appliance was reversed into him. In orthopaedic terms he was able to return to work normally after six months but he claimed he had suffered a psychiatric disorder. This was disputed but there was no suggestion he was a malingerer. The medical evidence from four psychiatrists led the judge to conclude that the claimant had not suffered from a post-traumatic stress disorder but he had suffered from psychiatric symptoms which the judge referred to as "anxiety" arising from the accident and the anxiety caused by prosecuting the claim against the Fire Brigade and his attempts to leave the Fire Brigade.

The Brigade appealed contending that the judge had fallen into error in awarding compensation beyond that attributable to the claimant's physical injuries and substituting "anxiety" for a true psychiatric condition. In any event, it was admitted that the evidential status of the medical reports relied upon was so unclear that a new trial should be ordered.

The Court of Appeal, allowing the appeal, held that if there was evidence that the psychiatric injury had been directly caused to the

---

[19] *Gumpo v. Church of Scientology Religious Education College Inc.* unreported, July 26, 1999. For more detailed discussion of these case management powers, see *Experts* Chapter and generally *Civil Procedure*, Vol. 1, The White Book Service 2000, 35.1.1.

[20] [1997] P.N.I.R. 263, CA.

[21] [1997] P.I.Q.R. P115, CA.

[22] [1995] P.I.Q.R. P27.

respondent short of the well-recognised condition of PTSD, then the judge would still have been justified in giving judgment for the respondent. However, it was impossible to divorce the respondent's psychiatric report that whatever disorder afflicted the respondent it was directly referable to the accident from the whole context of the expert's opinion which was rejected by the judge.

It is confusion of this nature which the expert witness protocols and the overriding duty of the expert to the court (Part 35.3) seek to avoid.

The independence of the judge in determining the weight to be attached to expert medical evidence was further reinforced in *Vernon v. Bosley (No.2)* where Stuart Smith L.J. observed, *per curiam*:

"The role of the expert medical witnesses is to inform the judge so as to guide him to the correct conclusions. It must be for the judge to gauge the weight and usefulness of such assistance as he is given and to reach his own conclusions accordingly. Expert witnesses are armed with the court's readiness to receive the expert evidence which it needs in order to reach a fully informed decision, whatever the nature of the topic may be, but their evidence ceases to be useful, and it may become counter-productive, when it is not marshalled by reference to the issues in the particular case and kept within the limits so fixed."

Reliance on Another Party's Report

29–26   There is no property in a witness and a party is therefore entitled to rely upon evidence disclosed by the opposing party. This can either be:

(a) by agreement with the opposing party; or

(b) by notice of intention to rely upon it as hearsay given under the Civil Evidence Act 1968 and subordinate rules of the court; or

(c) by the leave of the court in the form of deposition or witness statement; or

(d) by calling the maker.

If none of these procedures is followed, the courts are increasingly prepared to exercise their discretion to exclude such evidence: see, *e.g. Winchester Cigarette Machinery Co. Ltd v. Payne.*[23] However, the provisions of the Civil Evidence Act 1994 have widened considerably the scope of judicial discretion to admit hearsay evidence, and what evidence, hitherto excluded, will now be deemed to be receivable and admissible.

Reliance on the opposing party's evidence may become essential if, for example, the claimant or defendant's expert has failed to attend court or shortly before trial has changed his opinion. Often too, defendants are

---

[23] *The Times*, October 19, 1993.

driven to this tactic where they have been debarred from adducing their own medical evidence, and they are able to do so by virtue of the provisions of CPR Part 35.11 which provides that: "Where a party has disclosed an expert's report, any party may use that expert's report as evidence at the trial.[24]" Again, this is entirely consistent with the new culture of court-appointed experts and the overriding duty of the expert to the court.[25]

There is no requirement that in order to put such a report in evidence, it has to be agreed or the maker be called: see *Clarke v. LFCDA*[26] where the claimant without agreeing the defendant's engineer's report or calling the maker, relied upon the report to extent where it conceded primary liability for the accident without thereby accepting that part of the report which asserted a significant element of contributory negligence. This course was permitted by the judge who held that the terms of the Rule were quite clear and unambiguous.[27] This, too, is the understanding of the Woolf Committee who have specifically provided for use by one party of an expert report disclosed by another (Rule 35.11).

The Impact of Woolf and the Civil Procedure Rules

Although a medical examination represents a substantial part of a **29–27** personal injury case, medico-legal reports, prepared expressly for the purposes of litigation, are often based on examinations carried out a considerable time after the accident. It is in part this delay which was addressed by Woolf with emphasis upon the early instruction of experts and has been reflected in CPR. The overriding objective is intended to place the parties on an equal footing, saving costs and dealing with the case proportionately to the amount of money involved, the importance of the case, the complexity of the issues and the parties' financial position, ensuring the case is dealt with expeditiously taking full account of financial and court resource allocation.

The emphasis is upon early identification of the issues and facilitating and encouraging settlement or alternative dispute resolution (ADR). The general powers of management are set out at Part 3 and includes a stay (3.1(1)(f)) and (m) "take any other step or . . . order for the purpose of managing the case and furthering the overriding objective".

Requirements of a Medical Report and the Maker

The function of the report and the maker is to assist the court and the **29–28** provisions of Part 35 reflect the views expressed in Lord Woolf's Report[28]:

---

[24] Former RSC, Ord. 38, r. 42.
[25] For further discussion of the changing role of experts post-Woolf, see *The Expert and his Evidence*, Dr Walter Scott 2000 New Law Journal, May 26, 2000, p. 792.
[26] [1992] CLY.
[27] See generally "Using Opponents Expert Evidence", Allan Gore in Bulletin No. 35, July 1996, *Butterworth's Personal Injury Litigation Service*.
[28] Interim Report, Chap. 23; Final Report, chap. 13.

"There is widespread agreement with the criticisms I made in the interim report of the way in which expert evidence is used at present, especially the point that experts sometimes take on the role of partisan advocates instead of neutral fact finders and opinion givers.[29]"

Reference was made to the Court of Appeal in *Abbey National Mortgages plc v. Kerry Surveyors Nationwide Ltd and Ors*[30] where the Court of Appeal remarked:

"For whatever reason, and whether consciously or unconsciously, the fact is that expert witnesses instructed on behalf of parties to litigation often tend . . . to espouse the cause of those instructing them to a grater or lesser extent, on occasion becoming more partisan than the parties.[31]"

The intention is for the court to have complete control over the use of evidence using experts as independent advisers to the court and thereby countering allegations of lack of objectivity.

Part 35.10 of the CPR and Chapter 13, *Expert Evidence*, sets out the requirements for the content of an expert report addressing the problems of:

- the inclusion of irrelevant material;
- partisan views;
- straying beyond the field of professional competence;
- failure to address the real issues.

These matters are remarkably similar to those which are already addressed by experienced personal injury practitioners and which are set out earlier in this chapter at "*The Structure of the Report*".

It would seem therefore in the brave new world of civil litigation post-Woolf that the fears of bias and other objections which have conventionally led to refusal or the imposition of conditions upon examination by an opposing party's expert, are to become spectres of the past, deemed by the new case manager judges to be adequately addressed by providing that an expert must address his report to the court and not to any person from whom he has received instructions.

The Impact of the Human Rights Act 1998

29–29   The Human Rights Act 1998 received Royal Assent in November 1999 and came into force on October 2, 2000. Already, however, courts and public authorities have had regard to this and a massive increase in applications for judicial review is now anticipated.

---

[29] The Woolf Report: ACCESS TO JUSTICE, s.III, chap. 13.5.
[30] [1996] E.G.C.S. 23, CA.
[31] Chap. 13.26, *ibid.*

This Act incorporates the Articles of the ECHR. In considering the impact of this Act on the requirements for medical examination, reference should also be made to the parallel section in Chapter 25, *"Video Evidence."*

If a health authority or NHS Trust seeks a medical examination they will encounter the further difficulty that as a public authority section 6 of the Human Rights Act directly imposes upon them compliance with the European Convention on Human Rights 1953. Such compliance will also extend to bodies such as the Medical Protection Society and the Medical Defence Union, as well as insurance companies demanding such examination on behalf of defendants in road traffic accidents, industrial injury claims and class actions.

More recently it has been argued that the "horizontal" effect of the Human Rights Act as interpreted in recent case law from the European Court of Human Rights, leads to the ineluctable conclusion that the court accepts the conceptual possibility that the actions of private parties may comprise a violation of rights. Thus the way is open to the horizontal use of section 6 of the Act.[32]

There are two Convention rights which fall to be considered in this context: Article 6: the right to a fair trial and Article 8: the right to respect for a private and family life. The defendant will seek to rely upon the former and the claimant will invoke the latter.

Article 6 is a very powerful right: in *Moreiva de Azedo v. Portugal*[33] the court held that the "right to a fair trial holds so prominent a place in a democratic society that there can be no justification for interpreting Article 6(1) restrictively". This too appears to have been the view of the court in *Arrow Nominees Incorporated v. Blackledge*[34]

Yet when balancing the conflicting rights and prejudices of the parties in a request for a medical examination and the defendant's right to a fair trial, the justification arguably lies in Article 8, the right to respect for a private and family life? Moreover, there could be circumstances where the claimant could argue that the infringement of his privacy under Article 8 had the secondary effect of depriving *him* of a fair trial.

Whilst it has always been acknowledged that each side should have a reasonable opportunity to present its case without being at a significant disadvantage, the courts have equally accepted that a balancing exercise is required as between the respective parties' rights and interests. Equally, what is meant by "significant"? How essential is a yet further examination when there is objective medical assessment in the form of contemporaneous medical records and other expert reports?

---

[32] See Gareth Davies, *The "horizontal" effect of the Human Rights Act*, (2000) New Law Journal, p. 839 (June 2, 2000).
[33] (1990) 30 E.H.R.R. 721.
[34] *ibid.*

The "right" under Article 8 of the ECHR is "qualified" and *prima facie* interference with that right may be justified if it can be demonstrated that:

(a) the interference is "lawful";

(b) the interference serves a legitimate purpose;

(c) the interference is "necessary in a democratic society"; and

(d) the interference is not discriminatory.

"Fairness" is an undoubted tenet of these qualifications and the fairness of a hearing under Article 6 may depend on giving each party a fair opportunity to test the evidence of the other side.

Section 2 of the Act requires the court to have regard to existing caselaw—and *Edmeades* is an obvious example of this. However, the Act is also to be interpreted as a "living instrument" and thus, when weighing the individual merits of each case, caselaw is likely to provide little guidance. Ben Emmerson, Editor of HRLO observed that we will have to "engage in a form of lateral thinking in which precedent and established practice gives way to a superior system of constitutional human rights law."

The Respective Rights under Articles 6 and 8

29–30 It is axiomatic that in a democratic society, privacy remains the basic right of citizens. John Locke stated that "Every Man has a Property in his own Person. This no Body has any Right to but himself" and it is from this school of thought that laws concerning consent to medical treatment and examination have emerged. However, no right is absolute and all rights conflict with the rights of others.

There is an apparent conflict between a party's right to respect of his private and family life under Article 8 in his refusal to undergo a medical examination, and a party's right to a fair trial under Article 6 which requires such an examination to take place in order properly to test the opponent's case. A delicate balancing exercise would therefore seem to be required in order to meet the overriding objective under the CPR "to achieve justice".

It has been stated that the courts will be expected to interpret all legislation in a manner compatible with the Convention even where the dispute is between individuals.[35] Accordingly, until the recent decision in *Daniels v. Walker*, the expectation of most practitioners was that under the CPR the courts would take a pragmatic and sensible view and interpret Article 8(1) as providing a right which is qualified in the sense that it has to

---

[35] See the Lord Chancellor's address to the House of Lords in *Hansard*, col. 783 (November 24, 1997).

be seen and interpreted in context. Thus, as before, it would not be enough for the defendant to show that "interference" by subjecting a claimant to medical examination is "desirable" but "necessary" to achieve justice. This is entirely consistent with the "overriding objective" of the CPR.

In this regard it is interesting to note that in relation to public authorities, Article 8(2) provides that the public authority may only interfere in this right "in accordance with the law and (as) necessary in a democratic society in the interests of national security, public safety . . . for the protection of health or morals or for the protection of the rights and freedoms of others"

Using that proviso as a guide to interpretation of Article 8(1) a defendant may respectably argue that he has a right to be liable and/or to pay only that which is reasonable in accordance with established legal principles: in that case Article 8(1) should be interpreted so as to enable him to obtain evidence which will help him to achieve those aims. *i.e.* evidence that the claimant is "malingering".

However, Lord Woolf has recently made it very clear that the court should be "robust" in rejecting submissions based on Human Rights Act "rights" in arriving at case management decisions under the CPR. *Daniels v. Walker*[36] concerned the defendant's application for permission to instruct his own expert in the same discipline as a jointly instructed single expert who had already reported. The skeleton argument contained reference to the right to a fair trial under Article 6 of the ECHR. Lord Woolf observed:

"Article 6 has no possible relevance to this appeal. Quite apart from the fact that the (HR) Act is not in force, if the court is not going to be taken down blind alleys it is essential that counsel, and those who instruct counsel, take a responsible attitude as to when it is right to raise a HR point . . . Article 6 could not possibly have anything to add to the issue on this appeal. The provisions of the CPR . . . make it clear that the obligation on the court is to deal with cases justly. If having agreed to a joint expert's report a party subsequently wishes to call, evidence, and it would be unjust having regard to the overriding objective . . . not to allow that evidence, they must be allowed to call it . . . Expert issues are frequently determined on the basis of a court expert and the parties have to put up with it in the majority of situations. No-one suggests that the way matters are conducted in civil jurisdictions could contravene Article in the normal manner, nor could the proper use of the CPR . . . It would be unfortunate if case management decisions in this jurisdiction involved the need to refer to the learning of the European Court on Human Rights in order for them to be resolved. In my judgment, such cases as this do not require any consideration of HR issues, certainly issues under Article 6. It would be highly undesirable if the consideration of those issues was made more complex by the injection into them of Article 6 style arguments. I hope that judges will be robust in resisting any attempt to introduce those arguments."

---

[36] *The Times*, May 17, 2000, CA.

It would seem, therefore, that the jury remains out on what impact, if any, the Human Rights Act has—or will be permitted to have—upon decisions made pursuant to the CPR concerning the requirements for medical examination and the judicial balancing of the respective rights of the parties.

APPENDIX

FURTHER INFORMATION

Reports

European Human Rights Reports (EHRR) Decisions and Reports of the European Commission of Human Rights. (These are available from the libraries at Lincoln's Inn, Middle Temple and Gray's Inn.)	Sweet & Maxwell (DR)

Periodicals

European Human Rights Law Review (EHRLR)	Sweet & Maxwell
Human Rights Alerter	Sweet & Maxwell

Textbooks

Kier Starmer, European Human Rights Law Archbold, Chapter 16	LAG 1999
Wadham & Mountfield, Blackstones Guide to the Human Rights Act 1998 Lester & Pannick (eds), Human Rights Law and Practice	Butterworths 1999
D.J. Harris, M. O'Boyle and C. Warbrick, Law of the European Convention on Human Rights	Butterworths 1995

Some Website Addresses

www.beagle.org.uk/echr

www.dhcour.coe.fr/hudoc/default.asp

30. Video Evidence

Introduction

Video (televisual) evidence and the reports of Inquiry Agents are 30–01 increasingly being used in personal injury litigation: by claimants to demonstrate the extent of the disability and their needs resultant upon the material injury and by defendants to discredit the claimant's claim by showing to the court that the injuries are not as severe as the claimant may contend, that there is a functional overlay or that the claimant is frankly malingering.

In this Chapter it is proposed to examine:

(a) the admissibility of video evidence;

(b) the purpose of video evidence;

(c) when to use video evidence;

(d) the preparation of video evidence;

(e) the disclosure of video evidence;

(f) tactics for meeting video evidence;

(g) video evidence and the Civil Procedure Rules;

(h) the impact of the Human Rights Act.

Unless otherwise stated, "video evidence" encompasses "televisual evidence" and the written reports of Inquiry Agents.

The Admissibility of Video Evidence

Video evidence from either party is receivable in evidence following 30–02 prior disclosure unless a court is satisfied that there are special reasons to sanction non-disclosure before trial: Part 33.6 of the Civil Procedure Rules (CPR), previously RSC, Ord. 38, r. 5 (see *Disclosure* below). The maker must be available to give oral evidence if called upon to do so. More often than not, however, the claimant's legal advisers will agree that the video can be shown without the oral evidence of the maker, but seek to place a different interpretation upon it to that of the defence. Similar considerations apply to videos relied upon by claimants, but the emotional and legal problems created by covert surveillance do not arise in that situation.

More often than not, video evidence resulting from covert surveillance is fairly inconclusive: it is rare for a case to collapse entirely when a video film is disclosed. Nonetheless, it is sometimes of assistance for the medical experts on both sides to see how a particular claimant is walking or generally behaving away from the doctor's eye; sometimes this evidence can rebound on the defence if the claimant's medical expert is able to state authoritatively that the claimant's demeanour is consistent with the injury of which complaint is made.

Video surveillance evidence, however, is generally viewed as being somewhat distasteful, representing as it does, a significant invasion of the claimant's privacy particularly where any allegations of "malingering" prove to be without foundation. This aspect is particularly significant with the advent of the Human Rights Act 1998 which was fully implemented on October 2, 2000 (see *The Impact of the Human Rights Act* below). Increasingly, therefore, the courts' approach is that to be admissible in evidence, a video film and any Inquiry Agent's reports must be disclosed to the claimant before trial to give him an opportunity to consider the content, weigh the impact upon the merits of the case and determine how such evidence should be countered.

The Purpose of Video Evidence

30–03   Historically, visual aids have seldom been used by claimants in personal injury litigation: video evidence has largely been confined to rebuttal evidence adduced by defendants to demonstrate that a claimant is malingering or exaggerating. These visual aids, however, are increasingly useful in demonstrating the claimant's condition and prognosis; they give a developed impression of the reality of the claimant's condition and a graphic illustration of how the injuries and their sequelae have affected every aspect of the claimant's daily life and that of his family.

Claimants view covert video surveillance as unhelpful and unwarrantably intrusive, but defendants' insurers justify the often nefarious process of obtaining video evidence as an objective means of presenting the court either with unequivocal evidence of malingering or, in the absence of such evidence, with a balanced view of how a claimant is coping with his disability thereby going some way towards assisting the court in the assessment of all major heads of damages. In particular, in the larger claims, attention is focused not so much on general damages for pain, suffering and loss of amenity but upon past and future loss claims for earnings, care needs, domestic assistance, accommodation requirements and so forth.

Moreover, if malingering can be demonstrated, this has the additional advantage of seriously throwing into doubt the claimant's credibility as a witness on other issues including matters of liability.

30–04   Sometimes, video evidence is specifically aimed at liability issues, *e.g.* to show that a claimant was prepared to drink and drive on occasions subsequent to the accident and therefore had probably been prepared to do so on the occasion in question.

Increasingly, video evidence has come to be seen by defendants as an essential weapon in their armoury particularly where the claim carries a significant damages potential. The complexity of many back-injury claims, for example, where claimants additionally allege severe or almost complete incapacity by reason of Chronic Pain Syndrome and/or a Post Traumatic Stress Disorder, takes the medical evidence outwith the expertise of the orthopaedic and neurological experts into the more esoteric realm of psychology and psychiatry. So often such a development is viewed by insurers as a respectable gloss for malingering and they feel compelled to include video evidence in their preparation of the defence: malingering is no longer an element merely to be considered as part of an overall assessment, it now needs to be specifically excluded. Otherwise, many insurers will frankly not entertain these high claims, considering them to be fanciful and lacking an empirically established clinical foundation. There is a new intransigence towards "functional overlay" and "factitious symptomatology", leading to many more of these claims being contested.

Even in the present climate where, in accordance with Lord Woolf's recommendations, the Civil Procedure Rules actively encourage conciliation, mediation and compromise, there is little yielding in this stance in most insurers' claims departments. Indeed, this attitude is likely to become more rather than less entrenched with conditional fee agreements (CFAs) becoming commonplace following the withdrawal of legal aid from personal injury claims. This is particularly so now that the success fee and insurance premium are recoverable from the defendant.

When to Use Video Evidence

By the Claimant

In catastrophic injury claims and other injuries of maximum severity, a   30–05
well-prepared video sensitively and clearly demonstrating the impact of grievous injury upon a claimant, his family and carers, can assist considerably in the presentation of the case for trial, and make a significant difference to the quantification of a claim.

Where disclosed at an early stage a video will often result in an early and sensible settlement.

(i) The Advantages
These include: 30–06

    (a) The provision of a valuable insight into a day in the life of a catastrophically injured claimant with a clear demonstration of the daily difficulties encountered in mobility and in coping with the normal tasks of dressing, eating, exercise, etc., as well as the demands the handicap place on his carers.

(b) Assistance in persuading the court as to the appropriateness or a particular therapy or item of equipment, where this is disputed by the defendant: in *Coram (A Minor) v. Cornwall & Isles of Scilly HA*,[1] the claimant's physiotherapy expert recommended a small hydrotherapy treatment pool in the infant claimant's home as being medically advisable, and produced a documentary video film about hydrotherapy. The settlement figures approved by Tucker J. included provision for hydrotherapy and it is undoubtedly the case that the explanatory video led to the acceptance by the defence of the therapeutic need for this equipment. Since then hydrotherapy pools have been allowed in a number of cases, often by agreement. In another unreported case, a demonstration video about guide-dogs led to damages including the cost of obtaining, training and keeping a guide-dog.

(c) Assistance in demonstrating to the court certain technical procedures: in *Penney, Palmer and Cannon v. East Kent Health Authority*,[2] there was an alleged failure to spot abnormalities in the claimants' smear tests and to report those smears as at least borderline. A video was successfully used to demonstrate the system of histopathology-cytoscreening of smear tests for cervical cancer and, how if properly used, abnormal smears should not have been missed by the defendants.[3]

(d) Where a claimant is grievously injured, avoiding the need for him to attend court. This is particularly so where the claimant is not capable of preparing a witness statement or of giving oral evidence.

(e) Where it is anticipated that the claimant will be unlikely to survive until the date of trial, either by reason of the accident injury or otherwise. A video can be made in which the claimant sets out the circumstances giving rise to the negligence claim and which serves as

---

[1] April 16, 1996, Tucker J. reported in A.P.I.L. *Newsletter*, Vol. 6, issue 4, p. 15.

[2] [1999] M.I.C. 126 CA, Lord Woolf M.R. Lord Justice May and Lady Justice Hale.

[3] Other countries have shown a greater readiness to rely upon videos in this context than in England: *Denzin v. The Nutrasweet Company & Others* [1999] Medical Litigation Cases 70 (Australia, The Supreme Court of New South Wales (Common Law Division) Bruce J., February 22, 1999, was a very large product liability claim concerning intrauterine contraceptive (IUD) devices and an alleged link with pelvic inflammatory disease. The plaintiffs relied upon epidemiology, scientific analysis and clinical observations. They were unsuccessful and it may be instructive to note that the defendant's expert relied on video evidence of the IUD device and the fine copper wire which was considered to be the irritant. The video showed movement of the tail string but that the forces involved were insufficient to account for the alleged problems.

a visual proof of evidence. A video can also be used for quantum purposes, poignantly describing the effect of the accident upon the claimant and his family and what impact the knowledge of likely premature death has had upon his quality of life: see *Rose v. Duke*[3a] where in a clinical negligence claim brought by the widower, a 49 year old breast cancer victim made a videotape before her death describing the circumstances in which the missed diagnosis was made. She also described the impact upon her and her family of the knowledge that she only had a very short time to live, and the awareness that the defendant's misdiagnosis had resulted in the loss of a "window of opportunity" which with proper treatment would probably have resulted in a further ten years of life.

(f) Disclosure of the video can be accompanied by a claimant's "offer to settle": under Part 36 of the Civil Procedure Rules.[4] This may be the necessary prompt for a sensible compromise of the claim and may also be of assistance in the conferring between quantum experts that is now frequently ordered at the Case Management Conference.[5]

If either party intends to show a video as evidence, he must inform the court and provide the other party with a copy of the video or the opportunity to see it (if he asks) at least three weeks before the hearing. The court may decide not to take account of this evidence if these directions are not complied with: CPR Part 33.6(3) (see *Disclosure* below).

(ii) The Disadvantages

Editing of videos may, even unwittingly, present a distorted picture. 30–07 Wherever possible, therefore, a claimant should attend court in person and expand upon the matters shown in the video if called upon to do so. This also allows the defence to cross-examine upon the video and thus pre-empt adverse comment that the portrayal of the claimant is not accurate. Copies of all unedited film should be retained for production to the defence or the court, if so required.

Most judges are aware of the difficulties posed by careful editing, and in attaching weight to a video, do so in the context of the evidence of the various medical witnesses, including those instructed by the defence, as well as to the claimant's witness evidence from friends and relatives.

By the Defendant

Video evidence should not be considered in every serious personal injury 30–08 claim, but is likely to be of assistance where it is believed the claimant is malingering or exaggerating the effect of the injury, or not giving credit for

---

[3a] [2000] Medical Litigation Cases 0208 (June), Elizabether Steel J.
[4] Section III, Chap. 11, *Offers to Settle*.
[5] See CPR Part 35.12.

alternative earnings or earning capacity when maintaining a claim for loss of earnings or that he was compelled to take early retirement. It is also useful in providing a realistic picture of the likely care requirements where the claimant has presented a "Rolls Royce" package.

The suspicion of malingering is likely to arise in the following situations:

(a) Where there is an unresolved conflict on the findings of respective medical experts. A typical case is where a claimant has suffered a back injury and where the medical reports of one or both sides may comment upon the absence of organic findings supporting a complaint of disability which appears to be disproportionate to the apparently relatively minor nature of the original injury.

(b) Where the medical records, in particular those pre-accident, raise doubts as to whether certain symptoms and an alleged incapacity are entirely attributable to the accident. Using again the example of a back injury, claimants frequently deny any previous back problems whereas pre-accident general practitioner notes will show a number of consultations for back pain. Although the cross-examination opportunities from this inconsistency are self-evident, video evidence may be the clincher and avoid the expense of a trial.

(i) The Advantages

30–09 (a) Video evidence throws the extent of the claimant's disability into sharp focus and may have a significant impact upon the level of damages by demonstrating whether the apparently functional disability is genuine or whether the claimant is malingering.

(b) It may assist in a contested liability claim by casting doubt on the claimant's credibility.

(c) It assists in assessing the appropriate level of a Part 36 payment into court.

(d) It encourages early settlement.[6]

This is now of increasing importance in the current climate of personal injury claims, particularly with the emphasis on Alternative Disputes Resolution and the requirement for "proportionality".[7] Where the claim-

---

[6] See CPR Part 36.10, which provides that where a party makes an offer to settle before proceedings are begun, the court will take that offer into account when making any order as to costs.

[7] See generally CPR Part 1.4.10 concerning the "overriding objective". In low cost "Fast Track" claims (CPR Part 28), however, the defendant may not recover the costs of obtaining a video as this could be considered to be "disproportionate" to the overall value of the claim.

ant has not been entirely frank but does nonetheless have a genuine injury in respect of which damages will be awarded, early disclosure of video evidence may induce him to enter into earlier settlement than would otherwise be the case, with a resultant saving of costs. Even where a claimant is entirely honest, the knowledge that there is a video is unnerving and may render the claimant more amenable to settlement offers. This is particularly so where the claimant is proceeding under a Legal Expenses Protection Policy, where the insurers will be acutely aware that they will be at risk of a significant costs bill in the event of the defendants' Part 36 payment not being beaten at trial.[8]

Equally, CPR Part 36.21 contains punitive interest provisions on damages and costs, for defendants who proceed after receipt of a claimant's Part 36 offer, only to find that a larger sum is awarded at trial. There is, therefore, every incentive for defendants to make an attractive offer at an early stage of proceedings, and a video may tip the balance as to whether or not the claimant will accept this.

Such an offer combined with a video may also create difficulties for the claimant's legal advisers operating under a Conditional Fee Agreement (CFA). Previously, they would be unlikely to be unnerved by a covert video, the contents of many of which are fairly anodyne. In the present funding climate, however, a Part 36 payment offers the certainty of bread today rather than the possibility of jam tomorrow.[9]

Moreover, it is also likely that in the future defendants will seek to make **30–10** such offers on the understanding that the claimant's legal advisers' percentage uplift on any CFA is limited. Again, this is an incentive to the legal advisers, if not to the claimant himself, as there is always the risk, even where the claim is successful, that the costs assessor will significantly reduce the percentage uplift, having assessed the risks of litigation with the perfect vision of hindsight.

It is, therefore, essential for these advisers to view any such video with considerable care, seek the views of the relevant experts, and put firmly from their mind the possibility of financial loss or gain when advising the claimant on the accompanying offer.

   (e) It can be used retrospectively and advantageously even after the case has been fought and lost.

In Liverpool City Council v. Hill,[10] a claimant falsely claimed he tripped on a defective pavement and damaged his knee and was awarded £11,000 damages. Shortly thereafter, the Council carried out covert video sur-

---

[8] See CPR. Part 36.20.
[9] To the extent that even where the lawyers advise rejection of the offer, the legal expenses insurer may well insist on acceptance to ensure recovery of the "after the event" insurance premium and the costs expended to date.
[10] *The Times,* September 26, 1996, Liverpool County Court, H.H. Judge Hamilton.

veillance after his name appeared as a goalscorer for his Sunday football team in the local paper and six months after the original award he was ordered to repay the money with £1,100 interest. The judge commented: "There used to be a gibe 'drink is the ruin of the working classes' but now it might be said 'the video is the ruin of the cheating classes."

In *London Ambulance Service National Health Service Trust v. Swain*,[11] the claimant was awarded substantial damages but the hearing was then adjourned. Prior to the restored hearing the defendants obtained a video showing that she had grossly exaggerated her disability with the result that the defendants' appeal against the judge's award of general damages and loss of pension rights was allowed in part.[12]

More recently, a woman police constable took retirement from the police force on medical grounds, allegedly following a back injury caused by the defendant's negligence: she sought damages of £400,000 claiming that the injury had left her with persistent pain and severe limitation of movement in her neck and shoulder. However, a covert video showed her carrying heavy bags of shopping from the supermarket, lifting her children and manoeuvring a car without difficulty. Her claim that this merely illustrated that her neck was better in the mornings, tending to "get worse in the later part of the day", was rejected by the court. Her claims for future loss of earnings and loss of pension rights were dismissed, general damages of £2,000 were awarded and she was ordered to bear the costs of the three-day hearing.[13]

(ii) The Disadvantages

30–11   (a) Despite the moral high ground adopted by the Association of British Investigators in their Code of Ethics (below), videos are generally viewed with a certain amount of distaste and are contrary to the concept of open justice (see below, *The Impact of the Human Rights Act*).

    (b) The covert nature of video observation is normally such that a claimant is blithely oblivious of the hidden watcher and if he is honest and has given a full and frank account to his legal advisers and the various doctors, he has nothing to fear. This means that video evidence may rebound upon the defence if the claimant's doctors are able to say, as they often are, that the demeanour of a particular claimant and his way of walking, cleaning windows,

---

[11] [1999] M.L.C. 96.

[12] See too *Marchlewski v. Hunter Area Health Service* [1999] M.L.C. 93 (Australia: Sup. Ct. NSW, Dowd J. August 14, 1998) where the parents of a child born brain-damaged were shown by a video to have exaggerated their claimed exacerbated sensibilities in order to recover exemplary and/or aggravated damages.

[13] *Hayley Burton*, reported in the news section of *The Times*, April 14, 2000.

getting in and out of a car, etc., is entirely consistent with the material injury and its alleged consequences.

(c) Much of the distaste and dubious reputation of video evidence arises from the tactics in which some Inquiry Agents have indulged to obtain good "copy". Some of the tricks have included letting down a tyre to see if a claimant will attempt to change the wheel himself, video-filming a shopping expedition to see if the claimant will carry heavy bags and manipulate awkward and unwieldy supermarket trolleys, and spraying windows with muddy water to test whether a claimant will stretch and bend to clean them. Some agents even indulge in telephone calls requesting services such as catering, where it is believed the claimant is carrying on a business and not giving credit for earnings or earning capacity.

When these sort of tactics come to light and the claimant is shown to be genuine, a court will almost invariably regard all the claimant's claims far more benevolently than otherwise would be the case, and the defence may well find that the final bill is far higher than the insurer's reserve, and outweighs the benefits of obtaining expensive video evidence.

(d) Similarly, any blatant encroachment on the claimant's privacy where the allegation of malingering is held to be unfounded, could result in an indemnity costs order. Accordingly, such surveillance should only be advised where there is independent reliable evidence of possible malingering, *e.g.* a suggestion to this effect in the medical evidence. **30–12**

(e) In the absence of any express privacy laws in this country, video surveillance is not illegal unless it becomes so intrusive as to amount to the tort of harassment: see *Burris v. Asadani*.[14] In that case the court applied a balance of interests test between the alleged rights and interests of each party and it would seem that a new doctrine of "legitimate interests" has emerged, which is likely to be taken up in cases under the Human Rights Act (see below). The courts have yet to adjudicate upon the "legitimate [and claimed moral] interests" of a defendant's insurers in carrying out these investigations when balanced against the rights of an injured claimant to privacy and protection from intrusion by strangers. This, however, is an aspect of video surveillance in respect of which defendants and their advisers should be on their guard and is certain to arise under the Human Rights Act 1998 (see below).

---

[14] (Unreported), referred to in *Psychological assault and harrassment*, Tim Lawson-Cruttenden, [1996] New L.J. 1326.

The Preparation of Video Evidence

For the Claimant

30–13   In his final report on the civil justice system, Lord Woolf[15] described and deplored how:

> "A large litigation support industry, generating a multi-million pound fee income, has grown up among professions such as accountants, architects and others, and new professions have developed such as accident reconstruction and care experts."[16]

In fact, some of these "new professions" prepare videos of "A Day in the Life of [the Claimant]" which are of a very high quality. It is, however, important to treat these videos as confidential and copies should not be distributed without the claimant's consent to anyone other than the legal and medical advisers. At the end of the trial, all copies should be returned to the solicitors and not be retained as "training videos" (complete with the claimant's name and address on the opening credits), as has been known to happen with some organisations whose ethics on confidentiality are somewhat hazy.

Any video and supporting documentation must be carefully viewed before disclosure, ensuring that what it depicts is consistent with the narrative in the Statement of Case, witness statements and medical reports, and where it is not, investigating the discrepancies. An appropriate time to do this, if possible, is during conference, prior to disclosure of the expert evidence. Although RSC, Ord. 38, r. 5 provided for late disclosure of such evidence, it is tactically advantageous to disclose this at an earlier date, preferably when witness statements are exchanged. The emphasis on early disclosure has increased with the implementation of the recommendations of Woolf in the Civil Procedure Rules and the increased judicial involvement at the interlocutory stages in the judge's role as Case Manager.[17]

For the Defendant

30–14   It is unusual for video evidence adduced on behalf of the claimant and obtained with his consent and co-operation, to be contentious; occasionally the defence will demand to see the uncut version where the editing would appear to have been "economical with the truth", but this is rare. Not so,

---

[15] Woolf, *Access to Justice*. Final Report to the Lord Chancellor on the civil justice system in England and Wales, July 1996, HMSO.

[16] See Section III, Chap 13, *Expert Evidence*, p. 137.

[17] Indeed, CPR Part 33.6 which replaces Ord. 38, r. 5 lays down earlier time limits: see discussion at *Video Evidence under the CPR* below.

however, where this evidence is obtained covertly without the claimant's knowledge and certainly not with his consent.

Such evidence is usually obtained upon the instructions of the defendant's solicitors or insurers by Inquiry Agents who supply a contemporaneous surveillance record and sometimes, where appropriate, a transcript of any relevant conversation. Often, irritatingly, there is a voice-over describing in meticulous and tedious detail what the claimant is doing at the material time.

Many, but not all investigators, belong to the Association of British Investigators which has drawn up a Code of Ethics wherein they pledge, *inter alia*:

"1. To perform all professional duties in accordance with the highest moral principles and never be guilty of conduct which will bring reproach upon the profession of the private investigator and The Association of British Investigators.
2. To verify the credentials of clients and that they have lawful and moral reasons to instruct an investigation.
3. To respect the privacy of clients and the lawful confidence.
4. To ensure that services are adequately secure to protect privacy and to guard against inadvertent disclosure of private information.
5. To ensure that all employees and other persons paid to assist an investigation adhere to this code of Ethics and to accept responsibility therefor.
6. To conduct all investigations within the bounds of legality, morality and professional ethics.
7. To respect the best interest of our clients by maintaining the high standard of proficiency and reporting to our clients all the facts ascertained whether they be advantageous or detrimental, and nothing be withheld from the clients save by the dictates of Law.
8. To work together with all members of our Association towards the achievement of the highest professional objectives of the Association and to observe the precepts of truth, accuracy and prudence."

In many cases, unfortunately, this Code would appear to be honoured in its breach rather than in its observance. It is rare to hear a claimant agree that a covert video has been filmed "in accordance with the highest moral principles" or that an insurer has "moral reasons" to instigate the video investigation.

Disclosure

"Attacking the credit of a witness by dramatic confrontation in the witness box is **30–15** so much part of the English forensic tradition, so hallowed in history and fiction, that lawyers are naturally reluctant to be deprived of the chance to ambush the opposing party with some devastating piece of cross-examination. But times have changed, and the decision of this court in *Khan v. Armaguard* narrowly confines the discretion to permit such evidence not to be disclosed in accordance with the rules." *per* Hoffman L.J. in *Libby-Mills v. Commissioner of Police*.[18]

---

[18] [1995] P.I.Q.R. P324, CA.

The Rules of Procedure allow for disclosure to take place before trial and the emphasis has shifted under the CPR for *notice* of such intended disclosure to be given together with facilities for *inspection*. Previously, this was governed by RSC Ord. 38, r. 5 which provided:

"5. Unless, at or before the trial, the Court for special reasons otherwise orders, no plan, photograph or model shall be receivable in evidence at the trial of an action unless at least 10 days before the commencement of the trial the parties, other than the party producing it, have been given an opportunity to inspect it and to agree to the admission thereof without further proof."

This rule is now incorporated into the general rules of inspection and disclosure at CPR Part 33.6 which provides:

"Unless the court orders otherwise, no plan, photograph or model is receivable at trial unless the party intending to use such material 'as evidence of any fact' has given notice to other parties as required by the rule and given them an opportunity to inspect it and to agree its admission without further proof."

The wording is very similar but now contains specific provision for *notice* in addition to that for *inspection*. Unfortunately, CPR Practice Direction 33PD gives no guidance as to interpretation of this rule.

Notice of Disclosure and Inspection

30–16 "33.6(3) Unless the court orders otherwise the evidence shall not be receivable at a trial unless the party intending to put it in evidence has given notice to the other parties in accordance with this rule."

"33.6(4) Where the party intends to use the evidence as evidence of any fact then, except where paragraph (6) applies, he must give notice not later than the latest date for serving witness statements."

"33.6(5) He must give notice at least 21 days before the hearing at which he proposes to put in the evidence, if—

(a) there are not to be witness statements; or
(b) he intends to put in the evidence solely in order to disprove an allegation made in a witness statement."

"33.6(7) Where the evidence is being produce to the court for any reason other than as part of factual or expert evidence, he must give notice at least 21 days before the hearing at which he proposes to put in the evidence."

"33.6(8) Where a party has given notice that he intends to put in the evidence, he must give every other party an opportunity to inspect it and to agree to is admission without further proof."

These dual provisions for the giving of notice are likely to cause confusion although there has, as yet, been no reported case law. In circumstances where there are accompanying witness statements explaining the video, notice will be required at a relatively early stage of proceedings.[19] From the defendants' standpoint, however, there is the facility to withhold this notice until a later stage so that it may be tactically and effectively used to discredit matters set out in the claimants' witness statements. Part 33.6(5) enables him to do this. There has, of course, always been the facility to give notice earlier in proceedings and defendants have sometimes done so in order to force an early settlement or even withdrawal of the claim. The overriding objective under the CPR means that early notice is now increasingly desirable (see below at *Tactics for Disclosure*).

Withholding of Notice—"Ambush" at Trial

The incorporation of specific notice provisions raises the issue of **30–17** whether under the CPR, it remains open to the defendant to apply for an order directing that there be no notice or disclosure to the claimant before trial. A reading of Part 23 (General Rules about Applications for Court Orders) suggests that such an application can be made with or without notice.[20]

However, a direction dispensing without notice must be made, otherwise the video evidence "shall not be receivable" (Part 33.6(3)). A "half-way house" is theoretically possible whereby the claimant is put on notice that a video will be relied upon but disclosure or inspection is withheld. This, however, is most unlikely to arise in practice: if the court considers that the claimant should be aware of the existence of a video, the likelihood of him thereafter not being able to view this, is vanishingly small.

The other alternative, is that previously favoured by defendants, namely, to spring the video upon the claimant unexpectedly at trial. He can do so in one of two circumstances: firstly having obtained a court order without notice (*ex parte*) to be allowed to do so, or, even more rarely, by application to the trial judge for permission to call rebuttal evidence. However, the circumstances where this latter course is likely to be

---

[19] CPR r. 33.6(4).

[20] See Part 23.3(2)(b). Practice Direction (Applications) para. 3. lists the circumstances in which an application may be made without service of an application notice. Two of these are: "(2) where the overriding objective is best furthered by doing so" and "(4) with the permission of the court". These circumstances are considered further at Note 23.0.7, *Civil Procedure 2000*, Sweet & Maxwell. It is suggested, therefore, that if a defendant is able to persuade the court that the overriding objective will be best furthered by the claimant remaining in ignorance of either the *existence or content* of a video, then such an Order can still be made. However, the likelihood of this happening in practice must be extraordinarily rare given the present climate of openness in litigation and the emphasis being placed by the European Court on Human Rights on satisfying the requirements for a fair trial under Article 6 and safeguarding the claimant's rights under Article 8 of the Human Rights Act 1998 (see below).

permitted are becoming increasingly rare and circumscribed, reflecting the increasing emphasis on "openness" and "cards on the table" *per* Donaldson L.J. in *Naylor v. Preston Area Health Authority*.[21] This rarity is set to increase given the recognition of the rights of the individual under the Human Rights Act.

The Exercise of Discretion

30–18   It is arguable that the words "shall not be receivable" in CPR Part 33.6(3) are mandatory and binding upon the Court such that the Trial Judge retains no residual discretion to admit video evidence of which no previous notice has been given. It is submitted, however, that this cannot have been the intention of the Rules Committee as this would run contrary to the spirit of the "overriding objective" under Part 1 CPR. This requires the Judge to be able to exercise unfettered discretion in all procedural matters, in order to "achieve justice".

The Court therefore still has an inherent discretion to admit video evidence in circumstances where there has been no notice of the intention to adduce video evidence and/or inspection of the video contents. The exercise of this discretion has been considered by the Court of Appeal on a number of occasions in the last 15 years, and in the absence of any guidance from either the Practice Direction or the Courts since the CPR were implemented in April 1999, this Chapter will look at the position which applied under the former RSC, Ord. 38, r. 5.

(i) The Previous Approach

30–19   Prior to the amendment of the Rules of the Supreme Court, Ord 38, r. 5 in 1988, a claimant was often unaware before trial that a video had been obtained. Televisual evidence, photographs and allied Inquiry Agent evidence were frequently sprung upon unsuspecting claimants at the court door or during the course of trial as rebuttal evidence, following an apparently innocuous denial by a claimant under cross-examination concerning his ability to carry out gainful employment, housework or any other task by reason of his alleged injuries. Very occasionally the evidence was extremely effective: the claimant with the debilitating injury to his right knee and hip who is seen balancing on the offending leg beside the driver's door of an open-bonneted car, whilst the other leg is pumping the accelerator—one of many he was repairing in a flourishing car repair

---

[21] [1987] 2 All E.R. 353, CA. In this context, see the discussion below concerning the Court of Appeal's judgment in *Birch v. Hale Containers* [1996] P.I.Q.R. P307 CA. (Evans and Waite L.JJ. and Sir John May) Despite the fact that the defendant in that case had previously obtained an *ex parte* order for non-disclosure of the video, the Court was clearly unhappy with the "ambush" of the plaintiff at trial even though her conduct had little to commend it (see extracts from the judgment of Evans L.J. considered below).

business in the driveway of his house—whilst at the same time claiming full State benefits and total loss of future earnings and earning capacity. The presence at court of a representative from the Department of Social Security, tipped off by the Inquiry Agent, added further to the claimant's misery in failing to beat the payment into court.

Since October 1, 1989, latterly by virtue of RSC Ord. 38, r. 5,[22] and now under CPR Part 33.6, the defendant must apply at an interlocutory stage "without notice"[23] for an Order sanctioning the withholding of a document from disclosure where there is a serious allegation as to the claimant's bona fides. The onus lies upon the defendant to satisfy the court that an order for non-disclosure should be made. Whereas Ord. 38, r. 5 made specific provision for such application to be made "at least 10 days before trial", the absence of such time limit, reflects the wide Case Management powers now vested in the judiciary: it is likely that the courts will expect such applications to be made at a far earlier stage, and on notice (see above under *Notice of Disclosure* (at 30–16) *and Inspection* and below under *The Present Approach* at 30–20).

Before the decisions in *Digby v. Essex County Council*[24] and *Khan v. Armaguard*,[25] the courts varied in their approach to prior disclosure and there appeared to be no particular criteria applied in determining whether or not a claimant should be forewarned of such evidence before trial, each case being determined upon its own facts and the judge exercising a wide discretion. As late as 1988, in *McGuinness v. Kellogg Co of Great Britain Ltd*,[26] the Court of Appeal upheld the discretion of the lower court permitting a defendant not to disclose a video film of the claimant which showed him to be a malingerer. Neill L.J. gave guidance on the approach to the application of the exception in RSC Ord. 38 r. 5, but emphasised that where exceptional circumstances exist, the court still had a wide discretion to order non-disclosure.

(ii) The Present Approach

In Digby,[27] however, the Court of Appeal expressed preference for a **30–20** policy of openness and gave reasons for restricting *McGuinness*[28] and favouring a "cards on the table" approach. It was emphasised that normal procedure is to require prior disclosure and that it would require excep-

---

[22] Rules of the Supreme Court (Amendment No. 2) 1988 (S.I. 1988 No. 1340).
[23] See Part 23 and accompanying Practice Direction. In particular, Note 23.0.7, *Civil Procedure 2000*, Sweet & Maxwell, deals with those situations where applications without notice may be permitted although the application notice must still be filed (r. 23.1(1)).
[24] [1994] P.I.Q.R. P53, CA.
[25] [1994] 1 W.L.R. 1204, CA.
[26] [1988] 1 W.L.R. 913, CA.
[27] *ibid.*
[28] *ibid.*

tional circumstance to justify an order that such evidence may be adduced at trial without prior disclosure.[29]

In that case the claimant claimed that he had fallen and injured himself as a result of a pothole in the road. The medical evidence was that there was no organic cause for his symptoms but that there was likely to be a functional overlay. Neither of the two consultants who examined him, however, said in terms that he was malingering or dishonestly or deliberately exaggerating his symptoms. The defendant applied to adduce televisual evidence at the trial without prior disclosure fearing that the claimant might "as a result, be tempted to trim his evidence". This application was refused and Assistant Recorder Curl, in the course of his judgment, pointed out that special reasons were required for an order for non-disclosure which were that the claimant was said to be faking or grossly exaggerating his symptoms. It was not enough simply to say that the claimant's bona fides were in issue, because that occurs in so many cases to a larger or smaller extent. There had to be clear reasons to take it out of the normal run of cases.

The Court of Appeal upheld this refusal:

"The authorities make it plain that if there is a clear and unequivocal challenge to the bona fides of the plaintiff, and in particular if it is plainly alleged that he is malingering or grossly exaggerating his symptoms, that is a ground upon which the court may, indeed may even be likely to, exercise its discretion against disclosure" (*per* Sir Thomas Bingham, M.R.).

30–21 Simon Brown L.J. pointed out that withholding this evidence militates against encouraging settlement which is not in the public interest:

"The problems of acceding to a defendant's application to withhold material such as the video recording here are obvious. Such an order must inevitably give the defendant a powerful negotiation advantage. The plaintiff's advisers will be unable to value his case properly and confidently and advise him fully upon the advantages of settlement and the risks of litigation, fearful as they would always be that there was some skeleton in their client's cupboard, more troubling than he, for his part, was prepared to recognise . . . public policy generally commands a practice of cards on the table. It should be remembered that in personal injury cases, more perhaps than in most others, a plaintiff is likely, through the process of continuing medical questioning and examination, to have committed himself to a specific case. Logical analysis suggests therefore that if there is indeed video evidence plainly inconsistent with a plaintiff's already stated account of his injuries, disabilities and the like, it will generally already be too late for him to trim or tailor his evidence effectively.

Rather, the balance of risks seems to me to be likely to fall the other way: the risk that a plaintiff faced with the knowledge that there is undisclosed video

---

[29] Such circumstances would presumably include the qualifications to the right to respect for private and family life conferred by Article 8 of the European Convention on Human Rights (see *The Impact of the Human Rights Act* below).

evidence available to the defendant, may perhaps for understandable, psychological reasons, so far from exaggerating, positively minimise his complaints.

Save, therefore, in cases where malingering is clearly and categorically advanced as the basis for a non-disclosure order, where there can be demonstrated a plain risk of a plaintiff doctoring his evidence, and where that risk sufficiently outweighs a countervailing consideration . . . there should be only the rarest orders permitting non-disclosure."

In *Digby*, therefore, the order for disclosure was made based on the absence of any direct or unequivocal accusation of malingering. In *Khan*, however, the court went further in holding that even where "malingering" is clearly and categorically advanced, there should still be prior disclosure. This decision effectively outlaws "ambush by video" and provides for prior disclosure in all save very unusual cases distinguishable on their facts.

In his judgment, Rose L.J. placed considerable reliance upon three changes in the rules since *McGuinness* was decided, namely:

(a) exchange of witness statements has become the norm;

(b) automatic discovery has been provided for in personal injury cases unless there is a contrary direction (Ord. 25, r. 8(3)[30]); and

(c) the practice of "cards on the table" "has developed very considerably in the Queen's Bench Division".

"It is, as it seems to me, in the interest of the parties, the legal aid fund, and the efficient dispatch of business by the courts, that cases should be disposed of by settlement at an early stage. Almost always, in my view, this should mean that disclosure of video films . . . should be made, even in cases where the defendant's case is that the plaintiff is a malingerer" (*per* Rose L.J.).

The procedural position concerning the admissibility of video evidence **30–22** was reviewed in *Libby-Mills v. Commissioner of Police for the Metropolis*.[31] The defendant's case was that the plaintiff, an ex-marine and former police officer, was an out and out malingerer and that if the video was disclosed to him he would concoct a mala fides explanation, being described as a "plausible raconteur" by certain doctors who had examined him. In the spirit of compromise—which would find considerable favour in the current post-Woolf procedural climate—Otton J. (as he then was) proposed limited disclosure to the plaintiff's doctors and lawyers, but this invitation was declined by the defence. Otton J. then granted the defendant leave to adduce video evidence at the forthcoming trial without prior disclosure to the plaintiff.

On appeal, the common ground was that:

---

[30] Now CPR Part 31 and para. 2.10 of the Pre-Action Protocol for Personal Injury Claims.
[31] [1995] P.I.Q.R. P324, CA.

(a) the plaintiff's complaint was of a soft tissue injury with little physical sign of injury but a continuing history of complaint;

(b) the defendant challenged the plaintiff's bona fides; and

(c) there existed video evidence which was said to show the falsity of the plaintiff's account.

The plaintiff submitted was that there was nothing about these matters which placed the case in a rare category which would entitle the judge to grant the defendant leave not to disclose. The defence argued that to accede to this argument would be to legislate discretion out of existence.

The Court of Appeal considered the respective merits of the "open" approach of prior disclosure, and that where it is appropriate for leave to be given to dispense with production or inspection of material upon which the defendant intends to rely to demonstrate that the plaintiff is malingering. Allowing the appeal, Sir Thomas Bingham M.R. endorsed the approach in *Khan* and added:

> "I would accept that the result of authority is to confine within very narrow limits the discretion which exists under Order 38, r. 5. It is not, I think, useful to attempt to define the circumstances in which an order might properly be made in a personal injury case . . . the range of cases which can arise is infinite, and it may very well be that cases would arise in which it would be proper to make such an order even in a personal injury case. But for my part I have no doubt whatever that the correct approach is that laid down by Rose L.J. in *Khan's* case and that such orders should be very rare indeed. There appears to be nothing that distinguishes this case from what may be called 'ordinary cases' of this kind, and I can see no reason whatever for making a special order. In fact, I can see a number of disadvantages which would flow from it. It seems to me that in anything other than a very unusual situation it is highly desirable that no only the plaintiff's advisers but also the plaintiff himself should know the strength of the defence. Such information might lead to the withdrawal of the claim or certain advice being given to those who are financing it" (*per* Sir Thomas Bingham, M.R. at P327–P328).

30–23   This case, therefore, appeared decisively to have set narrow parameters for the exercise of this discretion only in *very rare* cases, in keeping with the "cards on the table" open approach to litigation and in anticipation of Woolf and the Human Rights Act.

However, in 1996 the Court of Appeal reviewed the whole issue of the exercise of discretion in these cases in their decision in *Birch v. Hales Containers Ltd,*[32] which was heard after *Libby-Mills*. In that case the defendants, in a personal injuries case, made covert video recordings of the plaintiff some weeks before trial showing that she was far more active than

---

[32] [1996] P.I.Q.R. P307 CA. (Evans and Waite L.JJ. and Sir John May).

she was later to claim in evidence. These recordings were properly "documents" which the defendants were obliged to disclose on discovery. They did not do so, however, but obtained an order *ex parte* under CCR, Ord. 38, r. 5, granting them leave to rely upon the video evidence without prior disclosure. No copy of the *ex parte* order was sent to the plaintiff's solicitors before trial although a payment into court of £55,000 had been made by the defendants. At trial before H.H. Judge Willis, the plaintiff's counsel was taken completely by surprise when the defendants sought to cross-examine the plaintiff on the video. By consent, the video was shown to the judge *de bene esse* without prejudice to a subsequent application by the plaintiff for an adjournment. The plaintiff's counsel sought the adjournment for the purpose of a re-hearing before a different judge who would not have seen the video, but this application was refused. The plaintiff's counsel then made it clear that she declined to take any further part in the proceedings and the plaintiff's medical expert, after seeing the video, indicated that he could no longer be or any assistance to the plaintiff. The trial judge proceeded to judgment and awarded the plaintiff only £2,000 and ordered that she pay the costs.

The plaintiff sought leave to appeal on three grounds against the original **30–24** non-disclosure order and on two grounds against the trial judge:

(a) that he did not have jurisdiction to make the non-disclosure order *ex parte*;

(b) that if he did have such jurisdiction he was wrong;

(c) that in any event he ought to have required the defendants to give notice of the order to the plaintiff's solicitors before the hearing of the action;

(d) that he ought not to have admitted the video into evidence; and

(e) that he wrongly refused the application to adjourn.

The plaintiff's submissions were that had she been aware of the existence of the video before trial, she would have had the opportunity to take the £55,000 out of court and, her medical expert might have been in a position to have given evidence of some assistance to her case if he had been given adequate notice of the video. As to costs, she submitted that the need for a trial only arose because of the defendants' failure to disclose the existence of a video, although this submission was not made before the trial judge.

It was held that once the judge had seen the evidence *de bene esse* the question of its formal admissibility became of very limited relevance and his decision to refuse an adjournment on that basis was not one of which the plaintiff could make legitimate complaint. The essential issue, therefore, was whether having seen this evidence the plaintiff should have been granted an adjournment to consider the implications of such evidence.

30–25   There seems little doubt from the judgment of Evans L.J. that he viewed the failure by the defendants to give prior disclosure of the film, or the fact of its existence, with considerable misgivings and that had the application for an adjournment been differently framed the trial judge might have been minded to accede to it. However, the plaintiff did not seek a short adjournment so that both counsel and the plaintiff's medical expert could reconsider the position in which they found themselves and as such, the issue of prior disclosure was not truly before the court, it was merely whether the judge should have continued to hear the case having viewed the video *de bene esse*. On this narrow point, the Court of Appeal considered that the trial judge could not be criticised for refusing the adjournment.

As to the failure to disclose the existence of the video film, Evans L.J. referred to the "movement in favour of a greater requirement on the defendants both to disclose and make available for inspection video recordings before the hearing" and how this had been confirmed by the judgment in *Khan* (which was not available at the time of the trial):

> "[*Khan*] goes so far as to indicate that the mere fact that the plaintiff is charged with malingering will not normally of itself provide special grounds for an order under Ord. 36, r. 5 such as was made here. Potentially therefore there is scope for argument in the present case as to what attitude this court should adopt now to a ruling that was made in November 1993 when the law was, as can now be seen, in a state of change. Ultimately, however, in my view, that is not a decisive or even an important fact for present purposes."[33]

The court considered that there was considerable force in the plaintiff's submission that but for the failure to disclose, no trial would have taken place but held that the fact that awareness of the existence of this evidence might have led to a different tactical approach by the plaintiff to the money in court was of marginal relevance:

> "Overall the concern of this court is with justice and justice means a result reflecting the true facts of the matter. The question ultimately therefore is whether the judgment as it exists can be shown arguably not to be a true reflection of the facts as they are now known."

Discussion

30–26   At first blush, the decisions in *Libby-Mills* and *Birch* appear irreconcilable. The wording of the requirement for prior disclosure as provided for in RSC, Ord. 38, r. 5 (and adopted by the CPR Part 33.6) is unequivocal:

> ". . . in accordance with modern practice which requires the exchange of material on which parties to litigation propose to rely before the trial so as to

---

[33] [1996] P.I.Q.R. P307 at P311–P312.

enable them to known what case they have to meet and ensure that appropriate judgments can be made about the respective strengths of the claim and the defence to it" (*per* Sir Thomas Bingham M.R. in *Libby-Mills* at page 325).

On the face of it, this would appear to be the substance of the plaintiff's submissions to the trial judge and before the Court of Appeal. However, the issue in *Birch* appeared to turn not so much upon the appropriateness of prior disclosure of video evidence but the scope of the adjournment sought from the trial judge after he had seen this evidence. Indeed, Evans L.J. specifically commented:

" . . . it seems to be that there is no material before the court . . . which would justify the inference that in the interests of justice this matter ought to be reopened . . . I would add only this, it was suggested to us . . . that leave should be refused on the simple ground that all that happened before the trial is now past history. There has been a trial and that therefore these difficulties are academic only. I would not be prepared to accept that submission for the reason already given which is shortly that this whole unfortunate catalogue began with an important failure by the defendants to comply with the rules as to discovery of the video recording."[34]

It seems, therefore, that the defendants were only allowed to escape censure both generally and in terms of costs because of the unfolding of subsequent events. Otherwise, despite having quite properly obtained an interlocutory order for non-disclosure, they were deemed to have been in breach of the rules by their "important failure to comply with the rules of discovery of the video recording". This can only mean that the Court of Appeal still considered the defendants to be under an obligation to disclose to the plaintiff's advisers that such evidence existed.

In future, therefore, it seems likely in similar circumstances that an **30–27** application for a short adjournment suitably phrased will be successful, particularly given the *notice* provisions contained in Part 33.6. Uncertainty as to the precise grounds upon which this adjournment was sought did create difficulties in this particular case[35]; moreover, the entire tenor of the plaintiff's complaints concerning this video was not that such video evidence was misleading or misrepresented the severity of her injuries: on the contrary, it was that had she been so much as aware of its existence, she would, so to speak, have taken the money and run. Beyond a rather weak point that, given time, her medical expert might have come up with some supportive evidence—highly unlikely, considering the uncompromising stance he took having seen the video—there was no suggestion that this case would have proceeded to trial or that the plaintiff would have been awarded a sum "approaching, even remotely, the figure of £55,000 which

---

[34] *ibid.* at P313–P314.
[35] *ibid.* at P310.

was in court".[36] Accordingly, so the plaintiff's argument ran, the unnecessary incurring of the costs of trial should be laid at the door of the defendants for not playing fairly!

Such reasoning certainly runs contrary to common sense and is morally and legally repugnant: it is unlikely to satisfy the overriding objective of "achieving justice"[37] with a just and equitable result and it certainly does not represent a "cards on the table" approach by the plaintiff. A payment into court is intended to protect both parties, not to be used simply as a bargaining counter by a greedy, and sometimes dishonest, plaintiff: she gambled and lost on the defendants' successful non-disclosure gambit.

Libby-Mills was not cited before the Court of Appeal in *Birch*, but in so far as the Court of Appeal in both cases expressly approved the approach of Rose L.J. in *Khan*, it cannot legitimately be argued that this decision was reached *per incuriam*. On the above analysis, therefore, *Birch* would seem to be a case the facts of which fall within the "very rare" cases envisaged by Rose L.J. in *Khan*, as approved by Bingham L.J. (as he then was) in *Libby-Mills* when commenting that the overwhelming majority of these were "ordinary cases" where an order for non-disclosure should not be made. Even then, the real issue of prior disclosure of video evidence, or the fact that such evidence existed, was clouded by the unfortunate nature of the application to adjourn made before the trial judge.

30–28   It seems, therefore, that the Court of Appeal still endorsed the "cards on the table" approach and disapproved of not disclosing the existence of the video evidence or the *ex parte* order. Indeed, although not stated explicitly, there appeared to be disapproval of a party seeking to obtain such orders *ex parte*: to comply with the rules, then and now under the CPR, such applications should be on notice and the claimant's advisers should be informed of the results.[38]

Claimants, however, should be warned that the mere fact they have not been informed that video evidence has been obtained is no guarantee that it has not been and, more importantly, may be the subject of an application without notice the existence of which has not been disclosed to the claimant's advisers, and that a court may subsequently be minded to allow such evidence in after only a short adjournment.

In such circumstances, it would be interesting to see whether the Court of Appeal would react in the same way in the event of a separate application by the plaintiff that the intrusive nature of the video evidence had been an infringement of her human rights under Article 8 of the Convention. One suspects that in such circumstances and for reasons similar to those given at the time, the Court would decide that the breach

---

[36] *ibid.* per Evans L.J.
[37] See CPR Part 1.
[38] This change of emphasis is reflected in the wording of Part 33.6 in that this provides that the consequence of a failure to give notice is that "the evidence shall not be receivable" unless the court orders otherwise (r. 33.6(3)).

of this right was justified by the qualifications to Article 8 (see *The Impact of the Human Rights Act* below). It is, however, only a matter of time before this issue is re-tested before the Court of Appeal.

It is submitted that, save for the most exceptional of circumstances, the days of trial by "ambush" are over. Henceforth the court's discretion will be applied sparingly and only in cases where 'exceptional circumstances' warrant the admission of previously undisclosed and non-notified video evidence. The court would have to be satisfied that "the overriding objective is best furthered" by admitting the evidence,[39] for example where there was unequivocal evidence of blatant malingering on a very large scale, where the video has only been obtained a matter of days before the substantive hearing.

Tactics for Disclosure

Even before *Woolf* both sides in personal injury litigation have looked **30–29** for early settlement or disposal of a claimant's claim and video evidence can be useful in this respect. Accordingly, given the increasingly complex position regarding funding and recovery of costs, it may be in the interests of both sides for such disclosure to take place earlier than hitherto has been the norm.

The encouragement throughout the CPR is for the parties to "set out their stalls" at an early stage in the litigation. Accordingly, it is sensible for notice to be given, or an application to withhold notice, to be made shortly after the close of pleadings. The notice provisions of Part 33.6 encourage this approach (see above *Notice of Disclosure and Inspection* at 30–16).

In practice, however, it is likely that such applications should be made, and will be encouraged to be made, at an even earlier stage than provided for by the CPR. An example of this can be found in the interpretation of the provisions concerning the Statement of Case at CPR Part 16. Part 16.5(2) provides that where there is a denial in the Defence of an allegation made in the Particulars of Claim, the defendant must give his reasons for denying the allegation (16.5(2)(a) and, if he has a different version to the claimant, must put this forward, *i.e.* plead a positive case (16.5(2)(b)).

Moreover, Practice Direction 16 at paragraph 9.2(1) provides that any allegation of fraud must be clearly set out, and PD 16 at paragraph 13.1 provides that where the dispute relates to medical evidence, the defendant must attach his own medical report to the Defence. These provisions, together with the Part 18 Request for Further Information, which can be made "at any time" during the proceedings, mean that the defendant is likely to be under an obligation to disclose the dispute as to the claimant's

---

[39] Practice Direction (Applications) para. 3(2).

bona fides earlier rather than later. In these circumstances it would be sensible to file his notice under CPR part 33.6, at the same time.

The Advantages of Early Disclosure

30–30   Video evidence adduced by the claimant in support of his claim has already been considered at *When to Use Video Evidence*.

As to disclosure of the defendant's video evidence, from the claimant's point of view this should be as early as possible and preferably before or, at the very least, at the time of exchange of witness statements (see r. 33.6(4)). Subsequent disclosure can result in embarrassment when tasks described as impossible in the statements are shown on the video to be performed with ease. This sometimes arises less through lack of probity on the part of the claimant than in slip-shod drafting or checking by the legal advisers of the claimant's witness statements, *e.g.* where the alleged inability genuinely occurred during the early stages of the claimant's recovery and there has been a failure to update the statement to record when it was that the claimant was able to resume that particular task such as gardening, shopping, emptying dustbins, etc. Sometimes, too, when claimants maintain that they "can't do" something, this means not that they are incapacitated but can no longer perform the task as they did pre-accident, or if they attempt it, the resultant cost is several hours of pain, only alleviated by rest which takes place out of sight of the video camera, *e.g.* a young mother pegging out clothes on the washing line but then lying down for a couple hours until the resultant pain wears off.

Precision is, therefore, required in the drafting of these statements in order to present an accurate picture of the *constraints* on a claimant performing certain tasks, rather than portraying this as an *inability* to do so.

Can the Claimant Compel Early Disclosure?

30–31   From the defendant's standpoint, it is usually procedurally advantageous to have as late disclosure as possible and hitherto the rules favoured this approach. It is arguable, however, that an Inquiry Agent's report is a statement of the oral evidence of a witness of fact and should therefore be exchanged at the same time as other non-expert witness evidence (see r. 33.6(4) and discussion at *Notice of Disclosure and Inspection* above). This is likely to be encouraged under CPR Case Management and provides the claimant with an appropriate opportunity to apply for sight of the video referred to in that report. Moreover, under RSC, Ord. 18, r. 12, a party was required to plead fraud with full particularity and this requirement is retained at Practice Direction 16, paragraph 9.2(1). An allegation of malingering is *ipso facto* an allegation that a claimant is acting fraudulently and should, therefore, be included in the Statement of Case.

Apart from any other consideration, the provisions of Part 16.5(2) now require the defendant to plead a properly particularised positive case: it is no longer acceptable simply to traverse the claimant's claim as to the nature and extent of his injury. A bare denial is likely to result in the defendant being debarred from adducing rebuttal evidence, including a video.

An allegation of malingering or at the very least functional overlay may in turn entitle a claimant to request further information (CPR Part 18) from the defendant as to the existence and content of a video although this may be regarded as a "fishing expedition". Previously, following the decision in *Det Danske Hedeselskabet v. K.D.M. International*[40] and *Hall v. Selvaco Ltd*,[41] it was rare in personal injury claims for a court to allow a request for further information prior to the exchange of witness statements. However, the culture of the CPR is for the Statements of Case to be made more effective and subject to "judicial scrutiny" at an early stage. Accordingly, as part of its responsibility for managing cases, the court will ensure that the parties plainly state the factual ingredients of their case so that the true nature and scope of the dispute can be identified. If, therefore, the issues cannot be readily identified from the pleadings, directions will be given with a view to rectifying this, including the requirement of a statement of the issues in dispute.[42] "The objective is to get the issues clarified quickly without the need for further exchanges between the parties in the form of the old requests for further and better particulars, notices to admit and interrogatories."[43]

However, it is often not until *after* the disclosure of witness statements and medical reports that the defence focus upon the possible advantages of obtaining video evidence in a particular case. Therefore, another approach would be for the claimant at the Case Management Conference to seek a debarring order in the event that notice of video evidence is not disclosed with other statements of fact. The court's extensive powers as to when and to what extent disclosure should take place, would arguably permit such an order to be made although this is most unlikely to occur in practice. Alternatively, the defendant is entitled to rely upon the provisions of Part 33.6(5) which allow him 21 clear days before the hearing at which he proposes to put in the evidence, to give notice in circumstances where there are not to be witness statements[44] or the evidence is intended solely to disprove an allegation made in a witness statement.[45]

---

[40] [1994] Lloyd's Rep. 534, Parker J.
[41] *The Times*, March 27, 1996, CA.
[42] See Woolf, interim report, pp. 116 *et seq.*
[43] Notes to 18.0.1, *Civil Procedure*, Vol. 1, Sweet & Maxwell.
[44] CPR part 33.6(5)(a).
[45] CPR part 33.6(5)(b).

Tactics for Meeting Video Evidence

30–32   The decisions in *Khan* and *Libby-Mills* mean that the use and effectiveness of video evidence requires a re-assessment by those acting both for claimants and defendants. Without the element of surprise, there has been a shift in the purpose and effectiveness of video evidence which enables claimants to be better prepared both in the anticipation and rebuttal of video evidence.

A similar shift in culture is now required by the respective rights conferred upon the parties by the Human Rights Act 1998.

By the Claimant

30–33 *(i) Anticipatory Tactics*

There are a number of ways in which being forewarned of video surveillance is to be forearmed:

(a) The negative and destructive emotions often experienced by claimants on discovering that they have been the subject of covert video surveillance, can to some extent be diffused if in cases where this is likely to happen, the claimant's legal advisers warn him in advance at an early stage in the litigation that the defendant is likely to embark on this investigation. The claimant should be encouraged to report any suspicions to his solicitors so that, where appropriate, objections can be made to the defendant in open correspondence and an application for disclosure of evidence made early in the proceedings, either at a Case Management Conference or by application under CPR Part 23 (see above).

(b) A claimant should be encouraged to keep a diary; in that way he may be able to point to artful editing of events on a given day.

(c) A counter-attack may be mounted by claiming that the taking of a video contravenes the claimant's right to respect for private and family life under Article 8 of the European Convention on Human Rights (see *Impact of the Human Rights Act* below).

(ii) After Disclosure of Video Evidence

30–34   When confronted by a video, the cardinal rule is not to panic but to make a careful evaluation of the film and any supporting documentation. Questions to consider:

(a) Is the subject of the film actually the claimant and not someone else, *e.g.* a twin brother/sister?

(b) Does the video present an accurate picture of the claimant's disability?

(c) Is what is shown consistent with the findings and opinion of the claimant's medical experts?

(d) Does the content and action shown accord with those matters deposed to in the claimant's own witness statement and those of other witnesses who have commented upon the claimant's injury and apparent resultant disability?

(e) Has there been misleading editing? A video might show that claimant moving apparently effortlessly from one strenuous task to another whereas the reality is that there may have been a considerable time lapse between the two activities. If the claimant has been encouraged to keep a diary, he may be able to recall performing the task shown *and* that thereafter he had to rest in bed. Evidence should be adduced in support of this, *e.g.* a friend or relative or a home visit from the general practitioner and/or contemporaneous entries in the GP notes.

(f) To what extent, if at all, is the claimant's case weakened/strengthened by this evidence? In *Hadler v. Cape Boards Ltd*,[46] the defendants sought to rely upon video evidence which had been edited and the accompanying Inquiry Agent's report contained subjective interpretation of the plaintiff's actions as shown on the film. The plaintiff applied at the pre-trial review that the report be amended as the "court sees fit" to remove the adverbs. The court acceded to this request (somewhat surprisingly—it may have been more appropriate to exclude the report altogether and let the video stand on its own) and made an order that within seven days the defendants were to disclose and provide for inspection all video evidence that they had obtained during the course of the proceedings. Thus, the plaintiff's solicitor was able to see the full extent of the video tapes obtained and counsel was properly briefed as to the likely cross-examination of the plaintiff.

(g) To what extent has the video infringed the claimant's right to respect for the private and family life? (Article 8 ECHR). A video of activities in a public place, such as a park or supermarket or at work is unlikely to be held to have been an infringement of this right. However, a video of the claimant in his own home, either filmed on private land or by a powerful telescopic lens from, say, across the street, may well be considered to be a clear breach of this right and could be excluded for this reason, despite the defendant's concomitant right to a fair trial under Article 6 of the Convention.[48a]

---

[46] [1996] A.P.I.L. Newsletter, Vol 6, Issue 2, p. 23, Mrs Recorder Matthews.

[48a] See however *Khan v. United Kingdom* (Application No. 3539 4/97) concerning a listening device attached covertly to a private house. Held that although a violation of the applicant's right under Article 8 the material obtained was relevant and reliable and did not render his trial unfair.

Steps to be taken:

30–35   (a) Before the claimant is shown the video, he and other witnesses should be questioned about matters revealed in the film. This allows an accurate assessment of the claimant's genuineness and effectiveness as a witness under cross-examination.

(b) The claimant should view the video in the presence of his solicitor to gauge his reactions. It is preferable to do this in conference: the video can be objectively analysed, problems arising calmly confronted and the claimant appropriately reassured, or—if the video proves to be his undoing—appropriately advised.

(c) The medical expert(s) should view the video at the earliest opportunity and be invited to comment upon it in writing. Such comment should be made with a view to disclosing the same to the defence. If possible, it is often helpful to have the medical expert present during Conference to comment and question the claimant upon certain aspects of the video as they relate to the expert's own findings upon examination, and the history he took from the claimant.

(d) If the claimant's doctors consider that the video is consistent with her injuries and complaints, it is tactically advantageous to seize the initiative and advise the defence that the claimant intends to rely upon the video at trial.[47]

(e) Consideration should be given as to how the video and the credibility of the maker may be attacked. This includes:

    (i) analysing the extent to which the overall impression of the tape has been "doctored" by careful editing;

    (ii) calling for sight of the original unedited film and if not available, seeking an Order that the maker file an affidavit deposing to why this is so: see *Hadler*[48]; and

    (iii) establishing whether the maker has indulged in any "agent provocateur" ploys, *e.g.* letting down a tyre. In one case a claimant's diary enabled her to recall that the garage mechanic who arrived to change the wheel in the supermarket car park, subsequently tested the tyre and found no evidence of any defect, but signs that the air valve had been deliberately released. A statement to this effect was obtained from him and sent to the defendant's solicitors with an accompanying letter

---

[47] *Note*: where the views of the experts differ as to the appropriate interpretation of the video, and if a *Discussion between experts* has been ordered, the areas of disagreement should be set out in their joint statement to the court: see CPR Part 35.12(3).

[48] *ibid.*

stating that the Inquiry Agent would be required to attend court as he had apparently filmed the entire incident!

An enquiry such as this in cross-examination, if met with a bare denial, can of course be taken no further as the claimant is unable other than by inference to establish the necessary evidential foundation to pursue that line of questioning. The intimation in correspondence, however, is usually enough where an investigator has indulged in such dubious and indeed illegal tactics. In the example given here, despite much filibustering, a significantly increased offer was made and a sensible and fair settlement achieved.

(f) Genuine claimants when they learn of the existence of a video, 30–36 frequently feel besmirched, intimidated and angered by what they believe is an unwarrantable intrusion into the intimacy of their everyday lives. For many, the discovery that they have been watched and may still be being watched whilst going about their daily and personal activities, is distinctly unnerving. Feelings akin to those experienced by the victims of stalkers have been recorded with claimants becoming frightened of going out and looking over their shoulder.[49]

It may well be that these emotions add to feelings of insecurity triggered by the accident injuries themselves and in this situation a claimant's advisers may make a virtue out of necessity by commissioning a further psychological report upon the psychological impact to a claimant on being made aware of video and/or Inquiry Agent surveillance. If it considered that the claimant has suffered an identifiable "psychological injury", *e.g. Page v. Smith*,[50] this then becomes part of the chain of causation from the original injury to be considered in the assessment of damages: a higher award may result. This is as yet untried ground as an enhanced award of this nature has yet to be made although, in *Smith v. LFCDA*,[51] McKinnon J. expressed himself very tempted to have done so "by reason of the fact that the claimant has had hanging over him the accusation of malingering although I am clear that that accusation should never have been made."

(g) Unreasonable and unwarrantable intrusive surveillance, does not prevent the claimant in certain circumstances seeking a Wasted Costs Order against the defendant's legal advisers (section 51(6) of the Supreme Court Act 1981 and CPR Part 44.14). Moreover they now have a discrete cause of action under section 7 of the Human

---

[49] Incidentally, should the behaviour of the video-operator be considered to amount to "stalking", a claimant now has a separate remedy under The Prevention of Harrassment Act 1997.
[50] [1995] P.I.Q.R. P329; [1996] A.C. 155, HL.
[51] [1990] QBD (unreported), McKinnon J., March 12, 1990.

Rights Act 1998 to sue within one year from the acts complained of.[52]

(h) In the event that the defendant makes an application for non-disclosure, (CPR Part 33.6) the claimant should consider inviting the court to view the video evidence before making an order: it may in fact be supportive of the claimant's case and, thus, the defence tactics to diminish the claimant's faith in his chances of success are defused. Again, however, in the present climate, an order dispensing with notice of disclosure is most unlikely to be made.

The Defendant

30–37 There is usually little contentious about a "Day in the Life of [a Claimant]" video and anticipatory tactics beyond awareness that such a video is likely to be made, are unnecessary. Upon disclosure, however, if the video appears to present a distorted impression of the claimant's disability, the defence can:

(a) seek disclosure of the unedited film;

(b) require the maker to attend court;

(c) apply to obtain their own video (this is extremely unusual);

(d) show this to their own quantum witnesses—occupational therapist, physiotherapist, care expert, etc., and obtain their written comments which should then be disclosed to the claimant with a view to this evidence being given orally at trial. It is also useful ammunition at any pre-trial meeting of experts. This is only likely to arise where the claimant himself is competent to give evidence and thus the video can be attacked in the course of cross-examination.

Video Evidence under the Civil Procedure Rules 1998

30–38 Video and enquiry agent evidence is only likely to be permitted in an exceptional case in Fast Track claims and on the Multi-Track is by court order only.[53] The application by the new rules has been considered in the body of this Chapter. For ease of reference they may be summarised as set out below.

---

[52] Section 8 deals with remedies against a public authority, within which definition some defendant insurers would fall. Practitioners are urged to familiarise themselves with the Act and the Strasbourg case law. It is not the remit of this Chapter to consider these in any detail.

[53] Note that Part 33.6 does not apply to cases allocated to the small claims track (r. 27.2(1)(d)).

The Civil Procedure Rules

(a) The defendant's obligations are set out in Part 16.5. A defendant **30–39** must give reasons for denying any allegation in the Statement of Case and under Part 16.5(2)(b), if he intends to prove a different version of events from that given by the claimant, *he must give his own version*. This may well be interpreted as disclosing the video at an early stage (see *Disclosure* above).

(b) Similarly, if a defendant is doubtful about the claimant's version of events (including, presumably his version of the severity of the disability) he must say why he is doubtful. Under Part 16.5(6), he must also state in specific terms why he disputes the claimants assessment of the value of his claim. Under draft rule 9(5), the defendant was also required to "identify in the defence any document which he considers to be necessary to his defence". This requirement does not appear to have been retained in the rules but an order to this effect undoubtedly comes within the wide remit of the court in the exercise of its Case Management powers.

(c) Evidence is governed by CPR Part 32 and includes powers to control evidence. Part 32.4 concerns the requirement to serve witness statements. The Final Report of Woolf expressed concern that witness statements had become "an elaborate, costly branch of legal drafting",[54] and the court has power to limit statements to certain issues or to order witness "summaries".[55] Although the practical approach is for "brief" witness statements, these presumably include statements concerning video evidence (see provisions at Part 33.6(4)) Further, failure to disclose a document in breach of a requirement to give standard disclosure may result in the draconian sanction of the case being struck out under Part 3.4(2)(c) although the courts have as a rule been reluctant to invoke this sanction in the interests of achieving justice (see *Biguzzi v. Rank Leisure plc*[56] and *Walsh v. Misseldene*[57]). Further, it has been suggested that to strike out a case where the failure to comply with Rule, Practice Direction or Court Order has not rendered a fair trial impossible (*pace* a failure to disclose a document which may not be considered on the facts to be fatal to the defendant's case) an Order striking out a case even for contumacious breach is likely to be a breach of Article 6 of the European Convention on Human Rights and Fundamental Freedoms (1953, Cmd 8969) as being a breach of the

---

[54] P.129.
[55] See CPR Part 32.9(3).
[56] [1994] 1 W.L.R. 1926; [1999] 4 All E.R. 934, CA.
[57] [2000] All E.R. (D) 26, CA.

Respondent's (claimant's) right to a determination of his civil rights and obligations at a fair and public hearing within a reasonable time by an independent tribunal: see *Arrow Nominees Incorporated v. Blackledge*[57a]

30–40   (d) Part 18 allows a party to seek from any other party "information about any matter which is in dispute in the proceedings"[58] and extends to any disputed matter even though the matter is not contained or referred to in the Statement of Case. Draft rule 35.2 provided that an Order compelling this information will be made providing "it is necessary in order to dispose fairly of the claim or to save costs". This specific requirement is not to be found in the CPR, but the consensus is that this and other mooted considerations, are consistent with the "overriding objective" stated in rule 1.1.[59] By an obvious extension of reasoning, it would seem that disclosure of video evidence clearly fulfils this criteria? These are matters which will be dealt with at the Case Management Conference (Part 3) when the forensically awake defendant will invoke Part 33.6(5) allowing him to defer notice of any such evidence until 21 days before the hearing.

    (e) As already discussed above under *Disclosure*, Part 33.6 contains new provisions to replace those under Ord. 38, r. 5, in particular in relation to *notice* of the intention to adduce video evidence:

    (f) Finally, there is now in place a Pre-action Protocol for Personal Injury Claims[60] the aims of which are to promote:

      (i) more pre-action contact between the parties;
      (ii) better and earlier exchange of information;
      (iii) better pre-action investigation by both sides;
      (iv) to put the parties in a position where they may be able to settle cases fairly and early without litigation;
      (v) to enable proceedings to run to the court's timetable and efficiently if litigation does become necessary.

Although primarily directed towards cases allocated to the Fast Track, "the spirit, if not the letter of the protocol, should still be followed for multi-track type claims".[61] Paragraph 2.7 sets out the requirements for the Letter of Claim and makes reference to the sanctions that can be imposed by the court for non-compliance with the Protocol. A defendant has three

---

[57a] December 8, 1999, Ch.D.
[58] CPR part 18.1(a).
[59] See Note at 18.1.5 on *Court's Discretion, Civil Procedure 2000*, Vol. 1, (Sweet & Maxwell, 2000).
[60] Set out at C2–1 *Civil Procedure 200*, Vol. 1, Sweet & Maxwell, p. 1304.
[61] See paragraph 2.4 of the Protocol.

months within which to investigate and respond to a claim before proceedings are issued (paragraph 2.8) the intention being to promote an early exchange of relevant information to help in clarifying or resolving issues in dispute (paragraph 2.10). It therefore would be tactically advisable and likely to result in considerable costs savings if defendants use their letter in response to state that they have a video which they are not prepared to disclose at this stage but which they will disclose at the appropriate time, with concomitant costs sanctions against the claimant, if the action is pursued. Alternatively, the existence of such a video would be a sensible explanation of why an otherwise apparently unreasonably low counter-offer is made.

Comment

The courts have interpreted these rules and the Protocol as mandating a **30–41** very wide exercise of judicial discretion. The norm in future, therefore, is for video evidence to be disclosed at an early stage. Accordingly, and despite the provision at Part 33.6(5), defendants should no longer proceed on the basis that they will either be allowed to give notice of the existence of a video or to produce one without prior notice, shortly before trial.

The Impact of the Human Rights Act 1998

The Human Rights Act 1998 received Royal Assent in November 1999 **30–42** and came into force on October 2, 2000. Prior to this date, however, courts and public authorities were expected to have regard to this and a massive increase in applications for judicial review is now anticipated in October 2000.

The general provisions of this Act and how these affect the criteria for the receivability of evidence, are considered in Chapter 29, *Medical Examination*.

This Act incorporates the Articles of the European Convention on Human Rights and is likely to have a substantial impact on the use of video evidence and covert surveillance in general. In particular, applications for the use of such evidence will be concerned with the qualified rights under Article 6 (the right to a fair trial) and Article 8 (the right to respect of private and family life). It is important to understand the nature and impact of these Convention Rights and the very fine balancing act required when:

(a) carrying out covert surveillance (unlike other Member States, *e.g.* France, the UK does not yet have a Privacy Law, but does Article 8 now suffice?); and

(b) seeking to adduce this evidence at trial.

Although section 2 of the Act requires the court to have regard to existing case law—and *Khan* and *Libby-Mills* are obvious candidates—the Act is also to be interpreted as a "living instrument". In this regard, when weighing the individual merits of each case, case law is likely to provide little guidance. For as Ben Emmerson, Editor of H.R.L.O. observed, we will have to "engage in a form of lateral thinking in which precedent and established practice gives way to a superior system of constitutional human rights law."

Section 3 of the Act allows the seeking of a declaration that the provision of primary legislation is incompatible with a Convention Right and this could lead to conflicting applications: by the claimant that the admission of a covertly obtained video is incompatible with his rights under Article 8; and by the defendants that the refusal of admissibility of the video conflicts with their rights under Article 6. This is particularly so where the overriding objective under the Civil Procedure Rules is "to achieve justice". This is, therefore, potentially both an ethical and legal tightrope.

However, the courts will be expected to interpret all legislation in a manner compatible with the Convention, even where the dispute is between individuals.[62]

The Respective Rights under Articles 6 and 8

30–43 It is difficult to lay down any clear guidance when part of the essential ethos of the Act is that it will be a "living instrument" which will, therefore, actively encourage "novel concepts" to be introduced into areas of procedure which have hitherto been accepted as soundly entrenched. Whilst, therefore, there is a "margin of appreciation" whereby it is conceded that a domestic court may be entitled to treat itself as better placed to evaluate the impact of Convention rights on its citizens than a Strasbourg decision on the same issue, a court is likely to be unwilling to depart from the fundamental rights set out in Articles 6 and 8. This is particularly so where the "object and purpose of the Convention as an instrument for the protection of human beings requires that is provisions be interpreted and applied so as to make its safeguards practical and effective" (see *Loizidou v. Turkey*[63]). The likely practical solution is that Convention rights should be interpreted and applied "proportionally" so as to allow a proper balance between competing interests. Therefore, any interference with a right guaranteed by the Convention will have to be justified by the public authority identifying its aim and objective and by reference to what is set out in the provisos to Articles 8 to 11 in which these rights are expressed in qualified terms. However, interference with those rights can only be justifiable if:

---

[62] (See the Lord Chancellor's address to the House of Lords, *Hansard*, 24/11/97, Col. 783).
[63] [1995] 20 E.H.H.R. 99.

(a) the interference is "lawful";

(b) it serves a legitimate purpose;

(c) the interference is "necessary in a democratic society"; and

(d) the interference is not discriminatory.

Defendants will, undoubtedly, argue that fairness and an even-handed approach to litigation means that they must be given the opportunity to "test" the claimant's evidence as to the extent of their disability. But given the rights conferred by Article 8, how will this be achieved in the context of the undoubted intrusion, some might say violation, of family life covert video surveillance causes? A cynic may argue that it is not an intrusion if the subject of the video surveillance is blissfully unaware that he is being filmed, particularly where the filming takes place in a public area such as a park or supermarket. The intrusion arises when the defendants admit to being in possession of this video, have viewed it with others, evaluated its probative value and are sufficiently impressed by the impact of the content to apply at the Case Management Conference for permission to rely on this evidence at trial.

On the other hand, the lack of respect must be simultaneous with the **30–44** commencement of, or the decision to carry out, surveillance however objective the prurience of the decision-maker. Therefore, if counsel advises video surveillance, his forensic antennae having been alerted to inconsistencies in the evidence (witness statements, medical reports, etc.) does this advice contravene Article 8? The answer is "probably", but counsel would be respecting his client's rights to a fair trial under Article 6.

One answer may be to seek leave to carry out covert surveillance. If so, can this be by one side alone (formerly *ex parte*)? Presumably not, as this would also interfere with the claimant's right to be heard on the issue and in breach of his rights under Article 6? On the other hand, if notice is given, it would be a bold tribunal which would grant permission, thereby giving rise to an impossible and blatantly unfair and stressful state of affairs whereby a claimant awaits trial knowing that at any time in any 24-hour period he may be being filmed. Indeed, surveillance of employees by their employers has already been challenged successfully under Article 8: *Niemitz v. Germany*.[64]

However, it should also be remembered that under Article 8(2) it is "immoral" to bring a false or bogus claim. This can apply equally to claimants and defendants. If the claimant's case is indeed bogus, that is clearly an infringement of the defendant's "rights".

The likely outcome of this argument is that the courts are likely to continue to take a pragmatic and sensible view, as indeed Lord Woolf has

---

[64] [1992] 16 E.H.H.R. 97.

done in the interpretation of the "strike out" provisions under the CPR (see *Walsh Misseldene*[65]). The probable approach will be to acknowledge the existence of the rights under Articles 6 and 8, but accept that both are qualified in the sense that they have to be seen in context, and within the parameters of the 'overiding objective' under CPR Part 1, to 'achieve justice'.

The Location of the Video Surveillance

30–45   If the surveillance is in a place that is inherently public, there is unlikely to be a breach of Article 8. However, surveillance on private land either by physical trespass by the cameraman or using a "paparazzi"-style long-range lens through windows over a high garden fence, will almost certainly be a breach of Article 8(1).[66] A likely grey area can be illustrated by a video of a claimant getting in or out of his car on his driveway: the place is private to the extent that the driveway is part of the claimant's home, but there is a "public" element in that by leaving his house the claimant has, arguably, waived his right to privacy as his actions may clearly be perceived from a public place, namely the pavement or roadway. Again, interpretation will turn upon the circumstances of each given case.

Public Authorities

30–46   Article 8(2) provides that the public authority may only interfere in this right "in accordance with the law and (as) necessary in a democratic society in the interests of national security, public safety . . . for the protection of health or morals or for the protection of the rights and freedoms of others". In *Niemitz v. Germany*,[67] it was held that secret surveillance was only permissible so far as strictly necessary for the protection of public institutions.

Using that proviso as a guide to interpretation of Article 8(1), a public authority defendant, such as an NHS Trust, may respectably argue that it has a right to be liable and/or to pay only that which is reasonable in accordance with established legal principles: in that case Article 8(1) should be interpreted so as to enable the defendant to obtain evidence which will help it to achieve those aims, *i.e.* evidence that the claimant is "malingering". In such circumstances, it is likely that in balancing the respective rights of the parties, the right to a fair trial under Article 6 will be seen as outweighing a claimant's feelings of outrage and infringements of his rights

---

[65] *ibid.*
[66] In this context it should not be forgotten that civil trespass is *not* in accordance with the law and thus is a breach of Article 8(1). In such circumstances it is not necessary to bring an action under Article 8(2).
[67] *ibid.* C.O.D.

under Article 8. However, in *Lord v. Debenture Trust ex parte BBC*,[68] Forbes L.J. considered Articles 6 and 8 and where the balance lay. He concluded that the degree of invasion is important and where this is significant, *e.g.* the use of false marketing devices to gain entry, the claimant's right under Article 8 is likely to take precedence.

---

[68] [1999] 472.

31. Offers to Settle and Payments into Court

Introduction

The coming into force of the Civil Procedure Rules 1998 (CPR), Practice **31–01** Directions (PD) and Pre-Action Protocols on April 26, 1999, has necessitated a complete revision of all matters pertaining to "offers to settle and "payments into court". This Chapter contains any analysis of the new provisions set out in the CPR and Practice Directions, up to and including "Update Number 17—July 1999". Thus, practitioners should ensure, when reading this Chapter, that there have been no amendments to the rules referred to, by any further "Updates".

Origins

Chapter 24 (Offers to Settle) of the Report, "Access to Justice", Lord **31–02** Woolf identified part of the policy of the report as being: " . . . *to develop measures which will encourage reasonable and early settlement of proceedings." He added:*

> "It is a curious feature of our present procedure, as reflected in the rules of court, that, although the majority of disputes end in a settlement, the rules are mainly directed towards preparation for trial. My aim is to increase the emphasis on resolution otherwise than by trial."

The recommendations contained within Chapter 24 are:

- The present practice of making payments into court should be replaced by a system which permits the parties to make an offer of settlement.
- Offers to settle can be made by a plaintiff as well as a defendant
- Offers to settle can relate to individual issues.
- Offers to settle can be made before commencement of proceedings.
- Offers to settle can result in substantially enhanced costs and interest being payable.
- The extent of entitlement to costs and interest in respect of an offer should be in the court's, discretion and should depend on the extent of disclosure by the parties.

These recommendations have now been translated into the detailed provisions of CPR Part 36 and its supplemental Practice Direction.

However, the "practice of making payments into court" was not replaced, as originally recommended, but rather supplemented by introducing formal detailed provisions relating to offers to settle claims ("Part 36 Offers"), and laying to rest the *Calderbank* letter. Amongst the innovative features of CPR Part 36, there is specific provision:

(a) that a Part 36 Offer (see below) may be made by any party, including a claimant, and

(b) that an offer to settle *before* proceedings are begun, which complies with CPR Part 36, rule 10, will be taken into account by the court when making any order as to costs.

Although there is nothing in CPR Part 36 which prevents a party making an offer to settle in whatever way he chooses, if that offer is not made in accordance with Part 36, it will only have the consequences specified in Part 36 if the court so orders.[1] Any Part 36 Offer will be treated as "without prejudice except as to costs",[2] and the fact that a Part 36 Payment has been made must not be communicated to the trial judge until all questions of liability and the amount of money to be awarded have been decided [CPR Part 36, rule 19(2)].[3] It is interesting to note that there is no express restriction on communicating a claimant's Part 36 Offer, but there can be no conceivable advantage in doing so.

Related provisions

31–03   Personal injury practitioners should be alert to the fact that, apart from CPR Part 36, there are other provisions relating to offers to settle and payments into court within the CPR:

(a) CPR Part 37 and its Practice Direction, Miscellaneous Provisions about Payments into Court, specifically:

(i) money paid into court under a court order;

(ii) Apportionment in proceedings under the Fatal Accidents Act 1976 and Law Reform (Miscellaneous Provisions) Act 1934.

(b) CPR, Part 20.3—a Part 20.3 Claim (*i.e.* a counterclaim or a claim for contribution or indemnity) is to be treated as a claim for the purposes, *inter alia*, of Part 36 (expressly noted in CPR Part 36, rule 1).

---

[1] CPR Part 36, r. 1(2).
[2] CPR Part 36, r. 19(1).
[3] CPR Part 36, r. 19(2).

(c) CPR Part 21.10—Compromise, etc., by or on behalf of a child or patient.

(d) CPR Part 44.3(4)(c)—in exercising its discretion as to costs the court must have regard to all the circumstances of the case including: "(c) any payment into court or admissible offer to settle made by a party which is drawn to the court's attention (whether or not made in accordance with Part 36)".

Application and Scope

The Civil Procedure Rules apply to all claims in which proceedings were 31–04 not commenced before April 26, 1999, and where a new step is to be taken in any proceedings in existence prior to that date. It is unlikely that the Practice Direction—Transitional Arrangements, supplementing CPR Part 51 will have any relevance to offers to settle or payments into court. Payment-out of money paid into court prior to April 26, 1999, is a "new step" and, thus, governed by the CPR.

The scope of the rules in CPR Part 36 is expressed to be about "*the consequences* where an offer to settle or payment into court is made in accordance with this Part".[4] Those consequences, namely the risk of financial penalties, were, under the old regime, rarely, if ever, borne by defendants. One of the overriding objectives of the CPR is "ensuring that the parties are on an equal footing".[5] The new regime introduces a system whereby any party to litigation can put the other at risk of financial penalty if the potential for a fair settlement is ignored or misjudged. It should be noted, however, that the Part 36 "consequences" do not apply to Small Claims Track cases "unless the court otherwise orders".[6]

CPR Part 36 is primarily concerned with Part 36 Payments and Part 36 Offers. Either can be made at any time *after* proceedings have started or in appeal proceedings. An offer made in accordance with the requirements of CPR Part 36, if made by way of an actual payment into court is a Part 36 Payment; otherwise it is a Part 36 Offer.[7] Logically, however, one should begin by considering the provisions that govern claims before commencement of proceedings.

The Pre-Action Offer

One of the pillars of the Woolf Reforms is the newly-conceived Pre- 31–05 action Protocol. At the time of writing, there are two: one relating to personal injury claims and the other to clinical disputes. The purpose of

---

[4] CPR Part 36, r. 1(b).
[5] CPR Part 1, r. 1(2)(a).
[6] CPR Part 36, r. 2(5).
[7] CPR Part 36, r. 2.

such protocols has been expressed to be, "To build on and increase the benefits of early but well-informed settlement which genuinely satisfy both parties to dispute."[8]

One of the expressed aims of the Protocol is "to put the parties in a position where they may be able to settle cases fairly and early without litigation". This aim is facilitated by the requirements of the Protocol which, if followed, should enable the parties to assess at least the relative merits of the claim, and, in many uncomplicated cases, the quantum of damages.

Although the Pre-Action Protocol for Personal Injury Claims does not expressly refer to "settlement offers", paragraph 2.13 of the Notes of Guidance states:

> "Parties and their legal representatives are encouraged to enter into discussions and/or negotiations prior to starting proceedings. The protocol does not specify when or how this might be done but parties should bear in mind that the courts increasingly take the view that litigation should be a last resort and that claims should not be issued prematurely when settlement is in reasonable prospect."

The objectives of the Pre-action Protocol have been given "teeth" in the provisions of CPR Part 36 r. 10. An offer to settle, by any party, made *prior* to the commencement of proceedings, will be (not "may be") taken into account when making orders as to costs after proceedings have begun. To secure the potential advantages that such a pre-action offer affords, that offer must:

(a) be expressed to be open for at least 21 days after the date it was made; and

(b) if made by a potential defendant, include an offer to pay the costs of the offeree up to the date 21 days after it was made.[9]

Futhermore, if the offeror is a defendant to a money claim, he must make a Part 36 Payment within 14 days of service of the claim form and such payment must be *no less than* the sum offered before proceedings commenced.[10] Once proceedings have commenced, an offeree may not accept a pre-action offer or a Part 36 Payment following upon it, without the permission of the court. The requirement for the court's permission appears to be necessary even if the Part 36 Payment is in a sum which exceeds the preceding pre-action offer, although why this should be so, is unclear.

There is no requirement that a claimant's pre-action offer should include provision for costs. It is unclear whether this is deliberate or an oversight.

---

[8] Introduction to the Pre-action Protocol for Personal Injury Claims, para. 1.1.
[9] CPR Part 36, r. 10(2).
[10] CPR Part 36, r. 10(3).

However, given the aims of the Protocol, it would appear to be sensible to include provision for costs in a claimant's offer. If provision is not included and the offer is accepted, the claimant will not recover costs. If provision for costs is included but the offer, including such provision, is rejected on the basis that it is outside the ambit of CPR Part 36(10), and the claimant then recovers more than he was, by his offer, prepared to accept by way of damages, it is considered unlikely that a court would not make an order penalising the defendant.

Defendant's Part 36 Offer

Any Part 36 Offer is made when it is received by the offeree[11]; any **31–06** improvement will be effective when its details are received by the offeree. Any part 36 offer (and, probably, any pre-action offer) may be the subject of a request by the offeror for clarification[12]—and see Part 23.

With two exceptions, an offer by a defendant to settle a money claim will not have the consequences set out in CPR, Part 36 (see below) unless the offer is made by way of a Part 36 Payment.

The two exceptions are:

(a) Part 36, rule 5(5) permits a Part 36 Offer to be made by reference to an *interim payment*;

(b) Part 36, rule 23 permits a Part 36 Offer by a defendant in cases where, if accepted, a Part 36 Payment or Offer would be a *compensation payment* as defined in section 1 of the Social Security (Recovery of Benefits) Act 1997, but only if:

    (i) at the time the defendant makes the offer he has applied for, but not received, a certificate of recoverable benefit; and

    (ii) he makes a Part 36 Payment not more than seven days after he receives the certificate.

Apart from the two exceptional cases noted in (a) and (b) above, in the context of personal injury litigation, the Part 36 Offer is likely to be used by a defendant primarily for the purpose of offers as to apportionment of liability. CPR Part 36, rule 5(4) specifically provides that "a defendant may make a Part 36 offer limited to accepting liability up to a specified proportion." Interestingly, as will be noted later, there is no similar provision in respect of a claimant.

The only other contexts in which the question of an "offer" arises, are:

- in the cases of claims for *provisional damages*. CPR Part 36, rule 7 deals with offers to settle claims including a claim for provisional

---

[11] CPR Part 36, r. 8(1).
[12] CPR Part 36, r. 9(2).

damages. If, as he may do, a defendant makes a Part 36 Payment in respect of such a claim, the payment notice must specify whether or not the defendant is offering to agree to the making of an award of provisional damages.

- in cases where a Part 36 Payment is expressed not to be inclusive or *interest*. In this case, CPR Part 36, rule 22(2) requires the Part 36 Payment notice to state "whether interest is offered and, if so, the amount offered, the rate or rates offered and the period or periods for which it is offered."

31–07   The *form* of a Part 36 Offer is provided for in CPR Part 36, rule 5:

(a) It must be in writing.

(b) It may relate to the whole or part of a claim "or to any issue that arises in it".

(c) It must expressly state to what it relates and whether it takes account of any counterclaim. Any offer will be treated as including all interest until the last date on which it could be accepted, unless the contrary is clearly specified (see above).

(d) If made *more than 21 days before trial*, it must be expressed to remain open for acceptance for 21 days from the date it is made *and* provide that after 21 days the offeree may only accept it if the parties agree the liability for costs *or* the court gives permission.

(e) If made *less than 21 days before trial*, it must be stated that the offeree may only accept it if the parties agree the liability for costs or the court gives permission.

(f) It must be signed by the offeror or his legal representative.[13] If made by a company, a person holding a senior position[14] may sign but must state the position he holds.[15]

A Part 36 Offer must be served on the offeree's legal representative.[16]

A Part 36 Offer may be withdrawn. Once withdrawn, the offer will not have the consequences set out in Part 36.[17]

Claimant's Part 36 Offer

31–08   A claimant's Part 36 Offer can be made at any time after proceedings have started[18] or in appeal proceedings and must be made in writing. It is effective when received by the defendant and must be served on the offeree's legal representative.

---

[13] PD, Part 36, para. 5.1(2).
[14] PD, Part 36, para. 5.6.
[15] PD, Part 36, para. 5.5.
[16] PD, Part 36, para. 11.1.
[17] CPR Part 36, r. 5(8).
[18] CPR Part 36, r. 2(4).

In personal injury litigation there are likely to be two situations in which a claimant will wish to consider making a Part 36 Offer, namely:

(a) an offer to accept a specified proportion of contributory negligence (if this issue arises); and

(b) an offer to accept a specific sum by way of damages, whether final or interim.

In the latter instance, there can be no "compensation payment" as defined in section 1 of the Social Security (Recovery of Benefits) Act 1997, unless and until the offer is accepted. It follows that any claimant's Part 36 Offer under (b) will, if accepted, be subject to deduction of relevant benefits. Consequently, claimant's advisers will need to consider the impact of deductible benefits before making a Part 36 Offer.

Part 36 Payment

A Part 36 Payment is made when written notice of the payment into court is served on the offeree.[19] It may relate to the whole claim or part of it or to any issue arising in it.[20] Except where a claimant is defendant to a counterclaim, there is no situation in personal injury litigation, in which a claimant would need to consider a Part 36 Payment; indeed CPR Part 36 makes no provision for acceptance of a claimant's Part 36 Payment only a claimant's Part 36 Offer.[21] **31–09**

If a defendant makes a Part 36 Payment he must file with the court a *Part 36 Payment Notice* (see Form N242A).

Such a notice must:

(a) state the amount of the payment;

(b) state whether it relates to the whole claim, part of it (and what part) or an issue (and what issue);

(c) state whether it takes into account any counterclaim;

(d) if there has been an interim payment, state whether this is taken into account;

(e) if not inclusive of interest, state whether interest is offered and, if so, the rate or rates offered and the period or periods for which it is offered[22];

---

[19] CPR Part 36, r. 8(2).
[20] CPR Part 36, r. 6(1).
[21] CPR Part 36, r. 12.
[22] For requirements (a)–(e), see CPR Part 36, r. 6.

(f) where benefits are to be deducted under the provisions of Schedule 2 of the Social Security (Recovery of Benefits) Act 1997, state:

    (i) the total amount represented by the "Part 36 Payment" (the gross compensation) and

    (ii) that the defendant has reduced this sum by a specified amount in accordance with section 8 of and Schedule 2 to the Act, naming the benefit and the amount and

    (iii) that the amount paid in (to be specified) is the net amount after deduction of the amount of benefit.[23]

Service of a Part 36 Payment Notice will be effected by the court unless the offerer tells the court that he will serve it, in which case the offeror must file a certificate of service [see CPR, Part 6 r. 10].[24]

Acceptance of a Part 36 Offer or Part 36 Payment

31–10   A Part 36 Offer or Part 36 Payment is accepted when notice of its acceptance is received by the offeror[25] (in respect of a Part 36 Payment, see Form N243).

A claimant may accept a defendant's Part 36 Offer or Part 36 Payment without needing the court's permission provided:

(a) the offer or payment was made not less than 21 days before the start of the trial, and

(b) written notice of acceptance is given to the defendant not later than 21 days after the offer or payment was made,[26]

otherwise the parties have to agree the liability for costs or acceptance can only be with the permission of the court which will make an order as to costs.[27] Where a claimant wishes to accept a Part 36 Offer made by one or more, but not all, of a number of defendants, then CPR Part 36, rule 17 applies.

A defendant may accept a claimant's Part 36 Offer without needing permission in precisely the same circumstances as a claimant may accept a defendant's offer or payment; if permission is required, as in the case of a claimant's acceptance, the court will make an order as to costs.

Where a Part 36 Offer or Part 36 Payment relates to a compromise by or on behalf of a *child or patient*,[28] it may only be accepted with he permission of the court, and no payment out can be made without a court order.[29]

---

[23] PD, Part 36, para. 10.
[24] CPR Part 6, r. 10.
[25] CPR Part 36, r. 8(5).
[26] CPR Part 36, r. 11(1).
[27] CPR Part 36, r. 11(1).
[28] CPR Part 21.
[29] CPR Part 36, r. 18.

If a Part 36 Offer or a Part 36 Payment is accepted, and relates to the whole of the claim, the claim will be stayed upon the terms of the offer; otherwise the stay be in respect of that part of any claim to which the offer relates with costs being determined by the court in default of agreement. Any stay will not affect the power of the court to enforce the terms of the Part 36 Offer, to deal with costs and to order payment out.[30]

The procedure for obtaining money out of court is detailed in PD, Part 36, para. 8.

Any alleged breach of the terms of an accepted offer can be dealt with by the court without the need to start a new claim (unless otherwise ordered).[31]

Costs and Other Consequences of Part 36 Offers or Payments

(a) Claimant Accepts a Defendant's Part 36 Offer or Part 36 Payment

If a Part 36 Offer or Part 36 Payment is accepted without the need for the court's permission, the claimant will be entitled to his costs of the proceedings on the standard basis, if not agreed, up to the date of serving notice of acceptance.[32]   31–11

If the offer or payment relates to *part* only of a claim and the claimant abandons the balance of his claim at the time of serving notice of acceptance, the claimant will be entitled to his costs (on a standard basis, if not agreed) of the proceedings up to the date of serving the notice of acceptance *unless the court orders otherwise.*

(b) Defendant Accepts a Claimant's Part 36 Offer

Where a claimant's Part 36 Offer is accepted without needing the court's permission, the claimant will be entitled to his costs of the proceedings up to the date upon which the defendant serves notice of acceptance.[33]   31–12

(c) Claimant Fails to do Better Than a Defendant's Part 36 Offer or Part 36 Payment

Unless it considers it unjust to do so, the court will order the claimant to pay any costs incurred by the defendant after the latest day on which the offer or payment could have been accepted without needing the court's   31–13

---

[30] CPR Part 36, r. 15.
[31] CPR Part 36, r. 15(6).
[32] CPR Part 36, r. 13(1) and (4).
[33] CPR Part 36, r. 14.

permission.³⁴ There are no specific criteria to assist in determining whether a costs order under this rule might be "unjust", but see (below) the provisions of CPR Part 36, rule 21(5).

(d) Claimant Does Better Than He Proposed in His Part 36 Offer

31–14   It is in this particular respect that the CPR introduces new penalties. *In addition* to awarding the claimant his costs on an *indemnity* basis from the latest date when the defendant could have accepted the offer without needing the court's permission, the court may also order *interest* on the whole, or part of, any sum of money (excluding interest) awarded to the claimant at a rate not exceeding 10 per cent above base rate for all, or some of, the period starting with the latest date on which the defendant could have accepted the offer without needing the permission of the court.³⁵ Such orders in respect of indemnity costs and interest *will be made* unless the court considers it unjust to do so³⁶; in considering whether it would be unjust to make such orders, the court will take into account:

- all the circumstances of the case;
- the terms of any Part 36 Offer;
- the stage at which a Part 36 Offer or Part 36 Payment was made;
- the information available to the parties when any offer or payment was made;
- the conduct of the parties with regard to giving or refusing to give information for the purpose of enabling the offer or payment to made or evaluated.³⁷

Note

31–15   Doubts as to the legality of the awarding of interest as a penalty, rather than as a compensatory payment, based upon the argument that the power to award interest is a matter of substantive law rather than procedural law (and thus not authorised by the Civil Procedure Act 1997), have been raised in an article in the *Journal of Personal Injury Litigation*.³⁸ The merit of the arguments advanced in support of such doubts will inevitably have to be tested. Editorial comment also raises doubt as to the legality of awarding interest as a penalty for failing to comply with a protocol "as this is imposed by a practice direction and not even a rule."³⁹

---

³⁴ CPR Part 36, r. 20(2).
³⁵ CPR Part 36, r. 21(2) and (3).
³⁶ CPR Part 36, r. 21(4).
³⁷ CPR Part 36, r. 21(5).
³⁸ "Awarding Interest Pursuant to Part 36.21(2) CPR—Is it Lawful?" [1999] J.I.P.L. 145.
³⁹ Editorial [1999] J.P.I.L. 81.

Clarification and Withdrawal of Offers and Payments

It has been noted (at para. 31–15 above) that the provision of informa- **31–16**
tion about offers and payments is particularly crucial to arguments which
may arise as to alleged injustice in making costs or interest penalty orders.
CPR Part 36, rule 9 makes specific provision for an offeree being able to
request the offeror to clarify the offer or payment notice, or, if necessary,
for the court to order such clarification (on application in accordance with
CPR Part 23 identifying the respects in which the terms of the offer or
payment are said to need clarification: Practice Direction, Part 36, paragraph 6).

Failure to seek clarification, where necessary, may thus prejudice any
later argument as to entitlement to costs or interest penalties.

A defendant who wishes to withdraw or reduce a Part 36 Payment must
obtain the court's permission[40] by making an application in accordance
with CPR Part 36, giving reasons.

Miscellaneous Provisions

(a) Practice Direction, Part 36, paragraph 11.2 provides for those cases **31–17**
where, in a claim arising out of an accident involving a motor car on
a road or in a public place, the damages claimed include a sum for
hospital expenses and the defendant or his insurer pays that sum to
the hospital under section 157 of the Road Traffic Act 1988. In such
cases, notice of that payment must be given to the court an all other
parties.

(b) As already mentioned, CPR Part 37 contains provisions relating to:
   (i) cases where money is paid into court under a court order;
   where a defendant makes a payment into court following an
   order under CPR Part 3, rules 1(3) or (5) (*e.g.* failure to comply
   with a rule, practice direction or relevant pre-action protocol),
   the defendant may choose to treat the whole or any part of the
   money paid into court as a Part 36 Payment. If so, he must file
   a Part 36 Notice Payment before CPR Part 36 will apply;
   (ii) proceedings under the Fatal Accidents Act 1976 and Law
   Reform (Miscellaneous Provisions) Act 1934, where the court
   is required to apportion money between the different claims
   when a single sum of money is paid into court in satisfaction of
   those claims and accepted.

Forms

The following specific forms relating to Part 36 Offers and Part 36 **31–18**
Payments are contained in the CPR:

---

[40] PD, Part 36, para. 3.4.

- *Form N242A*   Notice of Payment into court (in settlement—Part 36).

      This notice will need to be modified where an offer of provisional damages is made.[41] The form is also used where any notice of increase of a payment in is required.

- *Form 243*   Notice of Acceptance of payment into court (Part 36)

Comment

31–19   CPR Part 36 and associated provisions contain much that is familiar from the "old regime" and much that is new. Lord Woolf's original proposal that the "payment into court" be replaced by a system of "offers in settlement" was not adopted. Rather, the provisions relating to "offers to settle" have been grafted onto modified old rules of court, to formalise and extend the former use of *Calderbank* letters or informal settlement proposals. Notwithstanding the blend of "old" and "new", the provisions of CPR Part 36 represent a welcome adjustment in the balance of power afforded by the litigation tactic of offers and payments into court, with the introduction of clear and extended penalties for those who fail to consider properly the undoubted benefit of sensible settlement of claims, whether claimant, defendant or other party to proceedings.

---

[41] CPR Part 36, r. 7.

Section 4

FUNDING

32. Costs

Introduction

As Lord Woolf has observed, the change to the civil procedure relating **32–01** to costs, in particular the introduction of summary assessment of costs, is one of the most significant in the Civil Procedure Rules.[1] What follows is a summary of the rules about costs; where still relevant, decisions made under the old rules are cited in this text. They must, however, be treated with caution since they are no longer to be regarded as binding authority.

The General Rule

The general rule is that costs are in the discretion of the court which **32–02** shall have full power to determine by whom, to what extent, and when costs are to be paid.[2] The general rules for costs in the High Court and the county court are now set out in CPR Part 44.

The general rule is restated by CPR 44.3(2):

"(2) If the court decides to make an order about costs—
  (a) the general rule is that the unsuccessful party will be ordered to pay the costs of the successful party; but
  (b) the court may make a different order."

As Hoffmann L.J. observed in *McDonald v. Horn*,[3] referring to its predecessor RSC, Ord. 62, r. 3, this rule reflects a basic rule of English civil procedure, that a successful litigant has a prima facie right to his costs.

CPR 44–47 and their associated Practice Directions set out the specific rules about costs, in particular: the basis of assessment (CPR 44.4); factors to be taken into account in deciding the amount of costs (CPR 44.5); procedure for assessing costs (CPR 44.7); special situations (CPR 44.13); courts' powers in relation to misconduct (CPR 44.14); summary assessment procedure (PD44.4.3); fixed costs (CPR 45); Fast Track trial costs (CPR 46); procedure for detailed assessment of costs (CPR 47). These rules must be read with care by the practitioner, as their effect is wholly to replace the pre-existing rules for costs. Although many similarities and general principles relating to the entitlement to and recovery of costs are to

---

[1] CPR Costs Regime and the Bar—Seminar, July 19, 1999 at Lincoln's Inn.
[2] See Supreme Court Act 1981, s.51(1) and (3) and CPR r. 44.3(1).
[3] [1995] I.C.R. 685.

be noted, these are significant procedural changes which profoundly effect the way those principles will be applied by the court.

Entitlement to Assessment and Recovery

32–03   The "indemnity principle" is the backbone to an order for the recovery of costs. The principle is that a successful party cannot recover from the unsuccessful party a sum in excess of the successful party's liability to his solicitor. It was most recently considered by the Court of Appeal in *General of Berne Insurance Co. v. Jardine Reinsurance Management Ltd.*[4] May L.J. said (at 304):

> "The principle is simply that costs are normally to be paid in compensation for what the receiving party has or is obliged himself to pay. They are not punitive and should not enable the receiving party to make a profit".

Thus, a successful party is only entitled to recover those costs which he is (legally) obliged to pay his solicitor.[5]

Although the indemnity principle is overridden in certain cases of legally-aided parties by regulation 107b of the Civil Legal Aid (General) Regulations, it is not undermined merely because the successful litigant is a member of a trade union whose claim is being pursued with financial support from his union.[6] Once the client-solicitor relationship is established, there is a presumption that the client will be personally liable for the costs. That presumption can, however, be rebutted if it is established that there is an express or implied agreement, binding on the solicitor that the client would not have to pay those costs in any circumstances.[7] In *Bailey v. IBC Vehicles*,[8] the solicitors for a defendant in a personal injury action which had settled before trial objected to the hourly rate and mark up specified in the bill of costs submitted by the union on claimant's behalf and requested evidence to prove that there was no breach of the indemnity principle. The request was dismissed, but Judge J. indicated that in future, due to the growth of conditional fees and the increased interest in challenging such bills of costs, the extension of the client care letter and contentious business agreements, or a brief written explanation should normally be attached to the bill of costs in order to avoid unnecessary litigation.

---

[4] [1998] 2 All E.R. 301.
[5] *Gundry v. Sainsbury* [1910] 1 K.B. 645; but see the amendment to Supreme Court Act 1981, s.51, introduced by Access to Justice Act 1999, s.31.
[6] *See Adams v. London Improved Motor Coach Builders Ltd* [1921] K.B. 499; followed in *R. Miller (Raymond)* [1983] 1 W.L.R. 1056.
[7] See Lloyd J. in *R v. Miller (Raymond)* [1983] 3 W.L.R. 1056 at 1061.
[8] [1998] 3 All E.R. 570.

With the introduction of summary assessments of costs, and the potential for obtaining an order for costs at an interim hearing on behalf of a party whose personal liability for costs is contingent on the final outcome of the case, it is thought that some brief explanation of the entitlement to costs[9] should accompany the costs schedule. Save for the rules themselves, there is currently no published guidance on how and when the summary assessment of costs at an interim stage in proceedings ought to be conducted. If the personal liability for costs is contingent upon the final outcome of the case, there may be a strong argument for postponing the summary assessment.[10]

Exercise of Discretion

In exercising its discretion on costs the court is required to have regard 32–04 to all the circumstances[11] including:

(a) the conduct of all the parties;

(b) whether a party has succeeded on part of his case, even if he has not been wholly successful; and

(c) any payment into court, or admissible offer to settle made by a party which is drawn to the court's attention (whether or not made in accordance with Part 36).

Conduct of the Parties

"Conduct" is defined as including: 32–05

(a) conduct before as well as during the proceedings and the extent to which both parties followed any relevant pre-action protocol;

(b) whether it was reasonable for a party to raise, pursue or contest a particular allegation or issue;

(c) the manner in which a party has pursued or defended his case in relation to a particular allegation; and

(d) whether a claimant who has succeeded in his claim, in whole or in part, exaggerated his claim.[12]

---

[9] If solicitor and own client costs are claimed, then it ought to include sufficient details of base costs and percentage uplift to answer the court's enquiry under CPR 48.(2), see CPR 48.9.
[10] CPR PD 44.4.4.(1)(b).
[11] CPR 44.3(4).
[12] CPR 44.3(5).

CPR 44.3.6 sets out a non-exhaustive list of orders which the court may make.[13] CPR 44.3.8 provides that the court may order an amount to be paid on account before the costs are assessed. This power was recently considered in *Mars v. Teknowledge*,[14] where it was held by Jacob J. that the court should, on a rough and ready basis, normally order an interim payment of some lesser amount being such sum as that party would almost certainly collect. That case emphasises the principle aim of the CPR regime relating to costs, namely to bring home to the parties at an early stage in the proceedings both the costs and risks of litigation. In practice, an interim order for costs payable forthwith may frequently either stay or dispose of proceedings altogether.

Effect of Specific Costs Orders

32–06   CPR Part 44 sets out in tabular form, repeated below, the effect of specific orders which the court may make:

Term	Effect
• Costs • Costs in any event	The party in whose favour the order is made is entitled to the costs in respect of the part of the proceedings to which the order relates, whatever other costs orders are made in the proceedings.
• Costs in the case • Costs in the application	The party in whose favour the court makes an order for costs at the end of the proceedings is entitled to his costs of the part of the proceedings to which the order relates.
Costs reserved	The decision about costs is deferred to a later occasion, but if no later order is made the costs will be costs in the case.
Claimant's/defendants' costs in the case/application	If the party in whose favour the costs order is made is awarded costs at the end of the proceedings, that party is entitled to his costs of the part of the proceedings to which the order relates. If any other party is awarded costs at the end of the proceedings, the party in whose favour the costs order is made is not liable to pay the costs of any other party in respect of the part of the proceedings to which the order relates.

[13] See table below in text.
[14] *The Times*, July 8, 1999.

Term	Effect
Costs thrown away	Where, for example, a judgment or order is set aside, or the whole or part of any proceedings are adjourned, the party in whose favour the costs order is made is entitled to the costs which have been incurred as a consequence. This includes the costs of: (a) preparing for and attending any hearing at which the judgment or order which has been set aside was made; (b) preparing for and attending any hearing to set aside the judgment or order in question; (c) preparing for and attending any hearing at which the court orders the proceedings or the part in question to be adjourned; (d) any steps taken to enforce a judgment or order which has subsequently been set aside.
Costs of and caused by (an amendment)	Where, for example, the court makes this order on an application to attend a statement of case, the party in whose favour the costs order is made is entitled to the costs of preparing for and attending the application and the costs of any consequential amendment to his own statement of case.
Costs here and below	The party in whose favour the costs order is made is entitled not only to his costs in respect of the proceedings in which the court makes the order but also to his costs of the proceedings in any lower court.
No order as to costs	Each party is to bear its own costs of the part of the proceedings to which the order relates whatever costs order the court makes at the end of the proceedings.

Silence as to Costs

It is important to note the significant change in CPR 44.13 which provides **32–07** that:

> "Where the court makes an order which does not mention costs, no party is entitled to costs in relation to that order."

Time for Complying

A party must comply with an order for the payment of costs within 14 days **32–08** of:

    (a) the date of the judgment or order; or

(b) if detailed assessment is ordered, the date of the certificate of the detailed assessment.

Award of Costs: the Court's Discretion

Costs against Non-Parties—Aiden Shipping Co. Ltd v. Interbulk Ltd[15]

32–09   In the *Aiden Shipping* case, it was held that the discretionary power to award costs (SCA 1981, ss.51(1)) was in wide terms; there was no basis to imply a limitation to the effect that costs could only be ordered to be paid by parties to the proceedings. Balcombe L.J. in *Symphony Group v. Hodgson*[16] set out guiding principles which govern the exercise of discretion where an application is made for a non-party to pay costs of proceedings. It has been held that there is no statutory requirement or authority that "exceptional circumstances" are a necessary precondition for the exercise of the power,[17] nor that the relationship between a party and non-party need be an unusually close one.[18] A costs order can certainly be made against a non-party to proceedings, particularly where that person has a financial interest in the outcome and his involvement has not been justified but has been "wanton officious intermeddling".[19] For a fuller discussion of such orders and the principles involved see the Chapter on Wasted Costs hereafter, to which reference should be made; there is often an interrelationship between the two.

Where the court is considering making a costs order in favour of a non-party, that party must be added as a party for the purposes of costs only and must be given an opportunity to be heard.[20]

Materials for Exercising Discretion

32–10   (i) *General principle.* The discretion to make any order for costs must be exercised judicially in accordance with reason and justice.[21] The old authorities relating to the exercise of discretion as to costs are perhaps still helpful guiding authority. Thus, a successful claimant who recovers more than nominal damages should ordinarily have an order for costs against an

---

[15] [1986] A.C. 965, HL.
[16] [1994] Q.B. 179.
[17] *Globe Equities Ltd. v. Globe Legal Services and others*, The Times, April 14, 1999, CA.
[18] *Wiggins v. Richard Read (Transport) Ltd*, The Times, January 14, 1999, CA.
[19] *Nordstern Allegmeine Versicherungs AG v. Internav Ltd; Nordstern Allegmeine Versicherungs AG v. Katsamas*, The Times, June 8, 1999, CA following *Murphy v. Young & Co.'s Brewery Plc* [1997] 1 W.L.R. 1591.
[20] CPR 48.2(1).
[21] *Gupta v. Kitto*, The Times, November 23, 1998, if this principle needs authority.

unsuccessful defendant, subject to the other considerations to which the court is to have regard, in particular proportionality and the conduct of the parties.

Certainly under the older authorities it was wrong in principle for a judge to mark his disapproval of the way a successful claimant has conducted litigation by ordering him to pay the defendant's costs. In *Knight v. Clifton*,[22] it was held that in exceptional circumstances (but only then) the court had jurisdiction to award costs against a wholly successful defendant. This authority must now be seen in the light of the penal sanctions which may be imposed under the CPR where a claimant has done better than he has proposed in a Part 36 Offer[23] and the relevance of "conduct" in exercising the discretion on costs.

In the case of a wholly successful defendant, the judge should award him his costs unless there is evidence that he brought about the litigation, or has done something connected with the institution or conduct of the action calculated to occasion unnecessary litigation and expense, or has done some wrongful act in the course of the transaction of which the claimant complains.[24]

(ii) Failure to recover damages. Damage is of the essence of the tort of **32–11** negligence. Thus a claimant who fails to prove that the defendant's negligence caused damage loses his action. More than nominal damages must be recovered. A claimant who only recovers nominal damages is normally regarded as unsuccessful and liable to pay the defendant's costs.[25]

(iii) Separate issues. A notable change from earlier case law as at CPR **32–12** 44.3(5), which allows the court to assess the extent to which a party has been successful on each of the issues pursued.

(iv) Relevance of legal aid. The fact that the successful party has been in **32–13** receipt of legal aid and would not have a personal liability to pay his costs is *not* relevant to the exercise of discretion as to costs; to take account of the fact he is legally-aided is contrary to the Legal Aid Act 1988, s.31(1).[26]

(v) Late amendment. The general rule is that where a claimant makes a late **32–14** amendment, which substantially alters his case and without which the action would fail, a defendant is entitled to his costs down to the date of the amendment.[27]

(vi) Inflated claims: relevance of financial limits. Prior to the implementa- **32–15** tion of the CPR, the Court of Appeal had criticised improper inflation of a

---

[22] *Knight v. Clifton* [1971] Ch. 700, CA.
[23] CPR 36(1) and see para. 36–27 below.
[24] See Atkin L.J. in *Ritter v. Godfrey* [1920] K.B. 47.
[25] *Alltrans Express Ltd v. C.V.A. Holdings Ltd* [1984] 1 W.L.R. 394 (breach of contract).
[26] *Knight v. Lambeth LBC* [1995] C.L.Y., CA.
[27] *Beoco v. Alfa Laval Ltd* [1995] Q.B. 137, CA.

claim to a sum exceeding the relevant financial limit.[28] The test adopted in that case was whether the claimant could reasonably have expected to recover a sum in excess of the limit. With the raising of the small claims limit to £5,000, and the introduction of a Fast Track procedure with limitations on recovery of costs for cases less than £15,000 in value, it is thought that a similar test will apply to claimants who artificially inflate a claim in order to oust the prescribed Fast Track or small claims limits.

32–16 *(vii) Costs following allocation or reallocation.* CPR 44.11 deals with allocation and reallocation costs. Where a claim is allocated to a track and the court subsequently reallocates that claim to a different track then, unless the court orders otherwise, any special rules about costs applying:

(a) to the Fast Track will apply up to the date of reallocation; and

(b) to the second track will apply from the date of reallocation.

32–17 *(viii) Cases where costs orders are deemed to have been made.* In four specified circumstances under four separate rules, which provide for a right to costs, a costs order will be deemed to have been made on the standard basis. Those particular circumstances are set out in CPR 44.12, but are in summary: rule 3.7 (Defendant's right to costs where claim is struck out for non-payment of fees); rule 36.3(1) (Claimant's right to costs where he accepts defendant's Part 36 offer or Part 36 payment; rule 36(4) Claimant's right to costs where defendant accepts the claimant's Part 36 offer); and rule 38.6 (Defendant's right to costs where claimant discontinues).

32–18 *(ix) Courts' powers in relation to misconduct.* The courts' powers in relation to misconduct are set out at CPR 44.14. These matters are properly dealt with in the chapter relating to wasted costs.

32–19 *(x) Appeal against an order for costs.* Until section 54 of the Access to Justice Act 1999 comes into force, permission to appeal is not required against a summary assessment by the master or district judge. The rules for appeal against a detailed assessment are set out in CPR 47 and its associated Practice Direction.

Guiding Rules in Particular Circumstances

Interim Hearings

32–20 The costs of interim applications are in the discretion of the court and are subject to the same general principles already covered. Unless there is good reason not to do so, these costs will be summarily assessed at the

---

[28] *See Afzal v. Ford Motor Co. Ltd* [1994] 4 All E.R. 720, CA.

conclusion of the application and by reference to schedules of costs of the hearing prepared by both parties.

Pre-emptive Costs Orders

In the "most exceptional circumstances" the court may make an order **32–21** pre-empting the final outcome of the case in public interest cases. The "general rule" cited above is a formidable obstacle to any pre-emptive costs order as between adverse parties in ordinary litigation. It is difficult to imagine a case falling within the general principle in which it would be possible for a court properly to exercise its discretion in advance of the substantive decision.[29]

Lockley Orders

Where a party is legally aided, the court may, on an interim hearing, **32–22** order that costs awarded to the other party be set off against any damages or costs to which the legally aided party is or may become entitled. Where the legally-aided party is the receiving party of an order for costs, no summary assessment may be made. Conversely, where the legally-aided party is the paying party, it is proper to make a summary assessment of the costs and set off such costs against any award of damages and/or costs to which the legally-aided party is or may become entitled. The Court of Appeal in *Parr v. Smith*[30] has suggested that a preferable wording for an order *"not to be enforced without leave"* is an order that the determination of the assisted person's liability to pay be postponed in accordance with regulation 127b of the Civil Legal Aid (General) Regulations 1989. It is worth noting that CPR PD 44.4.9(2) provides that summary assessment is not by itself a determination of the assisted person's liability to pay those costs.[31]

Counterclaim and Set Off

Where a claimant recovers money on the claim and the defendant **32–23** recovers on his counterclaim, the general practice is to enter one judgment only for the balance in favour of the claimant, if he is the net winner. In such circumstances, the usual principles—costs to follow the event—will apply in respect of claim and counterclaim. This will, of course, be subject to the particular circumstances. Where in a traffic accident both parties were equally to blame and were awarded almost identical sums on the claim and counterclaim, the Court of Appeal made no order on either, as

---

[29] *R. v. Lord Chancellor, ex p. Child Poverty Action Group* [1999] 1 W.L.R. 349.
[30] [1995] 2 All E.R. 1031, CA.
[31] See Legal Aid Act 1988, s.17.

an order in favour of the claimant would have given him an unfair advantage.[32] Further, where a judge struck out part of a defendant's counterclaim and made an award of costs against him, it was, as a matter of principle, wrong for the judge to then make a further order staying proceedings relating to the remainder of the counterclaim until the defendant paid the costs awarded to the claimants.[33] CPR 40.13 provides that where the court gives judgment both *for* the claimant on his claim and *against* the claimant on a counterclaim, if there is a balance in favour of one of the parties, it may order the party whose judgment is for the lesser amount to pay the balance. In a case to which this rule applies, the court may make a separate order as to costs against each party.[34]

Part 20 Proceedings

32–24 *(i) General principles.* The court has always had power to make such order as to costs between the respective parties as the justice of the case may require.[35] Where the defendant reasonably brings in a Part 20 defendant and succeeds in the main action, he should usually recover against the claimant his costs of both the action and the Part 20 proceedings including those he has been ordered to pay to the Part 20 defendant, or, in a proper case, the claimant can be ordered to pay the Part 20 defendant's costs directly.[36] A successful Part 20 defendant is normally entitled to an order for costs against an unsuccessful Part 20 claimant even where the Part 20 claimant is legally aided.[37]

32–25 *(ii) Discontinuance.* No costs order is deemed to be made where a party discontinues third party or Part 20 proceedings. The Part 20 defendant must seek an order for his costs by application.

Multiple Parties

32–26 *(i) Co-defendants.* Where the claimant has reasonably sued two defendants in the alternative and succeeded against only one of them, the court may in its discretion order the unsuccessful defendant to pay the successful defendant's costs. This may be done:

(a) by an order that the unsuccessful defendant pay the successful defendant's costs direct, a "Sanderson Order";[38] or

---

[32] *Smith v. W.H. Smith & Sons Ltd* [1952] 1 All E.R. 528, CA.
[33] *Theakston v. Matthews, The Times*, April 13, 1998.
[34] See also CPR 46.3(6) in relation to Fast Track costs.
[35] *Edginton v. Clark* [1964] 1 Q.B. 367, CA.
[36] *LE Cattam Ltd v. A. Michaelides & Co.* [1958] 1 W.L.R. 717; *Thomas v. Times Book Co. Ltd* [1966] 1 W.L.R. 911.
[37] *Johnson v. Ribbons* [1977] 1 W.L.R. 1458, CA.
[38] *Sanderson v. Blythe Theatre Co.* [1903] 2 K.B. 533, CA.

(b) by an order that the claimant pay the successful defendant's costs and recover them from the unsuccessful defendant as part of the claimant's costs of the action, a "Bullock Order".[39]

The form of order is in the court's discretion. Where the claimant is insolvent or legally aided, a Sanderson order may be preferable. But where the unsuccessful defendant is insolvent, the successful defendant is not necessarily entitled to a Bullock or Sanderson order.[40]

Before the court can make either of the above orders it must be satisfied that the claimant acted reasonably in joining both defendants, *e.g.* where the claimant was a passenger injured in a vehicle in collision with another. In deciding whether to exercise such discretion the court will look at all the facts which the claimant knew or might reasonably have ascertained when he commenced proceedings.[41]

(ii) Joint tortfeasors. The Civil Liability (Contribution) Act 1978, which **32–27** provides for contribution between persons liable in respect of the same damage, by section 4 deprives the claimant of costs where more than one action is unnecessarily brought.

Part 36 Offers and Part 36 Payments

Costs orders in connection with Part 36 Payments and Part 36 Offers are **32–28** covered in Chapter 31.

Security for Costs

The High Court Rules in RSC, Ord. 23 have been re-enacted in CPR **32–29** Sch. 1, and by a new rule 1.A1 apply also the county court. The general principle is that no person shall be prevented from taking or defending proceedings as a result of his or her impecuniosity. In practice, there is unlikely to be any question of security having any part to play in personal injury actions at first instance. Even where the claimant is ordinarily resident abroad, the court should never exercise its discretion under RSC, Ord. 23, r.1, to order security to be given by an individual claimant resident in a Member State of the European Union in the absence of very cogent evidence of substantial difficulty in enforcing a judgment in the Member State.[42] If some special situation has arisen that might merit a possible application for security, then reference should be made to the detailed provisions of the rules.[43]

---

[39] *Bullock v. London General Omnibus Co.* [1907] 1 K.B. 264, CA.
[40] *Bankamerica Finance Ltd v. Nock* [1988] A.C. 1002; *Mayer v. Harte* [1960] 1 W.L.R. 770, CA.
[41] *Besterman v. British Motor Cab Co. Ltd* [1914] 3 K.B. 181.
[42] *Fitzgerald and Others v. Williams* [1996] 2 All E.R. 171, CA.
[43] RSC, Ord. 23.

Transfer of Proceedings

32–30 Subject to any order which may have been made by the original court, CPR 44.13(3)(4) provides that once a case is transferred the new court will deal with all questions as to costs, including the costs incurred before transfer.

Costs of Setting Aside Judgment

32–31 A claimant will normally be entitled to the costs of any application to set aside a regular judgment. The court may impose terms as to costs as a condition of setting judgment aside, *e.g.* the costs of the application and those thrown away. Where a judgment is irregular, the defendant is normally entitled to his costs of the application, but different considerations may apply, particularly if the irregularity was not the fault of the claimant.

Varying an Order for Costs

32–32 As under the old "slip rule", the court has power under CPR r.40.12(1) to correct any accidental slip or omission in any judgment or order. Normally, an order or judgment will be drawn up by the court. Until it is drawn up the court may recall or vary any order at any time.[44]

Appeals and Orders for Costs

32–33 By CPR r.44.13(2), a court dealing with a case on appeal may make orders relating to the proceedings giving rise to the appeal as well as the appeal itself. As a general rule, the successful appellant gets his costs of the appeal and below, and an unsuccessful appellant will have to pay the costs of the appeal. Where the appellant only succeeds in part or has succeeded only on a point not argued below or not raised in his notice of appeal, or has been guilty of objectionable conduct, he may well be deprived of some or all of his costs.[45]

Security for Costs of Appeal

32–34 See generally RSC, Ord. 59(5) re-enacted in Schedule 1 of CPR. Security for the costs of an appeal may be ordered where there are special circumstances which in the opinion of the court render it just to order security. While in the case of an individual claimant (as opposed to a

---

[44] *Hyde and Southbank Housing Association v. Kain*, *The Times* August 30, 1989, CA.
[45] CPR 44.3(5).

company) his impecuniosity is not grounds for an order for security below, the impecuniosity of a claimant is a ground for the award of security in the Court of Appeal: the appellant has already had the case determined after a trial and it is prima facie an injustice to allow an appeal by an impecunious appellant to proceed where the respondent will be unable to enforce an order for costs made in his favour by the Court of Appeal. The Court of Appeal, nonetheless, retains a discretion.

Appeals against Orders for Costs Only

Under RSC, Ord. 59, r. 1B, permission to appeal is required on an **32–35** appeal to the Court of Appeal against costs only.[46] Permission to appeal may be given to appeal or cross appeal by the court below, or by the Court of Appeal. Permission to appeal is not required where the order for costs against which an appeal is to be made is either against a non-party (*Aiden Shipping* type order)[47] or a wasted costs order against a legal representative.[48]

The first question will be whether the judge had material before him upon which he could exercise his discretion by making the order he did as to costs. The court will assume that he exercised his discretion unless satisfied that he did not do so. So it will not interfere where he gave reasons which are germane and not based on any false principle, nor where there are also other possible grounds for his discretion. But he must exercise it fairly. To succeed, therefore, on such an appeal the appellant must (in an area where the judge has a wide discretion) satisfy the court that the judge applied a false principle, or had no materials on which he could reasonably so exercise his discretion. Even where permission to appeal has been given, the court will not interfere unless there has been a manifest disregard of principle or misapprehension of the facts.[49] The same principles apply to an appeal to the judge against summary assessment for costs made by the master or district judge.

Appeal against detailed assessment

By CPR r. 47.21(1) no appeal may be brought against a detailed **32–36** assessment until written reasons have been obtained in accordance with CPR r. 47.23; and permission to appeal has been given (where necessary) under CPR r. 47.24; unless the Court otherwise orders. Permission to appeal is not required to appeal against:

---

[46] But see Access to Justice Act 1999, s.54.
[47] *Re Land and Property Trust Co. Ltd* [1991] 1 W.L.R. 601, CA.
[48] *Thompson v. Fraser* [1986] 1 W.L.R. 17, CA followed in *Wilson v. Kerry* [1993] 1 W.L.R. 963, CA.
[49] *Findlay v. Railway Executive* [1950] 2 All E.R. 550; *Alltrans Express Ltd v. C.V.A Holdings Ltd* [1984] 1 W.L.R. 394, CA.

(a) a decision of an authorised court officer; or

(b) a decision of a costs judge or a district judge to impose a sanction on a legal representative under CPR r. 44.14 (powers in relation to misconduct); or

(c) CPR r. 48.7 (wasted costs order).

A party who has a right to appeal does so by filing a notice of appeal.[50] The notice must be filed within 14 days after the court officer's reasons are served on the appellant; or if the court has directed that reasons need not be obtained, within seven days after the date of the decision appealed against.[51] On the appeal from an authorised court officer the court will:

(a) rehear the proceedings which gave rise to the decision appealed against; and

(b) make any orders and give such directions as it considers appropriate[52] on appeal from a costs judge or district judge,[53] if the court is satisfied that the appeal should be allowed, it may make any order and give such directions as it considers appropriate.[54]

Fixed Costs

32–37   A new system of fixed costs is set out in CPR r. 45, and supplemented by the associated Practice Direction, RSC, Ord. 62[55] and CCR, Ord. 38.[56] Fixed costs apply where the only claim is a claim for a specified sum of money and:

(a) judgment in default is obtained under CPR r. 12.4(1);

(b) judgment on an admission is obtained under CPR r. 14.4(3);

(c) judgment on an admission on part of the claim is obtained under CPR r. 14.5(6);

(d) summary judgment is given under CPR Part 24;

(e) the court has made an order to strike out a defence under CPR r. 3.4.(2)(a) as disclosing no reasonable grounds for defending the claims;

---

[50] CPR r. 47.24.
[51] CPR r. 47.25.
[52] CPR r. 47.25(2).
[53] CPR r. 47.26 1(a)–(b).
[54] CPR r. 47.26(2).
[55] CPR Sched. 1, App. 3.
[56] CPR Sched. 2, App. B.

(f) the only claim is a claim where the court gave a fixed date for the hearing when it issued the claim and judgment is given for the delivery of goods, and in either case the value of the claim exceeds £25.

RSC, Ord. 62, App. 3 to Sched. 1 to the CPR sets out the fixed costs in the High Court for: entering judgment in claims for the possession of land and additional costs for service; and taking certain enforcement proceedings.

CCR, Ord. 38, App. B to CPR Sched. 2 sets out fixed costs in county court cases for:

(a) money claims;

(b) claims for the recovery of land; and

(c) claims for the recovery of goods including goods covered under hire purchase agreements.

Summary Assessment of Costs

The rules on summary assessment embody the main principles underly- 32–38
ing the CPR. They serve a threefold purpose:

(a) to ensure that the successful party to an application or hearing is out of pocket in respectof their costs for as short a time as possible;

(b) to impress upon the parties both the risks and the costs of litigation and thereby encourage settlement; and

(c) to save the further costs of a detailed assessment.

CPR PD 44.4.4 sets out the new procedure for summary assessment. Generally, any interim application which is disposed of in less than one day will conclude with a summary assessment of costs unless there is good reason not to do so, *e.g.* where the paying party can show substantial grounds for disputing the sums claimed for costs that cannot be dealt with summarily or there is insufficient time.[57] It is the duty of the parties and their legal representatives to assist the judge in making a summary assessment of costs and to do so each party who claim costs *must* prepare a written statement of the costs he intends to claim showing separately in the form of a schedule:

(a) the number of hours to be claimed;

---

[57] CPR PD 44.4.4.(1)(b).

(b) the hourly rate to be claimed;

(c) the grade of fee earner;

(d) the amount and nature of any disbursement to be claimed;

(e) the amount of solicitor's costs to be claimed for attending or appearing at the hearing, and any VAT to be claimed on these amounts.[58]

The statement of costs must be filed at court and copies of it must be served on any party against whom an order for payment of those costs is intended to be sought. The schedule should be in the form annexed to (Practice Direction) 44; it must be served as soon as possible and in any event not later than 24 hours before the hearing.[59]

The failure by a party to comply with this direction is a matter to be taken into account by the court in deciding what order to make about costs, and about any further hearing or detailed assessment hearing that may be necessary as a result of that failure.[60]

32–39 The court may not make summary assessment of a receiving party who is an assisted person under the Legal Aid Act 1988; or of a receiving party who is a child or patient.[61]

On assessment the court must have regard to to all the circumstances including:

(a) conduct before and during proceedings;

(b) any efforts made to resolve the dispute;

(c) the amount or value of any property involved;

(d) the importance of the matter to all parties;

(e) the complexity, difficulty or novelty of the questions raised;

(f) the skill, effort, specialised knowledge and responsibility involved;

(g) the time spent on the case;

(h) the place where and circumstances in which work was done.[62]

No summary assessment of costs will be made if the parties have agreed the amount of costs payable.[63] In every case where an order for costs is made against a legally represented party (including an agreed order); and

---

[58] CPR PD 44.4.5.(2)(a).
[59] CPR PD 44.5(4).
[60] CPR PD 44.4.9(2).
[61] CPR PD 44.4.9(3).
[62] CPR r. 44.5(3).
[63] CPR PD 44.4.10.

the party is not present when the order is made, the party's solicitor must notify his client in writing of the costs order no later than seven days after the solicitor receives notice of the order.[64]

Fast Track Costs

CPR 46 deals with the amount of costs which the court may award as **32–40** the costs of an advocate for preparing for and appearing at the trial of a claim in the fast track. The following table shows the amount of Fast Track trial costs which the court may award (whether by summary or detailed assessment).[65]

Value of the Claim	Amount of Fast Track Trial Costs which the Court may award
Up to £3,000	£350
More than £3,000 but no more than £10,000	£500
More than £10,000	£750

The court does have power to award more, or less than the prescribed rates under CPR 46.3, in particular an additional £250 to a legal representative who attends the trial in addition to the advocate, and the court considers the legal representative's attendance necessary to assist the advocate.[66]

Where a defendant has made a counterclaim against the claimant, and (a) the claimant has succeeded on his claim; and (b) the defendant has succeeded on his counterclaim, the court will quantify the amount of the award of fast track trial costs to which:

(i) but for the counterclaim, the claimant would be entitled for succeeding on his claim; and

(ii) but for the claim, the defendant would be entitled to for succeeding on his counterclaim, and make one award of the difference, if any, to the party entitled to the higher award of costs.[67]

Improper or unreasonable conduct by a receiving party may result in the court awarding a party less than would otherwise be payable.[68] Conversely,

---

[64] CPR r. 44.2(iv)–(b).
[65] CPR r. 46.2(1).
[66] CPR r. 46.3(2)(b).
[67] CPR r. 46.3(6)(a)–(b).
[68] CPR r. 46.3(7).

where the paying party has behaved improperly during the trial the court may award such additional amount to the other party as it considers appropriate.[69]

Basis of Assessment

32–41   Costs (other than fixed fast track trial costs) are awarded either on the standard or the indemnity basis. The difference between an award under the standard or indemnity basis is now more significant than under the old rules because, whereas on an assessment on the standard basis the court must have regard to whether the costs were "proportionately and reasonably" incurred and "proportionate and reasonable in amount", the proportionality of the costs is ignored on the indemnity basis.[70]

There is little guidance on when indemnity costs should be ordered. In *Bowen-Jones v. Bowen-Jones*,[71] Knox J. declined to reappraise the old cases and adopted the approach of Brightman J. in respect of a predecessor to RSC, Ord. 76:

> "It is not the policy of the courts in hostile litigation to give the successful party an indemnity against the expense to which he has been put and, therefore, to compensate him for the loss which he has inevitably suffered, save in very special circumstances."[72]

Nonetheless, a typical case for indemnity costs would be against a contemnor[73] for persistent non-compliance with orders or the rules. Indemnity costs have been awarded against a defendant who failed to specifically plead that the claimant was a malingerer, such allegation amounting to an allegation of fraud which should have been specifically pleaded.[74] On the other hand, over vigorous of a breach of confidence action was held to be different from overt or deliberate dishonesty in its prosecution and not to attract an order for indemnity costs. The test appears to be that there must be misconduct in connection with the litigation whether in its actual conduct, or because of the nature of the underlying action, *e.g.* a finding of fraud.

Successful parties in receipt of legal aid are not entitled to an award on the indemnity basis from their unsuccessful opponents.[75] Regulation 197 of

---

[69] CPR r. 46.3(8).

[70] CPR r. 44.5(1)(a).

[71] [1986] 3 All E.R. 163.

[72] *Bartlett v. Barclays Bank Trust Co. Ltd (No. 2)* [1980] 2 All E.R. 92 at 98.

[73] See *Midland Marts Ltd. v. Hobday* [1989] 1 W.L.R. 1143.

[74] *Cooper v. P & O Stena Line Ltd*, *The Times*, February 8, 1999, applying *Bank or Baroda v. Panessar* [1987] Ch. 335; *Tharros Shipping Co. Ltd v. Bias Shipping Ltd* [1994] 1 Lloyd's Rep. 533; and *Wailes v. Stapleton Construction and Commercial Services Ltd* [1997] 2 Lloyd's Rep. 112.

[75] *Willis v. Redbridge Health Authority*, *The Times*, December 22, 1995, CA.

the Civil Legal Aid (General) Regulations 1989 provides that the costs paid to a solicitor to a legally-aided party out of the legal aid fund are to be taxed on a standard basis.

Detailed Assessment

Under the CPR, detailed assessment replaces what was formerly the **32–42** taxation of costs. It is governed by CPR 47 and the associated Practice Direction. The general rule is that the costs of any proceedings or any part of the proceedings are not to be assessed by the detailed procedure until the conclusion of the proceedings, but the court may order them to be assessed immediately.[76] Proceedings are concluded when the court has finally determined the matters in issue in the claim, whether or not there is an appeal.[77]

Within three months of the judgment, or the event whereby the right to detailed assessment arose a notice of commencement must be served on the paying party by the receiving party, together with the bill of costs. If proceedings are not commenced in time, CPR 47.8 provides sanctions for delay including the disallowance of all or part of the costs or interest payable. Within 21 days of service of the notice of commencement, the *paying* party must serve points of dispute in relation to the disputed items on the bill or costs. If no points of dispute are served, the receiving party may serve a request for a default costs certificate.[78]

The request for a hearing of the detailed assessment must be made by the receiving party after service of the points of dispute and, in any event, within three months of the expiry of the period for commencing the assessment proceedings. If such a request is not made, the paying party may apply for an order requiring the receiving party to make on failing which costs or interest may be disallowed in whole or in part.[79] An interim costs certificate may be issued by the court at any time after the filing of the request, and will generally include an order that the specified sum be paid.[80] Solicitor and own client costs are, unless the bill is paid out of the Legal Aid Fund, or pursuant to a conditional fee agreement, assessed on the indemnity basis.[81]

CPR 48.9 provides that on every assessment, (whether summary or detailed), of a solicitor's bill to a client where the solicitor and the client have entered into a conditional fee agreement, the client may apply for assessment of the base costs or for a percentage increase on or both. Where the assessment is for base costs, they are to be assessed in accordance with

---

[76] CPR 47(1).
[77] CPR PD 47 1.1(1).
[78] CPR 47.9.
[79] CPR 47.14.
[80] CPR 47.15.
[81] CPR 48.8.

CPR 48.8(2) as if the solicitor and his client had not entered into a conditional fee agreement. Where the client applies for assessment of a percentage increase, the court may reduce the percentage increase where it considers it to be disproportionate having regard to all the relevant factors as they reasonably appeared to the solicitor or counsel when the conditional fee agreement was made.

Even where a detailed assessment is ordered, the receiving party ought to apply for an interim payment of costs on account.[82]

Access to Justice

32–43   Practitioners should be aware of the impact of the Access to Justice Act 1999.[83] Section 29 provides for the recovery of insurance premiums by a successful party in respect of funding litigation on conditional fee or otherwise. Section 31 makes an amendment to section 51 of the Supreme Court Act 1981 allowing for rules to be made for securing that the amount awarded to a party in respect of costs to be paid to his legal representative is *not* limited to the amount that would have been payable to them had he hot been awarded costs. In other words, this amendment authorises departure from the indemnity principle. Section 54 deals makes it necessary to obtain permission to appeal from any order for costs.

Interest on Costs

32–44   The statutory interest on a judgment or order for the payment of costs runs from the date of the judgment or order, *not* from the date of the certificate quantifying the same or such other date as may be ordered as the date on which payment is to be made.[84] Interest payable pursuant to section 17 of the Judgments Act 1838 or section 74 of the County Courts Act 1984 on the costs deemed to have been made under CPR 44.12 begins to run from the date on which the event which gave rise to the entitlement to costs occurred.[85]

---

[82] See *Mars v. Teknowledge, The Times*, July 8, 1999.
[83] c.22.
[84] *Hunt v. RM Douglas Roofing* [1988] 3 All E.R. 823.
[85] CPR 44.12(2).

33. Wasted Costs and Costs Against Non Parties

Wasted Costs

The Jurisdiction

There are three possible heads of jurisdiction under which a legal 33–01 representative may be made personally liable for the costs of any proceedings in respect of acts or omissions committed in connection with such proceedings. Essentially, the jurisdiction is statutory, provided for by section 51(6) of the Supreme Court Act 1981 and it is pursuant to this provision that wasted costs orders within the strict definition of that term are made. The court also has limited jurisdiction to make an order for costs against a legal adviser personally, which limited additional jurisdiction arises under two heads. The first additional jurisdiction arises from the inherent jurisdiction of the High Court (only) and probably applies only to solicitors. The second area of additional jurisdiction arises under the general jurisdiction of the court as to costs contained in section 51(1) and (3) of the Supreme Court Act 1981, see generally *Hodgson v. Imperial Tobacco*.[1]

The second area of additional jurisdiction, section 51(1) and (3) of the Supreme Court Act 1981, cannot arise where a legal representative is acting only in that capacity in legal proceedings,[2] and is used ordinarily to obtain costs orders against non-parties (see below at para. 33–15). However, the Court of Appeal has held that there is jurisdiction to make a "wasted costs order" against a firm of solicitors being a non-party acting for a party to proceedings, where a benefit accrued to that firm from acting and where the firm had known that the client was not likely to be able to pay its costs.[3] The original application had been made under all three heads of jurisdiction, namely (i) section 51(6), (ii) the court's inherent jurisdiction, and (iii) under the general jurisdiction provided for by section 51(1) and (3). The judge had made a personal costs order in reliance on section 51(1) and (3), and the firm of solicitors in question were unsuccessful in their appeal against that order. *Globe Equities*, however, concerned a solicitor who had effectively become the client and was the driving force behind the litigation. He was not therefore acting only in the capacity of legal representative.

---

[1] [1998] 1 W.L.R. 1056, 1066.
[2] *ibid.*
[3] *Globe Equities Ltd v. Globe Legal Services Ltd; sub nom Globe Equities v. Kotrie and Others* T.L.R. April 14, 1999.

With the enactment of the Civil Procedure Rules (CPR), (in force from 26, April 1999) there is now a codified framework of rules applicable to the exercise of the statutory jurisdiction found in section 51(6), see CPR r. 48.7. Rule 48.7 is supplemented by the introductory Practice Direction to CPR Parts 43 to 48, applicable to costs applications generally and by Practice Direction 48, Costs—special cases which (see below) appears to lay down both substantive and procedural guidance. (Costs against non-parties are covered by CPR Part 48.2, see below).

The Supreme Court Act 1981, s.51(6) and (7)

33–02   The power to make a wasted costs order in the High Court and county court is found in the Supreme Court Act 1981, s.51(6) and (7).

The Supreme Court Act 1981, s.51 provides:

"(6) In any proceedings mentioned in sub-section (1),[4] the court may disallow, or, (as the case may be), order the legal or other representative concerned to meet, the whole of any wasted costs or such part of them as may be determined in accordance with the rules of court.

(7) In sub-section (6), 'Wasted Costs' means any costs incurred by a party—

(a) as a result of any improper, unreasonable or negligent act or omission on the part of any legal or other representative or any employee of such representative; or

b) which in the light of any such act or omission occurring after they were incurred, the court considers it unreasonable to expect that party to pay."

The Civil Procedure Rules

33–03   Rule 48.7 provides for the personal liability of legal representatives for costs. The rule was amended with effect from July 3, 2000 to provide as follows:

"48.7 Personal liability of legal representative for costs—wasted costs orders

"(1) this rule applies where the court is considering whether to make an order under Section 51(6) of the Supreme Court Act 1981 (court's power to disallow or (as the case may be) order a legal representative to meet, 'wasted costs').

(2) the court must give the legal representative a reasonable opportunity to attend a hearing to give reasons why it should not make such an order.

(3) (Initially this sub-rule provided that the court may direct that privileged documents are to be disclosed to the court and, if the court so directs, to the other party to the application for an order.)

---

[4] Sub-section (1) refers to "all proceedings in (a) the Civil Division of the Court of Appeal; (b) the High Court, and (c) any County Court".

(4) when the court makes a wasted costs order, it must specify the amount to be disallowed or paid.

(5) the court may direct that notice must be given to the legal representative's client, in such manner as the court may direct—

(a) of any proceedings under this rule; or

(b) of any order made under it against his legal representative.

(6) before making a wasted costs order, the court may direct a costs judge or a district judge to enquire into the matter and report to the court.

(7) the court may refer the question of wasted costs to a costs judge or a district judge, instead of making a wasted costs order.

Practice Direction—see practice direction—(costs—special cases) which supplements this part generally. See also practice direction (costs—introduction) which supplements Parts 43 to 48."

The Practice Direction to CPR Part 43 provides:

"1. This practice direction supplements Parts 43 to 48 of the Civil Procedure Rules. It applies to all proceedings to which those parts apply.

2. Section III of the Directions relating to Part 48 deals with transitional provisions affecting proceedings about costs which were pending before 26 April 1999.

3. Attention is drawn to the powers to make orders about costs conferred on the Supreme Court and any County Court by Section 51 of the Supreme Court Act 1981.

4. In these directions:
   'Counsel' means a barrister or other person who has a right of audience in relation to all proceedings in the High Court or in the County Court in which he is instructed to act.
   'Solicitor' means a solicitor of the Supreme Court or other person with a right of audience in relation to all proceedings, who is conducting the claim or defence (as the case may be) on behalf of the party to proceedings and, where the context admits, includes a patent agent.

5. In respect of any document which is required by these Practice Directions to be signed by a party or a legal representative of the Practice Direction supplementing Part 22 will apply and if the document in question was a statement of truth. (The Practice Direction supplementing Part 22 makes provision for cases in which the party is a child, a patient or a company or other corporation and cases in which a document is signed on behalf of a partnership)."

The Practice Direction to Part 48 provides: 33–04

53.1 Rule 48.7 deals with wasted costs orders against legal representatives. Such orders can be made at any stage in the proceedings up to and including the proceedings relating to the detailed assessment of costs. In general, applications for wasted costs are best left until the end of the trial.

53.2 The court may make a wasted costs order against a legal representative or of its own initiative.

53.3 A party may apply for a wasted costs order:

(a) of what the legal representative is alleged to have done or failed to do, and

(b) of the costs that he may be ordered to pay or which are sought against him.

The notice must be given at least 3 days before the hearing.

53.4 It is appropriate for the court to make a wasted costs order against the legal representative only if:

(1) he has acted improperly, unreasonably or negligently,

(2) his conduct has caused a party to incur unnecessary costs, and

(3) it is just in all the circumstances to order him to compensate that party for the whole or part of those costs.

53.5 The court will give directions about the procedure that will be followed in each case in order to ensure that the issue is dealt with in a way that is fair and as simple and summary as the circumstances permit.

53.6 As a general rule the court will consider whether to make a wasted costs order in two stages:

(1) In the first stage, the court must be satisfied:

(a) that it has before it evidence or other material which, if unanswered, would be likely to lead to a wasted costs order being made, and

(b) the wasted costs proceedings are justified notwithstanding the likely costs involved.

(2) At the second stage (even if the court is satisfied under paragraph (1)) the court will consider, after giving the legal representative an opportunity to put forward his case, whether it is appropriate to make a wasted costs order in accordance with paragraph 2.4 above.

[deleted with effect from 13 September 1999

53.7 Attention is drawn to rule 48.7(3) which gives the court power to direct that privileged documents be disclosed to the court and, if appropriate, to the other party to the application for the wasted costs order.]

53.8 On an application for a wasted costs order under Part 23 the court may proceed to the second stage described in paragraph 53.6 without first adjourning the hearing if it is satisfied that the legal representative has already had a reasonable opportunity to give reasons why the court should not make a wasted costs order. In other cases the court will adjourn the hearing before proceeding to the second stage.

53.9 On an application for a wasted costs order under Part 23 the application notice and any evidence in support must identify—

(1) what the legal representative is alleged to have done or failed to do; and

(2) the costs that he may be ordered to pay or which are sought against him.

53.10 A wasted costs order is an order—

(1) that the legal representative pay a specified sum in respect of costs to a party: or

(2) for costs relating to a specified sum or items of work to be disallowed.

*53.11 Attention is drawn to rule 44.3(a) (1) and (2) which respectively prevent the court from assessing any additional liability until the conclusion of the proceedings (or the part of the proceedings) to which the funding arrangement relates, and set out the orders the court may make at the conclusion of the proceedings.

Application in Practice

Orders can be made at any stage in the proceedings, including proceed- 33–05 ings relating to the detailed assessment of costs.[5] In general applications for wasted costs orders are probably best left until the end of proceedings. It is also open to the court to make a wasted costs order of its own initiative[6] (Practice Direction 53.2).

The Introductory Costs Practice Direction supplementing parts 43 to 48 applies to applications for wasted costs and sets out detailed provisions which need to be followed on any such application.

Where the court of its own initiative considers that a wasted costs order should be considered it must give the legal representative in question a reasonable opportunity to attend a hearing to give reasons why it should not make such an order.[7]

As a general rule (but apparently not inevitably), there are two stages to the process of obtaining a wasted costs order, whether instigated on the court's own initiative, or on application by a party. At the first stage, the court must be satisfied that it has before it evidence or other material which, if unanswered, would be likely to lead to a wasted costs order being made, *and that wasted costs proceedings are justified notwithstanding the likely costs involved* (Practice Direction 53.6(1)(b)).[8] The party applying for wasted costs needs to bear in mind the proportionality of the costs involved in wasted costs proceedings, see *A J Fahani v. Merc Property Ltd,*[9] where more time was spent on the wasted costs proceedings than on the substantive proceedings, and a wasted costs order was refused. If a party loses its application for wasted costs, then the normal rule will be that costs follow the event. Thus, the party seeking wasted costs would in fact end up paying the costs of the party against whom wasted costs were sought in relation to the satellite litigation. This is of particular importance where the wasted costs investigation may have been initiated by the court and subsequently pursued by a party.

The same judge should ideally hear the wasted costs application as heard 33–06 the substantive hearing, if practical, and the wasted costs proceedings should follow the substantive hearing as soon as possible, as the longer the

---

[5] PD, Part 48, 2.1.
[6] PD 2.2.
[7] CPR 48.7(2).
[8] PD, Section II (2.6).
[9] *The Times*, May 19, 1999.

time period between hearings the more that needs to explained to the judge.

The court may direct that notice be given to the legal representative's client in any manner as the court may direct of any proceedings for wasted costs. This assumes that the client is not present at the time.

The court will then give directions about the procedure that will be followed in each case in order to ensure that the issues are dealt with in a way that is fair and as simple and summary as circumstances permit (Practice Direction 53.5).[10]

At the second stage, the actual hearing for the application for wasted costs, the legal representative must be given an opportunity to state why a wasted costs order should not be made (CPR 48.7(2) and Practice Direction 53.6(2)(b)).[11]

The CPR as originally drafted provided, without specifying whether at stage 1 or stage 2, that the court could direct that privileged documents be disclosed to the court, and if the court so directed, to the other party to the application for an order, CPR 48.7(3).[12] In the first publication of the rules, attention was drawn to this power specifically in paragraph 2.7 of the Practice Direction to Part 48. This radical inroad into the common law rules of privilege has recently been declared (at first instance) to be *ultra vires*.[13] In addition, on August 27, 1999, the Lord Chancellor's Department issued amendments to the CPR, which amendments effect from September 13, 1999. The relevant paragraph of the Practice Direction to Part 48 (2.7) was deleted. The rule itself initially remained. Further amendments to the CPR taking effect from July 3, 2000 have now revoked the old Part 48.7(3).

Circumstances in which a Wasted Costs Order is Appropriate

33–07   It is appropriate for the court to make a wasted costs order against the legal representative only if the representative has acted improperly, unreasonably or negligently, his conduct has caused a party to incur unnecessary costs, and it is just in all the circumstances to order him to compensate that party for the whole or part of those costs. The leading explanation of what amounts to conduct justifying the making of a wasted costs order is found in *Ridehalgh v. Horsefield*[14] The extent to which courts will continue to have regard to past case law, or even to post-April 26,

---

[10] PD 2.5.
[11] CPR 48.7(2) and PD 2.6(b).
[12] CPR 48.7(3).
[13] *General Mediterranean Holdings SA v. Patel & Patel, The Times*, August 3, 1999.
[14] [1994] Ch. 205, CA.

1999 cases, following the enactment of the CPR, said to be a complete and self-contained code, is outside the scope of this Chapter. It seems unlikely that past principles will however simply fall by the wayside. The statutory basis for wasted costs has of course not changed.

"Improper" conduct covers, but is not confined to, conduct which would ordinarily justify disbarment, striking off, suspension from practice or other serious professional penalties. "Unreasonable" describes conduct which is vexatious, designed to harass the other side, rather than advance the resolution of the case; it makes no difference that the conduct was the product of excessive zeal rather than improper motives. However, it is not correct that conduct is *only* unreasonable if it is vexatious or designed to harass the other side.[15] Failure to agree substantially similar medical evidence in a minor personal injury case, necessitating the attendance at court of two expert witnesses, has been held to be unreasonable.[16] "Negligent" is not to be construed technically, but to denote failure to act with the competence reasonably expected of ordinary members of the profession.[17]

A solicitor who fails properly to instruct his advocate so that not all relevant matters are put before the court on an application to adjourn, exposes himself to a finding of unreasonable or negligent conduct.[18] Delay in the conduct of proceedings even though not leading to their dismissal, can also give rise to a wasted costs order.[19] A solicitor who learned of fraudulent conduct of his client and whose actions thereafter caused further costs to be wasted was liable for these.[20] A solicitor who commences an action does not thereby warrant that his client has a good cause of action but merely that he has a client who bears the name of a party to the proceedings and who has authorised them.[21] Failure to serve notice of discharge or revocation of Legal Aid does not permit of a reasonable explanation.[22]

The court in *Ridehalgh* made it plain at four points in its judgment that the threshold was whether the conduct in question was unjustifiable.[23] Failure to conduct a case economically or to abide by a Practice Direction will expose practitioners to a risk of wasted costs order.[24] It is to be expected that failure to comply with mandatory requirements of the CPR,

---

[15] *Jennifer Joseph v. Boyd & Hutchinson (a firm)*, January 13, 1999, Ch D (unreported).
[16] *Whittles (a firm), Joan Greenhoff v. J. Lyons & Co. Ltd*, June 30, 1998, CA (unreported).
[17] *Ridehalgh* at 232H and 233C, approving the test in *Saif Ali v. Sydney Mitchell & Co.* [1980] A.C. 198 at 218, 220.
[18] *Shah v. Singh* [1996] P.N.L.R. 84, CA.
[19] *Kilroy v. Kilroy* [1996] P.N.L.R. 67, CA.
[20] *R v. Liverpool City Council ex p. Horne* [1997] P.N.L.R. 95, DC.
[21] *Nelson v. Nelson* [1997] 1 W.L.R. 233, CA.
[22] *Re Stathams (Wasted Costs Order: Banks v. Woodhall Duckham Ltd & Others* [1997] P.I.Q.R. P464.
[23] *op.cit.* 226, 231, 236 and 237.
[24] *Practice Direction (Civil Litigation) Case Management* [1995] 1 W.L.R. 252.

the protocols, or even the new culture of the CPR, may, if there is no reasonable explanation, also be visited with a wasted costs order.

Hopeless cases

33–08   A legal representative is not to be held to have acted unreasonably, improperly, or negligently just because he acts for a party whose case is plainly doomed to fail. Courts should rarely, if ever, assume that a hopeless case is being litigated on the advice of the lawyers; clients are free to reject advice and to insist that their cases be litigated. The lawyer is there to present the case; it is for the judge and not the lawyers to judge it. Legal advisers are expected to continue to make their services available in a *"hopeless"* case where the litigant persists in pursuing the claim.[25] A properly-conducted case could appear reasonable and then turn out to be hopeless; accordingly, care should be exercised in finding that lawyers must have been acting improperly or unreasonably in a hopeless case. But a lawyer cannot lend assistance to a case which is an abuse of process, to use litigation for procedures or purposes for which they were not intended, or to pursue proceedings for reasons unconnected with success in the litigation of a case known to be dishonest. It is not entirely easy to distinguish by definition between the hopeless case and that which amounts to an abuse of process, but in practice it is not hard to say which it is. If there is any doubt, the legal representative is entitled to the benefit of it.

Relevance of funding from the Community Legal Service Fund; Impecunious Claimant; Conditional Fees

33–09   The courts must bear prominently in mind the peculiar vulnerability of lawyers representing assisted parties to applications for wasted costs orders because their clients are unlikely to meet any costs liability.[26] It would subvert the benevolent purposes of the community legal service if such representatives were subject to any unusual risk. They for their part must bear prominently in mind that their advice and conduct should not be tempered by the knowledge that their client is not the paymaster and so not in all probability liable for the costs to the other side.

Nor is there jurisdiction to make an order for costs against a lawyer solely on the ground that he acted without fee or under a conditional fee agreement.[27] Whether a solicitor is acting for remuneration or not does not alter the existence or nature of his duty to his client and the court, or affect

---

[25] *Brian Anthony Jones v. The Chief Constable of Bedfordshire Police*, July 30, 1999, CA (unreported).
[26] *Symphony Group plc v. Hodgson* [1994] Q.B. 179 at 194, CA.
[27] *Tolstoy-Miloslavsky v. Aldington* [1996] 1 W.L.R. 736 at 746, CA; *Hodgson & Others v. Imperial Tobacco* [1998] 1 W.L.R. 1056.

the absence of any duty to protect the opposing party in litigation from exposure to the expense of a hopeless claim. In neither case does he have to impose a pre-trial screen through which a litigant must pass.[28] The existence of a conditional fee agreement should make a legal adviser's position as a matter of law no worse, so far as being ordered to pay costs is concerned, than it would be if there were no CFAs. This is said to be unless, of course, the CFA is outside statutory protection.[29]

Reliance on Counsel

The guidance in *Locke v. Camberwell Health Authority*[30] was endorsed. **33–10** A solicitor does not abdicate his professional responsibility when he seeks the advice of counsel. He must apply his mind to the advice received. But the more specialist nature the advice sought, the more likely it is that it was reasonable to accept it and act on it. The solicitor is not allowed however to follow Counsel blindly or to ignore the glaringly obvious: see *Tolstoy-Miloslavsky v. Aldington.*[31]

Privilege

If the applicant's privileged communications are germane to an issue in **33–11** the application, to show what he would or would not have done had the other side not acted in the manner complained of, he can waive privilege; if he declines to do so adverse inferences can be drawn.

The respondent lawyers are in a difficult position. This is because privilege is not their's to waive. In the usual case, where waiver will not benefit their client, they be slow to advise him to waive his privilege, and they may well feel bound to advise their client to seek independent advice before doing so. The client in any event may be unwilling to waive privilege. Accordingly, the respondent lawyers are at a grave disadvantage in defending their conduct of the proceedings, unable to disclose what advice and warnings they gave, what instructions they received. It follows that the courts have to make allowance for the inability of the respondent lawyers to tell the whole story. Where there is room for doubt they are entitled to the benefit of it. It is only when, with all allowances made, a lawyer's conduct of proceedings was quite clearly unjustifiable that it could be appropriate to make a wasted costs order.[32]

Clients cannot rely on their legal privilege when they have acted fraudulently and the solicitor cannot connive in the use of such privilege to

---

[28] *Orchard v. S.E.E. Board* [1987] Q.B. 565, 572–574, CA.
[29] *Hodgson & Others v. Imperial Tobacco* [1998] 1 W.L.R. 1056.
[30] (1991) 1 Med.L.R. 249, CA.
[31] *op. cit.* at 747, 749 and 751.
[32] *Ridehalgh* at 237.

conceal fraudulent conduct.[33] It is also the case that not only are the respondents not permitted to disclose any privileged facts to the court, but since privilege is that of their client they should not reveal such matters to the lawyers retained to represent them on the application. Thus, they could not disclose to their own representatives their client's instructions, advice they gave, instructions to counsel or his advices, any correspondence or notes or communication with the client, witnesses or experts and so on. For further discussion of what may be disclosed (pre-CPR) see *Reg v. Horsham DC ex p. Wenman.*[34]

Rule 48.7(3) of the Civil Procedure Rules as originally drafted drove a coach and horses through the common law doctrine of legal professional privilege.

> *"(3) for the purposes of this rule, the court may direct that privileged documents are to be disclosed to the court and, if the court so directs, to the other party to the application for an order."*

The CPR provided very little guidance in relation to applications for a direction that a privileged documents be disclosed to the court. For example there was no requirement that the client himself actually has to be notified of an application. There was no guidance as to who should make such an application, or who should pay the costs of it? An applicant, where no disclosure of privileged documents is given, is met with the position that the respondent lawyers are entitled to the benefit of the doubt in relation to what advice and warnings they gave, and, accordingly, the applicant himself may be interested in privileged communications.

The respondent lawyers on the other hand who wish to blame either counsel or the client himself, may also have an obvious interest in wanting disclosure of privileged documents. Such problems are now academic. To the author's knowledge only one such order was ever made, at county court level, in *Harrison v. Zulver and Davies.*[35] Subsequently, the issue was fully aired before Mr Justice Toulson in *General Mediterranean Holdings FA* (Claimant) v. (1) *Ramanbhai Manibhai Patel* (2) *Kirit Kumar Ramanbhai Patel* (Defendants).[36]

33–12   In *Mediterranean Holdings*, the defendants' solicitors applied for a direction under CPR 48.7(3) that privileged documents containing statements made by the Defendants be disclosed to the court, and if so directed to the claimant. The defendant's solicitors were respondents to an application by the claimant for a wasted costs order against them. The defendants resisted the application on the grounds that: (i) CPR 48.7(3) was *ultra vires*; (ii) CPR 48.7(3) infringed Articles 6 and 8 of the European

---

[33] *op. cit.*
[34] [1994] 4 All E.R. 681 at 703, 704.
[35] May 21, 1999, H.H. Judge Rich Q.C.
[36] [1999] QBD, *The Times*, August 3, 1999.

Convention on Human Rights, such that even if *intra vires* the court should exercise its discretion by declining to make any order under it; and (iii) the application was in any event premature. The general words of paragraph 4 of Schedule 1 to the Civil Procedure Act 1997, provided that: "Civil Procedure Rules may modify the rules of evidence as they apply to proceedings in any court within the scope of the rules". The Law Society appeared in support of the defendants on grounds (i) and (ii).

Holding that rule 48.7 was *ultra vires*, Mr Justice Toulson found that the right to legal confidentiality arising between lawyer and client (save where the client was attempting to use the right for an unlawful purpose) was a matter of substantive law and not merely a rule of evidence, further it was a right of great constitutional importance within the common law, applying *R. v. Derby Magistrates Court ex p. B.*[37] The general words of paragraph 4 of Schedule 1 to the 1997 Act did not confer general power on the rule making bodies to abrogate or limit a person's right to legal confidentiality, since, first, fundamental principles of human rights could not be overridden by mere general words, and, secondly, this was especially so where the general words appeared in legislation which was not primary but subordinate. The language and structure of the Act did not suggest that Parliament had in mind the abolition or limitation of the right to legal confidentiality, accordingly CPR 48.7(3) was *ultra vires*. Further, even if CPR 48.7(3) was *intra vires*, the court would not have exercised its discretion to order disclosure since the defendants had a right to confidentiality under Article 8 of the Convention in respect of their communications with their solicitors; the right to a fair trial conferred by Article 6 did not give the right to interfere with another person's right to legal confidentiality; moreover, it was doubtful whether an order for the disclosure of privileged material for purposes of wasted costs application was a necessary and proportionate measure for the purposes of doing justice to the legal profession. Further, the court was not persuaded of the necessity towards disclosure and the present stage to enable the solicitors to properly conduct their defence. Accordingly, the application for a direction under 48.7(3) was refused.

There was no appeal in *Mediterranean Holdings*. The amendment to Practice Direction 48 deleting the reference to 48.7(3), did appear to suggest that the rule itself would be reconsidered and with effect from July 3, 2000 48.7(3) is finally revoked. The position of 48.7(3) in the limelight is over. Presumably, therefore, respondent lawyers can continue to claim the benefit of the doubt.

The Second and Third Stages of the Three-Stage Test

Even if the conduct of litigation has been improper, unreasonable or **33–13** negligent, this is not of itself sufficient to give rise to a wasted costs order. Thus, a finding of negligence does not mean that a wasted costs order has

---

[37] [1995] 3 W.L.R. 681.

to be made. Such use of the jurisdiction could result in satellite litigation which was as complex and expensive as the original litigation.[38] Obviously, the conduct complained of needs to have caused an applicant to incur unnecessary costs (48.7, 2.4(b)). In addition it must be just in all the circumstances to order a legal representative to bear all or part of the unnecessary costs.

Amount of Costs

33–14   A wasted cost order which does not specify the amount of costs to be awarded is said to be fatally flawed and it is not possible to vary or amend the order by adding a figure at a later date.[38a] The court when making a wasted costs order must direct that the legal representative pay a specified sum 48.7(4). But the Practice Direction at 53.9 allows alternatively for the court to specify that costs relating to a particular sum or items of work be disallowed.[39] The court also has power to direct that a costs judge or district judge to inquire into the matter report to the court before making a wasted costs order. This power of referring to a costs judge or a district judge also allows the court itself to refer the question of wasted costs instead of making a decision thereon and making a wasted costs order itself, CPR 48.7(6) and (7).[40] A wasted costs order which does not specify the amount of costs to be awarded is fatally flawed and it is not possible to vary or amend the order by adding a figure at a later date.

Costs Against Non-Parties

Generally

33–15   In *Aiden Shipping Co. Ltd v. Interbulk*,[41] it was held that the discretionary power to award costs[42] was in wide terms; there was no basis to imply a limitation to the effect that costs would only be ordered to be paid by the parties to proceedings. The Court of Appeal in *Symphony Group plc v. Hodgson*[43] has laid down principles to govern the exercise of discretion where an application is made for a non party to pay costs of proceedings.

Jurisdiction

An order against a non-party may be made under Section 51(1) and (3) of the Supreme Court Act 1981.

---

[38] *Dr Michael John Pelling v. Veronica Nana Bruce-Williams*, December 16, 1998, CA, Lord Woolf M.R., Brooke L.J. (unreported).
[38a] See re Harry Jagder & Co. (Wasted Costs Order) (No. 2 of 1999), The Times, August 12, 1999, CA.
[39] PD 2.8.
[40] CPR 48.7(6).
[41] [1986] A.C. 965, HL.
[42] Supreme Court Act 1981, s.51(1).
[43] [1994] Q.B. 179 at 192–194, CA.

The Civil Procedure Rules

CPR Part 48.2 applies to costs orders in favouir of or against non-parties. There is as yet no Practice Direction aimed specifically at this issue, but PD Costs, supplementing Parts 43 to 48 applies to all such applications.
Part 48.2 provides:

(1) Where the court is considering whether to exercise its power under section 51 of the Supreme Court Act 1981 (costs are in the discretion of the court) to make a costs order in favour of or against as person who is not a party to proceedings—

    (a) that person must be added as a paty to the proceedings for the purposes of costs only; and

    (b) he must be given a reasonable opportunity to attend a hearing at which the court will consider the matter further.

(2) This rule does not apply—

    (a) where the court is considering whether to

        (i) make an order against the Legal Services Commission:
        (ii) make a wasted costs order (as defined in 48.7); and

    (b) in proceedings to which rule 48.1 applies (pre-commencement disclosure and orders for disclosure against a person who is not a party).[43a]

Principles

An order against a non-party may be made under section 51(1) and (3) **33–16** of the Supreme Court Act 1981:

(1) It should not be made save in exceptional circumstances. The judge should treat any application for such an order with considerable caution.[44]

(2) It will be even more exceptional for an order for the payment of costs to be made against a non party, where the applicant has a cause of action against the non-party and could have joined him as a party in the original proceedings.

(3) Even if the applicant has good reason for not joining the non-party against whom he has a valid cause of action, he should warn him at the earliest opportunity of the possibility that he may seek an order for costs against him. At the very least this will be an opportunity to apply to be joined.

[43a] [1986] A.C. 965, HL.
[44] See *Re Land & Property Trust plc* [1991] 1 W.L.R. 601 at 604, CA.

(4) An application for payment of costs by a non-party should normally be determined by the trial judge.

(5) The fact that a trial judge may in the course of his judgment have expressed views on the conduct of a non-party constitutes neither bias nor the appearance of a bias.[45]

(6) The procedure for the determination of costs is summary. Subject to any relevant statutory exceptions, judicial findings are inadmissible as evidence of the facts upon which they were based in proceedings between one of the parties to the original proceedings and a stranger.

(7) The normal rule is that witnesses in proceedings enjoy immunity from any form of civil action in respect of evidence given during those proceedings.[46]

(8) The fact that an employee, or even a director or the managing director, of a company gives evidence in an action does not normally mean that the company is taking part in the action (to which it has not been joined), insofar as that is an allegation relied upon by the party who applied for an order for costs against a non-party company.

(9) The judge should be alert to the possibility that the application against a non-party is motivated by resentment of the inability to obtain an order for costs against a legally-aided litigant.[47]

The Court of Appeal[48] has rejected the submission that *Aiden Shipping* was authority for the proposition that the rationale of section 51(1), (3) was "to make the person substantially responsible for causing the costs to be incurred to bear them".

If, however, a third party:

(1) has a commercial interest in supporting the litigation, such as a trade union, insurer or other trade organisation, so as to render it just that they should be rendered liable; or

(2) has given an express or implied promise of indemnity to the claimant against his liability, if unsuccessful, for the defendant's costs, it might be right to make an order.

---

[45] See *Bahai v. Rashidian* [1985] 1 W.L.R. 1337 at 1342, 1346, CA; but otherwise where he has made findings against the unrepresented non-party; see *Re Freudiana Holdings Ltd, The Times*, December 4, 1995, CA.

[46] In *Sarra v. Sarra* [1994] 2 E.L.R. 880 an application for an order for costs against an expert witness was refused applying these principles.

[47] See also *Tolstoy-Miloslavsky v. Aldington* [1996] 1 W.L.R. 736 at 746, CA.

[48] *Taylor v. Pace Developments Limited* [1991] B.C.C. 406 at 409, CA.

In the absence of exceptional circumstances, this will not extend to making an order against a liquidator[49] or a legal expenses insurer.[50] However, insurers of a negligent defendant who caused an action against the defendant to be defended were held liable, both to indemnify the defendant to the limit of the insurance policy and to pay the costs of the action in which negligence was established. The liability for costs flowed from the insurer's decision that the action be defended. The Court said, in reality, the insurers were the defendants.[51] Costs were awarded against insurers for similar reasons in a first instance decision decided shortly after *T.G.A. Chapman, Pendennis Shipyard Ltd v. Margrathea (Pendennis) Ltd.*[52] Usually, however, costs will not be awarded against indemnity insurers in a sum which exceeds the limit of the indemnity.[52a]

The Court of Appeal considered the jurisdiction again in *Nordstern* **33–17** *Allgemeime Versicherungs AG v. Internav Ltd: Same v. Katsamas and Another.*[53] In considering the current test of maintenance, Lord Justice Waller referred to Lord Mustill's suggestion in *Giles v. Thompson*[54] that it was for the court to ask whether or not there was wanton and officious intermeddling with the disputes of others where the meddler had no interest, save a financial interest in the result. *Nordstern* makes plain that, whilst it was the case that where an agreement fell within the definition of champertous that would form a firm basis for exercising the section 51 jurisdiction against a non-party, the fact that an agreement did not fall within the strict definition of champerty would not lead to the conclusion that the jurisdiction should not be exercised under section 51. The Court also rejected a submission that a non-party's liability to pay needs to be secondary, holding that the jurisdiction to order costs against a non party provided by section 51 is not limited to those cases where a costs order has previously been made against a party to the litigation. Whilst section 51 of the 1981 Act had been replaced by section 4 of the Courts and Legal Services Act 1990, there was no suggestion in any of the subsequent cases that the change in language had produced any difference in the result.

An application for costs against a non-party under section 51 does not involve suing the non-party and the jurisdiction of the English court extends to the making of an order for costs against a non-party domiciled outside the jurisdiction where such a non-party, alleged to be the alter ego of a party to the proceedings, had such a connection with those proceedings that an order against him should be made. A non-party domiciled in a

---

[49] *Mettaloy Supplies Ltd (in liquidation) v. MA (UK) Ltd* [1997] 1 All E.R. 418, CA.
[50] *Murphy v. Young & Co.'s Brewery Limited* [1997] 1 All E.R. 518, CA.
[51] *T.G.A. Chapman Ltd v. Christopher, The Times,* July 21, 1997, CA.
[52] *The Times,* August 27, 1997.
[52a] *Cormack and Cormack v. The Excess Insurance Company Ltd, The Times,* March 30, 2000.
[53] *The Times,* June 8, 1999, CA.
[54] [1994] 1 A.C. 142, 164.

State party to the Convention on Jurisdiction and the Enforcement of Judgments in Civil and Commercial matters cannot thus require an applicant for costs to sue him in his home State. Even if an application for costs against a non-party does involve the non-party being sued, the non-party was sued as a third party to proceedings so that Article 6(2) applied as an exception to Article 2[55].

Where a legal representative acts solely in that capacity he is not subject to the section 51 (1) and (3) jurisdiction.[56] Section 51(1) and (3) will, however, operate against a legal representative who in reality is the client.[57]

---

[55] *National Justice Compania Naviera SA v. Prudential Assurance Co Ltd (No. 2), The Times,* October 15, 1999, CA.
[56] *Hodgson v. Imperial Tobacco* [1998] 1 W.L.R. 1056, 1066.
[57] *Globe Equities Ltd v. Globe Legal Services Ltd; sub nom Globe Equities v. Kotrie and Others,* T.L.R. April 14, 1999.

34. Conditional Fee Agreements

The Common Law

The common law governing contingent fees outside the scope of the Courts 34–01
and Legal Services Act 1990 as amended by the Access to Justice Act 1999 is
derived from the public policy relating to champerty and maintenance.

Maintenance is the financial support of litigation by a stranger without just
causes. "It is directed against wanton and officious meddling with the
disputes of others in which the (maintainer) has no interest whatsoever, and
where the assistance he rendered to one or the other is without justification
or excuse" per Fletcher Moulton L.J. in *British Cash and Parcel Conveyors
Ltd v. Lamson Store Service Co Ltd.* (1908) 1 K.B. 1006 and 1014. A just
cause for the maintenance would exist where the maintainer has a legitimate
interest in the outcome of the suit as a result of a financial or commercial
interest, or where social, family or other ties justify the maintainer in
supporting the litigation.

Champerty is maintenance with the addition that the maintainer acts for a
share of the proceeds of the litigation. It is unlawful unless permitted by
statue.

In Thai Trading Co. v. Taylor (1998) 2 W.L.R. 893, the Court of Appeal
held that there is nothing unlawful in a solicitor acting for a party to
litigation to agree to forgo all or part of his fee if he loses, provided he does
not seek to recover more than his ordinary profit costs and disbursements if
he wins.

Thai Trading was not followed in *Hughs v. Kingston upon Hull City
Council* (1992) 2 W.L.R. 1229 on the basis that the solicitor's Practice
Rules 1990 provided in rule 8 that such arrangements should not be
entered into and the Rules had the force of statute.

The Law Society changed its practice rule on January 7, 1999 to provide
that a solicitor should not enter into a fee arrangement unless authorised
by statute or common law.

In *Geraghty v. Awad Awwad* (unreported, CA November 25, 1999), the
Court of Appeal confirmed that conditional fee agreements entered into
before January 7, 1999 were unlawful unless sanctioned by statute and
complying with statutory requirements. The effect of the judgement is to
outlaw all conditional fee arrangements other than those authorised by
statute. May L.J. said, "Where Parliament has . . . modified the law by
which there is no present room for the court, by the application of what is
perceived to be public policy, to go beyond that which Parliament has
provided." It seems likely therefore that *Thai Trading* is no longer good
law and conditional fee agreements must comply with the statutory
provisions to be enforceable.

Statutory Provisions

34–02 Section 58 of the Courts and Legal Services Act 1990 in its original wording has been substituted by new wording set out in sections 27 and 28 of the Access to Justice Act 1999.

Section 58(1) as re-enacted provides that a conditional fee agreement shall not be unenforceable by reason only of the fact that it is a conditional fee agreement providing all the conditions of section 58 are satisfied. If they are not satisfied the conditional fee agreement is unenforceable.

A conditional fee agreement is an agreement with a person providing advocacy or litigation services which provides for his fees or expenses to be payable only in specified circumstances (usually that the litigation results in success). If the specified circumstances occur, then a success fee may be provided for and that will be an increase on the normal fee.

Conditional fee agreements are available in personal injury and clinical negligence actions and the maximum percentage by which the normal fees may be increased is 100 per cent (The Conditional Fee Agreements Order 2000 S.I. 2000 No. 823).

A conditional fee agreement must be in writing and the agreement must state the percentage by which the amount of the fees, which could be payable if it were not a conditional fee agreement, is to be increased (i.e. the percentage uplift which constitutes the success fee).

The section does not apply if the agreement is a non-contentious business agreement between solicitor and client under section 57 of the Solicitors Act 1974.

"Advocacy services and litigation services" includes any sort of proceedings for resolving disputed (and not just proceeding in court), whether commenced or contemplated.

The Access to Justice Act 1999 made an important change to the previous law in that it provides that a costs order made in any proceedings may include provision requiring payment by the other side of a success fee payable under a conditional fee agreement. Further, where an insurance policy has been taken out against the risk of incurring a liability in the proceedings (an "after the event" insurance), a costs order may include costs in respect of the premium of the policy (section 29).

This part of the Act came into force on April 1, 2000.

The Conditional Fee Agreements Regulations 2000[1]

34–03 These regulations came into force on April 1, 2000. Important changes were made regarding the necessary contents of a conditional fee agreement. Standard forms of agreement which predated April 1, 2000 will not be enforceable.

---

[1] S.I. 2000 No. 692.

A conditional fee agreement must be signed by the client and the legal representative unless it is an agreement between a legal representative and an additional legal representative (usually solicitor and counsel).

The requirements for the contents of conditional fee agreements are set out in Regulations 2,3 and 4 of the Regulations and are as follows:

Requirements for Contents of Conditional Fee Agreements: General

2 (1) A conditional fee agreement must specify

    (a) the particular proceedings or parts of them to which it relates (including whether it related to any appeal, counterclaim or proceedings to enforce a judgement or order),

    (b) the circumstances in which the legal representative's **fees** and expenses, or part of them, are payable,

    (c) what payment, if any, is due—

        (i) If those circumstances only partly occur,

        (ii) Irrespective of whether those circumstances occur, and

        (iii) On the termination of the agreement for any reason, and

    (d) the amounts which are payable in all the circumstances and cases specifies or the method to be used to calculate them and, in particular, whether the amounts are limited by reference to the damages which may be recovered on behalf of the client.

  (2) A conditional fee agreement to which regulation 4 applies must contain a statement that the requirements of that regulation which apply in the case of that agreement have been complied with.

Requirements for Contents of Conditional Fee Agreements Providing for Success Fees

3 (1) A conditional fee agreement which provided for a success fee—

    (a) must briefly specify the reasons for setting the percentage increase at a level stated in the agreement, and

    (b) must specify how mush of the percentage increase, if any, related to the cost to the legal representative of the postponement of the payment of his **fees** and expenses.

  (2) If the agreement relates to court proceedings, it must provide that where the percentage increase becomes payable as a result of those proceedings, then—

    (a) if—

        (i) any fees are assessed, and

        (ii) the legal representative or the client is required by the court to disclose to the court or any other person the reasons for setting the percentage increase at the level stated in the agreement,

    he may do so,

  (b) if—

        (i) any such **fees** are accessed, and

        (ii) any amount in respect of the percentage increase is disallowed on the assessment on the ground that the level at which the increase was set was unreasonable in view of facts which were or should have been known to the legal representative at the time it was set, that amount ceases to be payable under the agreement, unless the court is satisfied that it should continue to be so payable, and

  (c) if—

        (i) sub-paragraph (b) does not apply, and

        (ii) the legal representative agrees with any person liable as a result of the proceedings to pay fees subject to the percentage increase that a lower amount than the amount payable in accordance with the conditional fee agreement is to be paid instead, The amount payable under the conditional **fee** agreement in respect of those fees shall be reduced accordingly, unless the court is satisfies that the full amount should continue to be payable under it.

  (3) In this regulation "percentage increase" means the percentage by which the amount of the fees which would be payable if the agreement were not a conditional fee agreement is to be increased under the agreement.

Information to be Given Before Conditional fee Agreements Made

4. (1) Before a conditional fee agreement is made the legal representative must—

  (a) inform the client about the following matters, and

  (b) if the client requires any further explanation, advice or other information about any of those matters, provide such further explanation, advice or other information about them as the client may reasonably require.

  (2) Those matters are—

  (a) the circumstances in which the client may be liable to pay the costs of the legal representative in accordance with the agreement,

(b) the circumstances in which the client may seek assessment of the fees and expenses of the legal representative and the procedure for doing so,

(c) whether the legal representative considers that the client's risk of incurring liability for costs in respect of the proceedings to which agreement relates is insured against under an existing contract of insurance,

(d) whether other methods of financing those costs are available, and if so, how they apply to the client and the proceedings in question,

(e) whether the legal representative considers that any particular method of methods of financing any or all of those costs is appropriate and, if he considers that a contract of insurance is appropriate or recommends a particular such contract—

(i) his reasons for doing do, and
(ii) whether he has an interest in doing so.

(3) Before a conditional fee agreement is made, the legal representative must explain its effect to the client.

(4) In the case of an agreement where—

(a) the legal representative is a body to which section 30 of the Access to Justice Act 1999 (recovery where body undertakes to meet costs liabilities) applies, and

(b) there are no circumstances in which the client may be liable to pay any costs in respect of the proceedings, paragraph (1) does not apply.

(5) Information required to be given under paragraph (1) about the matter in paragraph 2(a) and (d) must be given orally (whether or not it is also given in writing), but information required to be so given about the matters in paragraph (2)(e) and the explanation required by paragraph (3) must be given both orally and in writing.

(6) This regulation does not apply in the case of an agreement between a legal representative and an additional legal representative.

General Effects of the Statutory Provisions

Counsel is free to choose whether or not he enters into a conditional fee 34–04 agreement and the cab rank principle does not apply.

The agreement must be in writing. Matters such as the definition of success, the obligations under the agreement, withdrawal from and termination of the agreement are all subjects for agreement between solicitor and counsel. A model form for a solicitor/counsel conditional fee agreement has been agreed between the Personal Injury Bar Association (PIBA) and the Association of Personal Injury Lawyers (APIL). A further returned agreement (which will be agreement 5) is under discussion at time of writing.

The agreement can be varied or redrafted in any way providing it complies with the statutory requirements above, although the Bar Council and PIBA recommend that the PIBA/APIL model is used.

In practice the percentage uplift will generally be the same as that in the solicitor and client agreement, but it does not have to be so, and there may well be cases where it should be different (e.g. where counsel enters into an agreement at a later time than the solicitor/client agreement and the risk has changed in the interim).

There is no statutory provision for a cap on the amount that can be recovered by way of a success fee except the 100 per cent uplift maximum. There is no need for the success fee to be capped or limited by reference to the level of damages recovered.

The lay client may take out insurance against incurring a liability for his own disbursements and for the other side's costs and the cost of the premium may be recovered as part of the cost order in the case (section 29 Access to Justice Act 1999).

"Except that a CFA enables solicitors and counsel to enter into an agreement which they would not otherwise be able to make, the existence of a CFA does not alter the relationship between the legal advisor and her client. The solicitor and counsel shall owe to the client exactly the same duties as he would owe the client if he had not entered into a CFA.

[He] remains under the same duty to his client and in performing his other responsibilities on behalf of the client. This extends to advising the client of what are the consequences to the client of the client entering into a CFA. The lawyer also still owes the same duties to the court . . . The lawyer, as long as he puts aside any consideration of his own interest, is entitled to advise the client about commencing, continuing and compromising proceedings, but the decision must be that of the client and not the lawyer. The lawyer has however the right, if the need should arise, to cease to act for a client under a CFA in the same way as a lawyer can cease to act in the event of there being a conventional retainer" per Lord Woolf in *Hodgson and others v. Imperial Tobacco Ltd and others* (1998) 1 W.L.R. 1056 at 1065.

The Claimants legal representatives are no more vulnerable to an order for costs against them personally in a case where there is a legally enforceable CFA than in any other case. A lawyer can be made personally liable for the costs of a party other than his client in certain circumstances, *e.g.* a wasted costs order but those circumstances are the same whether or not there is a CFA in existence.

Court Rules

Important changes to the CPR to take account of the new statutory **34–05** provisions were made by the Civil Procedure (Amendment No. 3) Rules 2000[2] and by new Practice Directions. The new rules came into force on July 3, 2000.

Under the new rules the court will not assess any "additional liability" (by which is meant "the percentage increase, the insurance premium or the additional amount in respect of provision made by a membership organisation") until the conclusion of the proceedings.

A party who seeks to recover an additional liability must provide information about the finding arrangement to the court and to other parties (CPR 44.15). The information to be given is set out in the Practice Direction of Section 19.4.

There is however no requirement to specify the amount of the additional liability or how it is calculated until it fails to be assessed (PD Section 19.1).

A claimant who has entered into a funding arrangement before starting proceedings must provide information to the court by filing notice when he issues the claim form and the information must be served on the other side with the claim form. If the funding arrangement is entered into later, a party must file and serve notice within 7 days of entering into the funding arrangement (PD section 19.2)

If the information given is no longer accurate, notice of the change must be given (PD section 19.3).

In assessing costs the court does not use the benefit of hindsight. It must have regard to the circumstances as they reasonably appeared when the funding arrangement was entered into.

In deciding whether a percentage increase is reasonable, relevant factors to take into account include the risk that no costs will be recovered (usually because the case is lost), the legal representative's liability for disbursements and what other methods of financing the costs were available to the receiving party.

To assist the court to make a summary assessment of an additional liability, a party seeking such costs must prepare and have available for the court a bundle of documents which must include a copy of: (1) the notice of the funding arrangement; (2) every estimate and statement of costs filed by him; and (3) the risk assessment prepared at the time when the relevant funding arrangement was entered into and on the basis of which the amount of the additional liability was fixed. A party may not recover any percentage increase if he has not complied with the Practice Direction or a court order to disclose the reasons for setting the percentage increase at the level stated in the conditional fee agreement.

---

[2] S.I. 2000 No. 1317.

Transitional Provisions

34–06 The Access to Justice Act 1999 (Transitional Provisions) Order 2000 prevents the Act or the new Regulations applying to agreements made before April 1, 2000, so that a success fee or insurance premium cannot be recovered from the other side in respect of those agreements. Further, where an agreement was entered into before April 1, 2000, a second or subsequent funding arrangement in respect of the claim does not give rise to an additional liability recoverable from the other side, so that an old agreement cannot simply be replaced by a new one.

However, if an agreement was entered into between April 1, and July 3, 2000, advantage can be taken of the new rules provided that the requirements of the new rules were complied with before July 31, 2000.

Assessing the Uplift

34–07 In order to maintain income and compensate for lost cases, the following formula can be used:

If the probability of success is x per cent, the conditional fee should be 100/x times the basic fee. So, for example, if the probability of success is 50 per cent, the calculation is 100 divided by 50 = twice the normal fee, *i.e.* an uplift of 100 per cent. The following table shows the effect on the uplift.

Chance of success	% Uplift
100	Nil
90	11
80	25
70	33
60	67
50	100 (maximum allowed)

These figures compensate solely for the uncertainty of outcome. They do not compensate for the outlay of any disbursements which the solicitor may fund nor for delay in remuneration and an increase in the uplift is appropriate to take account of these factors, although the other side will not have to pay any proportion of the increase attributable to the delay.

Patients and Minors

34–08 Cases concerning children and people under a disability can be conducted with a conditional fee agreement. It should be entered into by the litigation friend. Where a patient is already subject to the Court of Protection, the agreement should be considered with the receiver in consultation with the court. Since the terms of any settlement of a claim by a patient or minor has to be approved by the court, it would seem to be a wise precaution if a conditional fee agreement is to be entered into in these cases for an application to be made to the court for approval of the agreement unless the legal representative is prepared to act for a nil success fee. In an action on behalf of a successful patient or minor, the cost have to be assessed unless the court otherwise orders and the court may be willing to waive assessment without considering whether any success fee is reasonable.

35. The Impact of the Human Rights Act 1998 on Personal Injury Law and Practice

Introduction

It would be an understatement to say that British judges have not always **35–01** embraced European legislation and case law with much enthusiasm. Indeed, when the European Convention on Human Rights and Fundamental Freedoms was first drafted in 1949 by the Home Office, the then Lord Chancellor, Lord Jowett, called it a "half baked scheme to be administered by some unknown court the language of which was so 'vague and woolly' that it may mean almost anything".

Nevertheless, the United Kingdom was one of the founder members of **35–02** this Convention when it was adopted in 1950 and was the first country formally to accede.

At the time it was generally recognised that in due course domestic **35–03** legislation would incorporate the Convention directly into our law. That "due course" has taken almost exactly fifty years. Throughout that time, and even recently, the Convention has rarely merited mention in Courts or conversation.

The Human Rights Act 1998 ("the HRA") received the Royal Assent in **35–04** November 1999. It is to be implemented in full on October 2, 2000. There may still be practitioners in the field of personal injury and professional negligence who believe that the Act will have little or no impact on their field of work and that neither the Convention and Act is worth even cursory study. Perhaps they believe that neither the Convention nor the Act contains anything more than a series of well intentioned, anodyne and generalised expressions of broad principle all of which are already embraced by our legal system. They may even be encouraged in this approach by a superficial reading of the words of Lord Woolf in *Walker v. Daniels,* Times L.R. May 17, 2000 (see further below, para. 67).

We believe that this approach is at once mistaken and irresponsible. **35–05** Rather, we are certain that careful study of the Convention and the Act and even a little consideration of some of the commentary makes it plain that the HRA will have a substantial impact upon our litigation culture and practice.

Furthermore, the Bar may now have a golden opportunity to think and **35–06** actcreatively in the interpretation and application of the Convention, whilst following Lord Woolf's exhortation to do so "responsibly". We must also expect the Judges, whatever their historic prejudices may have been, to be prepared for such an approach. They have had extensive training through the Judicial Studies Board and the advice which they have received is to anticipate that 15% of all Court time will be allocated to Convention related issues. We suspect that that may be an exaggeration of reality but have no doubt that the whole issue of Human Rights is something that needs to be addressed by all practitioners as a discrete subject and not simply something to be picked up and fended off as and when it arises.

Structure and Summary

35–07   Section 1 of the HRA provides that the following Convention rights shall beincorporated:

> (i) Articles 2–12 and 14 of the Convention;
>
> (ii) Articles 1–3 of the First Protocol;
>
> (iii) Articles 1 and 2 of the Sixth Protocol;

and these are to be read in conjunction with Articles 16–18 of the Convention.

35–08   Schedule 1 of the HRA sets out these rights in detail. We summarise them here:

Article 2:	Right to life.
Article 3:	Prohibition of torture or inhuman or degrading treatment or punishment.
Article 4:	Prohibition of slavery and forced labour.
Article 5:	Liberty and security of the person etc.
Article 6:	Right to a fair trial.
Article 7:	Freedom from retrospective criminal offences to punishment.
Article 8:	Right to respect for private and family life.
Article 9:	Freedom of religion.
Article 10:	Freedom of expression.
Article 11:	Freedom of assembly and association.
Article 12:	Right to marry and to found a family.
Article 14:	Prohibition of discrimination in relation to Convention rights.

The First Protocol provides for:

Article 1:	Protection of property.

Article 2:   Right to education.
Article 3:   Right to free election.

The Sixth Protocol is concerned with the abolition of the death penalty.

The Convention of 1950 broke entirely new ground: for the first time, **35–09** individuals with grievances against Contracting States could petition an international body which took its decisions on the basis of its own legislative material—*i.e.* the Convention—and according to its own body of case law.

However, it was not until 1966 that the U.K. allowed individuals to **35–10** petition the Court in Strasbourg. The U.K. Parliament has in some circumstances taken account of the Convention directly by ensuring that certain primary and secondary legislation is consistent with it. This is certainly true of some modem family legislation but it is doubtful whether any Act of Parliament or Rules of Court—except perhaps the CPR in some respects—impacting directly upon personal injury legislation has been drafted with the Convention to the forefront of the author's consciousness.

Sooner or later we may well see a cultural change affecting our law and **35–11** practice. To be able to deal with it we shall all have to understand the nature and extent of Convention rights. To do so, in the view of Ben Emmerson, Q.C., the Editor of the Human Rights Law Review, we will have to "engage in a form of lateral thinking in which precedent and established practice gives way to a superior system of constitutional human rights law".

The Incorporation of the Convention by the HRA

The relevant provisions of the Convention are incorporated in three **35–12** ways:

(i) By Section 3 of the Act and by the requirement that "so far as it is possible to do so, primary legislation and subordinate legislation must be read and given effect in a way which is compatible with the Convention Rights". Section 2 of the HRA does not oblige Courts to follow earlier decisions: it obliges them to "take (them) into account". The concept here is that the Convention is a "living instrument" which is to be interpreted purposively and with imagination according to current social and political attitudes—see *Handyside v. U.K.* (1979–80) 1 E.H.R.R. 737. In following this approach, English Courts will have to look abroad to the views of Courts of other Member States in the Council of Europe all of which will form a part of a relevant body of material and even to judgments of other Courts with similar constitutional provisions—*e.g.* Australia, New Zealand, South Africa, Canada and India.

(ii) Sections 6 to 8 of the Act create new causes of action in relation to the acts or proposed acts of public authorities. Section 6 provides that it is "unlawful for a public authority to act in a way which is incompatible with a Convention right:" "public authority" as defined by Section 6(3) includes:

(a) a Court or Tribunal; and
(b) "any person certain of whose functions are functions of a public nature"

Section 7 of the Act gives a right to sue to any victim of an unlawful act, the limitation period for which proceedings is one year from the act complained of. Section 8 deals with remedies against a public authority.

(iii) The third way in which Convention issues will arise so as to affect personal injury practitioners is because the HRA enables a Court to make a declaration of incompatibility (as to which see generally Section 4 of the Act). This is principally directed at seeking a declaration that the provision of primary legislation is incompatible with a Convention right.

Application to "Public Authorities" and to Individuals

35–13   It is important to recognise that Section 6 of the Act directly imposes compliance with the Convention upon "public authorities". See also Section 6(3) and the definition of the term there. There can be no doubt that the Act will apply to any body whether it be statutory or non statutory which is exercising a public function. There will be many examples: local authorities, local education authorities, health authorities, NHS doctors, public utilities, privatised prison services and so forth. The definition of public authorities also includes Courts and Tribunals and it may be that they will also include bodies which exercise supervisory or disciplinary jurisdiction over those who perform public functions including disciplinary bodies and the professions (see *e.g. Philis v. Greece (No. 2)*. (1998) 25 E.H.R.R. 417).

35–14   The operation of the convention as between individuals and the State (in the form of a public authority) is known as "vertical" effect. However, the HRA will also have a significant "horizontal" effect between individuals. Courts will be expected to interpret all legislation in a manner compatible with the Convention, even where the dispute is between private individuals. The Lord Chancellor has said so in terms—see Hansard, November 24, 1997, col. 783. Other Convention rights (*e.g.* under Article 8) are specifically directed to individuals but those rights may well derive from corresponding duties owed by other individuals.

Interpretation

We have already seen that Section 2 of the Act is mandatory but requires 35–15 case law to be taken into account. Given that the Convention is to be interpreted as a "living instrument" practitioners may soon learn to argue about the application of novel concepts such as the "margin of appreciation". This may arise on the basis that a domestic court is entitled to treat itself as better placed to evaluate the impact of Convention rights on its citizens than a Strasbourg decision which deals with the same issue but in wholly different national circumstances. However the HRA is interpreted and applied, that interpretation has to be purposive and dynamic. To quote from *Loizidou v. Turkey* (1995) 20 E.H.R.R. 99 the "object and purpose of the Convention as an instrument for the protection of human beings requires that its provisions be interpreted and applied so as to make its safeguards practical and effective". The extent to which the doctrine of the "margin of appreciation" may or may not apply to our law, see Singh, Hunt and Demetriou writing in (1999) E.H.R.L.R. 15.

The principle of purposive interpretation is similar to the test applied by 35–16 the European Court of Justice in Luxembourg, when applying EC law (see the *Marleasing* case, referred to in the previous chapter). The difference in so far as there is one is that the English courts will apply a test set out in an English statute. Nevertheless, we consider that it is likely that the English courts will not differentiate in practice between what is possible for Human Rights and EC purposes, particularly since EC law must itself be interpreted in the light of Human Rights standards.

Just as this can be characterised as the "effectiveness" principle, so we 35–17 shall also have to learn the principle of "proportionality". This concept may have become familiar in recent times following the introduction of Civil Procedure Rules, but it underpins all relevant Strasbourg case law and, in short, requires that Convention rights should be interpreted and applied so as to allow a proper balance between competing interests: departure from Convention rights and principles will be unacceptable for a public authority unless primary legislation gives the authority no choice (see section 6). Section 3 requires that primary or secondary legislation must, so far as possible, be interpreted in a way compatible with the Convention. Any interference with a right guaranteed by the Convention will have to be justified by the public authority identifying its aim and objective (and, where necessary, by reference to what is set out in the provisos to Articles 8–11). This is a very different test from the familiar *Wednesbury* principle.

Summary of the Application of HRA Principles

It is certain that the HRA will have a substantial impact on our law and 35–18 practice we should remind ourselves of the three provisions discussed above:

(a) the interpretation section—Section 3(1),

(b) the power given to higher courts by Section 4 to make declarations of incompatibility, and

(c) the provision at Section 6 making it unlawful for a public authority to act other than in a way which is compatible with a Convention right.

35–19   The Convention rights are those provided for in the Articles of the Convention and the First Protocol. Some of those rights are absolutes and others, such as Articles 8 to 11, are expressed in qualified terms. Interference with these rights can only be justifiable if:

(a) the interference is "lawful";

(b) if that serves a legitimate purpose;

(c) if the interference is "necessary in a democratic society"; and

(d) the interference is not discriminatory.

35–20   If we are going to argue effectively about concepts such as "democratic necessity" and "public interest" we shall have to become familiar with the Strasbourg case law. Far from being based upon the somewhat rigid vertical structure with which we are familiar from the English law of precedent, it (in the words of Judge Martens, a former Judge of the European Court) is like "a living body of water, continuously open to changing currents". For a recent British example, see *Smith and Grady v. United Kingdom; Lustig-Prean and Beckett v. United Kingdom* (2000) 29 E.H.R.R. 493, 548.

35–21   We turn to consider the individual Convention rights and make a number of suggestions as to how they may prove to be relevant in our own practices.

Article 2: The Right to Life

35–22   All public authorities are duty-bound to protect life. This comment, it may be argued, might oblige them to provide a particular sort of life-saving treatment whatever the prospects of success and whatever the cost. In the case of a local authority, for example, which was also the landlord of Council property it might be argued that there is a duty to design or to modify that property in such a way as to ensure the maximum *possible* protection for a tenant. One of the authors of this chapter was involved in a case in which one of the allegations against a local authority qua landlord was that it failed to provide window catches on a fourth floor property when it had every reason to know that one of the children living in the flat was temperamentally inclined to climb and to jump out. Article 2 might have been relevant to the question of whether the local authority owed any duty of care and to the discharge of any duty.

Suppose that it is argued against a highway authority that it ought to **35–23** have provided a pedestrian crossing because of the known risks of that particular stretch of road or simply that the road or pavement should not have been in a dangerous condition, regardless of the system of maintenance, repair and inspection that it operated. Can it respond, in the light of Article 2, that it would have been too costly to do so or that it had other priorities? Perhaps not, since Article 2 is an absolute right. It is also easy to apply exactly the same analysis to a local authority/employer who might ordinarily seek to argue that a particular step would not have been "reasonably practicable" or which might otherwise have sought to justify action or inaction by reference to cost.

These illustrations demonstrate how Article 2 might be deployed against **35–24** a public authority which argues that it was entitled to decide what to do according to a cost/benefit analysis. But it may also be relevant to arguments about whether a public authority owes any duty of care in the first place.

In the context of medical negligence, the Courts may see a wide scope **35–25** for the dynamic development of the right to life. Not only may health authorities and NHS Trusts find it difficult to argue about lack of resources but the Convention rights may mean that the long-established *Bolam* test cannot survive. Others may go so far as to argue that the duty to provide care to preserve life is absolute and that, accordingly, it is unnecessary for a claimant to establish negligence at all. The argument would go that a public authority is required to make adequate provision for medical care and, if for whatever reason it has not done so, a breach of Article 2 has been established.

It is no answer to say that Article 2 is restricted to those cases where **35–26** actual loss of life has occurred. It has been interpreted so as to cover cases where injury has been sustained so long as loss of life was a possible consequence of the act or omission complained of.

In this chapter we are only seeking to give a few illustrations of what **35–27** issues may arise: the fertile imagination may soon breed others. For example, is the Government's failure (if so it be) to provide the public with accurate information about the true nature of the danger to life from BSE actionable under this Article—as to which one might look first at the claim in *LCB v. United Kingdom* (1999) 27 E.H.R.R. 212 where the Court had to consider a complaint that the parents of the applicant had not been warned by the Government of the potential danger of radiation during the Christmas Island nuclear testing programme. In the Court's judgment, the Court considered the issue of what information the Government should have provided: for another case involving similar considerations, see *Guerra v. Italy* (1998) 26 E.H.R.R. 357 where the Applicants, who lived close to a chemical factory, succeeded under Article 8 in relation to the lack of public information about the real hazards to their health.

Article 6: Right to a Fair Trial

35-28   Article 6(1) contains the following express rights: the right to i) a fair hearing, ii) a public hearing, iii) a hearing within a reasonable time, iv) a hearing by an independent and impartial tribunal, and v) the promulgation of a publicly declared judgment. We consider each in turn below.

35-29   These rights have been supplemented by further rights by virtue of the caselaw of the European Court of Human Rights. The European Court has expanded the right to a fair trial to cover a much broader scope of civil procedure and including the substantive law of negligence.

35-30   A good illustration of the application of the purposive interpretation of the obligation to provide a "fair and public hearing" is the case of *Moreiva de Azedo v. Portugal* (1991) 13 E.H.R.R. 721 where the European Court held that the "right to a fair trial holds so prominent a place in a democratic society that there can be no justification for interpreting Article 6(1) restrictively".

Fair Hearing and Equality of Arms

35-31   The fundamental principle which underlies this requirement is the concept of equality between the parties. It is one that we have seen under the CPR and Strasbourg case law makes it plain that each side should have a reasonable opportunity to present his case—including his evidence— without being at a significant disadvantage (*Dombo Beheer v. Netherlands* (1994) 18 E.H.R.R. 213, para 33). This extends to equal access to facilities (*Schuler-Zgraggen v. Switzerland* (1993) 16 E.H.R.R. 405).

35-32   The fairness of the hearing may depend on giving each party a fair opportunity to test the evidence of the other side. Can artificially imposed time limits (*e.g.* for cross-examination) satisfy that requirement? Will we have to reconsider the Court's use of its power to exclude evidence? In the case of single joint experts, which might have seemed another fertile ground for debate, consider what the Court of Appeal said in *Walker v. Daniels* and the basis upon which the existing CPR regime was justified.

35-33   The requirement of a fair hearing also imposes an obligation to provide a reasoned judgment in respect of any decision which is decisive of the outcome—see *Hadjianastassiou v. Greece* (1993) 16 E.H.R.R. 219; *Hiro Balani v. Spain* (1995) 19 E.H.R.R. 565; *Higgins v. France* (1999) 27 E.H.R.R. 703. It will probably be sufficient if the reasoned judgment consists at least of a clear (albeit brief) statement of reasons—*c.f. Stefan v. General Medical Council* [1999] 1 W.L.R. 1293.

Public Hearing

The Court will also have to consider what is meant by a public hearing. 35–34
In *Scarth v. United Kingdom* (1999) 27 E.H.R.R. CD 37 the Commission
declared it to be an admissible question that the lack of a public hearing in
County Court Small Claims cases constituted a violation of Article 6. After
that declaration, the U.K. Government conceded the point.

The requirement that a hearing should be in public means that what are 35–35
now called "private" (previously "Chambers") hearings cannot be secret. If
an interested party or even a casual member of the public asks to be
admitted to a hearing, it may be argued that it should be done.

Hearing within a Reasonable Time

There will also be an issue about excessive procedural delays and 35–36
particularly whether the toleration of such delays may constitute a violation of the right to have the "fair and public hearing within a reasonable
time". It may be that Article 6 is relied upon by defendants seeking to
strike out a claim on the basis that it has been too long in coming to trial.
On the other hand it is likely to be relied upon by either party in seeking to
oppose an application for the late admission of evidence.

The European Court of Human Rights will naturally assess the complex- 35–37
ity of the case when coming to a conclusion. The case of *Robins v. United
Kingdom* (1998) 26 E.H.R.R. 527 is instructive as to the length of delay
which may be considered unacceptable in normal, uncomplicated matters.
The case concerned an appeal on costs which was considered to be a
relatively straight forward matter. Delays of 10 months (caused by the
mistaken belief of the Legal Aid Board that the applicants had separated)
and 16 months (due to inaction by the Civil Appeals Office) were found to
be unreasonable and constituted a breach of Article 6(1). Where force of
circumstances requires a more speedy hearing, then a breach of Article 6
may arise, should proceedings be delayed (see *F.E. v. France* (2000) 29
E.H.R.R. 592 concerning a HIV victim infected by blood transfusion).

Hearing by an Independent and Impartial Tribunal

Article 6 also requires that the hearing should be "by an independent 35–38
and impartial tribunal established by law". This is a principle which has
been discussed in the Court of Appeal recently—see *Locobail* [2000] 2
W.L.R. 870. For an authority from the European Court, concerning a
judge who had also been involved in the legislative process, see *McGonnell
v. United Kingdom*, Times L.R. February 22, 2000 (Case No. 28488/95,
February 8, 2000). For recent authority on temporary Judges hearing civil

disputes, see *Clancy v. Caird,* Times L.R. May 9, 2000 and for a case on the right to legal assistance as a pre-requisite of fair trial, see *Magee v. United Kingdom,* Times L.R. June 20, 2000.

The Scope of Article 6(1): Substance Versus Procedure; Immunities

35–39   Personal injury litigation clearly falls within the scope of the Article in relation to the determination of civil rights and obligations, both as to the determination of liability and quantum. However, the Commission has held that compensation claims from a public fund do not fall within Article 6 (*Berler v. Germany No. 12624/87,* 62 DR 207 (1989); *B v. Netherlands No. 11098/84,* 43 DR 198 (1985); *Nordh v. Sweden No. 14225/88,* 69 DR 223 (1990)).

35–40   Article 6 is not concerned with ancillary proceedings which do not involve the determination of rights or obligations. Accordingly, disputes concerning interim relief, enforcement of judgments, or leave to appeal fall outside the right to a fair trial. The principal starting point concerning Article 6(1) is that the right to a fair trial does not involve an assessment of the merits of any case. Therefore a substantive rule which does not provide an individual with a right to bring a claim falls outside the scope of Article 6 (*H v. Belgium* (1988) 10 E.H.R.R. 339, para. 40). On the other hand, where a person is prevented from bringing a claim by virtue of a procedural rule, then Article 6(1) may apply. This distinction may be easier to conceive in theory than to apply in practice.

35–41   In *Powell and Rayner v. United Kingdom* ((1990) 12 E.H.R.R. 288 (Commission Opinion), 355 (Court Judgment)), the Commission held that the lack of a cause of action for trespass and nuisance in relation to aircraft overflight and noise did not raise any issues under Article 6(1). In the light of the decision of the Commission on admissibility, the Court declined to entertain the complaint under Article 6. (The Powell case has been followed more recently in *Hatton v. U.K.* (May 16, 2000, Case No. 36022/97, decision on admissibility)).

35–42   This may be contrasted with *Osman v. United Kingdom* ([1999] 1 F.L.R. 193; (2000) 29 E.H.R.R. 245) where the European Court of Human Rights did consider that the rule providing the police with immunity of suit against negligence claims was contrary to the Convention. In *Osman,* the United Kingdom accepted that the rule articulated in *Hill v. Chief Constable of West Yorkshire* [1989] A.C. 53 did not automatically prevent from the outset an action in negligence against the police, but rather allowed the domestic courts to make a considered assessment as to whether a particular case fell within or outside the immunity.

35–43   On that basis, the European Court of Human Rights held that the applicants were entitled to pray in aid Article 6(1). Further, on the merits, the European Court considered that the effect of the ruling of the Court of Appeal automatically excluding access to a court was disproportionate, given the facts of the case and the nature of the allegations made against the police.

The effect of the judgment of the European Court of Human Rights was **35–44** considered in the case of *Barrett v. Enfield LBC* [1999] P.I.Q.R. P272. Lord Browne-Wilkinson (with whom Lords Nolan and Steyn agreed) in a short but cogent speech dissected the logic of the *Osman* judgment, which he found "extremely difficult to understand". In fact their Lordships ruled in the *Barrett* case that there could in principle be a common law duty of care owed to a child taken into care by a local authority. However, Lord Browne-Wilkinson stated further, "[in] view of the decision in *Osman's* case it is now difficult to foretell what would be the result in the present case if we were to uphold the striking out order . . . In the present very unsatisfactory state of affairs, and bearing in mind that under the Human Rights Act 1998 Article 6 will shortly become part of English law, in such cases as these it is difficult to say that it is a clear and obvious case calling for a striking out." (at P278).

The effect of *Barrett* has been immediate. In *Gower v. LB Bromley* (July **35–45** 29, 1999, not yet reported) the Court of Appeal applied the three-fold test of *Caparo v. Dickman* [1990] 2 A.C. 605 to find that, on an application to strike out the claimant's case, it was both reasonably foreseeable and sufficiently proximate for there to be a duty of care owed by staff of a special needs school to a disabled child who alleged that he had suffered as a consequence of alleged negligence. The Court held that the question as to whether the third limb of *Caparo* was satisfied, namely whether it was fair just and reasonable to impose a duty of care, should be left to the trial judge after consideration of all the evidence. This case may be contrasted with *Palmer v. Tees Health Authority* [2000] P.I.Q.R. P1 (a personal injury claim decided shortly before the *Gower* case) in which the Court of Appeal ruled that where there was insufficient proximity to establish a duty of care, on the pleaded case, an action to strike out could succeed. The question of when it is appropriate, following *Osman* to strike out a case, or deal with liability on a preliminary point was further canvassed in *Kent v. Griffiths and London Ambulance Service* [2000] P.I.Q.R. P57. See also *Hale v. Simons* (on advocate's immunity) Times L.R. July 12, 2000.

Effective Access to a Court; Legal Aid

The first case in which the European Court of Human Rights articulated **35–46** a right of effective access to a court (both in law and in fact) was *Golder v. United Kingdom* (1979–80) 1 E.H.R.R. 524. This case concerned the rights of a prisoner to obtain access to a solicitor for the purpose of instituting libel proceedings. In principle, the applicant could obtain access to the

High Court to institute proceedings, however, in fact this right was restricted by the refusal of the prison authorities to permit him access to legal advice. The European Court of Human Rights held that what was to be guaranteed was effective access to a court which had been denied to the applicant.

35–47   A case of greater significance for personal injury practitioners in the light of the withdrawal of legal aid is *Airey v. Ireland* (1979–80) 2 E.H.R.R. 305. The applicant challenged the refusal to grant her legal aid in order to seek a decree of judicial separation from her husband. The European Court of Human Rights held that the possibility for the applicant to appear in person did not provide her with an effective right of access to a court. The Court recognised that it was not incumbent upon the state to provide legal aid for every dispute relating to a civil right. Nevertheless, the Court continued, "Article 6(1) may sometimes compel the State to provide for the assistance of a lawyer where such assistance proves indispensable for an effective access to court either because legal representation is rendered compulsory . . . or by reason of the complexity of the procedure or of the case".

35–48   *Stewart-Brady v. United Kingdom* (1997) 24 E.H.R.R. CD 38 was a case where the right to legal aid was refused. There, the Commission rejected a claim arising from a refusal to grant legal aid for an appeal against the striking out of an action on the grounds that there were no reasonable prospects of success and the costs were disproportionate to the amount claimed.

35–49   An interesting question will be whether, with the removal of Legal Aid, and the provision of alternative means of access to justice such as the Community Legal Service and/or Conditional Fee Agreements there will be adequate access to a Court. It is suggested that only in very serious or complex cases, or where the right to life is affected is it likely that the Courts will seriously entertain any challenge. For an example of a recent failure to pray in aid Article 6 in relation to a planning inquiry, see *R v. Secretary of State for the Environment, Transport and the Regions, ex parte Challenger,* CO/2048/2000, judgment of June 15, 2000.

Margin of Appreciation and Proportionality

35–50   Another English case which came before the European Court of Human Rights on the question of effective access to a court was *Fayed v. United Kingdom* (1994) 18 E.H.R.R. 393. The question of effective access arose in the context of proposed libel proceedings and the defence of qualified privilege of government inspectors in relation to allegations of fraud made in a report on the conduct of a company. The Court held that "the right of access to the courts secured by Article 6(1) is not absolute but may be subject to limitations" which may vary in time and place according to the needs and resources of the community and of individuals. The Court continued by stating that "the Contracting States enjoy a certain margin of appreciation, but the final decision as to observance of the Convention's requirements rests with the Court. It must be satisfied that the limitations applied do not restrict or reduce the access left to the individual in such a way or to such an extent that the very essence of the right is impaired". Any limitation "will not be compatible with Article 6(1) if it does not pursue a legitimate aim and if there is not a reasonable relationship of proportionality between the means employed and the aim sought to be achieved". The task of the Court was to strike "a fair balance between the demands of the general interests of the community and the requirements of the protection of the individual's fundamental rights".

Ashingdane v. United Kingdom, (1985) 7 E.H.R.R. 528 concerned a 35–51 mental patient who sought to challenge his continued detention in a secure mental hospital under the Mental Health Act 1959. One of the preconditions to bringing proceedings against the Secretary of State was the need for leave, which could only be granted by the High Court on "substantial grounds". The European Court held that the restriction had a legitimate aim and was proportionate.

Time limits have also been the subject of challenge in Strasbourg. 35–52 *Stubbings v. United Kingdom*, (1997) 23 E.H.R.R. 213 which concerned an unsuccessful challenge to the time limit of six years from age 18 years in relation to personal injury claims for childhood sexual abuse, indicates the width of the discretion left to the State. This may be compared with *Perez de Rada Cavanilles v. Spain*, (2000) 29 E.H.R.R. 109 where the European Court of Human Rights overturned the application of a very short time limit of three days governing the right to apply to set aside judgment.

Security for costs may also limit the right to access to a court. In *Tolstoy* 35–53 *Miloslavsky v. United Kingdom*, (1995) 20 E.H.R.R. 442 the European Court found no breach of Article 6 where the issue of security for costs arose in relation to an appeal to the Court of Appeal, whereas, in relation to first instance proceedings in *Ait-Mouhoub v. France*, [1998] H.R.C.D. 976 the European Court of Human Rights did intervene. In the latter case, the applicant, who had no resources, had applied for legal aid and had not received a reply from the legal aid office. The French court set as an amount of security the sum of 80,000 French francs. The European Court held that this was in breach of the applicant's rights under Article 6(1).

We consider that Article 6 is most likely to arise for consideration when 35–54 an English court exercises a discretion to grant access to a court, rather than as a discrete and separate right. However, issues of proportionality and justice must be viewed in a broad perspective in the light of the Convention and the Strasbourg case law.

Article 8: Right to Respect for Private Family Life

35–55   If the reader has got this far, he or she may by now have begun to get a taste for the imaginative interpretation and application of a simple principle which, on the face of it, is wholly uncontroversial. Of course everyone is entitled to "respect" for his private or family life. So what?

35–56   Perhaps the first and most obvious illustration of how this may matter in practice is in relation to disclosure. The current rules of disclosure, though now expressly limited to what is relevant, may be said to be too wide. Most of us have little or no hesitation in seeking or in providing all the medical records that exist in relation to a claim. In *MS v. Sweden* (1999) 28 E.H.R.R. 313, however, the issue was whether the applicant's medical history and medical records were part of her private life and whether she had waived her right to insist on that non disclosure simply because she had brought a personal injury action. In practice, a public authority will have to work hard to come within the proviso to Article 8(2). A private (*i.e.* non public) individual will need a different argument altogether.

35–57   Video evidence is bound to be controversial: at present, if the rules are complied with (and sometimes if they are not) a defendant commonly has absolutely no difficulty gaining admission of the video taken of the disabled claimant's "good day" gymnastics. This may change although we very much doubt that most such evidence can or should be excluded not only because of the qualified terms in which Article 8 is expressed but also because of the Defendant's absolute right to a fair trial under Article 6. It is, however, worth noting that in the context of employment the surveillance of employees by their employers has already been challenged successfully under Article 8—see *Niemitz v. Germany* (1993) 16 E.H.R.R. 97 and *Halford v. U.K.* (1997) 24 E.H.R.R. 523.

35–58   Another example is in relation to legal professional (and other) privilege—*see* Toulson J. in *General Mediterranean Holdings v. Patel* [1999] 3 A.E.R. 673. In that case, the disclosure of legally privileged material which would otherwise have been permitted under CPR Part 48.7(3) was held to be incompatible with Article 8.

35–59   In relation to the interpretation of Article 8, we expect the courts to take a pragmatic and sensible view and to interpret Article 8(1) as providing a right which is qualified in the sense that it has to be seen and interpreted in context. In relation to public authorities, of course, Article 8(2) provides that the public authority may only interfere in this right "in accordance with the law and (as) necessary in a democratic society in the interests of national security, public safety . . . for the protection of health or morals or for the protection of the rights and freedoms of others".

35–60   Using that proviso as a guide to interpretation of Article 8(1) a defendant may respectably argue that he has a right to be liable and/or to pay only that which is reasonable in accordance with established legal principles: in that case Article 8(1) should be interpreted so as to enable him to obtain evidence which will help him to achieve those aims.

Article 8 has also been interpreted so as to allow an applicant to 35–61 complain that the public authorities failed to provide relevant information about their health. The applicants in *Guerra v. Italy* (1998) 26 E.H.R.R. 357 lived close to a chemical factory which produced hazardous fumes. They contended that the failure to provide them with relevant information was an infringement of their right to respect for family life and the Court held, unanimously, that Article 8 had indeed been violated.

It may also be argued that a claimant can rely on Article 8 to refuse to 35–62 undergo a medical examination or testing by the defendant. This is a similar issue to that which we discussed above in relation to video evidence, and similar arguments will also arise. In practice, we expect the Courts' approach in the future to be hardly different from what happens at present.

Lastly, it is possible that Article 8 may arise in the context of claims for 35–63 care in major injury cases. One often hears a claimant seek to argue for a larger multiplier upon the basis that anything less would mean that the money will run out if the claimant lives longer than anticipated. In that case, it may be relevant to take into account the fact that a local authority might be in breach of Article 8 if it fails to provide adequate and suitable care for such a person—*c.f. R v. N and E Devon HA ex p. Coughlan* [2000] 2 W.L.R. 622.

We conclude by saying that the European case law on Article 8 35–64 emphasises that interference with these rights must not simply be desirable in the particular circumstances of the case: it must be shown to be necessary before it can be justified. Nevertheless some margin of appreciation is allowed and any "interference must, *inter alia*, correspond to a pressing social need, and be proportionate to the legitimate aim pursued"—see *Silver v. United Kingdom* (1983) 5 E.H.R.R. 344 and *Handyside v. United Kingdom* (1979–80) 1 E.H.R.R. 737, *Fayed v. United Kingdom* (1994) 18 E.H.R.R. 393 and *Sporrong v. Sweden* (1983) 5 E.H.R.R. 35.

View from the Bridge of the Court of Appeal

Two recent cases in the Court of Appeal indicate the likely approach of 35–65 the Courts when dealing with Human Rights points. The first case, *Williams v. Cowell* [2000] 1 W.L.R. 187 contains valuable guidance from Mummery L.J. as to what a Court will require when a Human Rights argument is raised. The second case sets out one (very senior) judge's view (Lord Woolf M.R., by chance) of the relevance of Article 6 to the CPR.

The conclusions of Mummery L.J. are worth citing in full: 35–66

"I would dismiss this appeal. It is possible, but probably unacceptable, to state the reasons for doing so in two short sentences: "The Act of 1993 does not apply to the appeal. Morison J. was entitled to exercise his discretion to refuse to hear the appeal in Wales or in Welsh in London."

It would have been possible, and quite definitely unacceptable, to use the material in 51 dividers assembled in two lever arch files of authorities to produce a judgment of 100 pages devoted mainly to explaining why the human rights material, although interesting and important in its various ways, was not needed to resolve the issues of construction and discretion. Perhaps there is a lesson for the future. The researches of Mr Allen and his juniors have been commendably thorough. No criticism of their industry or expertise is made. The hearing of the appeal was not unnecessarily prolonged. But when human rights points are taken there is a temptation to impress (and to oppress) the court with bulk and to turn a judicial hearing of a particular case into a human rights seminar. This temptation should be resisted. There should only be put before the court that part of the researched material which is reasonably required for the resolution of the particular appeal. It is not necessary to include all the treaty, convention, legislative, judicial, and periodical material which has been uncovered. In the interests of saving the legal costs of the parties and the time of the court, as well as for the conservation of the environment, self-restraint should be exercised to select what is reasonably required for counsel to develop the arguments and for the court to decide the case."

35–67   *Walker v. Daniels*, (judgment of May 3, 2000, Times L.R. May 17, 2000 (Lord Woolf M.R., Latham L.J.)) concerned the vexed question of the appropriate use of a single jointly instructed expert. Reliance was placed in the skeleton argument, in part, on Article 6. Lord Woolf stated as follows in rejecting this line of argument: "Article 6 has no possible relevance to this appeal . . . [I]f the court is not going to be taken down blind alleys it is essential that counsel, and those who instruct counsel, take a responsible attitude as to when it is right to raise a Human Rights Act point. (para 1.23) . . . Article 6 could not possibly have anything to add to the issue on this appeal. The provisions of the CPR, to which I have referred, make it clear that the obligation on the court is to deal with cases *justly* (original emphasis) (para. 1.24). It would be unfortunate if case management decisions in this jurisdiction involved the need to refer to the learning of the European Court on Human Rights in order for them to be resolved. In my judgment, cases such as this, do not require any consideration of human rights issues, certainly issues under Article 6. It would be highly undesirable if the consideration of those issues were made more complex by the injection of Article 6 style arguments. I hope that judges will be robust in resisting any attempt to introduce those arguments . . . When the 1998 Act becomes law, counsel will need to show self restraint if it is not to be discredited (para. 1.26)"

35–68   The result of the judgment of the Court of Appeal was to permit the Appellant some leeway, by not having to accept the imposition of a single joint expert without more—a solution which was not immediately obvious from a literal reading of the CPR. Arguably, the solution adopted reflected a proportionate weighing of the relevant interests of each party. To that extent, the CPR and Article 6 do not diverge. We consider that where a procedural judge is likely to make an order prohibiting a party from calling material evidence which causes a disproportionate impact on one party, then it will be appropriate in assessing what is "just" to apply a test which reflects the philosophy of the European Court on proportionality; in such circumstances Article 6 case law, where on point, will certainly be necessary background. (In the light of the comments in *Walker*, we would be interested to know whether a brave advocate succeeds before a Judge involved in drawing up the CPR in arguing that *McGonnell* applies—a case where Article 6 may well be relevant).

Written Material/Acknowledgments

We have read a number of papers which have provided a useful 35–66 commentary on the HRA and its implications as well as helping with many of the references included in this chapter: particularly, we would like to pay tribute to an article by Philip Havers Q.C. delivered at the AVMA Conference in 1999: Philip has also provided a valuable analysis on the impact of the Act in clinical negligence litigation which you will find in the new edition of Powers and Harris. Otherwise, we commend to you the "Civil Practitioner's Guide to the Human Rights Act 1998" written by Wendy Outhwaite and Marina Wheeler (published by Old Bailey Press). Other helpful material can be found in various text books and articles (see the Appendix for a list) but, as was the case with the CPR, there is in the end no substitute for reading the Act and for considering its text and possible interpretations yourselves.

Index